AF792460

2013
CyberArts

ARS ELECTRONICA

HATJE
CANTZ

Hannes Leopoldseder – Christine Schöpf – Gerfried Stocker

PRIX ARS ELECTRONICA

CyberArts 2013

International Compendium Prix Ars Electronica
Computer Animation / Film / VFX – Digital Musics & Sound Art – Hybrid Art – Interactive Art
Digital Communities – u19 – CREATE YOUR WORLD – [the next idea] voestalpine Art and Technology Grant
Prix Ars Electronica Collide@CERN Residency Award

CONTENTS

CONTENTS

10 Hannes Leopoldseder – **Quantum – On the Infinity of Data**
18 Christine Schöpf – **Prix Ars Electronica 2013**

COMPUTER ANIMATION / FILM / VFX

22 **A Quarter Past Human** – Statement of the Computer Animation / Film / VFX Jury
30 Forms – **Quayola, Memo Akten:** Golden Nica
36 Duku Spacemarines – **La Mécanique du Plastique**
40 Emma De Swaef, Marc James Roels / Beast Animation – **Oh Willy…**
44 Moritz Palnstorfer, Christian Schulze – **Ars Rata**
46 Kyle Mowat – **Ballpit**
48 Andrew Thomas Huang – **Björk—Mutual Chore**
50 Don Hertzfeldt – **It's Such a Beautiful Day**
52 Daniel Moshel – **MeTube: August sings Carmen "Habanera"**
54 Jérémy Clapin / Papy3D Productions – **Palmipedarium**
56 Kyra Buschor, Anna Habermehl, Constantin Paeplow – **Rollin' Safari**
58 Carl Burton – **Shelter**
60 Philipp Artus – **Snail Trail**
62 Chris Landreth – **Subconcious Password**
64 Te-Yu Liu – **The Carousel Family**
66 Nerdworking – **Under An Alias**

DIGITAL MUSICS & SOUND ART

70 **Blurring the Boundaries / Die Grenzen verwischen sich** – Statement of the Digital Musics & Sound Art Jury
74 Nicolas Bernier – **frequencies (a):** Golden Nica
78 [SjQ++] – **[SjQ++]**
82 Chris Carlson – **Borderlands Granular**
86 Typingmonkeys – **0b0000.tms**
88 Mark Malmberg – **Albireo2.1**
90 Michael Edwards – **altogether disproportionate**
92 Grischa Lichtenberger – **and IV (inertia)**
94 Simon Katan – **Cube with Magic Ribbons**
96 Suguru Goto – **Duali**
98 Roberto Pugliese – **Equilibrium Variant**
100 AGF (Antye Greie-Ripatti) – **Gedichterbe**
102 Nicolás Varchausky – **La Biblioteca Ciega**
104 Intermedia Chef – **The Half**
106 Yuri Suzuki – **The Sound of the Earth**
108 Robert Henke with students of the master's program Sound Studies at Berlin University of the Arts – **Works for Wave Field Synthesis**

HYBRID ART

112 **Undisciplined Art: From Low Tech to High Breed / Disziplinlose Kunst: Von der Niedrigtechnologie bis zur Hochzucht** - Statement of the Hybrid Art Jury
118 Koen Vanmechelens - **The Cosmopolitan Chicken Project—Diversity and Dualism:** Golden Nica
122 Tania Candiani - **Five Variations of Phonic Circumstances and a Pause**
126 Phil Ross - **Mycotecture**
130 Kuai Shen - **Oh!m1gas: biomimetic stridulation environment**
132 Matt Hope - **Breathing Bike**
134 David Glowacki with Phil Tew, Laura Kriefman, Joseph Hyde, Thomas Mitchell, Lisa May Thomas, Emma Harrie - **Hidden Fields**
136 Maja Smrekar - **HuMCC—Human Molecular Colonization Capacity**
138 Dmitry Gelfand, Evelina Domnitch - **Memory Vapor**
140 Mick Lorusso - **Microbial Schöppingen**
142 Sputniko! - **Nanohana Heels—Healing Fukushima**
144 Gilberto Esparza - **Nomadic Plants**
146 Chris Salter (in collaboration with Sofian Audry, Marije Baalman, Adam Basanta, Elio Bidinost and Thomas Spier) - **N_Polytope: Behaviors in Light and Sound after Iannis Xenakis**
148 Thomas Feuerstein - **Pancreas**
150 Paul Vanouse - **Suspect Inversion Center**
152 Louis-Philippe Demers - **The Blind Robot**

INTERACTIVE ART

156 **Interrogating Interaction** - Statement of the Interactive Art Jury
164 Michel Décosterd, André Décosterd / Cod.Act - **Pendulum Choir:** Golden Nica
168 rAndom International - **Rain Room**
170 Masaki Fujihata - **Voices of Aliveness**
172 Hernán Kerlleñevich, Mene Savasta Alsina - **AHORA. A song in the Hypertemporal Surface**
174 Daniel Rozin - **Angles Mirror**
176 Playmodes, MID - **Blaus**
178 Matt Richardson - **Descriptive Camera**
180 Dmitry & Elena Kawarga -**Down with Wrestlers with Systems and Mental Nonadapters!**
182 James Bridle - **Dronestagram**
184 Marnix de Nijs - **Exploded Views 2.0**
186 Olivier Bau, Yuri Suzuki, Ivan Poupyrev / Disney Research Pittsburgh - **Ishin-Den-Shin**
188 Neurowear - **Necomimi**
190 Perfume (Aa-Chan, Kashiyuka, Nocchi), Daito Manabe, Mikiko, Yasutaka Nakata, Satoshi Horii, Hiroyasu Kimura - **Perfume Global Site Project**
192 David Allan Rueter - **The Kuramoto Model (1,000 Fireflies)**
194 Rafael Lozano-Hemmer - **Voice Array**

DIGITAL COMMUNITIES

198 **The Muddy Camps of the Network Society / Die Niederungen der Netzwerk-Gesellschaft** - Statement of the Digital Communities Jury
200 **El Campo de Cebada:** Golden Nica
204 **Refugees United**
206 **Visualizing Palestine**
210 **African Digital Art Network**

212 **Casastristes**
214 **Indian Memory Project**
216 **I Paid a Bribe**
218 **Kyberia**
220 **Labmovel**
222 **Metropolitalia**
224 **NicoNicoGakkai Beta**
226 **Numbeo**
228 **oiga.me**
230 **Seeed Studio**
232 **The East Japan Earthquake Archive**
234 **Aaron Swartz** – Special Mention of the Jury

u19 – CREATE YOUR WORLD

238 **Three Days of Astonishment Jury Minutes: A Declaration of Love to the u19 Generation / Drei Tage des Staunens: Ein Juryprotokoll als Liebeserklärung an die u19-Generation** – Statement of the u19 – CREATE YOUR WORLD Jury
242 Dominik Koller – **Visual:Drumset:** Golden Nica
244 Isidor Dietrich – **Destino / facebook / BluCar / Nur Kreide**
246 HLFS Ursprung – **Soilution – Erde mit Zukunft**
248 Florian Bührle – **Feldversuche**
249 Sasan Hoseini, Arian Hoseini – **Lernprogramme für die Volkschule**
250 Elisabeth Bloder – **A Moving Picture**
251 Johannes Egger, Patrick Maier, Dražen Petrović, Simon Zigala / HTL Anichstraße Innsbruck – **Biogas für Burkina Faso**
252 Simon Stix – **Dictatorship of Perfection**
253 6B des Medienzweigs am BRG/ORG Henriettenplatz, Wien – **Gekommen um zu bleiben: Zur falschen Zeit im falschen Land**
254 4C / BRG Horn – **Kompositur**
255 Gabriel Krög – **Konstruktion eines Fortbewegungsmittels nach dem Vorbild einer Ameise**
256 Lena Sophia Wagner – **Massageschulranzen**
257 Informatikgruppe des BRG7 Kandlgasse – **Modern Media Guide**
258 HBLA für künstlerische Gestaltung Linz – **Schulgedächtnis – Eine interaktive Rauminstallation**
259 Michael Dunkel, Nikolaus Müller, Georg Schneider, Philipp Unger – **stop war—start thinking**

[the next idea] VOESTALPINE ART AND TECHNOLOGY GRANT

262 **Next Ideas** – Statement of the [the next idea] Jury
266 Marcelo Coelho, Skylar Tibbits, Natan Linder, Yoav Reches – **Hyperform:** [the next idea] voestalpine Art and Technology Grant
268 Martin Riddiford, Jim Reeves – **GravityLight**

PRIX ARS ELECTRONICA COLLIDE@CERN RESIDENCY AWARD

272 **Prix Ars Electronica Collide@CERN Residency Award** – Statement of the Collide@CERN Jury

280 Prix Ars Electronica 2013 – Jury
292 Prix Ars Electronica 2013 – Participants

PRIX ARS ELECTRONICA 2013

Quantum
On the Infinity of Data / Von der Unendlichkeit der Daten

Hannes Leopoldseder

If I close my eyes and think back to September 18, 1979, when the first Ars Electronica opened with the Linzer Klangwolke (Cloud of Sound), I can still hear Bruckner's "Eighth Symphony". I remember how an enormous crowd gathered to listen to the music in the Donaupark, and that some of the audience pulled down a glittery balloon that had been sent up for laser projections. I also remember hearing the raspy voice of the robot that gave the opening speech.

Then again, I also have an exact recollection of the shop window I was looking into when John F. Kennedy was murdered in Dallas at 8:30 pm (CET) on Friday, November 22, 1963. And I know where I was standing in the ORF Broadcasting Center in Vienna, where I was the news director, when terrorists attacked the World Trade Center in New York at 3:46 pm (CET) on Tuesday, September 11, 2001. A few minutes later we went on air, a live broadcast that ended up lasting 45 hours. Crucial events and experiences are indelibly imprinted on our minds.

The mind is also a perennial issue at Ars Electronica symposiums. Already in 1979, neurosurgeon Fritz Mundinger from the University of Freiburg gave a talk about computer technology and the brain – and the possibilities, limits and dangers. As Mundinger said: "With computer systems, images of arteries and sections of the brain may also be reconstructed and stored; and physiological data (stimulation response, evoked potentials) that has been obtained through stereotactic surgery, compared."[1]

In October of this year, 34 years after the first Ars Electronica, a significant new phase in data storage will be inaugurated. At this time, the US National Security Agency (NSA) will commence operations at a gigantic data and server complex in Bluffdale, Utah. Over an area of 30,000 m2, there will be servers that can handle massive amounts of information; a capacity of a yottabyte (1YB= 1024 bytes = 1,000,000,000,000,000 gigabytes) is to be reached by 2015. To grasp the dimension of this rather inconceivable computer storage unit, here is the order of these units by size: kilobyte, megabyte, gigabyte, terabyte, petabyte, exabyte, zettabyte and, last but not least, yottabyte.

The objective of this massive storage facility in Utah is to capture, store and analyze every form of

Wenn ich die Augen schließe und mich an die erste Ars Electronica erinnere, die am 18. September 1979 mit der Linzer Klangwolke eröffnet wurde, habe ich den Klang von Bruckners *Achter Sinfonie* im Ohr, ich erinnere mich, dass eine unübersehbare Menschenmenge im Donaupark der Musik lauschte, ein mit einem Laser bestrahlter Spiegelballon vom Publikum heruntergerissen wurde und ich den Roboter mit seiner krächzenden Eröffnungsrede hörte.

Ich erinnere mich aber auch genau an das Schaufenster, in das ich schaute, als John F. Kennedy an einem Freitag, 22. November 1963, um 20.30 in Dallas in Texas ermordet wurde, oder auch daran, an welchem Platz ich als Fernsehintendant im ORF Zentrum in Wien beim Terroranschlag auf das World Trade Center in New York, am Dienstag, 11. September, 15.46 Uhr gestanden bin. Ein paar Minuten später waren wir im TV live auf Sendung, eine Sendung, die 45 Stunden dauern sollte. Entscheidende Ereignisse und persönliche Erlebnisse graben sich tief in unser Gedächtnis ein.

Das Gehirn ist als Thema ein Dauerbrenner bei den Symposien der Ars Electronica. Bereits 1979 referierte der Neurochirurg Fritz Mundinger von der Albert-Ludwigs-Universität, Freiburg im Breisgau, über Computertechnik am Gehirn – Möglichkeiten, Grenzen, Gefahren. Mundinger: „Mit Computersystemen erfolgt auch eine Speicherung und Bildrekonstruktion von Gefäßen und Gehirnabschnitten und der Vergleich von mit der stereotaktischen Operation gewonnenen physiologischen Daten (Reizäußerungen, evozierte Potentiale)".[1]

Im Oktober dieses Jahres, 34 Jahre nach der ersten Ars Electronica, wird ein großer Schritt in der Speicherung von Daten erreicht. Die National Security Agency (NSA) wird in diesem Oktober einen gigantischen Daten-und Serverkomplex in Bluffdale, in Utah, USA, in Betrieb nehmen. Auf einer Fläche von 30.000 Quadratmeter befinden sich Server für Megadaten von einem Yottabyte (1YB = 10 hoch 24 Bytes = 1.000.000.000.000.000 GigaByte), 2015 soll diese Größe erreicht werden. Um diese kaum vorstellbare Speichereinheit begreifen zu können, hier die Reihenfolge nach Größenordnungen: Kilobyte, Megabyte, Gigabyte, Terabyte, Petabyte, Exabyte, Zettabyte und schließlich Yottabyte. Ziel des Megaspeichers in Utah ist es, jede Form von Kommunikation, private Emails, Handygespräche, Suchmaschinen jedwelcher Art, insbesondere Google, geheime Daten aus Wirtschaft und Politik aufzuzeichnen, zu speichern und auszuwerten. Das globale Informationsnetz des Pentagon, der „Global Information Grid", soll bis 2015

die Datenspeicherung auf Yottabytes (1024 Bytes) ausdehnen. Nach einer Analyse von Cisco muss die Speicherkapazität bis 2015 vervierfacht werden.[2]
Gus Hunt, der Technologiechef der CIA, sagte im März dieses Jahres bei einem Hearing: „We try to collect everything and hang on to it forever … It is nearly within our grasp to compute on all human generated information … Technology in this world is moving faster than government or law can keep up. It's moving faster I would argue than you can keep up: You should be asking the question of what are your rights and who owns your data."[3]
Edward Snowden, 30 Jahre, ehemaliger CIA-Mitarbeiter, hat mit seiner Aufdeckung von Prism, dem geheimen Überwachungsprogramm der USA, das Thema der weltweiten Datensammlung in den Vordergrund gerückt. Die USA behandeln ihn als Verbrecher, ihm droht im Falle der Verurteilung die Todesstrafe. Das von der NSA betriebene „Sicherheitsprogramm" Prism ermöglicht die weltweite Datenüberwachung, private Kommunikation, aber auch die Überwachung der Datenströme in allen populären Internetportalen der USA, von Google über Apple bis Microsoft, um nur drei aufzuzählen.
Ist damit Big Brother weltumspannend präsent geworden?
Wie bei jeder Technologie gilt auch bei Big Data: Sie kann zum Guten, aber auch zum Bösen eingesetzt werden. Die Rechenleistung der Computer ist ebenfalls in einem gewaltigen Anstieg.
Der schnellste Supercomputer der Welt wird Ende 2013 in China seinen Betrieb aufnehmen. Das geht aus der halbjährlichen Publikation um das Wettrennen der Supercomputer hervor, die Daten wurden am 17. Juni 2013 anlässlich der Internationalen Supercomputer Conference (ISC) in Leipzig publiziert. Die Nummer 1 ist „Tianhe-2" („Milchstraße 2") und präsentiert sich mit einer Rechenleistung von 33,86 PetaFlops (Billiarden Rechenschritte) pro Sekunde.
Sir Tim Berners-Lee bekannte in *WIRED*, es seien die Daten gewesen, die ihn zum World Wide Web gebracht hätten: „Originally, the acute frustration which led me to invent the World Wide Web in 1989 was all about documents. The frustration was that all kinds of documents were sitting in disks on machines … The WWW design offered a solution, and the world of linked documents exploded dramatically".[4]
In der Forschung verläuft die Entwicklung der Daten noch schneller: Die Sequenzierung von 10.000 Genomen bedeutet eine Datenmenge von 5 Petabyte. Die Datenrevolution vollzieht sich nicht nur in den vorhin angeführten

communication: private emails, mobile phone calls, search engines of all kinds (especially Google), as well as confidential data from the business world and politics. The Pentagon's "Global Information Grid" aims at expanding data storage to yottabytes by 2015. According to a report by Cisco, storage capacity needs to be quadrupled by 2014.[2]
At a hearing in March this year, the CIA's chief technology officer Gus Hunt said: "We try to collect everything and hang on to it forever. (…) It is nearly within our grasp to compute on all human generated information. (…) Technology in this world is moving faster than government or law can keep up. It's moving faster I would argue than you can keep up: You should be asking the question of what are your rights and who owns your data."[3]
Edward Snowden, a 30 year-old former CIA employee, has brought the topic of global data to center stage by exposing Prism, the US's secret surveillance program. The USA has labeled him a criminal and threatens to impose the death penalty if he is convicted. Prism, the NSA operated "security program", not only makes global data surveillance of private communication possible, but also the surveillance of data streams on popular US Internet portals – from Google and Apple to Microsoft, just to mention three.
Does this mean Big Brother is now watching us worldwide?
As with any technology, big data can be used not only to do good but also evil. And computing power is growing tremendously.
In late 2013, the fastest supercomputer in the world will go into operation in China, as could be read in a semi-annual publication on the race for supercomputers: on June 17, 2013, during the International Supercomputing Conference (ISC) in Leipzig, a list of the world's fastest supercomputers was released. Number one is the "Tianhe-2" (aka "Milky Way 2"); it has a processing speed of 33.86 petaflops (a quadrillion or one thousand billion operations per second).
As Sir Tim Berners-Lee explained in *WIRED*, it was the need to exchange data that gave him the idea for the World Wide Web: "Originally, the acute frustration which led me to invent the World Wide Web in 1989 was entirely about documents. The frustration was that all kinds of documents were sitting in disks on machines. (…) The WWW design

offered a solution, and the world of linked documents exploded dramatically."[4]

In the field of research, the development of data is even more rapid: sequencing 10,000 genomes involves a data volume of 5 petabytes. The data revolution is happening not only in these areas, but everywhere – in the life sciences and natural sciences, in our personal lives and thoughts. The data boom has already created a demand for more specialists. According to the consulting firm McKinsey, in five years up to 190,000 experts will be needed to analyze data, as well as about 1.5 million managers to deal with the data, and determine the consequences for products and markets.[5]

The demand for data scientists will be greater than ever before. They will become what quants were on Wall Street over the final decades of the 20th century. As Hal Varian, chief economist at Google, has said: "the sexy job in the next ten years will be statisticians".[6] This new data world will also generate new business models – in Stockholm, for instance, an innovative way of managing traffic has been developed that substantially reduces traveling time in the city center. Big data is also having an ever greater effect on politics.

"From Campaign War Room to Big-Data Broom" was the title of journalist Micah Cohan's report in the *New York Times* on the rapidly growing relevance of data in the political arena, especially prior to elections.[7] For years now, US data specialist Nate Silver has provided the most precise election forecasts; at the same time this mathematician, statistician and journalist has won a fortune at poker. His blog *FiveThirtyEight : Nat Silver's Political Calculus* has brought him a huge fan community, above all among politicians.

With big data, it is like with the advance of digitization into all realms of life. *Der Spiegel* reports in its cover story "Big Data Knows What Your Future Holds" of an incident in Santa Cruz, California, an incident that would have been viewed as merely anecdotal a few years ago: In one of the city's underground parking garages, a policeman observed a thief who was trying to break into a car. Yet before the thief could complete the job, the policeman arrested him. Important in this case is that the police officer had not been there by chance. That morning, a computer program had recommended he go there: an algorithm had

Bereichen, sondern überall, in den Lebenswissenschaften, in den Naturwissenschaften, in unserem Leben und Denken. Der Datenboom benötigt auch Menschen. Laut der Unternehmensberatung McKinsey fehlen in den USA in fünf Jahren bis zu 190.000 Experten für die Analyse von Daten und bis zu 1,5 Millionen Manager, die mit den Daten umgehen und für Produkte und Märkte die entsprechenden Konsequenzen ziehen können.[5]

Datenwissenschafter werden gefragter denn je sein. Sie sind das, was die „Quants" an der Wallstreet in den letzten Jahrzehnten des 20. Jahrhunderts waren. Hal Varian, Chefvolkswirt von Google: „Der attraktivste Job der nächsten zehn Jahre wird Statistiker sein".[6] Die neue Datenwelt wird neue Geschäftsmodelle ermöglichen, in Stockholm ist ein neues Verkehrsmanagement entstanden, durch das sich im Stadtkern die Fahrzeiten wesentlich verringert haben. Immer größer wird die Auswirkung von Big Data auf die Politik.

„From Campaign War Room to Big-Data Broom" titelt der Journalist Micah Cohan in der *New York Times*[7] seinen Bericht über die rapid steigende Relevanz von Daten im politischen Geschehen, insbesondere vor Wahlen. Der amerikanische Datenspezialist Nate Silver weist seit Jahren die präzisesten Wahlprognosen aus, gleichzeitig hat der Mathematiker, Statistiker, Journalist beim Pokern ein Vermögen gewonnen. Sein Blog *FiveThirtyEight : Nat Silver's Political Calculus* sichert ihm eine große Fangemeinde, vor allem unter Politikerinnen und Politikern.

Wie die fortschreitende Digitalisierung alle Lebensbereiche umfasst, so verhält es sich auch mit Big Data. *Der Spiegel* berichtet in seiner Coverstory „Die gesteuerte Zukunft" über ein chronikales Ereignis aus der kalifornischen Stadt Santa Cruz, das vor einigen Jahren noch als reine Anekdote gegolten hätte: In einer Tiefgarage der Stadt beobachtete ein Polizist einen Dieb, der gerade ein Auto knacken wollte. Dazu kam es nicht, der Polizist nahm den Autoknacker fest. Allerdings war der Polizist nicht zufällig an diesem Ort, sondern ein Computerprogramm hatte dies am Vormittag empfohlen: Ein Algorithmus hat errechnet, dass zu diesem Zeitpunkt an diesem Ort die höchste Wahrscheinlichkeit für ein kriminelles Delikt bestehe.[8]

Das Speichern der Mega-Daten ist aber nicht das einzige bestimmende Thema 2013, sondern gerade in diesem Jahr vollzieht sich in nahezu allen Bereichen der digitale Wandel in besonderer Ausprägung. Big Data führt auch zu Big Dog, einem Träger, aber auch einem gefährlichen Kämpfer aus der Werkstatt von Boston Dynamics. Der Roboter trägt 150 Kilo, wohin und zu welchem Zweck

auch immer. Eine Last mit Nahrung in unwirtliches Gebiet oder Dynamit zur Sprengung. Das Unternehmen Boston Dynamics bietet Roboter zu mannigfachen Aufgaben an, für militärische und zivile Zwecke.
Der Ire Noel Sharkey, Professor für Künstliche Intelligenz und Robotik an der Universität Sheffield, zählt zu den profiliertesten Kämpfern gegen Killerroboter. Sharkey startete seinen Feldzug gegen die Roboter 2007, als bereits 4.000 bewaffnete Schlachtfeld-Roboter im Irak stationiert waren. Der US-Kongress setzte sich zum Ziel, bis 2015 ein Drittel des Bodenkampfes mit unbemannten Roboter-Maschinen zu führen. Professor Sharkey führte seinen Kampf unermüdlich weiter. Am 23. April 2013 startete in London die „Campaign to stop Killer Robots", ein Report der Vereinten Nationen (UN) forderte ein globales Moratorium für die tödlichen autonomen Roboter, Waffensysteme, die Ziele auswählen und ohne menschliches Kommando töten können.[9]
Der Krieg mit Drohnen erweckt Abscheu, aber nicht überall, er findet auch Anhänger mit dem Argument: Kein Verlust von Menschenleben, der Pilot im Flugzeug drückt am Bildschirm auf den Knopf, er berührt den Joystick. Pervers: „Joy" heißt Freude und bringt den Tod. Byung-Chul Han, Professor für Philosophie und Kulturwissenschaft an der Universität der Künste in Berlin: „Die gezielte Tötung per Mausklick gleicht einer Menschenjagd, die brutaler und rücksichtsloser ist als die Jagd auf das Wild ... Man ‚spricht' das Wild an, bevor man es tötet. Tötung ohne Ansprache ist Mord."[10]
Roboter verändern nicht nur Kriege, sondern auch viele Bereiche unseres Alltags. Roboter sind und werden allgegenwärtig sein – in Supermärkten kassieren, Autos steuern, Texte schreiben, in Callcenters antworten, automatisch gleich im Handy übersetzen, mit Kindern spielen, Kranken und älteren Menschen Speisen reichen, Haare waschen, Medikamente sortieren, sich von Kindern knuddeln lassen wie Hiroshi Ishiguros *Telenoid* und vieles mehr.
Roboter und Digitalisierung werden unser privates Leben und den Alltag zunehmend verändern, aber auch dokumentieren. Bereits im Zweiten Weltkrieg entwarf Vannevar Bush die Idee eines „Memex"-Gerätes, das als eine Art Speichergerät das Gedächtnis erweitern sollte, Steve Mann filmte sein Leben und stellte es ins Netz, wie beim Ars Electronica Festival 1997 in Linz. Gordon Bell von Microsoft Research führte den analogen Plan von Vannevar Bush digital im Projekt *MyLifeBits* weiter und speicherte sieben Jahre seinen Alltag, mit Schriften, Fotos, Videos, Datum, Uhrzeit und Ort. Die Psychologin

calculated that the likelihood of a crime was greatest at this hour and this location.[8]
Nevertheless, mega data storage is not the only topical issue in 2013. Currently, new forms of digital change are occurring in almost all areas. For instance, big data has produced BigDog, a kind of vehicle and treacherous warrior developed by Boston Dynamics. This robot can move loads weighing up to 150 kilos to whatever destination, for whatever reason. It can transport objects to inhospitable regions and carry dynamite to blow up things. As an engineering company, Boston Dynamics specializes in robots that can do multiple tasks, for both military and civilian purposes.
Noel Sharkey, an Irish professor of artificial intelligence and robotics at the University of Sheffield, is one of the most renowned opponents of killer robots. Sharkey started his campaign against robots in 2007: at the time there were already about 4000 armed battlefield robots stationed in Iraq. The US congress had set itself the goal of making one-third of all ground combat vehicles unmanned robots by 2015. Professor Sharkey has tirelessly fought for a ban. In London, on April 23, 2013, the "Campaign to Stop Killer Robots" was launched; and a United Nations (UN) report called for a global moratorium on lethal autonomous robots – weapon systems that select targets and kill without humans directly issuing commands.[9]
Many people abhor the idea of waging war with drones, but not everyone. Advocates of drones argue that if they are used there is no loss of human life: the pilot of the plane has to just push a button on the screen or touch the joystick. How perverse to use the word "joy" when it brings death! Byung-Chul Han, professor for philosophy and cultural science at Berlin's University of the Arts remarks: "Targeted killing per mouse click is a manhunt more brutal and ruthless than hunting wild game. (...) In German hunting jargon, you "address" your target before killing it. Killing without doing so is murder."[10]
Robots are not only altering wars but also many areas of daily life. They are becoming ever more ubiquitous: one day they will take our cash in supermarkets, drive our cars, write our texts, answer our phones, translate for us on mobile devices, play with our children, deliver food to the sick and elderly, wash our hair, sort our medicines,

allow our kids to cuddle them (as with Hiroshi Ishiguro's *Telenoid*) and much more.
To an ever greater degree, robots and digitization are altering and archiving our personal lives and daily routines. Already during World War Two, Vannevar Bush had envisioned a "memex", a storage device that would extend people's memory. Steve Mann filmed his life and uploaded it to the web, as could be seen at the 1997 Ars Electronica Festival in Linz. Gordon Bell, from Microsoft Research, brought Vannevar Bush's vision to life in his digital project *MyLifeBits*. He stored his life for seven years, saving everything from documents, photos and videos to dates, times and places. Psychologist Sherry Turkle was greatly moved by the day she spent with Gordon Bell while researching for her book *Alone Together*. They looked through his archive – at the letters, e-mails, photos, notebooks, his MIT dissertation and many other things. "Bell", writes Sherry Turkle, "remains an enthusiast of life archiving but admits that it may be having unintended effects. For one thing, he suspects his project may be changing the nature of his memory. Bell describes a lack of curiosity about details of life that he can easily find in his life archive."[11]
As luck would have it, Memoto, a Swedish startup company, is putting its Lifelogging Camera on the market just in time for this year's Ars Electronica, whose theme is *TOTAL RECALL – The Evolution of Memory*: delivery starts in summer 2013 and the pre-order price is USD 279.00. Without needing to turn the camera on or off, it will automatically document your life, snapping a photo every 30 (!) seconds. If you want it to stop the flow of photos, you have to stick the camera into your pocket. The objective is to capture your life in photos. When you connect the camera to your computer, the pictures are automatically uploaded via a special app to Memoto's cloud service, which is being set up specifically for this purpose.
Memoto is another variation of Google Glass. In both cases, the question arises: Is it actually all right to record and store your environment without getting people's consent or should you have to ask each person whether you may photograph them? According to Memoto's founder Martin Källström, this is "the user's business". For him this invention is about finding "a way to re-experience our lives in the future while enjoying the present".[12]

Sherry Turkle verbrachte im Zuge der Recherche zu ihrem Buch *Verloren unter 100 Freunden* einen Tag mit Gordon Bell, der sie sehr bewegte. Sie betrachteten gemeinsam sein Archiv, die Briefe, E-Mails, Fotos, Notizbücher, seine MIT-Doktorarbeit, Briefe seiner Mutter und vieles mehr. „Bell", schreibt Sherry Turkle, „ist ein enthusiastischer Archivar seines Lebens, aber er gesteht ein, dass es unbeabsichtigte Nebenwirkungen haben könnte. So vermutet er zum Beispiel, dass sein Projekt das Wesen seines Gedächtnisses verändern könnte. Er beobachtet bei sich eine mangelnde Neugier auf Einzelheiten seines Lebens, die er mühelos im Archiv finden könnte."[11]
Durch Zufall kommt 2013, gerade recht zum Ars Electronica Thema *TOTAL RECALL – The Evolution of Memory* die Memoto Lifelogging Camera des schwedischen Startup-Unternehmens Memoto auf den Markt, Auslieferung Sommer 2013, Pre-order USD 279,00. Die Kamera dokumentiert automatisch den Alltag, ohne Ein-und-Ausschalten, die Kamera knipst alle 30 (!) Sekunden ein Bild, will man die Kamera abstellen, kann man sie nur in die Tasche stecken. Ziel ist es: das eigene Leben in Bildern festhalten. Über PC-Anschluss werden die Bilder durch eine spezielle Software in die eigens eingerichtete Memoto-Cloud gestellt.
Memoto ist eine andere Variante der Google-Brille. In beiden Fällen erhebt sich die Frage: Lässt sich die eigene Umwelt tatsächlich ohne Zustimmung speichern oder sollte jeweils bei Personen nachgefragt werden: Darf ich Sie fotografieren? Der Gründer von Memoto, Martin Källström: „Das ist Sache der Nutzer ... mir geht es darum, einen Weg zu finden, unser Leben in der Zukunft erneut zu erleben und dabei die Gegenwart zu genießen".[12]
Das Jahr 2013 ist auf dem Weg, das Jahr von Google zu werden. Die Digitalisierung des Wissens schreitet bei Google, trotz einzelner Rückschläge, von Jahr zu Jahr voran. Die Österreichische Nationalbibliothek ist an der Digitalisierung von Büchern sehr interessiert. Das Ziel von Generaldirektorin Johanna Rachinger: 2025 soll alles, zumindest die Mehrheit der Bücher online zugänglich sein. Besonders positiv zu bewerten ist, dass die Bücher nicht nur digitalisiert, sondern gleichzeitig per Texterkennungsprogramm erfasst werden, sodass sie durch ein Suchprogramm leicht zugänglich sind.
Die Digitalisierung verändert zunehmend den traditionellen Buchhandel durch E-Books und Self-Publishing, die deutschsprachigen Verlage haben die Geschwindigkeit des Wandels unterschätzt, nach 200 Jahren stellt Bertelsmann den *Brockhaus* ein. Im Feuilleton

von *FAZ-Online* vom 11. Juni 2013 liest es sich so: „Aus für *Brockhaus* – keine gedruckte Ausgabe mehr, Online-Aktualisierungen noch sechs Jahre, 300 Angestellte weniger: der Brockhaus gibt den Druck auf".[13] Der *Brockhaus* hat 200 Jahre die europäische Geschichte begleitet, Dichter, Schriftsteller und Denker, zwei Weltkriege überlebt, war aber letztlich nicht gerüstet für die Digitalisierung und ist an einem weltweiten digitalen Gratislexikon gescheitert. Vielen Printprodukten wird dieser radikale Medienbruch in den kommenden Jahrzehnten bevorstehen, es sei denn, sie setzen noch rechtzeitig kreative digitale Initiativen.

Die Websuche heißt bei den Usern seit langem einfach „googeln", seit 2004 gibt es das Verb auch im Duden. Dazu im Web Google Chrome und die Google Toolbar. Als Medien weist Google Folgende auf: Books, Bildersuche, News und Picasa. Unter Geo finden wir Google Earth und Panoramio, Fotos aus aller Welt. Die Spezialsuche führt zu Blogs, Scholar (wissenschaftliche Artikeln), Alerts. Kommunikation & Kooperation: Docs, Kalender, Übersetzer, Cloud Print, Gmail. Soziale Funktionen: Blogger, Groups, Hangouts.

Zu diesen Internetangeboten kommt 2013 das Experiment „Project Loon" – ein Ring von mehr als 1.000 Ballonen soll die Erde umrunden und vor allem den Menschen, die keinen Internetzugang haben, einen Netzempfang ermöglichen. Im Vordergrund steht „Google Glass", das voraussichtlich bahnbrechendste Medienprojekt seit langem – oder einer der größten Flops. Es braucht hier nicht mehr beschrieben werden, da seit Monaten eine weltweite Mediencoverage das Projekt erläutert, diskutiert, kritisiert. Ob Google Glass von Beginn an funktioniert, ist nicht von primärer Bedeutung, vielleicht funktioniert die Datenbrille nach einigen Jahren.

Das Entscheidende ist der transhumanistische Aspekt: Die Verschmelzung von Realem und Virtuellem. Zwei Menschen, über Kontinente getrennt, machen einen Klick und können dasselbe sehen. Für die Transhumanisten beginnt der Weg bei der Datenbrille und endet mit dem Biochip-Implantat im Gehirn, also mit direktem Anschluss im Cyberspace.

Damit beginnt eine neue Ära, eine Ära, die in der Literatur schon vielfach beschrieben wurde, von H.G. Wells, Julian Huxley, Ernst Jünger, Hans Morawec, Ray Kurzweil. Dan Brown hat als Bestsellerautor 200 Millionen Bücher verkauft. Diese Zahl wurde anlässlich der spektakulären Buchpremiere von *Inferno* am 14. Mai 2013 bekanntgegeben. Es ist bemerkenswert, dass in diesem Roman – der von den Kritikern des Feuilletons insgesamt wenig

2013 is on its way to becoming a Google year. Despite a few setbacks, the digitization of knowledge at Google is progressing from year to year. The Austrian National Library is particularly interested in digitizing books. General director Johanna Rachinger's goal: to make all the library's holdings – or at least the majority of its books – available online by 2025. Particularly positive here is that the books are not only to be digitized, but text recognition programs will be introduced that make them easy to access via search engines.

With e-books and self-publishing, digitization is radically altering the traditional book trade. German-language publishers underestimated the speed at which things were changing and so, after 200 years, Bertelsmann is discontinuing its prestigious *Brockhaus Encyclopedia*. In the feuilleton of *FAZ-Online* from June 11, 2013, this event was described as follows: "Over for *Brockhaus* – no more printed editions; online updates available for six more years only; 300 employees on their way out: *Brockhaus* to discontinue print version."[13] The *Brockhaus* has accompanied 200 years of European history, poets, writers and thinkers, survived two World Wars, but was ultimately not equipped for digitization and missed the boat when it came to establishing a worldwide digital encyclopedia, free of charge. Many print products are bound to face a similar fate in the coming decades, that is, unless they succeed in launching creative digital initiatives in time.

For ages now, when users search the web, they say they have "googled"; and since 2004 it has been an official verb in Duden dictionary (for the German language, the equivalent of Webster's or Oxford Dictionary; "to google" was added to these two in 2006). Online there is also Google Chrome and Google Toolbar. As media, Google now has the following categories: Books, Images, News and Picasa, among others. Under Geo Tools we find, e.g., Google Earth and Panoramio/Photos of the World. More specialized searches lead to Blogs, Scholar (with scientific articles) and Alerts; searches related to communications and cooperation lead to Docs, Calendar, Translator, Cloud Print and Gmail; and those related to social functions to Blogger, Groups and Hangouts.

In addition to these Internet services, in 2013, Google launched the experiment "Project Loon" –

a network of more than 1000 balloons that are to circle the earth and provide Internet access to those who have none. At the center of attention is "Google Glass", presumably one of the most groundbreaking media projects – or greatest flops – in ages. There's no need to describe it here, as for months now, the project has been explained, discussed and criticized in the media worldwide. Whether Google Glass works right away is not of major importance; it may, in fact, take several years before these data glasses actually work.
Decisive here is the transhumanist aspect: the fusion of real and virtual worlds. Two people, separated on different continents, can see the same thing at the click of a mouse. For transhumanists, it all starts with data glasses and ends with biochip implants in the brain – in other words, with a direct connection into cyberspace.
This is the start of a new era, one that has often been described in literature by authors like H.G. Wells, Julian Huxley, Ernst Jünger, Hans Morawec and Ray Kurzweil. Dan Brown is a best-selling author and has sold over 200 million books. This sales figure was announced at the spectacular premiere of *Inferno*, Brown's latest book, on May 14, 2013. Noteworthy here is that the protagonist of the novel – which critics across the board have either hardly appreciated or torn apart – is dedicated to transhumanism.
Stefan Sorgner, professor of medical ethics at the University of Erlangen-Nurnberg, is considered an expert for "new media ethics". This committed transhumanist sees the "brain pacemaker" as a further development of the "cardiac pacemaker". With its aid, it would be possible to treat Parkinson and depression more successfully. In an interview with Judith Innerhofer in *Die Zeit*, Sorgner added: "In the future, after a stroke, we may be able to replace parts of the brain with neural implants. Potential scenarios include everything from mind uploading to outsourcing of brain content to digital storage media (...) If needed, brain implants could be used to acquire a new foreign language or as a way to extend memory with access to knowledge online."[14]
While these ideas are frightening for some, others feel they will be able to reconcile themselves with them. In any case, one thing is clear: whether these visions become a partial or complete reality,

geschätzt bis verrissen wurde – der Protagonist dem Transhumanismus verpflichtet ist.
Stefan Sorgner, Professor für Medizinethik an der Universität Erlangen-Nürnberg, gilt als Experte für „ Ethik der Neuen Medien". Der bekennende Transhumanist sieht nach dem Herzschrittmacher als Weiterführung den „Hirnschrittmacher", mit dessen Hilfe bei der Behandlung von Parkinson und Depressionen große Erfolge erzielt werden könnten. Sorgner weiter in einem *Die Zeit*-Interview mit Judith Innerhofer: „Zukünftig können wir vielleicht Teile des Gehirns nach einem Schlaganfall durch neuronale Implantate ersetzen. Die Szenarien gehen dann bis zu Mind Uploading, also zu der Auslagerung unserer Gehirninhalte auf digitale Speichermedien ... Solche Medien könnten sich etwa nutzen lassen, um bei Bedarf eine neue Fremdsprache zu beherrschen oder auch als eine erweiterte Form des Gedächtnisses mit Zugriff auf das Wissen im Netz."[14]
Diese Vorstellungen sind für die einen erschreckend, andere wiederum können sich wohl mit diesen Gedankengängen anfreunden. Eines steht jedenfalls fest: Auch bei diesen Visionen, sollten sie teilweise oder ganz Wirklichkeit werden, sind Daten und Speicher eine der entscheidendsten Voraussetzungen.
„Quantum" wird für viele Begriffe verwendet: in der Wissenschaft, z. B. in der Astronomie, oder in der Spieleindustrie, z. B. als Firmenname. Ich möchte den Begriff „Quantum" als lateinischen Begriff benützen, hier heißt *quantum* einfach „wie viel". Wie viel Daten wird die Menschheit in diesem Jahrhundert benötigen, wenn das Wachstum so enorm ist wie in den letzten Jahren? Ist die Datenwelt ausdehnbar ins Unendliche, das durch keine Ziffer ausdrückbar ist außer durch das vom englischen Mathematiker John Wallis 1655 eingeführte Unendlichsymbol? Das Unendliche bleibt der direkten menschlichen Erfahrung unzugänglich.

1 Fritz Mundinger, *Ars Electronica Katalog 1979*, S. 38

2 James Bamford, The black box. Inside America's massive new surveillance centre, in: *WIRED*, 15.03.20123.

3 Gus Hunt on big data. In: *www.huffingtonpost.com/2013/03/20*

4 Tim Berners-Lee, Raw data, now! In: *WIRED*, 9. 11. 2012, *www.webfoundation.org/about/Sir-tim-berners-lee/*

5 Bernd Müller, Der ungehobene Schatz, in: *Technology Review* 3/2013, S. 72.

6 Hal Varian, *www.zeit.de/2013/02/Big-Data,seite-2*

7 Micah Cohen, From Compaign War Room to Big-Data Broom, In: *New York Times*, 10. Juni 2013

8 *Der Spiegel*, 20/2013, S.69

9 *www.stopkillerrobots.org*

10 Byung-Chul Han, Clausewitz im Drohnenkrieg, in: *Die Zeit*, 2012/47, S. 60

11 Sherry Turkle: *Verloren unter 100 Freunden. Wie wir in der digitalen Welt verkümmern*, 2012 München, S. 504.

12 *http://memoto.co* ; *Der Spiegel*, 18/2013, S. 111

13 *www.faz.net/aktuell/feuilleton/buecher*, 11. 06. 2013

14 *www.zeit.de/2013/20/transhumansismus-philosoph-stefan-sorgner*

a vital prerequisite for them, too, is data and how it is stored.

"Quantum" is used to designate many things: in science, e.g. astronomy, or for company names and products of the game industry. I would like to use the term "quantum" as it is used in Latin, where it simply means "how much". How much data are humans going to need in this century if growth continues at the same rate as it has over the past years? Can the data world be extended to infinity, which cannot be expressed by a number but only by the symbol introduced by the English mathematician John Wallis in 1655? No matter how things turn out, infinity will remain inaccessible to direct human experience.

1) Fritz Mundinger, *Ars Electronica Katalog 1979*, p. 38

2) James Bamford, "The black box. Inside America's massive new surveillance centre", in *WIRED*, March 30, 2012: *http://www.wired.co.uk/magazine/archive/2012/05/features/the-black-box*

3) "CIA's Gus Hunt on Big Data": *www.huffingtonpost.com/2013/03/20*

4) Tim Berners-Lee, "Raw data, now!" In *WIRED*, Nov. 9, 2012; *www.webfoundation.org/about/Sir-tim-berners-lee/*

5 Bernd Müller, "Der ungehobene Schatz", in *Technology Review* 3/2013, p. 72

6 Hal Varian, "The McKinsey Quarterly", January 2009: *http://www.mckinsey.com/insights/innovation/hal_varian_on_how_the_web_challenges_managers*

7 Micah Cohen, "From Campaign War Room to Big-Data Broom", in *New York Times*, June 19, 2013

8 "Living by the Numbers: Big Data Knows What Your Future Holds", Martin U. Müller, Marchel Rosenbach and Thomas Schulz, in *Der Spiegel Online International*: *http://www.spiegel.de/international/business/big-data-enables-companies-and-researchers-to-look-into-the-future-a-899964.html*

9 *www.stopkillerrobots.org* (accessed on July 4, 2013)

10 Byung-Chul Han, "Clausewitz im Drohnenkrieg", in *Die Zeit*, 2012/47, p. 60

11 Sherry Turkle: *Alone Together. Why We Expect More from Technology and Less from Each Other*, New York: 2011, p. 504

12 *http://memoto.co*; *Der Spiegel Online International*, May 3, 2013: *http://www.spiegel.de/international/europe/new-memoto-mini-camera-captures-life-in-30-second-snippets-a-897900.html*

13 *FAZ*, June 11, 2013: *http://www.faz.net/aktuell/feuilleton/buecher/themen/bertelsmann-gibt-lexikonsparte-auf-aus-fuer-brockhaus-12218510.html*

14 *http://www.zeit.de/2013/20/transhumanismus-philosoph-stefan-lorenz-sorgner*

Prix Ars Electronica 2013

Christine Schöpf

The Prix Ars Electronica, which was launched by ORF's Upper Austrian Regional Studio as a competition for computer art in 1987, proved from the start to be an enterprise with great potential. Already in its first years, it brought together different discipline—computer animation, computer graphics and computer music—and back then this was a completely new concept. Another quality involved its openness towards achievements from what were diverse and largely separate fields, such as science and research, and art and entertainment. Moreover, almost immediately it became clear that the Prix Ars Electronica had to be open to future developments. It had to be possible to introduce new categories as well as terminate others whose potential whose potential was no longer evident?

Today, in the 27th edition of Prix Ars Electronica, there are a total of seven (!) competition categories. Some of them have been fundamentally modified over the years, others are entirely new. In 1990, for instance, the category Interactive Art was introduced. And in 2004, with the rise of social media, the category www, which had been established in 1995, became Digital Communities. Computer Music was turned into Digital Musics in 1999 and then renamed Digital Musics & Sound Art in 2010. In 1998, a new category was set up with the u19 prize—for young people under 19. In 2004, another category was added: [the next idea]—voestalpine Art and Technology Grant, as a catchall for future-oriented concepts; and Hybrid Art, which was launched in 2007, as a category open to new forms of presentation, and with an emphasis on new projects resulting from collaborations between art, science and research. The most recent category, Collide@CERN, was established in 2011: it is an artist residency program at CERN, the European Organization for Nuclear Research, and the Ars Electronica Futurelab.

Der vom ORF-Landestudio Oberösterreich 1987 als Wettbewerb für Computerkunst gestartete Prix Ars Electronica erwies sich von Beginn an als ein Unternehmen mit Zukunftspotenzial. Bereits in den ersten Jahren vereinte er unterschiedliche Disziplinen – Computeranimation, Computergrafik und Computermusik –, was damals ein völlig neues Konzept darstellte. Ein weiteres Charakteristikum war die Offenheit für Leistungen aus unterschiedlichen und damals weitgehend getrennten Bereichen wie Wissenschaft und Forschung, Kunst und Entertainment. Darüber hinaus war von Anfang an klar, dass der Prix Ars Electronica auch offen auf zukünftige Entwicklungen reagieren sollte. Die Einführung neuer Kategorien sollte möglich sein, andere Kategorien, deren Potenzial nicht mehr schlüssig war, sollten beendet werden können.

Heute, also mit der 27. Ausgabe des Wettbewerbs, gibt es insgesamt sieben (!) Wettbewerbssparten, einige sind im Lauf der Jahre von Grund auf verändert worden, andere neu dazugekommen. 1990 wurde die Kategorie Interaktive Kunst eingeführt. Die 1995 begonnene Kategorie www wurde mit dem Aufkommen von Social Media 2004 zu Digital Communities, Computermusik wurde 1999 in Digital Musics und 2010 in Digital Musics &Sound Art umformuliert. Eine neue Sparte wurde 1998 mit dem u19-Jugendpreis für Unter-19-Jährige eingeführt. Ebenso neu dazu kamen 2004 [the next idea] – voestalpine Art and Technology Grant als Sammelbecken für zukunftsorientierte Ideenkonzepte und 2007 Hybrid Art als die Kategorie, die zum einen offen ist für neue Formen der Präsentation, vor allem aber das Augenmerk auf jene neuen Projekte richtet, die aus Kooperationen von Kunst, Wissenschaft und Forschung resultieren. Die jüngste, 2011 gestartete Kategorie ist „collide@CERN", ein Residency-Programm für Künstler am CERN, der Europäischen Organisation für Kernforschung, und im Ars Electronica Futurelab.

Warum dieser Blick zurück? Er soll verdeutlichen, dass der Prix Ars Electronica bereits in seiner Konzeption und seit seiner ersten Ausgabe ein Unternehmen ist, das sich der rapiden Entwicklung in der digitalen Kultur gestellt hat und dies über die Jahre auch kontinuierlich weiterverfolgt hat. Wie wohl kein anderer Wettbewerb liefert er in der Summe seiner jährlichen Ergebnisse von Anfang an ein aktuelles Abbild des Ist-Standes in den unterschiedlichen Kulturen und Gesellschaften.

4071 Projekte aus 73 Ländern wurden 2013 zum Wettbewerb eingereicht. Die Hauptpreise – das sind die Goldenen Nicas – gehen diesmal an Künstler und Künstlerinnen aus Kanada, Italien, der Türkei, der Schweiz, Spanien, Belgien und Österreich sowie der [the next idea] – voestalpine Art and Technology Grant an vier Visionäre aus Brasilien, den USA und Israel. Insgesamt € 117.000 gibt es in diesem Jahr an Preisgeldern.

Das langjährige Bestehen des Prix Ars Electronica wird kontinuierlich durch die öffentliche Hand wie auch durch Sponsoren aus der Wirtschaft gesichert. Unser Dank gilt vor allem der Stadt Linz, die seit 1979 das Festival Ars Electronica, den Prix Ars Electronica und das Ars Electronica Center finanziell trägt. Ebenso danken wir dem Land Oberösterreich für die kontinuierliche Unterstützung. Ein Sponsor der ersten Stunde ist die voestalpine, in den letzten Jahren mit der finanziellen Ausstattung des [the next idea] voestalpine Art and Technology Grant. Weiters danken wir Casinos Austria, Cubus, Cultur Contact Austria, Sony DAC und Linz AG für die langjährige Unterstützung und Kooperation.

Dokumentiert werden die Ergebnisse des Prix Ars Electronica alljährlich beim Ars Electronica Festival in Ausstellungen und Symposien, über das vorliegende Buch, die DVD und online über das Ars-Electronica-Archiv. Auch in internationalen Ausstellungen sind die Ergebnisse des jährlichen Prix Ars Electronica über den aktuellen Anlass hinaus einzusehen.

Why review all this? To illuminate the fact that, since its conception and very first edition, the Prix Ars Electronica has been an undertaking that has confronted and pursued the rapid development of digital culture over time. Unlike any other competition, the results taken as a whole provide an up-to-date picture of where things stand in very different cultures and societies each year.

4071 projects from 73 countries were submitted to the competition in 2013. The main awards—that is, the Golden Nicas in each category—are going this year to artists from Canada, Italy, Turkey, Switzerland, Spain, Belgium and Austria. The [the next idea]—voestalpine Art and Technology Grant has been awarded to four visionaries from Brazil, the USA and Israel. The prize money will total 117,000 euros in 2013.

The Prix Ars Electronica has been made possible by continuous funding from public facilities and institutions as well as sponsors from the industry. Above all our thanks go to the City of Linz, which since 1979, has financially backed the Ars Electronic Festival, Prix Ars Electronica, and the Ars Electronica Center. We are also grateful to the Province of Upper Austria for its untiring support. voest alpine has been a sponsor since day one, and in recent years has also funded [the next idea] voestalpine Art and Technology Grant. Last but not least our thanks go to Casinos Austria, Cubus, Cultur Contact Austria, Sony DAC and Linz AG for their years of support and cooperation.

Each year the winners of the Prix Ars Electronica are showcased in exhibitions and symposiums at the Ars Electronica Festival, as well as in this book, the accompanying DVD and online in the AEC archive. Following the annual events in Linz, the results of the Prix Ars Electronica 2013 will also be presented at international exhibitions.

COMPUTER ANIMATION / FILM / VFX

A Quarter Past Human

Tomek Bagiński, Chris Bregler, Suzanne Buchan, David O'Reilly, Anezka Sebek

Each of the subcategories of the notably expansive Computer Animation/Film/VFX category brings its own set of complexities and features, which are increasingly blending and merging with the others—perhaps unsurprisingly, almost all the works we saw used digital techniques to a greater or lesser degree. Computer animation is close to achieving its aspiration of being more real than real, and as such is moving towards visual effects, which are becoming increasingly "naturalized"; both can also be described as "animation we are not supposed to see." And even if the results aim to appear like a pre-digital "pure" animation film made with tangible media, they remain identified by tendencies towards narrative sensitivity and non-narrative, playful abstraction that, at their core, transmute human nature and experience. Hence this jury statement's title, which borrows from T. J. Bass's 1971 sci-fi novel about cultural genetics *Half Past Human*, where the human feeds the machine; in this Prix Ars category, the human still prevails over technology.

We observed some trends and developments in this year's submissions, and across all three modes it is clear that "state of the art" ain't what it used to be. Along with the push for realism, a persistent emergence of abstraction is changing what is "new." One example is the translation of very complex data sets into understandable, aesthetic and highly conceptual forms. The depiction of abstract forms in so many of the entries suggests a shift of form into conceptual art, a trend we can also observe with today's students, who are also trying to make sense of big data. On an arts-political level, because of processing and algorithmic data visualization processes, computer graphics and VFX tools are becoming more democratic and accessible, similar to what machinima and games engines made possible on a different aesthetic, one could say derivative, level.

This year saw more conceptual abstract animation from independent and emerging artists, previously the domain of established individuals and wealthy companies. While animation is usually understood as a mimetic-arts-based mode of film that focuses on storytelling, this year the "stories" were less narrative and anthropomorphically centered, and more about states of perception beyond "normal" and the life of "things," whether objects from the world or digitally created. There was a noticeable

Die Subkategorien der bemerkenswert expansiven Kategorie Computeranimation/Film/VFX haben je eigene Komplexitäten und Merkmale, die sich zunehmend mit anderen Kategorien vermischen und überschneiden; es überrascht vermutlich nicht, dass bei fast allen Arbeiten, die wir gesehen haben, in mehr oder minder großem Ausmaß digitale Techniken verwendet wurden. Die Computeranimation ist nahe daran, ihre Ambition, realer als die Realität zu sein, zu verwirklichen und nähert sich den Visuellen Effekten an, die zunehmend „naturalisiert" sind; man könnte beide auch als „Animationen, die wir nicht als solche wahrnehmen sollen" beschreiben. Und selbst wenn die Ergebnisse wie prädigitale „reine" Animationsfilme wirken wollen, die mit tangiblen Medien hergestellt wurden, bleiben sie durch Tendenzen zu narrativer Sensibilität und nicht-narrativer, verspielter Abstraktion erkennbar, die im Kern darauf abzielen, die menschliche Natur und Erfahrungswelt zu verwandeln. Daher der Titel dieses Statements der Jury, der an T. J. Bass' Science-Fiction-Roman *Half Past Human* (dt. Titel: *Die Ameisenkultur*) über kulturelle Genetik angelehnt ist, in dem der Mensch der Maschine ausgeliefert ist; in dieser Kategorie des Prix Ars Electronica hat der Mensch die Technologie noch im Griff.

Bei den diesjährigen Einreichungen waren einige Trends und Entwicklungen zu beobachten, wobei sich in allen drei Subkategorien deutlich zeigte, dass der „State of the Art" neu definiert wird. Neben einer Tendenz zu Realismus verändert die Omnipräsenz von Abstraktion die Definition dessen, was „neu" ist. Ein Beispiel dafür ist die Übersetzung sehr komplexer Datensätze in verständliche ästhetische und höchst konzeptuelle Formen. Die Darstellung abstrakter Formen in so vielen Einreichungen verweist auf einen Paradigmenwechsel hin zu konzeptueller Kunst, ein Trend, der sich auch bei heutigen Studenten beobachten lässt, die versuchen, den großen Datenmengen Sinn zu verleihen. Auf kunstpolitischer Ebene werden Computergrafik und VFX-Tools durch algorithmische Datenvisualisierungsprozesse demokratischer und leichter zugänglich, eine Entwicklung, die vergleichbar ist mit dem, was Machinima und Spiel-Engines auf einer anderen, man könnte sagen derivativen ästhetischen Ebene ermöglichten.

In diesem Jahr wurden mehr konzeptuelle abstrakte Animationen, die früher als Domäne etablierter Künstler und finanzkräftiger Firmen galten, von freischaffenden jungen Künstlern eingereicht. Während die Animation im Allgemeinen als eine auf den nachahmenden Künsten basierende Filmkunst verstanden wird, bei der das Geschichtenerzählen im Vordergrund steht, waren die „Geschichten“ dieses Jahr weniger narrativ und anthropomorph zentriert, sie handelten eher von Wahrnehmungsweisen abseits „des Normalen“ und vom Leben der „Dinge“, seien es reale Gegenstände oder digital kreierte. Weiters war eine bemerkenswerte Nostalgie nach alten Materialien, historischen Medien und Techniken zu beobachten, die mithilfe neuer Technologien verwandelt oder ironisch adaptiert wurden. Animierte Kurzfilme leiden, ungeachtet ihrer Thematik, nach wie vor unter einer gewissen Erwartungshaltung des Publikums, das Humor voraussetzt. Während einige Künstler nach wie vor „lustige“ Filme machen, gab es andere, die den Spaß auf eine neue Ebene hoben und unkonventionelle narrative Strukturen verwendeten.

Wir prüften eine sehr heterogene Zusammenstellung von 144 Filmen, die aus insgesamt – 775 eingereichten Filmen ausgewählt wurden – von experimentellen Arbeiten, Installationen und Werbespots bis hin zu Promoversionen von Spielen und Puppentrickfilmen. Einige Jurymitglieder waren überrascht über die wenigen Einreichungen seitens bekannter Vertreter der drei Subkategorien; anderen fiel die bescheidene Anzahl von qualitativ hochwertigen, Gaming-orientierten oder kommerziellen Arbeiten auf. Interessanterweise war die Mehrheit der ausgewählten Arbeiten experimenteller Art. Dies eröffnete einen diskursiven Raum für unsere Debatten, weil experimentelle Arbeiten den Balanceakt meistern, Regeln zu brechen und sie durch neue zu ersetzen, was, wenn es funktioniert, faszinierende Resultate zeitigt.

In dieser Kategorie, die unsere Vorstellungen und Gefühle auf dem Bildschirm darstellen kann, spiegeln sich in den jährlichen Einreichungen auch die Ängste der Gegenwart, in jüngerer Zeit etwa Klimawechsel, Krieg, globale Migration und Entfremdung der Jugendlichen. Statt solche Ängste in Geschichte und Subjektivität eingebettet zu sehen, entdeckten wir – insbesondere bei den CG-Arbeiten, ob sie nun auf Realismus abzielten oder nicht – eine Tendenz zu objektiver Exaktheit – vielleicht ein Ausdruck der Resignation. So bemerkte beispielsweise ein Juror, dass der Film *Forms*, so schön und bewegend er ist, auch eine an Riefenstahl erinnernde Glorifizierung sowohl der absoluten Perfektion menschlicher Bewegung als auch der Künstler im Stil des 21. Jahrhunderts ist, die durch die kühle Präzision der Daten und der Spitzentechnologie erzielt wurde. Andere von uns ausgewählte Einreichungen verwendeten ähnliche ästhetische Techniken, um eine konfuse Welt, die von Chaos und Kontrollmanie beherrscht ist und den Menschen keine Atempause lässt, zum Ausdruck zu bringen.

nostalgia for old materials, historical media and techniques that were transformed or ironized using new technologies. Animated shorts are still hampered by an audience expectation of humor, regardless of the subject matter. While artists continue to make “funny” films, there were a number that took funny into nuances of other areas of (human) concerns that made use of unconventional narrative structures.

We screened a very heterogeneous mix of 144 films pre-selected from a total of 775 films submitted, from experimental works, installations and adverts to games promos and puppet animation. Some of the jury were surprised at the lack of entries from well-known exponents of the three subcategories; others noticed the modest number of high-quality games-oriented or commercial works. Interestingly, the majority of the selection we worked with was experimental in nature. This made our task more discursive, because experimental works walk the difficult line of breaking rules and making new ones in their place, and when it works it can achieve compelling results.

In this prize category, which can depict what we imagine and feel *on screen*, contemporary anxieties are sometimes reflected in the overall annual submissions—recently this has been climate change, war, global migration and youth alienation. Instead of seeing such humane concerns embedded in story and subjectivity, we detected a shift towards clinical exactitude—perhaps as an expression of—especially in the CG works, whether they were aiming for realism or not. For instance, as beautiful and moving as it is, one juror observed that *Forms* is also a 21st century Riefenstahlesque glorification of both the absolute perfection of human movement and of the artists who made it, using the precision of cold data and high-end machines. Others we chose used similar aesthetics to express confusion of the world around us as chaotic, controlling and with no respite for the human.

A jury has the obvious goal of agreeing which works deserve awards, which of course is brutal by nature as most films will not be selected. Our result is not exactly what the best films are for an individual, but what a collective mind can agree upon. The varied backgrounds of the jury were a healthy mix of writers, teachers and practitioners with expertise in a range of commercial,

experimental and independent fields. But all of us are film lovers, and we were surprisingly in unison on many decisions, and open for discussion if not. Conversations were interspersed with exquisite observation, interjected pleas, and made pleasurable with delectable irony.
Supported by our jury's dedicated and talented Ars team, we quickly agreed a main criterion; that if a film can touch one's emotion, aesthetic senses, intellect and/or sense of humour (or any number of other things) it can be said to "work". We also decided that decisions were to be based purely on a work's merit, and not on an artist's background, art world position or production context. We first watched all works, and if one of the five members wanted a film to be considered it was kept. In a second round of this refined selection, we had in-depth discussions about each work's qualities; this was the stage where very worthy projects were excluded. Our most intense debates were during the first two days, which meant that the final decisions were for the most part unanimous, if not democratically decided.
The crux of the jury process this time pivoted on permeable distinctions between each juror's personal sensitivities and professional priorities. A few of us agreed that perhaps this lies in innate basic differences in disciplines of art and design, where art explores problems and conditions of the human and design attempts to solve those problems. For the latter, low tech and media archaeology are not always honored, whereas sleekness and savvy technology are. At the arts end, admiration is due to complex and perhaps so-called difficult works that address preverbal thought and emotions that are not easily expressed through logos and technology, and pay homage to the histories of the practice continuum they are part of (hence the "-esque" in some award texts). Our final selection included a number of works that elegantly walked both these lines.

Eine Jury hat die Aufgabe, sich darauf zu einigen, welche Arbeiten Auszeichnungen verdienen, was per definitionem etwas Brutales an sich hat, da die meisten Filme nicht in die engere Auswahl kommen. Unser Ergebnis sagt nichts darüber aus, welcher Film einem einzelnen Juror am besten gefallen hat, sondern auf welche Einreichung sich ein Kollektiv einigen konnte. Die Jury setzte sich aus Mitgliedern mit unterschiedlichen beruflichen Hintergründen zusammen und umfasste Autoren, Lehrer und Experten mit Kenntnissen in einer Reihe kommerzieller, experimenteller und unabhängiger Bereiche – gemeinsam ist uns allen, dass wir Filmliebhaber sind. Wir waren uns in unseren Entscheidungen überraschend oft einig und offen für Diskussionen, wenn dies nicht der Fall war. Die Gespräche waren aufgelockert durch Beobachtungen, Plädoyers und von feiner Ironie durchsetzt.
Eine zentrale Aufgabe im Rahmen des Auswahlverfahrens war diesmal eine nachvollziehbare Differenzierung zwischen den persönlichen Präferenzen und den beruflichen Prioritäten der einzelnen Juroren. Einige von uns kamen zu dem Schluss, dass diese Schwierigkeit in den grundlegenden Unterschieden zwischen den Disziplinen Kunst und Design begründet ist. Während die Kunst Probleme und Bedingungen des Menschseins zu ergründen sucht, versucht Design, solche Probleme zu lösen. Bei Design werden Lowtech und Medienarchäologie generell nicht geschätzt, Glätte und intelligente Technologie hingegen sehr wohl. In der Kunst favorisiert man komplexe und sogenannte schwierige Arbeiten, die Emotionen und präverbale Gedanken aufgreifen, welche durch den Logos und die Technologie nicht ausgedrückt werden können und eine Hommage an die Geschichte und das Kontinuum der Praxis sind, in die sie eingebunden sind (daher die Verweise auf andere Künstler in einigen Texten zu den Preisen). Unsere endgültige Auswahl beinhaltet eine Reihe von Arbeiten, die sich elegant auf beiden Ebenen bewegten.

GOLDENE NICA

Forms

Quayola, Memo Akten

Der durch seine Eleganz bestechende Animationsfilm *Forms* von Memo Akten und Davide Quagliola alias Quayola ist eine nicht narrative, emotional bewegende Abstraktion kinetischer Bewegungen. Seine Stärken sind die Gestaltung von etwas Schönem mit Effekten, die wie Motion Capture wirken, aber keine sind, und die gelungene Verbindung von Präzision und Überraschung, die mit Algorithmen und proprietären Programmen in der CG-Animation so selten gelingt. Seine Verdienste liegen in der puren Ästhetik von Bewegung, Farbe und Sound. Ungewöhnlich an dem Film ist, wie er die Zuseher zwischen einer distanzierten Beobachtung digitaler Eleganz und Momenten der Anerkennung menschlicher Höchstleistungen hin und her schwanken lässt. Dies ist eine Arbeit, auf die das Publikum bei der Vorführung möglicherweise körperlich reagieren wird (wie manche Juroren aus eigener Erfahrung wissen); die Entwicklung und Vollendung bestimmter Bewegungen in *Forms* kann unsere eigene Erfahrung körperlicher Strapazen und anstrengenden, beflügelnden Spiels widerspiegeln. *Forms* idealisiert die menschliche Gestalt und interpretiert die streng gebundenen und präzisen Bewegungen des Sports durch den Korpus großer Datenmengen. Wir waren fasziniert von dem Schwung und angenehm verblüfft durch die Abstraktion; der Soundtrack des metallischen Klickens akzentuierte die Übertragung der Bewegung in architektonische Formen aus Stabelementen.

AUSZEICHNUNGEN

Duku Spacemarines

La Mécanique du Plastique

Die raschen Übergänge von kruder Einfachheit zu visueller und narrativer Überspitzung erlebten wir als eine lustvolle Konfusion, die aus einem testosterongeladenen, explosiven Prozess resultiert. Spontane Kreativität, die mit Momenten überschäumender Ausgelassenheit gespickt ist, wird durch unterschiedliche Animationsstile visualisiert, wobei die Stilwechsel klug eingesetzt werden, um einen unverlässlichen Erzähler zu suggerieren. Mit *Duku Spacemarines* präsentiert das Kollektiv La Mécanique Du Plastique eine Entwicklungsgeschichte der Animation, die vom Vermächtnis der Strichmännchen bis zu realen und mythischen – urbanen Highend-Katastrophenszenarien reicht. Der Film erinnert uns daran, wie verspielt und variabel die Animation und ihre Techniken

GOLDEN NICA

Forms

Quayola, Memo Akten

Striking in its elegance, Memo Akten and Davide Quagliola's, aka Quayola's *Forms* is a non-narrative, viscerally moving abstraction of kinetics that is particularly strong for creating something beautiful out of what looks like motion capture, but is not—and its mix of precision and surprise is something that the algorithms and proprietary programs of CG animation so often fail to achieve. Its merits lie in the pure aesthetics of movement, color and sound. What is unusual is how it allows the viewer to oscillate between a distanced observation of digital elegance and moments of fleeting recognition of the apex of human performance. This is a work that an audience may respond to with their own bodies during screening (as some of the jury did); *Forms*' progression and completion of certain movements can mirror our own experience of physical exertion and of exhilarating, strenuous play. *Forms* idealizes human form, interpreting stringent and precise skilled sports movement through body "big data." We were fascinated by the momentum and pleasantly puzzled by the abstraction; we also found that the sound track of metallic clinking emphasized the translation of movement into rod-like architectural forms.

AWARDS OF DISTINCTION

Duku Spacemarines

La Mécanique du Plastique

Moving rapidly from crude simplicity to visual and narrative hyperbole, we experience a pleasurable confusion of testosterone-fuelled process under pressure. This spontaneous creativity, peppered with sparks of exuberant hilarity, is visualized by using different styles of animation, and cleverly uses shifting styles to reflect an unreliable narrator. With *Duku Spacemarines*, the collective La Mécanique Du Plastique suggests an animation evolution, from the legacy of stick figures to high-end urban disaster both real and mythical. It reminds us how playful and malleable the animated mode and its techniques can be and how experimental can also mean funny. Something intelligent is born from something stupid. We applaud the film's raison d'être of pure fun.

Oh Willy...

Emma De Swaef, Marc James Roels / Beast Animation

A somber, literally soft story, *Oh Willy...* uses traditional puppet animation techniques to enfold striking emotion into a conventionally linear but disenchanted fairytale. We were fascinated by Emma De Swaef, Marc James Roels and their team's huge commitment to style, which used tangible media of wool, fuzz and felt exclusively throughout; the textures are an apt metaphor for a world where everything is infantile, unstable and unsure. In a disarmingly unexpected narrative organization, Haneke-like characters silently suffer youth, death and aging, and the rites of passage of grief between a boy and his mom is the fuzzy embodiment of the nature/nurture dialectic. It is hard not to be affected by the warmth of the characters and the stunning visual cohesion of the textural world throughout this film. These days we look for the visceral, tactile, nostalgia or escape. This film gives us all of these, while relating a profoundly human story that is a feast for psychoanalytic interpretation. *Oh Willy...* takes puppet animation to a deeply philosophical and empathetic level—it is stop-motion's *Amour*, relieved with moments of tender humor.

HONORARY MENTIONS

Subconscious Password

Chris Landreth

Subconscious Password is a seriously self-ironic observation of ageing, friendship, the foibles of memory, and Freudian guilt structures. Moving from banal situations in apparent live-action, Chris Landreth flies us to the ends of the brain's dendrites and synapses in monstrous digital representations of childhood nightmares. The jury felt that the fluent visual effects blended seamlessly with CG animation represent the experience of a "senior moment," another milestone for Landreth as he continues to master visuality and technology to represent his favorite theme: the deeply subjective paranoia of correct social behavior.

Ars Rata

Moritz Palnstorfer, Christian Schulze

Moritz Palnstorfer and Christian Schulze's constantly transforming reflective sculptural meditation on volume, space and light both aligns to and

und wie vergnüglich experimentelle Erzählweisen sein können. Intelligentes entsteht aus weniger Intelligentem. Wir applaudieren einer Einstellung, die reinen Spaß als *raison d'être* des Films betrachtet.

Oh Willy...

Emma De Swaef, Marc James Roels / Beast Animation

Die skurrile „Soft-Story" *Oh Willy...* verwendet traditionelle Puppenanimationstechniken, um berührende Emotionen in einem konventionell linear erzählten, aber illusionslosen Märchen zu erwecken. Wir waren fasziniert von der Stilsicherheit des Teams um Emma De Swaef und Marc James Roels, das ausschließlich begreifbare Materialien wie Wolle, Fussel und Filz verwendete; diese Materialien sind eine stimmige Metapher für eine Welt, in der alles infantil, instabil und unsicher ist. In einer entwaffnend unvorhergesehenen narrativen Struktur leiden an Haneke erinnernde Figuren still an Jugend, Tod und Alter; Riten des Übergangs, etwa die Trauer eines Jungen um seine Mutter, werden von flaumigen Figuren als Dialektik von Anlage und Umwelt dargestellt. Man kann sich der Wärme, die von den Figuren ausgeht, und der erstaunlichen visuellen Kohärenz der texturalen Welt, die in diesem Film vorherrscht, schwer entziehen. Heute sehnen wir uns nach elementaren Emotionen, nach Greifbarem, Nostalgie und Ausstiegsszenarien. Dieser Film erfüllt all diese Sehnsüchte, während er gleichzeitig eine zutiefst menschliche Geschichte erzählt, die eine Fundgrube für psychoanalytische Interpretationen ist. *Oh Willy...* führt die Puppenanimation auf eine zutiefst philosophische und empathische Ebene – das *Amour* des Stop-Motion-Films, aufgelockert durch Momente zarten Humors.

ANERKENNUNGEN

Subconscious Password

Chris Landreth

Subconscious Password ist eine überaus selbstironische Auseinandersetzung mit dem Altern, der Freundschaft, mit Gedächtnisstörungen und Freud'schen Schuldmodellen. Ausgehend von banalen Situationen in Live-Action-Szenen katapultiert Chris Landreth uns in monströsen digitalen Darstellungen kindlicher Alpträume in die Welt der Dendriten und Synapsen. Die flüssig umgesetzten visuellen Effekte, die sich nahtlos mit der CG-Animation verbinden, repräsentieren nach Meinung der Jury überzeugend die Erfahrung „altersbedingter Gedächtnislücken". Ein weiterer Meilenstein für Landreth, der einmal mehr seine meisterhafte Beherrschung des Visuellen und der Technologie einsetzt, um sein Lieblingsthema zu bearbeiten: die zutiefst subjektive Paranoia vor korrektem Sozialverhalten.

Ars Rata

Moritz Palnstorfer, Christian Schulze

Moritz Palnstorfers und Christian Schulzes sich unablässig verwandelnde, skulpturale Meditation über Volumen, Raum und Licht verleugnet und stilisiert die Physik. Dieser Versuch einer Quadratur des Kreises im Bestreben nach digitalem Realismus verbindet gekonnt die Begrenzungen von architektonischen Formen und Volumen, Licht und Reflexionen sowie die nervöse Agonie einer polymorphen Kugel, die dem Raum, in dem sie eingebunden ist, entfliehen will. Der kreischend metallische, dröhnende Soundtrack unterstreicht akustisch die Verwandlung der Form, die zu ächzen und zu stöhnen scheint – man kann sich des Eindrucks nicht erwehren, dass Daten nicht in Schach zu halten sind.

The Carousel Family

Te-Yu Liu

Im Rahmen von Tropen und Figuren einer Jarryesken Sitcom aus den 50er Jahren und unter ungenierter Verwendung „roher" 3D-Computeranimation gibt Te-Yu Liu in seinem bizarren und höchst amüsanten Porträt einer Familie einen ungewöhnlichen Einblick in den Alltagstrott, der von Figuren mit Pferdeköpfen auf einer übergroßen Drehplatte dargestellt wird. Ob beim Essen, Schlafen, Baden oder Arbeiten, die Familie führt unermüdlich den unmöglichen Kampf gegen die Zentrifugalkraft. Die Metaphern in ihrer bisweilen kruden Animation sind ein unheimlicher Kommentar zu vertrauten Szenarien.

Shelter

Carl Burton

Shelter zeichnet sich dadurch aus, dass vertraute Haushaltsgegenstände dekonstruiert und in komplexe Himmelskörper verwandelt werden. Wir geraten in den Sog einer Geborgenheit vermittelnden Topografie, in der sich Holzobjekte und Erinnerungen verflechten und die in weiterer Folge einen surrealen und zunehmend traumähnlichen Kosmos eröffnet. Carl Burton entführt den Betrachter auf eine beeindruckend gestaltete Reise, die einer sehr individuellen kristallklaren Vision folgt.

Palmipedarium

Jérémy Clapin / Papy3D Productions

Die Interpretation der Nostalgie eines isolierten Jungen, der sich im Besitz eines Fantasievogels wähnt, durch 3D-Animation in einer düsteren entsättigten Tonalität und 2D-Ästhetik fand großen Anklang bei der Jury.

denies physics. This attempt at "squaring the circle" of aspirations to digital realism is a masterful mix of the limitations of architectural substance and volume, of light and reflections, and the itchy throes of a polymorphic sphere straining to escape while also contained. The screechily metallic, echoing soundtrack aurally underpins the shapeshifting form like groans, and there is a relentless impression that data cannot be contained.

The Carousel Family

Te-Yu Liu

Framed in the tropes of a 50s Jarryesque sitcom, and making unabashed use of "crude" 3D computer animation, Te-Yu Liu gives a particular insight into the daily grind in a bizarre and hilarious family portrait played out by horse-headed characters on an oversize "lazy susan" of life. Together, the family fights the impossible carousel's centrifugal force while eating, sleeping, bathing and working. The metaphors, while at times crudely animated, are eerie commentary on the familiar.

Shelter

Carl Burton

Shelter excels in taking familiar household objects and refracting them into complex celestial forms. In an ambience of safety, we recede into a woven, wooden topography of objects and memories, which then opens out into a surreal, massive and increasingly dreamlike cosmos. Carl Burton takes us on a finely crafted journey that is a crystal-clear vision of a single mind.

Palmipedarium

Jérémy Clapin / Papy3D Productions

The jury felt that Jérémy Clapin's use of 3D animation implemented with a somber 2D desaturated aesthetic beautifully interprets the nostalgic emotions of an isolated boy who gains the illusive ownership of a fantasy bird. As well, heightened emphasis on a balance between silence and natural sounds immerse the viewer in the noisy peace of the swamp, farm and woods and the rhythms of life and death.

Rollin' Safari

Kyra Buschor, Anna Habermehl, Constantin Paeplow

Humorously based on the unpredictable physics of an exercise ball, in *Rollin' Safari* Kyra Buschor, Anna Habermehl and Constantin Paeplow use animation principles of squash and stretch to gain a new dimension of hyperbole that makes predatory life impossible.

Snail Trail
Philipp Artus
Philipp Artus elevates the mundane movement of a gastropod in combination with the dynamics of a wheel to a poetic dance with saccadic, Kentridgesque ghost trails. The jury especially enjoyed the abstract motion, in stark chromatics, which develops rigid vectors into a sinuous calligraphic progression to culminate in a data visualization of its circular path. The soundtrack attacks our ears as it elastically drives the movement forward through its trace and retracing steps.

MeTube: August sings Carmen "Habanera"
Daniel Moshel
Daniel Moshel's wonderful, self-ironic comment on opera and disco, on everyday (online) "reality" and personal fantasy, makes clever use of visual effects and animation. Using retro analog, digital and cinematic wipes to move between who we are at home and who we secretly want to be, *MeTube* reveals a tour de force performance by August Schram of self-transformation, closet dressing and sadomasochistic play, which moves the viewer between the lead tenor's camp, deadpan displays of emotion and pleasure and oppressive domestic despair.

Under an Alias
Nerdworking
The jury chose Nerdworking's technically smart, site-specific installation for its palimpsesting of a building in Weimar with interpretations of the city's spectacular glory days and its eventual deterioration, destruction and complete erasure.

Ballpit
Kyle Mowat
As an exercise in the animation of physics taken to the extreme, the jury felt that Kyle Mowat's unique homage to early McLaren deserved mention because of its obscured use of digital methods in 2D and faux 3D abstractions. We especially enjoyed playful Fischli-Weissesque renditions of cause-and-effect, which unpredictably generates colorful toylike forms. It is life inside a psychedelic Rube Goldberg world, made richer by a flat pastel

Darüber hinaus lässt die Fokussierung auf die Balance von Stille und Naturgeräuschen den Betrachter in den von regem Treiben erfüllten Frieden eines Sumpfes, einer Farm und der Wälder eintauchen, in denen die Rhythmen von Leben und Tod spürbar sind.

Rollin' Safari
Kyra Buschor, Anna Habermehl, Constantin Paeplow
Kyra Buschor, Anna Habermehl und Constantin Paeplow verwenden in der Animation *Rollin' Safari*, die auf den unvorhersehbaren Eigenschaften eines Gymnastikballs basiert, auf humorvolle Weise die Animationsprinzipien des Squash und Stretch (Quetschen und Strecken), um eine neue Dimension der Übersteigerung zu eröffnen, die hier die Aufgabe hat, den Alltag von Raubtieren zu erschweren.

Snail Trail
Philipp Artus
Durch die Kombination mit der Dynamik eines Rads erhöht Philipp Artus die banale Bewegung eines Gastropoden zu einem poetischen Tanz, der sakkadische geisterhafte Spuren hinterlässt, die an Kentridge erinnern. Die Jury schätzte insbesondere die abstrakte Bewegung in zurückhaltenden Farben, bei der gebundene Vektoren in einen wellenförmig geschwungenen, kalligrafischen Verlauf gebracht werden, der in einer Datenvisualisierung der kreisförmigen Spur gipfelt. Der das Gehör attackierende Soundtrack treibt die Bewegung an und lässt sie elastisch vor- und zurückschnellen.

MeTube: August sings Carmen "Habanera"
Daniel Moshel
Daniel Moshels wunderbarer, selbstironischer Kommentar zu Oper und Disco, alltäglicher (Online-)Realität und persönlicher Fantasiewelt überzeugt durch den klugen Einsatz von visuellen Effekten und Animation. Mittels analoger und digitaler Schiebeblenden, die abwechselnd die Person, die man zu Hause ist, und die, die man insgeheim sein möchte, zeigen, präsentiert *MeTube* eine meisterhafte Performance von August Schram rund um Selbstveränderung, Kostümierung und sadomasochistische Spiele, die den Zuseher zwischen der trockenen, campy anmutenden Darbietung von Emotion und Leidenschaft und beklemmender häuslicher Tristesse pendeln lässt.

Under an Alias
Nerdworking
Die Jury entschied sich für die technisch überzeugende standortspezifische Installation von Nerdworking

aufgrund des Palimpsestierens eines Gebäudes in Weimar, wo auf Interpretationen der glorreichen Blütezeit der Stadt Darstellungen ihres schließlichen Verfalls, ihrer Zerstörung und kompletten Auslöschung folgen.

Ballpit
Kyle Mowat
Kyle Mowats einzigartige Hommage an den frühen Norman McLaren, eine ins Extrem gesteigerte Übung in der Animation organischer Formen, verdiente nach Meinung der Jury aufgrund der nicht zu erkennenden Verwendung digitaler 2D-Methoden und imitierter 3D-Abstraktionen eine Anerkennung. Wir schätzten insbesondere die an Fischli/Weiss erinnernde Umsetzung des Prinzips von Ursache und Wirkung, das hier auf unvorhersehbare Weise bunte spielzeugartige Formen hervorbringt. Der Film zeigt das Leben in einer psychedelischen Rube-Goldberg-Welt, die durch eine satte Pastellfarbgebung und einen Soundtrack-Mix aus klingelndem Glockenspiel und unheimlichen Stimmen Atmosphäre gewinnt.

Björk – Mutual Core
Andrew Thomas Huang
Bis zur Taille in Treibsand eingegraben, performt und interagiert Björk in Andrew Huangs Pop-Promo mit frei schwebenden animierten Skulpturen. Wir waren insbesondere von der Plastizität des Films beeindruckt, die so ausgeprägt ist, dass der Betrachter kaum noch zwischen realen und digital animierten Texturen und natürlichen Materialien unterscheiden kann – man meint geradezu, das Gesehene zu schmecken und zu riechen.

It's Such a Beautiful Day
Don Hertzfeldt
Wie opportun ist es, in einer Welt, in der elektronische Effekte für visuelle Highlights sorgen, 35-mm-Fotografie, fotochemischen Film und Strichmännchen einzusetzen? *It's Such a Beautiful Day*, eine weitere tiefgründige und idiosynkratische Arbeit von Don Hertzfeldt, zeichnet sich durch die kühne Ambition aus, eine komplexe und zutiefst menschliche Erfahrung mit bewusst beschränkten formalen und technischen Mitteln zu erzählen. Der von einem Erzähler, der zugleich allwissend, zärtlich, verwirrt und pragmatisch ist, kommentierte Film visualisiert Gedächtnisverlust auf beeindruckende Weise als Fragmentierung, Verblassen und Auflösung einer persönlichen Geschichte. Die hoffnungsvolle Visualisierung einer im wahrsten Sinn des Wortes allbekannten alltäglichen Erfahrung ist tröstlich für die Zuseher, die in diesem Film, der Sterblichkeit und Transzendenz thematisiert, ihr eigenes Leben wiedererkennen können.

palette and a soundtrack mix of tinkling chimes and eerie voices.

Björk—Mutual Core
Andrew Thomas Huang
Half submerged in an arid beachscape, in Andrew Huang's pop promo Bjork performs and interacts with suspended, animated sculptures. We were impressed by how the film's palpability leaves the viewer unsure of the distinction between real and digitally animated textures and natural materials, to the extent of feeling we could taste and smell them.

It's Such a Beautiful Day
Don Hertzfeldt
How appropriate is it to use 35mm photography, photochemical film and stick figures in a world where electronic visual effects are able to give us unimaginable eye-candy? Another profound and idiosyncratic work by Don Hertzfeldt, *It's Such a Beautiful Day* excels in its soaring ambition of telling a complex and deeply human experience using intentionally limited formal and technical means. Guided by a narrator who is at the same time omniscient, tender, puzzled and pragmatic, *It's Such a Beautiful Day* effectively visualizes memory loss as personal history fragments, fades and disappears. Its literally universal and hopeful visualization of an everyman's experience gives solace to viewers whose lives and families may be reflected in the subject—the interpretation of mortality and transcendence.

Forms

Quayola, Memo Akten

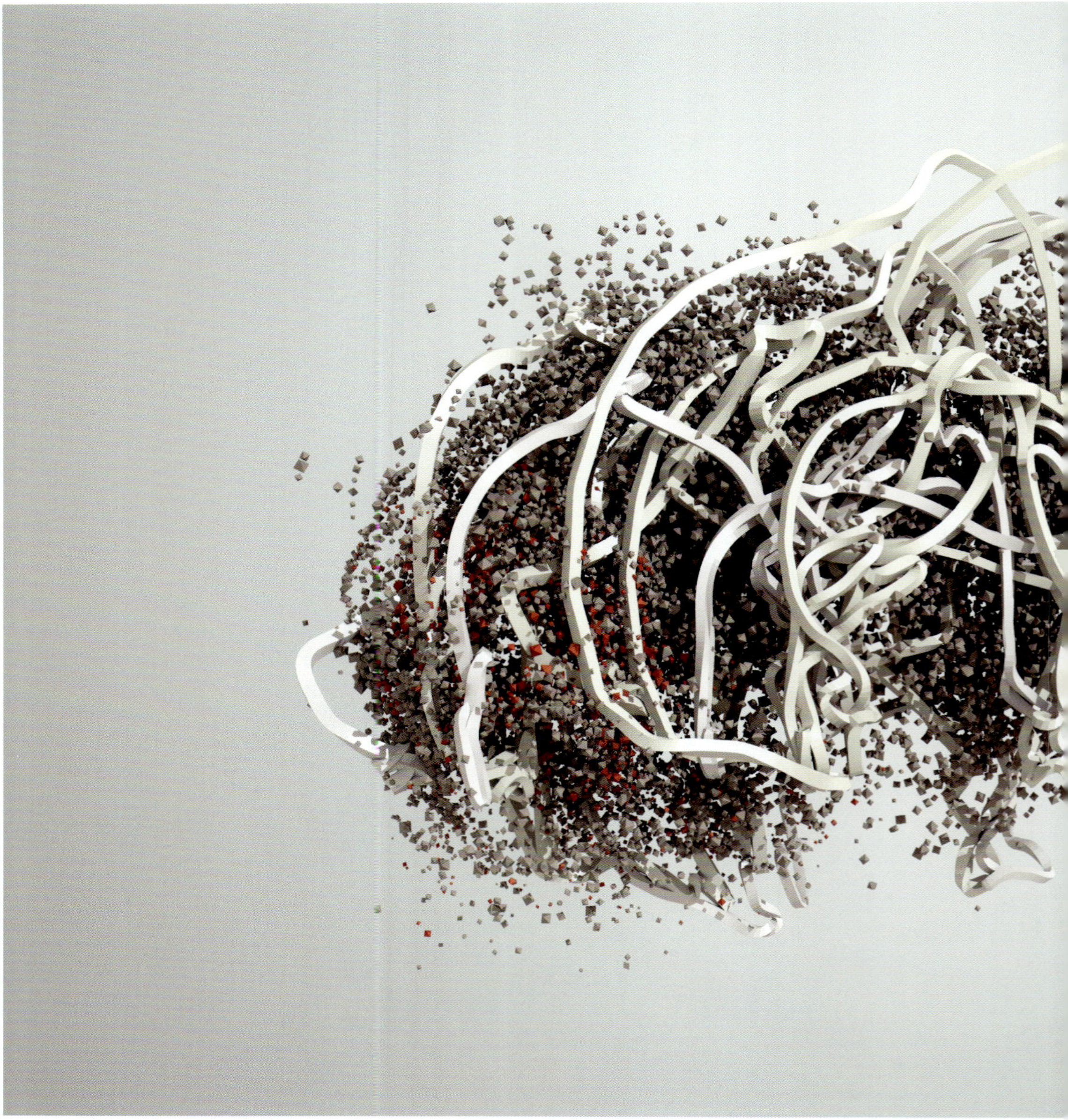

Forms is a collaboration between the visual artists Quayola and Memo Akten. A series of studies on human motion and its reverberations through space and time. It is inspired by the works of Eadweard Muybridge, Harold Edgerton Étienne-Jules Marey as well as by similarly inspired cubist

Forms, eine Studie menschlicher Bewegungen und ihrer Resonanz in Raum und Zeit, entstand in Zusammenarbeit der beiden bildenden Künstler Quayola und Memo Akten. Der Film ist beeinflusst von den Arbeiten von Eadweard Muybridge, Harold Edgerton, Étienne-Jules Marey, aber auch von kubistischen Werken wie Marcel

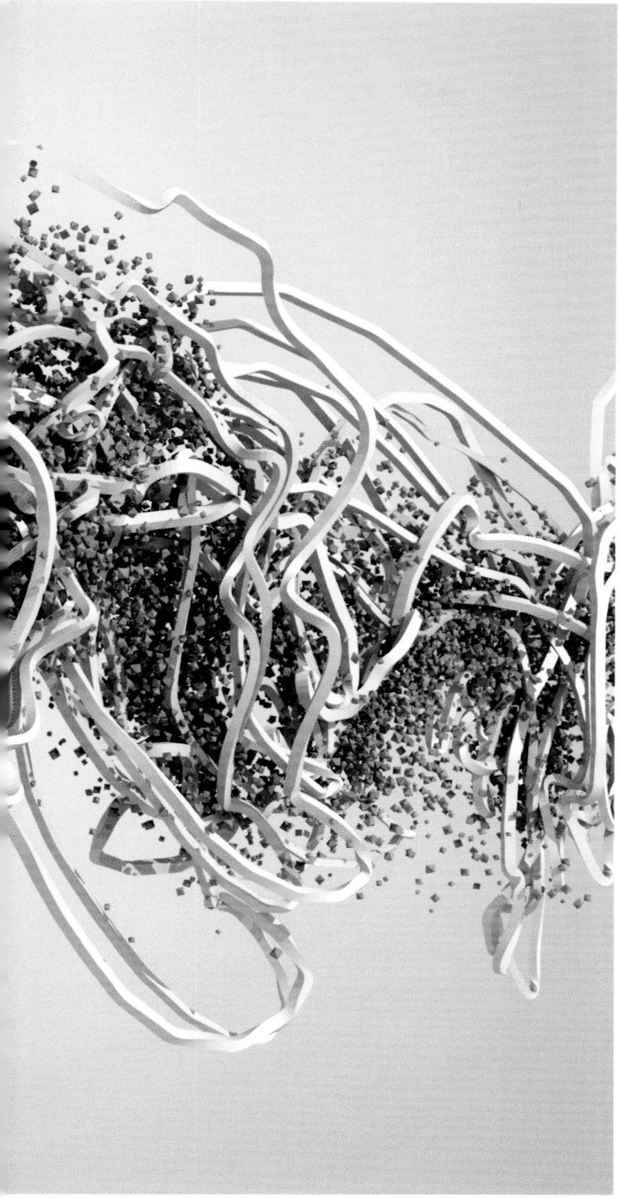

Duchamps *Akt eine Treppe herabsteigend Nr. 2*. Der Fokus liegt weniger auf wahrnehmbaren Bewegungsbahnen als auf der Erforschung von Extrapolationsverfahren zur Gestaltung abstrakter Formen und der Visualisierung verborgener Beziehungen – wie Kraft, Gleichgewicht, Anmut und Konflikt – zwischen dem Körper und seiner Umgebung.

works such as Marcel Duchamp's *Nude Descending a Staircase No.2*. Rather than focusing on observable trajectories, it explores techniques of extrapolation to sculpt abstract forms, visualizing unseen relationships—power, balance, grace and conflict—between the body and its surroundings.

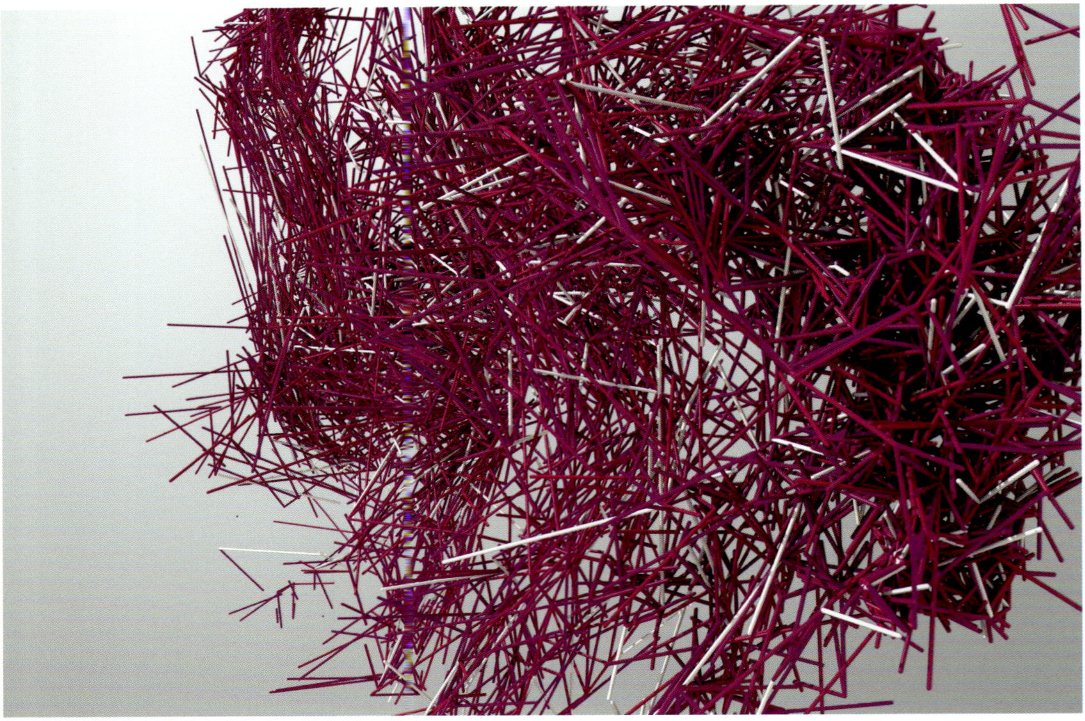

The project investigates athletes pushing their bodies to their extreme capabilities, their movements shaped by an evolutionary process targeting a winning performance. Traditionally a form of entertainment in today's society with an overpowering competitive edge, the disciplines are deconstructed and interrogated from an exclusively mechanical and aesthetic point of view, concentrating on the invisible forces generated by and influencing the movement.

The source for the study is footage from the Commonwealth Games. The process of transformation from live footage to abstract forms is exposed as part of the interactive multi-screen artwork to provide an insight into the evolution of the specially crafted world in which the athletes were placed.

Das Projekt setzt sich mit Athleten auseinander, die ihren Körper an seine Grenzen bringen, und deren Bewegungen von einem evolutionären Prozess hervorgebracht sind, der auf Erfolg ausgerichtet ist. Die sportlichen Disziplinen, die in der heutigen Gesellschaft traditionell eine von extremem Wettbewerb geprägte Form der Unterhaltung sind, werden dekonstruiert und aus einer rein mechanischen und ästhetischen Perspektive hinterfragt. Im Blickpunkt stehen die unsichtbaren Kräfte, die durch die Bewegung entstehen und diese beeinflussen.

Als Quellmaterial für die Studie wurden Filmaufnahmen von den Commonwealth-Spielen verwendet. Der Verwandlungsprozess von Live-Bildern in abstrakte Formen wird im Rahmen einer interaktiven Multi-Screen-Installation ausgestellt, die Einblick in die Entwicklung der außergewöhnlichen Welt gibt, in der die Athleten agieren.

Nexus Interactive Arts: production; Beccy McCray: producer; Jo Bierton – production manager; Matthias Kispert: sound design; Maxime Causeret: Houdini Developer; Raffael F J Ziegler (AKA Moco): 3D Animator; Katie Parnell: 3D Tracker; Eoin Coughlan: 3D Tracker; Mark Davies: 3D Tracking Supervisor. Commissioned by the National Media Museum for the *In The Blink of an Eye* Exhibition 2012; with the support of imove, part of the Cultural Olympiad programme. With thanks to BBC Motion Gallery and Commonwealth Games Federation

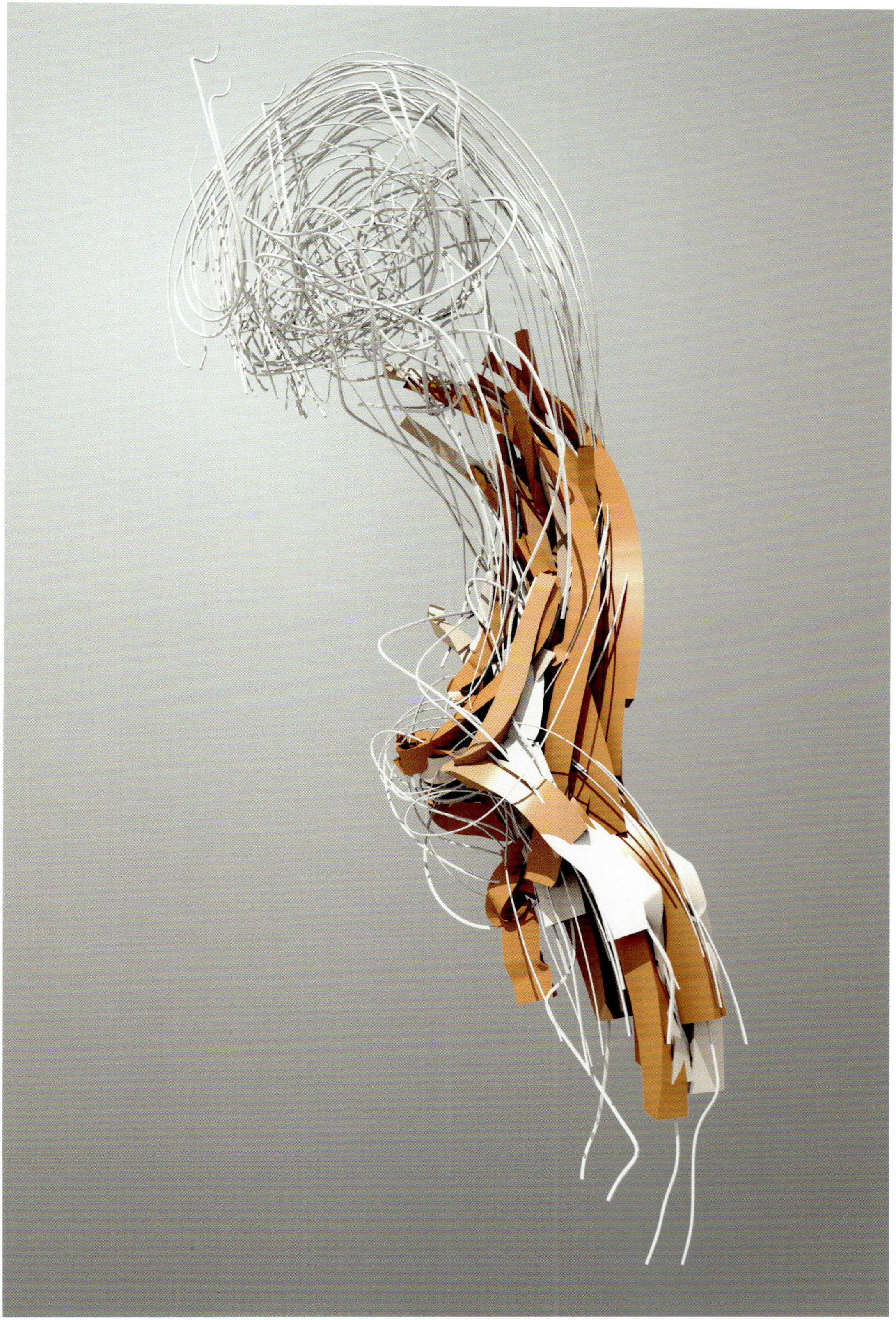

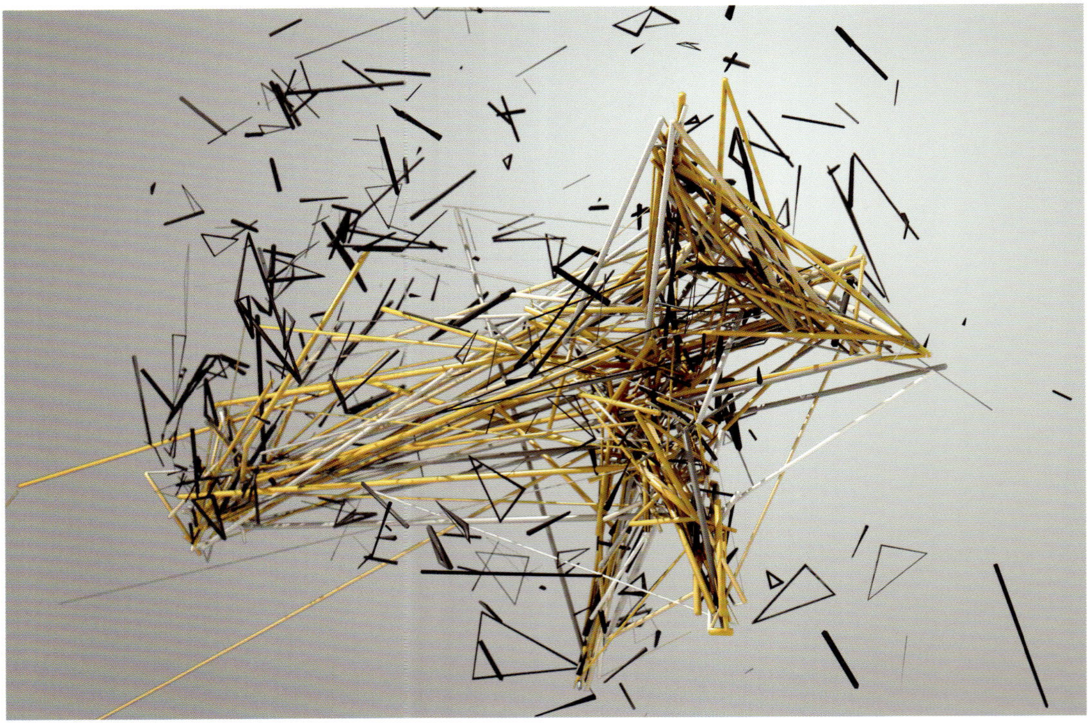

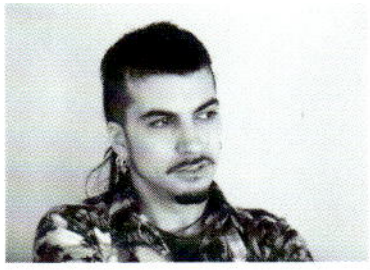

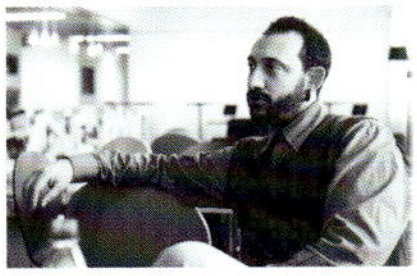

Quayola (IT). Regarded for his enigmatic video installations, Quayola creates hybrid spaces of animated painting and sculpture. Engaging a practice of audiovisual performance, drawing, photography and software programming, he explores a fine boundary between the real and the artificial. Special institutional commissions of Quayola's work have allowed him exceptionally rare access to the art and architecture of churches, theaters and museums in Europe, such as Notre Dame and the Vatican. In his work, original masterpieces and collections become raw canvas, as Quayola anchors a video-based exploration in a conversation about archives, collage, intellectual property and the appreciation of an object. **Memo Akten** (TR) is a visual artist, musician and engineer working at the intersection of art and science. His work covers a range of disciplines including installations, performances, films, music videos, online works and mobile applications. He is on the selection committee of ACM SIGGRAPH, computational consultant on the Architectural Association's Design Research Lab and one of the core contributors to the openFrameworks project. A strong supporter of open-source and a believer in the sharing of knowledge, he gives lectures and workshops around the world. In 2011 he co-founded Marshmallow Laser Feast, a collective of like-minded artists, designers and engineers. **Quayola** (IT), der vor allem für seine enigmatischen Videoinstallationen bekannt ist, kreiert hybride Räume aus animierten Gemälden und Skulpturen. In seiner künstlerischen Praxis, die audiovisuelle Performance, Zeichnung, Fotografie und Software-Programmierung umfasst, lotet er die schmale Grenze zwischen dem Realen und dem Künstlichen aus. Auftragsarbeiten von Institutionen ermöglichten ihm den nur wenigen Personen vorbehaltenen Zugriff auf Kunst und Architektur von Kirchen, Theatern und Museen in Europa, wie etwa Notre Dame und Vatikan. In seinen Arbeiten werden sowohl Originale von Meisterwerken als auch Sammlungen zu einer Projektionsfläche und von Quayola in einer videobasierten Analyse als Dialog über Archive, Collage, geistiges Eigentum und den Status eines Originals neu interpretiert. **Memo Akten** (TR) ist ein bildender Künstler, Musiker und Techniker, der an der Schnittstelle von Kunst und Wissenschaft arbeitet. Seine Arbeiten sind spartenübergreifend und umfassen Installationen, Performances, Filme, Musikvideos, Online-Produktionen und mobile Applikationen. Er ist im Award Committee von ACM SIGGRAPH, IT-Berater des Architectural Associations' Design Research Lab und einer der wichtigsten Unterstützer des openFrameworks-Projekts. Memo Akten ist ein engagierter Verfechter von Open Source und Wissenssharing und hält Vorträge und Workshops auf der ganzen Welt. 2011 war er Mitbegründer des Marshmallow Laser Feast, eines Kollektivs an der Schnittstelle von Kunst, Design und Technologie.

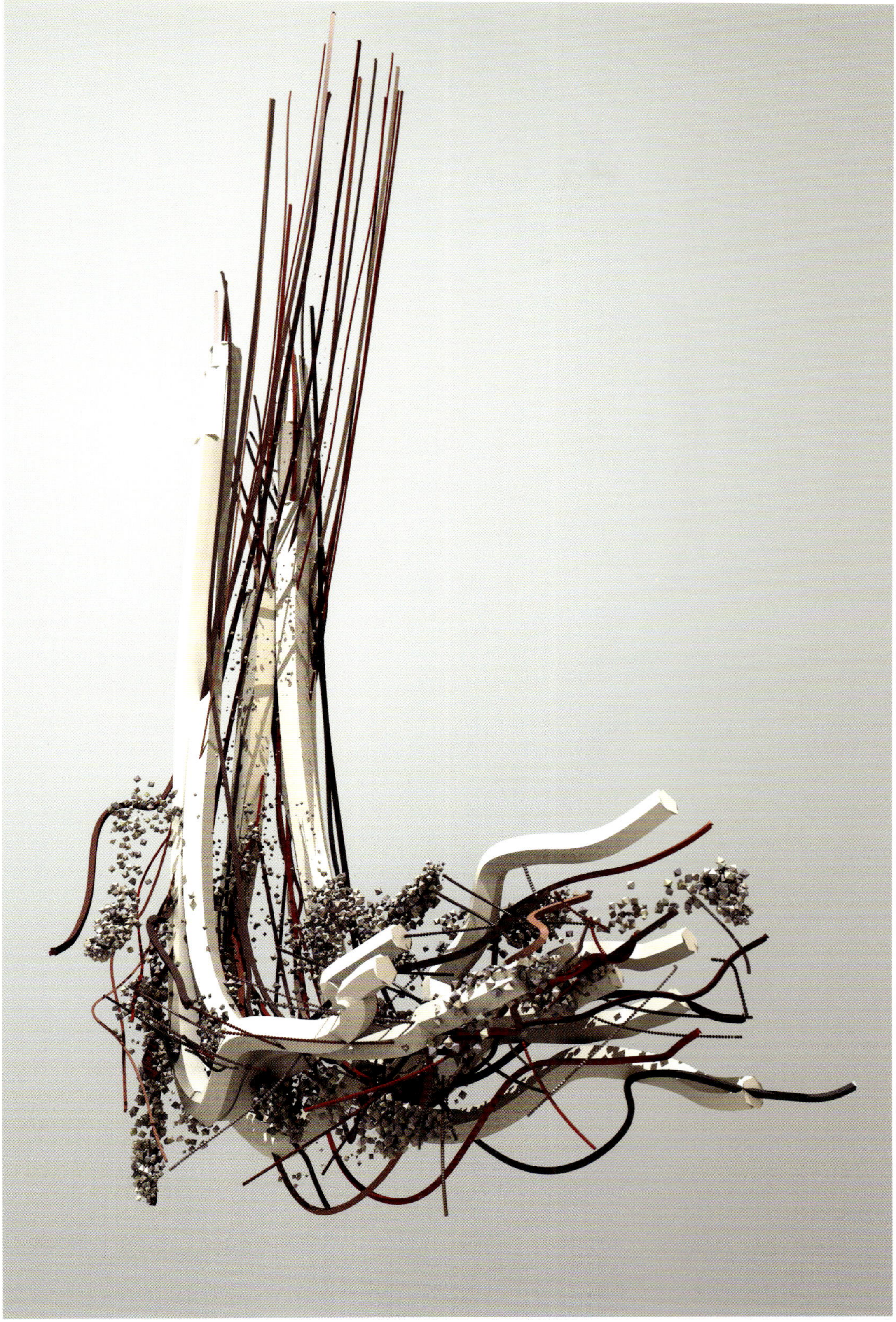

Duku Spacemarines

La Mécanique du Plastique

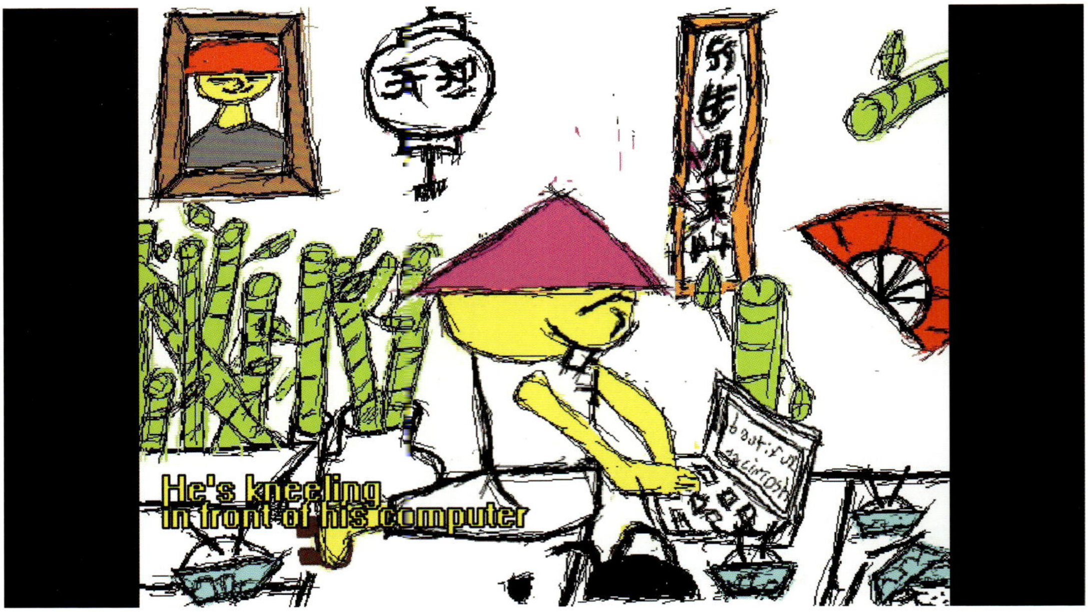

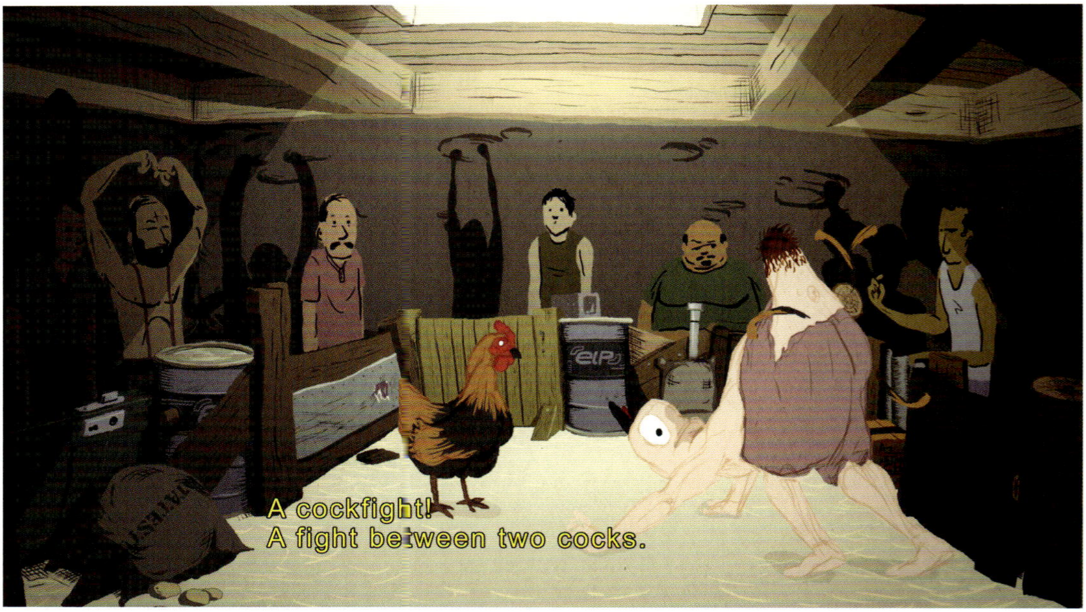

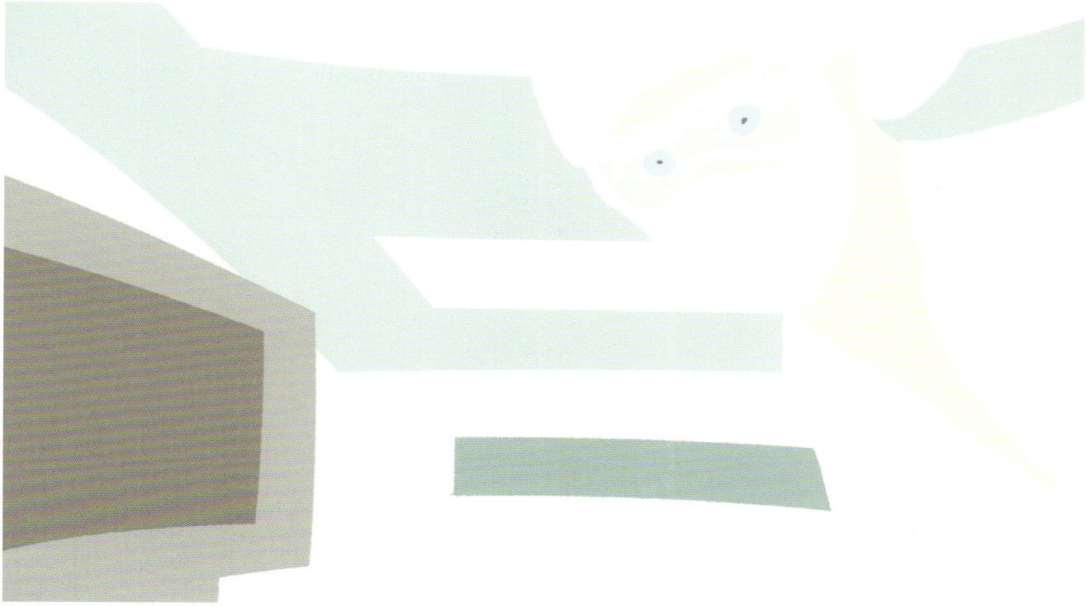

Duku Spacemarines ist ein animierter Kurzfilm über einen Moskito. Nein, eigentlich ist es die Geschichte eines Chinesen, der das kapitalistische System Amerikas hacken will. Oder doch ein Film über Hähne? Im Grunde ist es die Geschichte einer Geschichte. Basierend auf einem Drehbuch, das sich an Hollywood-Produktionen orientiert – mit Explosionen und allem, was dazugehört. Dem entspricht auch die Animation. Alles da, vom Glitch bis zum Blooming-Effekt. Was immer auch die Aussage sein mag, im Kino zählen visuelle Effekte.

Duku Spacemarines ist der Diplom-Film 2012 der Abteilung für digitale Kunst der Universität Paris 8 und wurde in einer typischen Pariser Wohnung mit Küche, Tisch und einem kleinen Wohnzimmer gedreht, in dem sich vier Computer, acht Bildschirme und vier junge Leute befinden, die sich La Mécanique du Plastique nennen.

Duku Spacemarines is a short animated film about a mosquito. No, it's rather the story of a Chinese man hacking the American capitalist system. Or is it about chickens? Actually it is the story of a story. A scenario that strives after the high standards of Hollywood, with explosions. And so the animation, from the glitch to the glow, never mind if there is nothing to say, cinema has visual effects.

Duku Spacemarines—a 2012 graduation film from the department of digital art of the University of Paris 8—was handmade in a typical Parisian apartment, with a table, a kitchen, and a small living-room filled with four computers, eight screens and four guys who go under the name of La Mécanique du Plastique.

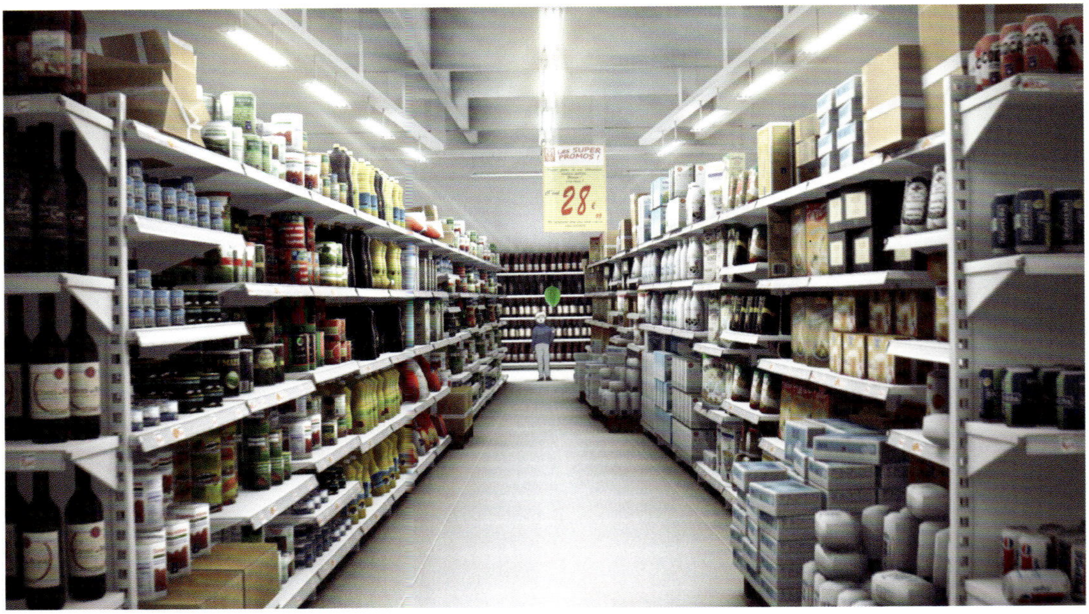
SUPER PROMOS !
28

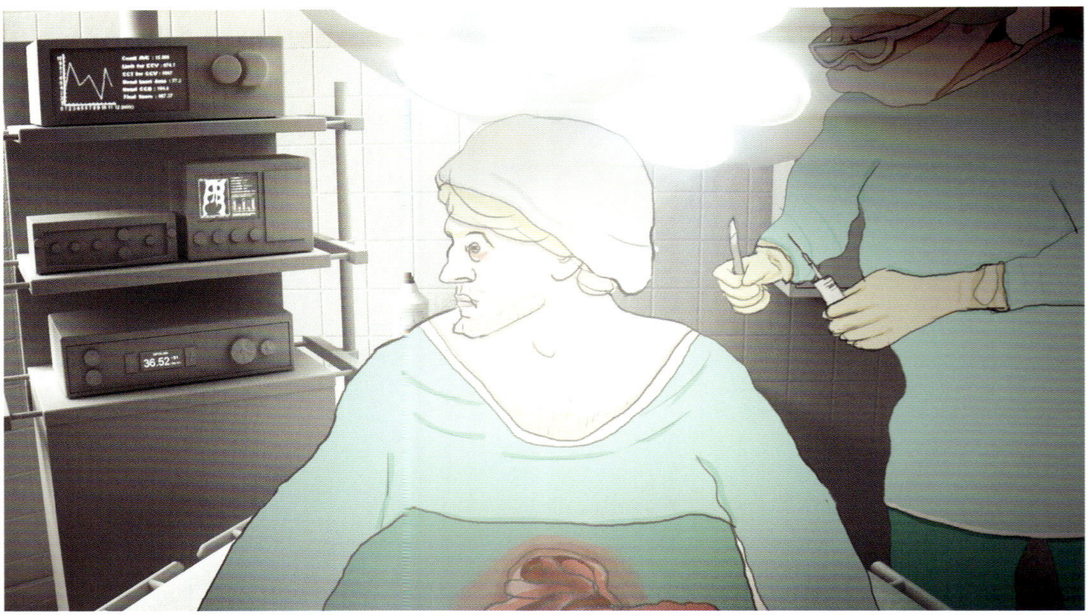
36.52

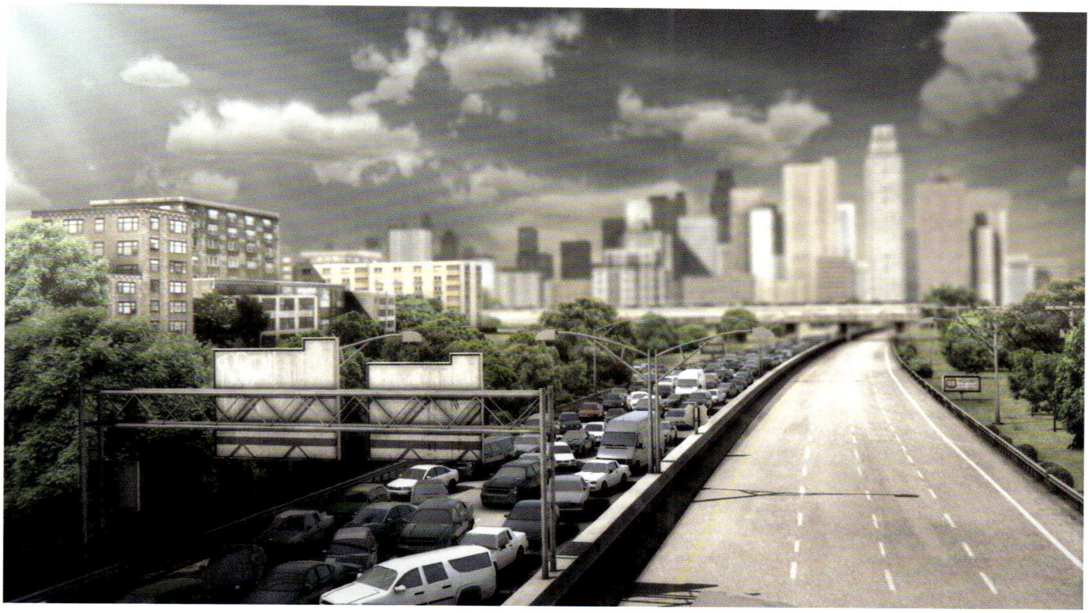

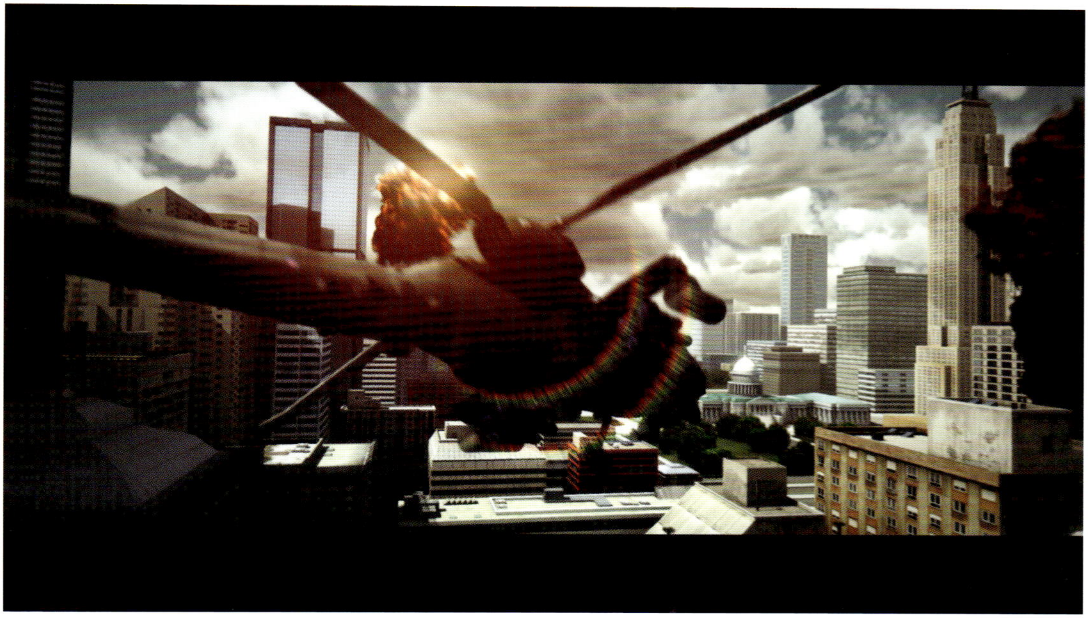

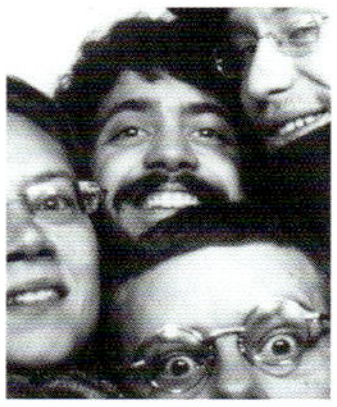

La Mécanique du Plastique (FR). As a collective of four French independent artists, La Mécanique du Plastique produce curious, short animated films mixing various techniques. After graduating in fine art, ancient Greek, computer science and computer graphics, our professional activities consist in programming, painting, music and digital art. **La Mécanique du Plastique** (FR), ein Kollektiv bestehend aus vier französischen Künstlern produziert kleine ausgefallene Animationsfilme, bei denen verschiedene Techniken kombiniert werden. Seit dem Abschluss unserer Studien in bildender Kunst, Altgriechisch, Informatik und Computergrafik widmen wir uns dem Programmieren, der Malerei, der Musik und digitaler Kunst.

Oh Willy...

Emma De Swaef, Marc James Roels / Beast Animation

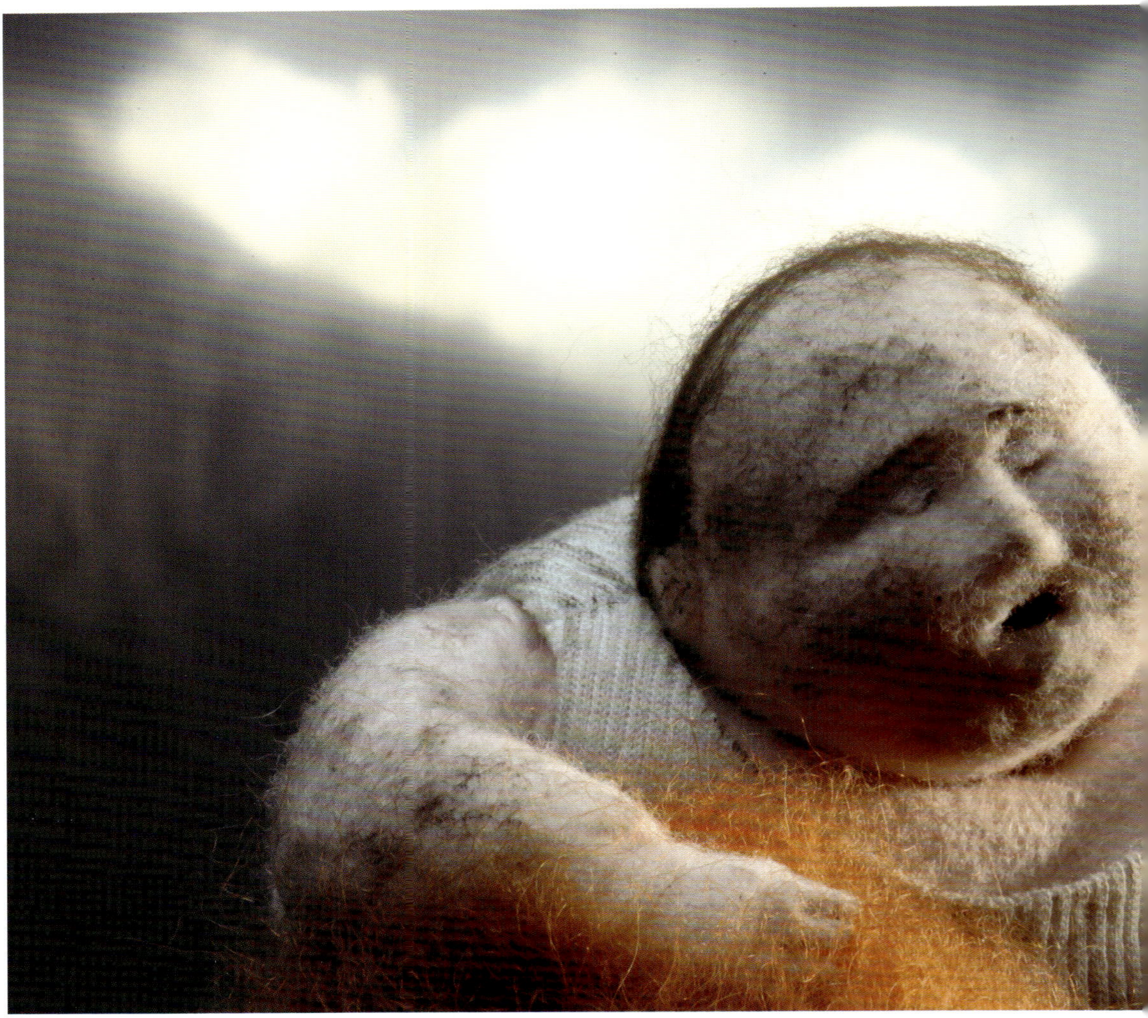

Fifty-something Willy returns to the naturist community where he spent his youth to visit his sick mother. When she dies shortly after he arrives, Willy is confronted with the choices he has made in his life. In confused sadness he flees into the forest. After a rough start, he finds the motherly protection of a big, gentle, hairy beast.

Der Mittfünfziger Willy kehrt in die Nudistenkommune zurück, in der er aufgewachsen ist, um seine kranke Mutter zu besuchen. Als sie kurz nach seiner Ankunft stirbt, lässt Willy sein Leben Revue passieren und wird mit den Entscheidungen konfrontiert, die seinen Weg bestimmt haben. Traurig und verwirrt flieht er in den Wald. Seine Verwandlung zum edlen Wilden gestaltet sich schwierig. Nach einem holprigen Start findet er mütterliche Geborgenheit bei einem großen, sanftmütigen Tier.

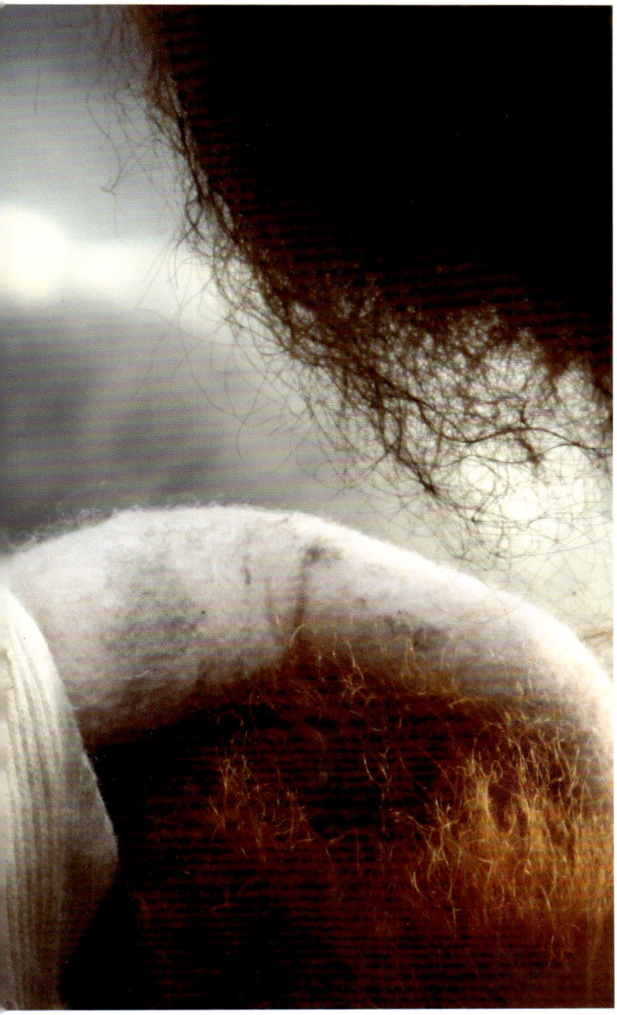

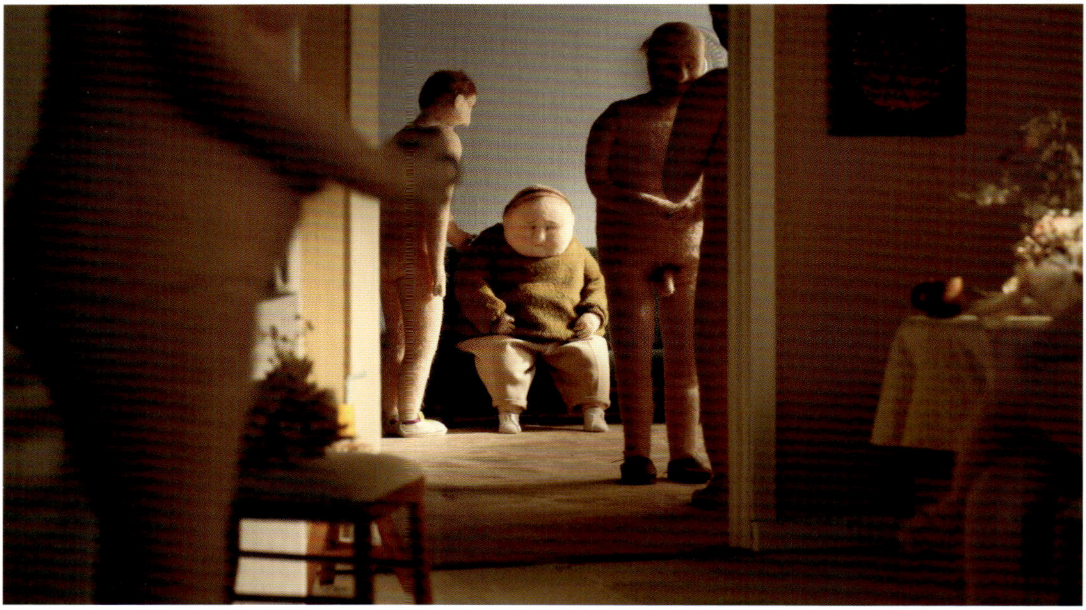

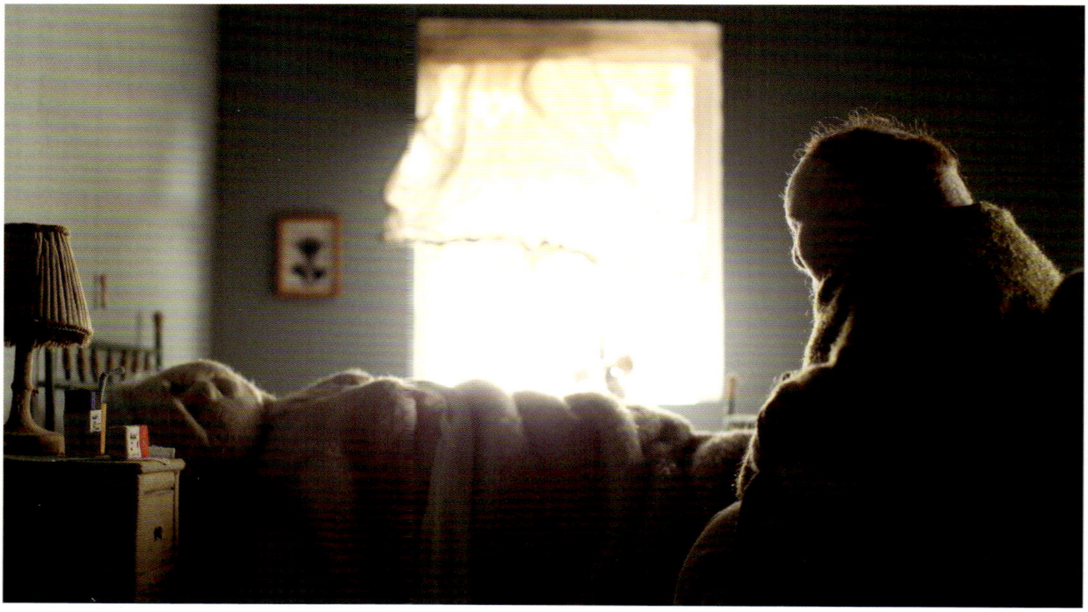

Directors: Emma De Swaef & Marc James Roels; co-production: Beast Animation; producers: Ben Tesseur & Nidia Santiago; animators: Andreas De Ridder, Alice Tambellini & Steven De Beul
With the support of the Flemish Audiovisual Fund (VAF). With the participation of France Télévisions, the Centre national du cinéma et de l'image animée–Contribution financière; with the support of Région Bretagne and the Netherlands Film Fund

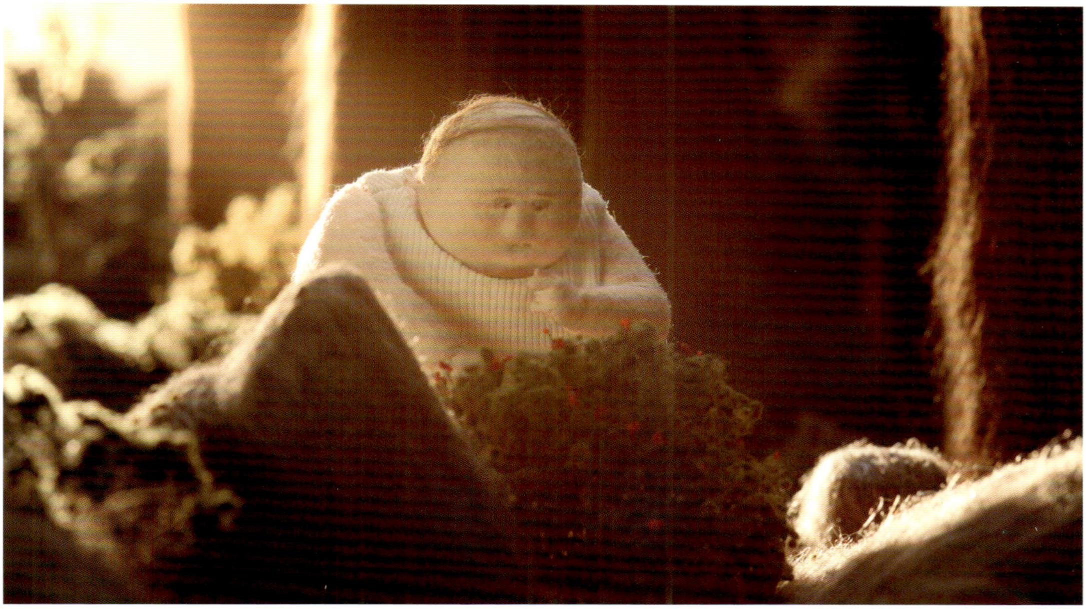

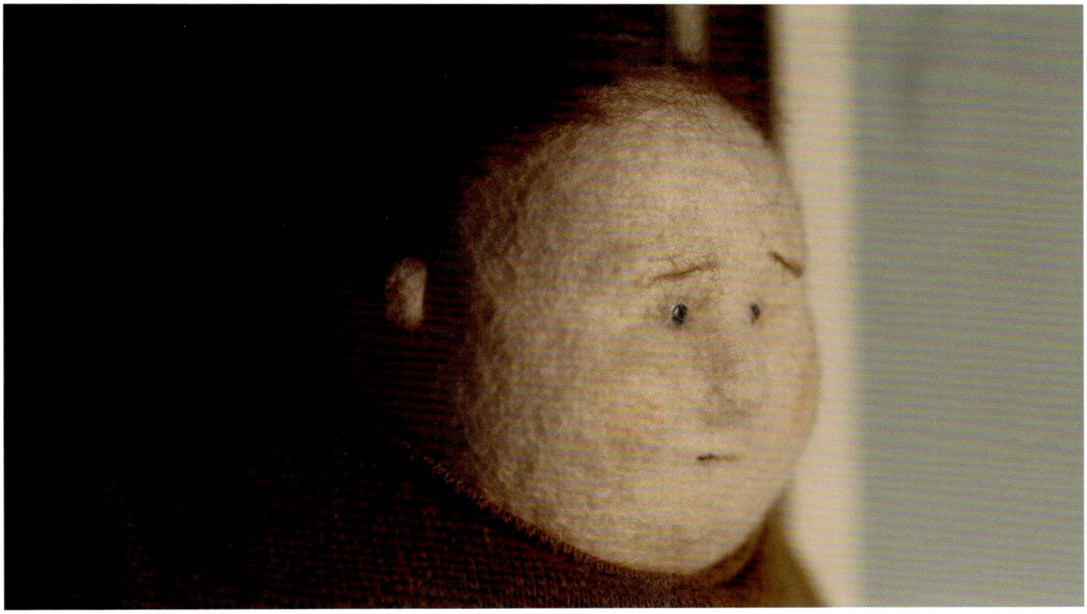

Emma De Swaef (BE) studied animation in Brussels and Gent. Since 2005 she has been making animations and documentaries. **Marc James Roels** (BE) studied animation in Gent. He makes commercials, animations and short fiction films. **Emma De Swaef** (BE) studierte Animation in Brüssel und Gent und produziert seit 2005 Animations- und Dokumentarfilme. **Marc James Roels** (BE) studierte Animation an der Kunsthochschule in Gent und macht Werbefilme, Animations- und Kurzfilme.

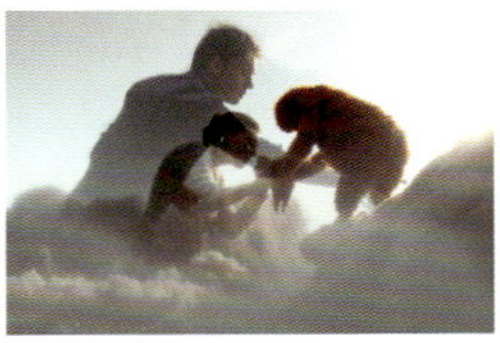

Ars Rata

Moritz Palnstorfer, Christian Schulze

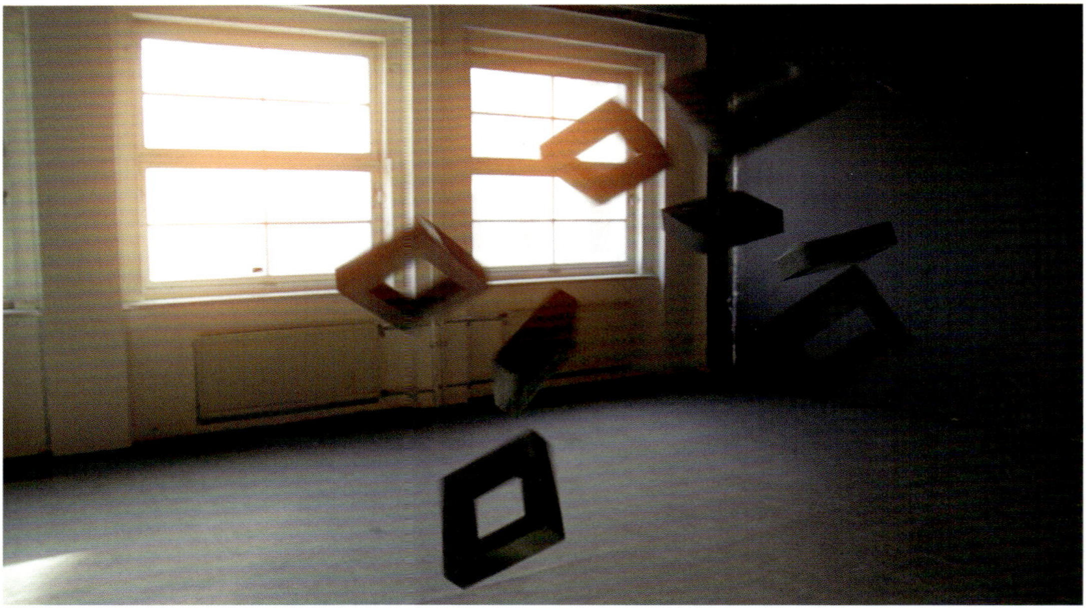

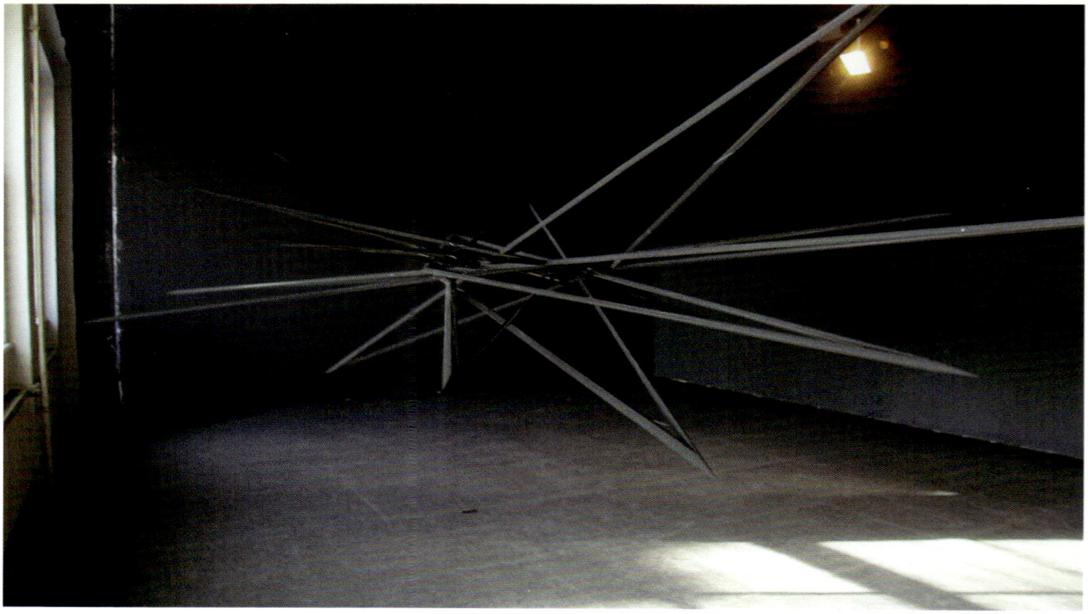

Produced by University of Applied Sciences Uppe⁻ Austria, Hagenberg Campus. Special thanks to Roland Keil and the staff of the degree program Digital Arts

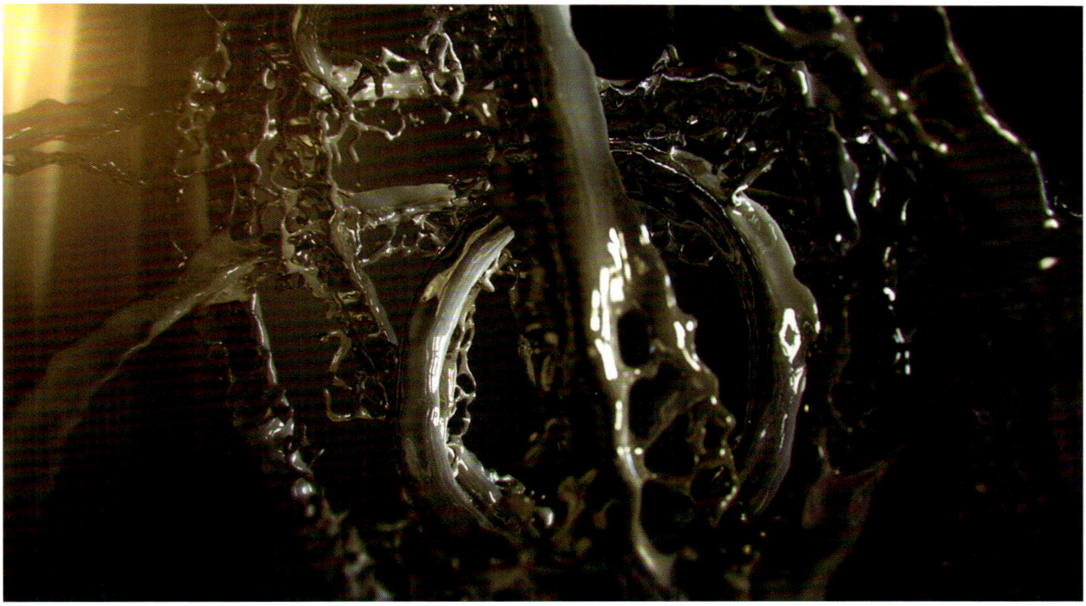

Ars Rata ist das Masterprojekt von Christian Schulze und Moritz Palnstorfer. Der Film zeigt das Leben einer Skulptur, die sich aus einer Kugel entwickelt und gegen den Raum ankämpft, der sie gefangen hält. Der Konflikt, der in der Auflösung der Skulptur gipfelt, ist als Computeranimation dargestellt, die in Videomaterial und zusätzliche computergenerierte Aufnahmen eingebettet ist.

Ars Rata is the master's project by Christian Schulze and Moritz Palnstorfer. The movie shows the life of a sculpture that evolves from a sphere and struggles with the room that imprisons it. This culminates in an existential disintegration of the sculpture. The conflict is depicted as a computer animation embedded in video footage and additional computer-generated shots.

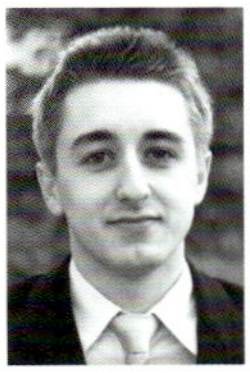

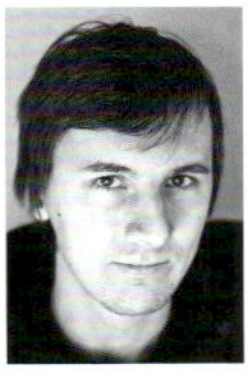

Moritz Palnstorfer (AT) is a visual-effects artist from Salzburg. He studied media technology and design (BSc) and digital arts (MA) at the Hagenberg Campus of the University of Applied Sciences Upper Austria. **Christian Schulze** (DE) studied computer science in media (BSc) at the Hochschule Harz (University of Applied Sciences) in Wernigerode and digital arts (MA) at the University of Applied Sciences Upper Austria in Hagenberg. His master's thesis deals with creative processes in terms of generative and interactive artworks. Since November 2012 Christian has been a freelance Nuke compositor and coder living in Berlin. **Moritz Palnstorfer** (AT) ist ein Visual-Effects-Künstler aus Salzburg. Er studierte Medientechnik und -design sowie Digital Arts an der FH OÖ Campus Hagenberg in Oberösterreich. **Christian Schulze** (DE) studierte Medieninformatik an der Hochschule Harz (Universität für angewandte Wissenschaften) in Wernigerode und Digital Arts an der Universität für Angewandte Kunst in Hagenberg, Oberösterreich. In seiner Master-Thesis setzte er sich mit kreativen Prozessen in der generativen und interaktiven Kunst auseinander. Seit November 2012 arbeitet Christian Schulze freiberuflich als Nuke Compositor und Programmierer in Berlin.

Ballpit

Kyle Mowat

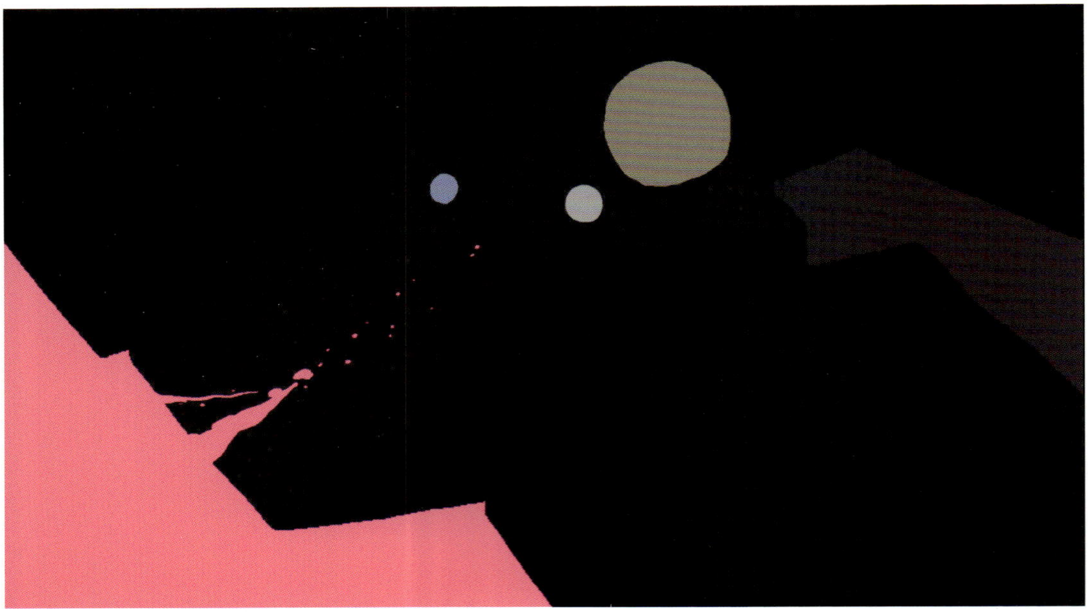

Ballpit is a short film that explores some of the concepts behind natural selection, things like adaptation to environmental changes, in an appealing and visually inventive way. The goal was to give the impression of life as a cycle in which the place of humans is only as a small part in a much larger process; a reminder of our relative insignificance.

Ballpit ist ein Kurzfilm, der sich mit Theorien zum Thema natürliche Selektion, etwa der Anpassung an sich verändernde Umweltbedingungen, auseinandersetzt. Die Intention dabei war, das Leben als Kreislauf darzustellen, in dem der Mensch nur ein Teil eines viel größeren Prozesses ist, und an unsere relative Bedeutungslosigkeit darin zu erinnern.

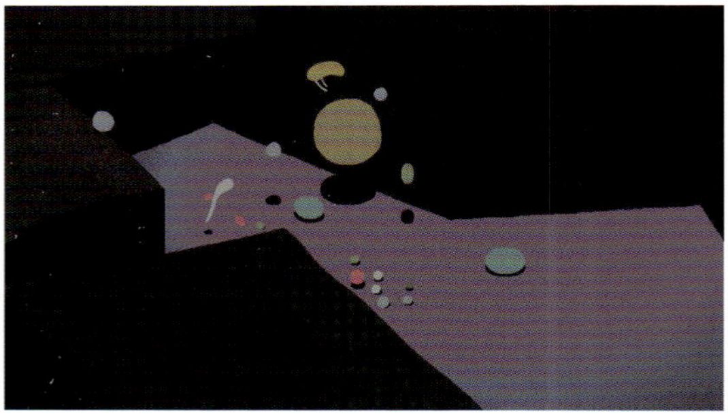

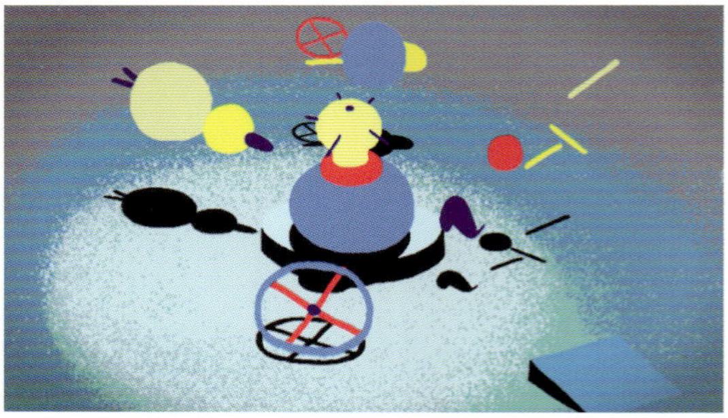

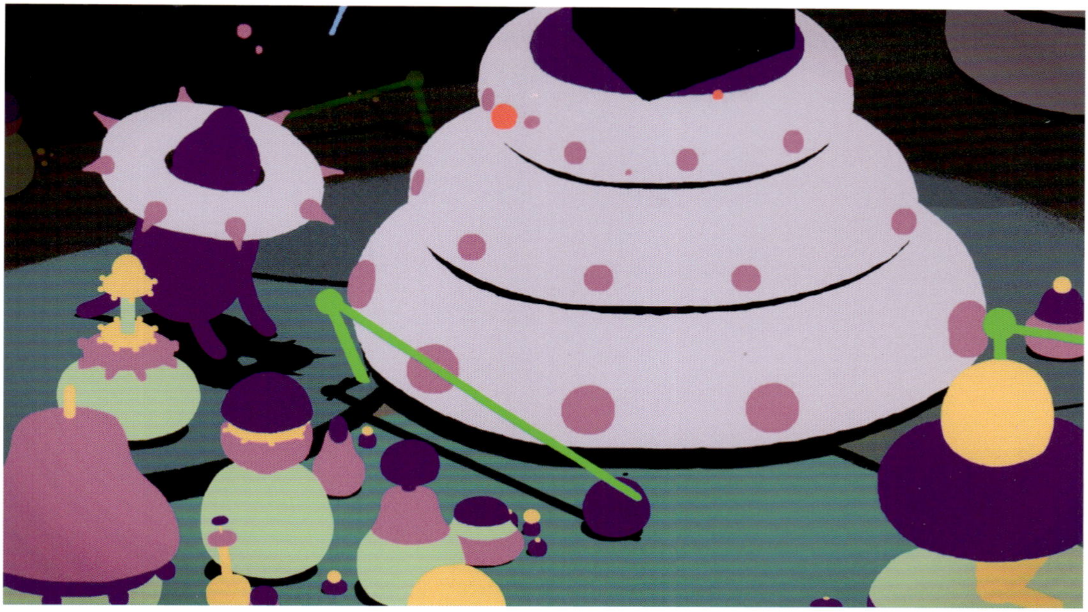

Am wichtigsten war mir eine positive Darstellung dieser Tatsache. Ich hoffte, etwas zu machen, das unsere Rolle in diesem unglaublichen und erstaunlichen Prozess anerkennt, statt unsere Bedeutungslosigkeit negativ zu akzentuieren.

Most of all I wanted to do this in a very positive sense. I hoped to make something that celebrates our place in such an incredible and astounding process rather than viewing our lack of importance as a negative.

Music by Lido Pimienta

Kyle Mowat (CA) is an animator designer and illustrator from Port Perry, Ontario, and a recent graduate from Sheridan's Bachelor of Applied Arts Animation program. *Ballpit* is Kyle's first film. **Kyle Mowat** (CA) ist ein Zeichner, Designer und Animationsfilmer aus Port Perry, Ontario, und absolvierte vor Kurzem das Studium Angewandte Kunst und Animation am Sheridan College. *Ballpit* ist sein erster Film.

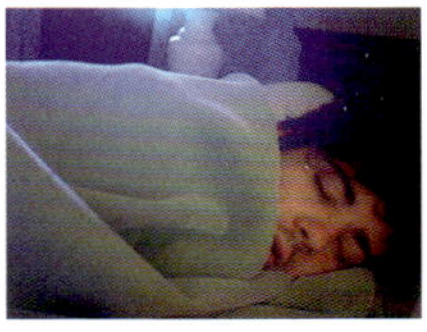

Björk—Mutual Chore

Andrew Thomas Huang

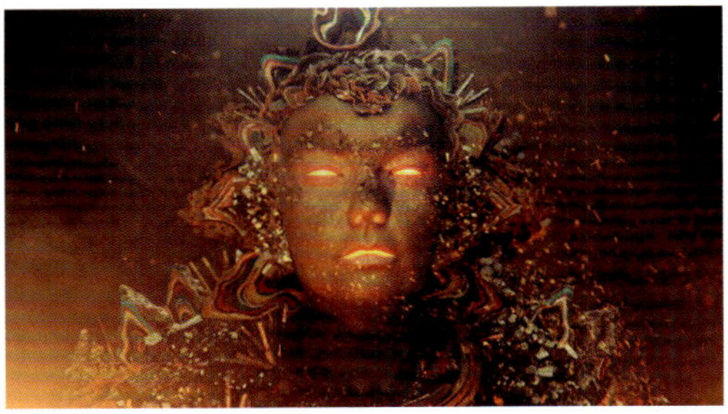

Björk's aesthetically stunning video for *Mutual Core* has been published through the Los Angeles Museum of Contemporary Art's new YouTube channel, MOCAtv. In addition to its standing as the ninth track on Björk's 2011 album *Biophilia*, *Mutual Core* is likely the first song in history to sing tectonic plate metaphors over a electronic beat.

Video director Andrew Thomas Huang, who recently earned accolades at the Cannes Lions New Directors Showcase, visually builds off of Björk's geological lyrical motifs by integrating the vocalist with the continually evolving sedimentary landscape.

After several minutes of a soft-synthesizer build-up, Björk erupts from the sand into a heavily distorted, pulsing chorus. Huang, not missing a beat, detonates a volcano to parallel Björk's lyrical passion.

On *Mutual Core*, Huang's film direction somehow matches the epic bombast that we have come to expect from Björk's songwriting—a seemingly impossible task!

Filming involved a combination of CGI effects, heavy makeup, and physical props manipulated like puppets against a green screen, and Huang says the direction was inspired by the volcanic surroundings of Iceland.

Björks ästhetisch hoch interessantes Video für *Mutual Core* wurde auf dem neuen YouTube-Kanal MOCAtv des Museum of Contemporary Art in Los Angeles präsentiert. Der neunte Track aus Björks 2011 erschienenem Album *Mutual Core* ist vermutlich der erste Song der Musikgeschichte, bei dem ein metaphorischer Text über tektonische Platten zu elektronischen Beats gesungen wird. Der Regisseur des Videos, Andrew Thomas Huang, der kürzlich beim New Directors Showcase in Cannes mehrfach ausgezeichnet wurde, setzt Björks lyrisch-geologische Motive visuell um, indem er die Sängerin inmitten einer sich ständig verändernden Landschaft zeigt, die aus Sedimenten vulkanischen Ursprungs gebildet ist.

Nach einem längeren Auftakt, der von Softsynthklängen getragen ist, bricht die im Treibsand vergrabene Björk in einen taumelnden, rhythmisch pulsierenden Gesang aus. Huang, der auf jeden einzelnen Takt eingeht, lässt synchron zu Björks lyrischer Leidenschaft einen Vulkan ausbrechen.

Er schaffte das scheinbar Unmögliche und setzte in seiner Regiearbeit für *Mutual Core* den epischen Bombast, den wir von Björks Songwriting erwarten, in kongenialen Bildern um.

Der Film arbeitet mit einer Kombination aus CGI-Effekten, aufwändigem Make-up und Requisiten, die wie Marionetten vor einem grünen Hintergrund bewegt wurden. Huang zufolge wurde die Bildsprache des Videos auch von der Vulkanlandschaft Islands beeinflusst.

http://www.youtube.com/watch?feature=player_embedded&v=ZM80F_J-QHE

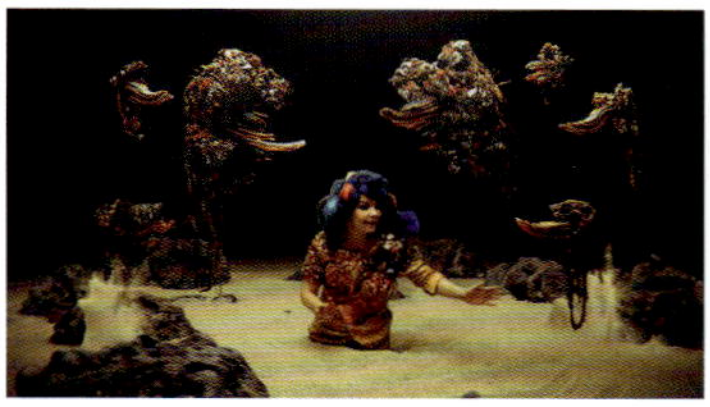
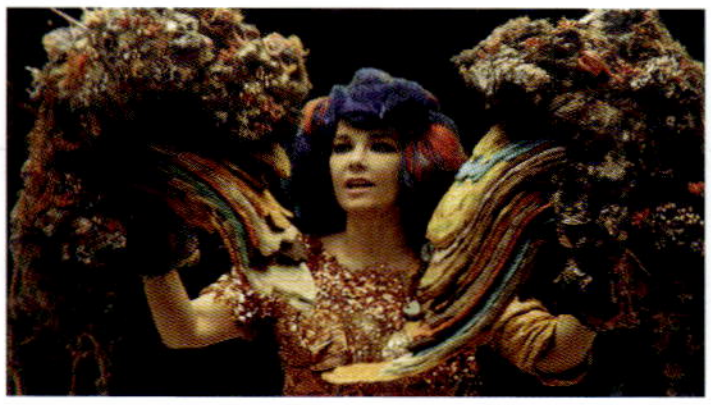
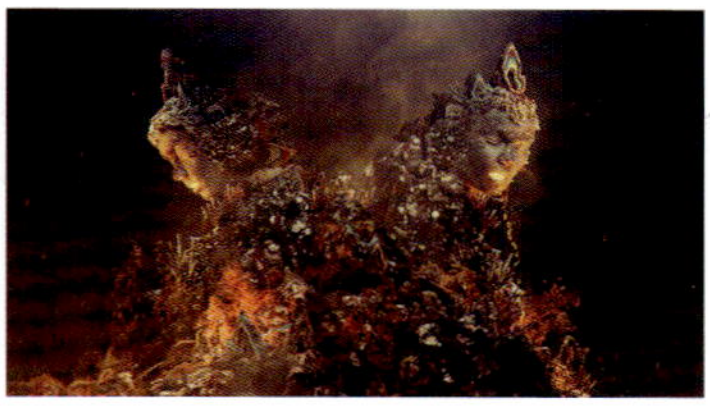

Directed by Andrew Thomas Huang, *http://www.andrewthomashuang.com*

Reykjavik Unit: producer: Árni Björn Helgason, director of photography: August Jakobsson, production designer: Gus Olafsson, hair & makeup artist: Frida Maria Hardardottir

Los Angeles Unit: director of photography: Laura Merians, production designer: Hugh Zeigler

VFX executive producer: David Lyons, lead CG supervisor: Michael Ranger, lead compositor: Lindsey Fry, FX technical director: Nico Sugleris, director's rep: LARK Creative

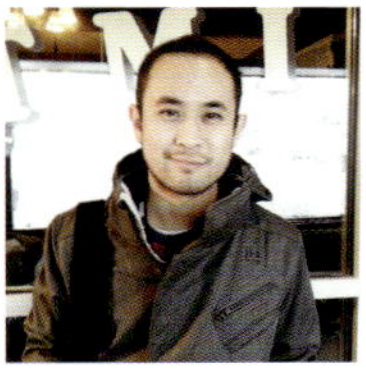

Andrew Thomas Huang (US) is a filmmaker and artist living in Los Angeles. His filmmaking career was preceded with a love of drawing and painting, paralleled with experimentation in animation, fashion and puppetry. These interests culminated in his short film *Solipsist*, which was honored at the Saatchi & Saatchi New Directors Showcase at Cannes Lions and won Best Experimental Short Film at the Slamdance Film Festival. The film caught the attention of Icelandic polymath Björk, leading Andrew to direct her music video for *Mutual Core*, premiering at the Museum of Contemporary Art, Los Angeles. Andrew's work has been showcased worldwide. He graduated with a degree in fine art and animation from the University of Southern California. **Andrew Thomas Huang** (US) lebt und arbeitet als Filmemacher und Künstler in Los Angeles. Vor seiner Karriere als Regisseur beschäftigte er sich mit Zeichnen und Malen und experimentierte in den Bereichen Animation, Mode und Marionettentheater. Diese unterschiedlichen Interessen konnte er in seinem Kurzfilm *Solipsist* bündeln, der beim Saatchi & Saatchi New Directors Showcase der Cannes Lions ausgezeichnet wurde und beim Slamdance Film Festival den Preis als bester experimenteller Kurzfilm bekam. Der Film erregte die Aufmerksamkeit der interdisziplinär arbeitenden isländischen Künstlerin Björk. Sie bekundete Interesse an einer Zusammenarbeit und ersuchte den Filmemacher, das Musikvideo für *Mutual Core* zu drehen. Der Videoclip wurde im Museum of Contemporary Art in Los Angeles präsentiert. Huang, dessen Arbeiten bereits weltweit gezeigt wurden, studierte Kunst und Animation an der University of Southern California.

It's Such a Beautiful Day

Don Hertzfeldt

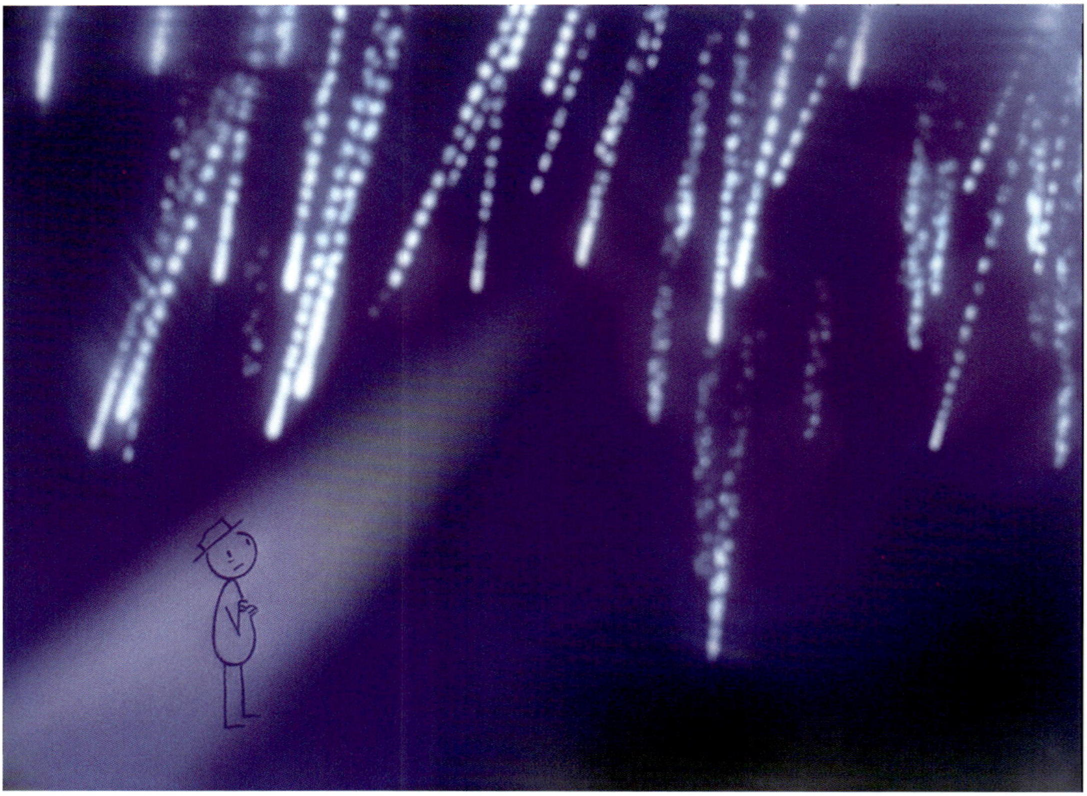

In this third and final chapter to Don Hertzfeldt's *Everything will be OK* trilogy, Bill finds himself struggling with memory loss.

Nearly two years in the making, the 23-minute *It's Such a Beautiful Day* is Don's longest, and most ambitious film to date: blending traditional animation, experimental optical effects, trick photography and new digital hybrids printed out one frame at a time, the movie was captured entirely on an antique 35mm animation stand. Built in the 1940s, it is one of the last surviving cameras of its kind still operating in America.

"The film follows an anxiety-stricken stick man named Bill for whom the mundane tasks of everyday life prove Earth-shatteringly momentous. We join him on a bittersweet existential odyssey which takes in dead birds, big onions, lunchbox messages, trains, manatees, leaf-blowers and the eventual death and rebirth of the known universe. The film is a pocket-sized epic, incorporating the blistering deadpan of Buster Keaton, the narrative

In diesem dritten und letzten Teil von Don Hertzfeldts Trilogie *Everything will be OK* hat Bill mit unerklärlichen Erinnerungslücken zu kämpfen.

Der 23-minütige Film *It's Such a Beautiful Day*, an dem Herztfeld fast zwei Jahre gearbeitet hat, ist sein bis jetzt umfangreichstes und ambitioniertestes Projekt: Der Film, in dem traditionelle Animation, Spezialeffekte, Trickfotografie und neue digital bearbeitete und einzeln ausgedruckte Hybridbilder kombiniert werden, wurde zur Gänze auf einem alten Tricktisch mit 35-mm-Kamera aus den 1940er Jahren aufgenommen, von dem nur noch wenige Exemplare in Amerika in Verwendung sind.

„Der Film folgt einem von Ängsten gepeinigten Strichmännchen namens Bill, für das die banalen Aufgaben des Alltags von weltbewegender Bedeutung sind. Wir begleiten Bill auf eine bittersüße existenzielle Odyssee, auf der wir mit toten Vögeln, riesigen Zwiebeln, Lunchbox-Sprüchen, Zügen, Seekühen, Laubbläsern und zuletzt mit Tod und Wiedergeburt unseres Universums konfrontiert werden. Der Film ist ein Heldenepos in Miniaturformat und vereint die stoische Ernsthaftigkeit von Buster Keaton,

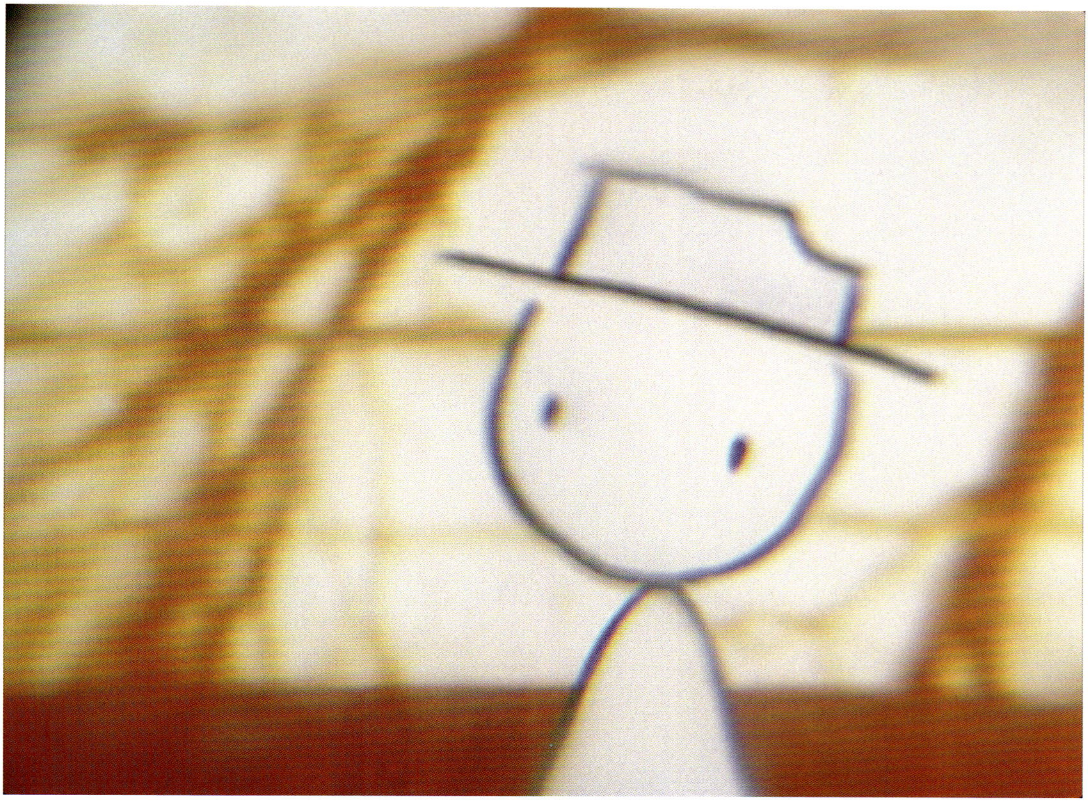

die narrativen Rückblenden von Charlie Kaufman, die kontemplative Zen-Ästhetik von Yazujiro Ozu und das grandiose philosophische Kino von Terrence Malicks." *(http://www.ica.org.uk/37391/Film/Its-Such-a-Beautiful-Day-The-Don-Hertzfeldt-Experience.html)*

back-flipping of Charlie Kaufman, the blissful Zen contemplation of Yazujiro Ozu and the grand philosophical investigations of Terrence Malick." *(http://www.ica.org.uk/37391/Film/Its-Such-a-Beautiful-Day-The-Don-Hertzfeldt-Experience.html)*

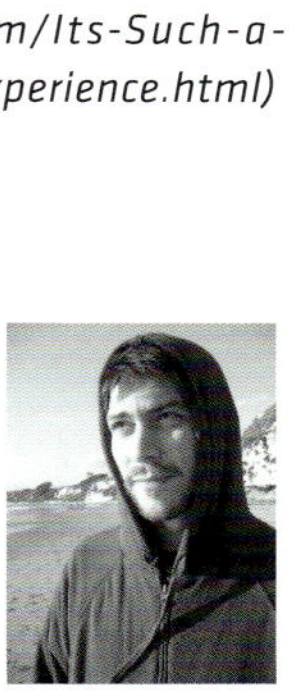

Don Hertzfeldt (US) is an Academy Award nominee whose animated films have screened around the world. Some notable honors include a Short Film Palme d'Or nomination at the 1999 Cannes Film Festival *(Billy's Balloon)*, a 2001 Oscar nomination for Best Animated Short *(Rejected)*, the Lawrence Kasdan Award for Best Narrative Film *(Everything will be OK)*, and Best Picture & Best Screenplay from the Fargo Film Festival *(I Am So Proud of You)*. In 2010, Don received the San Francisco International Film Festival's "Persistence of Vision" Lifetime Achievement Award at the age of 33. **Don Hertzfeldt** (US), dessen Animationsfilme auf der ganzen Welt gezeigt werden, wurde bereits mit einer Oscar-Nominierung gewürdigt. Zu seinen zahlreichen Auszeichnungen zählen die Nominierung für die goldene Palme in der Kategorie Kurzfilm beim Film-Festival von Cannes 1999 *(Billy's Balloon)*, 2001 die Oscar-Nominierung für den besten animierten Kurzfilm *(Rejected)*, der Lawrence Kasdan Award für den besten narrativen Film *(Everything will be OK)* sowie die Auszeichnung bester Film und bestes Drehbuch beim Fargo Film Festival *(I Am So Proud of You)*. 2010 erhielt Don Hertzfeld im Alter von 33 Jahren beim San Francisco International Film Festival den „Persistence of Vision Award" für sein Lebenswerk.

MeTube: August sings Carmen "Habanera"

Daniel Moshel

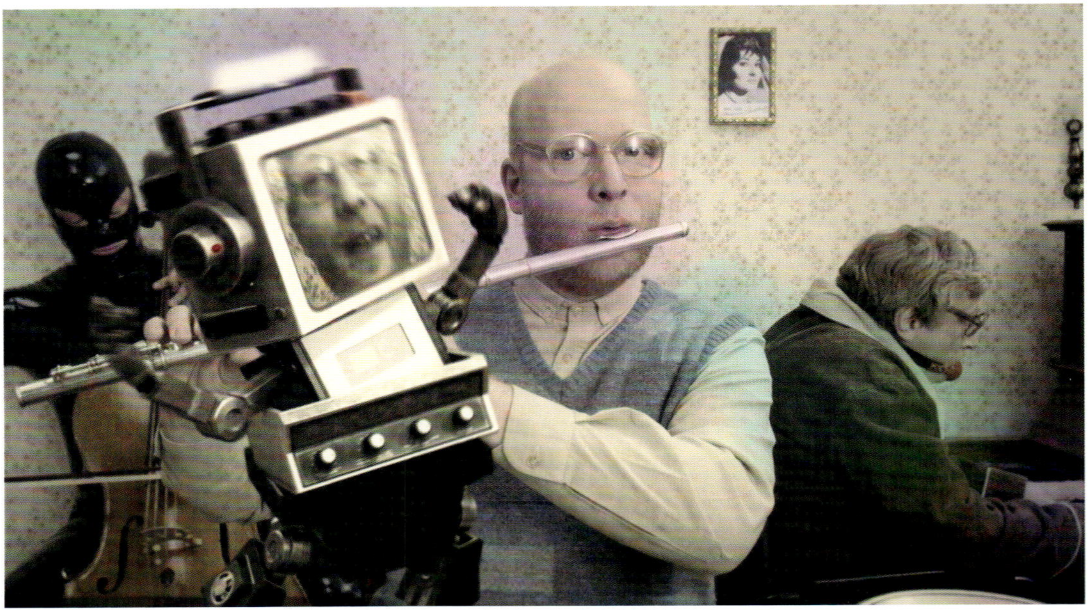

MeTube, a homage to thousands of ambitious YouTube users and video bloggers, gifted and less gifted self-promoters on the Internet, has attracted international attention. No less than George Bizet's "Habanera" from *Carmen* has been reinterpreted for *MeTube* and enhanced with electronic sounds. Behind the cross-over of musical styles are director Daniel Moshel as well as opera and oratorio tenor August Schram. Given Schram's fondness for oscillating between singing, art and new media, the film expert and the opera singer have merged their efforts. The result: a fusion of new media, classical opera singing interpreted in a modern manner and artistic, ingenious self-promotion laced with a dose of self-mockery.

MeTube, eine Hommage an Tausende ambitionierte YouTube-Nutzer und Video-Blogger, mehr oder minder begabte Selbstdarsteller im Internet, lässt international aufhorchen. Keine geringere Arie als George Bizets „Habanera" aus *Carmen* wurde für *MeTube* neu interpretiert und mit elektronischen Klängen unterlegt. Hinter dem Cross-over musikalischer Stilrichtungen stehen Regisseur Daniel Moshel sowie Opern- und Oratorientenor August Schram. Zu einer Zusammenarbeit der beiden kam es durch die Begeisterung des Opernsängers für interdisziplinäre Projekte an der Schnittstelle von Gesang, Kunst und Neuen Medien. Das Ergebnis: eine Verschmelzung von Neuen Medien und klassischem Operngesang in einer modernen Interpretation sowie eine originelle künstlerische Selbstdarstellung, versehen mit einer Prise Selbstironie.

Writer, director: Daniel Moshel; singing: August Schram; production: Moshel Film, August Schram; d.o.p.: Martin Bauer; editor: Christin Veith; production manager: Roland Pfannhauser; 3d concept art robot: Heri Irawan; 3d modelling/texturing/rendering: Michi Brandstetter; 3d animation: Christoph Schinko; compositing: Tommi Brandstetter; motion control: CMOCOS Vienna

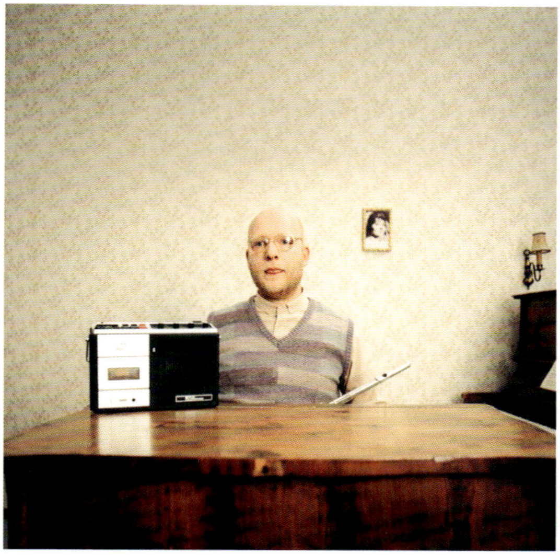

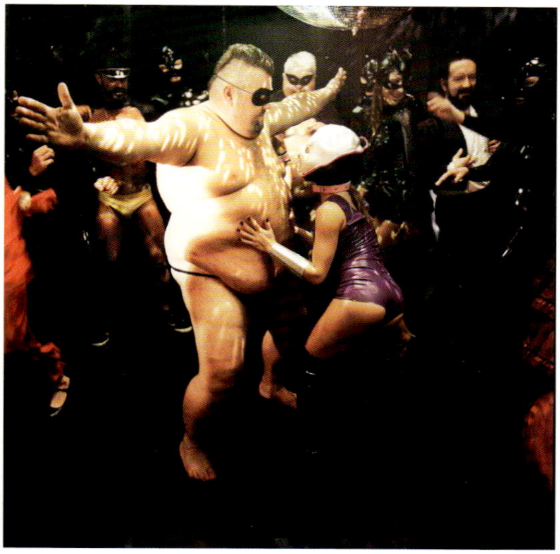

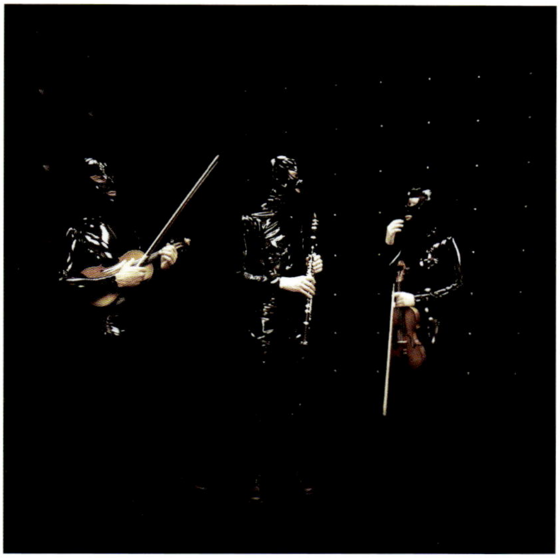

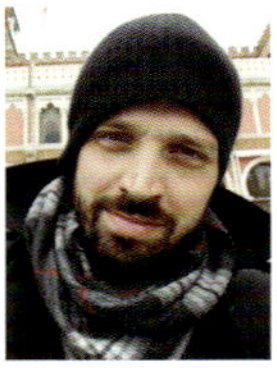

Daniel Moshel (DE), born in 1976, studied multimedia art at Salzburg University. Since 2003 he has been working as a freelance author/director/producer in Salzburg and Vienna. **Daniel Moshel** (DE), geb. 1976, studierte Multi Media Art an der FH Salzburg. Seit 2003 ist er selbstständig als Autor/Regisseur/Produzent in Salzburg und Wien tätig.

Palmipedarium

Jérémy Clapin / Papy3D Productions

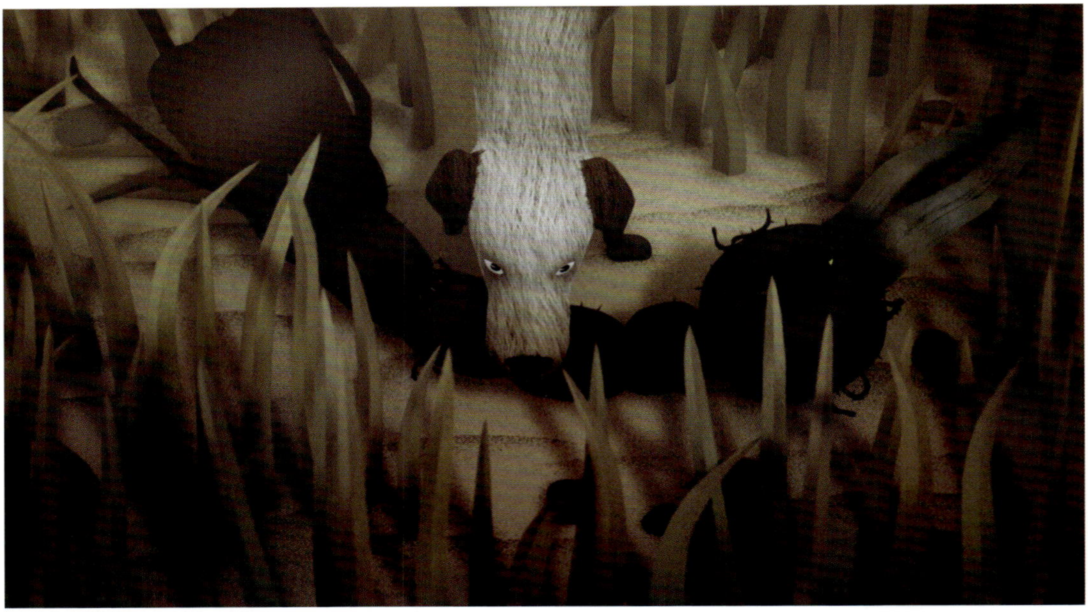

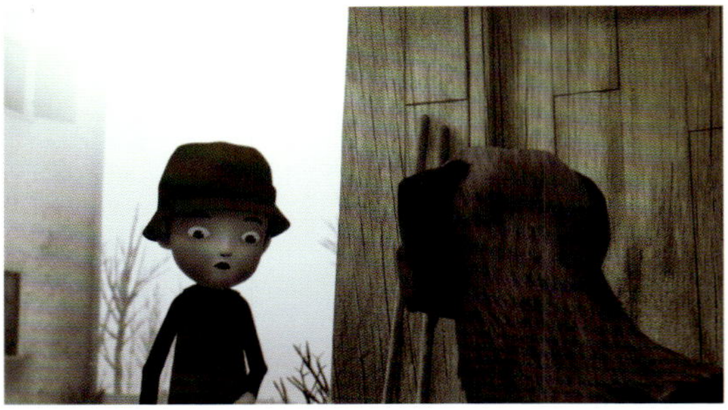

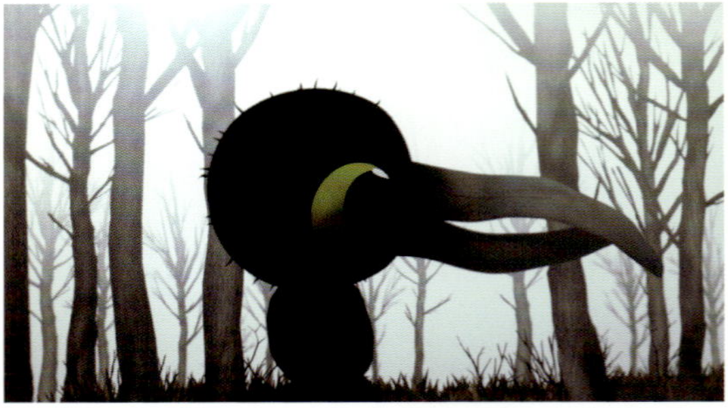

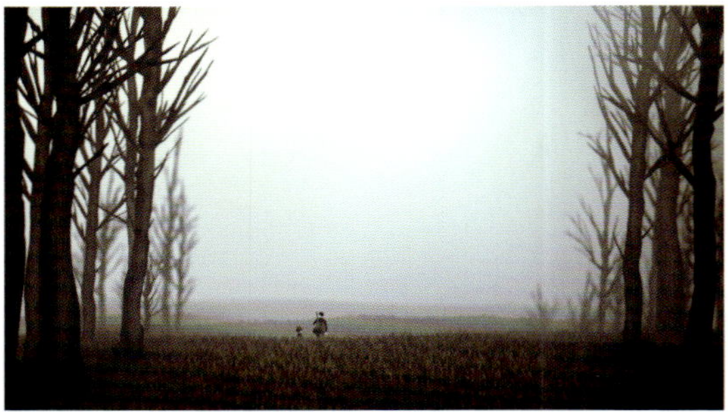

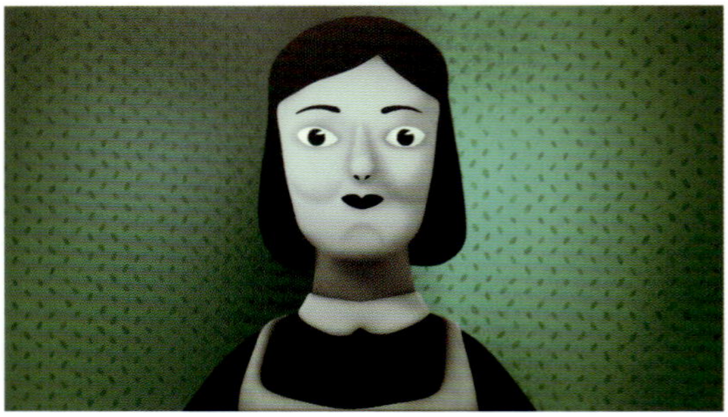

Producer: Richard Van Den Boom; executive producer: Jérémy Clapin; Music: François-Eudes Chanfrault; Technical director: Jean-François Sarazin (Vanilla Seed); Sound design and mix: Eric Lonni (Digital Salad). Supported by CNC, Arte, the Procirep/Angoa-Agicoa and the Val de Marne Council

Eigentlich kennt Simon Enten gut. Sie schnattern, fliegen, schwimmen – einige schlagen sogar Purzelbäume. Manchmal ist aber alles ganz schön verwirrend und Simon ratlos. Bei diesem neuen Film habe ich im Vergleich zu früheren Arbeiten einen anderen Regieansatz verfolgt. Ausgangspunkt war kein Konzept oder Handlungsaufbau, sondern der Wunsch, eine besondere Stimmung wiederzugeben: die Stimmung der Kindheit, Zerbrechlichkeit, Gefühle, die an ein sich ständig veränderndes Alltagsleben angepasst werden müssen. Der Protagonist des Films, Simon, ein sechsjähriges Kind, führt uns durch die Geschichte. Er reagiert so spontan, dass sich nie vorhersagen lässt, was er als nächstes tun wird. Er streift umher und zwingt uns, ihm zu folgen, wie ein Spielzeug, das an einer Schnur nachgezogen wird. Simon ist weder ein besonders nettes Kind noch ein Rabauke. Manchmal kann er grausam sein, gleich darauf zeigt er großes Einfühlungsvermögen. Sein innerer Konflikt wird von einem Monster personifiziert, das bisweilen auftaucht und das versonnene Kind verstört und in Aufruhr versetzt.
Palmipedarium wurde mit Open-Source-Software (Blender) realisiert.

Simon knows ducks quite well. They make noise, fly, swim, some even roll. Sometimes, it's a bit confusing and Simon gets lost.
I tried a different approach in directing this new film compared to my previous ones. The starting point was not a concept or a specific set-up, but a desire to picture a particular mood. Something about childhood, a frailty, feelings that must be adjusted to a shifting daily life. The film's main character, Simon, is a six-year-old child who guides us through the story. He reacts so spontaneously that nobody can predict what his next action will be. He moves around, forcing us to follow, like a toy pulled behind on a string. Simon is neither nice nor bad, but a bit of both. He can be cruel at times and immediately afterwards filled with empathy. Simon's inner conflict is embodied by the monster that comes to trouble the still, silent pool of the child's mind.
Palmipedarium was made using open-source software (Blender).

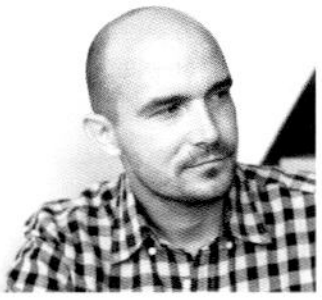

Jérémy Clapin (FR) received his degree at the Paris ENSAD in 1999. Since then he has worked in various fields: art direction, illustrator for editors and magazines, animator and independent director for commercials. In 2004, he directed his first animation short film, *A Backbone Tale*, which has won some fifteen international awards. In 2008, *Skhizein*, his second film, was nominated for the French Césars, shortlisted for the Oscars and won more than 90 festival awards. Since then he has directed many commercials, as well as the *Good Vibrations* short film for Acme Filmworks. In 2010, he joined Papy3D Productions. **Jérémy Clapin** (FR) schloss 1999 sein Studium an der Pariser ENSAD ab. Seither arbeitet er in verschiedenen Bereichen, u.a. als Art Director, Grafiker und Illustrator im Verlagswesen, als Animator und freier Regisseur für Werbefilme. 2004 inszenierte er seinen ersten Animationskurzfilm, *A Backbone Tale*, der an die fünfzehn internationale Auszeichnungen erhielt. Sein zweiter Film *Skhizein* wurde 2008 für den französischen Filmpreis César nominiert, kam auf die Shortlist für den Oscar und gewann mehr als 90 Preise bei diversen Festivals. Seither produzierte er zahlreiche Werbefilme sowie den Kurzfilm *Good Vibrations* für ACME Filmworks. 2010 schloss er sich Papy3D Productions an.

Rollin' Safari

Kyra Buschor, Anna Habermehl, Constantin Paeplow

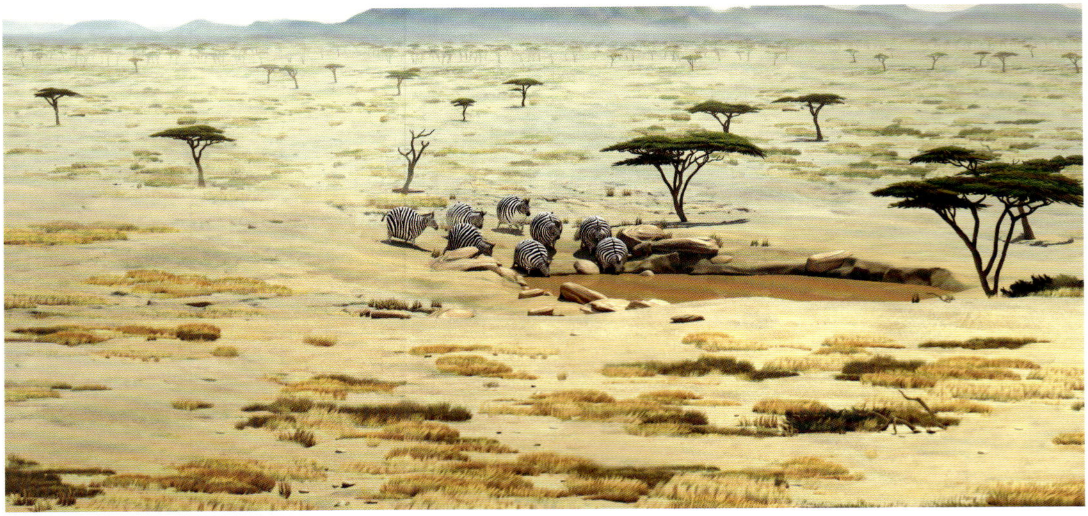

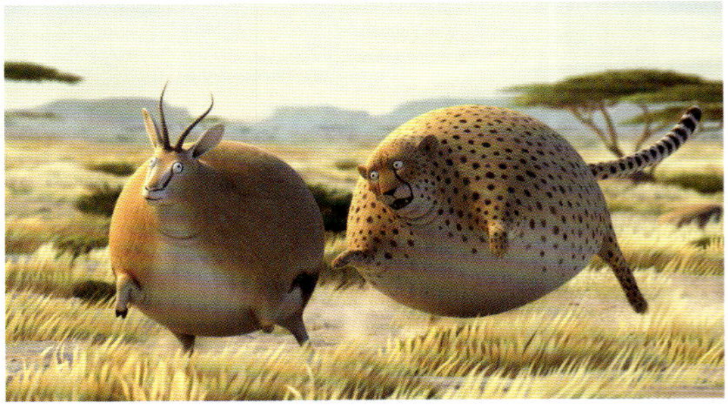

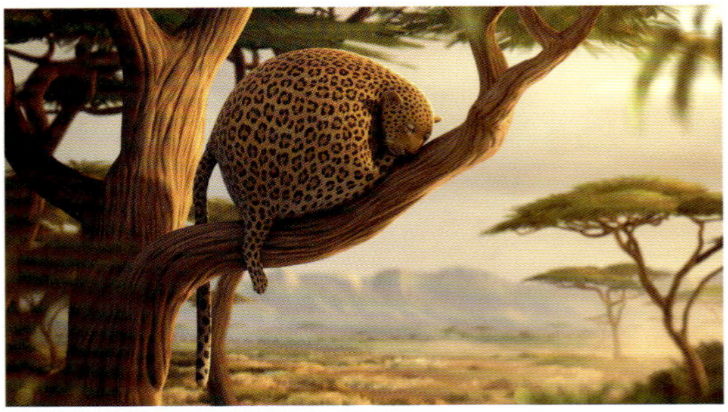

Rollin' Safari is a series of four short clips about bloated African animals that have huge difficulty living a normal life. The clips are a student project created by Constantin Paeplow, Kyra Buschor and Anna Habermehl and produced by Valentina Brüning and Anna Habermehl as trailers for the 2013 International Festival of Animated Film in Stuttgart.

Kyra and Constantin started brainstorming in October 2011, their initial idea being to tell the story of a hunter who comes across a fat, rolling deer that, because of its shape, is incapable of controlling itself. They imagined what a wildlife documentary would be like if all animals in it were round and what scenarios might occur. In November 2011 Anna Habermehl joined the team as the third director and together they decided

Rollin' Safari ist eine Reihe von vier kurzen Animationsfilmen über kugelig aufgeblasene afrikanische Tiere, die größte Schwierigkeiten haben, den Alltag zu bewältigen. Die Videoclips wurden im Rahmen eines Studentenprojekts von Constantin Paeplow, Kyra Buschor and Anna Habermehl realisiert und von Valentina Brüning und Anna Habermehl als Trailer für das Internationale Trickfilmfestival 2013 in Stuttgart produziert.

Kyra Buschor und Constantin Paeplow begannen im Oktober 2011 mit der Ideenfindung. Ausgangspunkt war die Überlegung, die Geschichte eines Jägers zu erzählen, der auf ein übergewichtiges Kugeltier trifft, das sich aufgrund seiner Form nicht in Kontrolle hat. Sie stellten sich vor, wie ein Dokumentarfilm über das Leben in der Wildnis aussehen würde und welche Szenarien sich ergeben könnten, wenn alle im Film vorkommenden Tiere rund wären. Im November 2011 stieß Anna Habermehl als dritte

Directors / animators: Kyra Buschor, Anna Habermehl, Constantin Päplow. Producers: Valentina Brüning, Anna Habermehl. Technical directors: Thomas Hartmann, Sascha Langer, David Kirchner, Markus Kranzler, Christoph Westphal

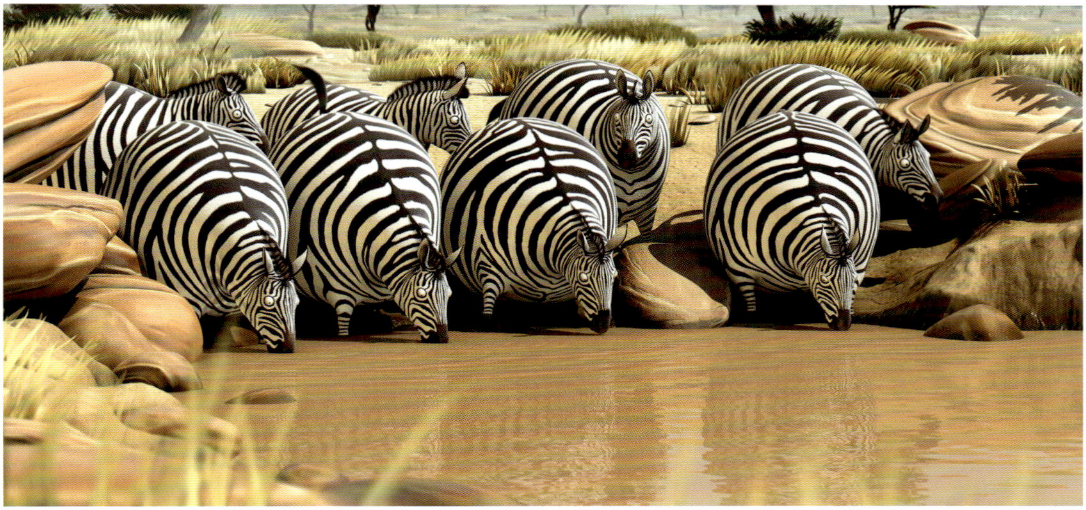

Regisseurin zum Team, gemeinsam beschlossen die Studenten, mehrere lustige Clips rund um kugelige Tiere zu produzieren. Inspirieren ließen sie sich dabei von zahlreichen populären Naturfilmen wie *Unser Planet*, *Planet Erde* oder Grzimeks *Serengeti darf nicht sterben*.

to produce several funny clips of various round animals. The directors' biggest inspiration was numerous popular wildlife documentaries as *Our Planet*, *Planet Earth* or Grzimek's *Serengeti Shall Not Die*.

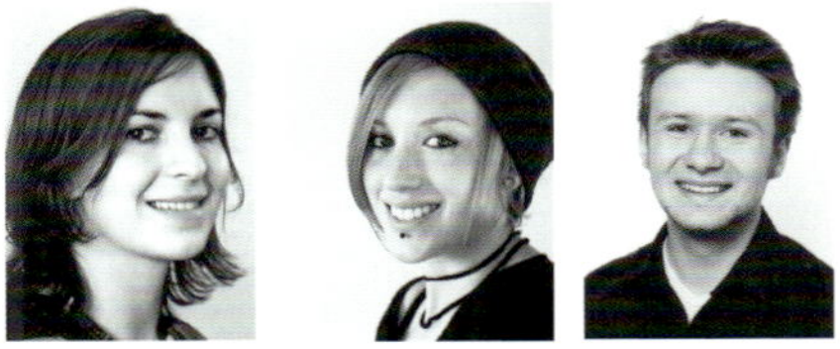

Kyra Buschor (CH), born 1987, finished the Liceo Artistico (German/Italian-speaking art school) and did internships in 3D animation at Los Banditos and the Digital Frame Studio. In October 2009 she started studying animation at the Baden-Württemberg Academy of Film. **Anna Habermehl** (DE), born 1986, began an apprenticeship as a media designer with Das Modular, a small media agency, in 2005. During her education she developed an affection for animated and moving pictures, and applied to the Baden-Württemberg Film Academy, where she has been studying since winter 2009. **Constantin Paeplow** (DE), born 1988, won the Young Talent Award for Animation in 2006 with his first animation film *Weltraumschrott*. In 2008 he started work as a freelancer, focusing on 3D animation and compositing on various productions. In October 2009 he started his course at the Baden-Württemberg Academy of Film, specializing in animation. **Kyra Buschor** (CH), geb. 1987, besuchte nach Abschluss der Sekundarschule das „Liceo Artistico", ein deutsch-italienisches Sprachgymnasium mit Schwerpunkt Kunst. Nach dem Abitur absolvierte sie zwei Praktika im Bereich 3D-Animation bei Los Banditos und im Digital-Frame-Studio in Stuttgart. Seit Herbst 2009 studiert sie Animation an der Filmakademie Baden-Württemberg. **Anna Habermehl** (DE), geb. 1986, entschied sich 2005 für ein Praktikum in einer kleinen Medienagentur. Während der Ausbildung zeigten sich deutliche Neigungen in Richtung Bewegtbild und Animation. Um sich beruflich fortzubilden, bewarb sie sich im Frühjahr 2009 an der Filmakademie Baden-Württemberg und studiert dort seit dem Wintersemester 2009/10 Animation. **Constantin Paeplow** (DE), geb. 1988, gewann 2006 mit seinem ersten Animationsfilm *Weltraumschrott* den Deutschen Nachwuchsfilmpreis. 2008 begann er als freiberuflicher 3D-Animator und Compositer, außerdem arbeitete er von 2008 bis 2010 als Freelancer bei der Trickompany an verschiedenen Animationsprojekten. Im Oktober 2009 begann er sein Studium zum 3D-Animator an der Filmakademie Baden-Württemberg.

Shelter
Carl Burton

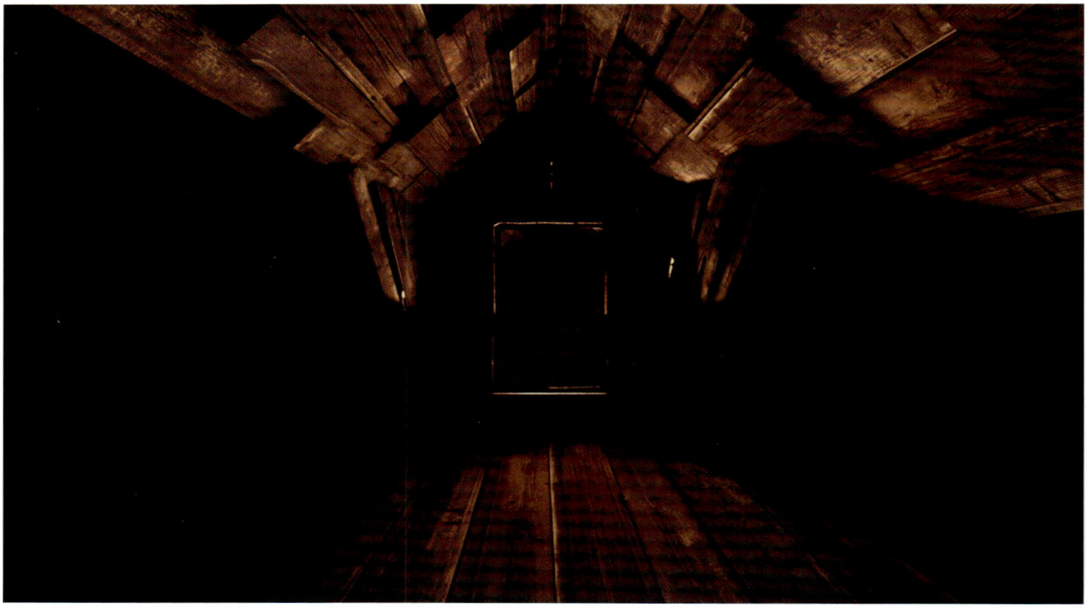

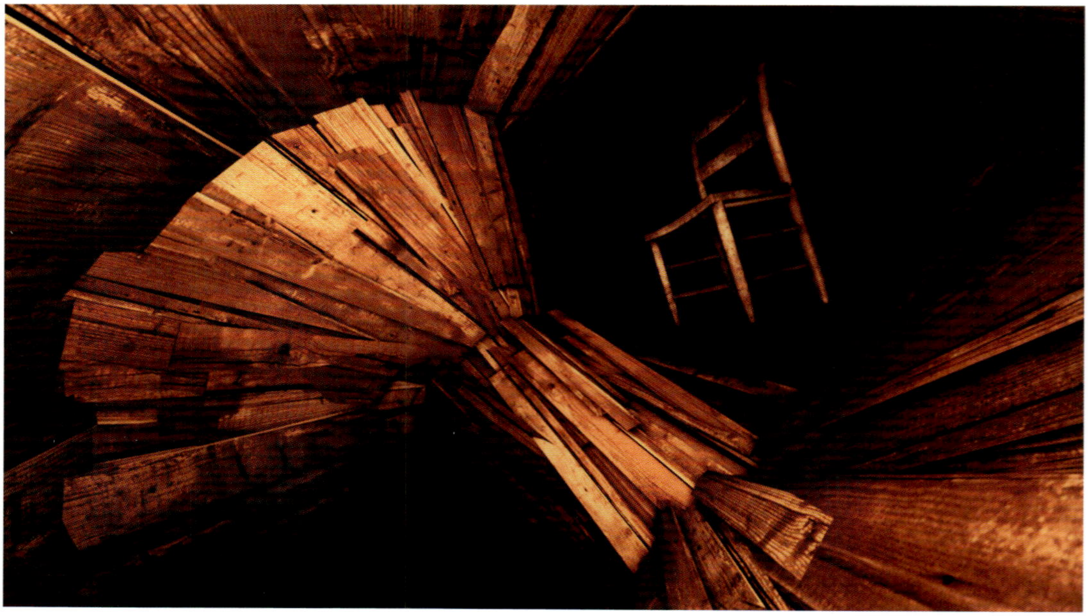

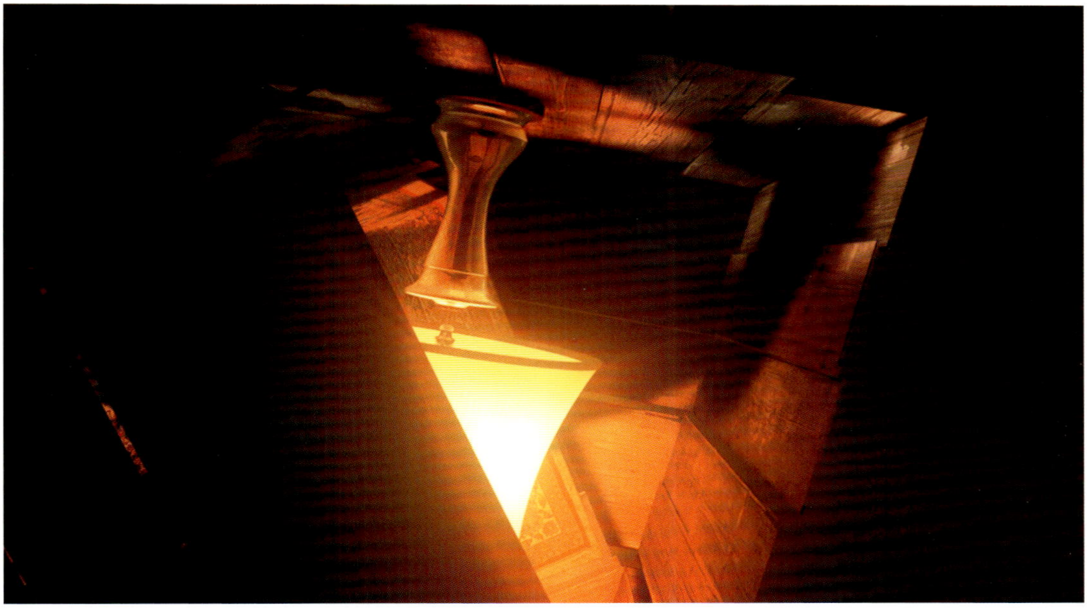

Während eines heftigen Regens erschließen sich auf einem Dachboden die Tiefen einer geheimnisvollen Welt. Vertraute Gegenstände bewegen sich durch ein stetig wachsendes Netzwerk komplexer Räume, die von atmosphärischen Klängen erfüllt sind. *Shelter* erhielt den Staff Pick des Filmportals Vimeo, war in der offiziellen Auswahl von Slamdance, SIGGRAPH Asia und VIS Vienna Independent Shorts und wurde als bester experimenteller Film beim Crossroads Film Festival ausgezeichnet.

A vast secret world is revealed inside an attic during a rainstorm. Familiar objects move through an ever-growing network of complex spaces alive with atmospheric sound. *Shelter* has been honored as a Vimeo Staff Pick, an official selection of Slamdance, SIGGRAPH Asia and VIS Vienna, and Best Experimental Film at the Crossroads Film Festival.

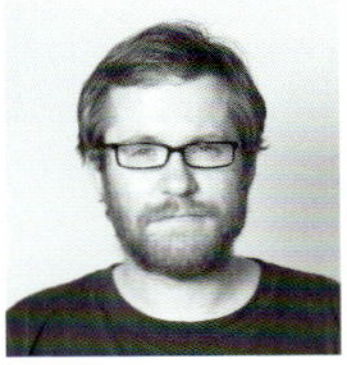

Carl Burton (US) received a BFA in fine art at the University of Illinois in Urbana-Champaign and an MFA at the University of California, San Diego, California. He now lives in New York City, working as an artist, animator and designer. **Carl Burton** (US) studierte bildende Kunst an der University of Illinois in Urbana-Champaign und an der University of California in San Diego, Kalifornien. Er lebt und arbeitet heute als Künstler, Animator und Designer in New York City.

Snail Trail

Philipp Artus

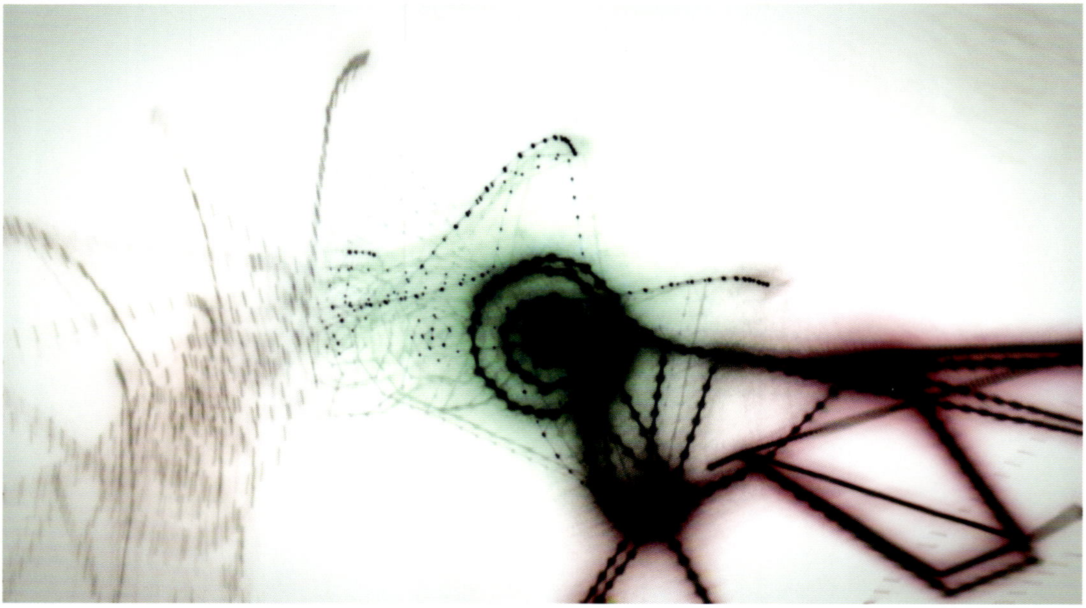

A snail invents the wheel and goes through a cultural evolution to finally get back to its origin.
The basic idea of the *Snail Trail* is inspired by processes of exponential acceleration, which can be observed at different levels. Thus the evolution of life proceeds at an extremely slow pace for more than three billion years, until it suddenly seems to explode in the Cambrian period. The tools of human beings progress relatively little during the Stone Age until there is a rapid cultural development during the Holocene.
Nowadays, a similar acceleration process is generated by the exchange of information through the Internet. From this perspective, the exponential spiral on a snail shell may almost appear like a miraculous wink of nature.
The animation is based on a laser sculpture *(https://vimeo.com/27659555)*, which has a somehow purer and darker feeling than the film. For me the challenge was to find the right tone for the film, to make it into something other than a mere copy of the laser installation. It took me some time to realize that I had to free my mind from the original character and to give space to an evolution. Finally, the film turned out much brighter and more colorful than I had imagined in the beginning.

Eine Schnecke erfindet das Rad und durchläuft eine kulturelle Entwicklung, bis sie schließlich zu ihren Ursprüngen zurückkehrt.
Die Grundidee von *Snail Trail* ist vom Modellansatz exponenzieller Wachstumsprozesse beeinflusst, die auf verschiedenen Ebenen beobachtet werden können. Die Evolution der Lebewesen verläuft über einen Zeitraum von mehr als drei Milliarden Jahren extrem langsam, bis sie im Kambrium plötzlich zu „explodieren" scheint. Die Werkzeuge des Menschen haben sich während der Steinzeit kaum weiterentwickelt, bis es im Holozän plötzlich zu einer rasanten kulturellen Entwicklung kommt.
Heute ist durch den Informationsaustausch im Internet ein ähnlicher Beschleunigungsprozess zu beobachten. Die exponenzielle Spirale auf dem Schneckenhaus erscheint, so gesehen, wie ein wundersames Augenzwinkern der Natur.
Die Animation basiert auf einer Laserskulptur *(https://vimeo.com/27659555)*, die reiner und dunkler wirkt als der Film. Für mich bestand die Herausforderung darin, den richtigen Farbton für den Film zu finden, der nicht nur eine Kopie der Laser-Installation, sondern ein eigenständiges Werk sein sollte. Es brauchte einige Zeit, bis mir klar wurde, dass ich mich vom ursprünglichen Konzept lösen und einer Entwicklung Raum geben musste. Schließlich wurde der Film viel heller und farbintensiver, als ich es mir zu Beginn vorgestellt hatte.

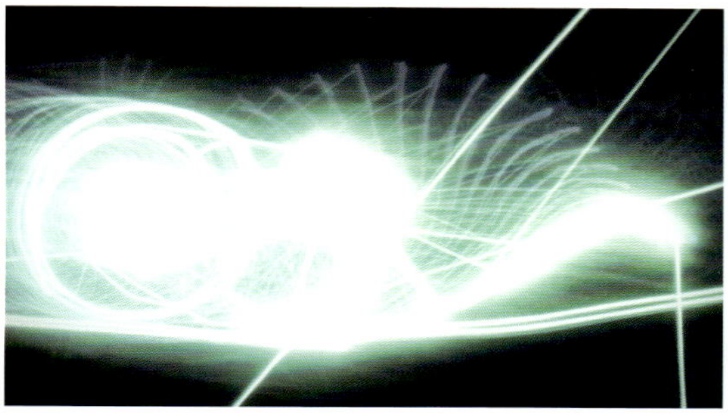
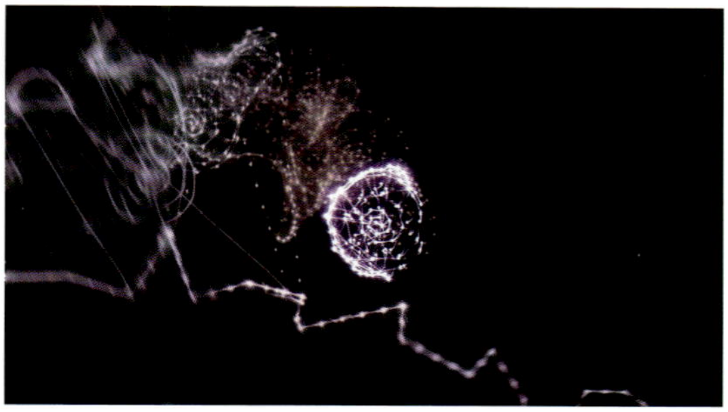
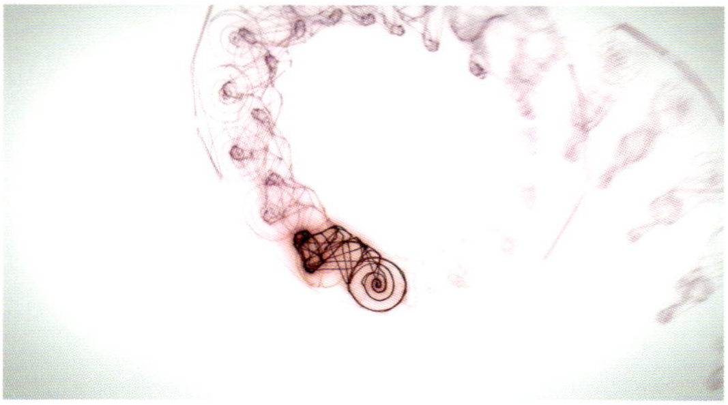
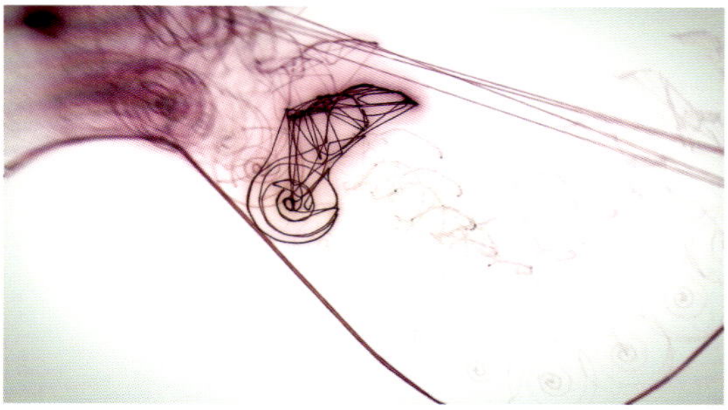
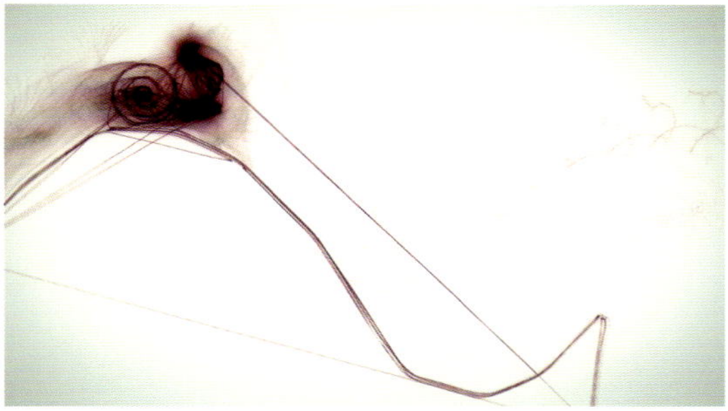
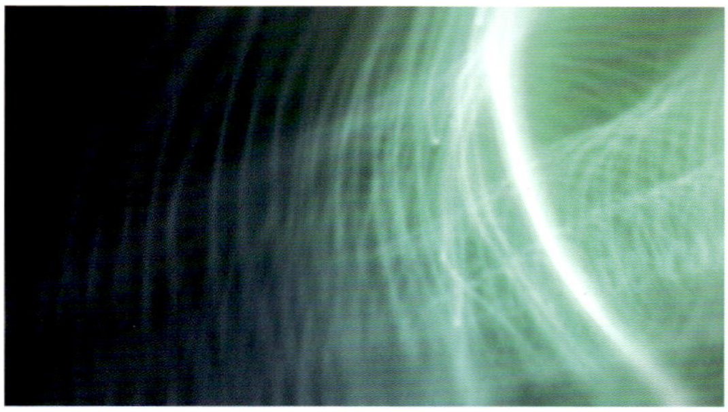

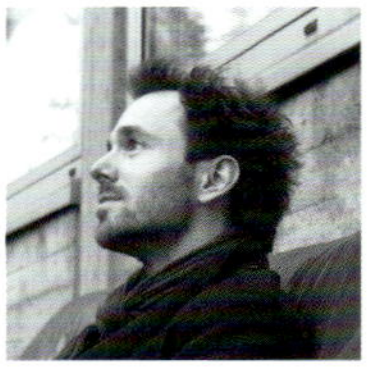

Philipp Artus (DE), born 1982, grew up in Bremen/Germany and began studying art at the École des Beaux Arts in Nantes, France. He continued his autodidactic studies of animation and music theory in Portugal and is currently finishing his graduation project at the Academy of Media Arts in Cologne, Germany. His experimental animations and site-specific installations explore the manifestations of life through movement, sound and imagery. He composes audiovisual experiences that unite playful elements with minimalist structures, timeless themes with contemporary observations, turbulent acceleration with contemplative silence. His projects have been shown in various museums, festivals and galleries around the world. **Philipp Artus** (DE), geb. 1982, wuchs in Bremen/Deutschland auf und studierte Kunst an der École des Beaux Arts in Nantes/Frankreich. Anschließend setzte er seine autodidaktischen Studien in den Bereichen Animation und Musiktheorie in Portugal fort. Derzeit arbeitet er an seinem Abschlussprojekt an der Akademie für Medienkunst in Köln. In seinen experimentellen Animationen und ortspezifischen Installationen untersucht er mittels Bewegung, Klang und Bildern die vielfältigen Manifestationen des Lebens. Er komponiert audiovisuelle Werke, die spielerische Elemente mit minimalistischen Strukturen, zeitlose Themen mit aktuellen Beobachtungen, turbulente Beschleunigung mit kontemplativer Stille verbinden. Seine Projekte wurden in verschiedenen Museen, Galerien und bei Festivals weltweit gezeigt.

Subconcious Password

Chris Landreth

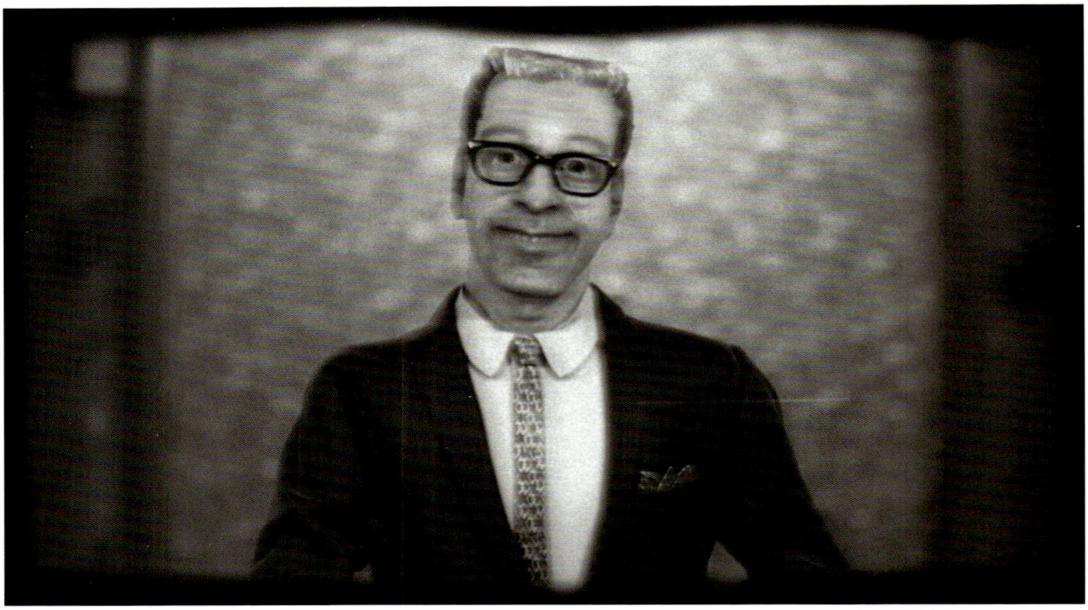

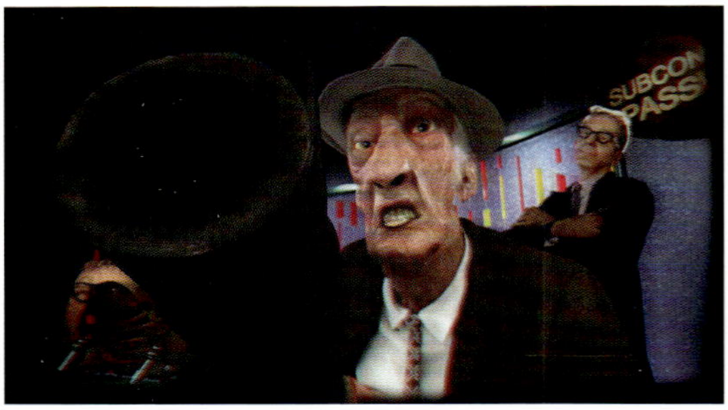

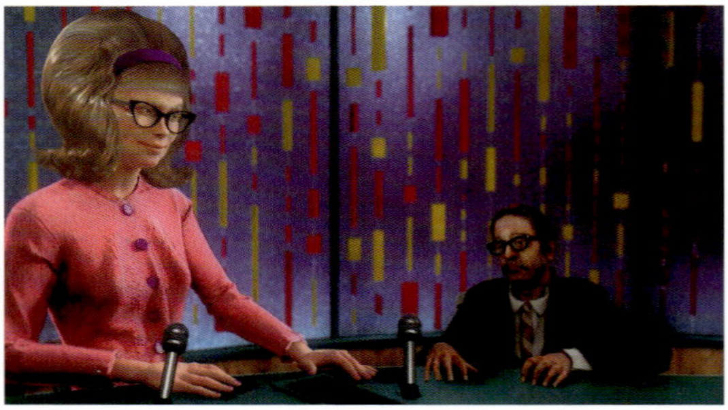

In the middle of a crowded bar Charles finds himself feeling increasingly desperate. The cause of his misery is an old friend he's just run into; his old friend ... you know ... what's-his-name ...

In *Subconscious Password*, Oscar-winning director Chris Landreth uses a common social gaffe—forgetting somebody's name—as the starting point for a mind-bending romp through the unconscious. Inspired by the classic TV game show *Password*, the film features a wealth of animated celebrity guests, plus Charles's mother and his childhood babysitter, who try (and try, and try) to prompt him to remember his friend's name. Charles, Landreth's alter ego, somehow fails to grasp even the most obvious clues. As his frustration increases, the film's 3D effects become more pronounced, mirroring his growing psychological

Im Gedränge einer überfüllten Bar wird Charles von Selbstzweifeln erfasst. Der Grund für sein Unbehagen ist, dass er gerade einem alten Freund begegnet ist, seinem alten Freund ... du weißt schon, wen ich meine ... wie heißt er noch?

In *Subconscious Password* verwendet Regisseur und Oscar-Gewinner Chris Landreth die allen vertraute peinliche Situation, dass einem der Name eines Bekannten entfallen ist, als Ausgangspunkt für eine fulminante Odyssee durch das Unbewusste. In dem von der von der TV-Spielshow *Password* inspirierten Film treten eine Reihe animierter Prominenter sowie Charles' Mutter und sein Babysitter auf, die alle wieder und wieder versuchen, seinem Gedächtnis auf die Sprünge zu helfen. Charles – Landreths Alter ego – schafft es aber, sogar die direktesten Hinweise nicht zu verstehen. In dem Maße, in dem sein Frustpegel steigt, werden die 3D-Effekte des Films,

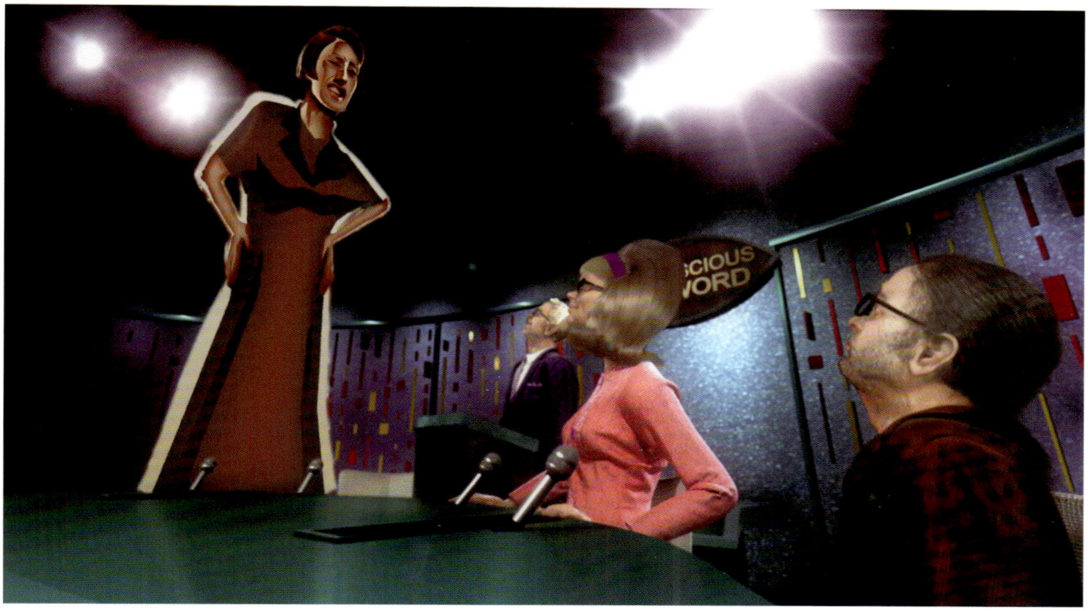

die den wachsenden psychischen Druck des Protagonisten spiegeln, ausgeprägter. Bis Charles schließlich klar wird, dass er sich in seine missliche Lage fügen muss.
Subconscious Password ist eine spielerische und respektlose Annäherung an eine vertraute Erfahrung. Der Film vermag zwar das Gedächtnis nicht zu verbessern, lässt einen aber nachsichtiger werden, wenn man sich mit der gefürchteten Frage quält: „Wie heißt er?", „Wie war doch sein Name?"

imbalance. Finally, he realizes he will simply have to surrender himself to his predicament.
Subconscious Password is a playful and irreverent take on a familiar experience. It may not help you jog your own memory, but it will make you more inclined to forgive yourself for struggling with the dreaded question: "What's his name? What's his name?"

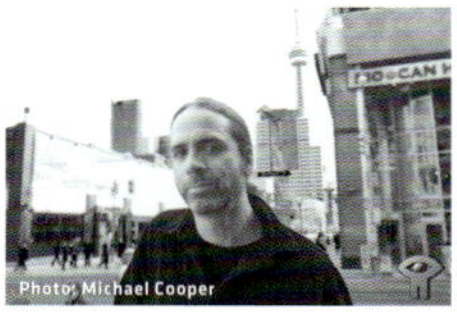
Photo: Michael Cooper

Chris Landreth (CA) is one of Canada's most celebrated animation directors, and the creator of a style he calls "psychorealism." Landreth studied theoretical and applied mechanics before taking up animation. His first short film, *The Listener*, was released in 1991. It was followed by the Oscar-nominated *The End* (1995) and the Genie winner *Bingo* (1996). In 2004, the NFB released Landreth's film *Ryan*, which won more than 60 awards, including the 2005 Academy Award for Best Animated Short Film. Landreth's animated short *The Spine* (2009) continued his exploration of the human psyche. It was nominated for a Genie and was named one of Canada's top ten films of the year by the Toronto International Film Festival. Striking a lighter tone than his earlier films, *Subconscious Password* continues to demonstrate his remarkable evolution as an artist. **Chris Landreth** (CA) ist einer der renommiertesten Animationsfilmemacher Kanadas und Begründer eines Stils, den er „Psychorealismus" nennt. Landreth studierte theoretische und angewandte Mechanik, bevor er sich der Animation zuwandte. Sein erster Kurzfilm, *The Listener*, erschien 1991. Es folgten der für den Oscar nominierte Film *The End* (1995) und der Gewinnerfilm des Genie Award *Bingo* (1996). 2004 brachte NFB (National Film Board of Canada) Landreths Film *Ryan* heraus, der mehr als 60 Auszeichnungen erhielt, darunter 2005 den Oscar für den besten animierten Kurzfilm. Mit *The Spine* (2009) setzte Landreth seine Erkundung der menschlichen Psyche fort. Der animierte Kurzfilm wurde für den Genie Award nominiert und beim Toronto International Film Festival unter die zehn besten Filme des Jahres gewählt. Der Film *Subconscious Password*, in dem Landreth einen leichteren Ton anschlägt als in früheren Arbeiten, zeigt eindrucksvoll die bemerkenswerte künstlerische Entwicklung des Regisseurs.

The Carousel Family

Te-Yu Liu

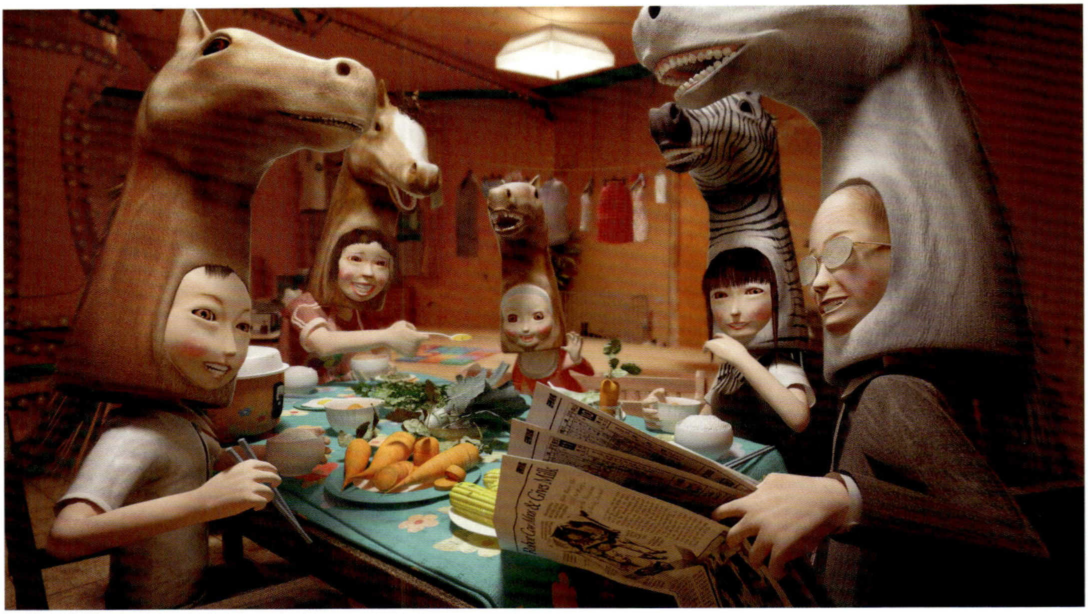

The Carousel Family is an animated comedy about a family living in a house that has been refurbished from a merry-go-round. Just like a real amusement ride, the floor in the house rotates when the music starts. So do the furniture and household goods. But electrical and sanitary equipment does not rotate, because they are fixed to the wall with pipes. The daily life of the family is busy with the rotation.
This animation is to commemorate my childhood memory, the excitement and satisfaction when I rode on a merry-go-round for the first time. It has kept rolling inside me ever since, and reminds me to enjoy the endless fun of daily life.

Die Animation *The Carousel Family* ist eine Komödie über eine Familie, die in einem Haus wohnt, das einmal ein Karussell war. Wie bei einer wirklichen Karussellfahrt dreht sich der Fußboden des Hauses, sobald die Musik einsetzt. Möbel und Inventar drehen sich mit. Nur die Elektrogeräte und die Sanitäranlage sind stabil an der Wand befestigt. Der turbulente Alltag der Familie dreht sich im wahrsten Sinn des Wortes im Kreis.
Diese Animation ist eine Hommage an meine Kindheit, an die Aufregung und das Glücksgefühl, als ich zum ersten Mal mit einem Karussell fuhr. Seit jenen Tagen dreht sich das Karussell in mir weiter und erinnert mich daran, dass der Spaß im Alltag nicht zu kurz kommen darf.

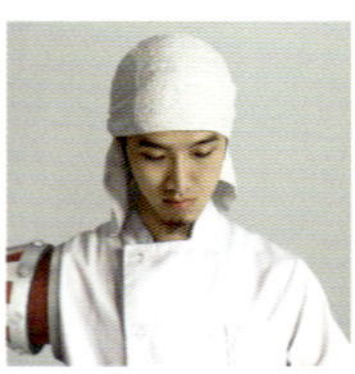

Te-Yu Liu (TW). *The Carousel Family* is my first animation. As an amateur breakdancer, I used to practice breakdancing in the railway station. So far I have attempted to create a visual style that combines realism and surrealism as the features of my works. I think art and design itself is somehow like dance—there must be a story to tell behind various visual clues. Good design always has a good story that affects people's emotions. One's life experience and expertise are all parts of this story. I hope this animation might recall the common life experience and childhood memories of the audience. For me this is the greatest satisfaction. **Te-Yu Liu** (TW). *The Carousel Family* ist mein erster Animationsfilm. Als Amateur-Breakdancer habe ich gerne auf Bahnhöfen getanzt. In meinen künstlerischen Arbeiten versuche ich eine Bildsprache zu entwickeln, deren herausragendes Merkmal es ist, Realismus und Surrealismus zu vereinen. Ich glaube, Kunst und Design haben Parallelen zum Tanz, die verschiedenen visuellen Anhaltspunkte müssen auf eine Geschichte verweisen. Auch gutes Design erzählt immer eine gute Geschichte, die die Emotionen der Menschen berührt. Die eigene Lebenserfahrung und das eigene Wissen sollten in eine solche Geschichte verwoben sein. Ich hoffe, dass diese Animation das Publikum an eigene Erfahrungen denken lässt und eigene Kindheitserinnerungen wachruft. Das wäre für mich der größte Erfolg.

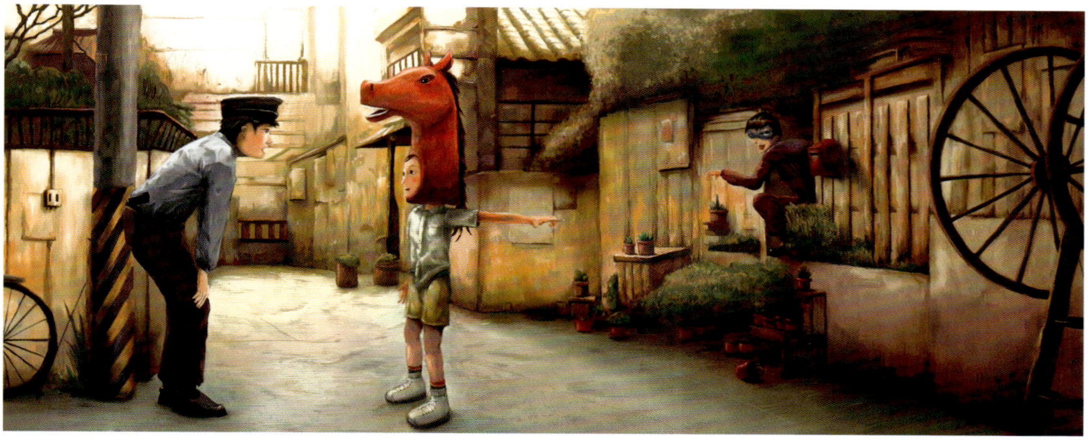

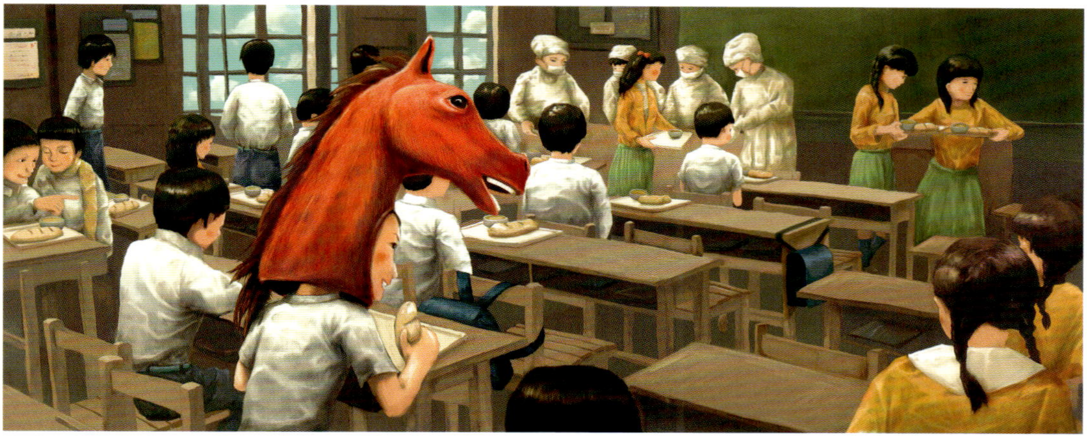

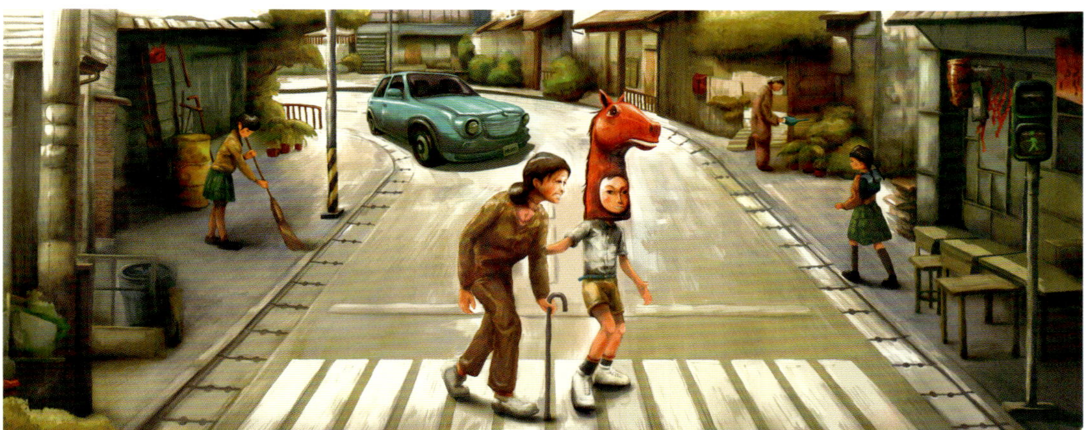

Animating / modeling / texturing / VFX / lighting / compositing: Te-Yu Liu; technical director: Shin-You Chen; original soundtrack: Rick Hu; ending credit soundtrack: Yu-Te Hsu; sound effect: Rick Hu; foley artist: Winnie Wang

Special thanks: Vick Wang / Jo-Yi Chen / Kuan-Hung Chen / Pu Chen / Wei-Chih Cho

Under An Alias

Nerdworking

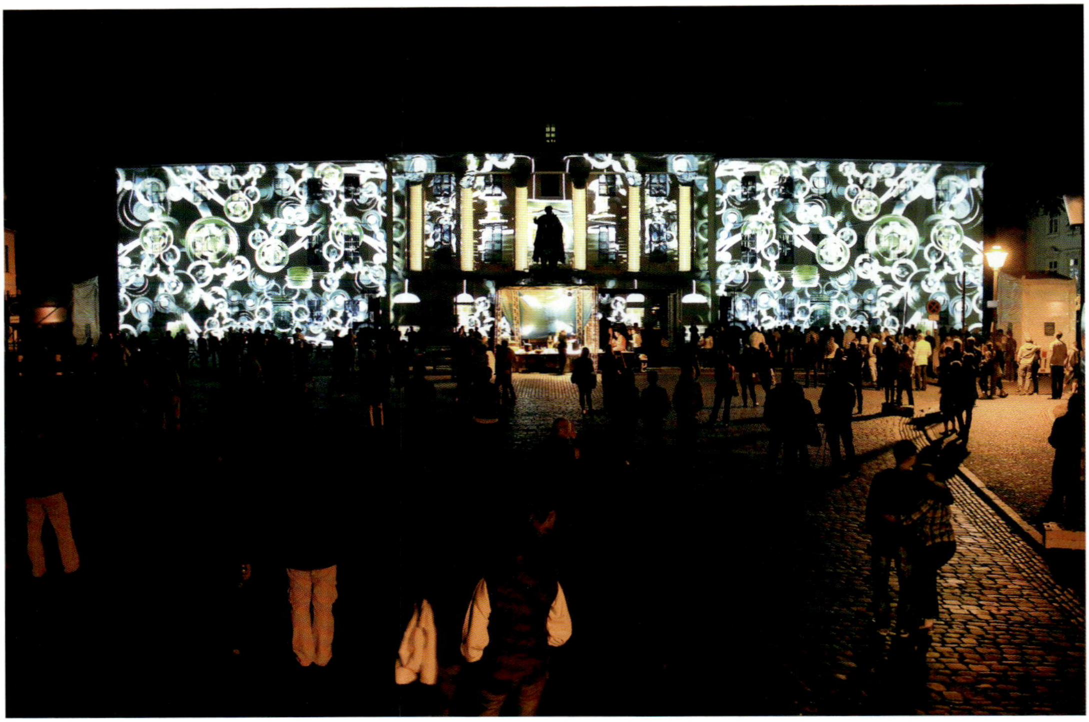

Under An Alias is the big new fairytale by Nerdworking, a digital historical expression. This time our story takes place in the small German town of Weimar. Weimar is a meeting and creation point for eminent intellectuals of our times. This is the town where Goethe wrote his masterpieces, where the music of Franz Liszt could be heard. This is where the German Republic was founded in 1919, whose legacy was subsequently marred by the establishment of a Nazi concentration camp here in 1937. Weimar, a city that currently merges art and architecture in the Bauhaus university, has

Under An Alias, die neue märchenhafte Inszenierung des Künstlerkollektivs Nerdworking, ist eine digitale Fassadenprojektion, die ein historisches Thema aufgreift. Diesmal ist unsere Geschichte in der kleinen deutschen Stadt Weimar angesiedelt. Weimar war und ist Treffpunkt und kreatives Zentrum bedeutender Intellektueller unserer Epoche: die Stadt, in der Goethe seine Meisterwerke schrieb, in der Franz Liszt wirkte und in der 1919 die erste deutsche Republik, die Weimarer Republik, ausgerufen wurde. In der Folge wurde die Geschichte Weimars von der Errichtung des Konzentrationslagers Buchenwald im Jahr 1937 überschattet. In

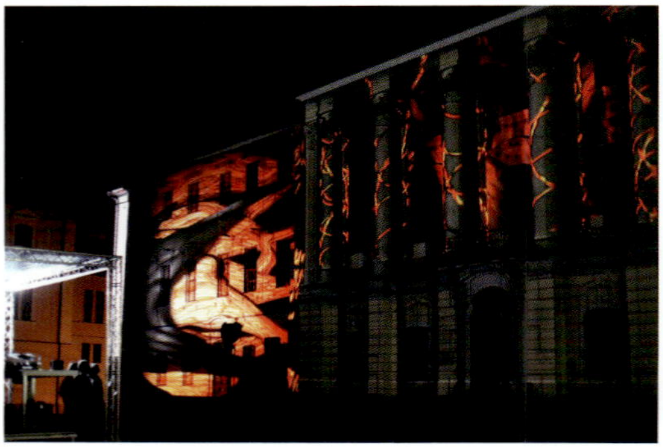

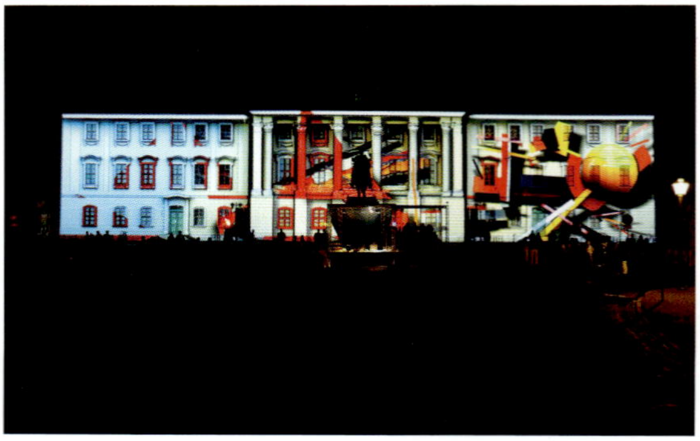

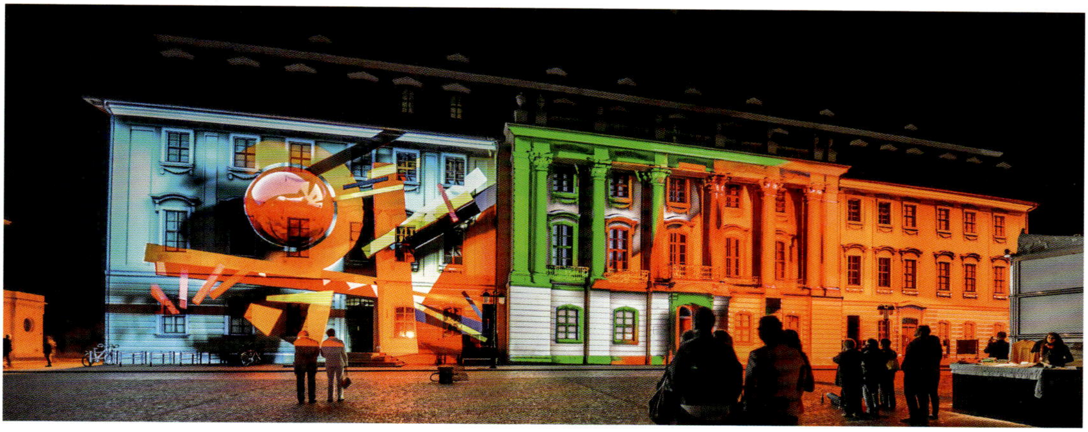

Weimar, einer Stadt, in der heute Kunst und Architektur in der Bauhaus-Universität eine Verbindung eingehen, finden sich noch viele nicht erzählte Geschichten. Weimars Geschichte neu zu überdenken, war für eine in Istanbul ansässige Künstlergruppe zwar ein schwieriges, aber äußerst lehrreiches Unterfangen und bot Nerdworking die Gelegenheit, eine Geschichte aus der Perspektive Außenstehender zu schildern.

Under An Alias entstand durch die Zusammenarbeit internationaler Künstler, die ausschließlich im Cyberspace kooperierten, und hatte als Hauptprogrammpunkt des Festivals „Genius Loci Weimar" Premiere. *Under An Alias* wurde von 10. bis 12. August im Fürstenhaus, der Franz-Liszt-Musikhochschule, jeden Abend von 20 Uhr bis in die frühen Morgenstunden, mehrmals gezeigt. Wir kamen zu dem Schluss, dass die Fassade dieses ikonischen Gebäudes die geeignetste Projektionsfläche für eine Analogie ist, deren erster Teil den Geist, den Spiritus loci, der Stadt veranschaulicht. Die folgenden Teile sind mit der Muskulatur und der Haut der Stadt vergleichbar. Die Fassadenprojektion ist eine Hommage an das Vermächtnis von Weimar und folgt chronologisch der Geschichte der Stadt.

many untold stories. Although difficult, telling Weimar's story was incredibly educational for an Istanbul-based group of artists. It gave an opportunity for Nerdworking to illustrate a story from another perspective. Dozens of people spent long hours immersing themselves the rich cultural background, while taking into consideration the opinions of previous researchers.

Under An Alias, created through the collaboration of international artists and working completely in cyberspace, made its debut as the main act of the Genius Loci Festival. *Under An Alias* was exhibited from 10 to 12 August at the Fürstenhaus, Franz Liszt Conservatory, every night several times a night from 8 p.m. until the early hours. We decided that there could be nothing more appropriate, than projecting the analogy onto this iconic building. The initial section of this tribute to the legacy of Weimar is the spirit, then the muscles then the skin. The story was based on the linear history of the city.

Nerdworking (TR) is an Istanbul-based art & science network founded in 2009 to research and to develop unique software and hardware for artistic, commercial, experimental interactive media works for the public space, fairs and performing arts. Nerdworking has many multidisciplinary artists, illustrators, designers, real-time animation designers, coders and mechatronics, robotics and electronics professionals. The team's core aim is to create new way to experience man-machine codes. **Nerdworking** (TR) ist ein in Istanbul ansässiges Künstlerkollektiv, das 2009 gegründet wurde, um Software und Hardware für künstlerische, kommerzielle, experimentelle und interaktive Medienarbeiten für den öffentlichen Raum, Messen und die Performing Arts zu erforschen und zu entwickeln. Das Netzwerk umfasst zahlreiche Künstler unterschiedlicher Disziplinen, u.a. Illustratoren, Designer, Echtzeit-Animationsdesigner, Programmierer, Mechatroniker, Robotertechniker und Elektroniker. Ziel des Teams ist es, neue Erfahrungen mit Interaktionen zwischen Mensch, Maschine und Codes zu schaffen.

DIGITAL MUSICS & SOUND ART

Blurring the Boundaries
Die Grenzen verwischen sich

Ludger Brümmer, Electric Indigo, Emre Erkal, Jeff Mills, Pamela Z

With the ever-increasing breadth of styles and genres and the sheer depth of possibilities that can be included under the rubric of "Digital Musics and Sound Art", it is clear that each of the many works considered for this category must be taken in individually. It is impossible to compare them one to the other, because they occupy such diverse territory. They each need to be regarded on their own terms and in their own specific contexts.

A case in point is Nicolas Bernier's *frequencies (a)*, the project we selected for this year's Prix Ars Electronica Golden Nica. This is a work of art that comprises music composition, sound installation, sculpture, design and performance within one piece, which the artist describes simply as "a sound performance." Even listening to the audio from the work sample without simultaneously viewing the visual presentation reveals the beauty and balance it possesses as just a sonic composition. When you add to that the visual impact of the highly sophisticated manufactured objects, the technical precision of their function and the minimal performance aesthetic that the artist employs in manipulating this beautifully crafted instrument, the work becomes unimpeachably convincing.

Bernier skillfully employs solenoids, driven by sequences from his computer, to strike a series of tuning forks with great precision while simultaneously triggering bursts of light that illuminate both the clear plexi armature and the artist himself as he performs relaxed, nonchalant tasks, imbuing the minimalist sound/light composition with a very seductive cinematic quality. The piece takes minimalism to a new level—distilling a clearly complex set of components down to a kind of simplicity and purity that is intelligent and tremendously moving. All these varied techniques and ideas are skillfully integrated into an extremely powerful artistic work that is sophisticated both in content and language.

By contrast, [SjQ++], which receives one of this year's Awards of Distinction, occupies a completely different kind of territory, even though it is also cross-disciplinary in its inclusion of live musical performance combined interactively with light (in this case, by way of projected images controlled by the actions of the performers). Although the beginning of the work is stark—consisting of short

Es versteht sich von selbst, dass mit der immer größer werdenden Bandbreite der Stilrichtungen und Genres und der unglaublichen Vielfalt an Möglichkeiten, die unter der Bezeichnung „Digital Musics and Sound Art" subsumiert werden können, jede der vielen Arbeiten, die in dieser Kategorie geprüft werden, individuell zu bewerten ist. Diese Arbeiten können unmöglich miteinander verglichen werden, weil sie so unterschiedliche Felder abdecken. Sie müssen jeweils nach eigenen Kriterien und in ihrem spezifischen Kontext betrachtet werden.

Ein typisches Beispiel dafür ist Nicolas Berniers Projekt *freqencies (a)*, das wir für die diesjährige Goldene Nica ausgewählt haben. Es ist ein Kunstwerk, das Musikkomposition, Soundinstallation, Skulptur, Design und Performance in einer Arbeit verbindet, die der Künstler schlicht als „Klangperformance" beschreibt. Auch wenn man nur die Tonaufnahme der Arbeitsprobe hört, ohne die visuelle Präsentation dazu zu sehen, offenbart sich die klangliche Schönheit und Ausgewogenheit der Komposition. Kommt dann noch die optische Wirkung der ausgefeilten und exquisit gefertigten Objekte, die technische Präzision der Funktionalität und die minimale Performanceästhetik, die der Künstler im Umgang mit diesem wunderschön gestalteten Instrument zeigt, hinzu, kann man sich der Faszination der Arbeit nicht entziehen.

Bernier schickt via Computer Sequenzen an Hubmagneten, um mit großer Präzision eine Reihe von Klanggabeln anzuschlagen, während er gleichzeitig gleißende Lichter pulsieren lässt. Diese beleuchten sowohl die Plexiglaswerkbank als auch den Künstler selbst, der entspannt performt und nonchalant agiert, was der minimalistischen Klang-Licht-Komposition eine verführerische filmische Dimension verleiht. Das Stück hebt Minimalismus auf eine neue Ebene – reduziert ein sehr komplexes Zusammenspiel von Komponenten auf eine Einfachheit und Essenz, die intelligent und unglaublich bewegend ist. Alle diese unterschiedlichen Techniken und Ideen sind gekonnt in eine äußerst starke künstlerische Arbeit integriert, die sowohl inhaltlich als auch formal sehr durchdacht ist.

Die Gruppe [SjQ++], die eine der diesjährigen Auszeichnungen erhält, betätigt sich in einem ganz anderen Feld, wenngleich auch sie durch die Kombination einer Live-Musikperformance mit visualisierten Klängen und Interaktionen (hier mittels projizierter Bilder, die durch die Aktionen der Performer gesteuert werden) multidisziplinär agiert. Obwohl die Arbeit mit kurzen Live-Sound-Impulsen, die weiße numerische Werte auf immersiven Projektionsflächen aufblinken lassen, reduziert beginnt und auf den ersten Blick einen ähnlichen Minimalismus suggeriert wie Berniers Werk, wird schnell klar, dass die Mitglieder von [SjQ++] ihr kühnes Konzept in eine ganz andere musikalische und visuelle Ästhetik einbetten. Vom Paradigma freier Improvisation ausgehend, bündelt das Ensemble seine Kräfte mit jenen der Maschine, um eine organische Medienkunst zu schaffen, die von einem einfachen Algorithmus vorgegeben und von Interaktionen gesteuert wird. Der musikalische und visuelle Dialog zwischen den Musikern und den Projektionen ist faszinierend und das Nebeneinander von „kreativer Musikästhetik und perfekt synchronisierten, computergenerierten, kühnen Bildern überraschend reizvoll.

Eine weitere Auszeichnung geht an Chris Carlsons Projekt *Borderlands Granular*, das wieder in ein völlig anderes Feld der digitalen Musik führt. Diese Arbeit ist weder eine Komposition noch eine Performance. Es handelt sich um ein digitales Musikinstrument in Form einer iPad-App, die entwickelt wurde, um Anwendern zu ermöglichen, mittels Granularsynthese Klänge in Echtzeit zu verwandeln. Diese Arbeit verlangt völlig andere Bewertungskriterien, weil wir es hier mit einem Instrument zu tun haben, das der Künstler mit der Absicht herstellte, dass *wir selbst* das Werk gestalten. Dennoch ist das jeweilige Ergebnis per definitionem in eine elaborierte Ästhetik eingebunden. Die frappierende Bedienerfreundlichkeit der Applikation, die äußerst komplexe Berechnungen der Granularsynthese in Echtzeit durchführt, ist überaus beeindruckend und ermöglicht dem Anwender, sich auf sehr spielerische Weise ganz auf den kreativen Prozess zu konzentrieren. Die Faszination dieser Software und der Benutzeroberfläche beruht insbesondere auf der transparenten Einheit von gestischer Interaktion und klarer, ansprechender optischer Darstellung, wodurch Anwender die vielfältigen nahtlos ineinandergreifenden Optionen intuitiv aktivieren können. Darüber hinaus würdigt die Jury die Tatsache, dass die Laptopversion Opensource-Software ist.

Die zwölf Projekte, denen wir Anerkennungen zusprachen, bestätigen die konstante Verbreiterung des Felds, das Digital Musics & Sound Art einnehmen. Wir entdeckten überzeugende Arbeiten von einer immensen Bandbreite, mit einem großen Spektrum an künstlerischen Ausdrucksmöglichkeiten und Fertigkeiten in den Bereichen Soundinstallation, elektroakustische Musikkomposition und Performance, Festmedien, Multimedia-Theater-Performances, Performance und Interfacedesign sowie Sound-Spatialisierungssysteme. Die ästhetischen und konzeptuellen Qualitäten der Arbeiten

bursts of live sound which trigger unison bursts of white, numeric material on immersive projection surfaces—and might superficially suggest a similar kind of minimalism as that seen in Bernier's work, it immediately becomes clear that the members of [SjQ++] use a very different musical and visual aesthetic to make their bold statement. Coming through a free improvisation paradigm, this ensemble joins forces with the machine to create an organic piece of media art that is directed by their interactions with one another and dictated by a simple algorithm. The musical and visual conversation between the musicians and the projections is compelling, and the juxtaposition of the "creative music" aesthetic with the perfectly synchronized, bold, computer-generated images is surprising and delightful.

Our other Award of Distinction goes to Chris Carlson's *Borderlands Granular*, a project that takes us, once again, to an entirely separate digital music territory. This work is neither a composition nor a performance. It is a digital musical instrument, in the form of an iPad app, designed to allow users to transform sounds in real time through granular synthesis. In this case, the work needs to be ingested in a very different way, because we are dealing with a tool that the artist made with the intention that we would be creating the work. And yet, by its very nature, it places everything that comes out of it within a certain, refined aesthetic space. The pre-eminent ease of handling the application while it performs extremely complex real-time computations of granular synthesis is truly impressive and allows the user to concentrate fully, and in a very playful way, on the creative process. What makes this piece of software and its interface so compelling is the transparent unity of gestural control with the clear and appealing visual representation of how the user is manipulating its multifaceted seamless operations. In addition, the jury appreciates the fact that the laptop version of this software is open-source.

The twelve projects on which we elected to bestow honorable mentions present further evidence of the ever-spreading breadth of territory covered by Digital Musics & Sound Art. We found strong work of immense range, skill and artistry in the areas of sound installation, electroacoustic music composition and performance, fixed media works, multimedia theatrical performance works, performance interface design and sound spatialization systems. And the aesthetics and intentions of the works were equally broad—encompassing social commentary and emotional triggers as well as elegantly abstract and minimal manipulations of sound, light and movement.

Among the sound installations and sonic sculptural objects, we were impressed by a number of varied projects. Roberto Pugliese's *Equilibrium Variant* takes advantage of the irresistible anthropomorphism inherent in a pair of robotic arms (one sporting a speaker as a "face" and the other a microphone), which brings to mind the kind of empathy elicited by the famous Pixar lamps. The sonic outcome of this carefully crafted piece is achieved via the feedback response of the pair's never-ending search for equilibrium. Meanwhile, Mark Malmberg's *Albireo2.1* can be considered somewhat zoomorphic. Solar-powered, bird-like "creatures" communicate wirelessly—sleeping by night and interacting by day—portraying the dynamics of an artificial ecology. Yuri Suzuki's *The Sound of the Earth* is a literal portrayal of the earth itself in the form of a spherical vinyl record inscribed with sampled sounds from around the globe. Suzuki explodes the idea of the flat disc into a three-dimensional globe fitted with a stylus that can actually traverse the surface of the "planet" to play back the sounds of the earth. While Suzuki's globe and Pugliese's yearning robotic couple elicited coos and chuckles from the jury, Intermedia Chef's *The Half* was more startling and sobering. With the martial tremor its 100 speaker cones displacing baking flour to spell out words in tumultuous clouds of dust, it reflects ambiguous feelings, displacement and alienation in the communities of a land like Korea split in two and thus adds a political dimension to its artistic value.

The approaches to musical performance span territory ranging from inventive, performative exploration of classical instrumentation combined with computer-based, algorithmic compositional techniques in Michael Edwards' *Altogether Disproportionate* to the elegant interface design and graphic/sonic performance of Simon Katan on his custom visual sequencer *Cube with Magic Ribbons*. And some of the most touching musical

waren ähnlich breit gefächert und reichten vom gesellschaftlichen Kommentar über emotionale Impulse bis hin zu elegant abstrakten, minimalen Manipulationen von Klang, Licht und Bewegung.

Bei den Soundinstallationen und Klangskulpturen beeindruckten uns eine Reihe sehr unterschiedlicher Projekte. Roberto Puglieses *Equilibrium Variant* profitiert von dem unwiderstehlichen Anthropomorphismus, der Roboterarmen anhaftet (einer trägt einen Lautsprecher, der an ein „Gesicht" denken lässt, der andere ein Mikrofon) und erinnert an die Art von Empathie, die von den berühmten Pixar-Lampen ausgelöst wird. Das klangliche Ergebnis dieses sorgsam austarierten Stücks wird durch die Feedbackreaktion der nie endenden Suche dieses Pärchens nach Gleichgewicht definiert. Mark Malmbergs *Albireo2.1* hingegen kann als etwas zoomorph beschrieben werden. Mit Solarenergie betriebene, vogelähnliche „Kreaturen" kommunizieren drahtlos – schlafen nachts und interagieren tagsüber – und repräsentieren die Dynamiken einer künstlichen Ökologie. Yuri Suzukis *The Sound of the Earth* ist ein Porträt der Erde in Form einer kugelförmigen Vinylplatte, in die gesampelte Sounds aus aller Welt eingeschrieben sind. Suzuki führt die Idee der flachen Schallplatte in einen dreidimensionalen Globus über, der mit einer Nadel versehen ist, welche die Oberfläche des „Planeten" überqueren kann, um die Klänge der Erde abzuspielen. Während Suzukis Globus und Puglieses sehnsüchtiges robotisches Pärchen die Jury erheiterten, löste *The Half* von Intermedia Chef Ernüchterung und Bestürzung aus. Die 100 Lautsprechermembranen, die mit einer martialisch anmutenden Erschütterung Backmehl aufwirbeln, um aus turbulenten Mehlwolken Worte zu bilden, spiegeln die ambivalenten Gefühle, die Entwurzelung und Entfremdung im geteilten Korea wider, wodurch dem künstlerischen Wert eine politische Dimension hinzugefügt wird.

Die Annäherungen an das Genre Musikperformance spannten einen Bogen von einer originellen performativen Auseinandersetzung mit klassischer Instrumentation und computerbasierten algorithmischen Kompositionstechniken in Michael Edwards *Altogether Disproportionate* bis zum eleganten Interface-Design und der auf einem visuellen Sequenzer kreierten grafischen/klanglichen Performance von Simon Katan *Cube with Magic Ribbons*. Einige der berührendsten musikalischen Performances wurden auf Tonträgern präsentiert, etwa Grischa Lichtenbergs höchst suggestive, ansteckend rhythmische Produktion *and VI (inertia)* und

Antye Greie-Ripattis (AGF) anspruchsvolle und komplexe elektronische Musikinterpretationen der deutschen Literaturgeschichte auf ihrem Album *Gedichterbe*.

Visuals, Theatralität und eine starke Interaktion zwischen Licht, Klang und Bewegung zeichnen eine Reihe weiterer Arbeiten aus. Nicolás Varchauskys Performance *La Biblioteca Ciega* verwendet ein breites Spektrum an Techniken, um ihre überwältigende Ausdruckskraft zu erzielen. Mit einem Orchester blinder Musiker, die verschiedenste Instrumente spielen, welche Licht in Klang verwandeln können, spiegelt das Stück manche Qualitäten von Berniers Performance/Installation wider, steckt aber in einer bewegenden theatralischen, raumspezifischen und geschichtsbezogenen Performance ein ganz anderes ästhetisches und klangliches Feld ab. Suguru Gotos *Duali* lotet die vielfältigen Möglichkeiten von Tanz, Motion-Capture-Systemen und interaktiven Medien aus, während Typingmonkeys in ihrer Echtzeit Audio/Video-Performance *0b0000.tms* in das komplexe Gebiet von Sound und Bild, das von zufälligen, computergenerierten numerischen Sequenzen gesteuert wird, einführen.

Mit einem seltenen Fokus auf den reinen Klang zog Robert Henke unsere Aufmerksamkeit auf die ausdrucksstarke und dynamische Verteilung virtueller Klangobjekte in einem Hörraum mittels Wellenfeldsynthese. Er teilt sich die Anerkennung mit seinen Studenten des Studiengangs Sound Studies der Universität der Künste Berlin für die schöne Sammlung *Works for Wave Field Synthesis*, die über eine Phalanx von 192 Lautsprechern in einer dreidimensionalen akustischen Klanginszenierung zu hören sind.

Die Jury war nach den drei Tagen, in denen sie sich durch ein so breites und abwechslungsreiches Terrain bewegt hatte, beeindruckt und aufgewühlt. Es war eine anstrengende Reise durch sehr unterschiedliche Welten, die spezifische Interpretationen verlangten, doch gab es eine Qualität, die allen Projekten, die ausgezeichnet wurden, gemeinsam war. Sie haben uns in irgendeiner Weise bewegt: Indem sie entweder an unsere Emotionen rührten oder uns zu denken gaben, lösten sie angeregte Diskussionen zwischen uns aus oder ließen uns zu einhelligen Entscheidungen kommen. Die Arbeiten, an die die zwölf Anerkennungen, die Auszeichnungen und die Goldenen Nica vergeben wurden, sind eine Bestätigung für und eine Hommage an die Verbreiterung dieses Felds und die Auflösung der Grenzen.

performances are presented in the form of recorded works, as is the case with Grischa Lichtenberger's highly imaginative, infectiously rhythmic *and VI (inertia)* and Antye Greie-Ripatti (AGF)'s sophisticated and elaborate electronic music interpretations of German poetry history in *Gedichterbe*.

Visuals, theatricality and strong interplay between light, sound and movement prevail in several of the works. Nicolás Varchausky's *La Biblioteca Ciega* employs a wide array of techniques to achieve its powerful expressiveness. Featuring an orchestra of blind musicians working with a battery of instruments designed to turn light into sound, the look of the piece echoes some of the qualities of Bernier's performance/installation but works an entirely different aesthetic and sonic territory in an emotive, theatrical, sight-specific and history-related performance. Suguru Goto's *Duali* taps the rich possibilities of dance, motion-capture systems and interactive media, while Typingmonkeys mine the intricate territory of sound and image controlled by random, computer-generated numeric sequences in their real-time audio/video performance *0b0000.tms*.

With a pure and rarified focus on sound itself, Robert Henke's work turns our attention to the expressive and dynamic placement of virtual sound objects within a listening space through wave field synthesis. He shares his Honorary Mention with his students at Berlin University of Arts' Sound Studies master's program for their beautiful collection of *Works for Wave Field Synthesis* diffused through a 192 loudspeaker array in exceptionally high spatial resolution.

This jury was challenged and stirred by the end of our three days of covering such wide and varied territory. It was a strenuous journey making sense of such wildly differing work, but there was one thing that all the projects we chose to honor had in common. They all moved us in some way. Either pulling at our emotions or making us think, the work sparked spirited arguments among us, or caused us to react strongly in unison. And between the twelve Honorary Mentions, the Awards of Distinction and the Golden Nica these works are an affirmation of and a tribute to the widening of this field's territory and the blurring of its boundaries.

frequencies (a)
Nicolas Bernier

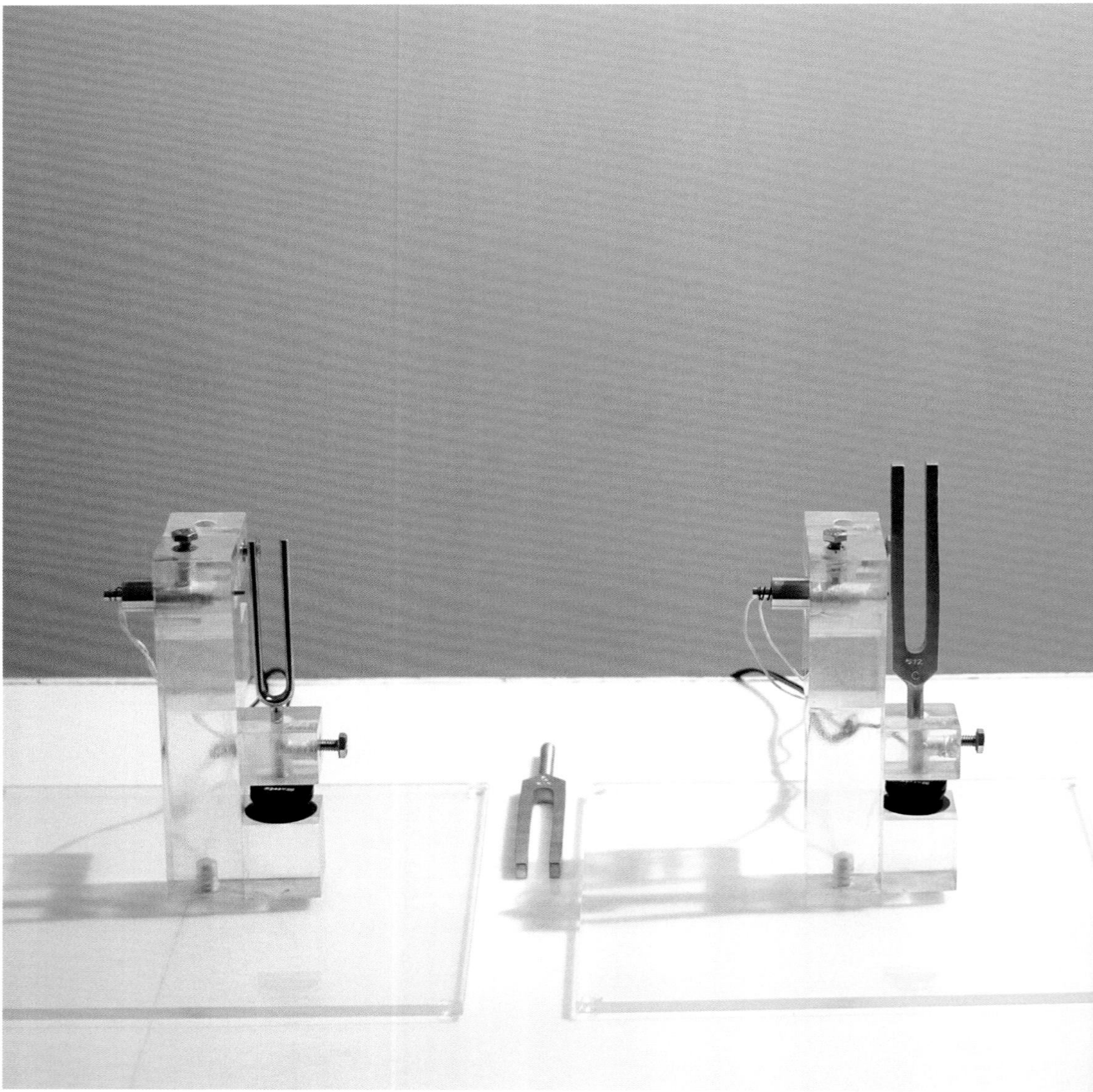

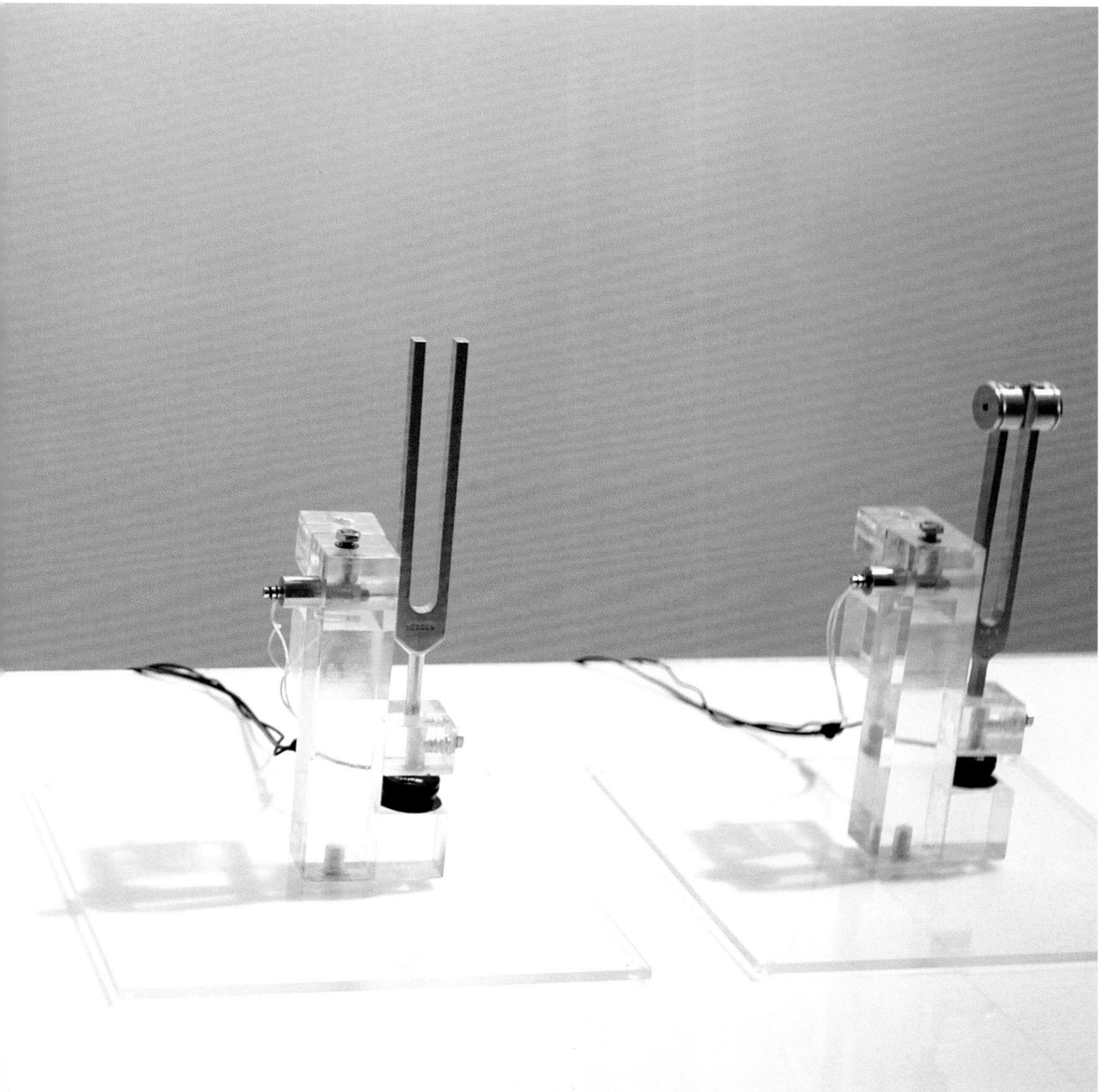

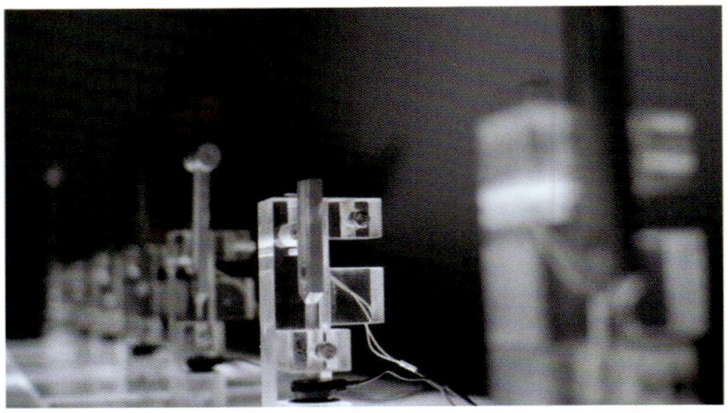
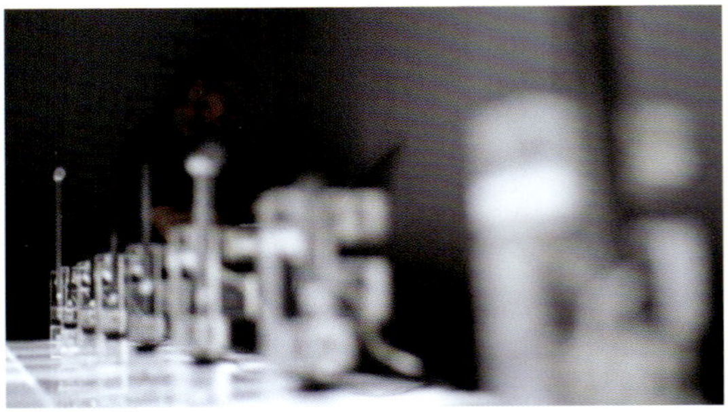
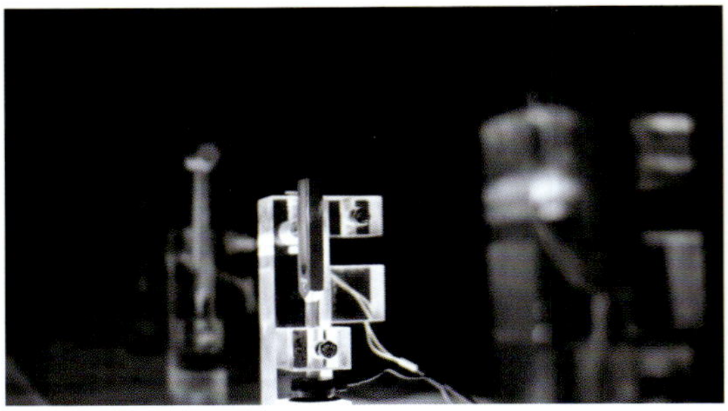
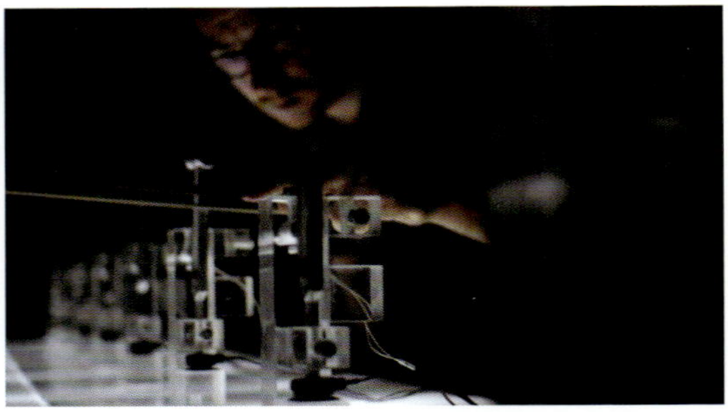
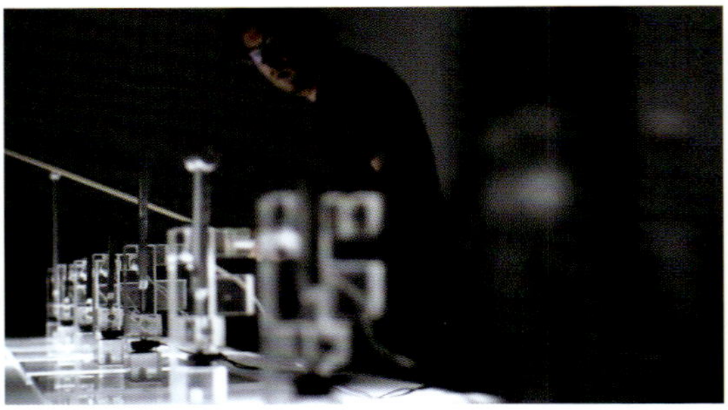
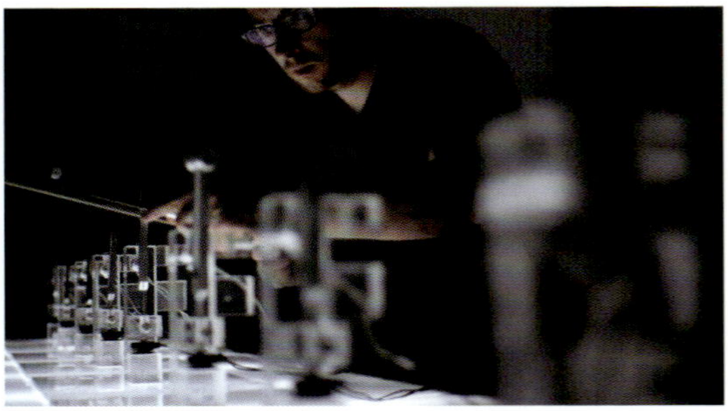
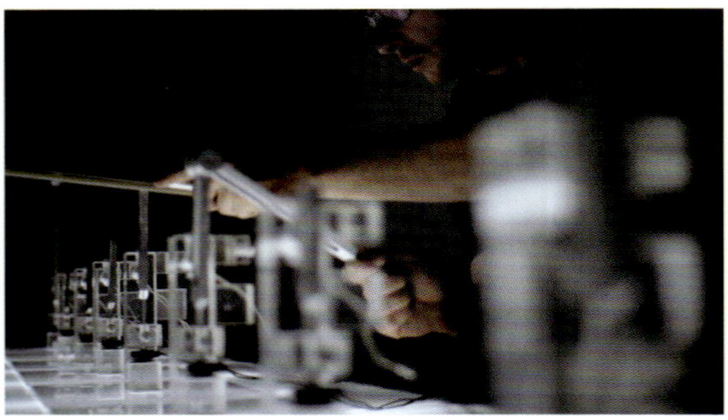
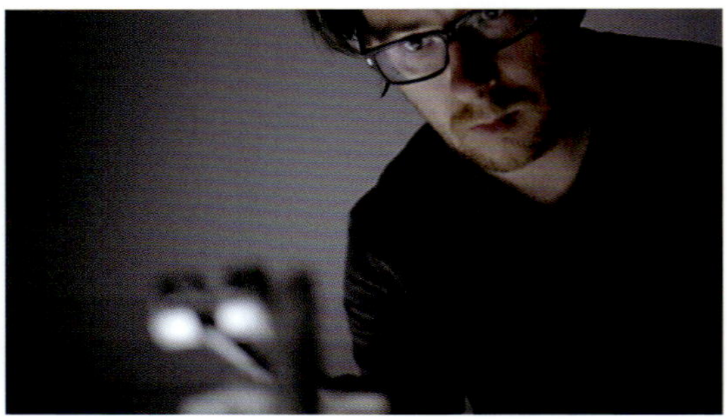

frequencies (a) is a sound performance combining the sound of mechanically triggered tuning forks with pure digital sound waves. The performer

frequencies (a) ist eine Klangperformance, die die klaren Töne von Stimmgabeln mit digitalen Klängen kombiniert. Mittels computergesteuerter Magnetventile löst der

Nicolas Bernier: audiovisual composition, concept, performance, programming, technical design and some electronics; Olivier Lefebvre: techical design; Laurent Loison: fabrication

Künstler präzise Schläge auf die Stimmgabeln aus. Synchron zu den Stimmgabeln pulsieren gleißende Lichter, die den Raum mit einer Komposition aus Licht und Ton erfüllen.
Ausgangspunkt der Komposition war eine akustische Stimmgabel – ein Objekt, das mich aus mehreren Gründen fasziniert: 1) Obwohl der Klang, den die Stimmgabel erzeugt, eindeutig akustisch ist, ähnelt er einem Sinuston und erinnert an die „primitiven" Experimente in der elektronischen Musik. 2) Die Stimmgabel wurde jahrhundertelang in der tonalen Instrumentalmusik verwendet und auch als wissenschaftliches Instrument eingesetzt, weshalb sie für mich auch ein Symbol für wissenschaftliche Forschung ist. 3) Sie ist nahezu im Verschwinden begriffen, da sie heute zunehmend durch elektronische Stimmgeräte ersetzt wird.
Stimmgabeln sind für mich das perfekte Instrument für Kompositionen, die einen Bogen zwischen elektronischer Musik und Akustik, zwischen Gegenwart und Vergangenheit spannen.
Nach einigen Jahren der Improvisation mit Stimmgabeln wollte ich eine Performance komponieren, die präziser ist, als Manipulationen an Objekten es ermöglichen. Ich habe daher einen Microcontroller verwendet, um ein Tempo und eine Präzision zu erreichen, die mittels menschlicher Manipulation nicht möglich wäre. Da das Stück wesentlich vom Minimalismus beeinflusst ist, habe ich einen Leuchttisch konstruiert, der an manche Werke des Minimalismus erinnern. Die Synchronisation ermöglicht eine Rückwirkung zwischen Sound und Visuellem.

triggers sequences from the computer, activating solenoids that hit the tuning forks very precisely. Streams of light burst synchronously with the forks, creating a not quite minimal sound and light composition.
The starting point the composition of this work was the acoustic tuning fork, an object that I find fascinating for many reasons: 1) while it is obviously acoustic, the sound it produces is quite close to the sine tone, reminiscent the "primitive" early electronic music experiments 2) tuning forks have been used for tonal instrumental music for centuries and have been used as a scientific instruments, so I see them as a symbol of research 3) We could almost say the object is approaching extinction, ironically being replaced today by electronic tuners.
For me, the tuning fork is the perfect object to compose in a way that draws a line between the electronic and the acoustics, between the present and the past.
After a couple of years of improvisation with tuning forks, I wanted to compose a performance that would be more precise than when I manipulate them myself, so this is why I used a micro-controller so I could have a velocity and a precision that would not be possible with human control. As the inspiration comes from minimalism, I then built a customized light table reminiscent of some minimalist works. This synchronization helps to produce a retroaction between the sound and the visual.

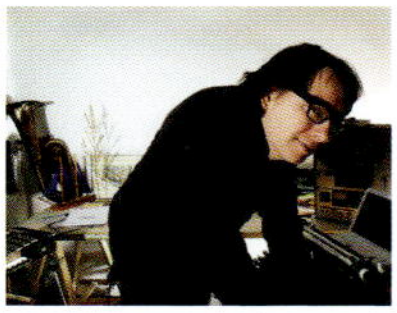

Nicolas Bernier (CA) creates sound performances, installations, musique concrète, live electronics, post-rock, noise improv an video art while also working with dance, theater, moving images and interdisciplinary contexts. In the midst of this eclecticism, his artistic concerns remain constant: the balance between the cerebral and the sensual and between organic sound sources and digital processing. The sound of Nicolas Bernier is somewhere between the old and the new. It is electronic music made from objects of the past: typewriters, old machines, tuning forks, soundscape memories and, yes, musical instruments. He is currently doing a PhD in sonic arts at the University of Huddersfield (UK) under the direction of Dr. Pierre Alexandre Tremblay and Dr. Monty Adkins. He is a member of Perte de Signal, a media-arts research and development center based in Montreal. **Nicolas Bernier** (CA) ist in den Bereichen Sound-Performance, Installationen, Musique concrète, Live-Elektronik, Post-Rock, Noise, Improv und Videokunst aktiv und arbeitet auch mit Tanz, Theater, Bewegtbild in interdisziplinären Zusammenhängen. Sein künstlerisches Anliegen bleibt in diesem Eklektizismus jedoch konstant: Es geht ihm stets um die Balance zwischen Rationalität und Sinnlichkeit, zwischen organischen Klangquellen und digitaler Bearbeitung. Der Sound von Nicolas Bernier bewegt sich im Spannungsfeld von Alt und Neu. Er macht elektronische Musik mit Gegenständen und Einflüssen der Vergangenheit wie Schreibmaschinen, Klanggabeln, alten Maschinen, klanglichen Erinnerungen und – ja, auch Musikinstrumenten. Bernier studiert derzeit Sonic Arts an der Forschungsstelle für Neue Musik der Universität Huddersfield (UK) unter der Leitung von Dr. Pierre Alexandre Tremblay und Dr. Monty Adkins. Er ist Mitglied von perte de signal, einem Produktionszentrum für Forschung und Entwicklung künstlerischer Projekte in Digitalkunst in Montreal.

[SjQ++]
[SjQ++]

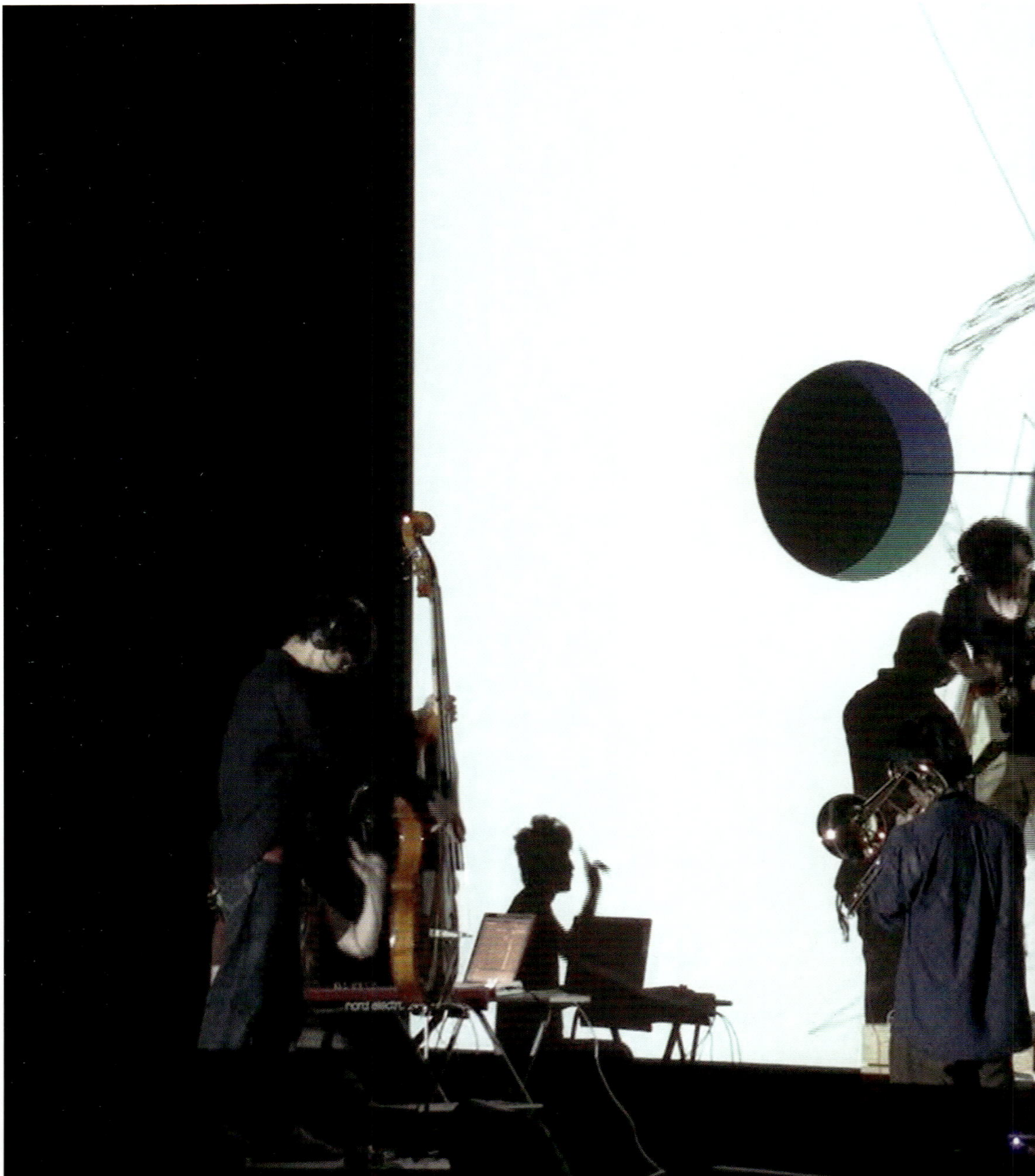

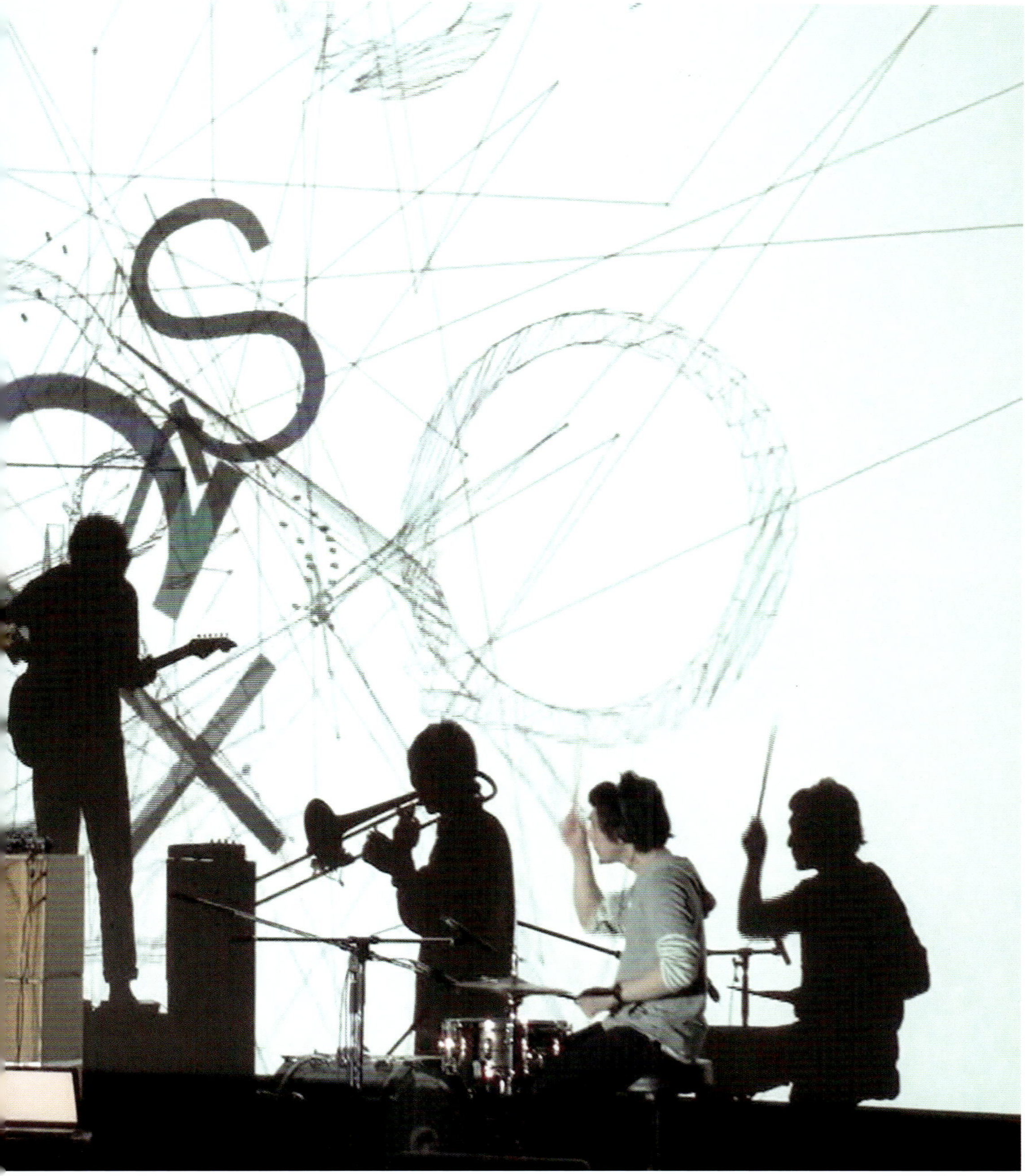

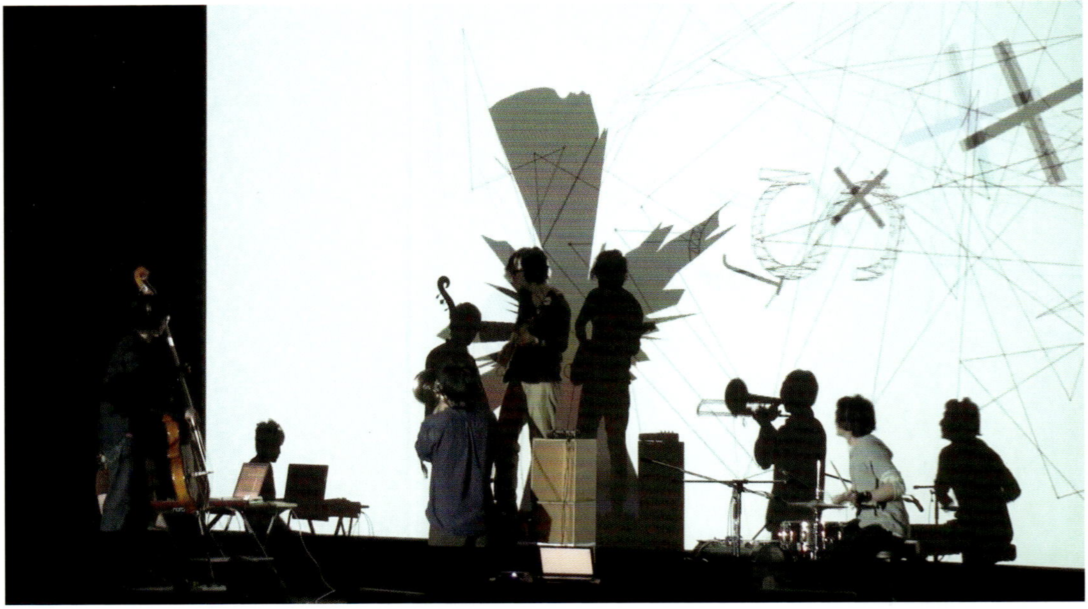

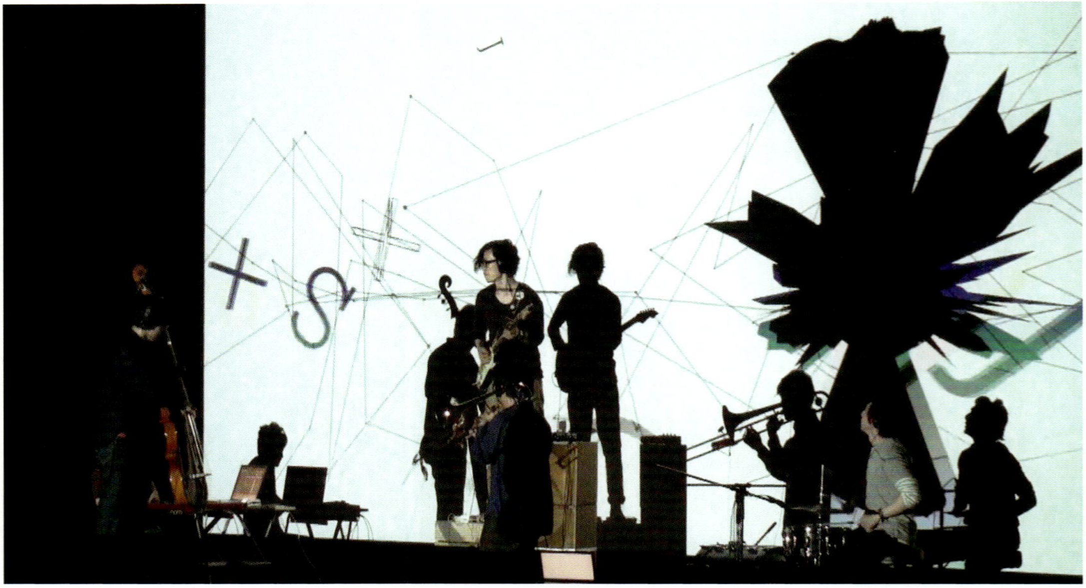

Piano / computer: Yuta Uozumi; trombone / computer: Tadashi Yonago; guitar: Isao Nakagaito; bass: Shuhei Otani; visual / computer: Ryo Kanda. Film : Shintaro Watanabe (at SuperDeluxe). Coordinator: cubicmusic / HEADZ

[SjQ++], ein audiovisuelles Projekt, komponiert mithilfe eines Multiagentensystems (MAS) Musik in Echtzeit. Das Multiagentensystem verfolgt einen Bottom-up-Ansatz und findet beispielsweise im Bereich der Computersimulation Anwendung. Die Agenten (Spieler) schaffen durch ihre Interaktionen Muster, die auf einer einfachen Regel beruhen. Bei *[SjQ++]* fungiert das Visuelle als Katalysator, der das Ensemble interagieren lässt. Das Verhalten der einzelnen Spieler wird auf Grundlage ihrer jeweiligen Sounddaten visualisiert.

Das System kann die Bedeutung von Klängen bearbeiten. So werden beispielsweise die Beziehungen zwischen den einzelnen Spielern durch Bewegungen der visualisierten Klänge miteinander in Verbindung gesetzt. Darüber hinaus lässt es die einzelnen Spieler mittels Animation kooperieren bzw. gegeneinander antreten. Durch die Steuerung des Interaktionsflusses kommt es zu einer dynamischen Performance. Das Publikum erlebt die Performance als untrennbares Ineinanderwirken von Klängen und visuellen Elementen. Die Klänge und Bilder werden nicht nur perfekt synchronisiert, sondern beeinflussen und verändern einander auch wechselseitig.

The audiovisual project *[SjQ++]* compose their music using a multi-agent system in real-time. A multi-agent system is a bottom-up method used in the field of computer simulation. The agents (players) create the patterns through their interactions based on a simple rule. In *[SjQ++]*, its visual image acts as a catalyst to make the ensemble interact. It visualizes the behavior of each player based on its sound data.

The system can manage the meaning of sound. For example, it connects each player's relations through motions of the sounds visualized. In addition, it uses animation to make each player cooperate/compete. Control of the interaction flow produces a dynamic performance. The audience experiences the performance of further indivisibility between the sound and the visual. Their sounds and visuals are synchronized perfectly by programming, and both are also affected by one another and change their performance accordingly.

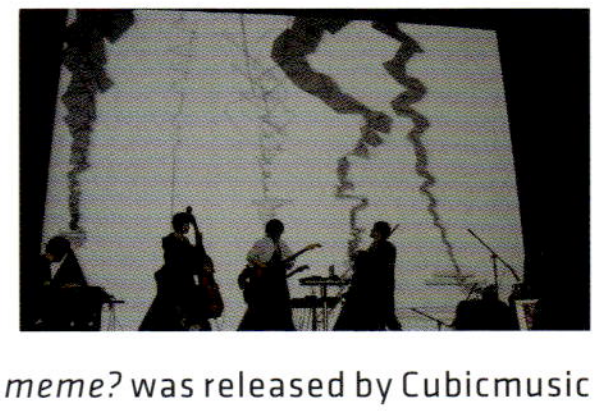

[SjQ++] (JP) is an audiovisual project established in Kyoto in 2012 by Yuta Uozumi (piano / computer), Tadashi Yonago (trombone / computer), Isao Nakagaito (guitar), Shuhei Otani (bass), Wataru Asada (drums) and Ryo Kanda (visual / computer). Originally they started an improvisational music project called *SjQ* in 2001. The following year their first piece *meme?* was released by Cubicmusic Japan. From 2012, the *[SjQ++]* audiovisual project was started with the participation of a visual artist (Ryo Kanda aka. Kezzardrix).

[SjQ++] (JP) ist ein audiovisuelles Projekt, das von Yuta Uozumi (E-Piano / Computer), Tadashi Yonago (Posaune / Computer), Isao Nakagaito (Gitarre), Shuhei Otani (Bass), Wataru Asada (Schlagzeug) und Ryo Kanda (Visuals / Computer) 2012 in Kyoto ins Leben gerufen wurde. 2001 starteten sie das Projekt für Improvisationsmusik *SjQ*. Im folgenden Jahr brachte das japanische Label Cubic Music ihre erste CD heraus. 2012 schloss sich der bildende Künstler Ryo Kanda alias Kezzardrix der Gruppe an, die sich nunmehr *[SjQ++]* nennt und audiovisuelle Projekte realisiert.

Borderlands Granular

Chris Carlson

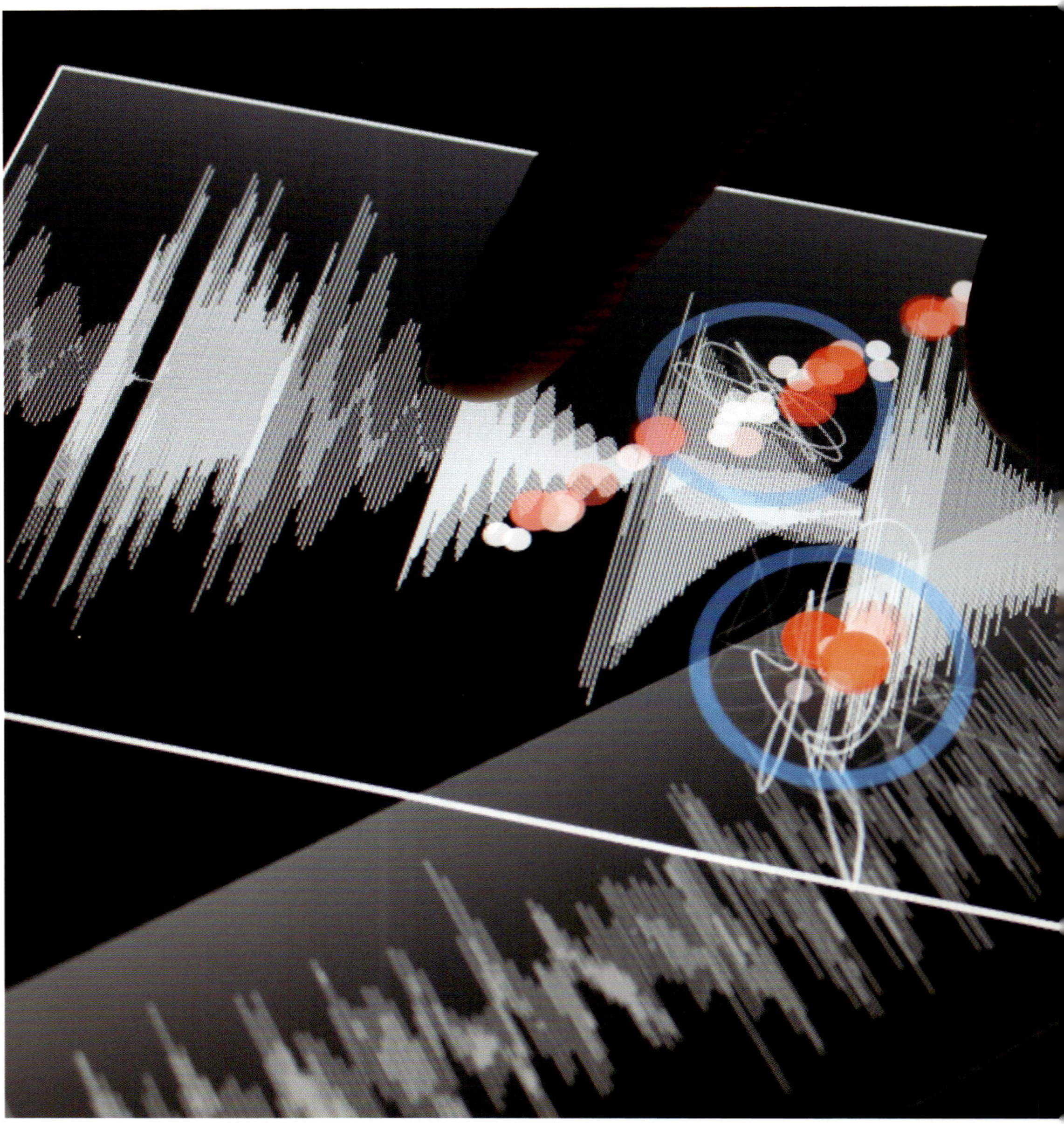

Borderlands Granular is a new musical instrument that allows users to explore, touch and transform sound with granular synthesis, a technique that involves the superposition of small fragments of sound, or grains, to create complex, evolving timbres and textures. The software enables flexible, real-time improvisation and is designed to

Borderlands Granular ist ein neues Musikinstrument, das Nutzern die Erforschung, Berührung und Veränderung von Klängen mittels Granularsynthese ermöglicht – einer Technik, die durch die Schichtung bzw. Überlappung von sehr kurzen „Soundschnipseln" oder „Grains" (Körner) komplexe, sich dynamisch verändernde Klangfarben und -strukturen erzeugt. Die Software unterstützt flexible

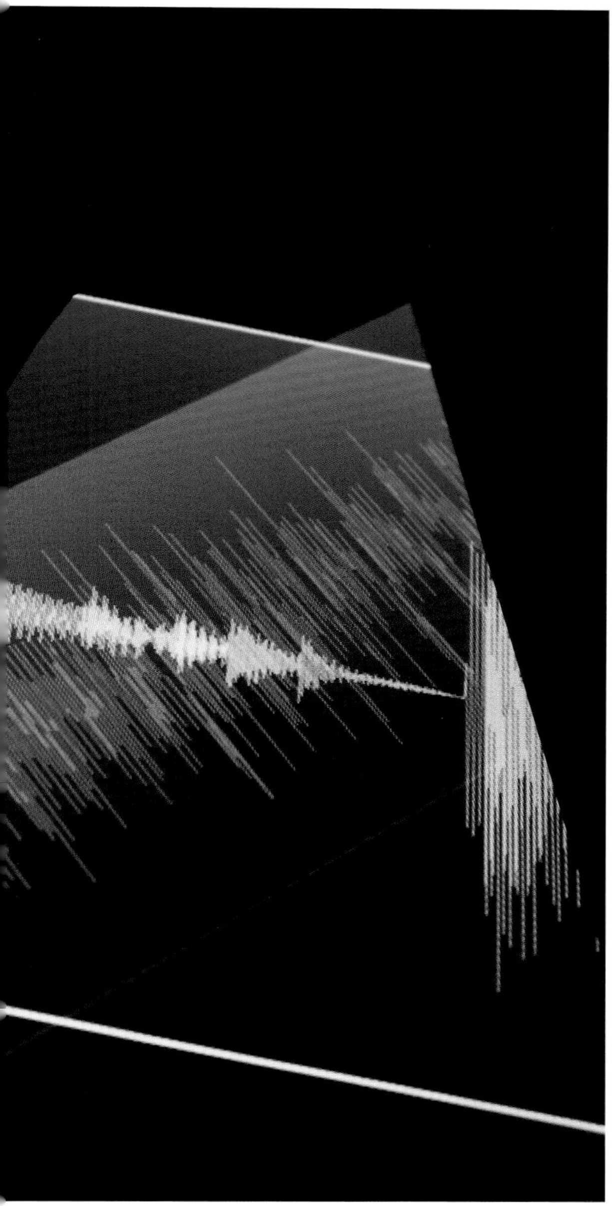

Improvisationen in Echtzeit und schafft die Voraussetzungen dafür, dass Anwender sich auf einem Grundlevel direkt mit Klangmaterial auseinandersetzen können. Der Anwender wird als Organisator von Klängen betrachtet, der gleichzeitig die Rolle des Kurators, Performers und Zuhörers einnimmt. Interaktion via Gesten und visuelles Feedback sind wichtiger als Knöpfe und Schieberegler,

allow users to directly engage with sonic material on a fundamental level. The user is envisioned as an organizer of sound, simultaneously assuming the roles of curator, performer and listener. Gestural interaction and visual feedback are emphasized through knobs and sliders to encourage a sculptural approach to making music and

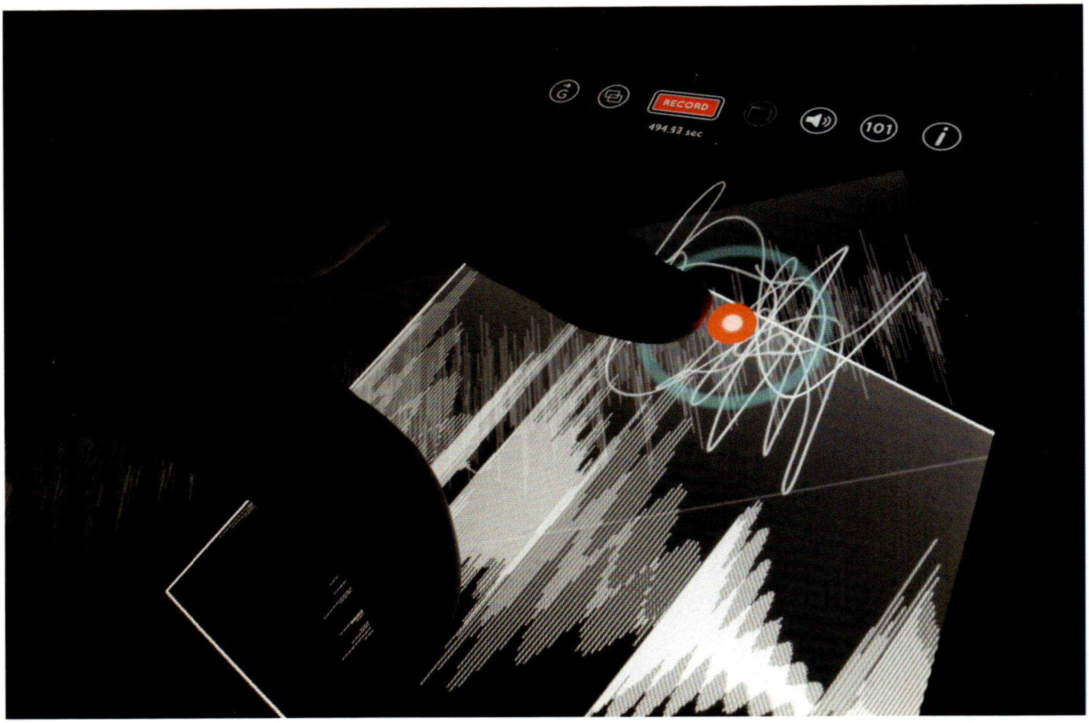

reinforce the malleability of audio. Users create, drag and throw pulsing collections of grains over a landscape of resizable audio files, dynamically and polyphonically sampling the waveforms beneath their fingertips. The iPad's built-in accelerometer may also be employed to shape sound with gravity. Performances may be recorded and saved to the user's computer or shared externally via SoundCloud.

Peter Kirn wrote a wonderful review of *Borderlands Granular* in an April 2012 post on the music technology blog *Create Digital Music*:

"How do you visualize the invisible? How do you expose a process with multiple parameters in a way that's straightforward and musically intuitive? Can messing about with granular sound feel like touching that sound—something untouchable? Music's ephemeral, unseeable quality, and

um einen skulpturalen Ansatz zum Musikmachen zu fördern und die Formbarkeit des Auditiven zu verstärken. Die Anwender kreieren pulsierende „Körner", ziehen und werfen sie über ein Feld aus Audiodateien und sampeln dynamische, polyphone Sounds mit ihren Fingerspitzen. Die Performer können auch den in das iPad integrierten Beschleunigungssensor verwenden, um einen tiefen vollen Klang zu erzielen und abschließend ihr Musikstück auf SoundCloud veröffentlichen, speichern und anderen Nutzern zugänglich machen.

Peter Kirn schrieb im April 2012 in einem Beitrag zum Musiktechnologie-Blog *Create Digital Music* ein wunderbares Review über *Borderlands Granular*:

„Wie visualisiert man das Unsichtbare? Wie kann man einen Prozess mit mehreren Parametern auf eine direkte Weise darstellen und eine musikalisch intuitive Herangehensweise bieten? Hat man beim Basteln mit Granular-Sound das Gefühl, Klänge – die an sich unantastbar sind

Supported by Stanford University's Center for Computer Research in Music and Acoustics (CCRMA) and a graduate fellowship from the Carmen Christensen Foundation. Thanks to Ge Wang, Mike Rotondo, and Jorge Herrera for their mentorship.
Menu icons and splash screen produced by Ben Nicholson. (http://www.bennicholsondesign.com)

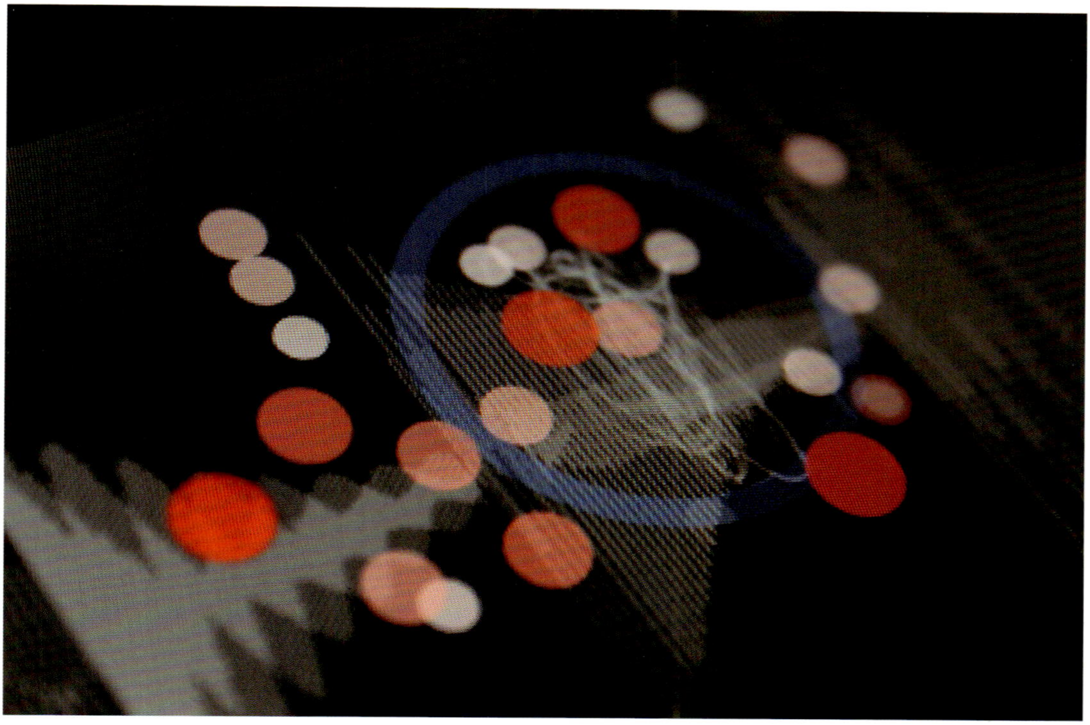

– zu berühren? Die Flüchtigkeit und Unsichtbarkeit von Musik und unsere abstrakte Annäherung an Klänge in der Computermusik sind Teil des Vergnügens, Musik zu machen. Dann damit herumzuexperimentieren, kann dieses Vergnügen erhöhen. Mit dem Design einer Benutzeroberfläche für ein granulares Playback-Instrument, das sich durch einfache Bedienung auszeichnet, löst der neue *Borderlands* für iPad und Desktop ein Problem, das vielen Computeranwendern vertraut ist." (Quelle: *http://createdigitalmusic.com/2012/04/borderlands*)

the ways we approach sound in computer music in similarly abstract ways, are part of the pleasure of making noise. But working out how to then design around that can be equally satisfying. That's why it's wonderful to see work like *Borderlands* for iPad and desktop. It solves a problem familiar to computer users—designing an interface for a granular playback instrument—but does so in a way that's uncommonly clear." (Source: *http://createdigitalmusic.com/2012/04/borderlands*)

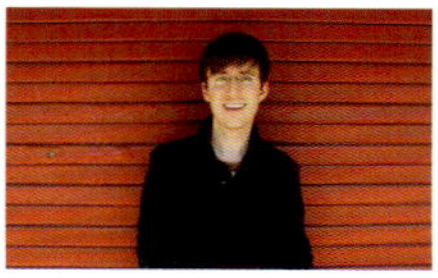

Chris Carlson (US) is an interactive developer who designs and builds immersive software and expressive interfaces. His work draws upon a breadth of experience in the areas of interactive audio, mobile music and physical computing and aims to inspire others to explore and create. He has an MA from Stanford University's Center for Computer Research in Music and Acoustics and a BSc in physics from James Madison University. *http://www.modulationindex.com* **Chris Carlson** (US) entwickelt und designt immersive Software und ausdrucksstarke Benutzeroberflächen. Er schöpft in seiner Arbeit aus Erfahrungen in den Bereichen interaktives Audio, Mobile Music und Physical Computing, wobei es sein primäres Anliegen ist, die Anwender zu inspirieren, selbst kreativ zu werden. Er studierte am Center for Computer Research in Music and Acoustics an der Stanford University und Physik an der James Madison University. *http://www.modulationindex.com*

0b0000.tms

Typingmonkeys

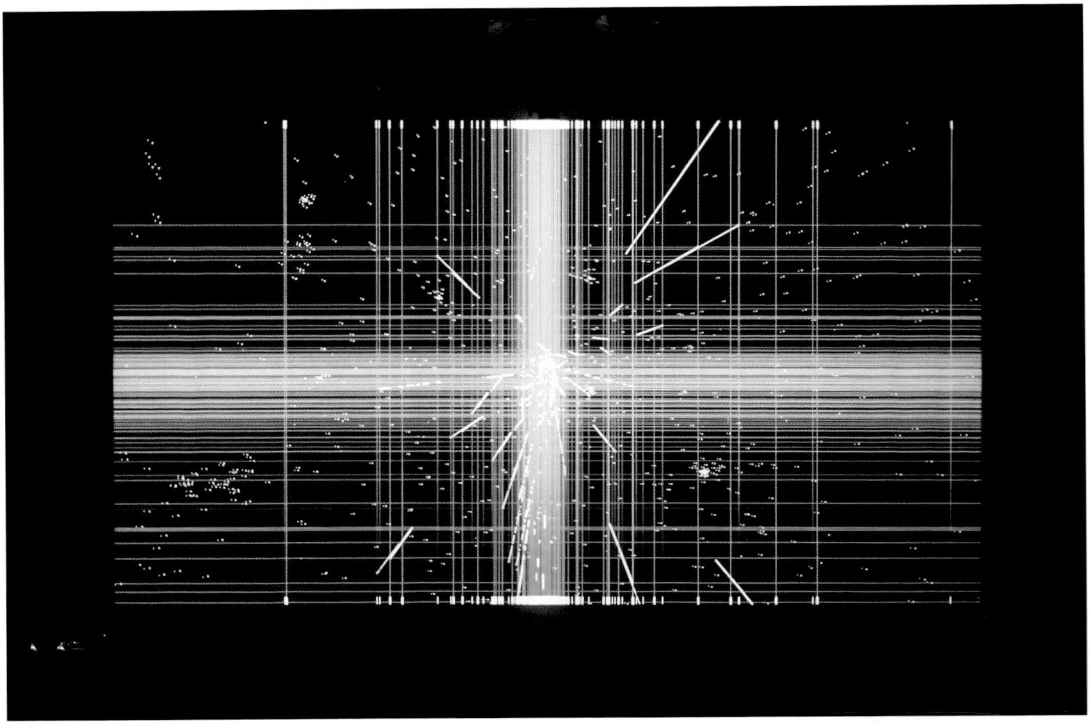

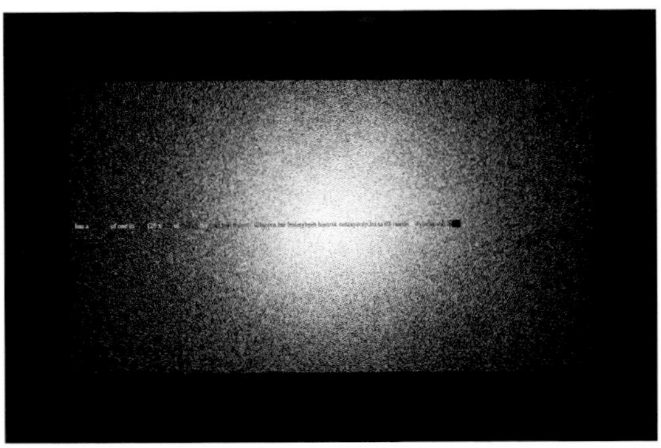

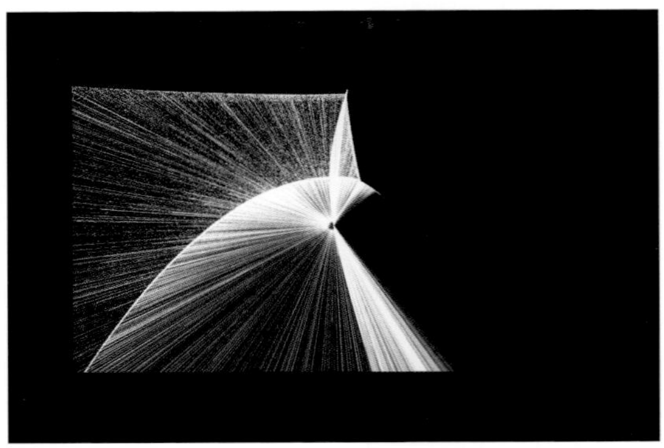

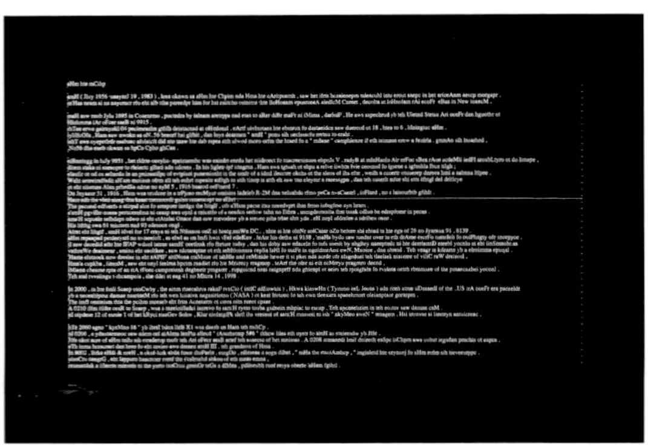

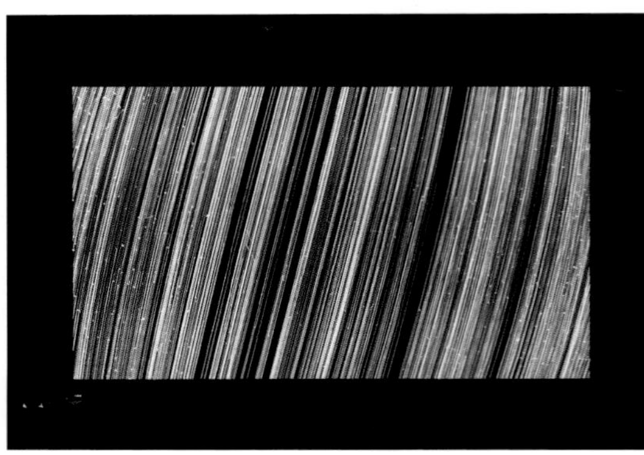

0b0000.tms ist eine audiovisuelle Performance mit Fokus auf Objektorientierung, Zufallsinitialisierung und Echtzeitverarbeitung. Es handelt sich um eine Reihe von Experimenten, die ein audiovisuelles Verständnis dessen ermöglichen sollen, wie auch kleinste Einheiten ein komplexes System generieren können.
Das „Infinite-Monkey-Theorem" (Theorem des endlos tippenden Affen) besagt, dass ein unendlich langer Satz, den Affen schreiben, die nach dem Zufallsprinzip auf einer Schreibmaschine Tasten anschlagen, jeden Satz, den es gibt bzw. geben könnte, beinhalten sollte. Einige Astrophysiker versuchen sogar den Ursprung des Universums durch dieses Gedankenexperiment zu erklären. Jedes System könne durch zufällige Aktionen generiert werden, wenn man unendlich viel Zeit bis zum Urknall zur Verfügung hätte. Eine andere Meinung besagt, dass der Affe nicht auf einem Textverarbeitungsprogramm tippen, sondern programmieren sollte. Demnach wäre ein Computerprogramm einfacher zu erstellen als ein für Menschen sinnvoller Satz.
Unser Name *Typingmonkeys* ist zwar als Parodie auf das „Infinite-Monkey-Theorem" zu verstehen, doch beschäftigen wir uns ernsthaft damit, die kleinsten Einheiten des Systems zu entwerfen und zu programmieren, um Menschen sinnvolle Erfahrungen zu ermöglichen.

0b0000.tms is an audio visual performance focusing on object-orientation, random initialization and real-time-processing. It is also a series of experiments to understand audiovisually how it is possible to construct a complex system from the smallest unit.
According to the "infinite monkey theorem," an infinitely-long sentence typewritten at random by a monkey should include every sentence that exists in the world or even that can exist in principle. Some astrophysicists seek to explain the beginning of the universe by this metaphor. It would be possible to generate any system by random operation if there were an infinitely-long period before the big bang. On the other hand, it is also suggested that the monkey should not use a word processor, but program a computer program as it would be easier to write a computer program than a meaningful sentence.
Our name, Typingmonkeys, is a parody of the "infinite monkey theorem", but we are actually "coding" to create a significant experience for human being by designing the smallest units of the system.

Photos: Hirotaka Hirabayashi

Typingmonkeys (JP) was formed in 2011 by Noguchi Kumiko and Hirakawa Norimichi. Utilizing computational capability the unit produces and controls a humanly impressible amount number of objects. The output sometimes makes no sense, like text typed by monkeys. **Typingmonkeys** (JP) wurde 2011 von Noguchi Kumiko und Hirakawa Norimichi gegründet. Die Gruppe produziert und steuert mithilfe rechnergestützter Methoden eine Vielzahl von Objekten. Wie von Affen getippte Texte ergibt das Ergebnis manchmal keinen Sinn.

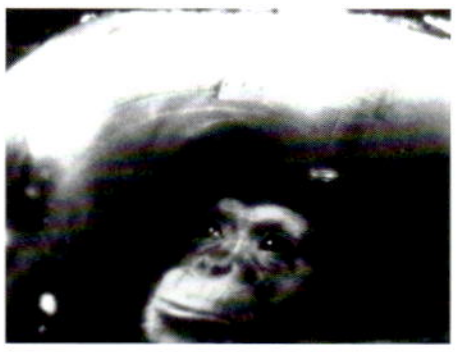

Albireo2.1

Mark Malmberg

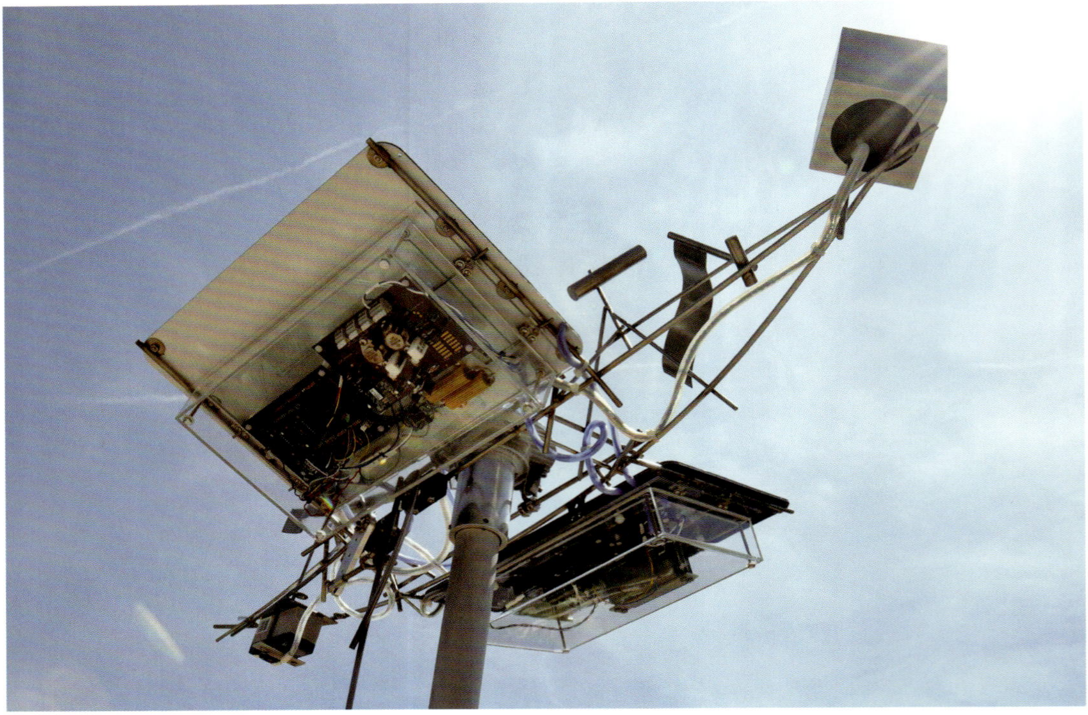

Albireo2.1 is a trio of robotic, bird-like creatures perched on top of poles, dancing, singing and chattering through the day. Wireless communication allows them to interact with each other improvisationally, both in motion and sound. Each is aware of its energy level as well as environmental variables and alters its behavior accordingly. They make different types of vocalization and respond to each other's sound choices by making variations of the same sound or by choosing another type of sound or action. Over a period of time one can observe subtle differences in the behavior of these creatures and see and hear them interacting with each other.

Albireo2.1 besteht aus drei vogelähnlichen Roboterfiguren, die auf Stangen befestigt sind und den ganzen Tag lang tanzen, singen und tirillieren. Drahtlose Kommunikation ermöglicht improvisierte Interaktionen mittels Bewegung und Klängen. Jede der Figuren reagiert auf ihr Energieniveau sowie auf Umgebungsvariablen und passt ihr Verhalten entsprechend an. Die Figuren stimmen unterschiedliche Töne an und reagieren auf die klanglichen Äußerungen der beiden anderen, indem sie deren Sound variieren oder durch andere Klänge und Aktionen konterkarieren. Nach einer Weile kann man subtile Unterschiede im Verhalten der Figuren erkennen und ihre Interaktionen sowohl optisch als auch akustisch wahrnehmen.

Special thanks to Phil Stone and Foundation for Contemporary Arts for their support.

Ich habe diese Figuren selbst gebaut und dafür selbst entworfene Leiterplatten und Arduino-Mikroprozessoren verwendet, die meinen eigenen Code nutzen. Ein Programm erzeugt die Klänge von Grund auf aus Rechtecksignalen, indem ein Ausgang zwischen 0 und 1 hin- und hergeschaltet wird. Das Timing dieses Zyklus wird algorithmisch verändert, um verschiedene Klangkategorien zu erzeugen, bei denen jeweils bestimmte Parameter mitschwingen, die sich geringfügig verändern, wenn ein bestimmter Klang vokalisiert wird.
Der Klangteppich, den diese Figuren ausbreiten, ist so konzipiert, dass er auch mit der Überlagerung der urbanen Geräuschkulisse und Klängen der Natur interagiert. Die zur Gänze durch Solarenergie betriebenen Figuren von *Albireo* erwachen mit dem Sonnenlicht, begrüßen den Tag pfeifend und trällernd und begeben sich bei Einbruch der Dunkelheit mit zarten digitalen Schnarchlauten zur Ruhe.

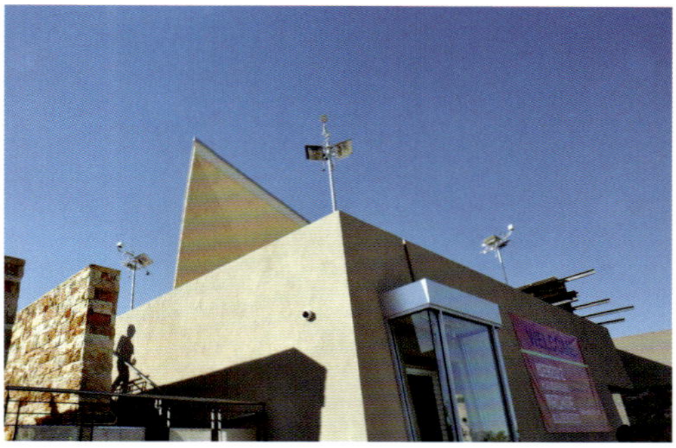

These creatures are hand-built by myself, with circuit boards of my own design, using Arduino microprocessors running my own code. The sounds are programmed from scratch with square waves generated by switching an output pin between 0 and 1. The timing of this cycle is modified algorithmically to form different categories of sounds, each with a certain envelope of parameters, but changing slightly each time the particular sound type is vocalized.
The soundscape created by these creatures is designed to interact comfortably within the overlap between urban sounds and those of nature. Powered completely by the sun, the creatures of *Albireo* awaken to the sun with whistles and warbles, and at the end of the day they have a bit of a digital snore as they fall asleep.

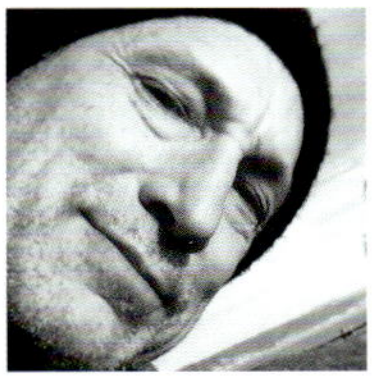

Mark Malmberg (US), born 1953, earned a BFA in sculpture from Carnegie-Mellon University in 1977. He entered the world of computer graphics in 1988 when he joined fledgling studio Xaos Inc. in San Francisco, California. Unique in its field, Xaos developed proprietary software to specialize in organic, fluid animation not otherwise possible at the time. In early 1989, Malmberg took the role of Creative Director at Xaos, which he held for ten years. Over the years, Malmberg has been recognized nationally and internationally for his animation design and directing work. Over the past decade he has returned to his roots as a sculptor. Pioneering a new sound/sculptural genre, he is currently producing hand-built solar-powered robotic mobiles. **Mark Malmberg** (US), geb. 1953, schloss 1977 sein Studium der Bildhauerei an der Carnegie-Mellon University ab. Die Welt der Computergrafik entdeckte er 1988, als er in das aufstrebende Unternehmen Xaos Inc. in San Francisco, Kalifornien, eintrat. Xaos entwickelte als einziges Unternehmen der Branche proprietäre Software für organische, flüssig ablaufende Animationen, deren Realisierung damals anderweitig nicht möglich war. Von 1989 bis 1999 war Malmberg Creative Director von Xaos. Mittlerweile ist er national und international als Animationsdesigner und Regisseur anerkannt. In den letzten zehn Jahren kehrte er zu seinen Wurzeln zurück und beschäftigte sich wieder mit Bildhauerei. Er leistete Pionierarbeit im neuen Genre der Klangskulpturen und kreiert derzeit handgefertigte, solarbetriebene Roboter-Mobiles.

altogether disproportionate

Michael Edwards

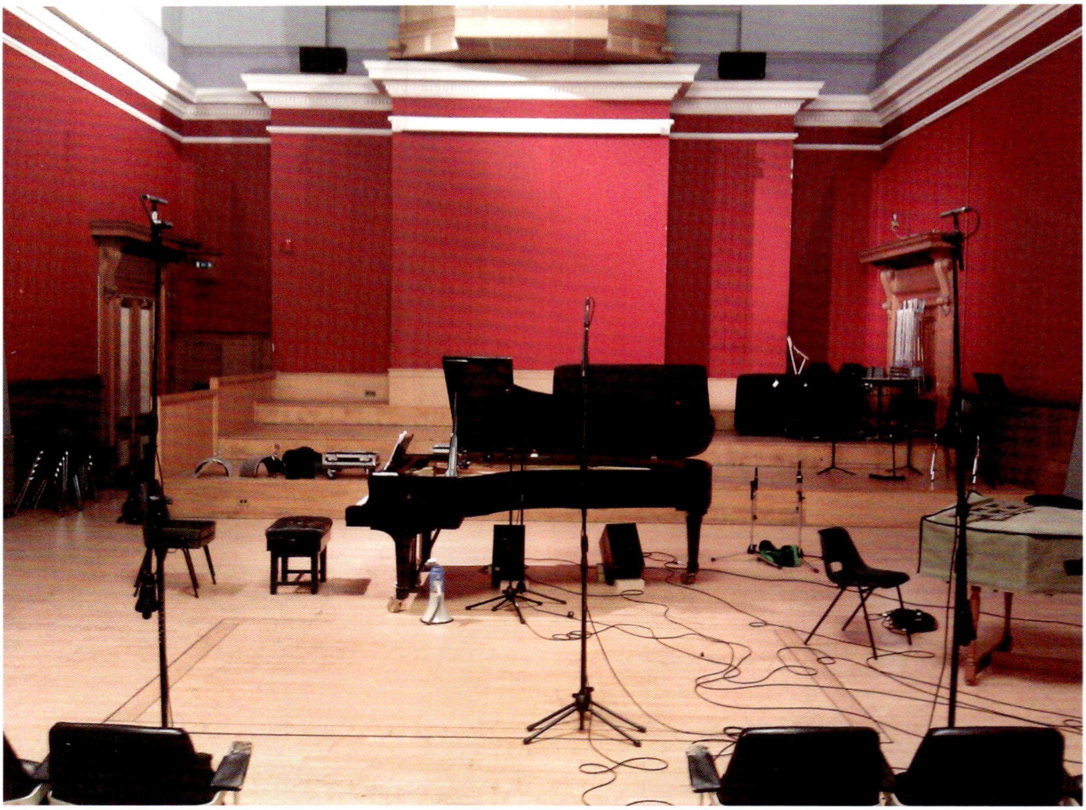

Algorithmically generated from beginning to end using my own 13-year-old algorithmic composition software project, *altogether disproportionate* employs a new technique developed especially for this piece. Using what I call rhythm chains, all the material is generated from two small sets of nine

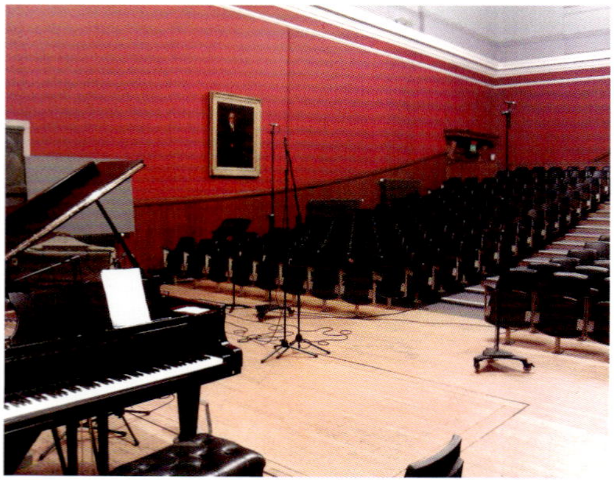

altogether disproportionate wurde zur Gänze mit meiner dreizehn Jahre alten Software Algorithmic Composition generiert, wobei eine neue Technik, die eigens für dieses Stück entwickelt wurde, genutzt wurde. Das gesamte Material wird mit Rhythmusketten, wie ich sie nenne, aus zwei kleinen Sets zu je neun rhythmischen Gruppen erzeugt, die jeweils nur einen Taktschlag dauern, begleitet von langsameren kontrapunktischen rhythmischen Gruppen von zwei oder drei Schlägen Länge. Obwohl die Rhythmen an sich sehr einfach sind, können die metrischen Gruppierungen, die durch den Verkettungsprozess entstehen, insbesondere bei den hohen Tempi (es beginnt mit 176 Beats pro Minute), eine beträchtlich höhere Komplexität erreichen, als das Material vermuten ließe. Auch die Harmonie wird algorithmisch erzeugt, wobei Ringmodulationstechniken eingesetzt werden, die aus dem Bereich der (analogen) Signalverarbeitung entlehnt sind. Im Prinzip erzeuge ich Summen- und Differenzklänge aus den harmonischen Partialtönen einer einzelnen Tonstufe, um harmonisches Klangmaterial zu kreieren, das häufig grundlegend tonal

ist, obwohl es nicht auf konventionelle oder funktionelle Weise verwendet wird.
Die Algorithmen bestimmen sowohl das mit dem Live-Piano als auch das mit dem Computer erstellte Klangmaterial, wodurch die Grundstruktur vereinheitlicht wird und eine Klangwelt entsteht, in der elektronische und akustische Materialien zum Klang eines Super-Pianos verschmelzen, das gleichzeitig präpariert (im Sinne von Cage, Cowell etc.) und unpräpariert ist.

Michael Edwards: composition, programming, recording, mix, master; Per Rundberg: piano

rhythmic groups, each lasting only one beat, along with accompanying slower contrapuntal rhythmic groups lasting two or three beats. Though the rhythms themselves are very simple, the metrical groupings created by the chaining process can become considerably more complex than the materials would imply at face value, especially at the high tempi indicated (we start at 176 beats per minute).

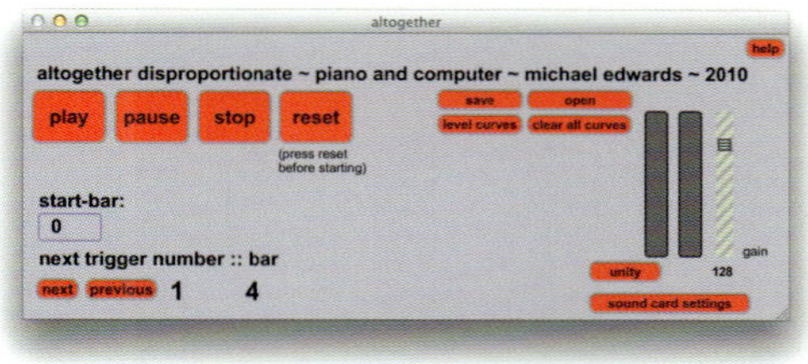

Harmony is also algorithmically generated, using ring modulation techniques borrowed from the realm of (analog) signal processing. Essentially I generate sum and difference tones from the harmonic partials of a single pitch to create harmonic material that is often fundamentally tonal, though not used in a conventional or functional manner.
The algorithms determine both the live piano and computer-generated sound material, thus unifying their structural base and creating a sound world where the electronic and acoustic materials are often blended into a super-piano, which is simultaneously prepared (in the sense of Cage, Cowell, etc.) and unprepared.

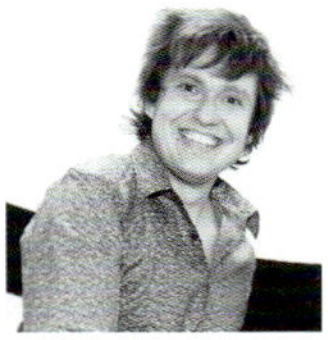

Michael Edwards (UK), born 1968, studied oboe then composition at Bristol University with Adrian Beaumont (1986-91), privately with Gwyn Pritchard, and computer music with John Chowning at CCRMA, Stanford University (1991-96). He was consultant software engineer in Silicon Valley (1996-97), visiting professor at the Mozarteum University Salzburg (1997-2002), and is currently a reader at the University of Edinburgh. His compositional interests lie in the development of algorithmic composition structures for instrumental music and the integration of these within similarly generated computer-processed sound structures and live electronics. He is also active as an improviser on laptop, saxophones and MIDI wind controller. **Michael Edwards** (UK), geb. 1968, studierte Oboe und Komposition bei Adrian Beaumont an der Universität Bristol (1986–1991). Es folgten Privatstudien bei Gwyn Pritchard und das Studium der Computermusik bei John Chowning am CCRMA, Universität Stanford (1991–1996). Er arbeitete als Software-Spezialist im Silicon Valley (1996–1997), war Gastprofessor an der Universität Mozarteum Salzburg (1997–2002) und ist derzeit Lektor an der Universität Edinburgh. Seine kompositorischen Interessen liegen in der Entwicklung algorithmischer Kompositionsstrukturen für Instrumentalmusik und der Integration derselben in elektronisch generierten Klangstrukturen und Live-Elektronik. Er hat sich auch als Improvisator auf dem Laptop, mit Saxofonen und MIDI-Controller einen Namen gemacht.

and IV (inertia)

Grischa Lichtenberger

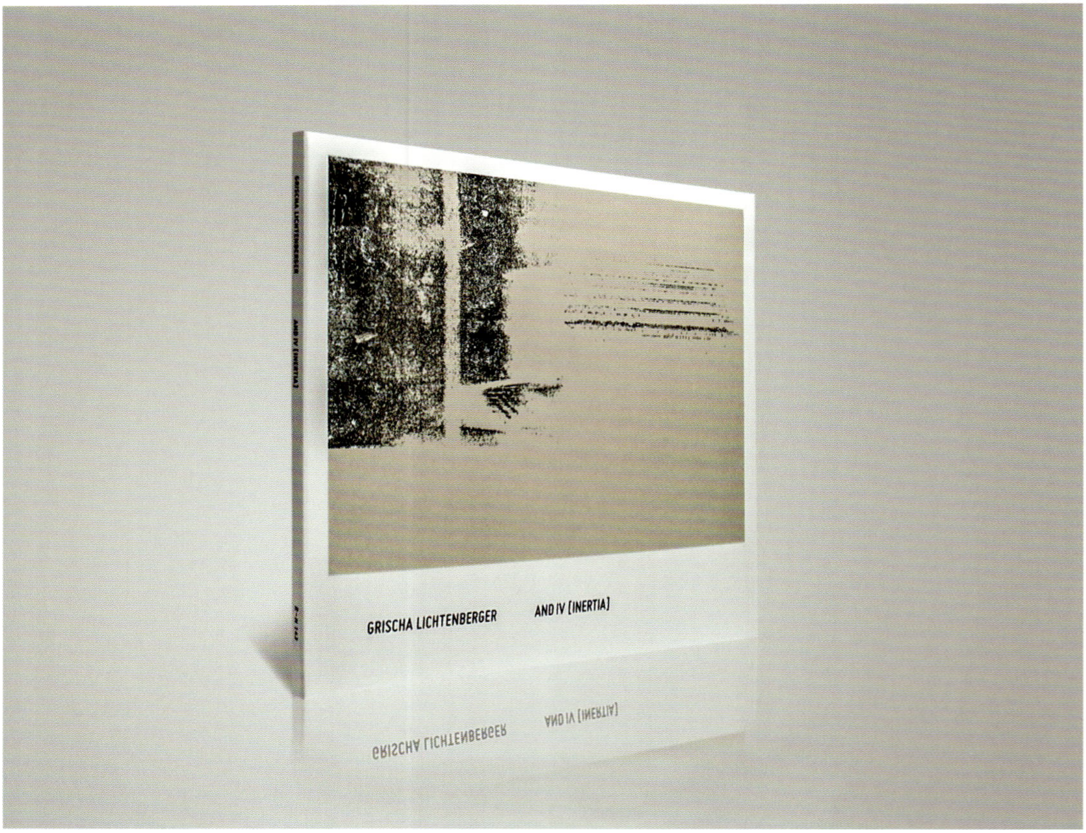

"The title *and IV (inertia)* refers to a fictionalized successor to the Baksan Neutrino Observatory in the Caucasus. First it was an idea for a novel, based on the consideration that it is impossible to deal with the topic of a *lebensraum* such as Berlin without being hit by stylization—so I had to experiment with strategies of fiction."

For his musical production, Grischa Lichtenberger uses field recordings of his environment, which are manipulated and broken down to their bare essentials until only fragments are left. Apart from

„Der Titel *and IV (inertia)* bezieht sich auf ein fiktives Nachfolgemodell des im Kaukasus befindlichen Baksan-Neutrinoteleskops. Zunächst war es eine Idee für einen Roman, die von der Überlegung ausging, dass es unmöglich ist, sich thematisch mit einem Lebensraum wie Berlin zu beschäftigen, ohne Klischees anheimzufallen – ich musste also mit fiktionalen Strategien experimentieren."

Grischa Lichtenberg verwendet für seine musikalische Produktion Feldaufnahmen seiner Umgebung, die manipuliert und auf das Wesentliche reduziert werden, bis nur Fragmente übrig bleiben. Abgesehen von analogen Quellen benutzt er auch digitale Klangdaten, die ähnlich gedreht und gewendet werden, bis die Grenzen zwischen Analogem und Digitalem verschwimmen. Das Arrangement dieser Partikel ergibt einen eher rauen und brachialen maschinenhaften Cut-up-Sound mit einer ungewöhnlichen Dynamik – nämlich fast keiner. Es hat den Anschein, als ob die 21 Tracks nur aus einem äußerst reduzierten Satz von Elementen bestünden, die aber virtuos und mit einer großen Variatonsbreite neu arrangiert wurden.

Gebrochene Beats und tröpfelnde Basslinien verweisen auf Downbeat-Tracks, rumpeln und lassen einen über ihren fehlenden Rhythmus stolpern, bis sie schließlich den zugrunde liegenden Groove wieder aufnehmen. Ebenso sind schroffe technoide Elemente integriert. Im zweiten Teil der Aufnahme ist auch Raum für neue Entwicklungen, in denen eher introvertierte und luftig leichte Melodieansätze in den Vordergrund treten.

Lichtenbergers Album *and IV (inertia)* entspricht seiner sonstigen künstlerischen Arbeit, die auch Disziplinen wie Installation und Malerei umfasst. Hinter all seinen Werken ist eine künstlerische Grundhaltung zu erkennen. So abstrakt seine Musik klingen mag, trägt sie doch immer eine persönliche Handschrift. Insofern ist *and IV (inertia)* die konsequente Weiterführung eines Konzepts, das Lichenberger bereits in *~treibgut* verfolgte, nämlich „Aspekte der Legitimation künstlerischer Arbeit in Verbindung mit der konkreten Lebenssituation zu definieren".

analog sources, he also uses digital sound data, which is likewise turned and twisted until the boundaries between analog and digital are blurred. The arrangement of these atomic elements results in a rather rough and brutal machine-like cut-up sound with outstanding dynamics—almost none. It seems like that the 21 tracks consist only of a minimal set of elements, but which are rearranged in a virtuoso way and with a high degree of variation.

Broken beats and dribbling basses allude to downbeat tunes, allow one to stumble because of their arhythmicity, to eventually take up the underlying groove again. Equally, there are fierce and harsh techno elements. And towards the second part of the record there is also room for new developments where more introverted and airy songs take over.

Lichtenberger's musical production on *and IV (inertia)* is in line with his general artistic work, which also comprises other artistic genres such as installations and paintings. There is a mental attitude behind all this, and while the music sounds abstract, one may still identify his personal note. In this way *and IV* is the extension of a concept he already started with his *~treibgut* EP, "to define aspects of legitimation for an artistic work in engagement with the concreteness of one's living situation."

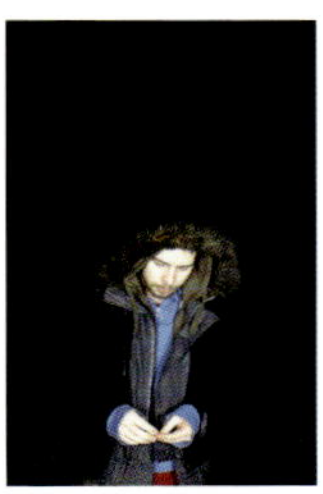

Grischa Lichtenberger (DE), born in 1983. Starting in 2006, Lichtenberger decided to rethink the artistic process from scratch—its ethical legitimization and its epistemological backgrounds—all in regard to the concreteness of the biographical situation in its landscape and history. Since 2008 Grischa Lichtenberger has lived in Berlin. In 2009 he released his debut EP *~treibgut ununbium* on the German label raster-noton. *~treibgut* is a system of references to the river Rhine—working as a motto for varied expressions: installations, videos, music, painting and drawings. With the new "supertitle" *andyrchie iv* he tries to take forward the idea of revaluating the reference to landscape as "the place we live in." **Grischa Lichtenberger** (DE), geb. 1983, beschloss 2006, den künstlerischen Prozess – seine ethische Legitimation und epistemologischen Hintergründe – im Kontext einer konkreten biografischen, von der jeweiligen Landschaft und Geschichte geprägten Situation von Grund auf neu zu überdenken. Seit 2008 lebt er in Berlin. 2009 brachte er seine Debüt-EP *~treibgut ununbium* bei dem deutschen Label raster-noton heraus. *~treibgut* ist getragen von Referenzen an den Rhein, der als Leitmotiv für verschiedene künstlerische Ausdrucksformen dient: Installationen, Videos, Musik, Malerei und Zeichnung. Mit dem neuen „Übertitel" *andyrchie iv* versuchte er die Idee weiterzuentwickeln und die Referenz an die Landschaft als „Lebensraum" neu zu interpretieren.

Cube with Magic Ribbons

Simon Katan

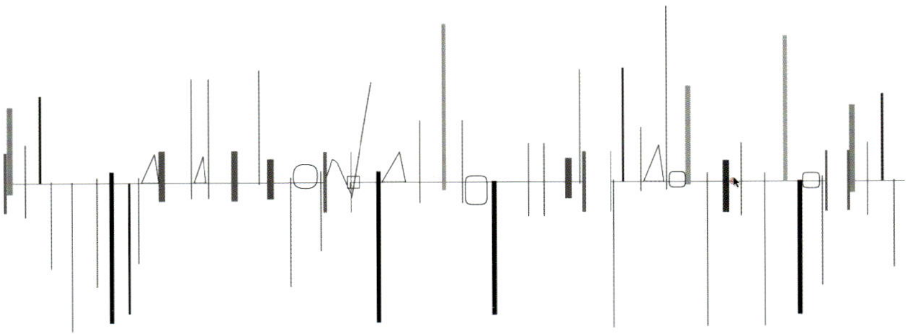

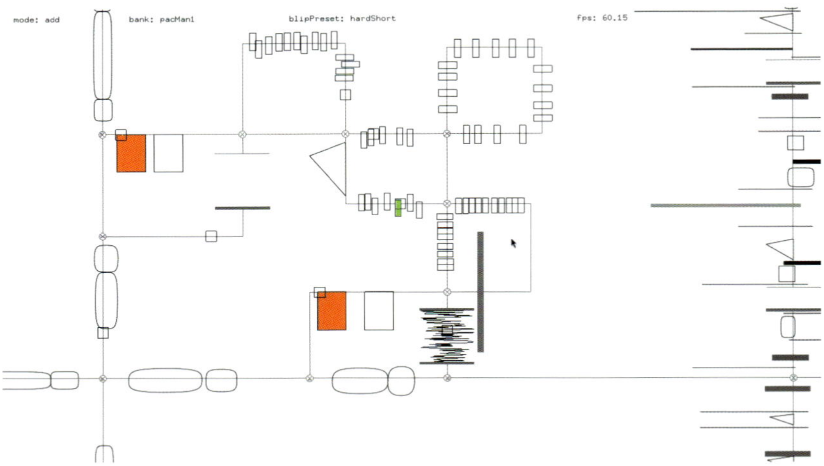

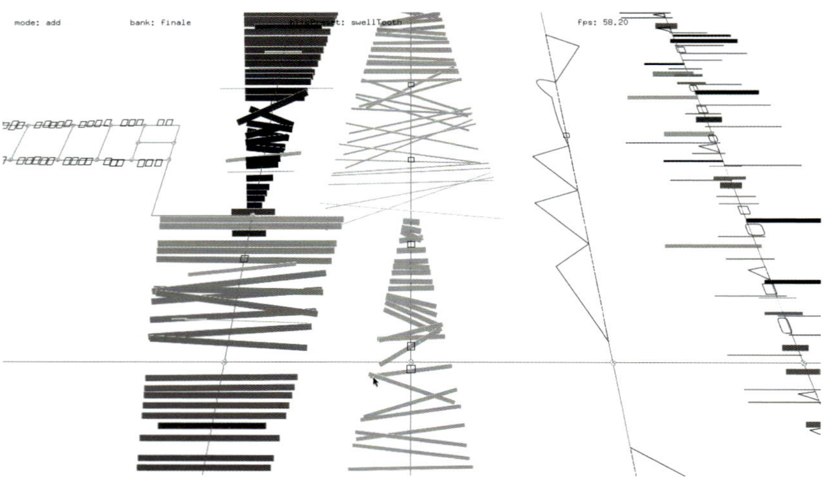

Cube with Magic Ribbons ist eine am Computer erstellte Komposition aus Bildern und Synthesizerklängen für Live-Performance. Das Stück ist nach einer Zeichnung von M.C. Escher mit einer Vielzahl widersprüchlicher Perspektiven benannt, aber auch von den labyrinthischen Räumen in den zweidimensionalen Grafiken früher Computerspiele wie Asteroids und Pac-Man beeinflusst. Es wurde mit dem speziell angefertigten visuellen Sequenzer SoundCircuit kreiert, der – statt ein konventionelles DAW-Layout zu verwenden – mehrere virtuelle Tonköpfe auf Spuren, die frei miteinander verbunden werden können, durch einen zweidimensionalen labyrinthischen Raum wandern lässt. Wenn sich die Tonköpfe durch das daraus resultierende Netzwerk bewegen, nimmt die topologische Anordnung der Spuren direkten Einfluss auf die Makro-Form der Musik. Darüber hinaus erweist sich das Stück in dem Maße, in dem es diesen verwirrenden Raum erschließt, als zunehmend flexibel und komplex, bleibt dabei aber kompromisslos an die musikalische Form gebunden.

Cube with Magic Ribbons is a computer-visual and synthesized-sound composition for live performance. The piece takes its title from a drawing by M.C. Escher, which is rich in contradictory perspectives, but it is also inspired by the wrapped spaces found in the two-dimensional graphics of early computer games such as Asteroids and Pac-Man. It was created using a custom visual sequencer, SoundCircuit, which rather than employing a conventional DAW layout, allows multiple virtual tape heads to travel through a two-dimensional wrapped space along tracks that can be freely interconnected. As the tape heads travel through the resultant network, the topological layout of the tracks comes to directly influence the macro form of the music. Furthermore, as the piece unfolds the nature of this already confusing space reveals itself to be increasingly elastic and complex, yet inexorably intertwined with the musical form.

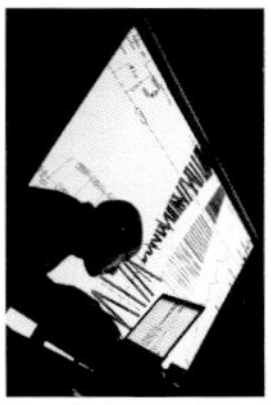

Simon Katan (UK) is an artist and coder with a background in composition who combines electronic music, live animation, interaction and social gaming. His work incorporates hidden mechanisms, emergent behavior, paradox, self-reference, inconsistency, abstract humor, absurdity and wonder. He makes software that creates musical odysseys by exploring animated worlds and design games in which the players unwittingly become performers of bizarre and occasionally daft rites. He especially enjoys connecting these two worlds using technology. Simon recently completed a PhD in audiovisual co-dependency at Brunel University. **Simon Katan** (UK) ist Künstler und Programmierer mit einer Ausbildung in Komposition, der in seiner künstlerischen Praxis elektronische Musik, Live-Animation, Interaktion und Social Gaming verbindet. Seine Arbeiten implizieren verborgene Mechanismen, emergentes Verhalten, Paradoxa, Selbstreferenzialität, Widerspruch, abstrakten Humor und wundersame Absurdität. Er entwickelt Software, die musikalische Odysseen ermöglicht, indem er animierte Welten und Spiele entwirft, in denen die Spieler unbewusst skurrile und mitunter unsinnige Riten vollziehen. Ein besonderer Anreiz besteht für ihn darin, diese beiden Welten mittels Technologie zu verbinden. Simon Katan promovierte vor Kurzem an der Brunel-Universität in London mit einer Dissertation über audiovisuelle Kodependenz.

Duali

Suguru Goto

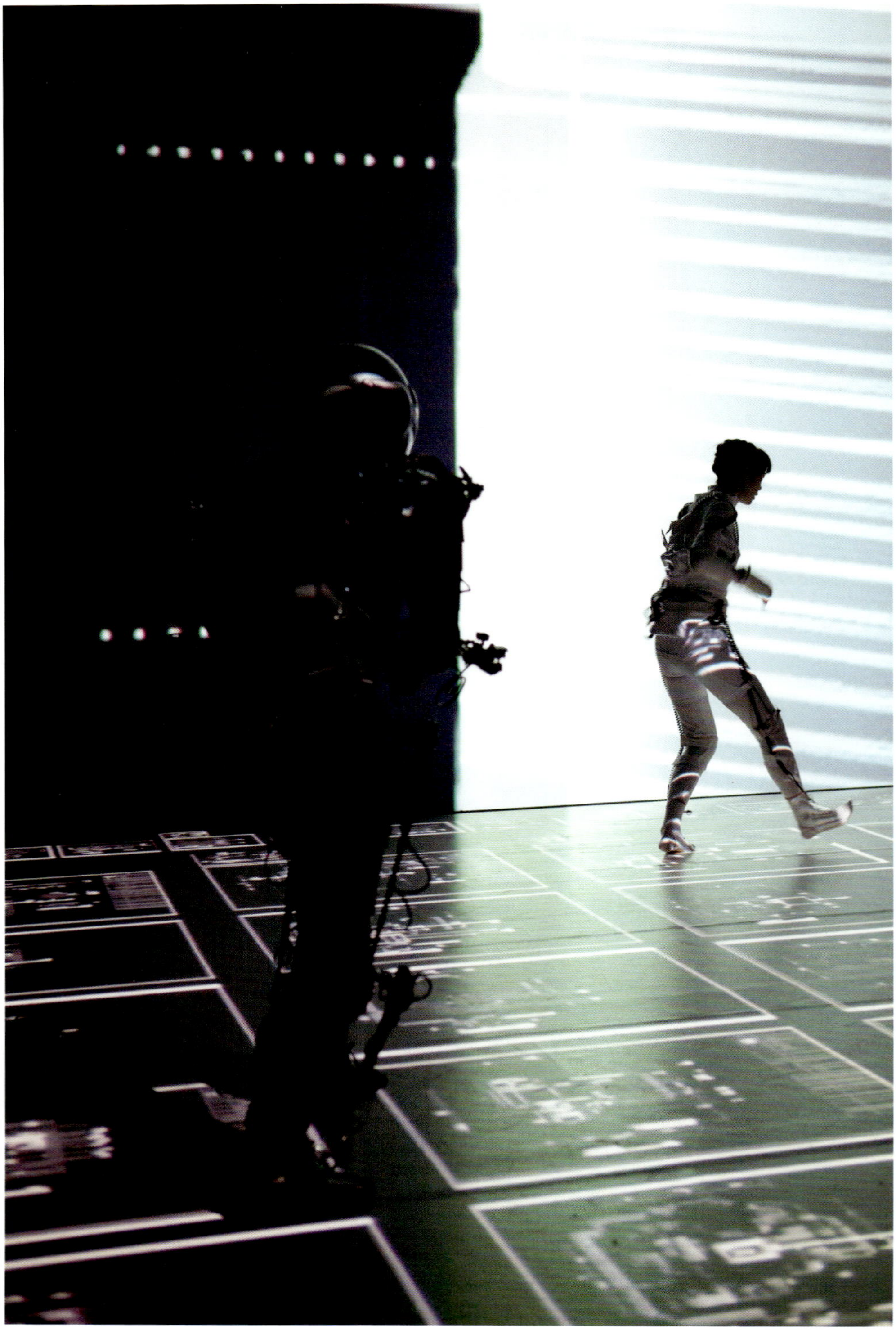

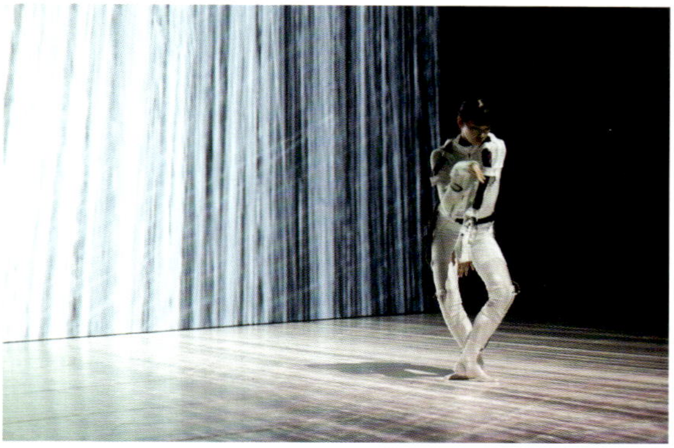

The idea of *Duali* is based upon the idea of performance in the context of new media, dance, music and images. However, it does not really belong to any one style. The special system which includes motion capture system and wirelsss system is developed by the artist. Utilizing this, the work explores the extension of the potentialities in the relationship between man and machine. This performance particularly exploits the interaction between the the body of the performers, the video images of their bodies, and the image and architectural/lightning-like image on stage, which can transform in real time thanks to a body suit.
The work is based upon the concepts of dualism. None of them are intended to be superior or inferior; however, both interact with one another and give rise to different contexts. For example, with the two dancers (who seem to be opposite characters) it expresses the interaction between the video representation and the real bodies presented on stage.

Das Konzept von *Duali* basiert auf der Idee einer Performance im Kontext von Neuen Medien, Tanz, Musik und Bildern, wobei das Stück keinem Genre wirklich zuzuordnen ist. Die Technik, die ein Motion-Capture-Verfahren und ein drahtloses System umfasst, wurde vom Künstler selbst entwickelt. Die Arbeit lotet eine Erweiterung der Möglichkeiten in der Beziehung von Mensch und Maschine aus. Die Performance beruht insbesondere auf den Interaktionen zwischen dem Körper der Performer, den Videobildern ihrer Körper und dem architektonisch anmutenden, blitzartigen Bildern auf der Bühne, die mithilfe eines speziellen Catsuits in Echtzeit verändert werden können.
Diese Arbeit geht vom Konzept des Dualismus aus. Keiner der Akteure wird als überlegen oder unterlegen betrachtet, die beiden interagieren miteinander und bringen durch ihr Aufeinandereinwirken neue Konstellationen hervor. Die beiden Tänzer, die unterschiedliche Charaktere verkörpern, bringen auch die Interaktion zwischen der Videorepräsentation und den wirklichen Körpern, die auf der Bühne agieren, zum Ausdruck.

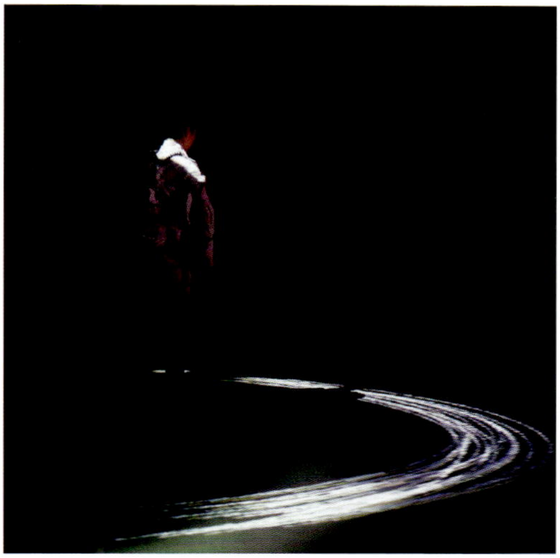

Photos by TranSonic2012, Center for Art and Technology, TNUA

Suguru Goto (JP) is a composer/performer, an inventor and a media artist. He is deeply involved in technical experimentation in the artistic field and in the extension of existing potentialities in the man-machine relationship. In his work, new technologies are mixed in interactive installations and experimental performances; he has invented virtual music instruments that create an interface for communication between human movements and the computer; sound and video images are controlled by virtual music instruments in real time through computers. **Suguru Goto** (JP) ist Komponist, Performer, Erfinder und Medienkünstler. Er beschäftigt sich intensiv mit technischen Experimenten im künstlerischen Bereich sowie mit der Erweiterung bestehender Möglichkeiten der Beziehung von Mensch und Maschine. In seinen Arbeiten kombiniert er neue Technologien in interaktiven Installationen und experimentellen Performance. Er hat virtuelle Musikinstrumente erfunden, die eine Schnittstelle für die Kommunikation zwischen menschlichen Bewegungen und Computer kreieren, wobei Sound und Videobilder von virtuellen Musikinstrumenten in Echtzeit via Computer gesteuert werden.

Equilibrium Variant

Roberto Pugliese

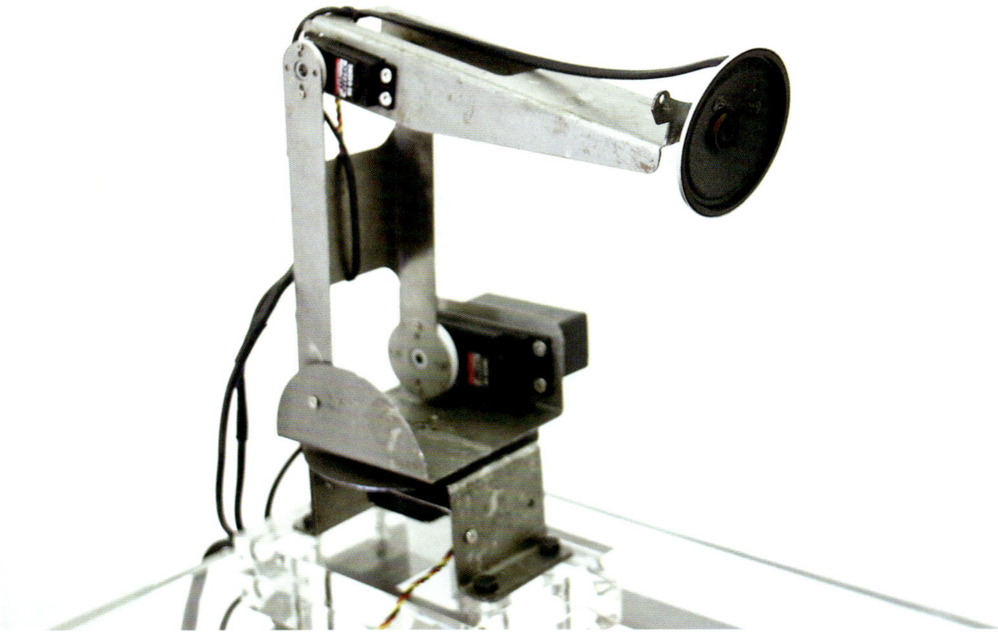

Equilibrium Variant is intended to explore the occurrence of the Larsen effect (also known as feedback) through the use of mobile devices in three-dimensional space. The distinctive screech of the Larsen effect typically occurs when a microphone catches the sound emitted by a speaker. It starts when the microphone is located too close to the speaker and interferes with its frequency. The microphone amplifies and reproduces the speaker's frequency at an ever-increasing width, virtually unlimited though in practice stopped by the amplifier's clip. Two mechanical arms are mounted on a stand. At the end of one arm there is a microphone, at the end of the other there is a speaker. Software manages the position of the arms dynamically and ensures that the distance between the microphone and the speaker never causes the amplifier to clip. In this way, the system tends to reach an equilibrium that is physically impossible to attain. The struggle for balance creates an acoustic and visual dimension that is never the same: the frequency of feedback and the movements of the mechanical arms are

Equilibrium Variant versucht, den Larsen-Effekt (auch bekannt als akustische Rückkoppelung oder Feedback) mittels Verwendung mobiler Geräte im dreidimensionalen Raum zu erforschen. Das charakteristische Pfeifgeräusch des Larsen-Effekts tritt im Allgemeinen dann auf, wenn sich ein Mikrofon zu nahe bei einem Lautsprecher befindet, in dessen Frequenzbereich kommt und ein vom Lautsprecher ausgegebenes Signal aufnimmt. Das Mikrofon gibt die Frequenz des Lautsprechers wieder und verstärkt sie, wobei sich die Tonrückkoppelung theoretisch endlos aufschaukeln kann, in der Praxis aber durch das Clipping des Verstärkers gestoppt wird.

Auf einem Plexiglastisch sind zwei mechanische Hebelarme angebracht. Am Ende des einen befindet sich ein Mikrofon und am Ende des anderen ein Lautsprecher. Eine Software steuert den dynamischen Positionswechsel der Hebelarme und sorgt dafür, dass die Distanz zwischen Mikrofon und Lautsprecher so ist, dass kein Clipping entsteht. Auf diese Weise erreicht das System ein Gleichgewicht, das physikalisch unmöglich zu erreichen ist. Das Ringen um das Gleichgewicht lässt eine neue akustische und visuelle Dimension entstehen, die nie gleich bleibt: Die Frequenz des Feedbacks

und die Bewegungen der mechanischen Hebelarme sind immer unterschiedlich und verändern sich in Echtzeit. In der Biologie bezeichnet Feedback die Fähigkeit eines Systems zur Selbstregulation, wobei die Anpassung an veränderte Rahmenbedingungen berücksichtigt wird. Alle Lebewesen verfügen über diese Fähigkeit.
Dieses Projekt führt das Phänomen mittels Sound in die Welt der Kybernetik ein. Der Sound lässt alle Bewegungen extrem harmonisch und natürlich wirken und die mechanischen Hebelarme bewegen sich kreatürlich wie Lebewesen, etwa wie zwei kämpfende oder umeinander werbende Tieren. Das System wird zu einem biomechanischen Organismus, der ein Eigenleben hat und auf Anforderungen von außen reagiert.

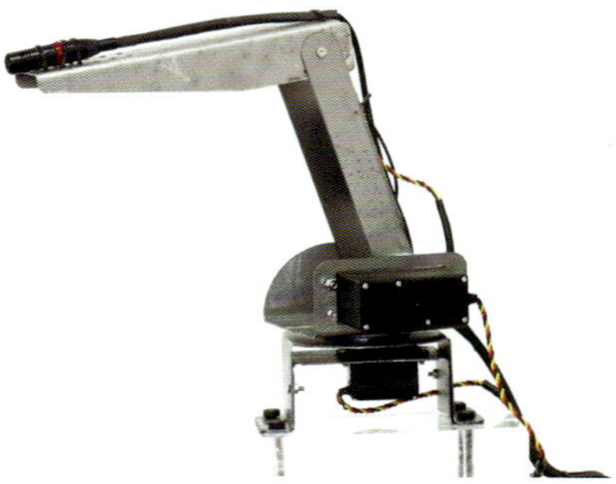

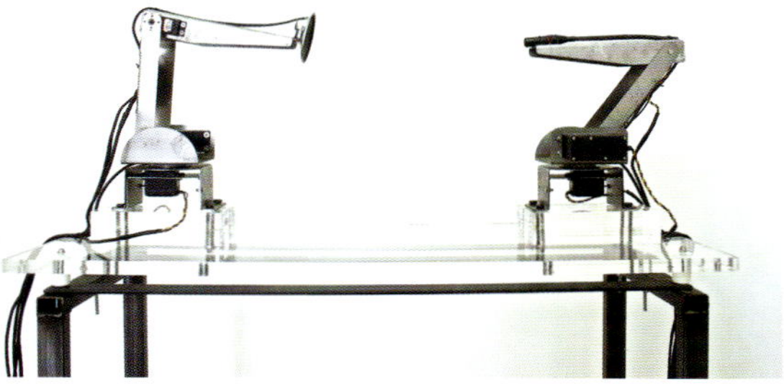

always different and change in real time. In nature, the phenomenon of feedback is the capacity of a system to regulate itself, taking into account the effects of certain modifications to its features. All living beings experience this condition.
This project introduces this phenomenon into the world of cybernetics through the use of sound. Sound makes all the movements extremely harmonic and natural, and the mechanical arms show a movement pattern that is similar to the behavior of living beings, such as two animals fighting or courting. The system changes into a biomechanical organism that has its own life and reacts to external influences.

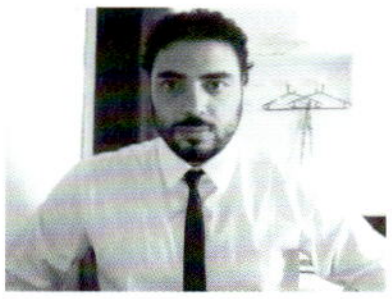

Roberto Pugliese (IT), born 1982, divides his time between teaching (musical systems and electro-acoustic and informatics laboratory), playing music and realizing sound installations. His research primarily derives its energy from two artistic currents—of sound art and of kinetic and programmed art. Using software-controlled mechanical tools that interact among themselves, with the environment that surrounds them and with the observer, he aims to examine new areas of research in sound phenomena, to analyze the processes that the human psyche uses to differentiate structures of natural origin from artificial ones (acoustic as well as visual), to discover the relationship between man and technology and the relationship between art and technology without ever losing sight of the visual aspect. **Roberto Pugliese** (IT), geb. 1982, unterrichtet musikalisch-digitale Systeme und Elektroakustik und macht Klanginstallationen und Musik. Seine Arbeit ist von zwei künstlerischen Richtungen geprägt: Sound-Art sowie kinetischer und programmierter Kunst. Durch die Verwendung Software-gesteuerter Apparaturen, die miteinander, mit der Umgebung und dem Betrachter interagieren, möchte er neue Forschungsansätze zu Klangphänomenen ausloten und die Prozesse analysieren, die in der menschliche Psyche ablaufen, um Strukturen natürlichen Ursprungs von artifiziellen (sowohl akustischen als auch visuellen) zu unterscheiden. Auf diese Weise rückt er die Beziehung zwischen Mensch und Technik sowie zwischen Kunst und Technik in den Blickpunkt, ohne dabei den visuellen Aspekt aus den Augen zu verlieren.

Gedichterbe

AGF (Antye Greie-Ripatti)

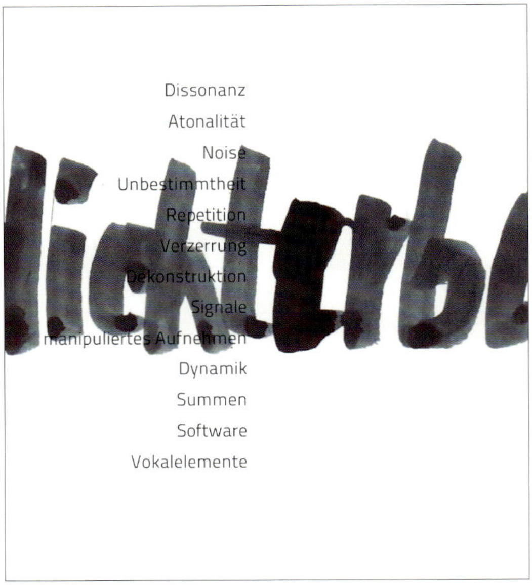

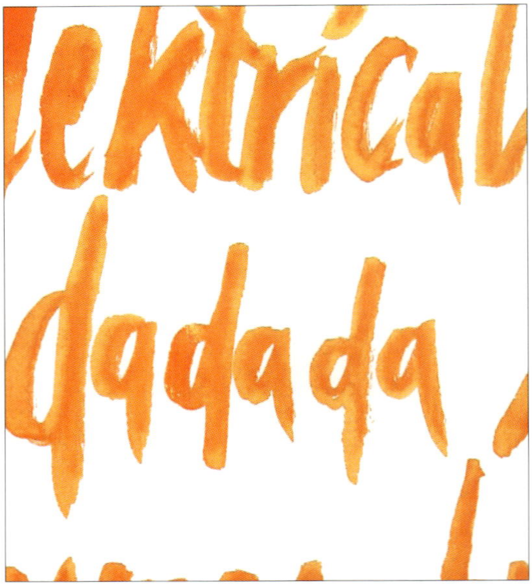

Gedichterbe investigates German poetry and the heritage of the German language within electronic music and society. Starting with the first known female German poet, Frau Ava (11th century), until today's "wunderkind" poet Ann Cotten (born 1982), poets are chosen from the Romantic period of the 18th century via Jewish poets of the 20th century to poets from both Germanies after WW II.

Personalities from the German electronic music scene help AGF to interpret the poems, and the collaborators range from the famous techno DJ Ellen Allien, the underground avant-garde legend Gudrun Gut, the prolific German Rapper Pyranja, Berlin's electronic star Barbara Morgenstern, Cobra Killer's scandalous Gina D'Orio and more.

AGF presents poets and poems that are close to her heart. Specifically, she investigates and interprets the relation to sound and music. So what does this sound like? Can Quio rap Frau Ava? Do Friedrich Schiller and Günderode stand the test of time ? Can Else Lasker-Schüler and Paul Celan inspire us today?

Gedichterbe setzt sich mit deutscher Dichtung, dem Vermächtnis der deutschen Sprache und ihrem Einfluss auf die elektronische Musik sowie gesellschaftliche Entwicklungen auseinander. Die Künstlerin spannt einen Bogen von der ersten namentlich bekannten deutschen Dichterin Frau Ava (11. Jahrhundert) bis zum heutigen „Wunderkind" der Literaturszene, der Schriftstellerin Ann Cotten (geb. 1982). Dazwischen finden sich Dichter der Romantik aus dem 18. Jahrhundert ebenso wie jüdische Poeten des 20. Jahrhunderts und Autoren der Nachkriegszeit aus den beiden Hälften Deutschlands.

Prominente Akteure aus der deutschen Elektronik-Szene unterstützten AGF bei der Interpretation der Gedichte: Techno-DJ Ellen Allien, Underground-Avantgarde-Legende Gudrun Gut, der produktive deutsche Rapper Pyranja, Berlins Electronic-Star Barbara Morgenstern, die skandalöse Gina D'Oro von Cobra Killer und viele mehr.

AGF stellt Poeten und Gedichte vor, die ihr am Herzen liegen, wobei insbesondere die Beziehung zum Klang und zur Musik hinterfragt und interpretiert wird. Wie klingt das? Kann Quio Texte von Frau Ava rappen? Haben die Werke Friedrich Schillers und von Karoline von Günderode dem Prüfstein der Zeit standgehalten? Können uns Else Laske-Schüler und Paul Celan heute noch inspirieren?

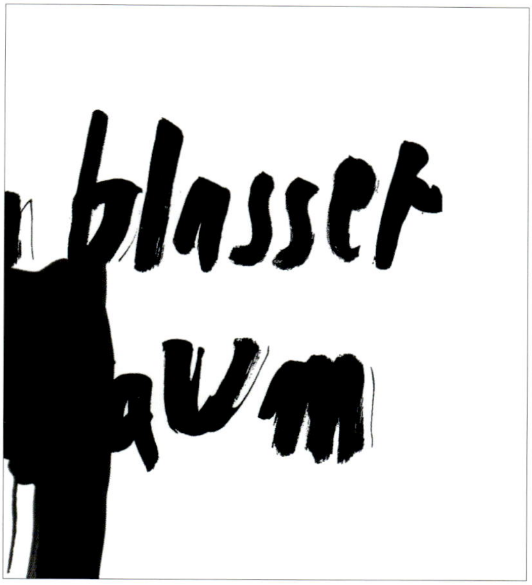

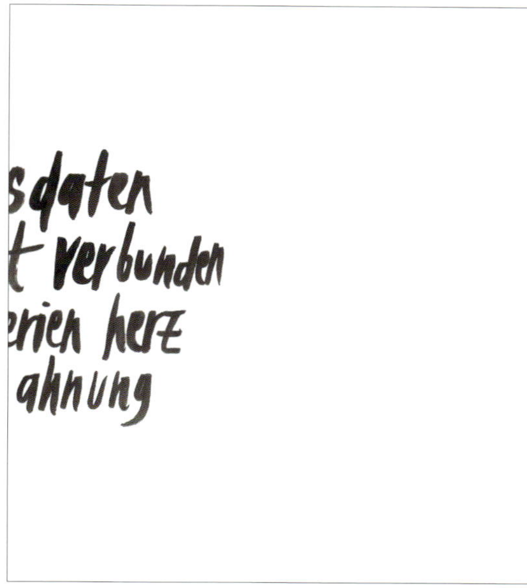

Die Musik ist auf radikale Weise modern, zeitgenössisch und minimalistisch und unterstützt die Poesie und die Geschichte, die sie umgibt. Der historische Text wird mittels digitaler Sound-Technologie und Ästhetik interpretiert. Manchmal sind die Gedichte dekonstruiert, mit Cut-Up-Technik bis zur Unkenntlichkeit bearbeitet. Manchmal sind die Gedichte pur und rein, manchmal fehlen die Worte vollkommen und die Musik spricht für den interpretierten Poeten.
Im umfangreichen CD-Booklet (70 Min.) finden sich zahlreiche kalligrafische Zeichnungen von AGF und ein begleitender Text in deutscher Sprache von Christine Lang über Sprache und Klang im Kontext dieser Arbeit.

The music is radically modern and contemporarily minimalistic, supporting the poetry as well as the history around it. The historical text is interpreted via digital sound technology and aesthetics. Sometimes poems are deconstructed and cut-up and processed to the point of non-recognition; sometimes the poems stand there pure and sometimes words are entirely missing and music speaks for the poet who is being interpreted.
The voluminous CD Book (70 min) includes numerous calligraphic drawings by AGF and an extended scientific text in German by Christine Lang about language and sound in the context of this work.

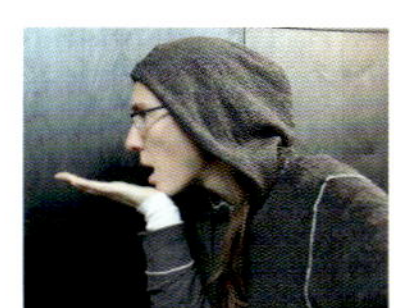

AGF (DE) is the artist name of Antye Greie-Ripatti, a vocalist, digital songwriter, producer, performer, e-poet, calligrapher, digital media artist and curator. She is known for artistic exploration of digital technology through the deconstruction of language and communication. Her poetry, which she converts into electronic music, calligraphy and digital media, has been presented on records, live performances and sound installations in museums, auditoriums, theaters, concert halls and clubs in Europe, America and Asia. **AGF** (DE) ist der Künstlername der Sängerin, digitalen Komponistin, Produzentin, Performerin, E-Poetin, Kalligrafin, Medienkünstlerin und Kuratorin Antye Greie-Ripatti. Sie wurde bekannt durch ihre künstlerische Auseinandersetzung mit der Dekonstruktion von Sprache und Kommunikation mithilfe von digitaler Technologie. Ihre poetischen Arbeiten, die sie mittels elektronischer Musik, Kalligrafie und digitaler Medien umsetzt, wurden auf CDs, bei Live-Auftritten und Sound-Installationen in Museen, Auditorien, Theatern, Konzerthallen in Europa, Amerika und Asien präsentiert.

La Biblioteca Ciega

Nicolás Varchausky

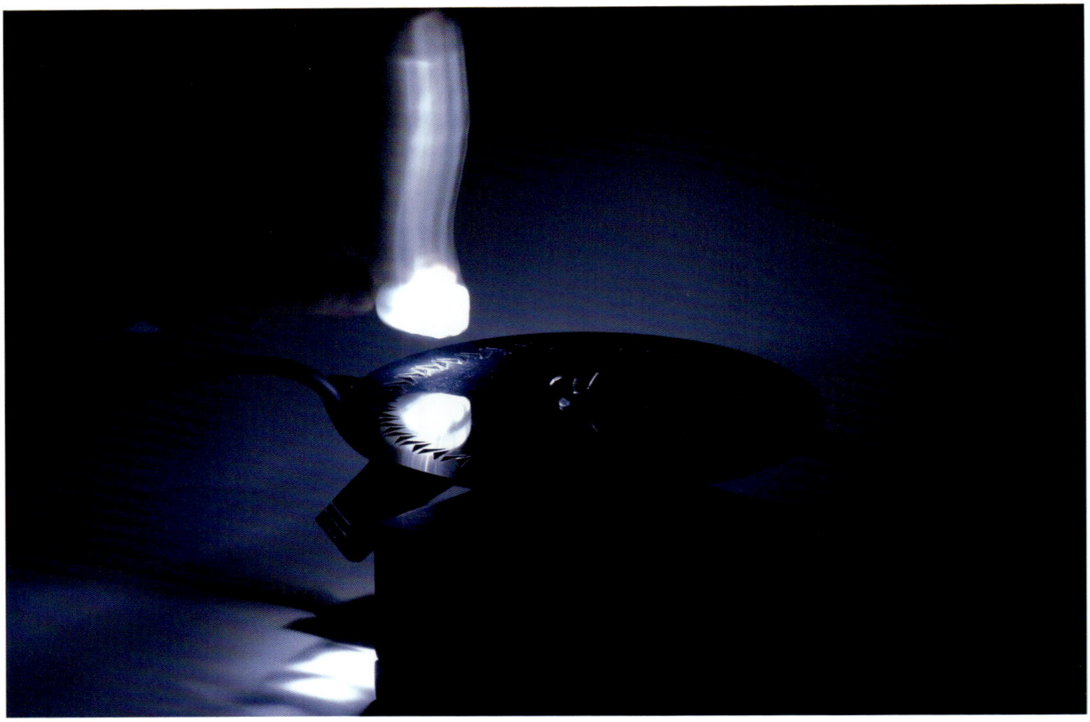

In 1955 the Argentinian writer Jorge Luis Borges was appointed Director of the National Library at a time when he was losing his sight completely. In his *Poem of the Gifts*, he reflects on the magnificent irony of simultaneously being given "the books and the night." *La Biblioteca Ciega* (the Blind Library) is a site-specific sound art performance composed for the very reading room of the library where Borges stood sightless, surrounded by books.

La Biblioteca Ciega uses a series of custom-made instruments that turn light into sound. Mechatronic optical turntables, sonic back-lights and light-bars were designed and built by the artist and then played by members of the Banda Sinfónica de Ciegos, an orchestra of blind musicians. The bars of light turn on and off in chaotic patterns controlled by the performer, generating complex waveforms. The turntables use a belt-and-pulley system activated by a hand crank that spins an acrylic disc. Each of the discs has a different sound-wave form carved out by a laser cutter. The performer plays the disc by spinning it and bringing a small flashlight closer to the perforated groove. Underneath it, a light sensor reads the

1955, gerade als er zum Leiter der argentinischen Nationalbibliothek ernannt wurde, erblindete der argentinische Schriftsteller Jorge Luis Borges. In seinem *Gedicht von den Gaben* schreibt er über die Ironie, dass ihm zugleich „die Bücher und die Nacht" gegeben wurden. *La Biblioteca Ciega* (Die blinde Bibliothek) ist eine standortspezifische Klangkunst-Performance, die für den Lesesaal jener Bibliothek komponiert wurde, in der Borges von Büchern umgeben war, die er nicht sehen konnte.

Für *La Biblioteca Ciega* wurde eine Reihe von Instrumenten speziell angefertigt, die Licht in Klang verwandeln. Der Künstler entwarf und konstruierte mechatronische optische Plattenteller, akustische Backlights und Leuchtstäbe, die von Mitgliedern der Banda Sinfónica de Ciegos, einem aus blinden Musikern bestehenden Orchester, gespielt werden. Die Lichtstäbe blinken in chaotischen Mustern, die vom Performer gesteuert werden, wodurch komplexe Wellenformen entstehen.

Für die Plattenteller wird ein Riemenantrieb verwendet, der mittels einer Handkurbel angetrieben wird, die eine Acrylscheibe in Drehung versetzt. Jede dieser Scheiben verfügt über eine andere mittels Laserschnitt erstellte Klangwellenform. Der Performer spielt die Scheibe,

indem er sie dreht und eine kleine Lampe näher an die perforierte Rille bringt. Darunter liest ein Lichtsensor die Intensitätsschwankungen des Lichts aus, das durch die Aussparungen dringt. Ein elektronischer Schaltkreis nimmt diese Schwankungen auf und verwandelt sie in Spannungsdifferenzen, anders gesagt in ein analoges Klangsignal. Die Backlights produzieren auf ähnliche Weise Klänge, wobei die Aussparungen hier linear sind.
Ein Computer verwandelt diese analogen Signale mit der Software SuperCollider in Echtzeit und spatialisiert sie durch ein Ambisonics-Verfahren mit acht Kanälen, das das Publikum in ein Klangbad taucht. Durch das Experimentieren mit alternativen Methoden der Klangeinschreibung wird *La Biblioteca Ciega* zu einer klanglichen Reflexion über Lesen und Schreiben.
In Borges dunkler Bibliothek lesen uns blinde Musiker einen Text vor, die in Licht und Schatten geschrieben ist, einer Sprache, die nur durch die Interaktion zwischen Mensch und Maschine verständlich wird.

Performed by Cristian Alderete, Javier Cabanellas and Marcela Chavez (members of Banda Sinfónica de Ciegos). Composition, instruments design and live electronics by Nicolás Varchausky. Commissioned by Secretaría de Cultura de la Nación Argentina. With support from DXARTS (University of Washington) and Universidad Nacional de Quilmes.

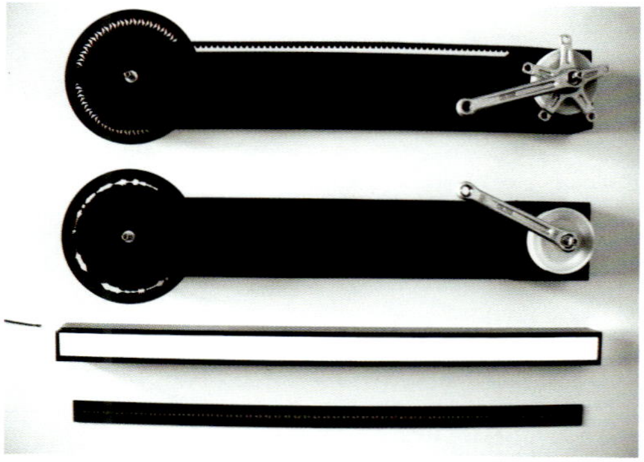

fluctuations of light as it passes through the cutouts. An electronic circuit takes these fluctuations and turns them into voltage differences, in other words, into an analog sound signal. The backlights produce sound in a similar way, but the waveform cutouts are linear.
A computer transforms these analog signals in real time using the SuperCollider software and spatializes them through an eight-channel ambisonic array that surrounds the audience, creating an immersive sonic experience. By experimenting with alternative methods of sound inscription, *La Biblioteca Ciega* becomes a sonic speculation on reading and writing.
In Borges's darkened library, blind musicians read to us a passage written in light and shadow, a language that can only be heard through the interaction between humans and machines.

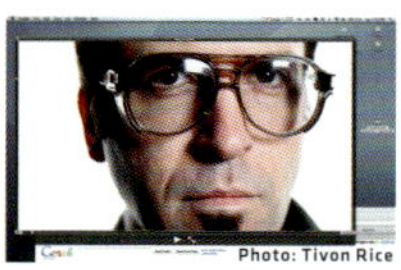
Photo: Tivon Rice

Nicolás Varchausky (AR), born 1973, is a composer, performer and researcher. His work explores the relations between sound, space, memory and spoken word within technological environments. He has a degree in electroacoustic music composition from the Universidad de Quilmes (UNQ, Argentina), where he works as an assistant professor. Since 1999, his artistic production has been oriented not only on electronic and instrumental music composition but also on sound-art projects, performance, interactive installations and site-specific projects in public spaces. He teaches courses on electronic music composition, sound design, sound, music & drama and the SuperCollider software. He directs the research project SAETAS (Sistemas Algorítmicos de Espacio y Tiempo en el Arte Sonoro, UNQ) on systems aesthetics in sound art. He has also taught at the Universidad de Buenos Aires, UBA, the electronic arts degree at the Universidad Tres de Febrero and at the Fundación Universidad del Cine. **Nicolás Varchausky** (AR), geb. 1973, ist Komponist, Performer und Forscher. In seinen Arbeiten setzt er sich mit Klang, Raum, Gedächtnis und dem gesprochene Wort in technologischen Zusammenhängen auseinander. Er studierte Elektroakustik-Komposition an der Universidad de Quilmes in Argentinien, wo er als Dozent tätig ist. Seit 1999 orientiert sich seine künstlerische Produktion nicht nur an der Komposition von elektronischer und Instrumentalmusik, sondern auch an Klangkunstprojekten, Performance, interaktiven Installationen und standortspezifischen Projekten im öffentlichen Raum. Er unterrichtet elektronische Komposition, Sound Design, Klangkunst, Musik und Schauspiel und SuperCollider-Software. Darüber hinaus leitet er das Forschungsprojekt S.A.E.T.A.S. (Sistemas Algorítmicos de Espacio y Tiempo en el Arte Sonoro, Universidad Nacional de Quilmes) über ästhetische Systeme in der Klangkunst und unterrichtete auch an der Universidad de Buenos Aires, Elektronische Kunst an der Universidad Tres de Febrero sowie an der Fundación Universidad del Cine.

The Half

Intermedia Chef

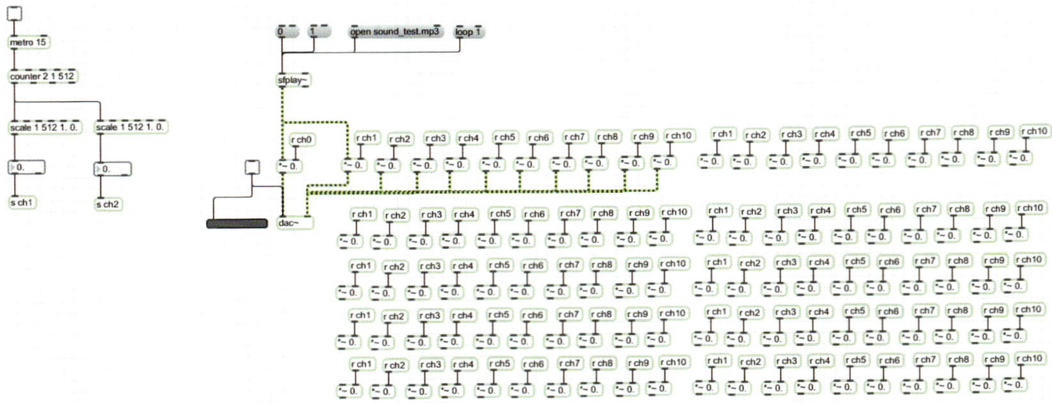

The artist group Intermedia Chef captures the experience of South Korea's younger generation through our sound installation work, *The Half*. We are speaking up about the ambiguity we feel towards North Koreans, a feeling that is based on our history of division, which started at the end of World War II, and the political gridlock that ensures we remain divided. The Korean War changed many things and the saddest is 60 years of separation between families who have not yet reunited.

One member of our group, Jaewan Choi, has personally experienced this historic tragedy. Knowing about his grandfather's brother in North Hamgyong province, Choi also wonders about the rest of his family members in the other half. Whatever sympathy or longing we have regarding reuniting both halves of the country, we are supposed to view people in North Korea as national enemies. This is what we have all learned through our education and life experience, including our mandatory military service. This contradiction between our emotional attitude and social background is the basis of our sound installation *The Half*.

Als Künstlergruppe Intermedia Chef versuchen wir in der Sound-Installation *The Half*, das Lebensgefühl der Jugend Südkoreas zu vermitteln. Wir thematisieren die ambivalenten Gefühle, die wir gegenüber Nordkoreanern empfinden und die auf die Geschichte der Teilung nach dem Zweiten Weltkrieg zurückzuführen sind, sowie die festgefahrene Politik, die dafür verantwortlich ist, dass diese Teilung andauert. Der Koreakrieg hat vieles verändert, wobei das Traurigste wohl ist, dass Familien seit sechzig Jahren getrennt voneinander leben müssen.

Jaewan Choi, ein Mitglied unserer Gruppe, hat die Auswirkungen dieser historischen Tragödie persönlich erlebt. Er weiß, dass der Bruder seines Großvaters in der Provinz Nord-Hamgyong lebt und sorgt sich um den Verbleib der übrigen Familienmitglieder in „der anderen Hälfte". Ungeachtet unserer Sympathien oder der Sehnsucht nach der Wiedervereinigung der beiden Hälften wurde uns in der Schule, durch unsere Erfahrungen und nicht zuletzt beim Militärdienst beigebracht, die Menschen in Nordkorea als nationale Feinde zu betrachten. Dieser Widerspruch zwischen unserer emotionalen Einstellung und dem gesellschaftlichen Hintergrund ist das Thema unserer Sound-Installation *The Half*.

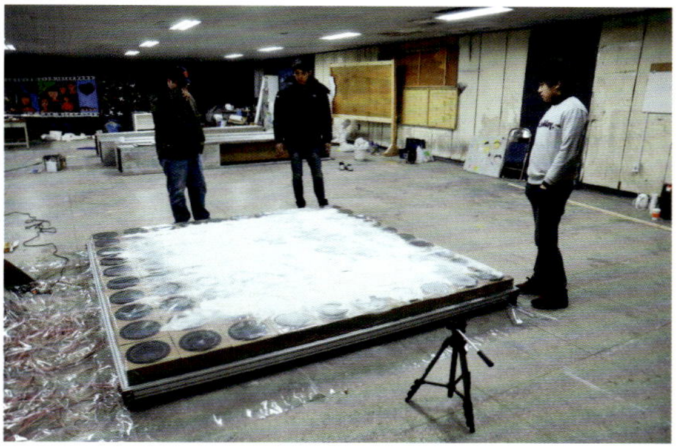

Zunächst führten unsere Diskussionen über die Visualisierung der spezifischen historischen Hintergründe zu frustrierenden und unklaren Ergebnissen. Dann kamen wir auf die Idee, eine kinetische 3D-Typografie zu verwenden, um unsere kreativen Vorstellungen in einer klaren und deutlichen Bildsprache umzusetzen. Wir kreierten eine 25 Buchstaben umfassende, pixelartige Typografie, die aus hundert Lautsprechern besteht, welche aus dem Archivmaterial von Massenmedien Schallwellen produzieren. Diese Schallwellen werden mithilfe von Mehl sichtbar gemacht. Schließlich verbinden sich die Buchstaben zu dem Satz „Growing Gap Between the Halves" (Wachsende Kluft zwischen den Hälften). Die Arbeit beinhaltet eine Botschaft der beiden getrennten ethnischen Gruppen und transportiert darüber hinaus die Erfahrung der Isolation in den beiden Ländern. Trotz der eindeutigen Aussage vermittelt das Werk auch die Unsicherheit und Ambiguität, die wir gegenüber der anderen Hälfte empfinden.

In the first place, our discussions about visualizing the specific historical background had always ended up in frustrating and unclear conclusions. Then we decided to use 3D kinetic typography to make our creative ideas visually clear and effective. We created a 25-letter pixelated typography made from 100 speaker units, which produce sound waves with archived mass media material. The sound waves become visible by the use of flour, and eventually the letters spell out the sentence "Growing Gap Between the Halves." The complete work connotes a message of the divided ethnic groups and isolated experience in two different countries. Despite the clear message, the work still includes the slight uncertainty and ambiguity we feel towards the other half. And this is what we ultimately try to address with our project.

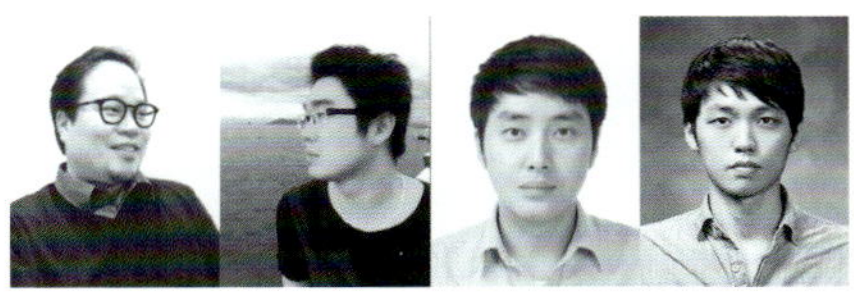

Intermedia Chef (Jaewan Choi, Dongjo Kim, Wonchul Lee and Jinhyung Park) (KR). From diverse academic and professional backgrounds, they first met each other at Data+ Lab. in the Graduate School of Advanced Imaging Science, Multimedia and Film, Chung-Ang University (GSAIM). They were interested in interdisciplinary research based on digital interaction and its application and were trying to explore dynamic artwork generated by computer-controlled sound in the aspect of data visualization leading sound waves to a physical source. Furthermore, they are aiming to turn the sound-wave energy into a kinetic type of visual art. Die Mitglieder der Gruppe **Intermedia Chef** (Jaewan Choi, Dongjo Kim, Wonchul Lee und Jinhyung Park) (KR), die einen unterschiedlichen akademischen und beruflichen Werdegang haben, begegneten sich am DATA+ Lab. der Graduate School of Advanced Imaging Science, Multimedia and Film der Universität Chung-Ang (GSAIM). Ihr gemeinsames Interesse galt der interdisziplinären Forschung basierend auf digitaler Interaktion und deren Anwendung. Sie setzen sich mit dynamischer Kunst auseinander, die durch computergesteuerten Sound unter dem Aspekt der Datenvisualisierung entsteht und die Energie der Schallwellen auf physikalische Quellen zurückführt. Ihr Ziel ist, dass die Schallwellenenergie sich als eine kinetische Form visueller Kunst manifestiert.

The Sound of the Earth

Yuri Suzuki

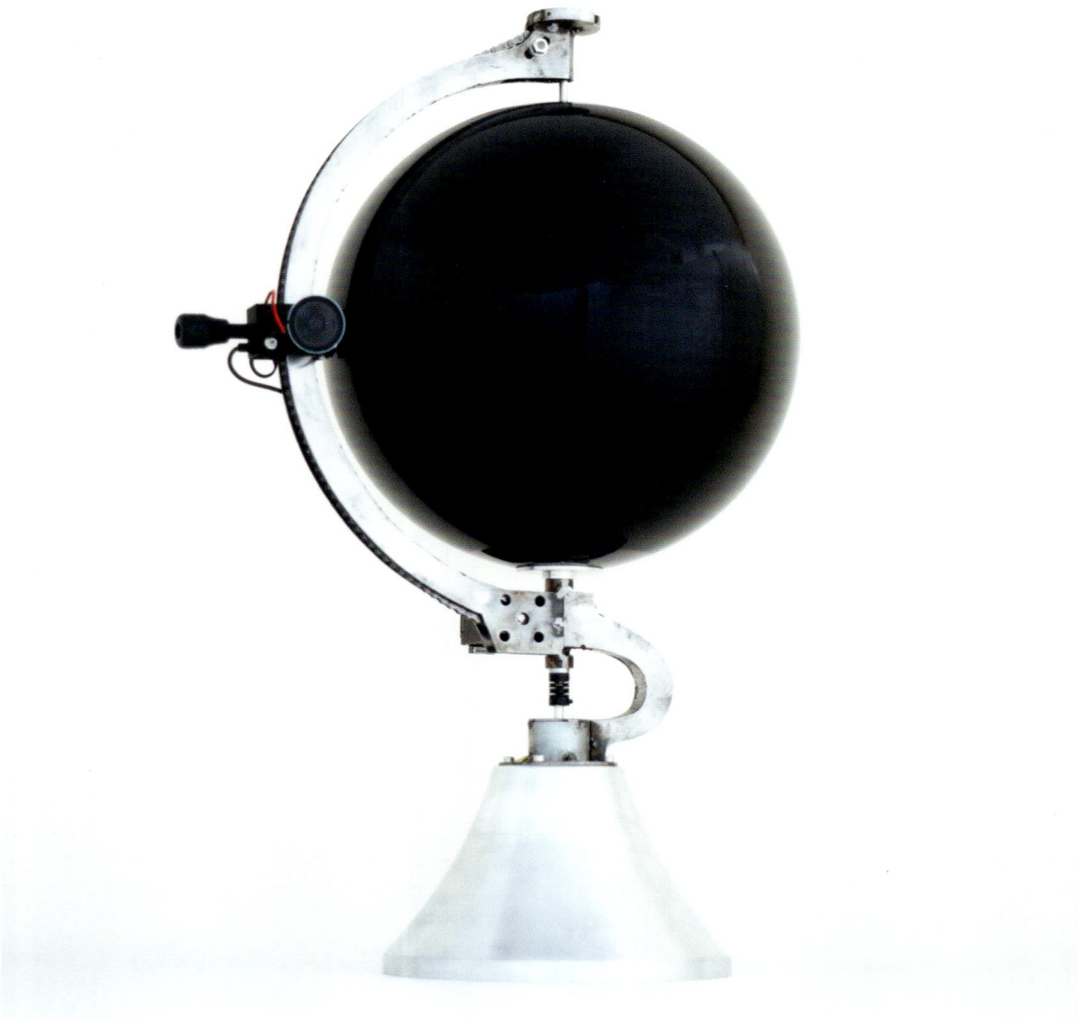

The Sound of the Earth is a spherical vinyl record and record player that can play back the sounds stored on it. The surface of the globe is engraved just like a normal vinyl but recording the sound in 3D instead of a flat surface—the grooves representing the outlines of the geographic land mass.

The Sound of the Earth besteht aus einem Schallplatten-Globus und einem Plattenspieler, der die darauf gespeicherten Klänge wiedergibt. Die Oberfläche des Globus ist wie eine Vinylschallplatte geprägt, wobei die Signale auf einer dreidimensionalen statt einer flachen Oberfläche gespeichert sind. Die Rillen repräsentieren die Umrisse der geografischen Gebiete.

Concept collaboration: Yoshihiro Katsumata; hardware development: KIMURA (Tasco Inc) / Akichika Tanaka; sound programming: Bengt Sjölén. Special thanks to Vestax.

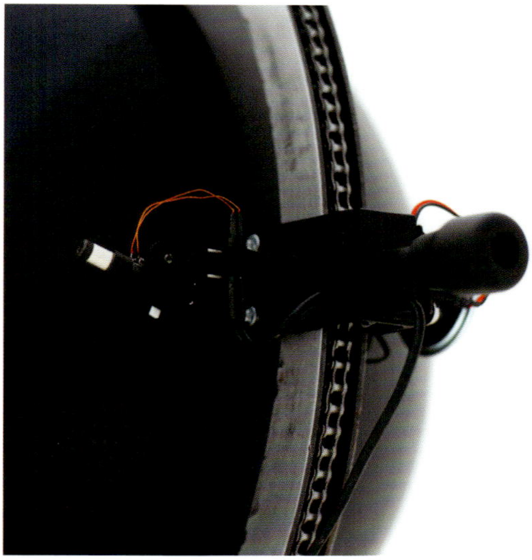

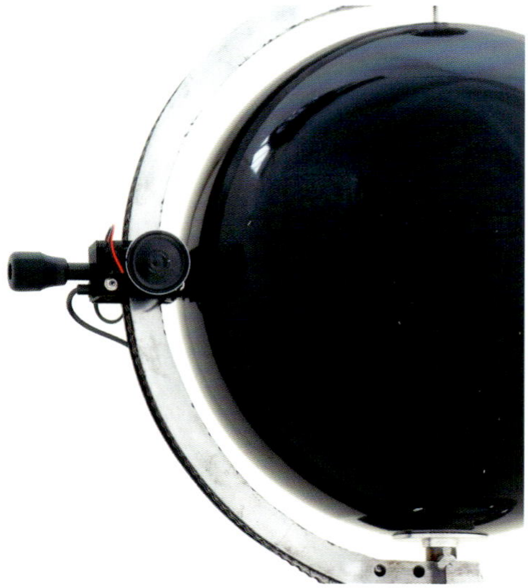

Jedes Land auf der Schallplatte ist mit einem anderen Sound vertreten. Wenn die Nadel das jeweilige Land passiert, werden Feldaufnahmen abgespielt, die Yuri Suzuki auf der ganzen Welt im Lauf von vier Jahren aufgenommen hat: traditionelle Volksmusik, Nationalhymnen, Straßenmusik und Gesprächsaufnahmen.
Der Plattenspieler verfügt über eine Rollenkette, um die Nadel vom Nord- zum Südpol zu bewegen. Eine Reise rund um den Globus dauert etwa dreißig Minuten. Die Nadel hat einen kleinen Lautsprecher und Verstärker integriert, die die Klänge wiedergeben. Da sich der Plattenspieler in einer Spirale um die Erde bewegt, werden „die Klänge der Erde" in Fragmente aufgesplittet, die man hören kann, wenn die Nadel über den jeweiligen Breitengrad läuft.

Each country on the disk is engraved with a different sound; as the needle passes over it plays field recordings collected by Yuri Suzuki from around the world over the course of four years—traditional folk music, national anthems, popular music and spoken broadcasts.
The record player uses a bush roller chain to move the stylus from the north pole to the south pole. A full journey across the earth takes around 30 minutes. The stylus has a small speaker and an amplifier to generate sound. As the record player moves across the earth in a spiral, the *Sounds of the Earth* are split into fragments which you hear as the stylus moves over the seas and borders of the world.

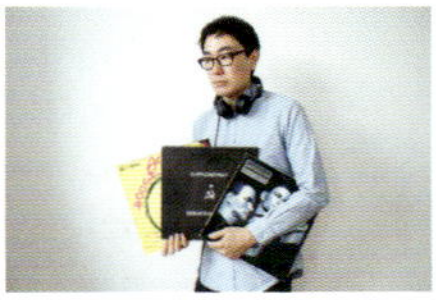

Yuri Suzuki (JP/UK), born 1980, is a sound artist, designer and electronic musician who produces work that explores the realms of sound through exquisitely designed pieces. Between 1999 and 2005 he worked for the Japanese art unit Maywa Denki, where he developed a strong interest in music and technology. In 2005 he moved to London to study at the Royal College of Art. After his graduation in 2008 he opened his own studio in London. Suzuki's work raises questions of the relation between sound and people and how music and sound affect people's minds. **Yuri Suzuki** (JP/UK), geb. 1980, ist Klangkünstler, Designer und Elektronik-Musiker und setzt sich in exquisit komponierten Stücken mit der Welt der Klänge auseinander. Von 1999 bis 2005 arbeitete er für die japanische Kunstfactory Maywa Denki und entdeckte sein großes Interesse an Musik und Technologie. 2005 ging er nach London, um am Royal College of Art zu studieren. Nach Abschluss seines Studiums im Jahr 2008 eröffnete er sein Studio in London. Suzukis Arbeit hinterfragt die Beziehung zwischen Klang und Mensch und die Auswirkung von Musik und Klängen auf den Menschen.

Works for Wave Field Synthesis

Robert Henke with students of the master's program Sound Studies at Berlin University of the Arts

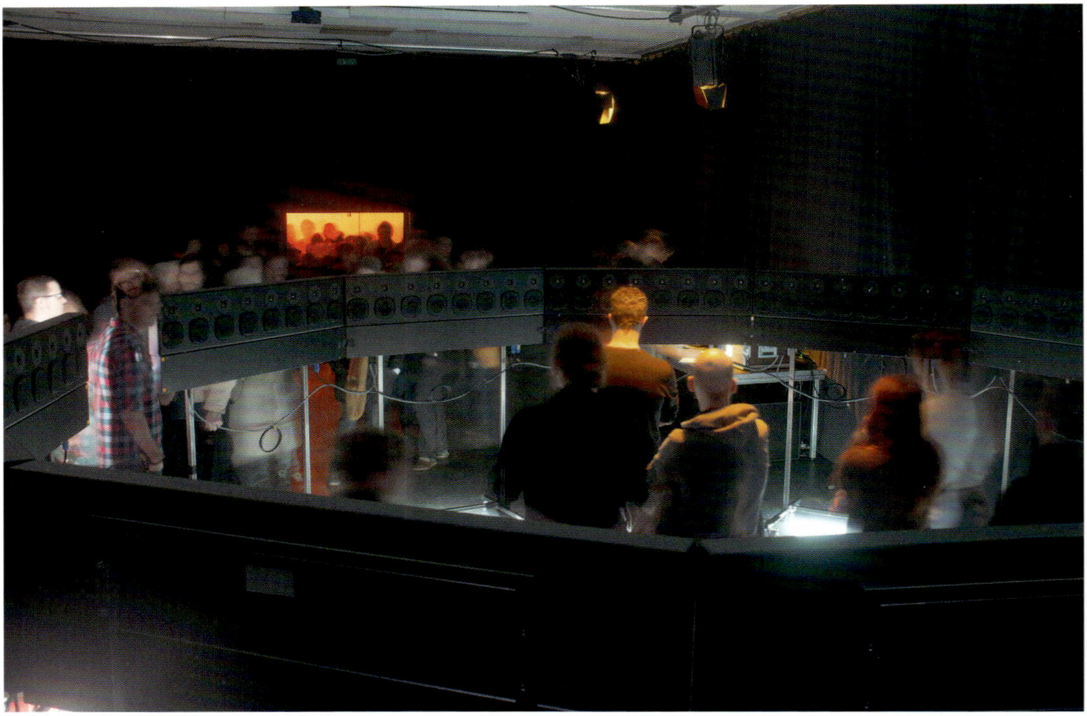

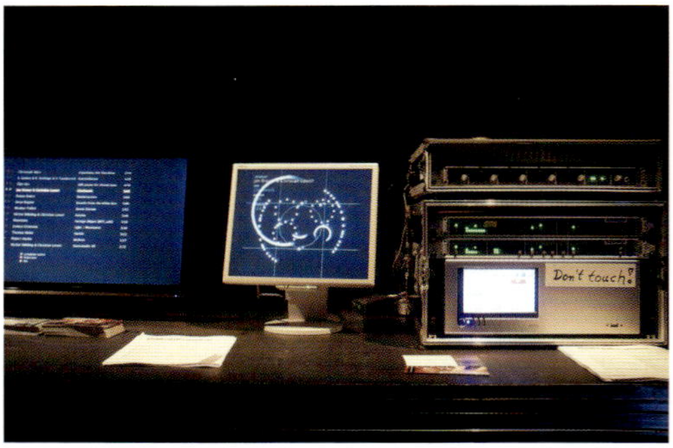

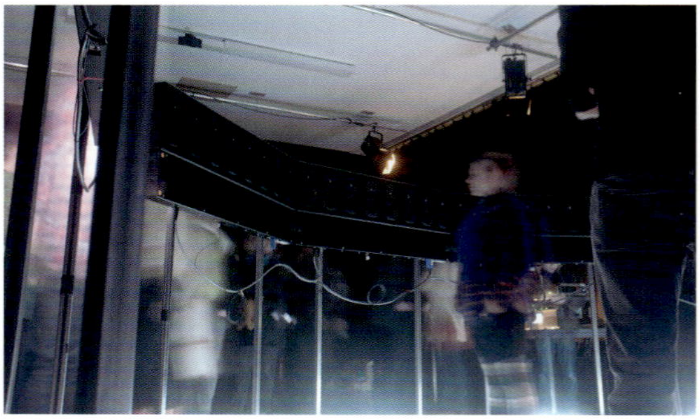

Works for Wave Field Synthesis is a collection of works for an array of 192 loudspeakers, created by Robert Henke and his students of the master's program Sound Studies at Berlin University of the Arts on the occasion of the first public display of the system during the CTM Festival in Berlin, 2013. Wave Field Synthesis (WFS) is a relatively new and computationally expensive surround-sound technique that makes it possible to dynamically place

Works for Wave Field Synthesis ist eine Sammlung von Stücken für einen Ring aus 192 Lautsprechern, komponiert von Robert Henke und seinen StudentInnen des Fachbereichs Soundstudies an der Universität der Künste, Berlin, erstmals präsentiert beim CTM Festival 2013. Wellenfeld Synthese (WFS) ist ein relativ neues und rechenintensives Mehrkanal-Verfahren, welches es erlaubt, Klangquellen mit großer Präzision im Raum zu bewegen. Bis zu 64 Quellen können in Echtzeit innerhalb

Student works by Christoph März, Edgardo Gómez, Rafael Santiago, Volodymyr Taranovych, Silje Nes, Jan Brauer, Christian Losert, Dusan Bracic, Anna Bogner, Nicolas Probst, Michel Wähling, Jessica Ekomane and Thomas Maier. Composed and implemented December 2012.

und außerhalb des Ringes platziert werden. Das Publikum kann sich während der Wiedergabe der Stücke frei bewegen und diese nicht nur als lineare zeitliche, sondern auch als räumliche Kompositionen aus verschiedenen Hörpositionen erfahren. Die Wiedergabe der Werke als kontinuierlicher Loop unterstützt diese Rezeptionshaltung. *Works for Wave Field Synthesis* kann daher sowohl als Reihe von Kompositionen als auch als Installation interpretiert werden.

Die technischen Details, inklusive der nötigen Computer und die Anzeigen der Bewegungsabläufe werden als integraler Bestandteil der Installation betrachtet, und befinden sich außerhalb des Ringes. Diese Präsentation erlaubt es den RezipientInnen sich entweder vollständig auf die auditive Erfahrung zu konzentrieren oder sich in die technischen und konzeptionellen Aspekte der Stücke zu vertiefen, welche oft unmittelbar aus den grafischen Details der Bewegungen ersichtlich werden.

virtual sound objects with extremely fine spatial resolution in the listening space. Up to 64 sonic objects can be positioned in real time inside and outside the ring of speakers, whilst the audience has the chance to walk around and explore the works not only as linear developments over time but also as sonic architecture that depends on the listener's position.

The pieces run as a loop, and visitors are encouraged to walk in and out of the speaker ring, to get different sonic perspectives. Thus, for the creators, the work is considered to be in the middle between composition and installation. The technological details, including the rendering computers and the visualization displays are considered as essential part of the installation, allowing the audience to either entirely focus on the audible part of the works or dive into the technical aspects or the conceptual background, which often becomes very clear when looking at the traces of movements as shown in the real-time display located outside the ring.

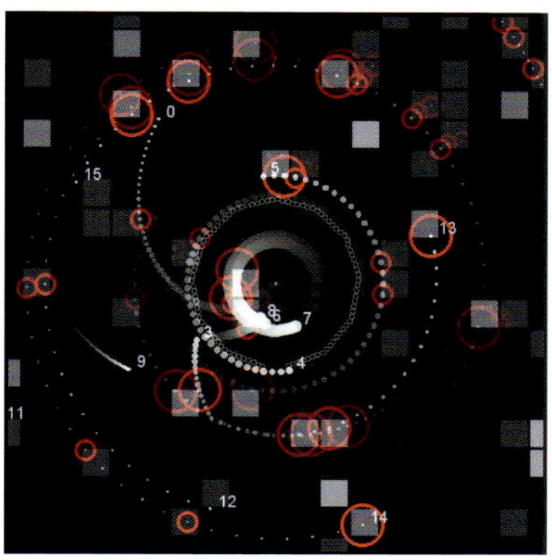

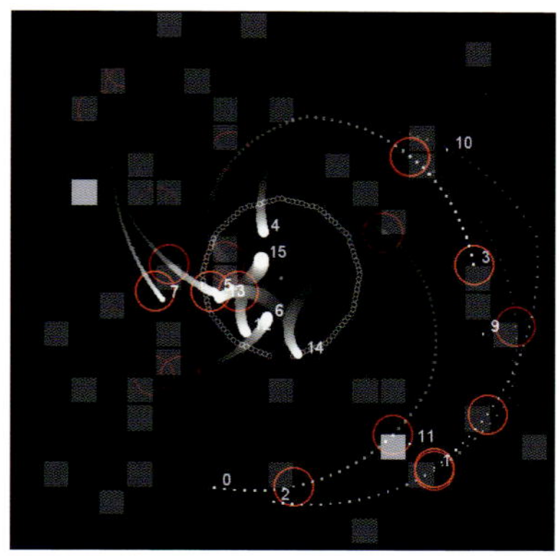

Robert Henke (DE) builds and operates machines to produce art. He pairs archaic concepts with computer science in order to explore new aesthetic territories between composition, performance and installation. He is a pioneer of multichannel sound, using methods and systems like wave field synthesis and ambisonics to create situations of total immersion, expanding the sonic experience of his performances beyond of what can be reproduced in stereo. He has been central to the development of Ableton Live, which became the standard tool for electronic music production and completely redefined the performance practice of electronic music. He holds a professorship in sound design at the Berlin University of Arts. For 2013 he has been selected as Mohr Visiting Artist at Stanford University, teaching a class at the Center for Computer Research in Music and Acoustics (CCRMA).

Robert Henkes (DE) audiovisuelle Arbeiten im Grenzbereich von Konzert und Installation verbinden archaische Konzepte mit neuer Technologie. Er nutzt Methoden wie ambisonics und Wellenfeldsynthese, um zeitlose Momente völliger auditiver Immersion zu schaffen, welche sich in Stereo so nicht verwirklichen lassen. Robert Henke ist Mitentwickler der Musiksoftware Ableton Live und ist Professor an der Universität der Künste, Berlin. Im Frühjahr 2013 wurde er als Mohr Visiting Artist an das Center for Computer Research in Music and Acoustics (CCRMA) der Stanford University berufen.

HYBRID ART

Undisciplined Art: From Low Tech to High Breed
Disziplinlose Kunst: Von der Niedrigtechnologie bis zur Hochzucht

Andrea Grover, Jens Hauser, Jurij Krpan, Arthur I. Miller, Karin Ohlenschläger

In its seventh year (itch) of existence, the Hybrid Art category unfolded once again as an important indicator of techno-cultural phenomena that currently preoccupy artists with regard to their chosen methods, media and content. This shape-shifting grouping is one that "naturally" mutates and evolves from year-to-year, making it all the more elusive to define and categorize. Described by Ars Electronica as an arena where the "primary emphasis is on the process of fusing different media and genres into new forms of artistic expression as well as the act of transcending the boundaries between art and research, art and social/political activism, [and] art and pop culture." As such, Hybrid Art is a catchall for aesthetic output that falls between disciplines, or rather work that is "non-disciplinary" or "undisciplined" (the latter, a double entendre that emphasizes the category's wild child unruliness). Hybrid's inherent *in-betweeness* constitutes a veritable tango for jurors—it demands that they be conversant and discerning within many branches of knowledge, beyond even the global diversity of possible appreciations of artistic and aesthetic quality alone.

Accordingly, there were discussions and tangos within the jury as to the degree to which accurate translations of scientific concepts into artistic forms could—and should—be imperative criteria for the evaluation of Hybrid Art works. While it is true that the current talk and hype around "artistic research" and "sci-art" sets the framework to see such projects through the lens of scientific rigor, the jury decided by a majority to equally acknowledge subversion, *mise-en-abyme* and reverse engineering.

Within this sprawling category and among the huge scope of practices that Hybrid Art normally entails, a few tendencies in particular were revealed to the jury. One has been the ever-growing interest and

Auch im (verflixten) siebenten Jahr ihres Bestehens hat sich die Kategorie Hybrid Art wieder als wichtiger Indikator techno-kultureller Phänomene erwiesen, die KünstlerInnen heute umtreiben – methodisch, medial und inhaltlich. Diese metamorphe Kategorie ist eine, die sich naturgemäß von Jahr zu Jahr verändert und weiterentwickelt, was es umso schwerer macht, sie zu definieren und festzuschreiben. Im Vordergrund stehen bei ihr laut Eigendefinition der Ars Electronica „die Verbindung von unterschiedlichen Medien und Genres zu neuen künstlerischen Ausdrucksformen sowie das Überschreiten der Grenzen von Kunst zu Forschung, zu sozialem und politischem Engagement, aber auch zu popkulturellen Bereichen". So gesehen ist Hybrid Art ein Sammelbegriff für alles Disziplinenübergreifende, keiner Disziplin Zuordenbare oder Disziplinlose (wobei letzteres in seiner Doppeldeutigkeit auch auf die kindliche Unbändigkeit der Kategorie verweist). Dieses konstitutive Dazwischensein der Hybrid Art verlangt den JurorInnen einen ziemlichen Spagat ab, kommt doch zur globalen Vielfalt in der Bewertung rein künstlerischer und ästhetischer Qualitäten noch die Notwendigkeit, in vielen Wissensgebieten bewandert und urteilsfähig zu sein.

So wurde etwa in der Jury heftig darüber diskutiert, wie weit die exakte Übersetzung wissenschaftlicher Konzepte in künstlerische Formen als entscheidendes Kriterium für die Bewertung von Hybrid-Arbeiten herangezogen werden könnte und sollte. Doch auch wenn die gegenwärtige Debatte und der Hype um „künstlerische Forschung" und „Sci-Art" nahelegt, derartige Projekte unter dem Aspekt wissenschaftlicher Strenge zu betrachten, war schließlich eine Mehrheit der Jury dafür, auch Subversion, *mise-en-abyme* und *Reverse Engineering* zu berücksichtigen.

In dieser wild wuchernden Kategorie und der damit seit jeher einhergehenden Fülle an Praktiken zeichneten sich für die Jury gleichwohl einige Tendenzen ab. Eine davon ist das stetig wachsende Interesse an der Darstellung

und am Ausdruck von *Leben(digkeit)* sowie die Vielfalt medienkünstlerischer Ansätze dazu. Kennzeichnend dafür war die Zunahme an Projekten, die mit biotechnologischen Konzepten und Systemen arbeiten. Waren Kunstformen aus diesem Bereich seit jeher stark repräsentiert, so zeigt sich am diesjährigen Profil eine Verschiebung, die für die Beseitigung solch rudimentärer Ordnungskategorien wie „Biokunst" spricht. *Leben(digkeit)* umfasst heute ein breites Spektrum an Praktiken, die von der molekularen bis zur ökologischen Ebene reichen, und verweist auf die Notwendigkeit einer verfeinerten Taxonomie in dieser anbrechenden neuen Do-it-yourself und Eigenanbau-Ära.
Eine weitere Tendenz ließe sich als *Rückkehr zum Analogen* umschreiben. Die breite Vielfalt der verwendeten und untersuchten materiellen Medien scheint von einem allgemeinen Hang zur Re-Analogisierung zu zeugen; als typische Cluster zeichneten sich u. a. Vinylplatten, Ferrofluide, analoge Morphogenese, Kinetik, technisch erzeugter Medienlärm, Zeichenmaschinen, Maschinentexte und absurde Apparaturen ab. Damit verbunden war ein Trend zum Aufbrechen technologischer Lock-in-Phänomene, der in einem weiteren Sinn als *Reverse Evolution* bezeichnet werden könnte. Solche Projekte waren gekennzeichnet vom Versuch, die Uhr zurückzudrehen, z. B. Auswirkungen des Klimawandels und andere Umweltschäden rückgängig zu machen, durch Zuchtwahl entstandene Arten rückzuzüchten, Kommunikationstechnologien aufzuschließen, die die Form menschlicher Beziehungen bestimmen, technisch einfache grüne Alternativmaterialien zu entwickeln und eine Art *Zurück-aufs-Land-2.0*-Bewegung ins Leben zu rufen. Handelt es sich hier vielleicht um eine künstlerische Reaktion auf das, was Friedrich Kittler anstrebte, nämlich den Humanwissenschaften „ihr medientechnisches Apriori" nachzuweisen, um eine umgekehrte Evolution, die sich mit dem Problem auseinandersetzt, dass technische Medien das Denken sowie kulturelle Muster und Neigungen bestimmen statt ihnen zu folgen?

diversity in media artistic concepts to stage and express *(a)liveness*. This notable observation was marked by the increase in number of projects that deal with biotechnological concepts and systems. While art forms in this realm have already been abundantly present in this category, this year's profile indicates an additional shift toward abolishing the use of rudimentary organizational terms such as "bio art." *(A)liveness* now entails a broad spectrum of practices from the molecular to the ecological scale, and it indicates a need for a more nuanced taxonomy in this emerging neo-DIY *grow-your-own* era.
Another tendency can be described as a *return to the analog*. The wide range of material media employed and questioned seemed to testify to a wider trend of re-analogization; among the typical clusters that appeared there were vinyl records, ferrofluids, analog morphogenesis, kinetics, technically produced media noise, drawing machines, machine texts and absurd contraptions. Related to the analog trend was that of undoing "technological lock-in," which in a wider sense could be referred to as *reverse evolution*. These projects were marked by efforts to turn back the clock—for example, the impulse to undo the effects of climate change and environmental damage, reverse-engineer selectively bred species, unlock the communication technologies that shape human relationships, develop low-tech alternative green materials, and generate a kind-of *Back to the Land 2.0* movement. Could this be an artistic response to what Friedrich Kittler once addressed as a need to prove to the human sciences their "technological-media a priori," a reverse evolution that addresses the problem that technological media of all kinds determine rather than follow thought, cultural patterns and predispositions?

Recent technologies continue to have their luster and attraction to artists: the jury further identified new and highly sophisticated approaches to the existing field of *data visualization*, now encompassing neuro-aesthetics and physics—the latter seen in projects where invisible phenomena such as cosmic rays and energy fields are measured and made perceptible and, in some cases, interactive.
Still other artists invoked the *technological uncanny*, charting the relationship between new technologies and the emergence of superstitions and irrational beliefs. And lastly, more than a few artists' projects applied or translated the language of one subject to another. For example, there were instances of words translated into data and vice versa, poetry generated by code, and gesture translated into energy—a kind of reclaiming of the right to *techno-romanticism* while working within fields that privilege empiricism. This plurality of methodologies and refusal to specialize—from low tech to high breed—is what continues to make the Hybrid Art category the most mercurial of Prix Ars Electronica.

GOLDEN NICA

The Cosmopolitan Chicken Project
Koen Vanmechelen
The *Cosmopolitan Chicken Project* (CCP) is a worldwide crossbreeding program with chicken breeds from different countries, which Koen Vanmechelen started in 1999. The artist took this omnipresent domesticated animal *(Gallus gallus)* as a metaphor for humanity *(la condition humaine)* and its social and cultural dynamics. In 2011 he presented the 15th generation of hybrids—the "Mechelese Fayoumi" at the Venice Biennial. The Poulet de Senegal from Africa constituted the 16th generation in 2012, while the 17th generation with contribution of Slovenian Styrian rooster hatched at Kapelica Gallery Ljubljana in April 2013.

Gleichzeitig haben neueste Technologien für KünstlerInnen nach wie vor ihren Reiz. Die Jury konnte z. B. neue hoch komplexe Ansätze auf dem altvertrauten Gebiet der *Datenvisualisierung* verzeichnen, die sich auf die Felder der Neuroästhetik und der Physik erstrecken. Letzteres z. B. in Projekten, in denen unsichtbare Phänomene wie kosmische Strahlung und Energiefelder gemessen und sichtbar gemacht – und in manchen Fällen sogar interaktiv angesprochen – werden.
Andere KünstlerInnen wiederum beschwören das *technologische Unheimliche*, indem sie der Beziehung zwischen neuen Technologien und dem Auftreten abergläubischer und irrationaler Vorstellungen nachspürten. Und nicht zuletzt gab es auch eine beträchtliche Menge an Projekten, die die Sprache eines Gegenstandsbereichs auf einen anderen übertrug. Da wurden zum Bespiel Wörter in Daten übersetzt und umgekehrt, Poesie mittels Code generiert und Gesten in Energie umgewandelt – in einer Art Behauptung des Rechts auf *Technoromantik*, auch wenn man in Gebieten arbeitet, die sich auf die Empirie berufen. Eben diese Methodenvielfalt und hartnäckige Spezialisierungsverweigerung – von der Niedrigtechnologie bis zur Hochzucht – macht die Kategorie Hybrid Art immer noch zur sprunghaftesten Kategorie des Prix Ars Electronica.

GOLDENE NICA

The Cosmopolitan Chicken Project
Koen Vanmechelen
Das *Cosmopolitan Chicken Project* (CCP) ist ein von Koen Vanmechelen seit 1999 betriebenes Kreuzungsprogramm mit Zuchthühnersorten aus verschiedenen Ländern der Welt. Der Künstler begreift das weltweit verbreitete Haushuhn *(Gallus gallus)* als Metapher für die *conditio humana* und ihre soziokulturelle Dynamik. 2011 stellte er auf der Biennale von Venedig die 15. Hybridengeneration – das „Mechelse Fayoumi" – vor. Aus seiner Kreuzung mit dem Poulet de Senegal entstand 2012 die 16. Generation, und im April 2013 wurde in der Galerija Kapelica in Ljubljana die 17. ausgebrütet – das „Mechelse Styrian",

hervorgegangen aus der Verbindung mit einem slowenisch-steirischen Hahn.
Ausgangspunkt für all diese Arten war einmal das Bankivahuhn, das in den Ausläufern des Himalaya lebende Wildhuhn. Der Mensch hat diese Art domestiziert, über die ganze Welt verbreitet und zu lokalen Arten weitergezüchtet, die typische Merkmale ihrer jeweiligen Kultur widerspiegeln. Die so entstandenen Arten bilden lauter künstlich geschaffene Endpunkte, oft sogar im buchstäblichen Sinn, weil sie unfruchtbar wurden und die „reine Rasse" damit zu existieren aufhörte. Dagegen möchte Vanmechelen all diese Züchtungen beenden, indem er sie wieder zu einem neuen Ausgangspunkt zurückkreuzt, und liefert damit ein Beispiel für das Prinzip schöpferischer Zerstörung.
Im Verlauf des jahrelangen Kreuzungsprozesses entdeckte Vanmechelen, dass jede weitere Hybridengeneration widerstandsfähiger, langlebiger, weniger krankheitsanfällig und weniger aggressiv ist. Genetische Vielfalt ist ein wichtiger Faktor für lebensfähige Populationen. Die einmalige Versuchsanordnung des CCP bietet Wissenschaftlern zudem eine interessante Gelegenheit, die genetische Diversität zwischen verschiedenen Arten und die Auswirkungen des Kreuzens zu untersuchen. Daraus entstand das *Cosmopolitan Chicken Research Projekt* (CCRP), eine künstlerisch-wissenschaftliche Zusammenarbeit mit dem Humangenetiker Professor Jean-Jacques Cassiman.
Dem CCP geht es allerdings nicht um die Rekonstruktion eines Urhuhns. Es will nicht in die Vergangenheit zurück, sondern steht im Gegenteil für die Zukunft. Es ist der Beginn einer neuen Form permanenter Evolution, eines *perpetuum mobile* genetischer Diversifikation. Im Fokus des Projekts steht weder die Henne noch das Ei, sondern der Prozess des Kreuzens und die dadurch erzeugte Vielfalt. Als interdisziplinäre künstlerische Praxis entmystifiziert es die Rolle der Biotechnologie und zeigt, dass der menschlichen Zivilisation die „Formung der Natur" in die Wiege gelegt ist. Das *Cosmopolitan Chicken* hält uns einen Spiegel vor. Kreuzen ist eine praktische, aber auch eine philosophische Notwendigkeit, wenn nicht sogar eine moralische Pflicht. Das CCP vereint Kunst,

The starting point for all these species was once the red jungle fowl, the original chicken that lived in the foothills of the Himalayas. Humans took this chicken, spread it all over the world and produced an indigenous breed, one that reflects typical cultural characteristic of their community. These descendant breeds are all man-made endpoints, even sometimes literally so, in the sense that they became infertile and the "pure race" ceased to exist. In contrast, Vanmechelen wants to end all these breeds by blending them back into a new starting point, providing a chicken-breeding example of the principle of creative destruction.
After so many years of their cross-breeding, Vanmechelen in contrast found that each successive generation of hybrids is more resilient, lives longer, is less susceptible to disease and exhibits less aggressive behavior. Genetic diversity is critical for viable populations. The unique CCP set-up provides scientists, for example, with an interesting model to investigate the genetic diversity between breeds and makes it possible to assess the consequences of cross-breeding. Out of this arose the CCRP, an artistic, genetic project and an alliance between human geneticist professor Jean-Jacques Cassiman and artist Koen Vanmechelen.
But the CCP does not aim to reconstitute the proto-chicken. It does not want to return to the past. On the contrary, it symbolizes the future. It is the starting point of a new form of evolution that will never end, a *perpetuum mobile* of genetic diversification. The core of the project is neither chicken nor egg, but crossbreeding and the diversity that comes from it. As interdisciplinary artistic activity it is demystifying the role of biotechnology while showing that "designing nature" lies in the cradle of human civilization. The *Cosmopolitan Chicken* holds up a mirror to us. Cross-breeding is a practical but also a philosophical necessity, if not a moral duty. The CCP involves a symbiosis of art, science, philosophy, politics and ethics. It is the artist's way of reflecting on the existential

questions of individual identity and life, and it touches on contemporary issues regarding globalization, racism, genetic modification and cloning by providing a subtle critique of a society where the ideology of cultural diversity in its extreme consequences can be oppressive, racist, chauvinistic and nationalistic.

AWARDS OF DISTINCTION

Five Variations of Phonic Circumstances and a Pause

Tania Candiani

The first award of distinction goes to Tania Candiani's sophisticated media archeological labyrinth *Five Variations of Phonic Circumstances and a Pause*, which was site-specifically produced for the Laboratorio Arte Alameda, located in a former church and hotspot of the Inquisition in Mexico City. Several extremely elaborate mechanical, musical and visual devices were created within a collaborative community approach involving local sound artists and public writers. These variations embody trans-historical communication models while continuously reversing their logical thread. Within the specter of technically induced "glocalization," Candiani draws with great sensitivity on the particular Mexican context, while tangibly staging how technologies of all times have dictated relationships between orality and literacy, and created subsequent relationships of power. The jury was impressed by the artist's ability to create machines, experiences and creative situations of tension by providing a fine assemblage of metanarrativity: organs imitate voices instead of vice-versa; destabilizing pianolas turn the first binary mechanisms for recording music into quasi-digital noise machines; a robotic embroidery machine

Wissenschaft, Philosophie, Politik und Ethik. Es ist Vanmechelens Art und Weise, über existenzielle Fragen der individuellen Identität und des Lebens nachzudenken. Überdies berührt es auch Gegenwartsprobleme wie Globalisierung, Rassismus, Genmodifikation und Klonen, übt es doch subtil Kritik an einer Gesellschaft, in der die Ideologie kultureller Vielfalt im Extremfall in Repression, Rassismus, Chauvinismus oder Nationalismus umschlagen kann.

AUSZEICHNUNGEN

Five Variations of Phonic Circumstances and a Pause

Tania Candiani

Die erste Auszeichnung geht an Tania Candianis komplexes medienarchäologisches Labyrinth *Five Variations of Phonic Circumstances and a Pause*, ein ortsspezifisches Projekt für das Laboratorio Arte Alameda, das in einer ehemaligen Kirche, einem Brennpunkt der Inquisition in Mexiko, untergebracht ist. In einem kollaborativen, lokale KlangkünstlerInnen und öffentliche SchreiberInnen einbeziehenden Ansatz entstanden eine Reihe kunstvoller und aufwändiger mechanischer, musikalischer und visueller Apparaturen. Es sind Variationen transhistorischer Kommunikationsmodelle, die zugleich deren logische Entwicklung umkehren. Vor dem Hintergrund einer technisch induzierten „Glokalisierung" und unter feinfühliger Einbeziehung des spezifisch mexikanischen Kontexts macht Candiani sinnlich greifbar, wie Technologien zu allen Zeiten die Beziehung zwischen Mündlichkeit und Schriftlichkeit diktiert und damit Machtverhältnisse begründet haben. Die Jury war beeindruckt von der Fähigkeit der Künstlerin, mit Maschinen Erfahrungen und kreative Spannungsfelder zu erzeugen, indem sie diese in ein feines metanarratives Geflecht einwebt: Orgeln ahmen menschliche Stimmen nach; irritierende Pianolas verwandeln die ersten binären Musikaufzeichnungsgeräte in quasi digitale Noise-Maschinen; ein

Stickroboter gibt die Beichten von BesucherInnen wieder, aber in verschlüsselter, unentzifferbarer Form; vor Ort arbeitende öffentliche Schreiber zeigen, wie schon der Vermittlungsakt zwischen einem menschlichen Medium und einer Schreibmaschine den Text zu einer technischen Erfindung macht. Candiani entwirft eine kunstvoll gearbeitete Genealogie des Automaten. Ihre poetische Archäologie wirft ein vermeintlich anachronistisches, tatsächlich aber radikal zeitgenössisches Licht auf die Politik hinter den „neuen Medien".

Mycotecture
Phil Ross

Die zweite Auszeichnung geht an Phil Ross' Versuchsreihe *Mycotecture*, seine Experimente zur Züchtung von Architektur und Möbeln aus Pilzen. Ross' obsessive, seit nunmehr zwanzig Jahren betriebene Forschung begann mit dem Versuch, den glänzenden Lackporling *(Ganoderma lucidum)* dazu zu bringen, skulpturale Formen auszubilden. Dessen Myzelien werden wegen ihrer antikarzinogenen, anti-mikrobiellen, antiviralen und immuntherapeutischen Eigenschaften in der chinesischen Medizin seit über 2000 Jahren kultiviert und als Heilmittel eingesetzt. Haupttriebfeder für Ross' Forschung ist die Vorstellung einer Architektur, die aus biologisch restlos abbaubaren, ungiftigen, feuerfesten, wasser- und schimmelresistenten Baumaterialien besteht, die praktisch unbegrenzt nachwachsen und auch noch gesund sind. Seine Pilzziegel sind „härter als Beton" und wärmedämmender als Glasfasermatten. Ross begreift seine Myzelgebilde sowohl als Material für Kunst als auch für Architektur, sieht aber noch viele weitere Anwendungsmöglichkeiten: Seiner Meinung nach eignet sich der glänzende Lackporling als Rohmaterial für Kunststoffe, Batterien, Computer und sogar Zellgewebe. Seine eleganten Gebilde stehen erst am Anfang dessen, was Ross und andere für eine bevorstehende Revolution halten. „Die Zukunft gehört dem Pilz", sagt er.

translates visitors' confessions and makes them visible but, encoded, undecipherable; commissioned public writers show how the mediating act of a simple human medium and a typewriter already makes a published text into a technological invention. Candiani proposes a finely crafted genealogy of automatons. Her poetic archeology indirectly shines a supposedly anachronistic but radically contemporary light on the underlying politics of "new media."

Mycotecture
Phil Ross

The second award of distinction goes to Phil Ross's *Mycotecture* series, an experiment in growing architecture and furniture from mushrooms. Ross's obsessive research extends over two decades and began with an interest in generating sculptural forms from *Ganoderma lucidum*, commonly known as reishi or lingzi mushrooms. These mycelia have been cultivated and prescribed in Chinese medicine for over 2000 years and are noted for their anti-carcinogenic, anti-microbial, anti-viral and immunotherapeutic properties. The notion of constructing architecture from entirely biodegradable, non-toxic, fireproof, water- and mold-resistant materials that are in seemingly unlimited supply and good for you is what propels Ross in his research. His *Mycotecture* bricks are "stronger than concrete" and trap more heat than fiberglass insulation. Ross sees his mycelium structures as both art and architectural materials, but with many possible applications: he suggests that reishi mushrooms hold the potential to provide raw material for plastics, batteries, computers, and even tissue generation. His elegant structures are just the beginning of what Ross and others believe is a fungal revolution, or as he puts it, "The future is fungal."

The Cosmopolitan Chicken Project—Diversity and Dualism

Koen Vanmechelen

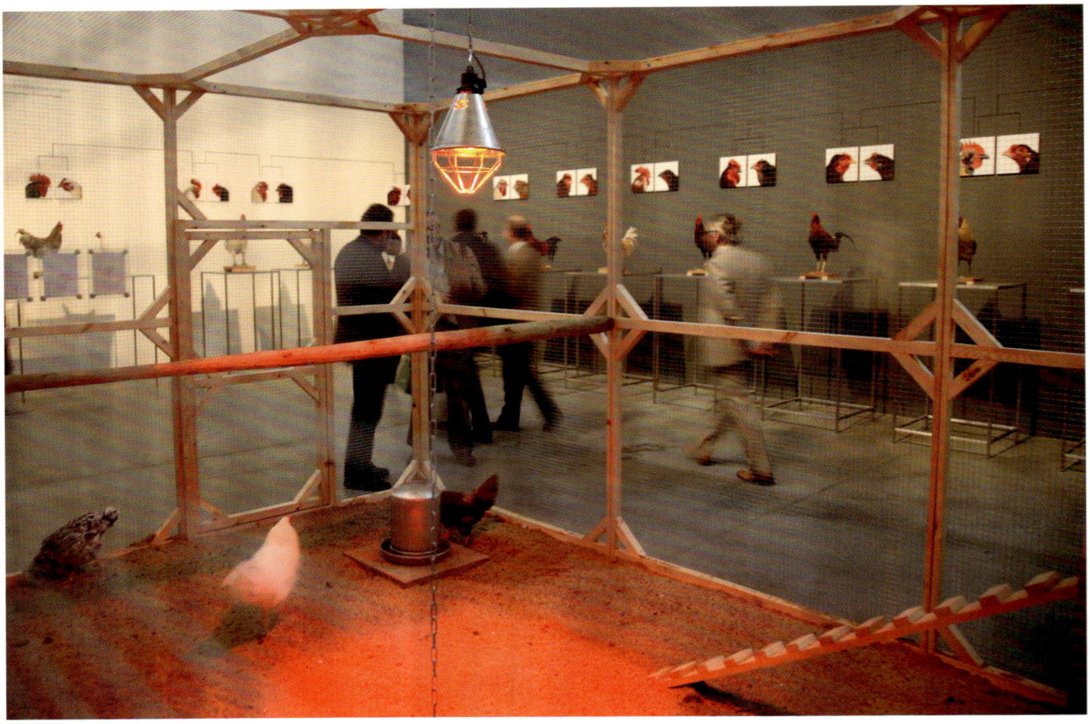

The *Cosmopolitan Chicken Project* (CCP, 1999) is a global, transdisciplinary and transtemporal examination of the themes of biocultural diversity and identity through the interplay of art, science and beauty. In the CCP Koen Vanmechelen crossbreeds chicken breeds from different countries.

Vanmechelen's ultimate goal is the creation of a Cosmopolitan Chicken carrying the genes of all the planet's chicken breeds. The starting point for all these species was once the red junglefowl, the original chicken that lives at the feet of the Himalayas. Humans took this chicken, spread it all over the world and made an indigenous breed, shaped to reflect the typical cultural characteristics of its community. While these native breeds

Das *Cosmopolitan Chicken Project* (CCP, 1999) ist eine globale, transdisziplinäre und transtemporale Untersuchung biokultureller Diversität und Identität, die Kunst, Wissenschaft und Ästhetik miteinander verbindet. Im Rahmen des CCP kreuzt Koen Vanmechelen Hühnersorten verschiedener Länder.

Vanmechelens Ziel ist die Schaffung eines kosmopolitischen Huhns, das Gene von sämtlichen Hühnersorten der Welt in sich trägt. Der Ursprung all dieser Arten war das Bankivahuhn, das auch heute noch an den Ausläufern des Himalaya lebende Wildhuhn. Der Mensch hat diese Art domestiziert, über die ganze Welt verbreitet und zu lokalen Arten weitergezüchtet, die typische Merkmale ihrer jeweiligen Kultur widerspiegeln. Handelt es sich bei diesen einheimischen Arten um evolutionäre

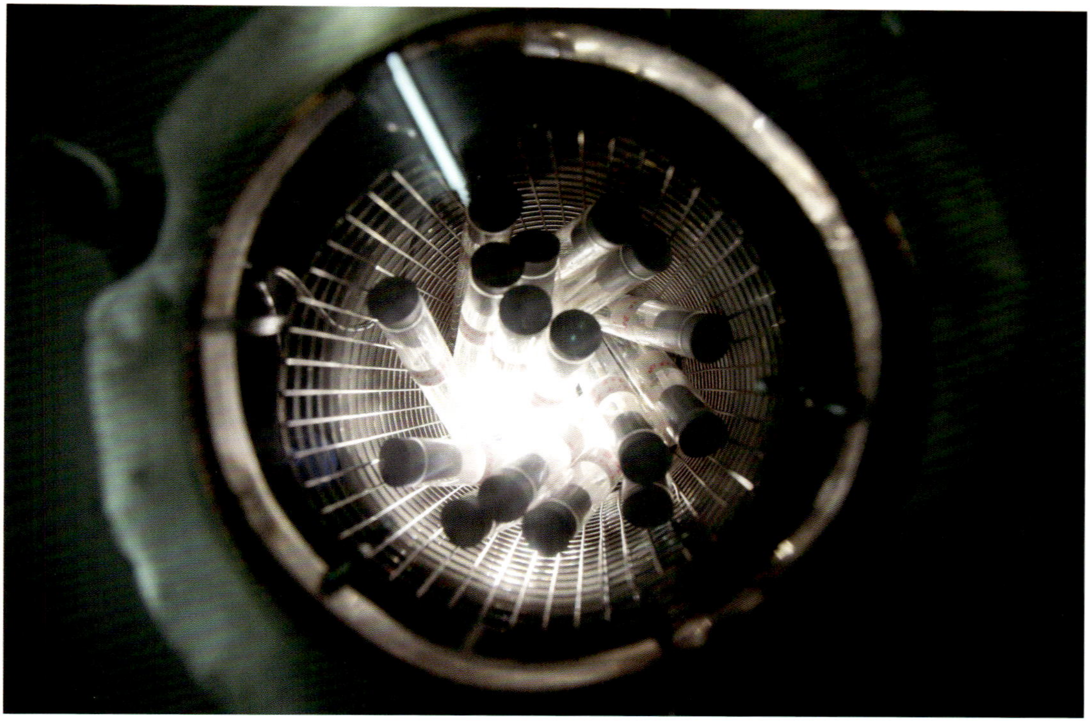

Sackgassen oder Endpunkte (in einigen Fällen sogar buchstäblich, weil sie unfruchtbar sind), so sind Vanmechelens Hybriden Lösungen. Sein Huhn ist mehr als bloß ein domestiziertes Tier, es ist Kunst. Es dient als Metapher für das menschliche Tier und seine Beziehung zur biologischen und kulturellen Vielfalt der Erde.

Bei den seit vielen Jahren durchgeführten Kreuzungen hat sich gezeigt, dass die Hybriden von Generation zu Generation „besser" werden. Sie sind widerstandsfähiger, langlebiger, weniger krankheitsanfällig und weniger aggressiv. Das *Cosmopolitan Chicken Research Project* (CCRP), das verschiedene CCP-Hybriden untersucht, zeigt darüber hinaus, dass genetische Vielfalt ein wichtiges Moment ist. Bisher hat dieses Forschungsprojekt die Hypothese des Künstlers erhärtet, dass die Kreuzung

are evolutionary dead-ends (even sometimes literally so, in the sense that they are infertile), Vanmechelen's hybrids are solutions. Much more than a mere domesticated animal, the chicken is art in itself. It serves as a metaphor for the human animal and its relationship with the biological and cultural diversity of the planet.

Many years of crossbreeding has proved that each successive generation of hybrids is "better." They are more resilient, live longer, are less susceptible to diseases and exhibit less aggressive behavior. The *Cosmopolitan Chicken Research Project* (CCRP), which studies the various CCP hybrids, also proves that genetic diversity is essential. So far, this research has found support for the artist's

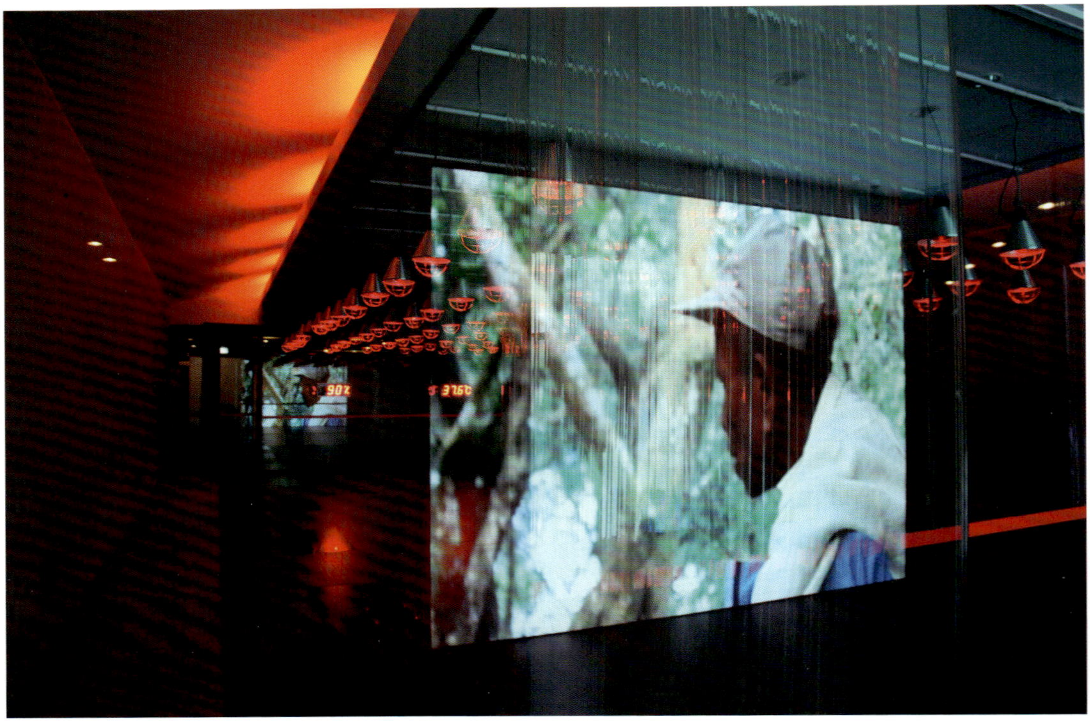

hypotheses that the crossing of different races leads to greater diversity. It is also a fact that the fertility and life span have increased.

The diversity that characterizes Vanmechelen's work is also visible in the media he uses, from more traditional (painting, photography) to innovate techniques (genome visualization). It further involves a symbiosis of art, science, philosophy, politics and ethics and deals with topics such as globalization, racism, genetic modification and cloning. It is the artist's way of reflecting on the existential questions of individual identity and life.

The core of the project is therefore neither the chicken nor its egg, but the process of crossbreeding and the diversity this creates. "The CCP is a mirror. Every organism needs another organism to survive," says Vanmechelen.

unterschiedlicher Rassen zu mehr Diversität führt. Fest steht auch, dass es zu einer Steigerung der Fruchtbarkeit und Lebensspanne gekommen ist.

Die Diversität, um die es in Vanmechelens Werk geht, spiegelt sich auch in den von ihm verwendeten Medien, die von Malerei und Fotografie bis zur Genomvisualisierung reichen. Überdies ist das Projekt eine Symbiose aus Kunst, Wissenschaft, Philosophie, Politik und Ethik, die Themen wie Globalisierung, Rassismus, Genmodifikation und Klonen berührt. Es ist Vanmechelens Art, über existenzielle Fragen wie Individualität und Leben nachzudenken.

Im Mittelpunkt des Projekts steht also weder die Henne noch das Ei, sondern der Prozess des Kreuzens und die dadurch erzeugte Diversität. „Das CCP ist ein Spiegel. Jeder Organismus braucht zum Überleben einen anderen Organismus", sagt Vanmechelen.

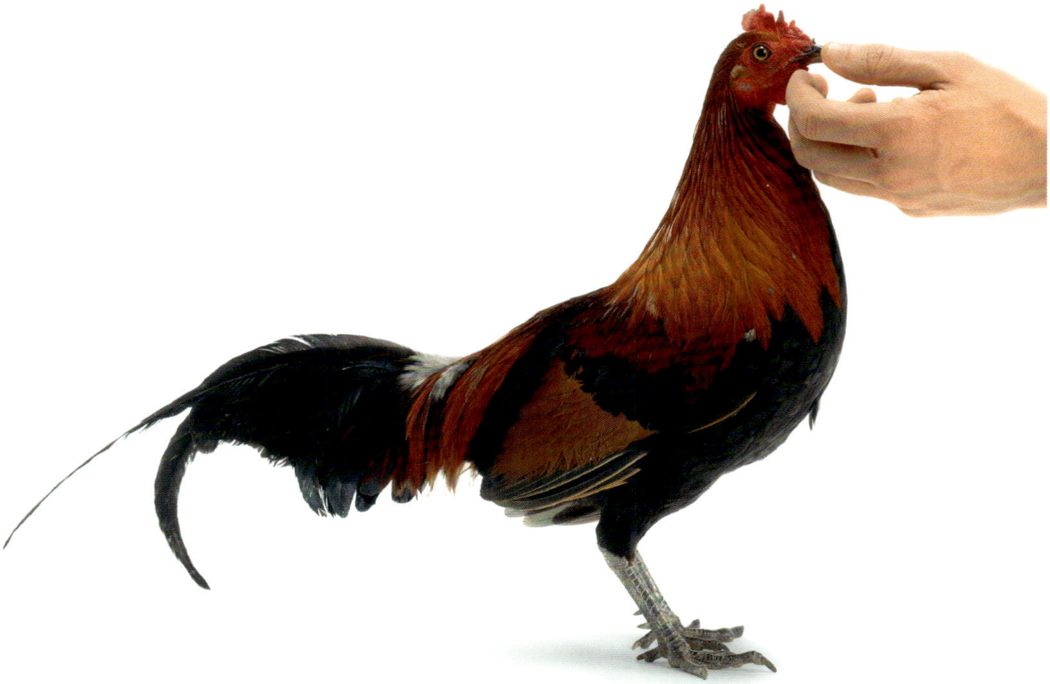

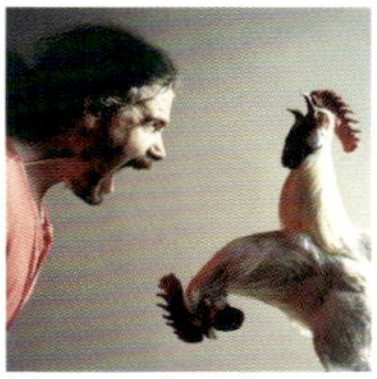

Koen Vanmechelen (BE), born 1965, is an internationally renowned, conceptual artist. His groundbreaking work deals with diversity and identity. Over the past decade Vanmechelen has collaborated with scientists from different disciplines. This earned him an honorary doctorate at the University of Hasselt. Vanmechelen uses a plethora of artistic tools for his work—from painting and video to installations, sculpture and glass—which includes three projects. These are: the *Cosmopolitan Chicken Research Project* (CCP), the wooden statue *Cosmogolem* and the fertility project *Walking Egg*. Vanmechelen has presented his work on almost all continents. His work was also shown at the Biennales of Venice, Moscow, Dakar and Poznan and at the Shanghai World Expo 2010. **Koen Vanmechelen** (BE), geb. 1965, ist ein international bekannter Konzeptkünstler. Zentrale Themen seines bahnbrechenden Werks sind Diversität und Identität. Seit zehn Jahren arbeitet Vanmechelen dabei mit Wissenschaftlern aus den verschiedensten Fachbereichen zusammen, was ihm ein Ehrendoktorat der Universität Hasselt eingetragen hat. In seinem Werk, das u.a. das *Cosmopolitan Chicken Research Project* (CCP), die Holzstatue *Cosmogolem* und das Fertilitätsprojekt *Walking Egg* umfasst, benutzt er eine Fülle künstlerischer Techniken von Malerei und Video bis hin zur Installation, Bildhauerei und Glasbearbeitung. Vanmechelens Arbeiten wurden auf fast allen Erdteilen gezeigt und waren auf den Biennalen von Venedig, Moskau, Dakar und Poznan sowie auf der Expo 2010 in Shanghai zu sehen.

Five Variations of Phonic Circumstances and a Pause

Tania Candiani

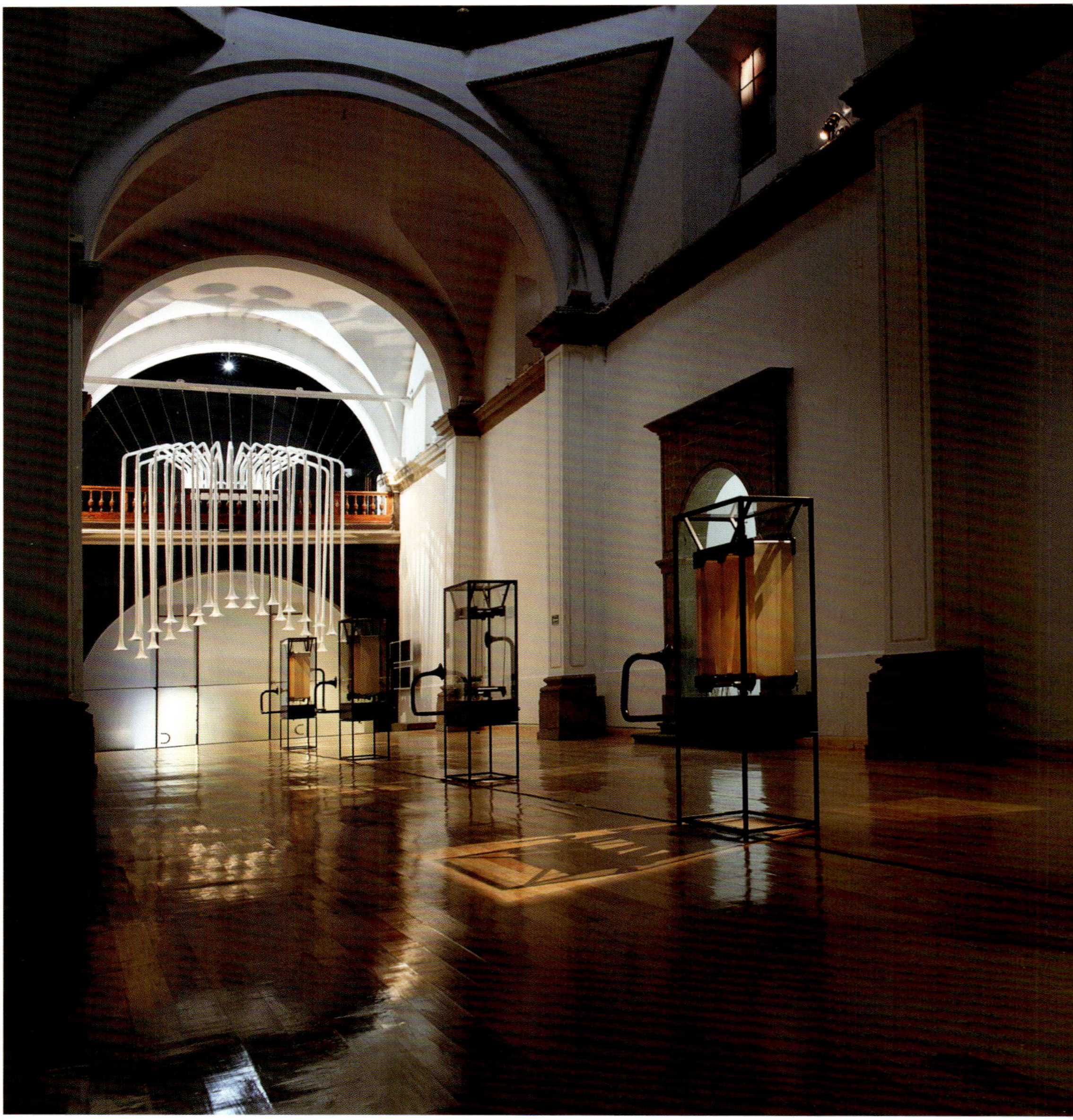

The conceptual axis of the project *Five Variations of Phonic Circumstances and a Pause* is rooted in poetic actions regarding machines, language, codification and the audible texture of narration. Each work, in its singularity, positions itself as an organ forming part of a larger complex system: a discourse surrounding the culture of listening—the audible, acoustic technologies, the gesticulation

Die konzeptuelle Achse des Projekts *Five Variations of Phonic Circumstances and a Pause* ruht auf poetischen Aktionen mit Maschinen, Sprache, Kodifizierung und der Audiotextur des Erzählens. Die einzelnen Arbeiten verstehen sich jeweils als Organe eines größeren komplexen Ganzen: eines Diskurses rund um die Kultur des Hörens – den Bereich des Akustischen und seiner Technologien, der Gestik des Erzählens, der Lautgestalt der Stimme.

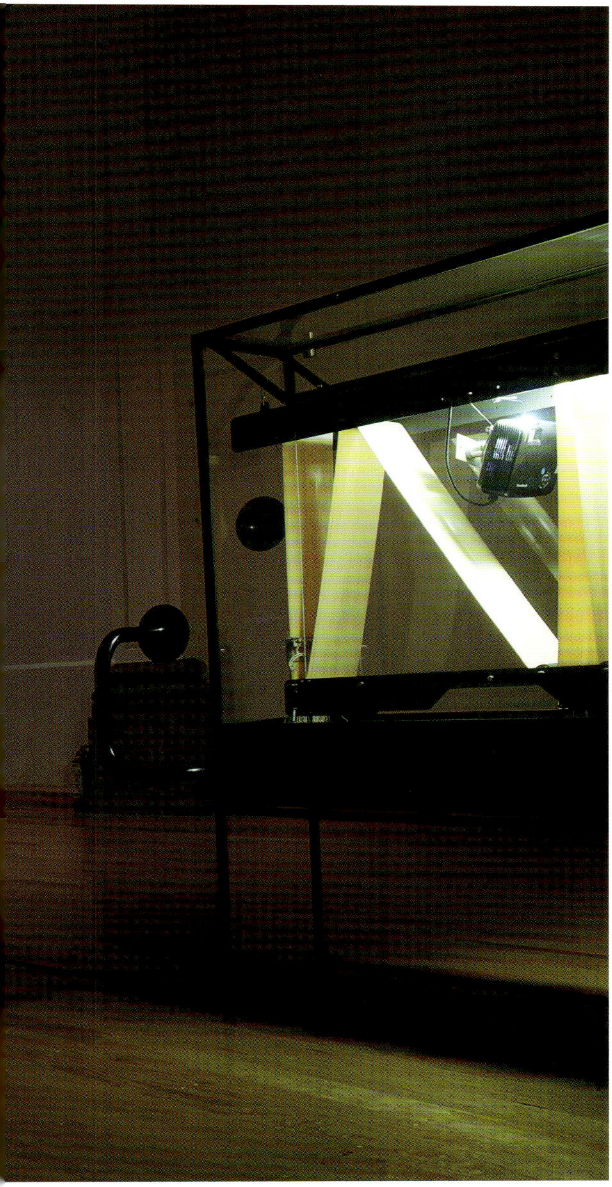

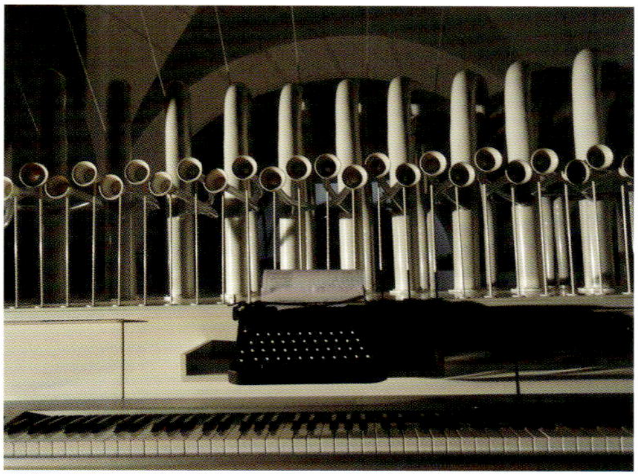

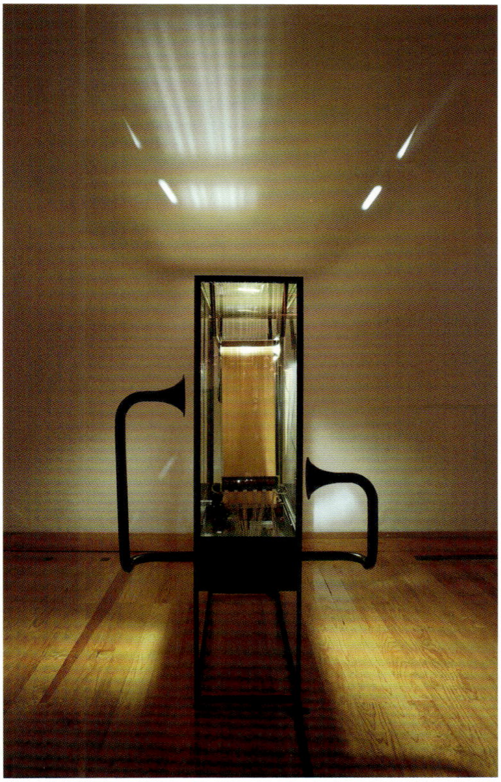

„Poetische Aktionen mit Maschinen" referiert hier auf die Variationen, die durch Phänomene wie die Kodifizierung der Sprache hervorgerufen werden – die Verschlüsselung des mündlichen Ausdrucks durch bestimmte, mit technischen Innovationen und der Funktion bestimmter Geräte verbundene Umstände, ein Prozess, der sowohl die Spannung der erzählenden Stimme als auch des hörenden Systems erhöht. Was all diese Sprechmaschinen und

of narration, the audible texture of the voice. In speaking of "poetic actions in regard to machines," I am referring to variations that occur through phenomena such as the codification of language, the encryption of the orality of the expression in particular circumstances, involving the innovation of machines and the functions of specific devices, tensing the voice that narrates as much

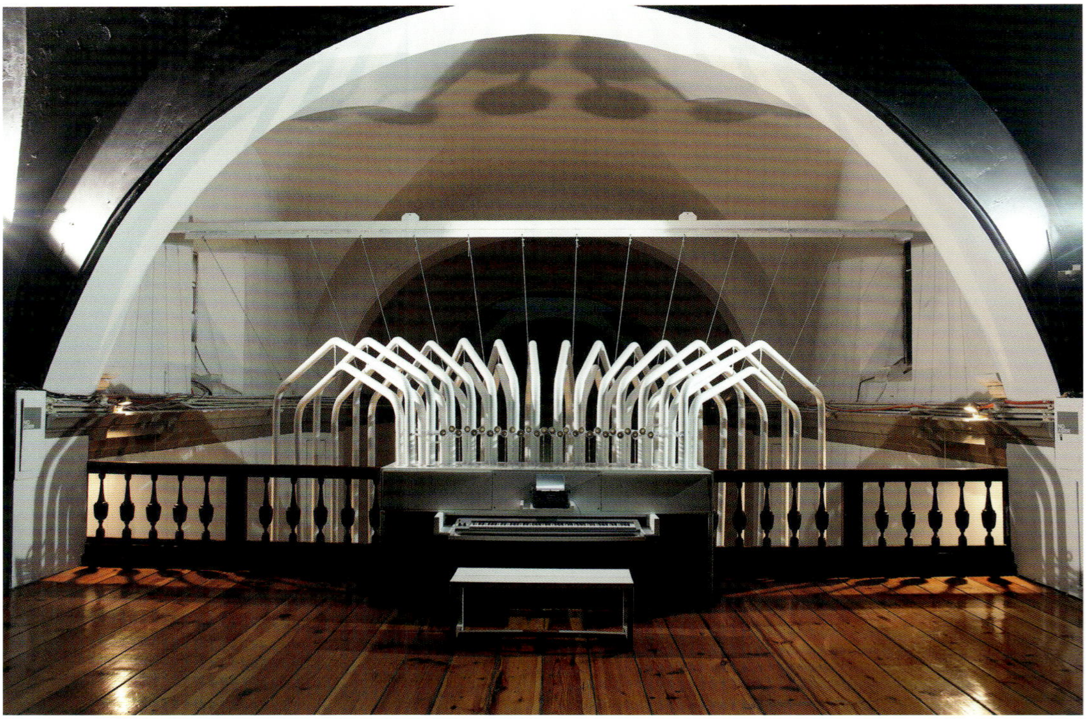

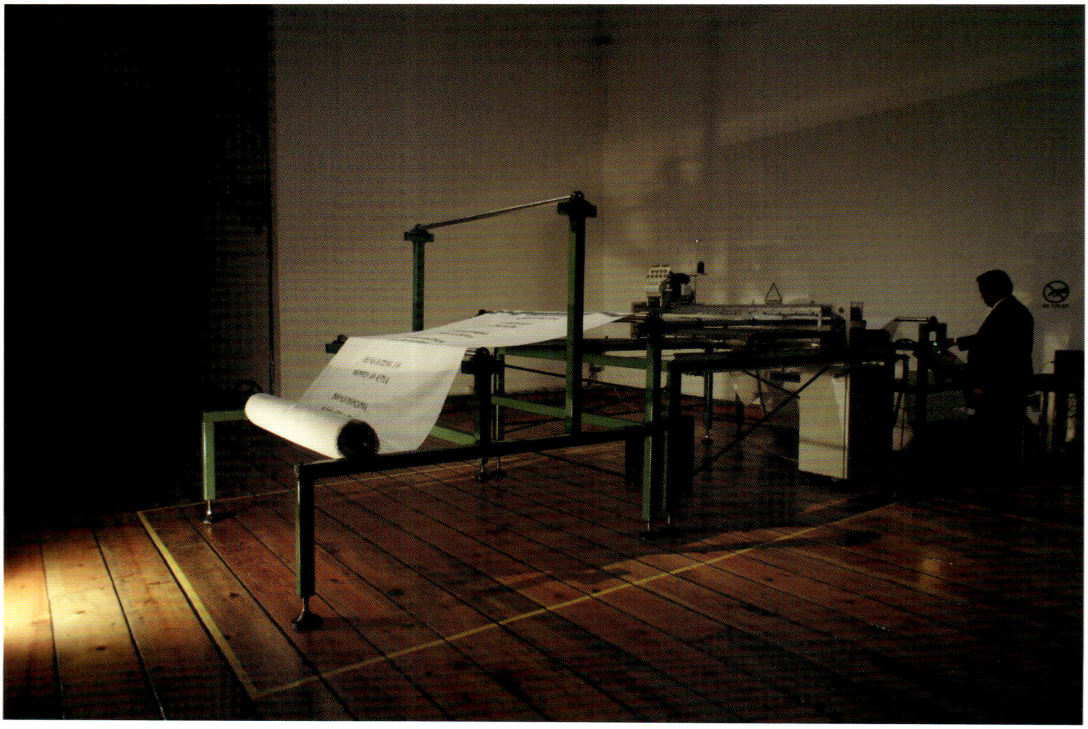

Hörsysteme miteinander verbindet, ist ihre Teilhabe an der Genealogie der Automaten und die jeder Archäologie der Science-Fiction zugrundeliegende Sehnsucht.
Die Maschinen von *Five Variations of Phonic Circumstances and a Pause* haben allesamt die Funktion, Klänge, oder genauer gesagt, phonische Umstände, zu verarbeiten. Jede von ihnen thematisiert und erweitert eine bestimmte mit Maschinen, Instrumenten oder Technologien verbundene Vorstellung und unterzieht deren Klang- oder Lauteigenschaften einer der im Titel erwähnten Variationen.
Ziel der Maschinen ist die Übersetzung und Interpretation von Klangereignissen – Geräuschen, mündlichen Äußerungen, Lesungen, Erzählungen, Gemurmel, Heimlichkeiten, Musik – durch ihre Verschiebung von einem akustischen Register in ein anderes, ihre Umwandlung in Text und Code.
Die Geräte sind irgendwo zwischen Science-Fiction, viktorianischer Dampfmaschinentechnik und den neuesten Errungenschaften der KI- und Spracherkennungstechnologie angesiedelt.
Die fünf Variationen verweisen durchgehend auf eine Reihe von Kommunikationsmodellen und Formattransformationen, die ein Spannungsverhältnis zwischen wissenschaftlicher Erkenntnis und menschlichem Faktor entstehen lassen und die Entfremdungserfahrung hervorheben, die mit dem heutigen breiten Einsatz von Medien verbunden ist.

as the systems that listens. The narrative behind each one of these speaking machines and listening systems is found in the link they share with the genealogy of automatons and a desire implied in an archeology of science fiction.
The machines of *Five Variations of Phonic Circumstances and a Pause* are constituted as mechanisms whose particular use is processing sounds or, more precisely, phonic circumstances.
Each of them contains and expands a type of imaginary associated with machines, instruments and specific technologies whose sonorous/phonetic quality is exposed to one of the eponymous variations.
The machines' goal is to translate and interpret sound events–noises, orality, readings, narrations, murmurs, secrets, music–by changing them from one phonic register to another, transmuting them into text and code. These devices lie somewhere between science fiction, Victorian steam technology and the latest artificial-intelligence and speech recognition technologies. The five variations refer constantly to a number of communication models and format transformations, which create tension in the relationship between scientific knowledge and the human factor and additionally emphasize the dislocation experience present in the contemporary media's expansive range.

Curator: Karla Jasso. Laboratorio Arte Alameda

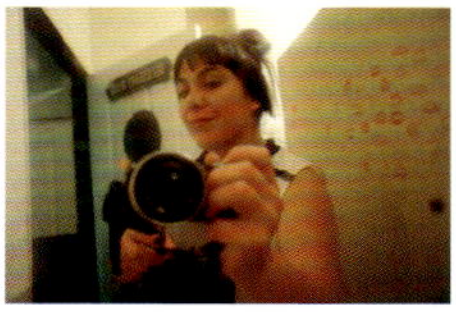

Tania Candiani (MX). The starting point for her research processes is language, text, the political implications of the domestic, of what is public and private, and of "the others." Her translation strategies among systems–linguistic, visual and phonic–and practices generate equivalences and associations, where there is a constant nostalgia for the obsolete that makes us consider the discursive content of artifacts and of former projections of future. As one of her fields of interest, the production of works in collaboration with inhabitants of defined sites aims at an exploration of language as everyday knowledge, and at the revelation of urban rituals when faced with an expressly generated circumstance. Tania Candiani has been a Guggenheim scholarship fellow in the creative arts category and part of the National System of Creators since 2012. **Tania Candiani** (MX). Ausgangspunkte für ihre Forschungen sind Sprache, Text sowie die politischen Implikationen des Eigenen, des Begriffs von öffentlich und privat, des Anderen. Ihre Strategie der Übersetzung zwischen Systemen – Sprache, Bild, Klang – und Praktiken schafft Äquivalenzen und Assoziationen, die oft gekennzeichnet sind von einer Sehnsucht nach dem Obsoleten und die Aufmerksamkeit auf die diskursiven Inhalte von Artefakten und früheren Zukunftsprojektionen lenkt. Ihr Interesse an der Entwicklung von Arbeiten zusammen mit den Bewohnern der jeweiligen Schauplätze zielt auf die Erforschung von Sprache als Alltagswissen und die Enthüllung urbaner Rituale durch Konfrontation mit eigens hergestellten Situationen. Tania Candiani war Guggenheim-Stipendiatin im Sektor Kunst und ist seit 2012 Teil des Sistema Nacional de Creadores de Arte.

Mycotecture

Phil Ross

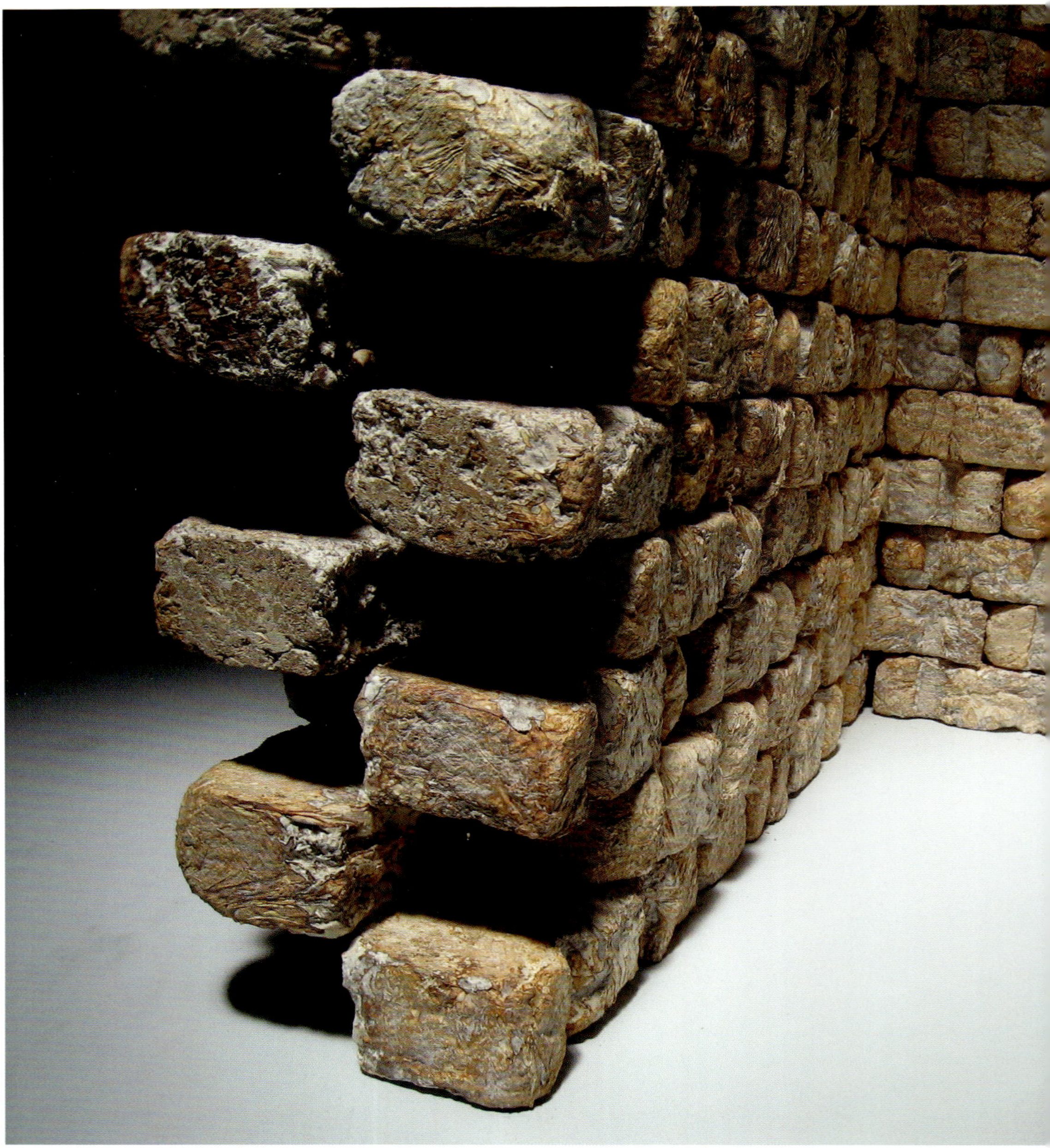

In the early 1990s I began growing a series of sculptural artworks using living fungus as an artistic material. These artworks were created by infusing live fungal cells into a pulverized-cellulose-based medium (sawdust). The sawdust serves as both food and framework for the

In den frühen 1990er Jahren begann ich eine Reihe skulpturaler Arbeiten aus lebenden Pilzen zu schaffen oder, besser gesagt, zu züchten. Die Arbeiten entstanden durch das Einbringen lebender Pilzzellen in ein pulverisiertes Zellulosemedium (Sägemehl), das dem Organismus gleichermaßen als Gerüst wie als Nahrung dient.

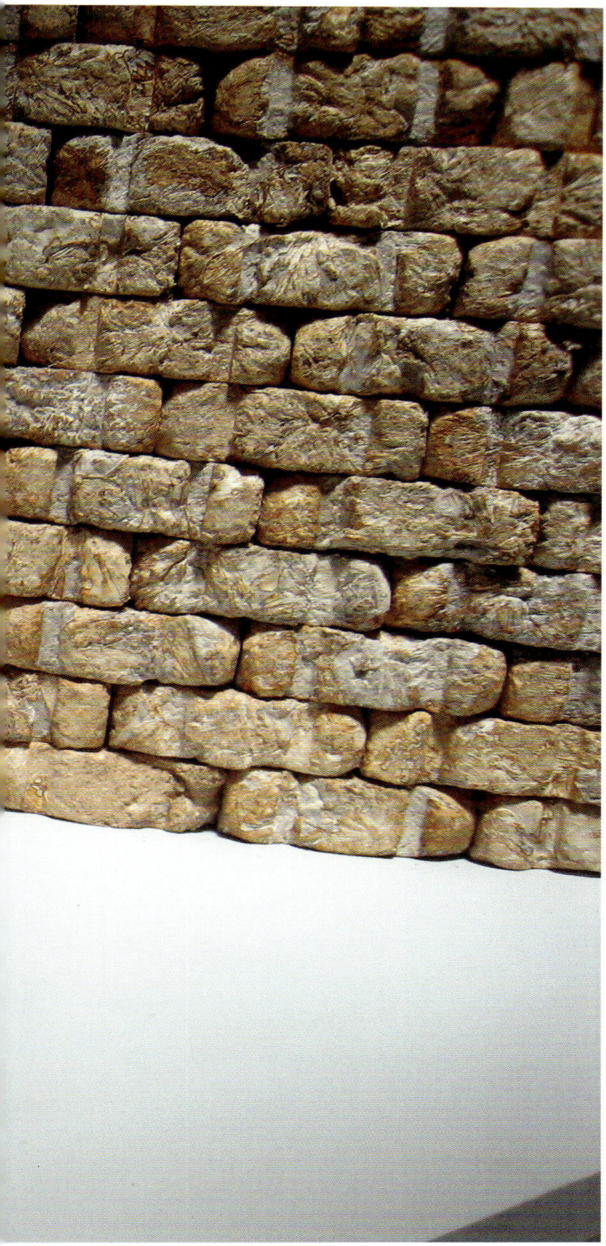

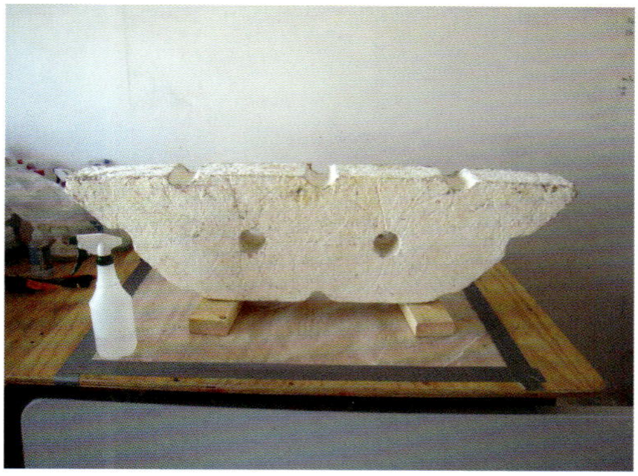

Innerhalb einer Woche verfestigt sich diese Verbindung aufgrund der natürlichen Neigung des Pilzes, aus kleineren Gewebeteilen ein größeres Ganzes zu bilden. Ähnlich wie Gips nimmt Pilzgewebe die Form eines jeden Behälters an, in den es eingebracht wird, und im getrockneten Zustand wird daraus ein leichtes und stabiles Material;

organism to grow on, and in about a week this aggregate solidifies as a result of the fungi's natural tendency to join together smaller pieces of its tissue into a larger constituent whole. Like plaster, fungal tissue will take on the form of any container it is molded within, and once dried out it becomes

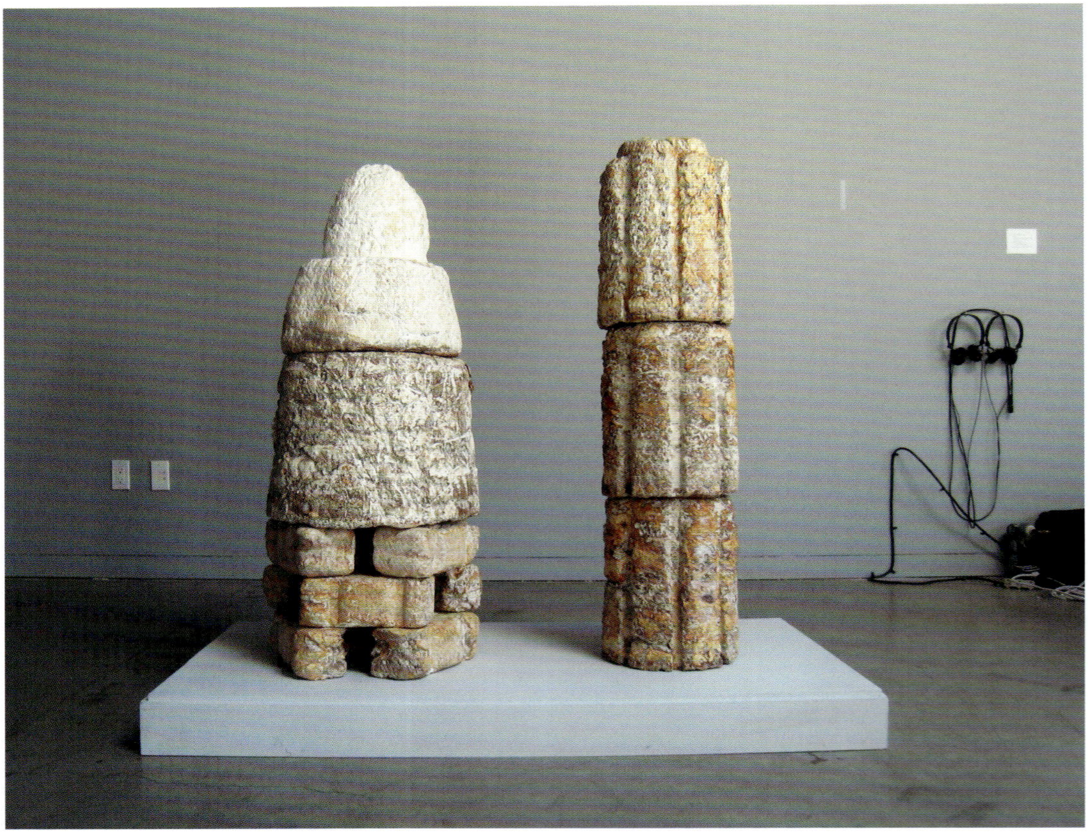

a lightweight and strong material. While incredibly durable, the material can readily be broken down through benign organic processes and incorporated back into the world. In addition to being an interesting material with which to grow artwork, fungi have the potential to replace many materials that are currently made using petroleum-based products.

Over the years I have experimented with this fungal material to grow a diverse range of objects, and in 2009 I received a commission from the Kunsthalle Dusseldorf to grow a two-cubic-meter teahouse for their EatArt exhibition. The architectural folly presented in the museum was a demonstration of how fungi might be used as a renewable building resource, and was the proof of concept toward the ambition of growing a much larger structure in the same manner. Since the EatArt exhibition I have continued my material tests and experiments and

ein Material, das sich trotz seiner enormen Haltbarkeit leicht wieder mittels unschädlicher organischer Prozesse abbauen und in die Natur zurückführen lässt. Pilze sind aber nicht nur ein interessantes Material für die Schaffung von Kunstwerken, sie haben auch das Potenzial, viele der Materialien zu ersetzen, die derzeit auf Erdölbasis hergestellt werden.

Im Lauf meiner jahrelangen Experimente habe ich aus diesem Pilzmaterial die unterschiedlichsten Objekte gezüchtet. 2009 wurde ich von der Kunsthalle Düsseldorf beauftragt, für die dortige EatArt-Ausstellung ein zwei Kubikmeter großes Teehaus zu schaffen. Der im Museum präsentierte Zierbau demonstrierte die Einsatzmöglichkeit von Pilzen als erneuerbares Baumaterial und war der Machbarkeitsnachweis für das Ziel, mit derselben Methode ein viel größeres Gebäude zu errichten. Seit der EatArt-Ausstellung habe ich meine Materialversuche und Experimente fortgeführt und im letzten Jahr habe ich in San Francisco eine Reihe organischer Möbel

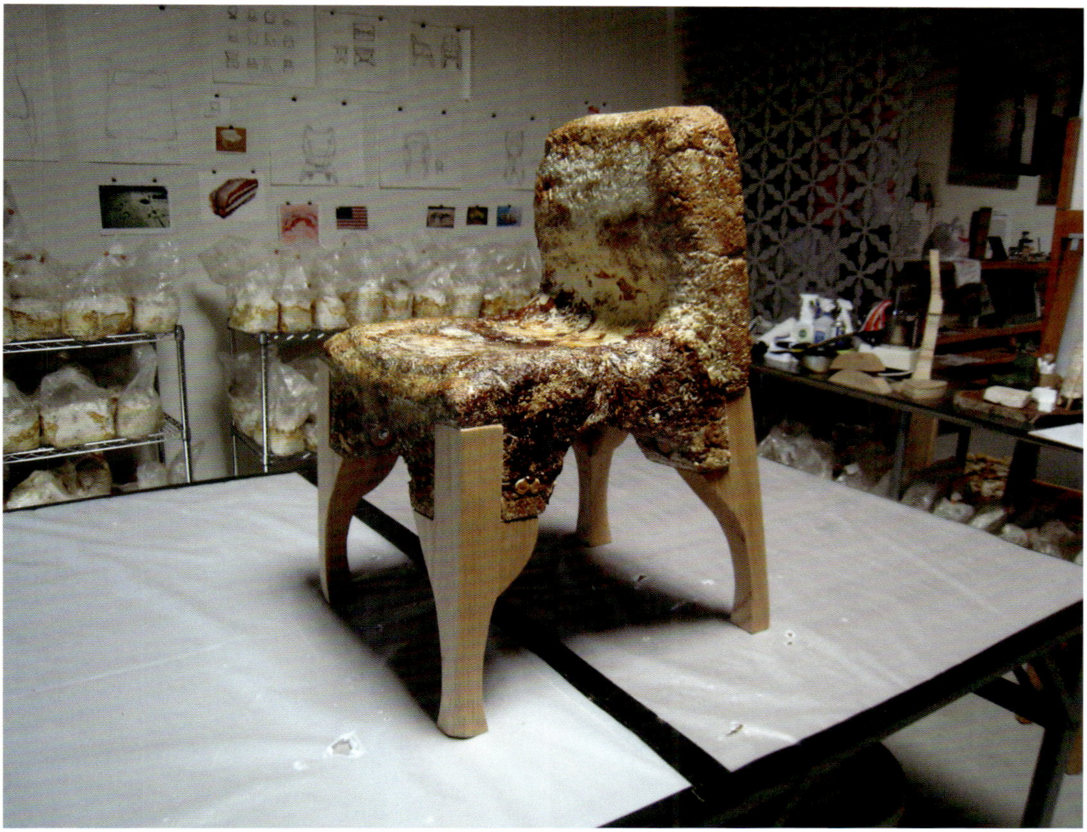

gezüchtet, die zeigen, dass das Material eine Menge weiterer kreativer Anwendungsmöglichkeiten besitzt.

in this past year have created a series of locally grown organic furniture here in San Francisco to demonstrate how this material might be used in a range of creative applications.

Lead Engineer: Michael Sgambellone

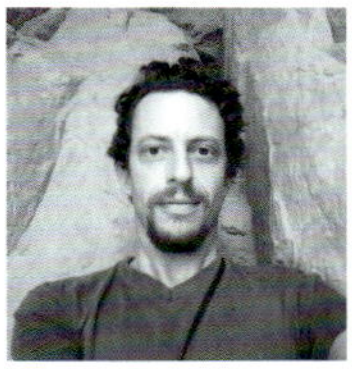

Phil Ross (US) is an artist, educator and inventor whose creative work is focused on the relationships between human beings, technology and the greater living environment. From 2001–2008 Philip was a visiting lecturer at Stanford University, UC Berkeley and the San Francisco Art Institute. In 2008 Philip joined the University of San Francisco's Department of Art and Architecture as an assistant professor. Philip has been a vital contributor to the emerging Bay Area maker culture of open scientific practice and informal science education through the numerous classes, workshops and lectures that he has offered on DIY biology over the past ten years. Phil received his BFA in sculpture from the San Francisco Art Institute in 1991, and an MFA from Stanford University in 2000. **Phil Ross** (US) ist Künstler, Lehrer und Erfinder, dessen kreative Arbeiten um das Verhältnis zwischen Mensch, Technologie und Lebenswelt kreisen. Von 2001 bis 2008 war er Gastdozent an der Stanford University, an der UC Berkeley und am San Francisco Art Institute. 2008 wurde er Assistenzprofessor am Institut für Kunst und Architektur der University of San Francisco. Ross hat in den vergangenen zehn Jahren mit zahlreichen Kursen, Workshops und Vorträgen über DIY-Biologie wesentlich zur aufstrebenden Maker-Kultur einer offenen wissenschaftlichen Praxis und informellen wissenschaftlichen Ausbildung in der Bay Area beigetragen. Er hält einen BFA in Bildhauerei vom San Francisco Art Institute (1991) und einen MFA von der Stanford Universität (2000).

Oh!m1gas: biomimetic stridulation environment

Kuai Shen

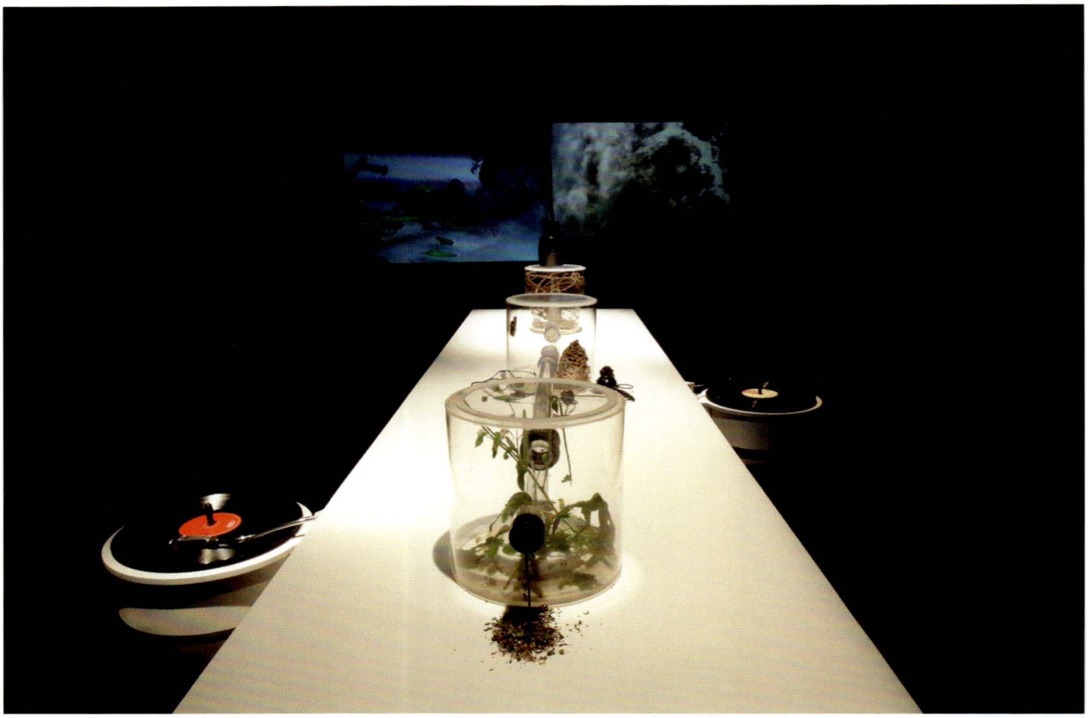

The *Oh!m1gas: biomimetic stridulation environment* is an artistic research and audiovisual installation that approaches the self-organization in ants as a cybernetic system with emergent manifestations. *Oh!m1gas* 'is based on a do-it-yourself approach to bioacoustics, measuring the vibratory sounds and mapping the activity of an ant colony and their relation to the artificial ecosystem where they live. By means of contact microphones and video surveillance interfaced with the computer, which feeds this bio-data to two turntables, the life of the ant colony emerges as a soundscape of scratching effects.

The activity of an ant colony is observed, archiving the ants' movements and sounds inside a digital matrix. A pair of turntables constantly reacts to the changes that emerge from the colony (e.g., recruiting units for defense, task allocation when rebuilding the nest or organizing the harvesting of vegetation), thus spinning vinyl records that produce scratching sounds similar to the original stridulations (rubbing noises produced by body parts) of some ants. Leafcutter ants use the stridulatory organ, human DJs use the turntable: a reactive soundscape that reveals the connection between

Oh!m1gas: biomimetic stridulation environment ist ein künstlerisches Forschungsprojekt und eine audiovisuelle Installation, die die Selbstorganisation von Ameisen als kybernetisches System mit Emergenzen auffasst. *Oh!m1gas* misst – basierend auf einem bioakustischen DIY-Ansatz – die Vibrationsgeräusche einer Ameisenkolonie und in einem künstlichen Ökosystem und zeichnet deren Aktivitäten auf. Die mithilfe von Kontaktmikrofonen und Videokameras erhobenen Biodaten werden über einen Computer an zwei Plattenspieler

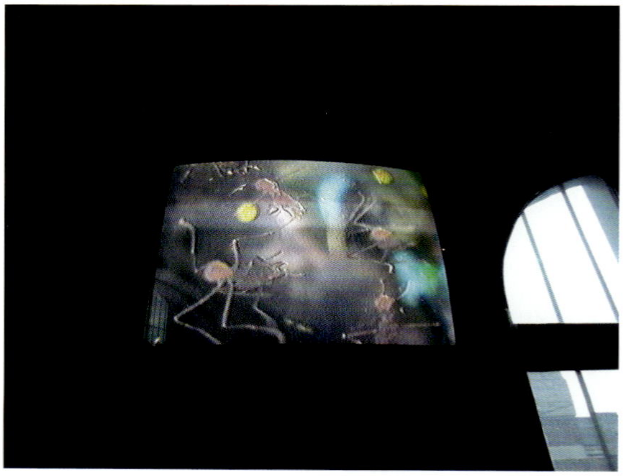

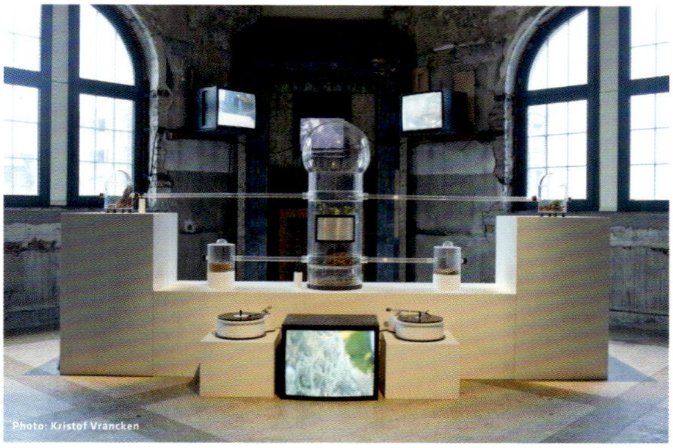

scratching as an aesthetic expression created by human culture and the stridulation phenomena of leafcutter ants as a modulation mechanism for communication.
I believe we can learn from the way the ants construct their miniature ecosystems. Like them, we can apply an experimental design approach based on self-organization, where sounds and physical interaction promote and consolidate the interaction of life.

geschickt, wo das Leben der Ameisenkolonie als Soundscape aus Scratch-Effekten in Erscheinung tritt.
Die Aktivität der Ameisenkolonie wird beobachtet und ihre Bewegungen und Geräusche in einer digitalen Matrix abgelegt. Die beiden Plattenteller werden durch die in der Kolonie auftretenden Veränderungen (z. B. die Rekrutierung von Verteidigungskräften, die Aufgabenverteilung bei der Umbildung des Baus oder die Organisation der Pflanzenernte), in Drehung versetzt und rufen auf den darauf liegenden Vinylplatten Scratch-Sounds hervor, die den (durch Reibung von Körperteilen entstehenden) Stridulationsgeräuschen mancher Ameisen ähneln. Blattschneiderameisen machen mit dem Stridulationsorgan, was menschliche DJs mit dem Plattenteller machen. So entsteht eine reaktive Soundscape, die eine Beziehung zwischen Scratching als künstlerischem Ausdruck des Menschen und dem Stridulationsphänomen als Modulationsmechanismus in der Kommunikation von Blattschneiderameisen herstellt.
Ich bin überzeugt, dass wir von der Art, wie Ameisen ihre kleinen Ökosysteme organisieren, etwas lernen können. Gleich ihnen können wir einen auf Selbstorganisation beruhenden experimentellen Designansatz wählen, in dem Geräusche und physische Interaktion die Wechselbeziehungen des Lebens fördern und stabilisieren.

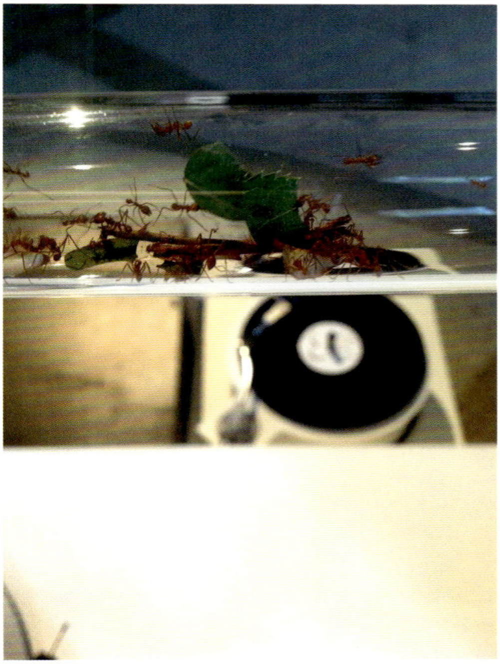

Kuai Shen (EC/DE) was born in Guayaquil, Ecuador. He has a BA in digital arts from the University of San Francisco de Quito, a diploma in media arts with honors from the Academy of Media Arts in Cologne, and he recently finished an interdisciplinary research in game design and development at the University of Applied Sciences Cologne. He has exhibited in well-known international media art festivals, galleries and biennials worldwide. Kuai Shen's publication on his research on ants has been published in *Biologically-Inspired Computing for the Arts*, a reader on data visualization, and in the *Leonardo* MIT journal for the Siggraph. **Kuai Shen** (EC/DE), geb.in Guayaquil, Ecuador, studierte Digital Arts an der Universidad San Francisco de Quito sowie Medienkunst/Audiovisuelle Medien an der Kunsthochschule für Medien Köln. Vor kurzem beendete er ein interdisziplinäres Forschungsprojekt in Gamedesign und Game-Entwicklung an der Fachhochschule Köln. Seine Arbeiten wurden weltweit auf renommierten Medienkunstfestivals, Biennalen und in Galerien gezeigt. Kuai Shens Publikationen über seine Ameisenforschung sind in *Biologically-Inspired Computing for the Arts*, einem Reader über Datenvisualisierung, und in der MIT-Zeitschrift *Leonardo* erschienen.

Breathing Bike

Matt Hope

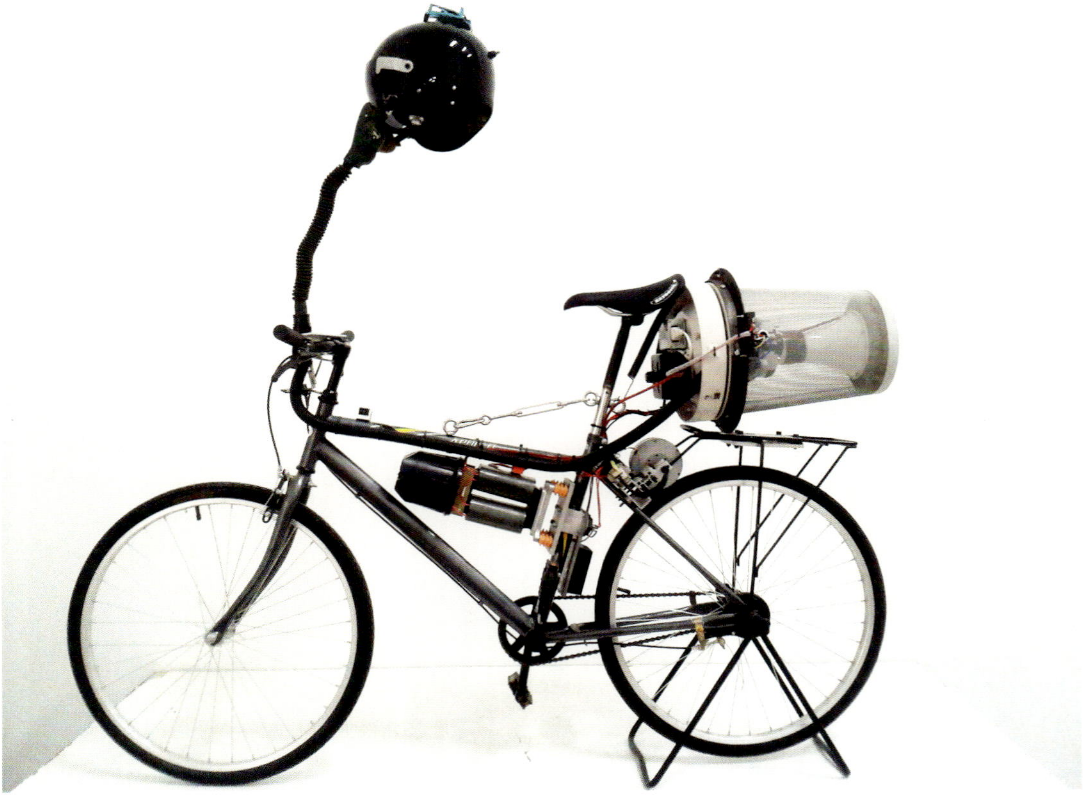

The Breathing Bike is a prototype air-cleaning bicycle made in reaction to Beijing's ongoing air quality dilemma. The bike is composed of a mixture of domestic and industrial detritus found in the artist's studio, assembled onto the frame of China's cheapest supermarket bicycle, "The Apollo". As a hybrid artwork, it uses functional elements grafted together to talk about the current state of the built environment.

As the wheels turn, a wind generator in direct contact with the rear tyre begins to produces an electrical current. This electricity is fed through a series of industrial transformers to a static electric air-cleaning system that pumps filtered air to the rider via a fighter pilots respirator.

The Breathing Bike comes to form a kind of dystopian bricolage through the use of ultra-cheap shortlived products and their subverted use. An IKEA "Dokument" waste paper bin, found the world over in both homes and offices serves to filter large pieces of debris from being sucked

Das *Breathing Bike* ist der Prototyp eines luftreinigenden Fahrrads, das als Antwort auf das fortdauernde Luftverschmutzungsproblem in Beijing entstanden ist. Die zur Gänze aus Haushalts- und Industrieartikeln aus dem Atelier des Künstlers erbaute Vorrichtung ist auf den Rahmen eines der billigsten Fahrräder Chinas, eines „Apollo", montiert. Als hybrides Kunstwerk äußert es sich durch eine wilde Aneinanderreihung von Funktionsgegenständen zum gegenwärtigen Zustand unserer gebauten Umwelt.

Setzt sich das Fahrrad in Bewegung, beginnt ein direkt auf dem Hinterrad laufender Windgenerator elektrischen Strom zu erzeugen. Dieser wird über eine Reihe von Industrietransformatoren zu einem elektrostatischen Luftreinigungssystem geleitet, das die gefilterte Luft über die Sauerstoffmaske eines Kampfpiloten zum Fahrer befördert.

Durch die subversive Verwendung ultrabilliger, kurzlebiger Industrieprodukte wird das *Breathing Bike* zu einer Art dystopischer Bricolage. Ein „Dokument"-Papierkorb von IKEA, wie er auf der ganzen Welt in Wohnungen

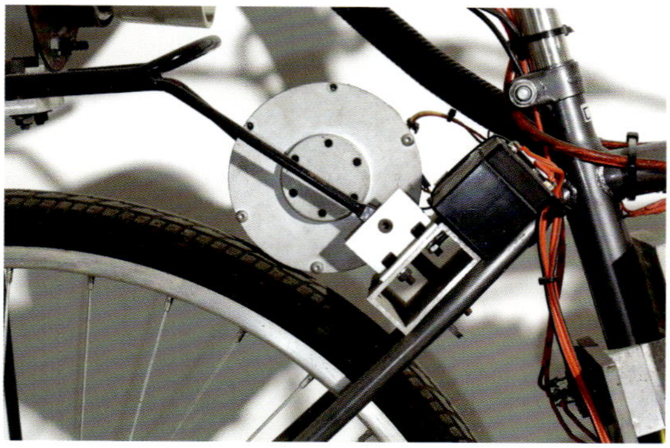

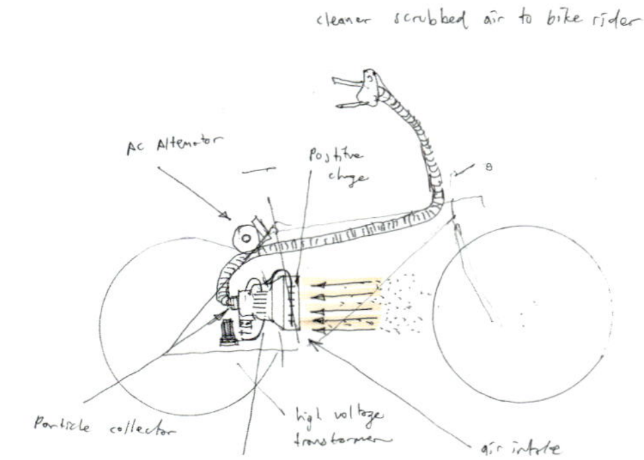

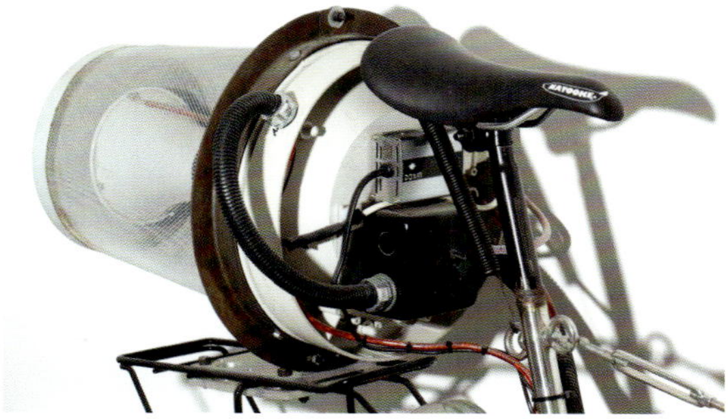

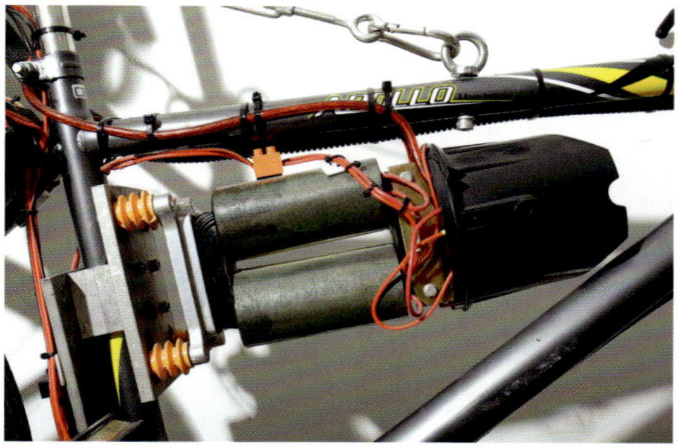

Photographer: © 2013 Amanda Anderson

und Büros Verwendung findet, dient dazu, größere Teile abzuhalten und den Fahrer vor der Hochspannung zu schützen. Die industrielle Produktion derartiger Artikel ist mit ihrem hohen Energieverbrauch und ihrem Streben nach raschen Gewinnen zweifellos einer der Hauptbeiträger zur Luftverschmutzung.
Das *Breathing Bike* thematisiert das Paradoxon von Chinas halsbrecherischem Wachstum durch eine Kontrastierung des Industriellen und Privaten mit der Nutzung seiner Gebrauchsgegenstände. Das Ganze wird angetrieben von der Verausgabung des menschlichen Körpers und ist aufgepfropft auf das sozialistische Chassis von Chinas rasant schwindender Vergangenheit: das Fahrrad.

in and to protect the rider from the high voltage electricity. The industrial production of these very products, with their high energy comsumption and striving for rapid profits, is no doubt a major contributor to the air degradation itself.
The Breathing Bike attempts to address the paradox of China break neck speed of development by juxtaposing the industrial and domestic with the use of its functional components, powered via the human exertion of the body. Framed onto the socialist chassis of Chinas ever disappearing past – the bicycle.

Matt Hope (UK), born 1976, is a British artist who lives and works in Caochangdi, an arts district in Beijing, China. He is known for elaborate kinetic art and sound art constructions that utilize the large-scale manufacturing factories in China. **Matt Hope** (UK), geb. 1976, ist ein britischer Künstler. Er lebt und arbeitet im Künstlerviertel Caochangdi in Beijing und ist bekannt für seine elaborierten kinetischen und klangkünstlerischen Arbeiten, die die großindustriellen Fabrikationsmöglichkeiten in China nutzen.

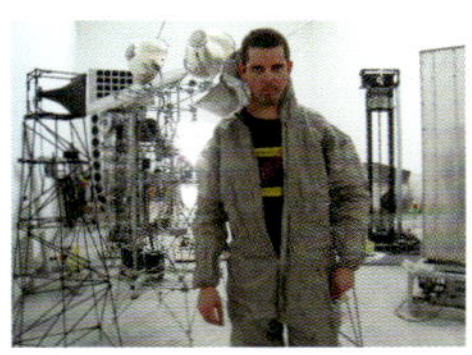

Hidden Fields

David Glowacki with Phil Tew, Laura Kriefman, Joseph Hyde, Thomas Mitchell, Lisa May Thomas, Emma Harrie

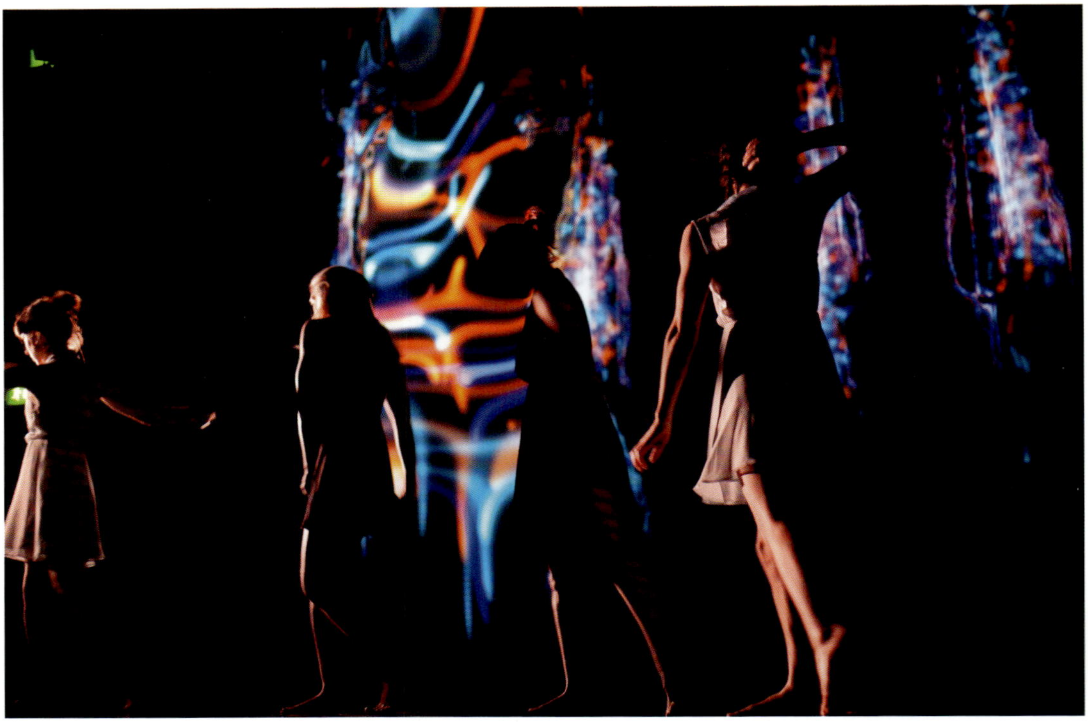

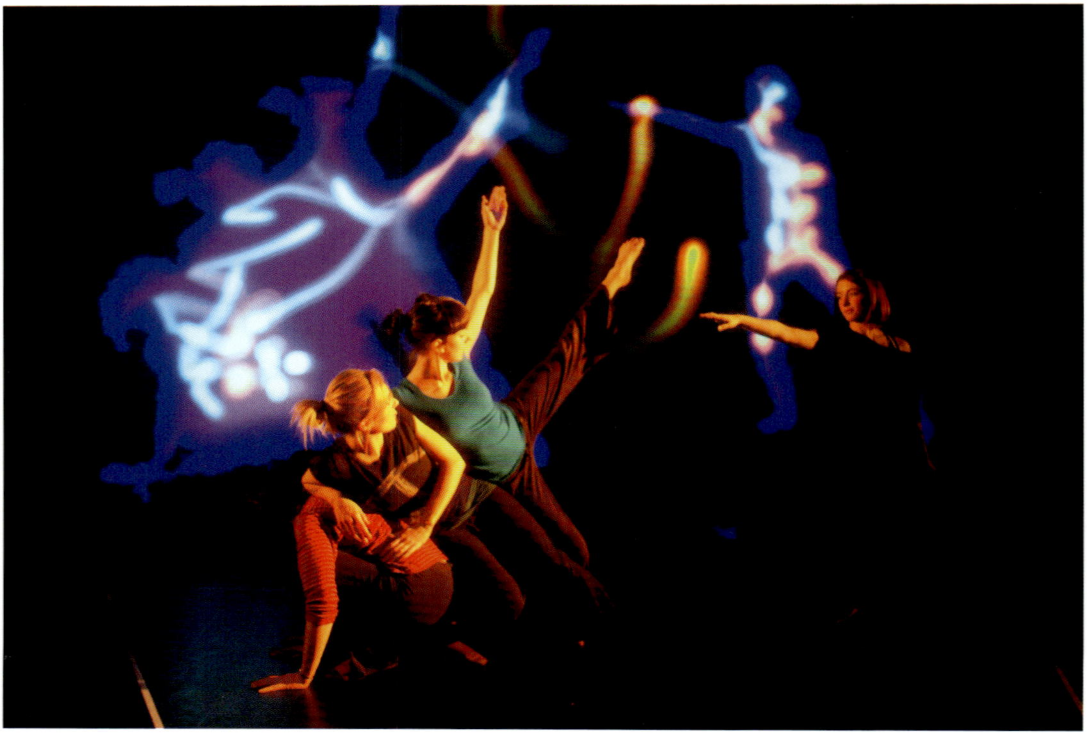

http://danceroom-spec.com/
http://vimeo.com/48764930

Hidden Fields ist die erste Tanzshow der Welt, die auf Algorithmen und Mathematik aus der Quantenphysik beruht. Sie ist das Ergebnis einer einmaligen wissenschaftlich-künstlerischen Zusammenarbeit, die breite internationale Resonanz und ein großes Presseecho erfuhr. *Hidden Fields* verbindet 3D-Bildbearbeitung, Quantendynamik, Gaming, Tanz und Menschen zu einer erweiterten Tanzperformance, die zeigt, wie unsere Energiefelder mit der uns umgebenden und sonst unsichtbaren Welt der Atome interagieren. Die Verschmelzung von strenger Wissenschaft, generierten Soundscapes und schön anzusehenden interaktiven Visuals hat zur Entwicklung einer neuen Choreografiesprache geführt, die die Grenzen unseres Verhältnisses zu präziser Bewegung, Wissenschaft, Raumwahrnehmung und Kunst verschiebt.
Hidden Fields arbeitet mit der von David Glowacki in Zusammenarbeit mit anderen entwickelten Soft- und Hardwareplattform danceroom Spectrosopy (dS). dS setzt menschliche Bewegungen streng physikalisch in Klänge und Bilder um. Die Bewegungen werden mit einer Reihe von 3D-Kameras erfasst und an einen speziell gefertigten Supercomputer geschickt, wo sie eine Software als Energiefelder interpretiert. Die Energiefelder (oder Energie-„Avatare") der Personen werden in Echtzeit auf einen riesigen Bildschirm projiziert. Innerhalb dieser Avatare bewegen sich flüssig Tausende projizierter Partikel umher, die die Milliarden Atome repräsentieren, von denen wir ständig umgeben sind. Mithilfe von dS können Menschen bei der physischen Bewegung im Raum mit diesen Atomen interagieren – sie einfangen, wegschieben, austauschen und mit ihnen tanzen.

Hidden Fields is the world's first ever dance show driven by algorithms and mathematics from quantum dynamics. It is the result of a unique sci-art collaboration that has attracted significant international attention and press coverage. Fusing 3D imaging, rigorous quantum dynamics, gaming, dance and people, *Hidden Fields* is an augmented dance performance that shows how our energy fields interact with the otherwise invisible atomic world around us. Its fusion of rigorous science, generative soundscapes and beautiful interactive visuals has led to the development of a new choreographic language that pushes the boundaries of our relationship with precise movement, science, spatial awareness and art.
Hidden Fields uses the danceroom Spectrosopy (dS) software and hardware platform developed by David Glowacki and collaborators. dS uses rigorous physics to create sounds and images from people's movements. Using a set of 3D cameras, people's movements are captured and fed to a custom-built supercomputer, where a software program interprets them as energy fields. In real time, people's energy fields (or energy "avatars") are projected onto a giant screen. Moving fluidly within people's energy avatars are thousands of projected particles that represent the billions of atoms that are always around us but too small for our eyes to see. As people move within the physical space, dS enables them to use their "energy fields" to interact with these atoms—catching, pushing, sharing and dancing with them.

Project lead: David Glowacki; digital artist: Phil Tew; choreographer: Laura Kriefman; music tech and composition: Joseph Hyde and Thomas Mitchell; contemporary dancers: Lisa May Thomas and Emma Harrie

David Glowacki (US) is a scientist, author, philosopher, and inventor. He has published across a range of subjects. His scientific research straddles the boundary where physics meets chemistry—where classical effects are fading out and quantum effects are just kicking in. dS is motivated by his desire to reveal our connection to the beautiful and subtle microscopic world. He has a PhD in physical chemistry. **David Glowacki** (US) ist Wissenschaftler, Autor, Philosoph und Erfinder. Seine Publikationen behandeln eine ganze Reihe von Themen, seine wissenschaftliche Forschungsarbeit gilt vor allem der Schnittstelle von Physik und Chemie – dort wo klassische Effekte verschwinden und erste Quanteneffekte auftreten. dS wird vom Wunsch motiviert, unsere Verbindung mit dem herrlichen und subtilen Mikrokosmos zu zeigen. Glowacki ist Doktor in physikalischer Chemie.

HuMCC—Human Molecular Colonization Capacity

Maja Smrekar

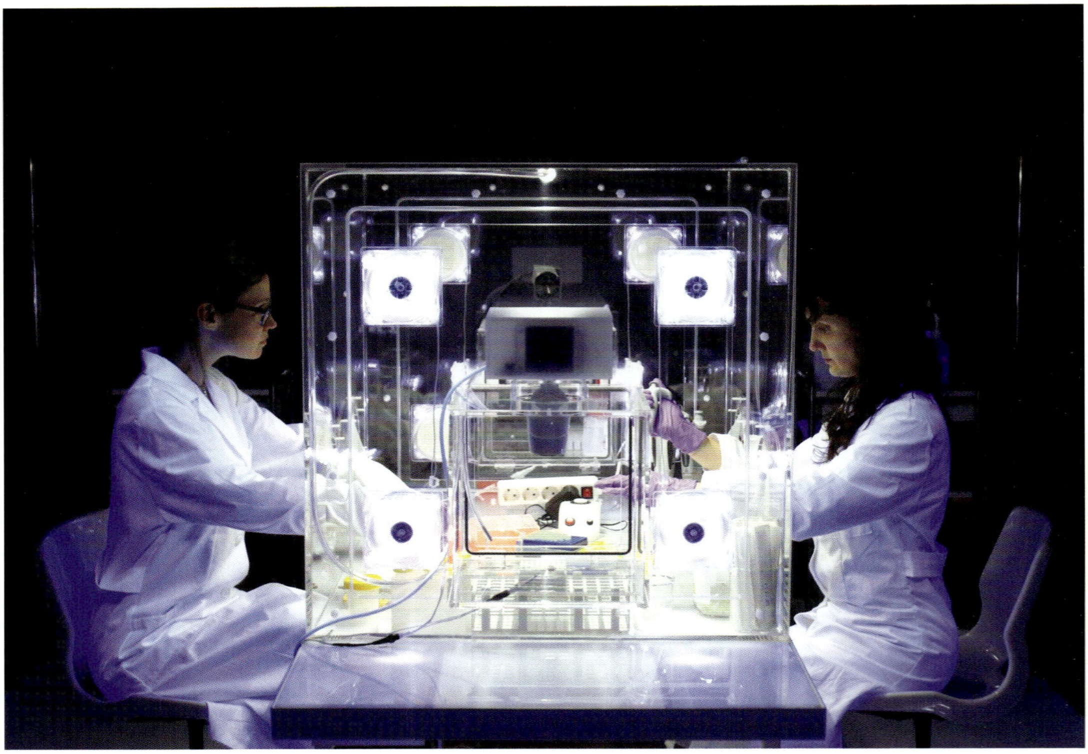

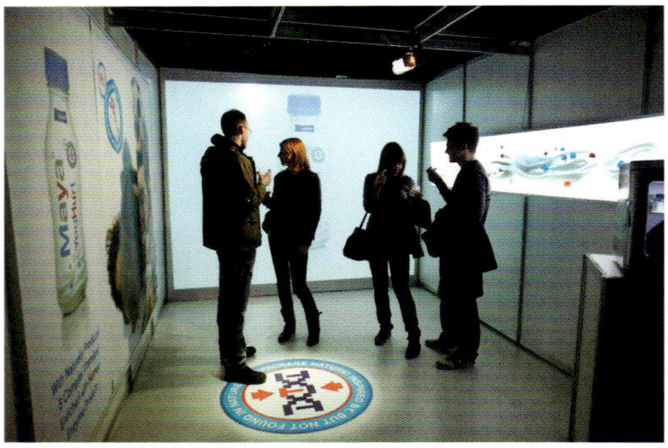

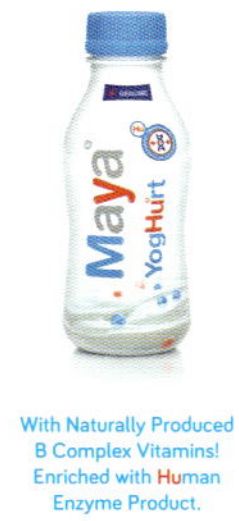

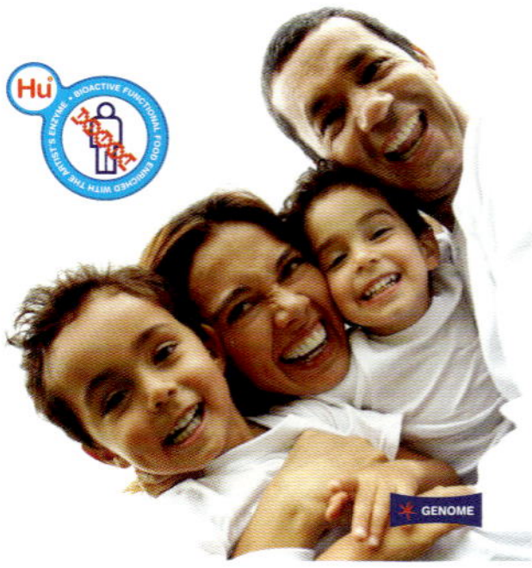

Food prices are going to rise in the future due to lack of production capacity, which decreases inversely with the global population growth. The food industry is exploring new possibilities and alternative capacities for future food production within the fields of synthetic biology and biotechnology. The *HuMCC—Human Molecular Colonization Capacity* project focuses on the food industry's biotechnology production, and in its final form is represented as a highly designed yoghurt package, containing the product of

Die Nahrungsmittelpreise werden in Zukunft steigen, weil die Produktionskapazitäten mit dem globalen Bevölkerungswachstum abnehmen. Die Nahrungsmittelindustrie sucht daher auf dem Gebiet der synthetischen Biologie und Biotechnologie nach alternativen Möglichkeiten und Produktionskapazitäten. Das Projekt *HuMCC – Human Molecular Colonization Capacity* beschäftigt sich mit dieser biotechnologischen Produktion der Nahrungsmittelindustrie und nimmt in seiner Endgestalt die Form eines Joghurts an, das das Produkt eines Enzyms der Künstlerin enthält und öffentlich zum Konsum angeboten wird, während seine Verpackung zugleich als Hybridkunst-Readymade in einer Galerie ausgestellt wird. Das Projekt ist eine sozialdarwinistische Versuchsanordnung, umgesetzt im Bereich der industriellen Nahrungsmittelproduktion. Es paraphrasiert die von Marx erforschte Verschwendung der Produktivkräfte, die Ausbeutung von Arbeitszeit durch technische Innovationswellen, um der tendenziell sinkenden Profitrate bei wachsender Kapitalakkumulation entgegenzuwirken. Das wird hier an der Produktion von Milchsäure (einem der meistverwendeten Zusätze in der heutigen Nahrungsmittelindustrie) durch einen genetisch veränderten Mikroorganismus gezeigt, der aus dem Code eines Gens der Künstlerin und dessen Kombination mit dem eines Hefegens synthetisiert wurde.

Das Projekt entspricht dem Paradigma von *Soylent Green*, wo die Angst vor der ökologischen Katastrophe in eine subtile Kritik am Kannibalismus des organisierten Kapitals umschlägt: die Konzerne benutzen Menschen nicht nur buchstäblich dazu, sich am Leben zu erhalten, die Menschen begehren diese Produkte auch noch! „Maya Yoghurt" ist ein taktisches Medium, ein Mittel, um die Bevölkerung unter Druck zu setzen – der unaufhörliche Drang des Kapitals, sich immer weiter zu entwickeln, auch wenn das (sublime) Dosen an Kannibalismus beinhaltet.

Brand identity and web design: Atelje.Balant
Executed in cooperation with the Institute of Biochemistry, Medical Faculty, University of Ljubljana, Slovenia. Co-worker (molecular biology): Dr. Metka Lenassi, co-worker (molecular gastronomy): Tilen Konte; co-worker (biotechnology): Špela Petrič. Special thanks: Dr. Ana Plemenitaš.
Production: Kapelica Gallery—Zavod K6/4, Ljubljana.
Supported by Ministry of Culture / Republic of Slovenia and Municipality of Ljubljana.

an artist's enzyme, which is offered for public consumption while at the same time the package is represented as a hybrid-art readymade object exhibited in a gallery. The project stands as a social darwinism experience paraphrased within the realm of the industrial food-chain process.

The *HuMCC* project paraphrases a concept for the waste of productive forces explored by Marx, who established a connection between rising levels of accumulation of capital and the tendency of the rate of profit to fall, related to the exploitation of labor time—by new waves of technological innovation. This is shown by the genetically transformed microorganism producing lactic acid (as one of the most-used additives in the contemporary food industry) after being synthetically designed by the code of the artist's gene composed with the code of a yeast gene and transformed back into the same microorganism.

The project is therefore located in the *Soylent Green* paradigm where the fear of ecological cataclysm turns into a subtle critique of corporate cannibalism: not only are corporations actually using people to continue to maintain themselves in their own lives but these same people are simultaneously yearning for those products! "Maya Yoghurt" is an overidentification tactical media product as means of producing pressure on the population—this infinite desire of capital to continue developing regardless of whether that would include even (sublime) levels of cannibalism.

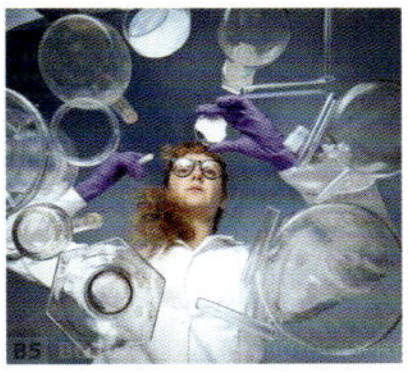

Maja Smrekar (SI), born 1978, 2005 graduated at the Sculpture Department of Fine Art Academy in Ljubljana and is currently finishing an MA at the New Media Department. Her main interest is in the phenomenology of perception, which she first started researching through space phenomena by composing live videos with other artists in various collaborations in interactive sound/visual projects. Her projects have researched frequency phenomena through biofeedback and telematic presence in relation to the body, privacy and the (inter-)subjective perception of space. In the last two years she has been developing projects within the field of bioart with the focus on living organisms. **Maja Smrekar** (SI), geb. 1978, absolvierte ein Studium der Bildhauerei an der Akademie für Bildende Kunst Ljubljana (2005) und schließt dort gerade einen Master im Fach Neue Medien ab. Ihr Hauptarbeitsgebiet ist die Phänomenologie der Wahrnehmung, wobei sie sich zunächst – vor allem durch Live-Videoarbeiten in interaktiven Klang-/Bildprojekten zusammen mit verschiedenen anderen Künstlern – räumlichen Phänomenen widmete. Weitere Projekte beschäftigten sich mit Frequenzphänomenen durch Biofeedback und Telepräsenz mit Bezug auf den Körper, die Privatsphäre und die (inter)subjektive Raumwahrnehmung. In den letzten zwei Jahren entwickelte sie Biokunstprojekte mit einem Fokus auf lebende Organismen.

Memory Vapor

Dmitry Gelfand, Evelina Domnitch

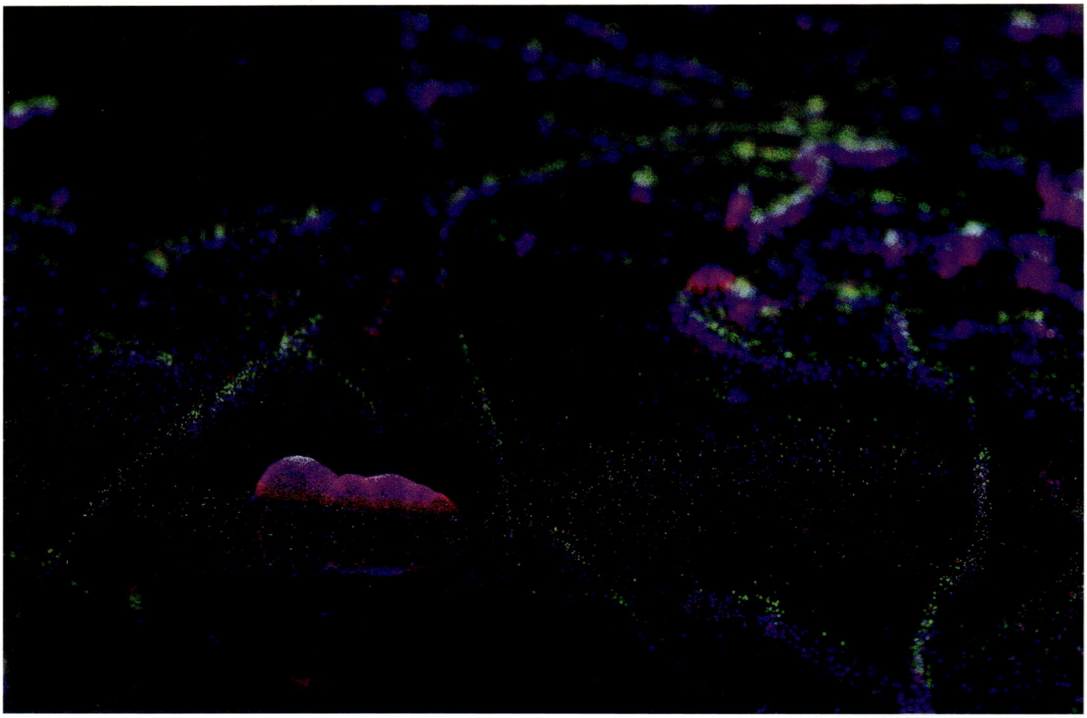

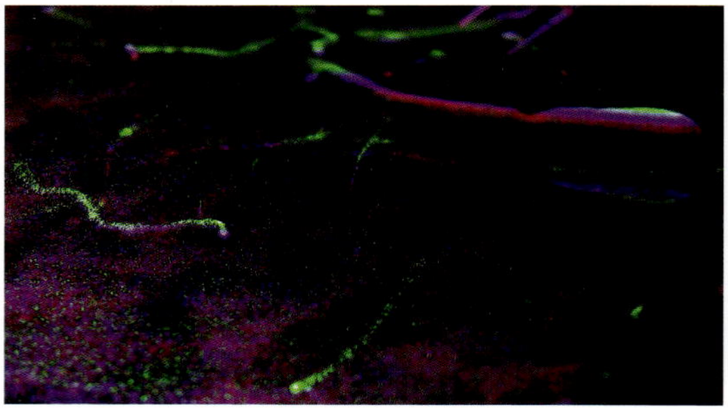

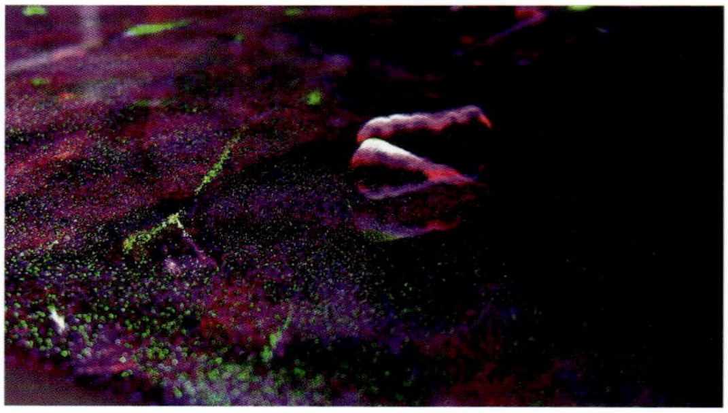

As you are reading this text your body is being penetrated by thousands of charge carriers arriving from all possible directions of outer space. Although these subatomic messengers, known as cosmic rays, are too small and too fast to be seen, they leave macroscopic condensation trails in the cryogenic environment of a cloud chamber. Though initially intended for studying the nucleation of atmospheric clouds, the cloud chamber accidentally led to the pivotal discovery of cosmic rays and to the birth of particle physics.

Während Sie diesen Text lesen, wird Ihr Körper von Tausenden Ladungsträgern durchdrungen, die aus allen Richtungen des Weltalls auf sie einprasseln. Diese gemeinhin als kosmische Strahlung bekannten subatomaren Boten sind zwar zu klein und schnell, um sie direkt sehen zu können, sie hinterlassen aber in der kalten Umgebung einer Nebelkammer makroskopische Kondensstreifen. Ursprünglich zur Untersuchung des Nukleationsprozesses von Wolken entwickelt, führte die Nebelkammer zufällig zur Entdeckung kosmischer Strahlen und zur Geburt der Teilchenphysik.

Memory Vapor besteht aus einer 1 x 1 Meter messenden Nebelkammer, auf die elektrische und magnetischer Felder einwirken, sodass sie auch zum Teilchenbeschleuniger wird. Auf dem Boden der Kammer verdampft flüssiges Ethanol zu einer dünnen Wolke, sobald die Temperatur auf -200° C fällt. Zur Kühlung werden acht Liter Flüssigstickstoff direkt unter der Kammer verwendet.
Unser künstlerischer Beitrag besteht in der Einführung einer pulsierenden weißen Laserebene, die die Spuren der ionisierten Nuklei, Myonen, Elektronen, Positronen und Antiprotonen zum Leuchten bringt. Der Laser macht jedes Mikrotröpfchen der flüchtigen Kondensstreifen zu einer lichterfüllten Linse. Das Licht ist im Tröpfchen gefangen wie der Schall im Flüstergewölbe einer Kathedrale. Mit der Häufung der Reflexionen wird das Licht verstärkt und das Tröpfchen zum Laserresonator. Das Pulsieren des Lasers bewirkt auch ein anderes Zeitgefühl: So wie ein fliegendes Geschoss mithilfe rascher Lichtblitze fotografiert werden kann, kann hier die mikrotemporale Dynamik vom bloßen Auge erfasst werden und bedarf keines Aufzeichnungsmediums. Die raumzeitliche Wahrnehmung der Teilchenspuren wird enorm gestreckt und ruft einen ungewöhnlichen Eindruck von irisierender Tiefe hervor. Nur durch solch unvermittelte und erweiterte Erfahrungen können Betrachter in eine direkte Verbindung mit der Quantenrealität treten.

Supported by Studiolab and the Amsterdam Fund for the Arts

Memory Vapor comprises a one-cubic-meter cloud chamber to which electric and magnetic fields are applied, making it also a particle accelerator. At the bottom of the chamber, once the temperature drops to -200° C liquid ethanol begins to evaporate into a thin cloud. The cooling is achieved with eight liters of liquid nitrogen placed directly below the chamber.
Our unique artistic contribution lies in the use of a pulsating white laser sheet to illuminate the tracks of ionized nuclei, muons, electrons, positrons and antiprotons. The laser turns each micro-droplet of these ephemeral condensation trails into a luminous lens. The light is trapped in the droplet just like sound is trapped in the whispering chambers of Gothic cathedrals. As reflections accumulate, the light is amplified, turning the droplet into a laser cavity. The pulsation of the laser also incites a sense of altered temporality: in the same way that a flying bullet can be photographed with rapid flashes of light, the naked eye can register such micro-temporal dynamics without any need for a recording medium. As a result, the spatio-temporal perception of particle tracks is vastly enhanced—an unusual sensation of iridescent depth emerges. The observer's instantaneous connection with quantum reality can only be truly achieved through unmediated and expanded experience.

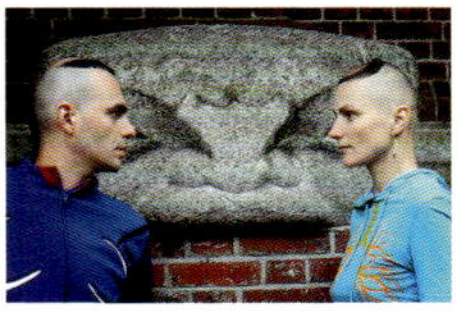

Dmitry Gelfand (RU), born 1974, and **Evelina Domnitch** (BEL), born 1972, create sensory immersion environments that merge physics, chemistry and computer science with uncanny philosophical practices. The artists employ current findings, particularly in the domain of mesoscopics, to investigate questions of perception and perpetuity. The duo have collaborated with numerous scientific research facilities, including the Drittes Physikalisches Institut (Goettingen University, Germany), the Institute of Advanced Sciences and Technologies (Japan), and the Vrije Universiteit (the Netherlands). They are recipients of the Japan Media Arts Excellence Prize (2007). Since 2009, they have been active members of Synergetica Laboratory in Amsterdam. Since 2011 they have been teaching at the ArtScience Interfaculty of the Royal Academy of Art (KABK) in the Hague, the Netherlands. **Dmitry Gelfand** (RU), geb. 1974, und **Evelina Domnitch** (BEL), geb. 1972, schaffen sinnlich-immersive Environments, in denen sie Physik, Chemie und Computerwissenschaften mit unheimlichen philosophischen Verfahren verbinden. Auf der Grundlage neuester wissenschaftlicher Erkenntnisse, vor allem im mesoskopischen Bereich, untersuchen sie Fragen der Wahrnehmung und der Stetigkeit. Das Duo hat mit zahlreichen Forschungseinrichtungen wie dem Dritten Physikalischen Institut der Universität Göttingen (DE), dem Institute of Advanced Sciences and Technologies (JP) und der Vrije Universiteit (NL) zusammengearbeitet. 2007 wurden sie mit dem Japan Media Arts Excellence Prize ausgezeichnet. Seit 2009 sind sie aktive Mitglieder des Synergetica Lab in Amsterdam und seit 2011 unterrichten sie an der ArtScience Interfakultät der königlichen Kunstakademie (KABK) in Den Haag (NL).

Microbial Schöppingen

Mick Lorusso

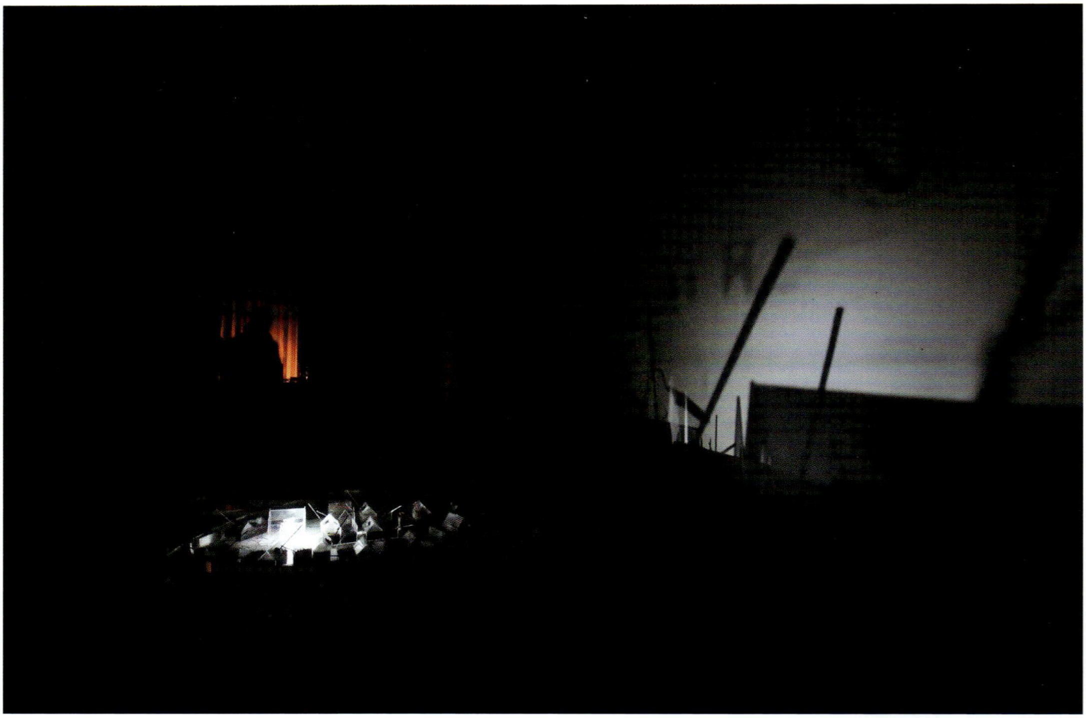

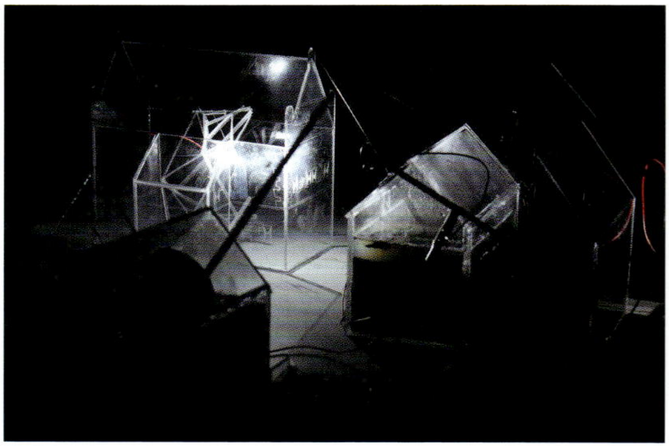

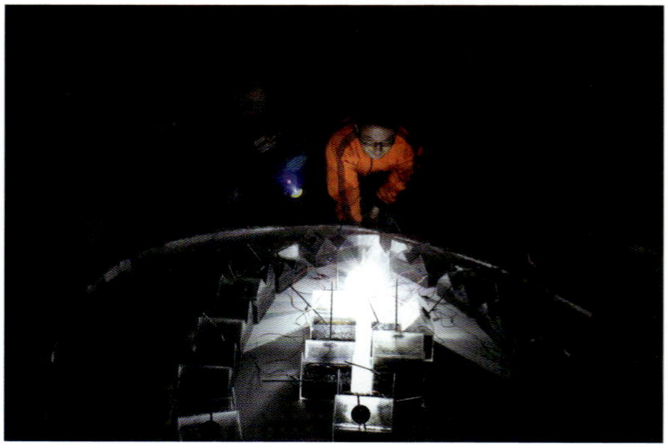

Microbial Schöppingen, a model based on an old German village, acts as a parallel town where communities of bacteria inhabit Plexiglas houses where they work together to create light. These anaerobic bacteria make an electrical current as they break down food scraps (mostly sugars and carbohydrates) into smaller molecules and ions. The technology is known as a microbial fuel cell (MFC), and in *Microbial Schöppingen* each MFC

Microbial Schöppingen ist eine nach einem historischen deutschen Dorf modellierte Parallelwelt, deren Plexiglashäuser von Bakterienkulturen bewohnt werden, die gemeinsam Licht produzieren. Die anaeroben Bakterien erzeugen beim Verstoffwechseln ihrer Nährstoffe (vorwiegend Zucker und Kohlenhydrate) Strom – mit einer Technologie, die als mikrobielle Brennstoffzelle (MBZ) bekannt ist. In *Microbial Schöppingen* besteht jede mikrobielle Brennstoffzelle aus einem anaeroben

Anodenhaus, das über eine Protonen-Austausch-Membran mit einem aeroben Kathodenhaus verbunden ist. Die Häuser sind miteinander verschaltet und betreiben eine helle weiße Leuchtdiode im Alten Rathaus. Live-Schattenspiele in dem auf die Wand geworfenen Licht rufen spielerisch die mikrobiellen Bewohner der Häuser ins Bewusstsein. Das Projekt erinnert an die Fähigkeit allen Lebens zur Nutzung und Umwandlung von Energie.
Auch wenn Bakterien meist negativ konnotiert sind, so sind sie doch größtenteils unsere engsten Verbündeten und Gefährten. *Microbial Schöppingen* ist eine Reflexion über Mikrobenverbände, die viele besondere Fähigkeiten und Gesellschaften ausgebildet haben und sogar in der Lage sind, sich mit unseren Technologien zu verbinden.
Von den Forschern am Laboratory of Microbial Ecology and Technology (LabMET) in Gent, die mir geholfen haben, die Effizienz meiner mikrobiellen Brennstoffzellen zu verbessern, habe ich viel über neue Anwendungsmöglichkeiten mikrobieller Technologien erfahren: die Herstellung biologischer Treib- und Kunststoffe, die Stromversorgung für Meeressensoren, die Abwasserreinigung bei gleichzeitiger Energiegewinnung. Orientieren wir uns an diesen älteren Arten unseres Planeten, werden wir vermutlich noch viele elegante Lösungen für den Umgang mit der ökologischen und sozialen Krise der Gegenwart finden.

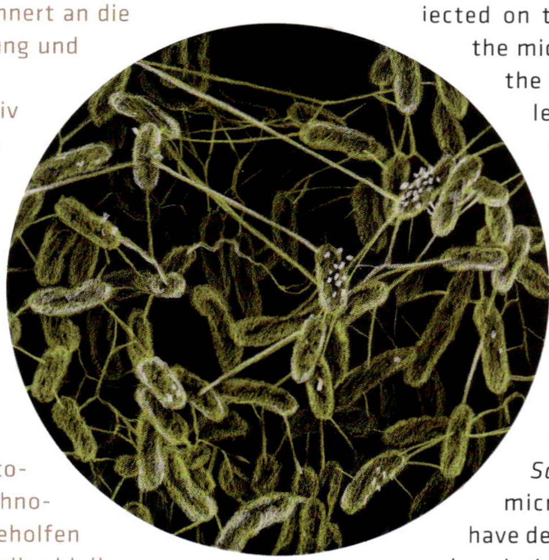

consists of an anaerobic anode house connected to an oxygenated cathode house via a proton-exchange membrane. The houses are wired together to power a bright white LED placed in the Plexiglas Altes Rathaus (Old Town Hall). Live shadow puppet performances in the light projected on the wall playfully imagine the microbial community living in the houses. On a fundamental level, *Microbial Schöppingen* reminds us of the versatility that all life has in harnessing and transforming energy.
While bacteria often have a negative connotation, in reality the majority of bacteria are our closest allies and companions. *Microbial Schöppingen* reflects on the microbial communities that have developed many special skills and societies, and can even interface with our technologies in unique ways.
The researchers at the Laboratory of Microbial Ecology and Technology (LabMET) in Gent, who helped me make these microbial fuel cells function more efficiently have introduced me to many different applications that microbial technologies can have: making biofuels and plastics, recharging offshore ocean sensors and cleaning wastewater while producing energy. If we look to these other, more ancient species on our planet for guidance we may find many beautiful suggestions of how to deal with our current ecological and social crises.

Sponsored by the Stiftung Schöppingen Künstlerdorf
Scientific advisors: LabMET

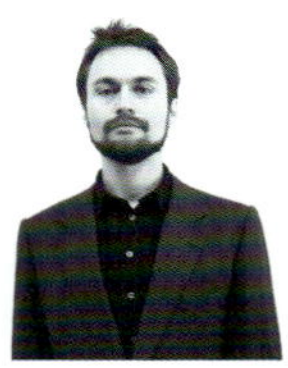

Mick Lorusso (US/MX) is an interdisciplinary artist based in Mexico City. Through sculpture, drawing, installations and interactions he re-examines energy as a mysterious force that keeps us alive, runs our technologies and interconnects the microscopic to the galactic. His current work with microbial technologies reintegrates his pre-college interest in microbiology and bioremediation, which he researched as an intern at the University of Utah. He has an MFA in sculpture from the San Francisco Art Institute and a BA from Colorado College, and has exhibited in Germany, Mexico and throughout the western states of the US.

Mick Lorusso (US/MX) ist ein interdisziplinärer Künstler mit Sitz in Mexico City. In Form von Skulpturen, Zeichnungen, Installationen und Interaktionen untersucht er Energie als geheimnisvolle Kraft, die uns am Leben erhält, unsere Technologien antreibt und das Mikroskopische mit dem Galaktischen verbindet. Seine aktuellen Arbeiten mit mikrobiellen Technologien knüpfen an sein früheres Interesse an Mikrobiologie und Bioremediation an, das er als Schülerpraktikant an der University of Utah verfolgte. Er hat einen Masterabschluss in Bildhauerei vom San Francisco Art Institute und einen Bachelor of Arts vom Colorado College. Seine Arbeiten wurden in Deutschland, Mexiko und im gesamten Westen der USA ausgestellt.

Nanohana Heels—Healing Fukushima

Sputniko!

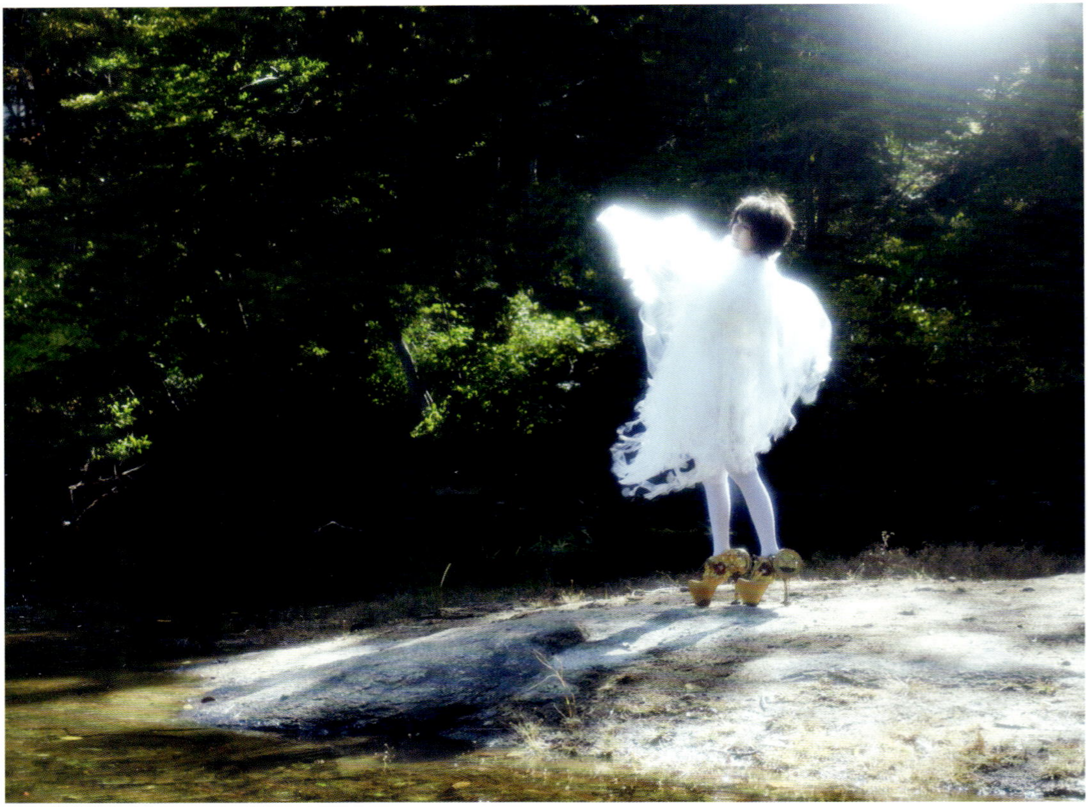

Nanohana Heels, created in collaboration with shoe designer Masaya Kushino, is a pair of shoes that plant rapeseed (Nanohana) in the soil through their mechanical heels. Using the heels, rapeseed is automatically planted as the wearer walks.

Experiments by Belarusian scientists have shown that rapeseed flowers absorb radioactive substances such as caesium-137 and strontium-90 from the soil. These radionuclides are stored in the flowers' stalks and seed coats, but not in the seeds themselves—which is fortunate, because the seeds can safely be turned into canola oil, the most popular source of biodiesel. In the 2000s this discovery led to the planting of rapeseed by the Ukraine and Belarus governments in over 50,000 hectares of Chernobyl-affected land, in a move to revive the area's agriculture industry, which had been wiped out by the 1986 nuclear accident.

Nanohana Heels, entwickelt in Zusammenarbeit mit dem Schuhdesigner Masaya Kushino, ist ein mit mechanischen Absätzen versehenes Paar Schuhe, mit dem die Trägerin beim Gehen automatisch Rapssamen *(nanohana)* aussät.

Weißrussische Wissenschaftler haben herausgefunden, dass Rapsblüten radioaktive Substanzen wie Caesium-137 und Strontium-90 aus dem Boden aufnehmen. Diese Radionuklide werden in den Stielen und Samenschalen der Pflanze abgelagert, nicht aber in den Samen selbst – sodass sich die Samen so problemlos zu Rapsöl verarbeiten lassen, dem häufigsten Ausgangsmaterial für Biodiesel. Aufgrund dieser Entdeckung ließen die Regierungen der Ukraine und Weißrusslands in den 2000er Jahren auf über 50.000 Hektar des durch den Reaktorunfall von Tschernobyl verseuchten Landes Raps anbauen, um die Landwirtschaft der Gegend wiederzubeleben.

Shoe Design: Masaya Kushino (JP), film: Visitor Studio (UK), model making: KIMURA (JP) / Naoki Kawamoto (JP); photography: Naoki Ishikaza, Takuya Shima (JP)

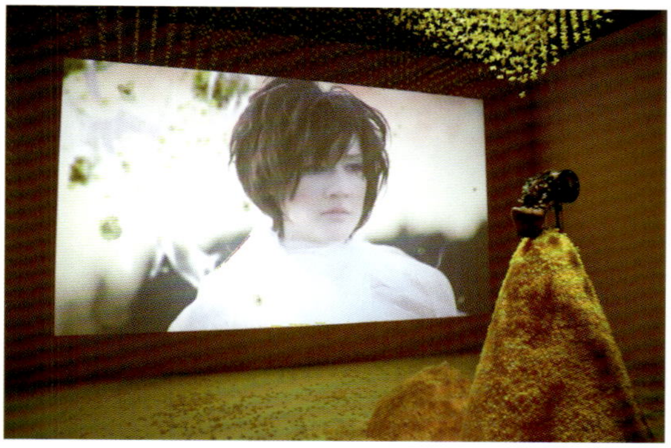

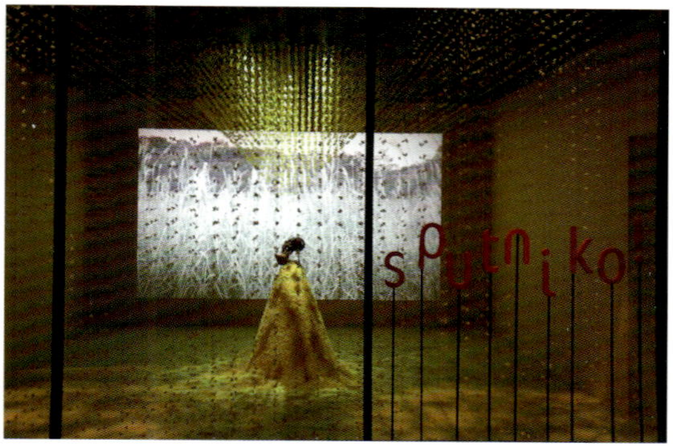

Das schwere Atomunglück, das sich im März 2011 in Fukushima, Japan, ereignete, hatte ebenfalls verheerende Auswirkungen auf das Leben der lokalen Bevölkerung. Auch in Fukushima hat es inzwischen verschiedene Bewegungen gegeben, die sich für die Anpflanzung von Raps einsetzen, um das verseuchte Land zu dekontaminieren. Eine davon ist z. B. das *Nanohana Project Network*, das Versammlungen und Workshops zum Thema abhält. Mit dem Projekt *Nanohana Heels* wollten wir dazu beitragen, der Diskussion über den Wiederaufbau von Fukushima und die Zukunft der Atomenergie breitere Aufmerksamkeit zu verschaffen.

In March 2011, Fukushima, Japan, also suffered a devastating nuclear power plant accident, which is hugely affecting the lives of many local residents today. Since the earthquake, there have also been movements to plant rapeseed in Fukushima, to de-contaminate the affected land. For example, the *Nanohana Project Network* is actively holding summits and workshops in Fukushima on the topic. The *Nanohana Heels* project has been developed in the hope of being a catalyst to further spread discussion on the rebuilding of Fukushima and on the future of nuclear energy.

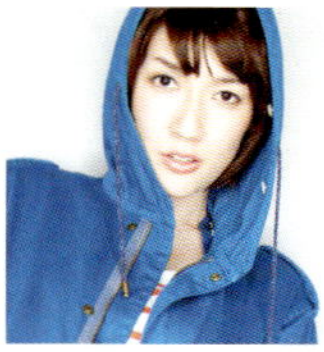

Sputniko! (JP/UK). Her multimedia artworks explore the intersections of technology, feminism and pop culture. Produced through research and investigative cooperation with scientists, her works are critical speculations on possible futures of humanity and technology. She is currently a guest professor at Kobe Design University and is the youngest advisor for the METI (Ministry of Economy Trade and Industry) *Cool Japan* project, representing the voice of young creatives in Japan. Sputniko! also advises for Recruit's Media Technology Lab and is currently directing a project commissioned by Adachi ward, which has the highest rate of poverty and crime of all 23 wards of Tokyo, aimed at reinvigorating the creative scene of the Adachi area. **Sputniko!** (JP/UK). Ihre Multimedia-Arbeiten operieren an der Schnittstelle zwischen Technologie, Feminismus und Popkultur. Auf Forschung und investigativen Kooperationen mit Wissenschaftlern beruhend, stellt sie kritische Spekulationen über die Zukunft der Menschheit und der Technik an. Sputniko! ist derzeit Gastprofessorin an der Designuniversität Kobe und die jüngste Beraterin des vom METI (Ministerium für Wirtschaft, Handel und Industrie) initiierten Projekts *Cool Japan*, einer Vertretung junger japanischer Kreativer. Sputniko! arbeitet überdies als Beraterin für das Recruit Media Technology Lab und leitet ein vom tokioter Stadtbezirk Adachi, dem Viertel mit der höchsten Armuts- und Kriminalitätsrate in der Stadt, in Auftrag gegebenes Projekt zur Stärkung der lokalen Kreativszene.

Nomadic Plants

Gilberto Esparza

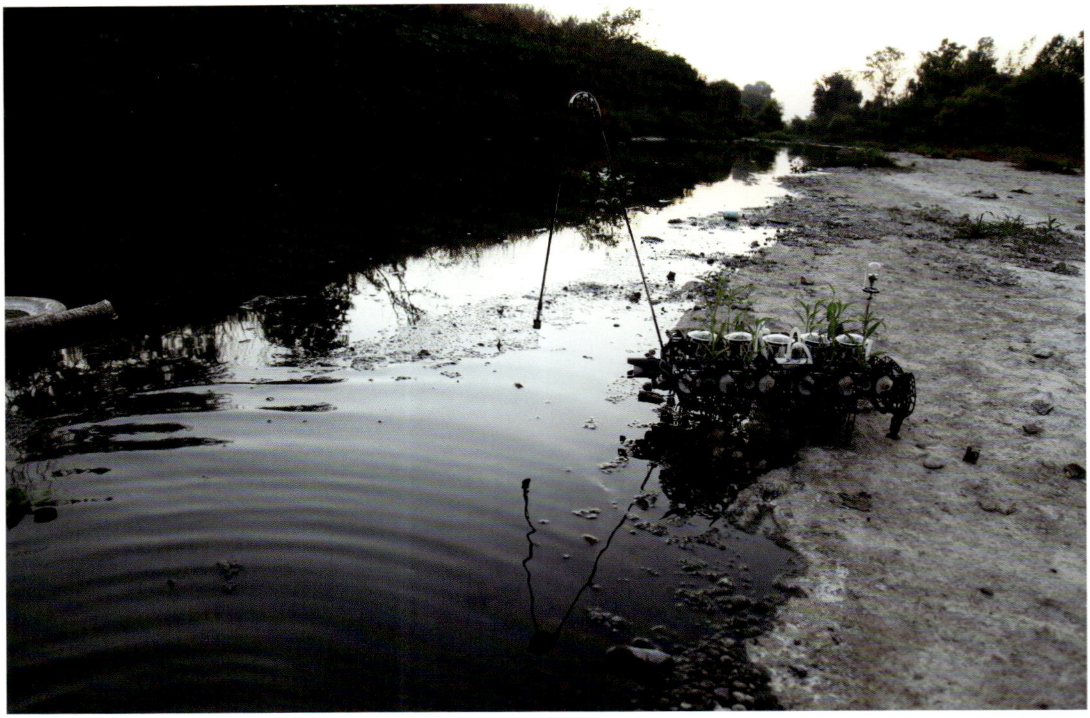

Nomadic Plants is a research project resulting from the situation of some rivers that have been contaminated by large amounts of industrial and domestic waste, which turns the water into a center of infection affecting communities and ecosystems.
The project not only highlights but also seeks to analyze how we manage the waste we generate and how we can convert it into nutrients and energy in order to improve the quality of the water in rivers. This research project takes the form of a new species that operates as an antibody to keep an ecosystem in balance. It consists of an autonomous robot that lives in symbiosis with microorganisms and native plants. This species, developed to transform waste into electricity, oxygen, clean water, nutrients and life, can survive on the banks of polluted rivers.

Nomadic Plants ist ein Forschungsprojekt, das eine Antwort auf die Situation einiger Flüsse sucht, deren durch Industrie- und Hausabfälle verseuchtes Wasser zu einem Infektionsherd für Gemeinden und Ökosysteme geworden ist.
Das Projekt weist nicht nur auf unseren Umgang mit dem von uns produzierten Abfall hin, sondern versucht auch zu analysieren, wie wir ihn in Nährstoffe und Energie umwandeln und damit die Wasserqualität unserer Flüsse verbessern können. Das Ganze geschieht in Form einer neuen, als Antikörper operierenden Spezies, die das Ökosystem im Gleichgewicht hält. Sie besteht aus einem autonomen, in Symbiose mit Mikroorganismen und einheimischen Pflanzenarten lebenden Roboter. Ausgestattet mit der Fähigkeit, Abfälle in Strom, Sauerstoff, sauberes Wasser, Nährstoffe und Leben umzuwandeln, ist sie imstande, in den Uferzonen verschmutzter Flüsse zu überleben.

Supported by Second prize, Vida 13.0 de Fundación Telefonica, Fundación/Colección Jumex; Fundación Bancomer; Universidad de Guanajuato Campus Irapuato – Salamanca; support Program Production and Research in Art and Media 2009, Centro Multimedia, Centro Nacional de las Artes; Fondo Nacional para la Cultura y las Artes; LABoral, Centro de arte y creación industrial; Centro Párrag; Laboratorio de Arte Alameda

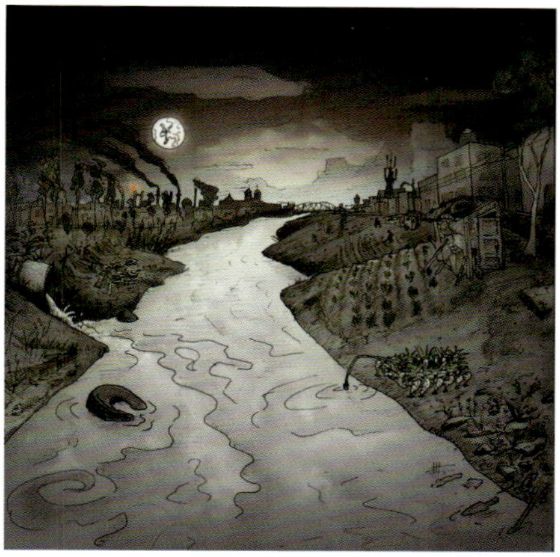

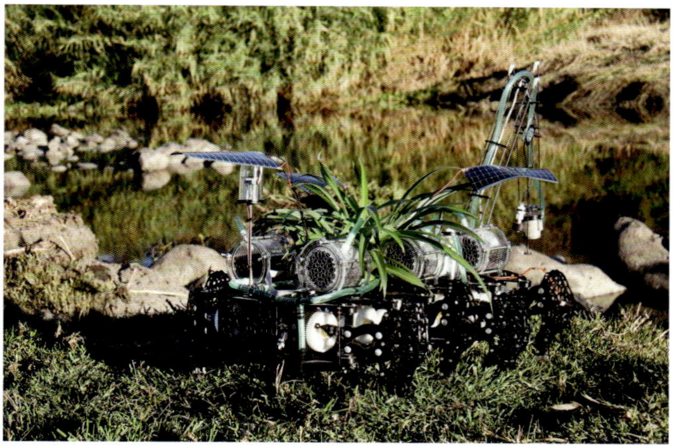

Der Stoffkreislauf der nomadischen Fabrik beginnt mit der Suche nach verschmutztem Wasser. Sie saugt es auf und befördert es zu einer Batterie mikrobieller Brennstoffzellen. Diese beschleunigen den biologischen Zersetzungsprozess, um sauberes Wasser für die Feuchtbiotope zu gewinnen, in denen Pflanzen und Bakterien wachsen, die das elektronische System mit Strom versorgen. Dieser Kreislauf kontrolliert das Ökosystem und hält es im Gleichgewicht. Dazu kommt eine Gruppe von Photovoltaikzellen, die den Fortbewegungsapparat des Roboters speist. Sobald er genug Energie getankt hat, erwacht er und macht sich auf Nahrungssuche. Ist das Wasser stärker verschmutzt, gibt er Laute von sich.

The metabolic cycle of the *Nomadic Plant* starts when it finds contaminated water. It sucks up the liquid and carries it to a set of microbial fuel cells. These cells accelerate the biodegradation processes to clean the water that feeds the wetlands, where plants grow along with bacteria, providing power to the electronic system. The circuits monitor and keep the ecosystem in balance, while another group of photovoltaic cells feed the robot's locomotion system. Once it has accumulated enough energy, the body wakes up and sets off in search of food. When pollution levels in the water are higher, the *Nomadic Plant* expresses itself through sound.

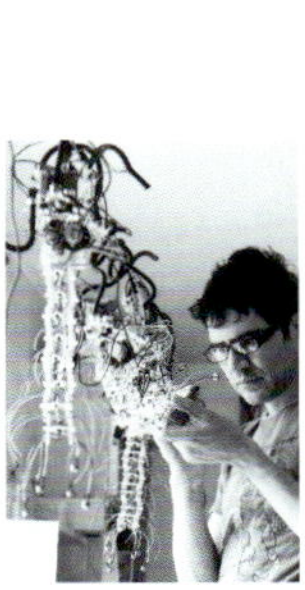

Gilberto Esparza (MEX), born 1975, has a BFA from the University of Guanajuato and an MFA from the Polytechnic University of Valencia, Spain. He has been artist in residence in the New Media Research Center in Mexico City and the Noordkaap project space in of Dordrecht, the Netherlands. His work is an inquiry into the effects of technology on social relations and economic phenomena as well as their impact on the environment and the urban structure. It is linked to an ongoing research process into alternative types of energy. His practice employs recycling consumer technology on a path between the analog and the digital.

Gilberto Esparza (MEX), geb. 1975, studierte Kunst an der Universidad de Guanajuato (BFA) und an der Universidad Politècnica de Valencia (MFA). Er war Artist-in-Residence am Centro Mulitmedia in Mexico City und am Noordkaap Projectspace in Dordrecht. In seinen Arbeiten beschäftigt er sich mit den Auswirkungen der Technologie auf soziale und wirtschaftliche Verhältnisse sowie ihren Folgen für die natürliche und urbane Umwelt. Damit verbunden ist auch eine ständige Erkundung alternativer Energieformen. In seinen Arbeiten recycelt er häufig Konsumtechnologie im Zwischenbereich zwischen analog und digital.

N_Polytope: Behaviors in Light and Sound after Iannis Xenakis

Chris Salter (in collaboration with Sofian Audry, Marije Baalman, Adam Basanta, Elio Bidinost and Thomas Spier)

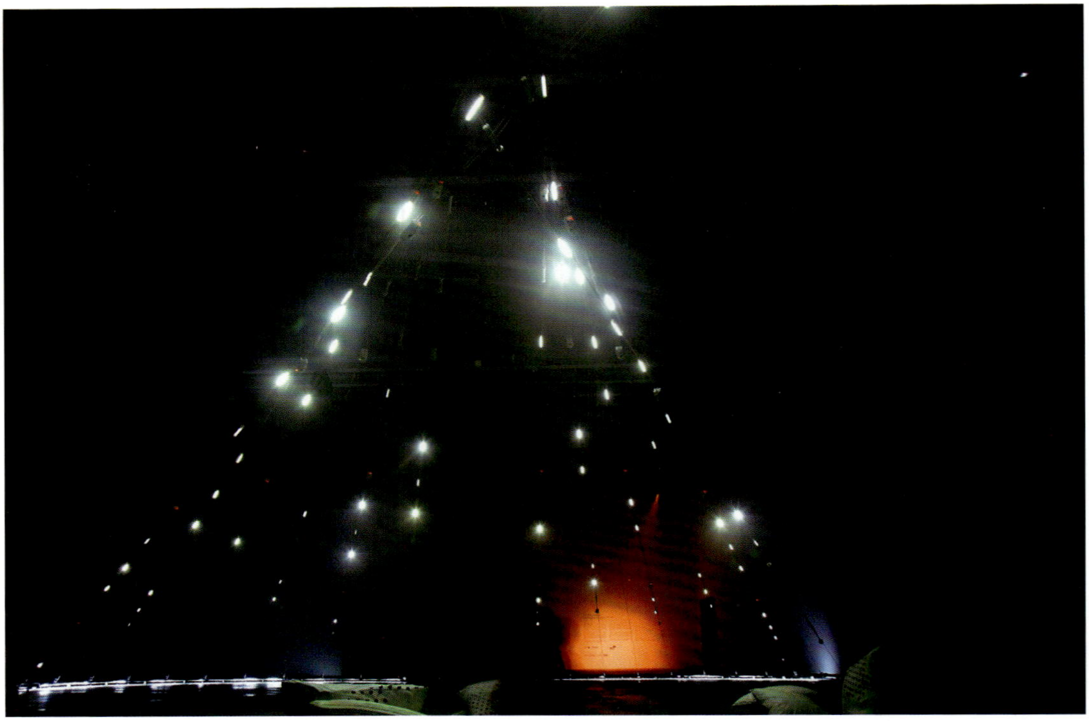

N_Polytope: Behaviors in Light and Sound after Iannis Xenakis is a spectacular light and sound performance installation combining LED lighting, lasers, sound, wireless sensors and machine-learning software, inspired by composer Iannis Xenakis' radical 1960s-1970s works called *Polytopes* (from the Greek *poly*, many and *topos*, space). *N_Polytope* both re-imagines Xenakis' research into probabilistic/stochastic systems with new techniques and explores how these techniques also exemplify our own historical moment of extreme instability. The work runs both as a 15-minute performance and in a continuously evolving installation mode.
The system interacts with itself, steered through a custom-developed wireless sensor network with software-utilizing machine-learning techniques, specifically from the research area of reinforcement learning in which software learning agents interact with their environment in order to achieve a goal. Physically, 150 ten-watt LEDs and 50 tiny speakers are suspended on 24, 20+ m stretched aircraft cables, which form a ruled surface. While the behavior of the LEDs creates a changing space of bursting points, the colored lasers that bounce off

N_Polytope: Behaviors in Light and Sound after Iannis Xenakis ist eine von Jannis Xenakis' radikalen *Polytope*-Kompositionen aus den 1960er und 1970er Jahren inspirierte spektakuläre Licht- und Klangperformance bzw. -installation, die mit einer Kombination aus LED-Leuchten, Lasern, Ton, drahtlosen Sensoren und maschineller Lernsoftware arbeitet. *N_Polytope* re-imaginiert Xenakis' Untersuchungen probabilistischer/stochastischer Systeme mit neuen Techniken und ergründet zugleich, inwiefern diese Techniken für unsere eigene extrem instabile historische Epoche stehen. Das Stück kann sowohl als 15-minütige Performance als auch als sich kontinuierlich entwickelnde Installation laufen.
Gesteuert durch ein speziell für den Zweck entwickeltes drahtloses Sensornetzwerk mit Software-gestützten maschinellen Lerntechniken, interagiert das System mit sich selbst. Das Lernsystem stammt aus dem Bereich des verstärkenden Lernens, bei dem Software-Lernagenten mit ihrer Umwelt interagieren, um ein bestimmtes Ziel zu erreichen. Im physischen Raum sind 150 Zehn-Watt-LEDs und 50 Minilautsprecher über 24 gespannte, eine Regelfläche bildende Flugzeugseile von 20+ Meter Länge verteilt. Während die LEDs einen sich ständig verändernden Raum aufblitzender Punkte schaffen, erzeugen die

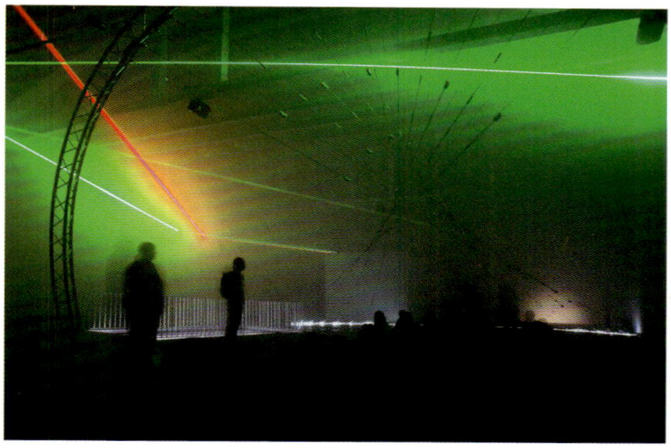

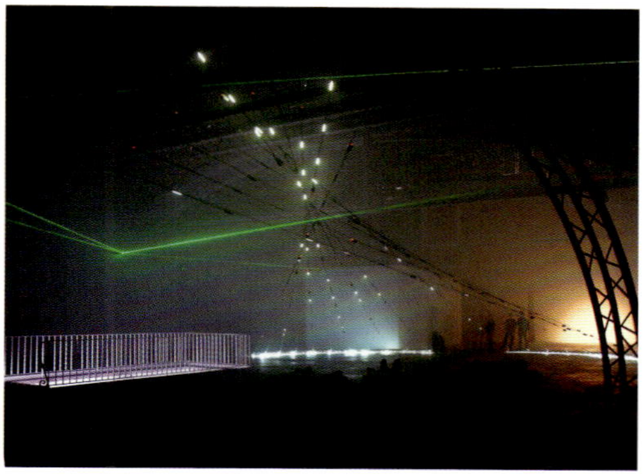

von festen und beweglichen Spiegeln reflektierten farbigen Laser flüchtige Architekturen aus Linien und Formen. Der mehrkanalige Ton aus den Minilautsprechern und der weiteren Umgebung, der einen Kontrapunkt zur Szenografie bildet, wechselt zwischen kargen Natursounds und dichten elektronischen Texturen. In ihrer Verteilung über das Gerüst aus Seilen verhält sich das Netzwerk der Lautsprecher-Winzlinge wie aus vielen kleinen Elementen (Grains) zusammengesetzte Klanggebilde; es erzeugt Schwärme von kleinen Soundpartikeln, die einem Feld voller Zikaden oder einer Anhäufung von Insekten gleichen – und damit auch mit der stochastischen Bewegung von Massenstrukturen verwandt sind, für die sich Xenakis interessierte. *N_Polytope* entfaltet sich als ein teils vorherbestimmtes, teils unvorhersehbares Ereignis, das ständig zwischen Ordnung und Unordnung, Ausgeglichenheit und Chaos changiert.

the surface of fixed and changing mirrors generate fleeting architectures of lines and shapes. Counterpointing the visual scenography, multichannel audio from the small speakers as well as the larger environment shifts between sparse natural and dense electronic textures. Across the architectural cable structure, the network of tiny speakers produces the behavior of mass sonic structures made up of many small elements (sonic grains) creating swarms of tiny sounds that resemble a field of cicadas or masses of insects–akin to Xenakis' interest in the stochastic movement of mass structures. Thus the overall course of *N_Polytope* is that of an event that is partially scripted and partially indeterminate, thus enabling the performance to continually move between order and disorder, tranquility and chaos.

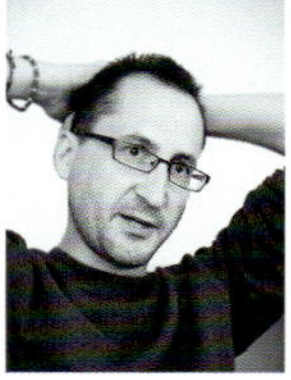

Chris Salter (US/CA) is an artist, the Director of Hexagram-Concordia Centre for Research-Creation in Media Arts and Technology and the Associate Professor for Design and Computation Arts. Salter studied economics and philosophy at Emory University and received his PhD in the area of theater, with a second concentration from Stanford University in computer-generated sound. After collaborating with Peter Sellars and William Forsythe / Ballett Frankfurt, he co-founded and directed the art and research organization Sponge (1997–2003). His solo and collaborative work has been seen at major international exhibitions and festivals in over a dozen countries. He is the author of *Entangled: Technology and the Transformation of Performance* (MIT Press, 2010). **Chris Salter** (US/CA) ist Künstler, Leiter des Hexagram-Concordia Centre for Research-Creation in Media Arts and Technology und Associate Professor für Design und Computerkunst. Er studierte Ökonomie und Philosophie an der Emory University und promovierte in Theaterwissenschaften. Ein zweiter Studienschwerpunkt war computergenerierte Musik an der Standford Universität. Nach Mitarbeit bei Peter Sellars und William Forsythe / Ballett Frankfurt gründete er zusammen mit anderen die Kunst- und Forschungsorganisation Sponge (1997 – 2003), die er auch leitete. Seine Einzelarbeiten und Kooperationen waren auf wichtigen internationalen Ausstellungen und Festivals in über einem Dutzend Ländern zu sehen. Salter ist Autor von *Entangled: Technology and the Transformation of Performance* (MIT Press, 2010).

Pancreas

Thomas Feuerstein

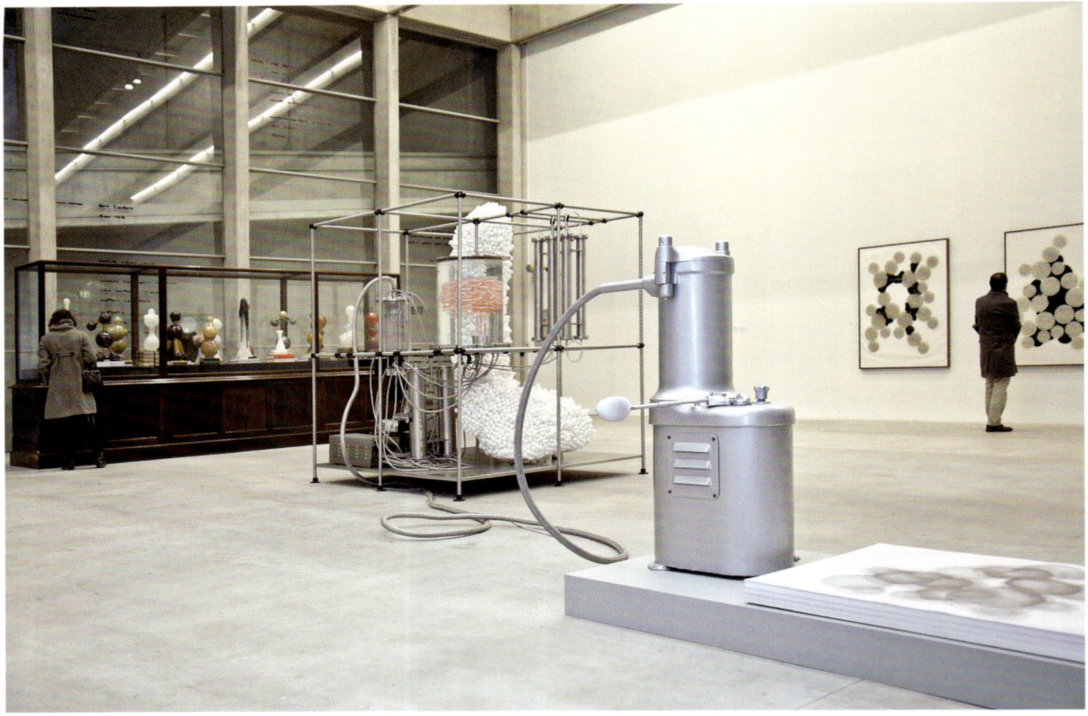

The processual sculpture *Pancreas* transforms books into sugar (glucose) that feeds human brain cells. The books' paper is shredded, soaked in water, and pressed into an artificial intestine (a fermenter) in which bacteria break the cellulose down into glucose. After filtering and purifying, the glucose is fed to the cells growing inside a glass tank (a brain in a vat). The feeding of the artificial brain follows a strict diet: the brain food consists exclusively of Hegel's *Phenomenology of Spirit*.

Die prozessuale Skulptur *Pancreas* verwandelt Bücher in Zucker (Glukose), der wiederum als Nahrung für menschliche Gehirnzellen dient. Das Papier der Bücher wird geschreddert, in Wasser eingeweicht und in einen künstlichen Darm (Biofermenter) gepresst, wo Bakterien die Zellulose zu Glukose zerlegen. Nach ihrer Filterung und Reinigung wird die Glukose an die in einem Glasbehälter wachsenden Gehirnzellen verfüttert. Dabei ist das künstliche Gehirn auf eine strenge Diät gesetzt: Seine Nahrung besteht ausschließlich aus Hegels *Phänomenologie des Geistes*.

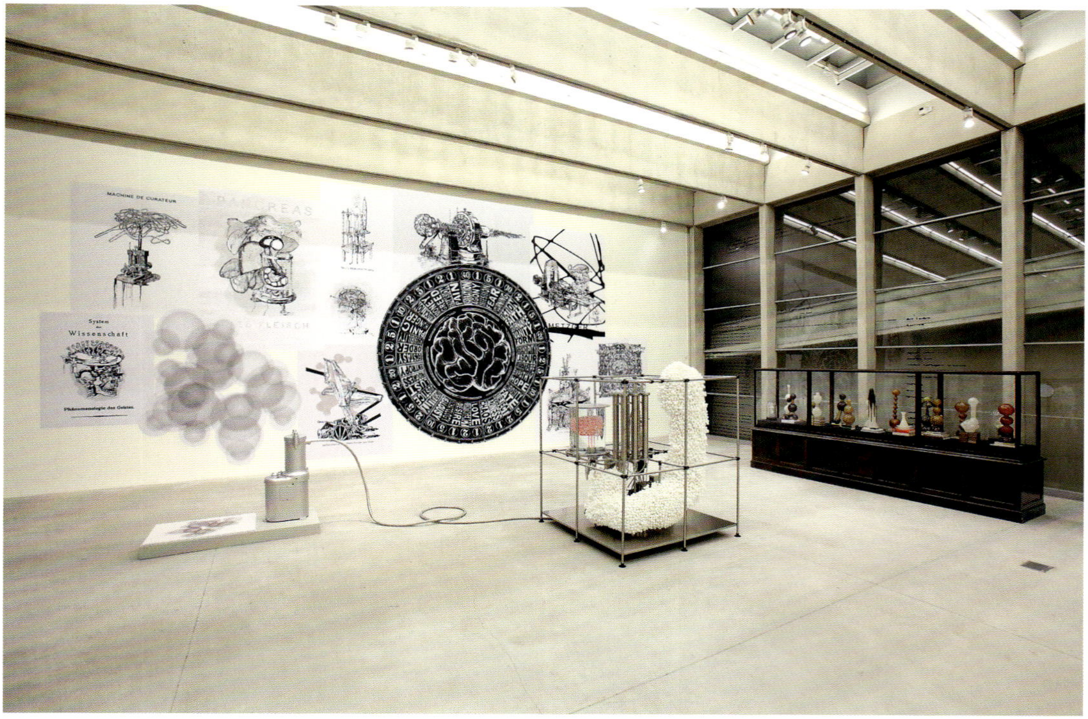

Pancreas ist eine pataphysische Maschine, die mithilfe von Biotechnologien Literatur und Bücher, also Symbole und Daten, in Materie und Fleisch übersetzt. Glukose, ein universaler Treibstoff allen Lebens, von dem sich sämtliche Zellen, insbesondere aber Gehirnzellen, ernähren, wird hier zum künstlerischen Material für eine Skulptur (griech. *pánkreas*, *pán* = „alles", *kréas* = „Fleisch").

Pancreas is a pataphysical machine that uses biotechnologies in order to translate language and books, that is symbols and data, into matter and flesh. Glucose, as a universal fuel of life, which all cells, especially brain cells, feed on, becomes the artistic material for *Pancreas* (Gr. *pánkreas*, *pán* = all, *kréas* = flesh).

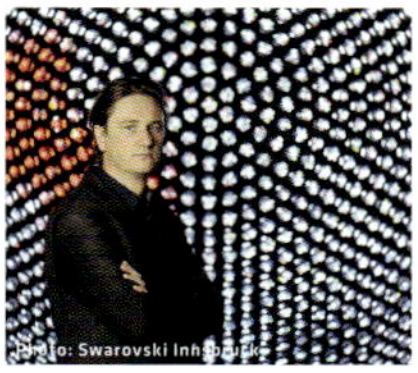

Thomas Feuerstein (AT) was born in 1968. From 1987 to 1995 he studied art history and philosophy at the University of Innsbruck. From 1992 to 1994 he and Klaus Strickner co-edited the magazine *Medien.Kunst.Passagen.* In 1992 he founded the office for intermedia communication transfer and medien.kunst.tirol art association. Since 1997 he has been a lecturer and visiting professor at the University of Applied Arts Vienna, Bern University of the Arts, the F+F School for Art and Media Design Zurich, the University of Applied Sciences Vorarlberg–InterMedia Studies, the Mozarteum University Salzburg and the University of Innsbruck. **Thomas Feuerstein** (AT), geb. 1968, studierte von 1987 bis 1995 Kunstgeschichte und Philosophie an der Universität Innsbruck. Von 1992 bis 1994 gab er gemeinsam mit Klaus Strickner die Zeitschrift *Medien.Kunst.Passagen* heraus. 1992 gründete er das Büro für intermedialen Kommunikationstransfer und den Kunstverein medien.kunst.tirol. Seit 1997 Lehraufträge und Gastprofessuren an der Universität für angewandte Kunst Wien, der Hochschule der Künste Bern, der F+F Schule für Kunst und Mediendesign Zürich, der Fachhochschule Vorarlberg Studiengang Intermedia, dem Mozarteum Salzburg und der Universität Innsbruck.

Suspect Inversion Center

Paul Vanouse

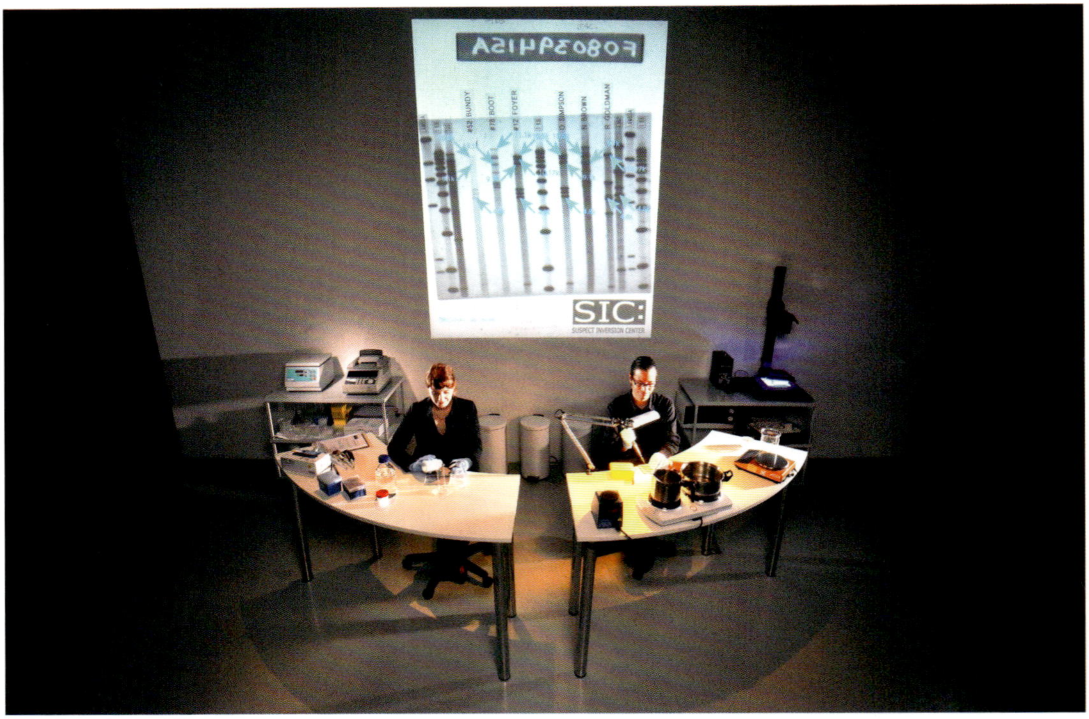

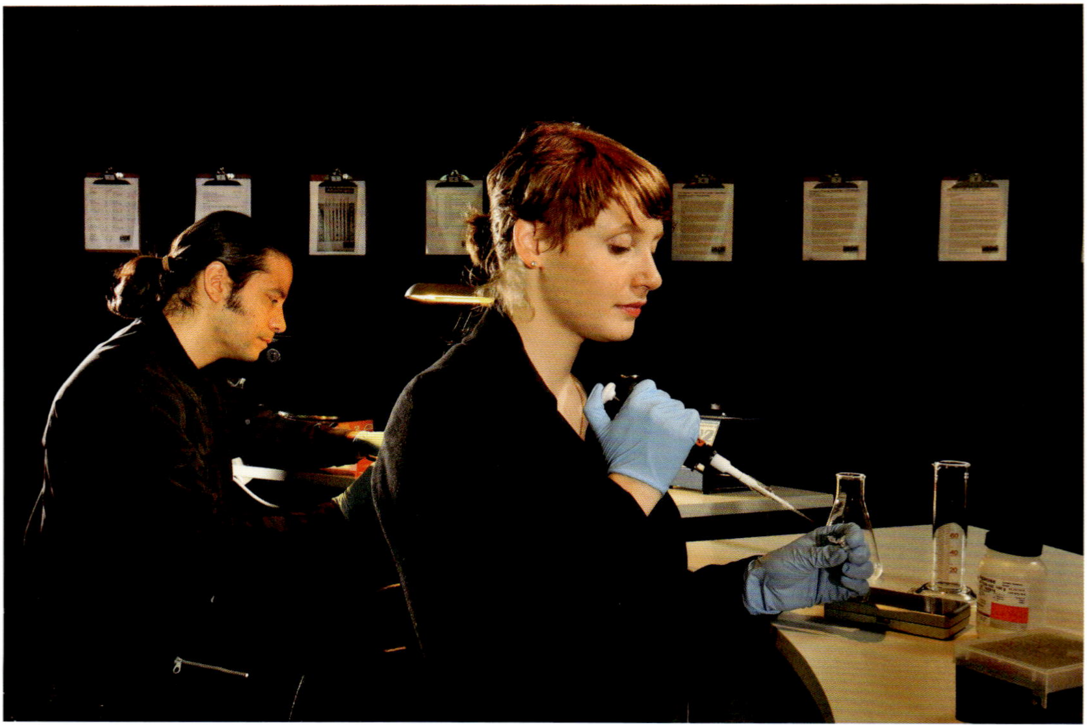

Das *Suspect Inversion Center* (SIC) ist ein offenes Arbeitslabor, in dem der Künstler Paul Vanouse und seine Assistentin Kerry Sheehan DNA-Beweismaterial vom Mordprozess gegen O.J. Simpson aus dem Jahr 1995 nachbilden – und zwar aus der DNA des Künstlers. Die Installation besteht aus zwei halbkreisförmig angeordneten Labortischen und Regalen mit allen notwendigen Utensilien für die Tätigkeit des *Suspect Inversion Center*. Vanouse und Sheehan gehen während der gesamten Galerieöffnungszeiten unter den Augen des Publikums ihrer Arbeit nach. Ist diese abgeschlossen und das Bild der Original-DNA einigermaßen genau rekonstruiert, werden die nachgebaute Kopie und das Original nebeneinander ausgestellt, zusammen mit den chemischen „Rezepten" zur Erzeugung dieser Bilder. Das SIC lädt das Publikum ein, sämtliche Schritte der Laborarbeit mitzuverfolgen und mit den Experimentatoren zu interagieren. „Nach über zwei Jahren Arbeit an der Reproduktion dieses Bildes hat sich nun im März 2013 ein erster Erfolg eingestellt. Wir wollen weitere Reproduktionen mit anderen Bildgebungsverfahren herstellen und noch bessere Ergebnisse erzielen, die wir dann auf der Website veröffentlichen."

Mit dem *Suspect Inversion Center* verleiht Vanouse seiner DNA nicht nur das Aussehen der ursprünglichen DNA des mutmaßlichen Täters, sondern bildet mit ihr das gesamte historische DNA-Dokument nach, wobei er jede Komponente des offiziellen DNA-Artefakts einer genauen Prüfung unterzieht. Die Geschichte der Kunst ist voll von solchen bewussten Reproduktionen: von Kopien alter Meister zu Studienzwecken, über Kunstfälschungen bis zu den Appropriationen der Pop Art und der Postmoderne, die natürlich alle ganz anders konnotiert sind und sich ganz unterschiedlich auf das „Original" auswirken.

Supported by Ernst Schering Foundation and Beall Center, UC Irvine

Suspect Inversion Center (SIC) is an open working laboratory where artist Paul Vanouse and assistant Kerry Sheehan recreate DNA evidence from the 1995 OJ Simpson murder trial: using the artist's own DNA. The installation consists of semicircular lab tables and shelves containing all the necessary equipment to perform the activities of the Suspect Inversion Center. Vanouse and Sheehan continuously perform the work, during daily gallery operations, witnessed by visitors to the exhibition. When the work is complete and the original DNA image has been reasonably accurately reproduced, the "reverse-engineered" copy and the original are displayed side by side, along with the full chemical "recipes" used to create the images. SIC invites the audience to observe each step of the laboratory process and interact with the experimenters. "After more than two years of working to reproduce this image the first success took place in March 2013. We will be continuing this month to make additional reproductions with alternate imaging technologies, with the aim of improving even further—I will be posting these on the website."

In *Suspect Inversion Center*, Vanouse is not simply making his DNA look like the original suspect DNA, but using his own DNA to recreate an entire historical DNA document by scrutinizing every component of the authoritative DNA artifact. The history of art is replete with such intentional reproduction: from students' copying a master's painting, to art forgeries, to pop and postmodern appropriation, but of course each has radically different connotations and affects upon the "original".

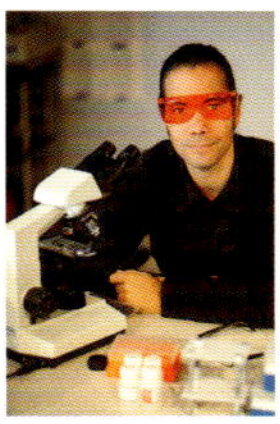

Paul Vanouse (US) has been working in emerging media forms since 1990. Interdisciplinarity and impassioned amateurism guide his art practice. His electronic cinema, biological experiments and interactive installations have been exhibited in over 20 countries. For the past decade, Vanouse has been engaged with forcing the arcane codes of scientific communication into a broader cultural language. Vanouse is a professor of visual studies at the University at Buffalo, NY. He holds a BFA from the University at Buffalo (1990) and an MFA from Carnegie Mellon University (1996). **Paul Vanouse** (US) arbeitet seit 1990 mit neu entstehenden Medien, wobei sein künstlerisches Schaffen von Interdisziplinarität und leidenschaftlichem Dilettantentum gekennzeichnet sind. Sein elektronisches Kino, seine biologischen Experimente und seine interaktiven Installationen sind in über 20 Ländern ausgestellt worden. Im letzten Jahrzehnt hat er hauptsächlich daran gearbeitet, die arkanen Codes wissenschaftlicher Kommunikation in eine allgemein verständliche kulturelle Sprache zu übersetzen. Vanouse ist Professor für Visual Studies an der University at Buffalo, NY. Er studierte Kunst an der University at Buffalo (BFA, 1990) und an der Carnegie Mellon University (MFA, 1996).

The Blind Robot

Louis-Philippe Demers

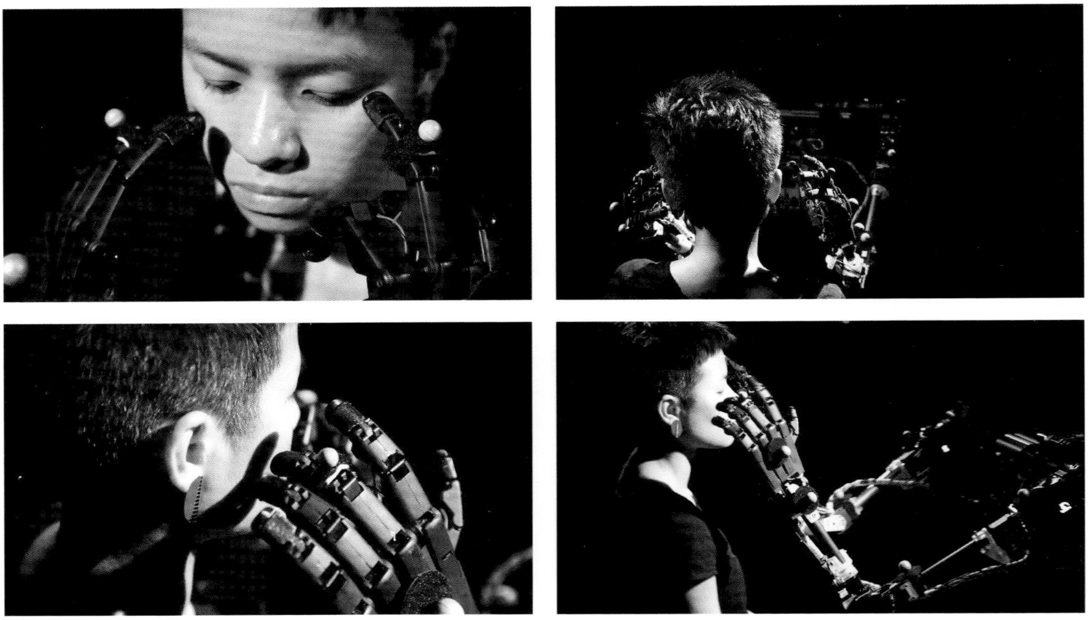

With *The Blind Robot*, the aim is to further understand the degrees of engagement, whether intellectual, emotional or physical, that are generated when a social robot intimately touches a person. Initially, *The Blind Robot* is a minimalistic piece of mechanical engineering. The rationale is to start from a recent known cultural artifact—the robot arm—and transform it from a high precision tool into a fragile, imprecise and emotionally loaded agent.

The Blind Robot dient dazu, ein besseres Verständnis der intellektuellen, emotionalen und/oder körperlichen Beteiligung zu gewinnen, die im Spiel ist, wenn ein soziales Roboter eine Person auf intime Weise berührt. *The Blind Robot* ist zunächst ein minimalistisches Stück mechatronischer Ingenieurskunst. Es geht darum, ein erst seit Kurzem bekanntes kulturelles Artefakt – den Roboterarm – von einem kalten Präzisionsinstrument in einen zarten, vagen, gefühlsbesetzten Akteur zu verwandeln.

Mechatronics: Dennis Low; programming: Vineet Kuruvila. Support: Start Up Grant and MOE Tier1 Grant (Nanyang Technological University)

The Blind Robot ist ein typischer Roboterarm mit einer fein gegliederten Hand. In der Installation sollen Besucher vor dieser Maschine Platz nehmen und mit ihr in einen nonverbalen Dialog eintreten. Der Roboter tastet sorgfältig den Körper des Besuchers – vor allem Gesicht und Oberkörper – ab, nicht unähnlich einem Blinden, der auf diese Weise versucht, eine Person oder einen Gegenstand zu erkennen. Anschließend produziert die Maschine auf einem Monitor oder einer Projektionsfläche eine visuelle Darstellung dessen, was ihre Finger „gesehen" haben.

The Blind Robot bezieht sich direkt auf die Arbeiten Merleau-Pontys und sein Beispiel des den Körper erweiternden Blindenstocks. Feenberg kommt in seiner Analyse von Merleau-Pontys Blindenstock zu dem Schluss, dass dieser nicht nur dazu dient, die Welt zu begreifen, sondern den Blinden auch als Blinden enthüllt. Genau diesen Aspekt macht sich *The Blind Robot* zunutze: Er versucht, eine emphatische Situation und eine Neigung zur Anteilnahme herzustellen.

Überdies spielt der blinde Roboter auch auf den Schachtürken *(Mechanical Turk)* an. Er strahlt Intentionalität aus und wird zu einem Turing-Test von Handlungsmacht und künstlichem Leben. Der Roboter hat die komplexe Aufgabe, Menschen zärtlich zu berühren, wozu derzeit kaum ein Roboter in der Lage ist. Wir haben unsere Hypothese kürzlich durch Tests an über 100 Personen verifizieren können. Die fiktive soziale Rolle (des Blinden) verstärkt den Akt des Berührens und den Akteurcharakter des Roboters durch die entstehende emotionale Verbindung zwischen Mensch und Roboter.

The Blind Robot comprises a typical robotic arm equipped with an articulated hand. In this installation, visitors are invited to sit in the front of this machine and engage into a non-verbal dialogue with it. The robot delicately explores the body—mostly the face and upper body—of the visitor in a manner that recalls what blind people do to recognize a person or an object. On a nearby screen or projection the machine then produces a visual rendering of what its fingertips have "seen."

The Blind Robot is a direct reference to the works of Merleau-Ponty and his example of the body extension of the blind man's cane. When Feenberg analyzes Merleau-Ponty's blind man's cane, he concludes that the cane does more than sense the world; it also reveals the blind man as blind. It is this very aspect that the *Blind Robot* exploits: to create an empathic situation and a positive predisposition to the engagement.

Furthermore, *The Blind Robot* is a direct allusion the chess-playing "Mechanical Turk". *The Blind Robot* emanates a sense of intentionality and it becomes a Turing test of agency and perceived artificial life. *The Blind Robot* has the complex task of touching people softly, something achieved by hardly any contemporary robots. We recently verified this hypothesis by testing the robot with more than 100 people. The fictitious social role (a blind person) augments the act of touching and the robot's agency via the potential of the created emotional connection between the human visitor and the robot.

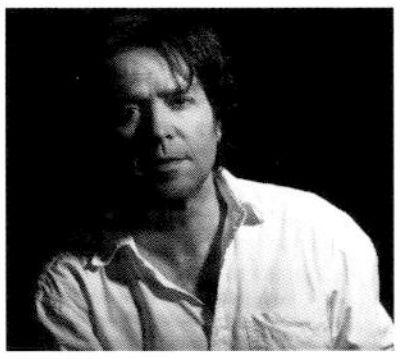

Louis-Philippe Demers (CA/SG) makes large-scale installations and performances. His main areas of work are entertainment robotics and interaction design. Over the past two decades, he has participated in more than 70 artistic and stage productions and has built more than 300 machines. His projects can be found in theater, opera, subway stations, art museums, science museums, music events and trade shows. Demers' works have been featured at major venues worldwide. He was Professor of Digital Media and Exhibit Design/Scenography at the Karlsruhe University of Arts and Design. Since then he has joined the Interaction and Entertainment Research Center and the recently founded School of Art, Design and Media at Nanyang Technological University (Singapore). **Louis-Philippe Demers** (CA/SG) macht groß angelegte Installationen und Performances. Seine Arbeitsschwerpunkte sind Unterhaltungsrobotik und Interaktionsdesign. Im Lauf der letzten 20 Jahre hat er an über 70 Kunst- und Bühnenwerken mitgewirkt und über 300 Maschinen gebaut. Seine Projekte und Werke sind in Theatern, Opernhäusern, U-Bahnstationen, Kunstmuseen, Technikmuseen, Musikveranstaltungen und Handelsmessen zu finden und waren an führenden Veranstaltungsorten in der ganzen Welt zu sehen. Er war Professor für Digitale Medien und Ausstellungsdesign/Szenografie an der Hochschule für Gestaltung in Karlsruhe. Mittlerweile arbeitet er am Interaction and Entertainment Research Centre und lehrt an der neu gegründeten School of Art, Design and Media an der Nanyang Technological University in Singapur.

INTERACTIVE ART

Interrogating Interaction

José Luis de Vicente, Mariano Sardón, Olga Shishko, Jer Thorp, Maholo Uchida

Every year the more than 500 projects submitted to the Interactive Art category in the Prix Ars Electronica bring with them the opportunity and the obligation to question what this artistic space might mean today. How should the category be defined if it is to remain a useful concept? To what extent can the set of criteria laboriously developed throughout the many years of previous Golden Nicas, Distinctions and Mentions still be applied in a productive manner (and if it deserves to be preserved)?

Some things we know for sure. Interactivity should no longer be defined by a specific formal language prescribed by the vocabulary of the 1990s. Today, most of all, it is a set of strategies that can be situated in multiple contexts, within the art world and outside of it. A testament to this is the diversity in the origins of the projects submitted, which forces us to make choices among items as fundamentally different as an emerging technology demo, an innovative product, a social-activism intervention and a carefully thought out artwork. This remains a sign of the category's identity, and it is always the starting point of long, engaging conversations inside the room at the Ars Electronica Center that becomes our home for three long days.

It is always a risky exercise to make bold, ambitious claims about the state of the discipline using submitted projects as evidence. But it is impossible not to draw conclusions when going through this vast number of references. Besides, there is probably no better annual survey than this one anyway.

With this in mind, we are quite certain that 2013 was not a paradigm-shifting year; the best projects were developed by names with a considerable previous body of work, continuing their personal trajectories and paths of research. It seems no coincidence that some of the biggest names in the field or figures of undeniable historical importance are among the awards.

An ongoing theme seemed to be the dialog with the arts, a growing engagement with different traditions and practices beyond the limits of what we call new media art. We found less explicitly political projects than in previous years and more well-rounded, exquisitely finished projects that can exist successfully in a gallery setting.

Über 500 eingereichte Projekte in der Kategorie Interactive Art bringen jedes Jahr aufs Neue die Gelegenheit und Verpflichtung mit sich, nach der jeweiligen Bedeutung dieses künstlerischen Raums zu fragen: Wie ist die Kategorie zu definieren, wenn sie weiter brauchbar und sinnvoll sein soll? Und in welchem Maß sind die Kriterien, die im Lauf der Jahre anhand früherer Goldener Nicas, Auszeichnungen und Anerkennungen herausgearbeitet wurden, immer noch produktiv verwendbar (und verdienen sie es, überhaupt beibehalten zu werden)?

Ein paar Dinge stehen immerhin fest. Interaktivität ist nicht mehr durch eine bestimmte formale Sprache definierbar, deren Vokabular in den 1990er Jahren festgelegt wurde. Sie besteht heute in erster Linie aus einer Reihe von Strategien, die in verschiedenen Kontexten – innerhalb und außerhalb der Kunstwelt – Anwendung finden. Ein Beleg dafür ist die Vielfalt der Herkunftsbereiche, aus denen die eingereichten Projekte stammen und die uns nötigt, eine Auswahl aus Arbeiten zu treffen, die so grundlegend verschieden sind wie die Demo einer neu entstehenden Technologie, ein innovatives Produkt, eine soziale Intervention oder ein sorgfältig konzipiertes Kunstwerk. Das bleibt auch weiterhin ein Kennzeichen der Kategorie, das Jahr für Jahr den Ausgangspunkt für lange, eingehende Diskussionen in jenem Raum des Ars Electronica Center bildet, der für drei Tage zu unserer Wohnung wird.

Es ist immer riskant, aufgrund der Einreichungen des jeweiligen Jahres kühne, weitreichende Behauptungen über den Zustand der ganzen Disziplin aufzustellen; es ist aber auch unmöglich, beim Durchforsten dieser Vielzahl an Arbeiten *keine* Schlussfolgerungen zu ziehen. Im Übrigen gibt es vermutlich ohnedies keinen besseren Jahresüberblick.

Vor diesem Hintergrund sind wir uns einigermaßen sicher, dass der Jahrgang 2013 keinen Paradigmenwechsel mit sich bringt. Die besten Projekte kamen von Leuten, die bereits auf ein eindrucksvolles Werk zurückblicken und ihre persönlichen Entwicklungslinien und Forschungswege weiterverfolgen. Nicht zufällig befinden sich unter den Ausgezeichneten einige der größten Namen auf dem Gebiet bzw. Figuren, deren historische Bedeutung außer Frage steht.

Ein Thema, das weiter Konjunktur hat, scheint uns der Dialog mit den Künsten zu sein, die zunehmende Auseinandersetzung mit verschiedenen Traditionen und Praktiken jenseits der sogenannten Medienkunst. Es gab weniger explizit politische Projekte als in früheren

Jahren und mehr wohl durchdachte, exquisit ausgeführte Arbeiten, die sich in jeder Galerieumgebung behaupten können.
Strategien, die sich in den letzten fünf Jahren als produktiv erwiesen haben, sind auch weiterhin gut für interessante Ideen: die Sprache des Gadget in Japan, die Methodik des Crowdsourcing und kollaborative Arbeiten im großen Maßstab, die Umgebung des „Social Web" als ein Kontext, der weiterer Hinterfragung und Kritik bedarf. Dazu kommt natürlich die gelegentliche Vorführung einer neuen Technologie, die, auch wenn sie erst im Entstehen begriffen ist, neue imaginative Möglichkeitsräume eröffnet.

GOLDENE NICA

Pendulum Choir

Michel Décosterd, André Décosterd

Im herausragenden *Pendulum Choir* überschneiden sich gleich mehrere Sprachen und Traditionen. Es ist also nicht überraschend, dass ihn das Publikum auf ganz unterschiedliche Weise rezipiert. Teils Performance, teils Musikkomposition, teils dynamische Mensch-Maschine-Installation, vermitteln die neun Sänger und 18 hydraulischen Zylinder, die das System bilden, eine völlig neue ästhetische Erfahrung und bieten einen denkwürdigen Anblick.
Klang, Bewegung und Skulpturalität sind Schlüsselelemente im Werk der Brüder Michel und André Décosterd. Das Projekt setzt einerseits ihre bisherige Forschungstätigkeit fort, beschäftigt sich aber andererseits auch mit noch unerforschten Beziehungen zwischen dem Organischen und dem Mechanischen.
In der Arbeit stehen die neun Sänger des Chors auf sich autonom bewegenden hydraulischen Plattformen. Während sie singen, verändern sich Position und Neigung ihrer Körper. Das wirkt sich unmittelbar auf die Qualität und Klangfarbe ihrer Stimmen aus, weil die Schwerkraft die Lage ihrer inneren Organe beeinflusst.
Ziel dieser symbiotischen Beziehung zwischen den Sängern und der mechanischen Konstruktion ist es, die Rolle der Bewegung für die menschliche Stimme zu ergründen, und zugleich ein „lebendes Organ" (bzw. eine lebende Orgel) zu schaffen. Das reicht bis zum Thema der Komposition – *Atem* – und bis zu ihrer Aufführung, bei der die neun A-Capella-Stimmen mittels Klangsynthese erweitert werden.

Strategies that have been productive in the last five years continue to provide interesting ideas: the language of the gadget in Japan, crowdsourcing methods and collaborative works that exist on a massive scale, the environment of the social web as a context that still needs to be interrogated and contested. And of course, the occasional display of a new technology that, while incipient, opens up new spaces of possibility in the imagination.

GOLDEN NICA

Pendulum Choir

Michel Décosterd, André Décosterd

The outstanding *Pendulum Choir* exists at the crossroads of several languages and traditions, so it is not surprising that each member of an audience would approach it differently. Part performance piece, part music composition, part human-computer dynamic installation, the nine vocalists and eighteen hydraulic jacks that make up the system produce both an unprecedented aesthetic experience and a memorable vision.
Sound, movement and the sculptural are the key elements in the work of the brothers Michel and André Décosterd. This project continues their ongoing research while focusing on possible unexplored relationships between the organic and the mechanical.
In the work, a choir of nine singers is supported by hydraulic platforms that move autonomously. As they operate, the position and inclination of the singers' bodies changes. This has a direct effect on the quality and color of their voices, as gravity changes the position of their internal organs.
The aim of this symbiotic relationship between the singers and the mechanical structure was to explore the role that movement could have in the human voice, building a "living organ." This extends to the theme of the composition, revolving around the topic of "breath," and to the same performance, in which the nine a capella voices are augmented by a sound-synthesiser.

AWARDS OF DISTINCTION

Rain Room

rAndom International

A crowd pleaser, surely, but also an amazing conceptual and technical achievement, rAndom International's *Rain Room* is a success on every possible level. Building on the principles of the language of reactive interaction as practiced over the last two decades, the installation takes these further and creates a magical immersive experience that will be hard to forget for all those who have tried it.

The visitor is invited to enter a hundred-square-meter room where water is constantly pouring from the ceiling. As they walk around the space, the audience will notice that water keeps falling everywhere around them but not on the precise spot where they are standing. Once visitors understand the rules of this environment, they cannot help "playing the room," testing the limits of the system and trying different movements and positions. While the project incorporates important technical breakthroughs, the formal elegance of the *Rain Room* and its playful character connect it with classic pieces in the history of interaction, making it a truly timeless piece of art that transcends the technologies it uses to operate.

Voices of Aliveness

Masaki Fujihata

Masaki Fuhijata's *Voices of Aliveness* is a sculpture of voices conceived as a "meta-monument" built of collective memory. Following on his previous series of *Field-Works* projects, Fujihata set up a bicycle track at La Martiniere, in Nantes, and recruited volunteers to shout as they rode round it. Masaki's experiment uses bicycles equipped with a GPS unit and a video camera that captures the rider's face. As participants ride, traces of their paths and shouts are recorded and stored in a database. Masaki later uses these to create an online visualization in which all participants' paths appear as a tower-like "time tunnel," a structure of collected shouting that rises skywards.

The resulting process has a strong human dimension; a very clear intention to create a testimony of humankind, a reservoir of voices that balances the technology involved in the process and the

AUSZEICHNUNGEN

Rain Room

rAndom International

Ein Publikumsrenner, aber auch eine erstaunliche konzeptuelle und technische Leistung. *Rain Room* von rAndom International ist ein Erfolg auf ganzer Linie. Die Sprache der reaktiven Interaktion aufgreifend und weiterführend, wie sie in den letzten zwei Jahrzehnten gepflogen wurde, vermittelt diese Installation eine magische Immersionserfahrung, die jenen, die sie gemacht haben, wohl für immer unvergesslich bleiben wird.

Die AusstellungsbesucherInnen sind eingeladen, einen hundert Quadratmeter großen Raum zu betreten, in dem ständig Wasser von der Decke fällt. Folgen sie der Einladung, merken sie bald, dass das Wasser überall um sie herunterfällt, außer an der Stelle, wo sie sich selbst aufhalten. Wenn die in dem Environment geltenden Regeln klar sind, kann das Publikum nicht umhin, „mit dem Raum zu spielen", die Grenzen des Systems auszuloten und verschiedene Bewegungen und Positionen auszuprobieren. Wiewohl das Projekt wichtige technische Neuerungen miteinbezieht, erinnern seine formale Eleganz und sein spielerischer Charakter eher an klassische Arbeiten in der Geschichte der Interaktion. Damit ist *Rain Room* ein wahrhaft zeitloses Kunstwerk, das die ihm zugrundeliegenden Technologien transzendiert.

Voices of Aliveness

Masaki Fujihata

Masaki Fuhijatas *Voices of Aliveness* ist eine Stimmenskulptur, ein aus kollektiven Erinnerungen errichtetes „Metamonument". Anknüpfend an seine frühere Serie von *Field-Works*, richtete Fujihata in La Martinière bei Nantes eine Fahrradroute ein und rekrutierte Freiwillige, die sie befahren und sich dabei die Seele aus dem Leib schreien sollten.

Die Fahrräder in Masakis Experiment sind mit GPS und einer Videokamera ausgestattet, die das Gesicht des jeweiligen Fahrers oder der Fahrerin aufnimmt. Ihre Fahrtwege und Schreie werden aufgezeichnet und in einer Datenbank gespeichert. Daraus schafft Masaki später eine Online-Visualisierung, in der die Bewegungsspuren sämtlicher TeilnehmerInnen als turmförmiger „Zeittunnel" angeordnet sind, ein himmelwärts strebendes Gebilde aus gesammelten Schreien.

Der ganze Prozess hat eine zutiefst menschliche Dimension; es geht darum, ein Zeugnis der Menschheit, ein

Reservoir von Stimmen zu schaffen, das ein Gegengewicht zur Technologie und zu den konzeptuellen Aspekten der Arbeit bildet. Die Arbeit ist humorvoll und geht unter die Haut.

ANERKENNUNGEN

AHORA. A song in the Hypertemporal Surface

Hernán Kerlleñevich, Mene Savasta Alsina

Ein von den KünstlerInnen vorher komponiertes und aufgeführtes Musikstück wird in viele verschiedene kleine Stücke zerschnitten und auf im Raum verteilte Lautsprecher aufgeteilt. Die einzelnen Klänge werden dann durch das Umhergehen der BesucherInnen im Raum abgerufen. So entsteht ein von der Interaktion des Publikums abhängiges Klanggebilde aus verschiedenen stehenden Klängen. Das Musikstück wird durch die wechselnde Dynamik im Ausstellungsraum fortwährend neu zusammengesetzt, wobei die kollektive Intervention des Publikums einen integralen Bestandteil des Kompositionsprozesses bildet.

Angles Mirror

Daniel Rozin

Daniel Rozins Spiegelserie ist möglicherweise eine der bedeutendsten Werkgruppen, die die Kommunikation zwischen einem User und einem digitalen System in ihrer reinsten und einfachsten Form untersuchen. Rozins Projekte sind unterschiedliche Formalisierungen ein- und derselben Geste: Ein User tritt einer computergesteuerten Fläche gegenüber, der Computer erkennt seine Präsenz und verändert die Fläche dergestalt, dass sie seine Umrisse wiedergibt. Seit dem bahnbrechenden *Wooden Mirror* von 1999 hat der Künstler unzählige Permutationen dieser Idee geschaffen, aber der *Angles Mirror* ragt darunter als ein besonders kraftvolles und einzigartiges Exemplar hervor. Eine einfache kinetische Fläche aus kleinen mechanischen Zeigern bildet ein System, das faszinierend zu beobachten ist und dem man sich nicht entziehen kann.

Blaus

MID, Playmodes

Die ortsspezifische Installation *Blaus* ist ein interessantes Beispiel dafür, wie ein „toter" Raum mittels einfacher und erschwinglicher Technologien in einen hybrides immersives Environment verwandelt werden kann. In

conceptual aspects of the piece. The complete work has humor and a deep emotional impact.

HONORARY MENTIONS

AHORA. A song in the Hypertemporal Surface

Hernán Kerlleñevich, Mene Savasta Alsina

A music composition previously written and performed by the project's authors is broken into several different small pieces, which are then assigned to loudspeakers spread around the room. The sounds are triggered as the user moves around the room. The resulting experience is a sound structure produced by several sounds depending on the interaction of people in space. The music is then constantly rewritten through the shifting dynamic of the gallery, with the collective intervention of an audience, which is a key contributor to the process.

Angles Mirror

Daniel Rozin

Daniel Rozin's mirror series could very well be one of the most important bodies of work investigating the purest, most simple form of communication between a user and a digital system. Rozin's projects explore different formalizations of the same gesture: a user faces a surface controlled by a computer, the computer recognizes the user's presence and the surface is transformed to reproduce an outline of them. Since his iconic *Wooden Mirror* in 1999, the artist has produced countless permutations of the idea, but the *Angles Mirror* is one of the most powerful and singular. A simple, kinetic surface made up of small mechanical arms constitutes a system that becomes fascinating to watch and engage with.

Blaus

MID, Playmodes

The site-specific installation *Blaus* is an interesting example of how simple, affordable technologies can be deployed to transform a "dead" space into a hybrid immersive environment. Taking over a giant 18th century water tank that is currently part of Girona's history museum, Playmodes used motorized laser beams, mirrors and RGB lighting to transform visitors' perception of the building, effectively creating new geometries and spatial relations. Sound also played an important role, as the acoustics of the space were studied to develop a music and sound design that factored in the architectural characteristics of the room.

Descriptive Camera

Matt Richardson

The *Descriptive Camera* could easily overlooked as a one-liner joke, a simplistic idea not worthy of much analysis. But it is the simple fact that the idea can be implemented without effort becomes completely fascinating and has important implications. Matt Richardson's project consists of a networked photographic camera that also includes a thermal printer. When the user points it at an object or scene and takes a picture, the camera sends the image taken to Amazon's Mechanical Turk system, where humans are recruited to perform simple repetitive tasks for small amounts of money. Minutes later, a written description of the image will be received by the camera and produced on the thermal printer. The description, written by an anonymous person, is the only information that the camera outputs, as we will not be able to see the picture taken.

Down with Wrestlers with Systems and Mental Nonadapters!

Dmitry & Elena Kawarga

Dmitry Kawarga's work deals with ideas of biomorphism, a term and a small branch in art history that was very much influenced and formed by Hans Arp. Going beyond this concept, Kawarga developed this interactive installation for the Dada Moscow show. The project evokes a very powerful sense of society's fascination for machines and technology in the period before WW1, and it also shows the brutal consequences of that fascination.

Kawarga has created a machine that takes the idea of social models totally to the point of absurdity, creating an evolving structure of conveyor belts, treadmills, surveillance cameras and figurines.

einem riesigen, heute zum Historischen Museum von Girona gehörenden Wasserreservoir aus dem 18. Jahrhundert veränderte Playmodes mithilfe von bewegten Laserstrahlen, Spiegeln und RGB-Leuchten die Wahrnehmung des Bauwerks, indem es buchstäblich neue Geometrien und räumliche Relationen schuf. Eine besondere Rolle kam dabei auch dem Klang zu, da Musik und Sounddesign auf einer genauen Analyse der Raumakustik beruhten und damit die Eigenfrequenzen des Raums miteinbezogen.

Descriptive Camera

Matt Richardson

Descriptive Camera könnte leicht als bloßer Gag abgetan werden, eine simple Idee, über die sich nicht weiter nachzudenken lohnt. Aber schon der Umstand, dass die Idee ohne großen Aufwand umsetzbar ist, nimmt einen bald sehr dafür ein und hat nicht zu unterschätzende Implikationen. Matt Richardsons Arbeit besteht aus einer Fotokamera, die zusätzlich mit einem Thermodrucker ausgestattet ist. Macht der User damit eine Aufnahme von einem Objekt oder einer Szene, sendet die Kamera das Bild an den Amazon-Dienst Mechanical Turk, wo Menschen gegen geringe Bezahlung zur Ausführung einfacher repetitiver Tätigkeiten angeworben werden. Minuten später erhält die Kamera eine schriftliche Bildbeschreibung zurück und gibt sie über den Thermodrucker aus. Die von der anonymen Person verfasste Beschreibung ist die einzige Information, die die Kamera liefert. Die Aufnahme selbst bekommt man nicht zu sehen.

Down with Wrestlers with Systems and Mental Nonadapters!

Dmitry & Elena Kawarga

Das Werk von Dmitry Kawarga dreht sich vornehmlich um Ideen des Biomorphismus, eine von Hans Arp begründete und von ihm beeinflusste kunstgeschichtliche Strömung. Mit der Entwicklung dieser interaktiven Installation für die Ausstellung „Dada Moskow" erweitert Kawarga dieses Konzept. Das Projekt beschwört eindringlich die Maschinen- und Technikbegeisterung der Gesellschaft vor dem Ersten Weltkrieg, aber auch deren brutale Folgen. Mit seinem sich nach und nach erschließenden System aus Fließbändern, Tretmühlen, Überwachungskameras und Figurinen hat er eine Maschine geschaffen, die die Idee eines Gesellschaftsmodells ins Absurde übersteigert.

Dronestagram
James Bridle

Dronestagram ist eines der wichtigsten künstlerischen Artefakte, die im Zusammenhang mit James Bridles bekannter Untersuchung der sogenannten „New Aesthetic" entstanden ist, einer im Entstehen begriffenen visuellen Kultur, die aus maschinellem Sehen, Computerartefakten und Computerglitches sowie der Allgegenwart der Netzwerklogik hervorgeht. (Drohnen, das Thema des Projekts, sind übrigens ein Inbild der „New Aesthetic".) Bei *Dronestagram* werden Daten über Schauplätze und Opfer von Drohnenangriffen im Nahen Osten – hauptsächlich gesammelt vom Bureau of Investigative Journalism – mit Satellitenaufnahmen der Gegenden verknüpft, wo die Angriffe stattgefunden haben. Diese Bild- und Textströme werden zum Inhalt der Instagram- und Tumblr-Accounts, die dem Projekt seinen Namen geben. Das Projekt erzeugt eine Spannung zwischen den vertrauten und banalen Informationen, die die Timelines unserer sozialen Medien füllen, und den dramatischen Ereignissen, die meist im Verborgenen bleiben, geheim gehalten und im Ungewissen gelassen werden.

Exploded Views 2.0
Marnix de Nijs

Schon in früheren Arbeiten hat sich Marnix de Nijs mit der digitalen Repräsentation urbaner Umwelten in immersiven, navigierbaren Installationen beschäftigt. In *Exploded Views 2.0* kehrt er zu diesem wiederkehrenden Motiv zurück, allerdings mit einer neuen Technik, die interessante Implikationen aufwirft. In der Arbeit erscheinen Städte als Punktwolken, die der Betrachter oder die Betrachterin in unterschiedlichen Richtungen durchstreifen kann. Die Punktwolken entstehen durch die Aggregation und Analyse von Bildern, die auf die populärsten sozialen Medien hochgeladen wurden. So wird *Exploded Views 2.0* zu einer Repräsentation der Welt, die durch das kollektive Handeln Tausender InternetnutzerInnen zustande kommt.

Ishin-Den-Shin
Olivier Bau, Yuri Suzuki, Ivan Poupyrev / Disney Research Pittsburgh

Haptik und Akustik, Intimität und Körperlichkeit werden in *Ishin-Den-Shin* auf überraschende Art und Weise verbunden. Die von Künstlern, Designern und Technikern bei Disney Research entwickelte Installation stellt mit ihrer

Dronestagram
James Bridle

Dronestagram is one of the most relevant artistic artifacts produced by James Bridle's famous investigation into what he has called the New Aesthetic, an emerging visual culture produced by machine vision, computer artifacts and glitches and the ubiquity of the logic of the network. (Drones, the subject of the project, are the most iconic element in the New Aesthetic). For Dronestagram, data on the location and casualties of drone strikes in the Middle East—collected mostly by the Bureau of Investigative Journalism—is combined with satellite photography of the area where impacts took place. This stream of images and texts becomes the content of the Instagram and Tumblr accounts from which the project takes its name. It creates a powerful tension between the familiar and banal information that usually makes up the timelines of our social-media services and dramatic events that remain mostly hidden, shrouded in secrecy and uncertainty.

Exploded Views 2.0
Marnix de Nijs

In his previous work Marnix de Nijs has explored the digital representation of urban environments through immersive, navigable installations. In *Exploded Views 2.0* he returns to this recurring theme while using a novel technique with interesting implications. In this work, cities appear as point clouds that the visitor can navigate in various directions. The point clouds are produced by aggregating and analyzing the images that are uploaded by the users of the most popular social-media services. In this way, *Exploded Views 2.0* becomes a representation of the world as captured and portrayed by the collective action of thousands of Internet users.

Ishin-Den-Shin
Olivier Bau, Yuri Suzuki, Ivan Poupyrev / Disney Research Pittsburgh

In *Ishin-Den-Shin* touch and sound, intimacy and the body are connected in unexpected, surprising ways. The installation, developed by artists, designers and engineers at Disney Research, makes a notable contribution to interface research, exploring the transformation of sounds into electric signals that can be passed from body to body by touch and reconstructed by the inner ear. A wireless mike allows participants to record a sound. When the user touches another participant while holding the mike, the sound is transformed into an electric current that the skin can feel. If the first user touches the ear of another participant, the recording will be revealed, as the sound is "whispered" and heard as an inner voice only by the listener.

Necomimi
Neurowear
This brain-scanning device that reads cerebral activity and uses the information to control artificial limbs is not a critical design project or even an example of Japanese device art. It is an actual, wearable product that is being commercialized as a fashion statement. *Necomini* consists in two artificial bunny ears that the user can wear, controlled by a brainwave interface. As our state of mind is decoded and read by the interface—focused, tired or relaxed—the ears move autonomously, amplifying our expressivity and providing more information about our current mood. *Necomini* hints at the possibility of an emerging posthuman pop culture that could start appearing on the streets of cities all over the world.

Perfume Global Site Project
Perfume (Aa-Chan, Kashiyuka, Nocchi), Daito Manabe, Mikiko, Yasutaka Nakata, Satoshi Horii, Hiroyasu Kimura

The *Perfume Global Site Project* is an interesting example of the ongoing paradigm shifts in contemporary culture being produced by the dynamics of online participation and the ethics and aesthetics of "openness." For the international launch of Perfume's career—a well-established pop trio in Japan—motion-capture data of the band's latest on-stage choreography was released. Fans all over the world produced hundreds of derived projects, from animation pieces to fan videos. Closing the circle of the dialog between the band and their

Umwandlung von Klängen in elektrische Signale, die durch Berührung von Körper zu Körper übertragen und vom Innenohr wieder rekonstruiert werden können, einen bemerkenswerten Beitrag zur Interface-Forschung dar. Mit einem speziell präparierten Mikro können NutzerInnen etwas aufnehmen. Berührt die aufnehmende Person, während sie das Mikrofon in Händen hält, eine andere Person, wird ihre Äußerung in Form eines elektrischen Signals, das durch die Haut perzipierbar ist, weitergegeben. Berührt die betreffende Person das Ohr der zweiten Person, wird das Aufgenommene für sie hörbar. Es wird quasi „weitergeflüstert", da es nur als innere Stimme zu hören ist.

Necomimi
Neurowear
Dieses „Hirnlesegerät", das Informationen über die Gehirnaktivität zur Steuerung künstlicher Organe verwendet, ist weder ein kritisches Designprojekt noch ein Beispiel japanischer Device Art, sondern ein tatsächlich existierendes, als Modeartikel vermarktetes Wearable-Produkt. *Necomini* besteht aus zwei künstlichen, von einen Hirnwelleninterface gesteuerten Katzenohren. Die Lektüre und Entzifferung unseres Bewusstseinszustands durch das Interface – als konzentriert, müde oder entspannt – wird in Ohrenbewegungen übersetzt, die unsere Ausdrucksfähigkeit erhöhen und mehr über unsere gegenwärtige Stimmung verraten. In den *Necomini* kündigt sich vielleicht eine posthumane Popkultur an, die schon bald weltweit in den Straßen der Städte auftauchen könnte.

Perfume Global Site Project
Perfume (Aa-Chan, Kashiyuka, Nocchi), Daito Manabe, Mikiko, Yasutaka Nakata, Satoshi Horii, Hiroyasu Kimura

Das *Perfume Global Site Project* ist ein interessantes Beispiel für den unablässigen Paradigmenwechsel in der zeitgenössischen Kultur, der durch die Dynamik der Online-Partizipation und die Ethik und Ästhetik der „Offenheit" zustande kommt. Zum Start der internationalen Karriere des in Japan gut etablierten Pop-Trios Perfume wurden die Motion-Capture-Daten von der neuesten Bühnenchoreografie der Band veröffentlicht. Fans aus der ganzen Welt entwickelten daraus Hunderte – von Animationsarbeiten bis zu Fan-Videos reichende

– Projekte. Mit der späteren Einbindung dieser Projekte in die Live-Shows von Perfume schloss sich der Dialog zwischen der Band und ihren Fans zum Kreis.

The Kuramoto Model (1,000 Fireflies)

David Allan Rueter

Die „Crowd" als Material für Performance-Arbeiten wird allmählich zu einer gut etablierten zeitgenössischen Strategie. Das beim Northern Sparks Festival in Minneapolis durchgeführte Projekt *The Kuramoto Model* nutzt die „Crowd" sowohl für die Produktion (Finanzierung über Kickstarter) als auch für die Umsetzung. Grundlage des Projekts sind mit Mikrocontrollern und Funkmodulen ausgestattete LED-Leuchten, die sich fernsynchronisieren können. Tausend davon wurden an RadfahrerInnen verteilt, die das Projekt über Crowdfunding mitfinanziert hatten. Diese unternahmen dann am Abend des Festivals eine gemeinsame Ausfahrt, bei der sie die Geräte trugen. Während die Menge dahinfuhr, blinkten die LEDs in synchronen, am Verhalten von Glühwürmchen orientierten Mustern und Rhythmen.

Voice Array

Rafael Lozano-Hemmer

In dieser herausragenden Arbeit verwickelt Rafael Lozano-Hemmer das Publikum in ein Spiel mit Mehrstimmigkeit und Lichtmustern, das von ganz einfachen Prinzipien ausgeht, aber ein faszinierendes, einnehmendes Erlebnis vermittelt. Wer daran teilhaben will, spricht in eine Sprechanlage, die sein Stimmmuster automatisch in Lichtblitze übersetzt – ein einmaliges Blinkmuster, das als Loop in der ersten Leuchte des *Array* gespeichert wird. Jede neue Äußerung schiebt alle vorangegangenen um eine Stelle weiter, sodass am Ende der akkumulierte Klang aller 288 früheren Aufnahmen zu hören ist, was eine klare und starke Einbeziehung der TeilnehmerInnen zur Folge hat. Ein interessantes Merkmal der Arbeit ist, dass sie in manchen Situationen zu einem Spiegelbild davor stehender Menschenansammlungen wird und gleichsam das Gemurmel der Menge einfängt und wiedergibt. Die Dynamik der Arbeit konfrontiert das Publikum mit dem Unvorhersehbaren. Das Publikum kann die Klang- und Lichtgestalt, die es hervorbringt, nicht genau vorherbestimmen, fühlt sich aber bemüßigt, seine Möglichkeiten als Gestaltungsmittel zu ergründen.

followers, these projects were later incorporated in Perfume's live shows.

The Kuramoto Model (1,000 Fireflies)

David Allan Rueter

The crowd as material for a performance piece is becoming a well-established contemporary strategy. *The Kuramoto Model*, held in the context of the Northern Sparks festival in Minneapolis, uses the crowd for the production of the project (funded through Kickstarter) and for its own staging. The project relies on LED devices with microcontrollers and radios that can synchronize with each other at a distance. A thousand of these were distributed among cyclists who supported the crowd-funded project. These then rode together on the night of the festival, wearing their LED devices. The LEDs blinked as the crowd moved, creating synchronous patterns and rhythms, inspired by the behavior of fireflies.

Voice Array

Rafael Lozano-Hemmer

In this outstanding work, Rafael Lozano-Hemmer proposes a game of polyphonies and light patterns to the audience, which, starting from very simple principles, becomes a fascinating and engaging experience. Participants speak into an intercom that automatically translates their voice patterns into flashes of light. Their unique blinking pattern is stored as a loop in the first light of the array. Each new recording pushes all the previous ones down a position, and gradually one can hear the cumulative sound of the 288 previous recordings generating a clear and strong engagement with participants. A very interesting characteristic of the work is that in certain situations it mirrors all the people standing in front of it, capturing and reflecting the murmur of the crowd. The sound and light of dynamics of the work allow participants to experience the unpredictable. Spectators cannot precisely determine the sound and light structure the piece generates, but they feel compelled to explore its possibilities as creative tool.

Pendulum Choir

Michel Décosterd, André Décosterd / Cod.Act

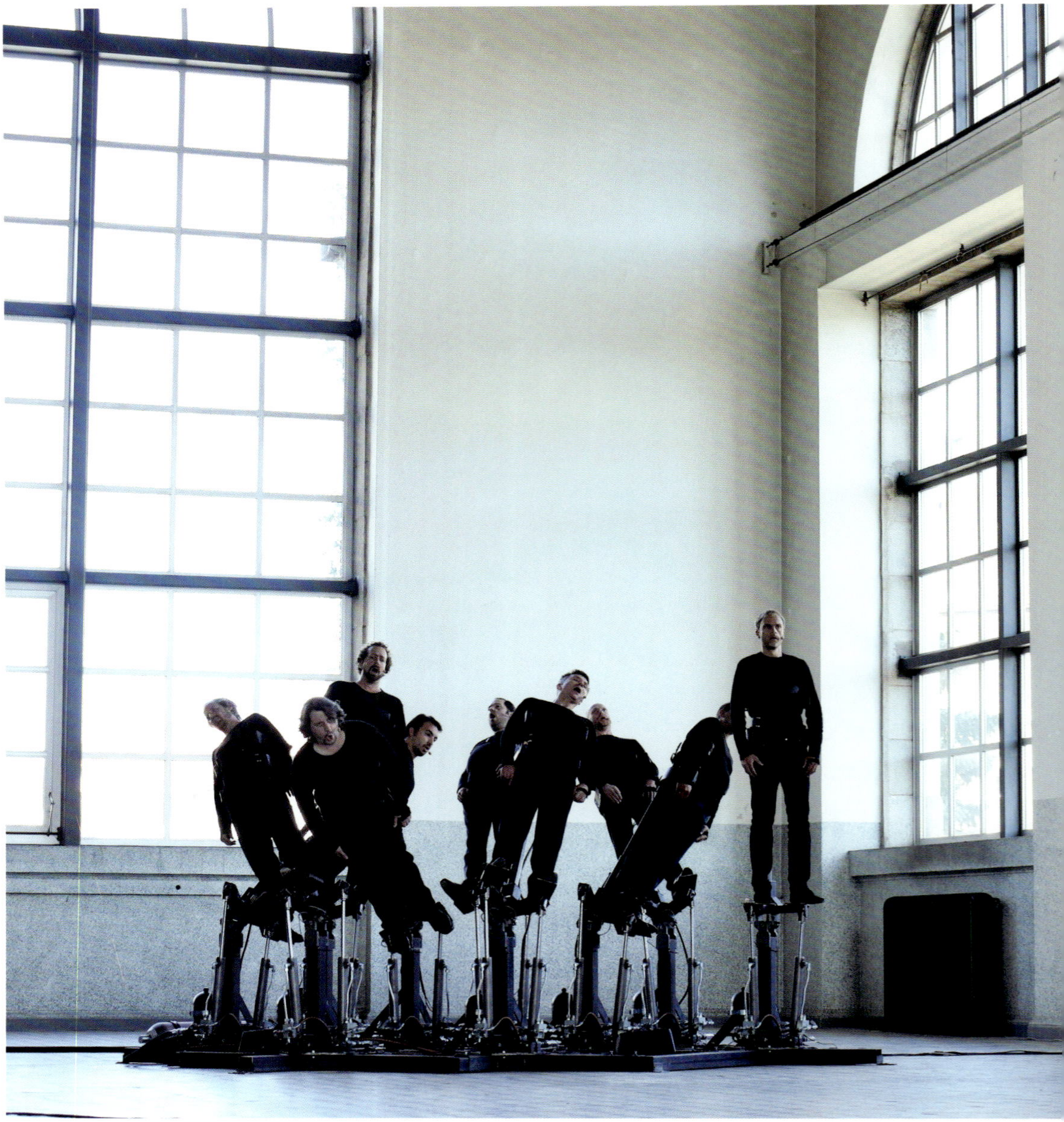

Pendulum Choir is an original choral piece for nine a cappella voices and 18 hydraulic jacks. The choir stands on tilting platforms, constituting a living, sonorous body. That body expresses itself through

Pendulum Choir ist ein Chorstück für neun A-Capella-Stimmen und 18 hydraulische Zylinder. Die Sänger stehen auf Kipppodesten, die zusammen einen lebenden Klangkörper bilden. Dieser Körper drückt sich durch

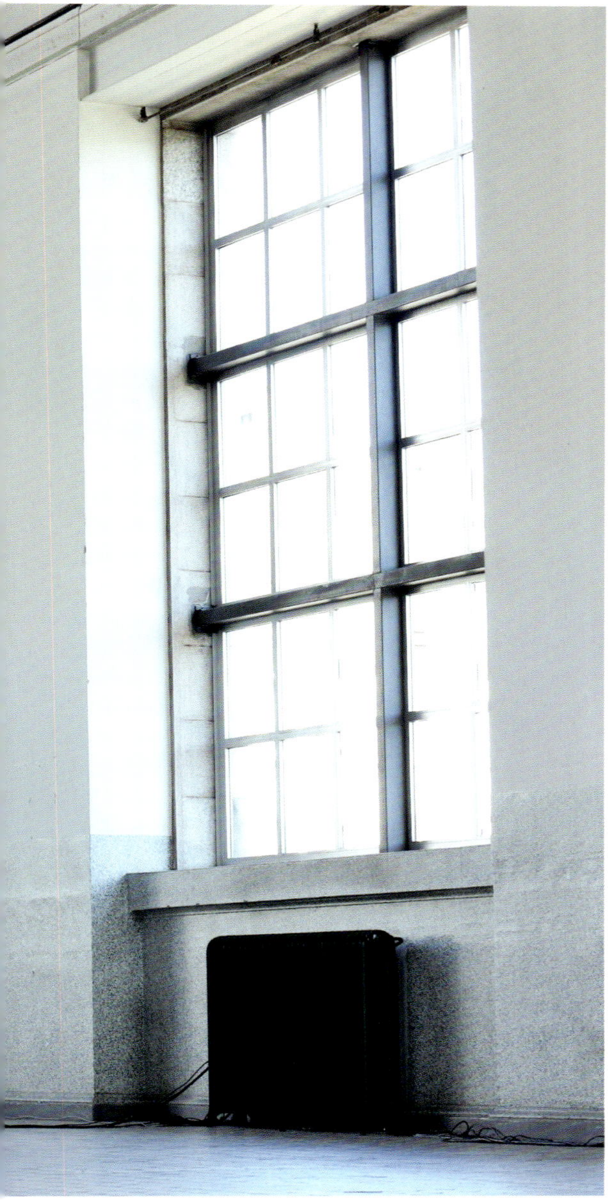

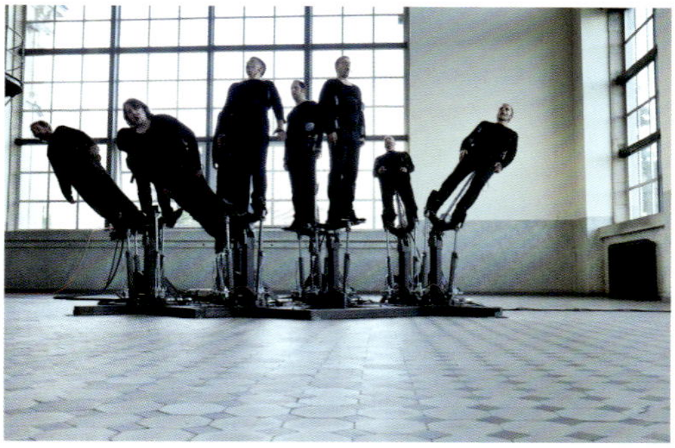

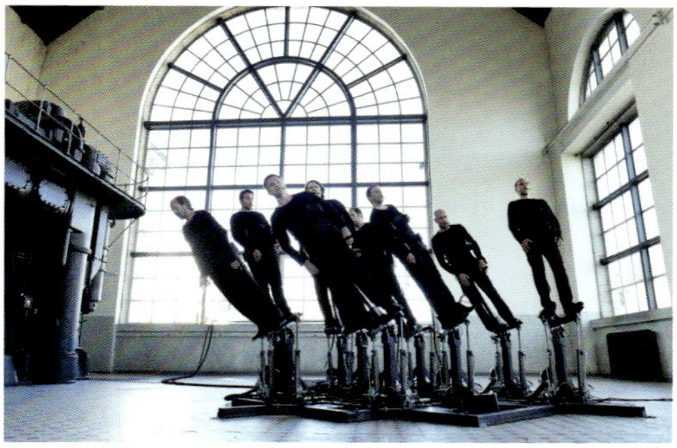

Photos: Xavier Voirol

verschiedene physische Zustände aus. Seine Plastizität hängt mit seiner Sonorität zusammen. Diese pendelt zwischen abstrakten, repetitiven, lyrischen und narrativen Klängen. Die Körper und Stimmen der Sänger

various physical states. Its plasticity varies at the mercy of its sonority. It varies between abstract sounds, repetitive sounds and lyrical or narrative sounds. The bodies of the singers and their voices play with and against gravity. They brush against and avoid each other, creating subtle vocal polyphonies. Or, supported by electronic sounds, they break their cohesion and burst into lyrical flight or fold up into an obsessional and dark ritual. The organ travels from life to death in a robotic allegory where the technological complexity and the lyricism of the moving bodies combine into a work with Promethean accents.

In 2006 we created *ex pharao*, a rewriting of the opera *Moses und Aaron* by Arnold Schönberg. It was rewritten in the form of a new orchestral piece in which visitors can modify the sound and dramaturgic parameters in real time. These modifications are operated by means of a mechanical installation. The visitor is simultaneously the orchestra conductor and one of the actors of the opera.

With *Pendulum Choir* we continue our research on the possible relations and interactions between orchestral music and movement. In this new production, we concentrate on an a cappella work.

Within the continuum of our research, the idea of creating a moving choir came from our intention to instigate a relation between movement and sound that was as close fitting and natural as possible. In *Pendulum Choir*, the mechanical set-up engenders physical constraints on the singers and, as a consequence, on the way they sing. This creates new and unexpected sonorities, a plastic parameter that we decided to incorporate in the musical writing. Similarly, we sought to include phenomena due to gravity, gravity forces, and acceleration forces on the singers. These phenomena are well-known in mechanics but still foreign to musical compositions.

The concept of a mass of sonorous and moving human bodies, going through a natural distortion under the effect of physical forces brings to mind a living organ. It evokes a muscle or a living organism emitting sounds in relation to its distortions.

In order to write a plastic and musical piece that has homogeneity, we used the representation of a lung. Each singer represents one of the lung's alveoli. The flux of air going through the organ becomes sonorous, as sung by the singers. The theme of the musical piece is the breath.

The link between the bodies of the singers is plastic, elastic. The movement of the choir constantly challenges the cohesion of the voices and their density. The sound material of breath

kämpfen und spielen mit der Schwerkraft. Sich aufeinander zu und voneinander weg neigend, schaffen sie subtile vokale Polyphonien. Oder sie geben, unterstützt von elektronischen Klängen, ihren Zusammenhalt auf und brechen in lyrische Höhenflüge aus oder verschränken sich in einem obsessiven, düsteren Ritual. Das Gesamte ist eine Reise vom Leben zum Tod in einer robotischen Allegorie, in der sich technische Komplexität und der Lyrismus bewegter Körper zu einem Werk mit prometheischen Akzenten vereinen.

2006 versuchten wir mit *ex pharao* eine Neufassung von Arnold Schönbergs Oper *Moses und Aaron*. Sie nahm die Form eines Orchesterstücks an, bei dem das Publikum in Echtzeit Klang und dramaturgische Parameter modifizieren konnte. Die Modifikationen erfolgten mithilfe einer mechanischen Konstruktion. Der/die ZuhörerIn war zugleich Dirigent des Orchesters und eine der Figuren der Oper. Mit *Pendulum Choir* führen wir unsere Recherche über mögliche Beziehungen und Interaktionen zwischen orchestraler Musik und Bewegung fort, diesmal im Bereich „a cappella".

Die Idee, einen bewegten Chor zu schaffen, ergab sich im Rahmen unserer Forschung aus dem Bestreben, eine möglichst stimmige und natürliche Beziehung zwischen Bewegung und Klang herzustellen. Bei *Pendulum Choir* unterwirft die mechanische Konstruktion die Sänger körperlichen Einschränkungen und wirkt sich damit auch auf deren Gesang aus. Auf diese Weise entstehen neue, unerwartete Klangqualitäten, ein plastisches Moment, das wir in die Partitur mit einbeziehen wollten. Ebenso wollten wir die Auswirkungen von Schwerkraft und Beschleunigung auf die Sänger einbeziehen, Phänomene, die zwar gut aus der Mechanik bekannt sind, aber in der Musik noch keine Berücksichtigung gefunden haben.

Die Idee eines Gebildes aus klingenden und bewegten menschlichen Körpern, das sich unter Einwirkung physischer Kräfte auf natürliche Weise verformt, erinnert an ein lebendes Organ – einen Muskel, der in Abhängigkeit von seinen Verformungen Klänge von sich gibt.

Um ein homogenes plastisches Musikstück zu schaffen, legten wir ihm das Bild einer Lunge zugrunde. Jeder Sänger ist ein Lungenbläschen. Die durch das Organ strömende Luft nimmt im Gesang der Sänger Klanggestalt an. Der Atem ist auch Thema des Stücks.

Die Verbindung zwischen den Sängerkörpern ist plastisch-elastisch. Die Bewegung des Chors stellt ständig den Zusammenklang und die Verdichtung der Stimmen infrage. Das Klangmaterial des Atems ist im Grunde abstrakt und repetitiv, kann aber auch als verbal und narrativ gesehen werden. Der Chor haucht den Atem aus und singt das Aushauchen zugleich. Er bewegt sich vom

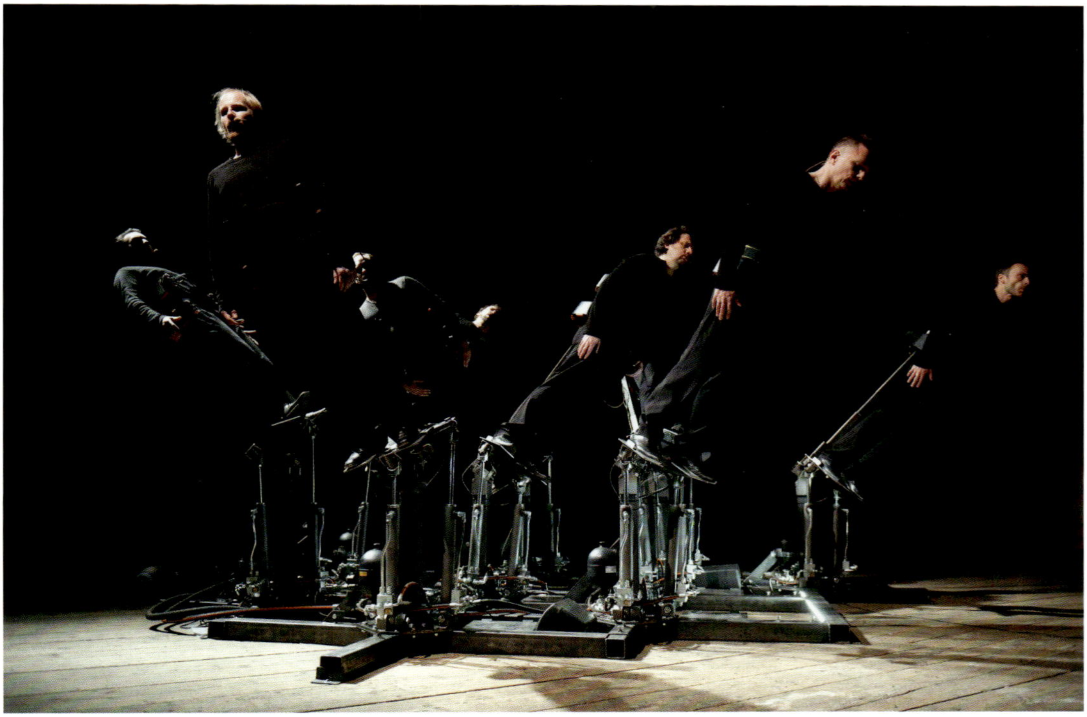

Leben zum Tod, schnaubt, ringt nach Luft, verliert das Gleichgewicht, während er vom Gefühl des letzten Atemzugs auf dem Weg zur Hölle berichtet. Dieser Teil beruht auf Gedichten von Vergil, Ovid und Horaz. Die Bewegungen verstärken die Erzählung. Das Werk entfaltet sich zwischen Abstraktion und Lyrismus.

is basically abstract and repetitive, but it can also be considered as verbal and narrative. The choir blows and sings the breath. It travels from life to death, exhales, suffocates, loses its equilibrium while recounting its sensation of the last breath on its descent to hell. This musical part is based on poems from Virgil, Ovid and Horace. The movements support the narrative. The work evolves between abstraction and lyricism.

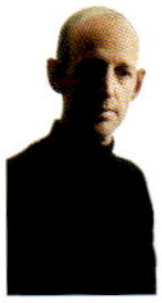

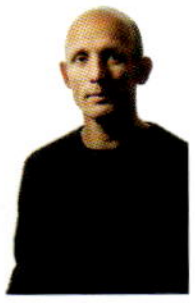

Michel Décosterd (CH), born 1969, worked as architect in Berlin and Weimar (D, 1994–96). Since 1997 he has been working in plastic arts and in architecture and develops and constructs sound machines. **André Décosterd** (CH), born 1967. 1984/88 apprenticeship in organ building. Since 1997 has been working as a musician and composer. Specializes in computer programming of musical applications. Studies composition systems specific to contemporary music, in particular logarithmic composition. Carries out research on the interaction between man and machines. Produces musical works for contemporary ensembles and for the theater. Teaches in the Ejma. In 1997 Michel and André founded the group Cod.Act. Since its inception, Cod.Act has collaborated with Jacques Décosterd (1936), an engineer in the fields of industrial computer sciences and automation systems. **Michel Décosterd** (CH), geb. 1969, arbeitete zunächst als Architekt in Berlin und Weimar (1994–96). Seit 1997 ist er im Bereich Bildhauerei und Architektur tätig und entwickelt und konstruiert Klangmaschinen. **André Décosterd** (CH), geb. 1967, absolvierte 1984–88 eine Orgelbauerlehre. Seit 1997 arbeitet er als Musiker und Komponist. Er spezialisiert sich auf Programmierung von Musikapplikationen. Auseinandersetzung mit typisch zeitgenössischen Kompositionssystemen, insbesondere logarithmischer Komposition und Forschungen zur Mensch-Maschinen-Interaktion. Schreibt musikalische Werke für zeitgenössische Ensembles und fürs Theater und lehrt an der Ejma in Lausanne. 1997 gründeten Michel und André die Gruppe Cod.Act, die von Beginn an mit Jacques Décosterd (1936), einem aus der Industrie kommenden Computer- und Automatisierungstechniker, zusammenarbeitet.

Rain Room
rAndom International

http://random-international.com/work/rainroom/

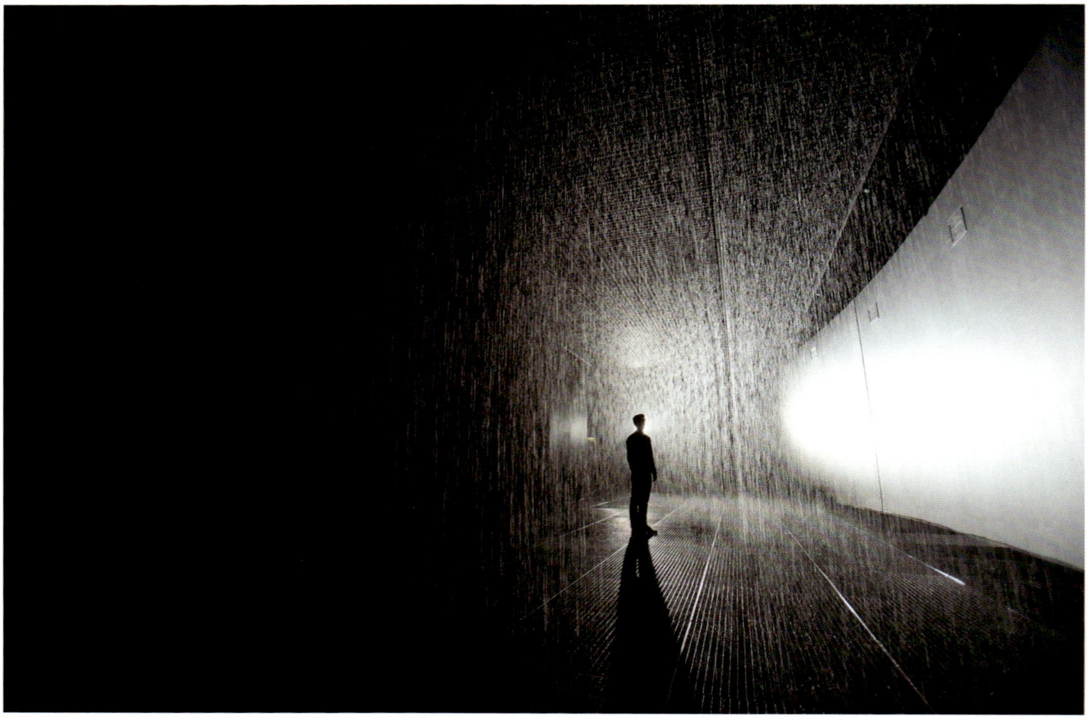

Rain Room is a 100-square-meter field of falling water through which it is possible to walk, trusting that a path can be navigated without being drenched in the process. As you progress through the exhibition space, the sound of water and a suggestion of moisture fill the air, before you are confronted by a carefully choreographed downpour that responds to your movements and presence.

Rain Room ist ein 100 Quadratmeter großes Feld aus herabstürzendem Wasser, durch das man gehen kann, ohne nass zu werden, wenn man darauf vertraut, dass dies möglich ist. In einem von Wassergeräuschen und Feuchtigkeit erfüllten Raum treffen die BesucherInnen auf einen sorgfältig choreografierten Regenguss, der auf die eigene Präsenz und die eigenen Bewegungen reagiert.

Rain Room has been made possible through the generous support of the Maxine and Stuart Frankel Foundation for Art, Barbican. Video by Gramafilm, music by Max Richter.

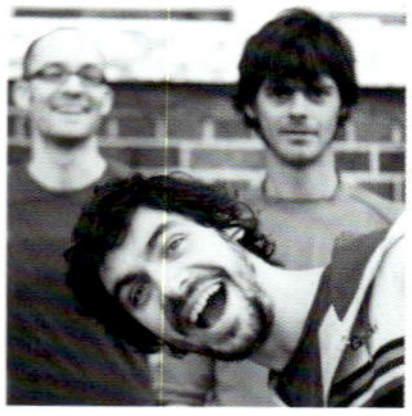

rAndom International (UK) create artworks and installations that explore behavior and interaction, often using light and movement. Founded in 2005 by Stuart Wood, Florian Ortkrass and Hannes Koch, the studio utilizes raw fragments of artificial intelligence to encourage relationships between the converging worlds of animate and inanimate. The studio is based in a converted warehouse in Chelsea, London, and today includes a growing team of diverse talent. **rAndom International** (UK) schaffen – meist mit Licht und Bewegung – Kunstwerke und Installationen zur Untersuchung von Verhaltens- und Interaktionsformen. Das 2005 von Stuart Wood, Florian Ortkrass und Hannes Koch gegründete Studio nutzt Rohfragmente künstlicher Intelligenz, um Beziehungen zwischen belebter und unbelebter Welt herzustellen. Das Studio mit Sitz in einem umgebauten Lagerhaus in Chelsea, London, besteht heute aus einem wachsenden Team unterschiedlichster Talente.

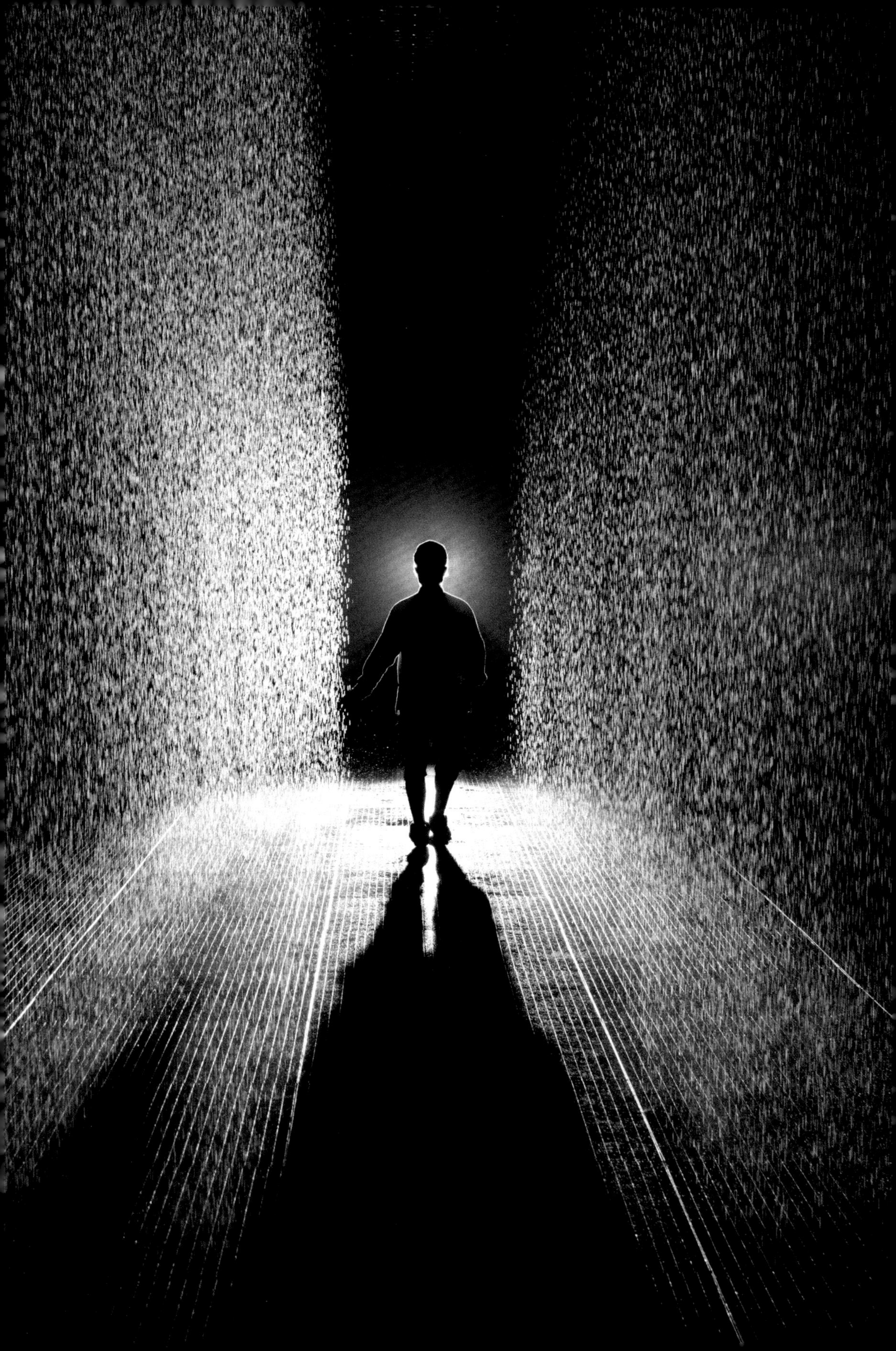

Voices of Aliveness

Masaki Fujihata

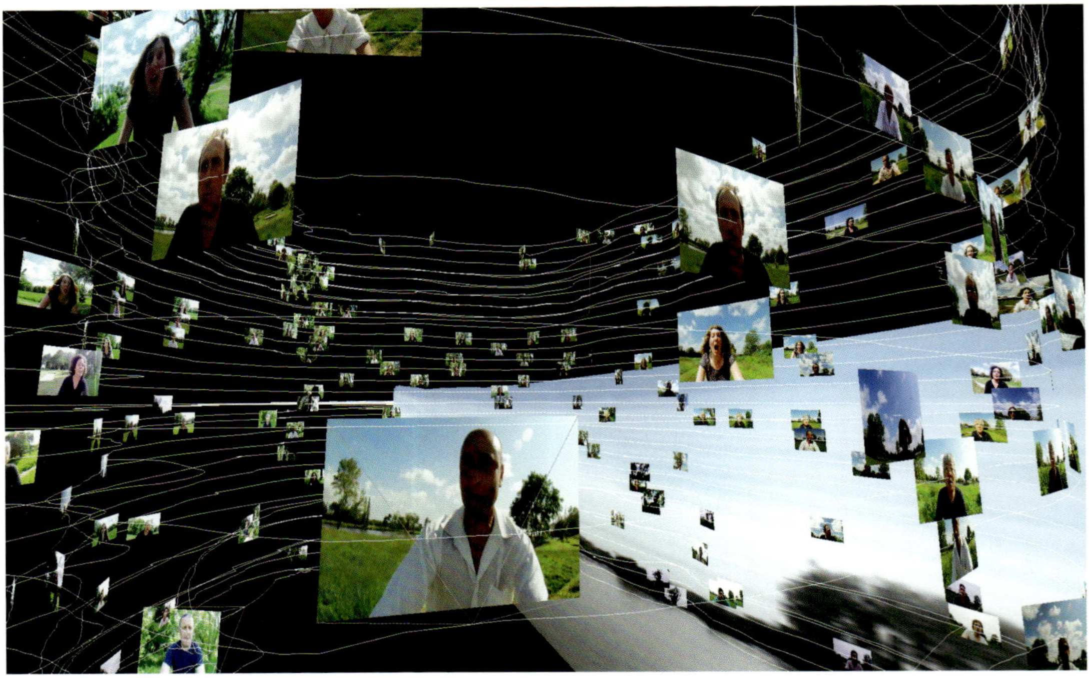

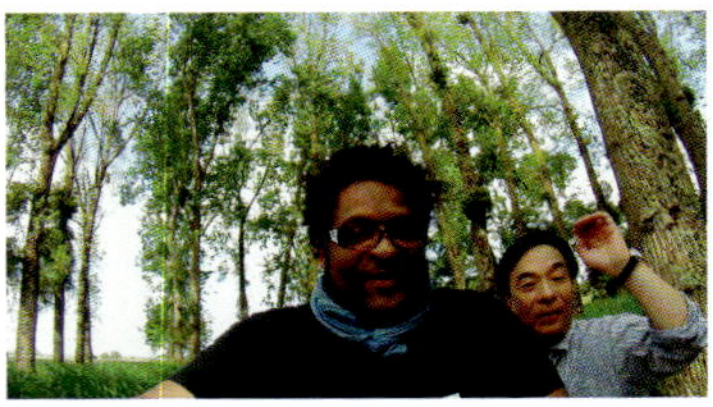

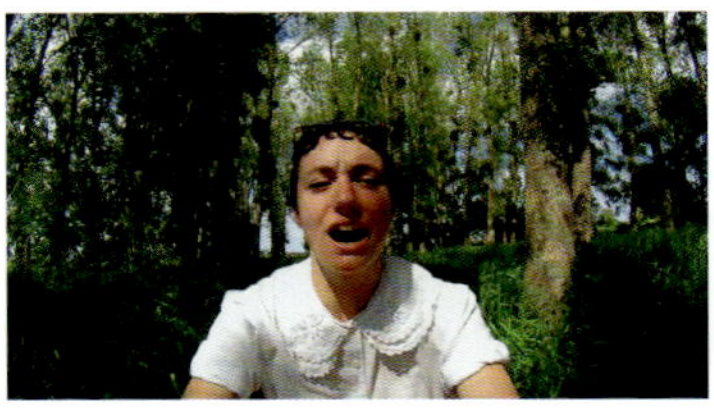

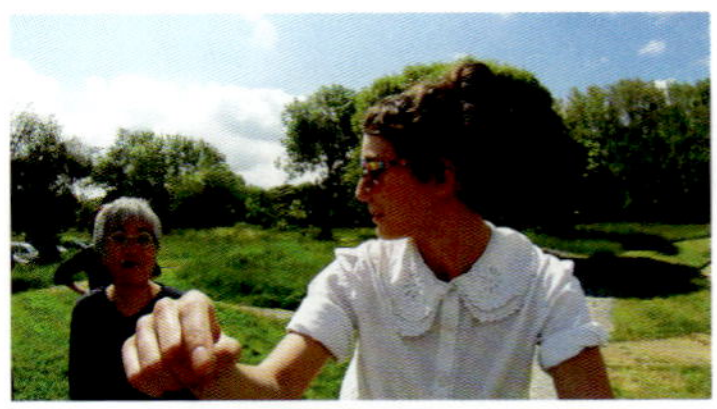

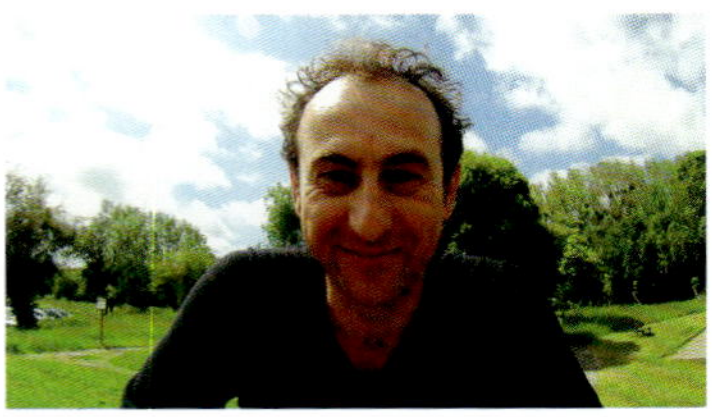

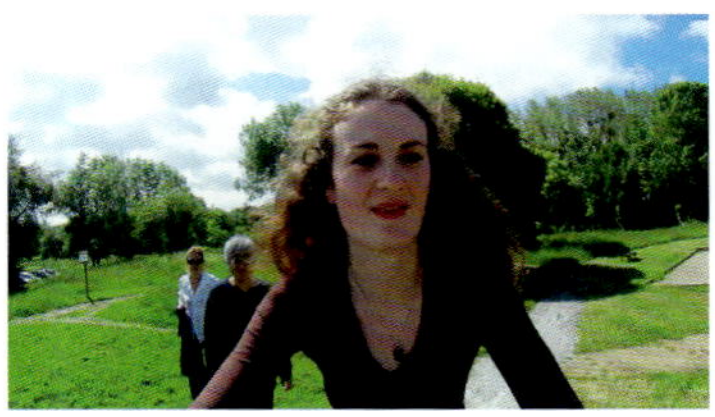

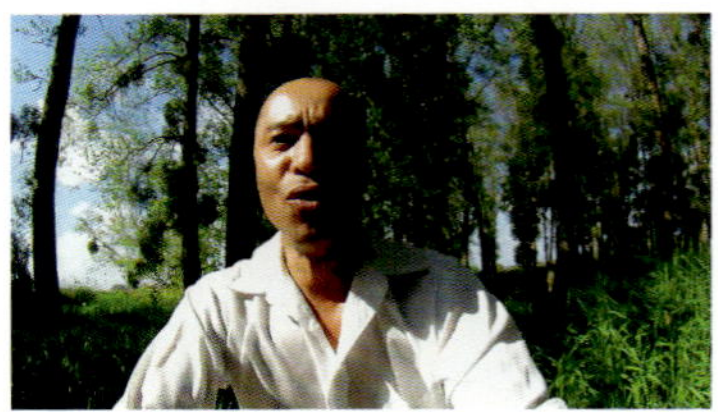

Project commissioned by L'école supérieure des beaux-arts de Nantes Métropole. Music and sound direction: Yasuaki Shimizu. Technical support: Takeshi Kawashima. Production realized by ESBA, Nantes Metropole.

Voices of Aliveness schickt Leute mit dem Fahrrad auf eine speziell für das Projekt vorbereitete Strecke – den sogenannten „shouting circuit" – und bittet sie, sich dabei die Seele aus dem Leib zu schreien. Die Fahrräder sind mit einem GPS-Logger und einer Videokamera ausgestattet. Die Wegstrecke und die Schreie der TeilnehmerInnen werden aufgezeichnet und im Cyberspace in Form eines Rings wiedergegeben.
Voices of Aliveness ist eine Sammlung dieser Fahrwege und Schreie: eine Stimmenskulptur, ein aus einem kollektiven Gedächtnis erbautes „Metamonument". Die gesammelten ringförmigen Bewegungsspuren der TeilnehmerInnen werden zu einem „Zeittunnel" übereinander getürmt – einen gen Himmel gerichteten Cybertunnel aus Schreien. Das Ganze wird im Web dokumentiert.
Das Projekt verbindet den realen mit dem virtuellen Raum. Es fragt, wie wir unserem Leben, unserem Lebensgefühl, unserer Aktivität im virtuellen Raum Ausdruck verleihen können, aber auch, wie wir unsere Taten als kollektives Gedächtnis ins Internet bringen können. Die einzige Möglichkeit ist, ein neues Ausdrucksmittel zu erfinden und unsere Kreativität zu entwickeln. Die Schreie der TeilnehmerInnen bilden den Schlüssel zur Verbindung von Technologie und Erinnerung.

Voices of Aliveness invites people to ride a bicycle on a special path called the "shouting circuit" prepared exclusively for this project and asks them to shout out loud. The bicycles are equipped with a GPS recorder and a video camera. As participants ride the bicycle, traces of their path and shouts are transformed in cyberspace into the shape of ring.
Voices of Aliveness is a collection of the shouts of the participants. It is a sculpture of voices. It is a "meta-monument" made of collective memory. The collected rings from each participant are compiled to form a tower-like "time tunnel"—a cyber tunnel of collected shouting that extends toward the heavens. The experience is documented on the Web.
The project connects real space with virtual space. It asks how we can give expression to our lives, our sense of being alive and our activities in virtual space, as well as how we can convey our actions as collective memory to the Internet. Our only option is to invent a new means of expression and develop our creativity. The participants' shouts are the key to connecting technology and memory.

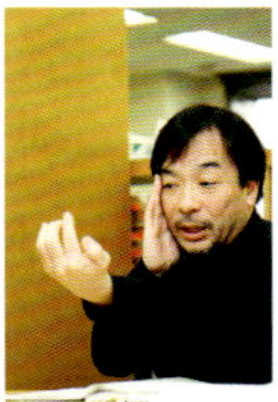

Masaki Fujihata (JP), born 1956, started out in the 1980s working in the fields of computer graphics and animation. Subsequently, in tandem with the dramatic developments in digital technologies, he began pursuing their possibilities in artistic expression, boldly moving into uncharted territory in the world of art. His works, imbued with the special features unique to the newest technologies in interactive art, virtual reality and networking, raised a variety of issues that had never emerged in earlier media of expression. In his every endeavor, his stance, to see through to the core essence, always remains constant, however, as he earnestly probes fundamental questions to do, for example, with human perception and awareness and why humans communicate.
Masaki Fujihata (JP), geb. 1956, begann in den 1980er Jahren im Bereich Computergrafik und Animation. Mit der rasanten Entwicklung der Digitaltechnik erweiterte er deren Möglichkeiten nach und nach auf die Ebene künstlerischen Ausdrucks und stieß dabei oft in unerforschtes Gelände vor. Seine mit den neuesten Methoden interaktiver Kunst, virtueller Realität und Netzwerktechnik operierenden Werke beschäftigten sich mit einer Reihe von so noch nie behandelten Themen, die frischen Wind in die Kunst brachten. Bei all seinen Projekten hielt er jedoch stets daran fest, den innersten Kern der Dinge zu ergründen, geht es ihm doch um fundamentale Fragen wie menschliche Wahrnehmung, Bewusstsein und Kommunikation.

AHORA. A song in the Hypertemporal Surface

Hernán Kerlleñevich, Mene Savasta Alsina

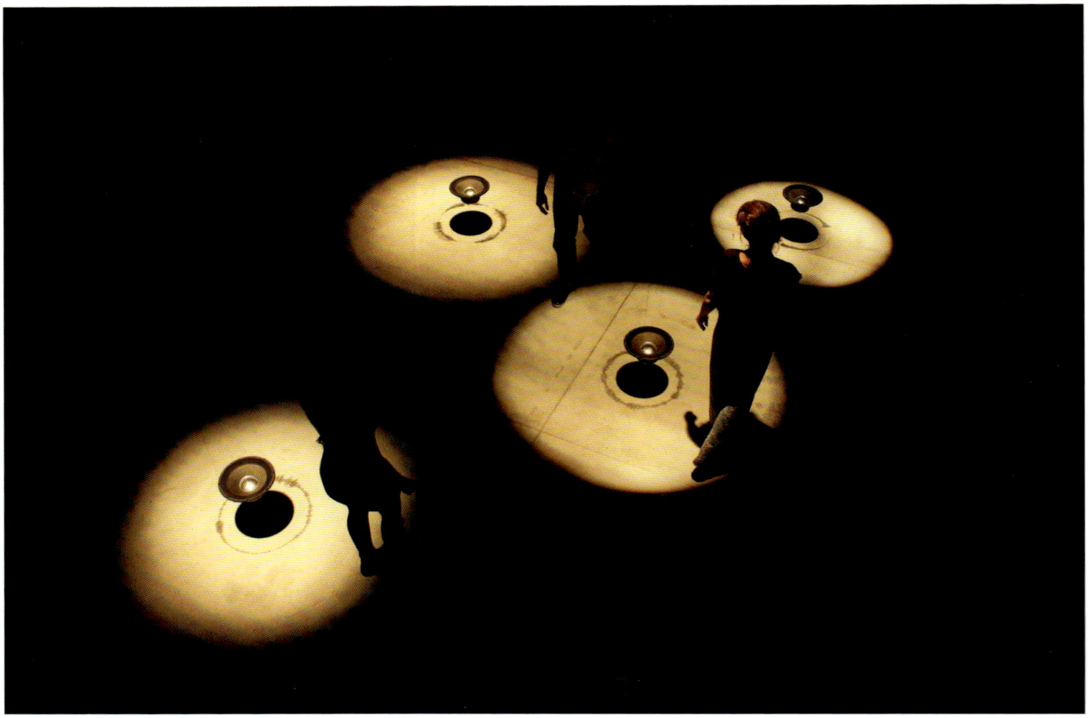

AHORA is an interactive song, composed and installed in the *Hypertemporal Surface*. As temporal solids, its sounds exist potentially unfolded on the floor, waiting for someone to make them sound in response to the path they take.
The *Hypertemporal Surface* is a software environment developed for musical composition in space. It makes it possible to "install sounds" in space. In other words, it lets us map time into space. As every moment of the original duration of sounds is anchored to a specific spatial coordinate, moving through space is literally moving through time. Anyone who walks inside this room evokes the potential times of the composition in a particular way; the song is rewritten with every new path.
AHORA, as the compositional environment that hosts it, proposes a reflection about the relationship between time and space, about the idea of all times coexisting simultaneously in the same plane, and that it is the observer who updates them, bringing order and meaning.

AHORA ist ein in der *Hypertemporal Surface* installierter und komponierter interaktiver Song. Seine einzelnen Klangelemente liegen als zeitliche Festkörper unentfaltet auf dem Boden herum und warten darauf, dass eine umherstreifende Person sie durch ihre Schritte zum Erklingen bringt.
Die *Hypertemporal Surface* ist eine Software-Umgebung zur Erstellung von Kompositionen im Raum. Sie ermöglicht die „Installation" von Klängen im Raum, das heißt, die Abbildung von Zeit auf den Raum. Da jeder einzelne Moment des ursprünglichen Klangablaufs mit einer bestimmten Raumkoordinate gekoppelt ist, bewegt man sich auf seinem Weg durch den Raum buchstäblich durch die Zeit. Wer in dem Raum herumgeht, ruft auf je eigene Weise die potenziellen Zeiten der Komposition auf; das Stück wird mit jedem neuen Weg neu geschrieben.
AHORA setzt als Kompositionsumgebung eine Reflexion über das Verhältnis von Raum und Zeit in Gang, über die Vorstellung, dass alle Zeiten gleichzeitig auf einer Ebene existieren, und dass es der Betrachter/Hörer ist, der sie aktualisiert, in eine Ordnung bringt und ihnen Bedeutung verleiht.

Sound materials: OPERADORA (Mene Savasta Alsina, Hernán Kerlleñevich and Santiago Martínez); realization of sensing system: Pablo E. Riera; realization of sensing system: Pablo E. Riera

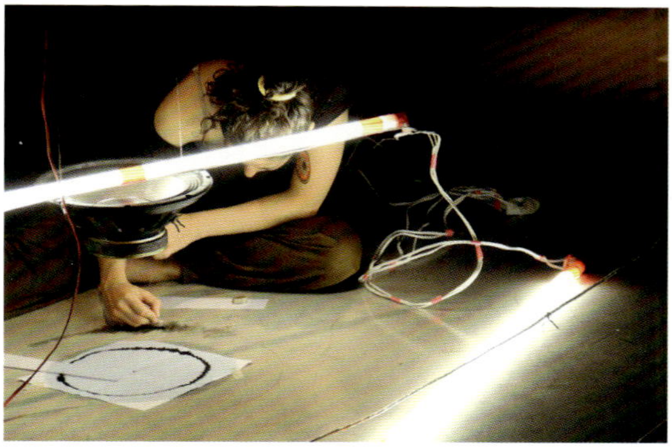
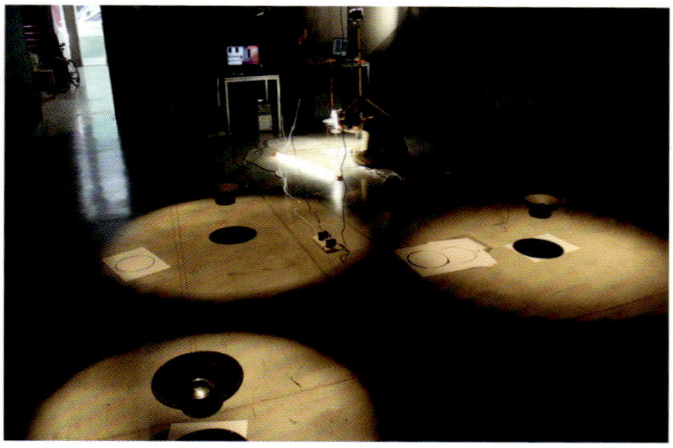

Die Arbeit folgt einem räumlichen Kompositionsprinzip. Die Verteilung von vier Klangebenen im Raum, die jeweils einem Lautsprecher zugeordnet sind, legt die Interaktionsmöglichkeiten für das Musikstück fest. Die Position der Person im Raum steuert einen persönlichen Zeitcursor für sämtliche Klänge. Nähert sich die Person dem Lautsprecher, steigt die Lautstärke, der jeweils zu hörende Moment hängt vom Winkel ab, in dem sie dazu steht. Steht die Person still, bleibt auch die Zeit stehen. Nur durch das Herumgehen in der Installation lässt sich die immanente Zeitlichkeit jedes Klangs erfahren. Nur wer die Fläche durchstreift, kann mit seinen Ohren die räumliche Morphologie dieser vom Musikprojekt *Operadora* geschaffenen Klänge erfassen.

This work is based on a spatial composition principle. The distribution in space of four sound layers, each one belonging to a speaker, sets up the interaction possibilities for this musical piece. The position of the observer in the room controls a personal time cursor for all the sounds. If the viewer approaches the speaker, the volume rises and the instants that are heard depend on the angular position. If they stand still, time stops. Only by walking through the installation it is possible to know the immanent temporality of each sound. Only someone who walks through the Surface is capable of revealing, with their ears, the spatial morphology of these sounds created by *Operadora*, our musical project.

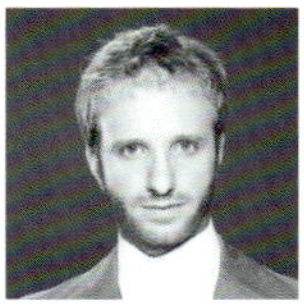
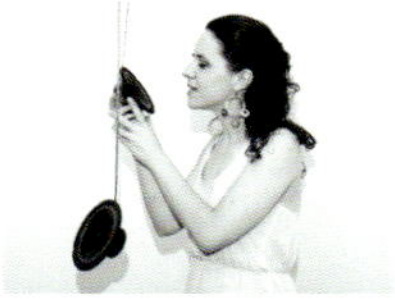

Hernán Kerlleñevich (AR) is a sound artist, electro-acoustic composer and musician. His production includes electro-acoustic works, installations and multi-channel sound interventions, audio postproduction and music for media. He designs interfaces and programs environments for real-time music creation. He is a professor of computer music and sound design and teaches at UNQ, FUC and UNTREF. **Mene Savasta Alsina** (AR) is a sound artist, musician and art historian whose research and production is in the field of sound art, performing and doing installations. As a composer and performer she participates of musical projects such as *Operadora*, *El Tronador* and *Música Destructiva*. She is a founding member of the art collective Marder. She teaches the history of visual arts at several universities. **Hernán Kerlleñevich** (AR) ist Klangkünstler, elektroakustischer Komponist und Musiker. Sein Werk umfasst elektroakustische Stücke, Installationen und mehrkanalige Klanginterventionen, Audio-Postproduction und Musik für Medien. Er entwirft Interfaces und programmiert Environments zum Musizieren in Echtzeit. Er lehrt Computermusik und Sounddesign an der Universidad Nacional de Quilmes, der Fundación Universidad del Cine und der Universidad Nacional de Tres de Febrero. **Mene Savasta Alsina** (AR) ist Klangkünstlerin, Musikerin und Kunsthistorikerin mit den Forschungs- und Arbeitsschwerpunkten Klangkunst, Live-Musik und Installationen. Als Komponistin und Live-Musikerin ist sie an mehreren Musikprojekten wie z. B. *Operadora*, *El Tronador* und *Música Destructiva* beteiligt. Sie ist Gründungsmitglied des Künstlerkollektivs Marder. Seit 2005 unterrichtet sie Kunstgeschichte an mehreren Universitäten.

Angles Mirror

Daniel Rozin

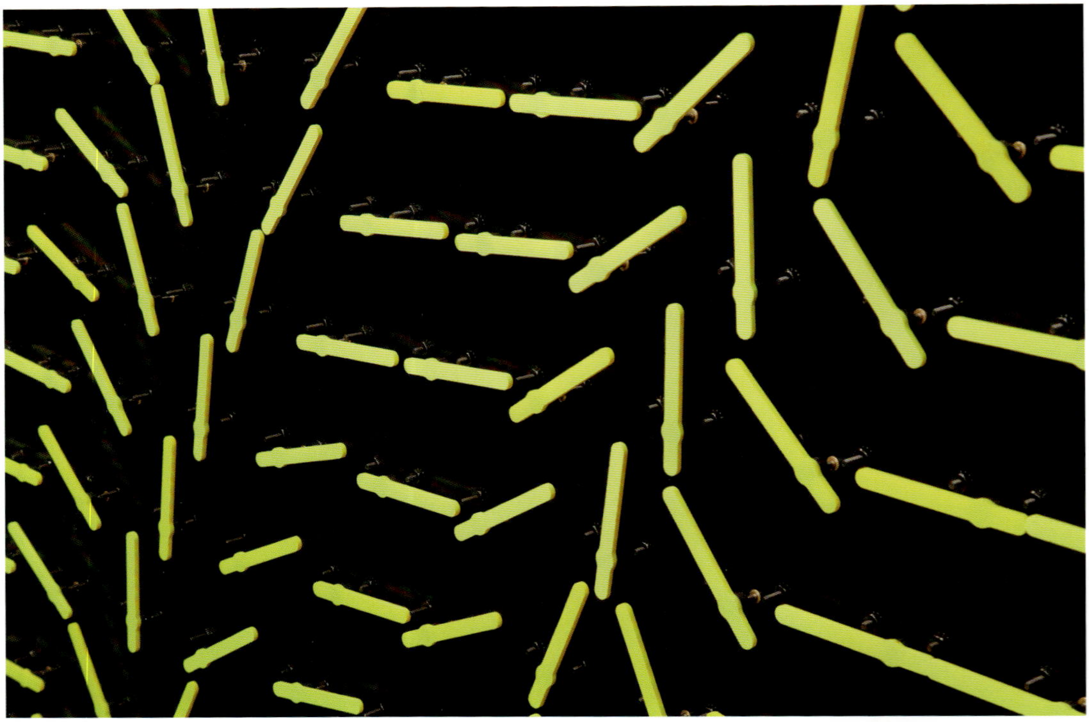

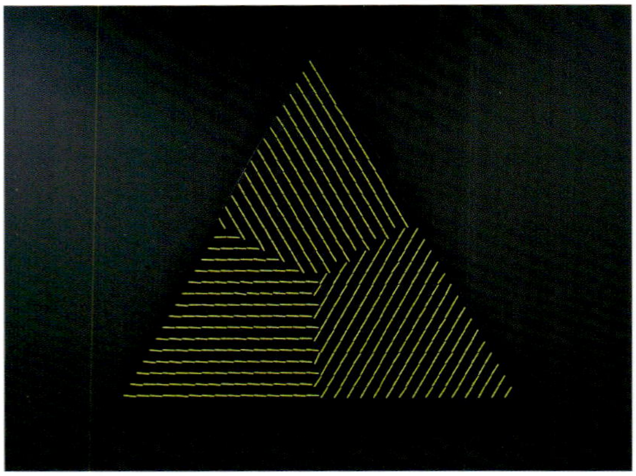

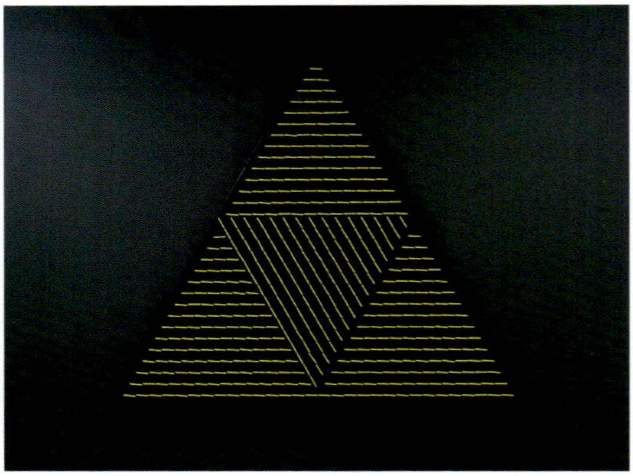

Since the late 1990s, Rozin's constructions have investigated the psychological and optical cues inherent in image building, such as pattern and the materiality of the picture plane. In a departure from the traditional rectilinear grid, Rozin's 2012-13 series of work proposes another geometric basis of image creation. His *Angles* series focuses on rotational systems of orientation. These works celebrate the polar or angular notations of pictographic information.

Mit seinen Konstruktionen untersucht Rozin seit Ende der 1990er Jahre die psychologischen und optischen Grundlagen der Bilderzeugung wie z. B. Muster und Materialität der Bildfläche. In seiner 2012–13 entstandenen Serie *Angles* unterbreitet der Künstler nun eine neue, vom üblichen Rechteckraster abweichende Form der geometrischen Bilderzeugung: eine, die auf Rotation beruht. Es sind Arbeiten, die piktografische Informationen polar bzw. in Form von Winkeln notieren.

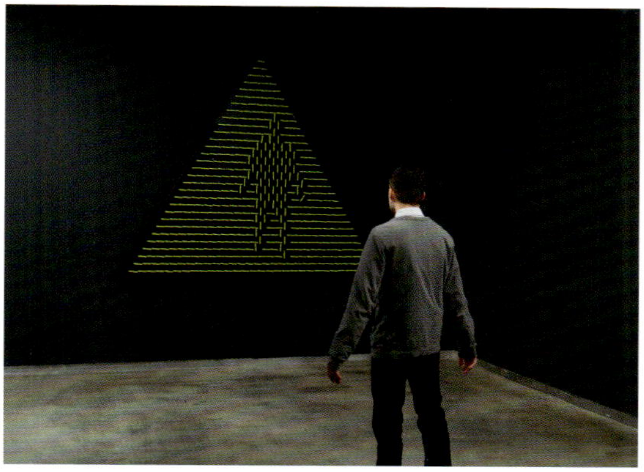 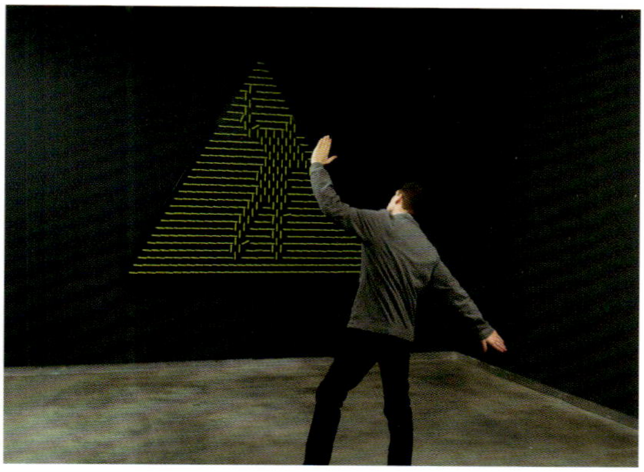

Der *Angles Mirror* baut das Bild nicht mehr aus verschiedenen Hell- und Dunkelwerten auf, sondern stützt sich auf ein System linearer Rotation, das die Neigung der Kontur eines Objekts anzeigt. Die an der Wand angebrachte Skulptur besteht aus einem scharfkantigen dreieckigen Stahlblock, der mit gelben, drehbaren Zeigern übersät ist. Als isometrisches Raster bevorzugt die Struktur Muster und Winkel, die in einem gleichseitigen Dreieck vorkommen. Die Zeiger, die ihre Helligkeit nicht verändern können, bilden das von einer Kamera aufgenommene Spiegelbild in Form von unterschiedlichen Neigungswinkeln ab. Der den Betrachtenden umgebende negative Raum wird in horizontale Linien übersetzt.
Anstelle eines fotorealistischen Bildes wird die dreidimensionale Bewegung einer Figur wiedergegeben, der optische Fluss visualisiert, der sich aus der Distanzveränderung zur Skulptur ergibt. Mit der Vor- und Rückbewegung des Betrachtenden entsteht eine nuancierte Kontur, die unsere Art der Raumwahrnehmung verändert. Die Bewegungsabfolge auf der Bildfläche des *Angles Mirror* wird z. T. durch das Publikum bestimmt. Bewegt es sich von der Skulptur weg oder betrachtet sie aus der Distanz, bilden sich darauf eine Reihe vordefinierter Bilder und Übergänge aus.

The *Angles Mirror* rejects the idea of building a picture based on relative lightness and darkness. Instead, it explores a system of linear rotation that indicates the direction of an object's contour. A wall-mounted sculpture, the *Angles Mirror* is a sharp triangular block of steel, dotted with yellow, pivoting indicator arms. Based on the isometric grid, its structure favors the patterns and angles found in an equilateral triangle. The arms, which cannot change brightness or luminosity, use input from a camera and reconstruct the view with areas of varying angles. The negative space surrounding a viewer is translated into horizontal lines on the picture plane. Rather than creating a photorealistic image, the three-dimensional movement of a figure is represented, visualizing optical flow as the viewer's proximity to the sculpture changes. A nuanced contour results, as the viewer shifts back and forth, altering the way the structure of space is perceived. In the *Angles Mirror*, the sequence of movement across the picture plane is directed in part by its audience. When the viewer walks away from the work, or chooses to view the sculpture from a distance, a series of predefined images and transitions cover the object's surface.

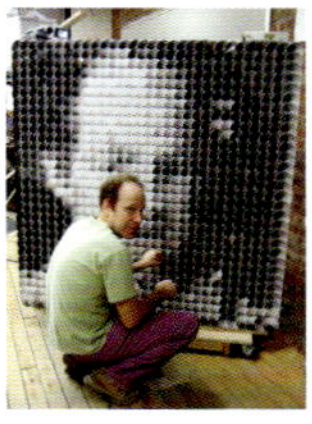

Daniel Rozin (US) creates interactive installations and sculptures that have the unique ability to change and respond to the presence of a viewer. His best-known works respond in real time and recreate a live visual representation of the viewer's likeness, staging the audience as an active and creative part of his art projects. Since the late 1990s, his constructions have also investigated the psychological and optical cues inherent in image building. **Daniel Rozin** (US) schafft interaktive Installationen und Skulpturen, die auf die Gegenwart des Betrachtenden reagieren und sich mit ihr verändern. Seine bekanntesten Arbeiten schaffen in Echtzeit ein Abbild des Betrachtenden und machen damit das Publikum zu einem aktiven und kreativen Teil seiner Kunstprojekte. Mit seinen Konstruktionen untersucht Rozin seit Ende der 1990er Jahre die psychologischen und optischen Grundelemente der Bilderzeugung.

Blaus

Playmodes, MID

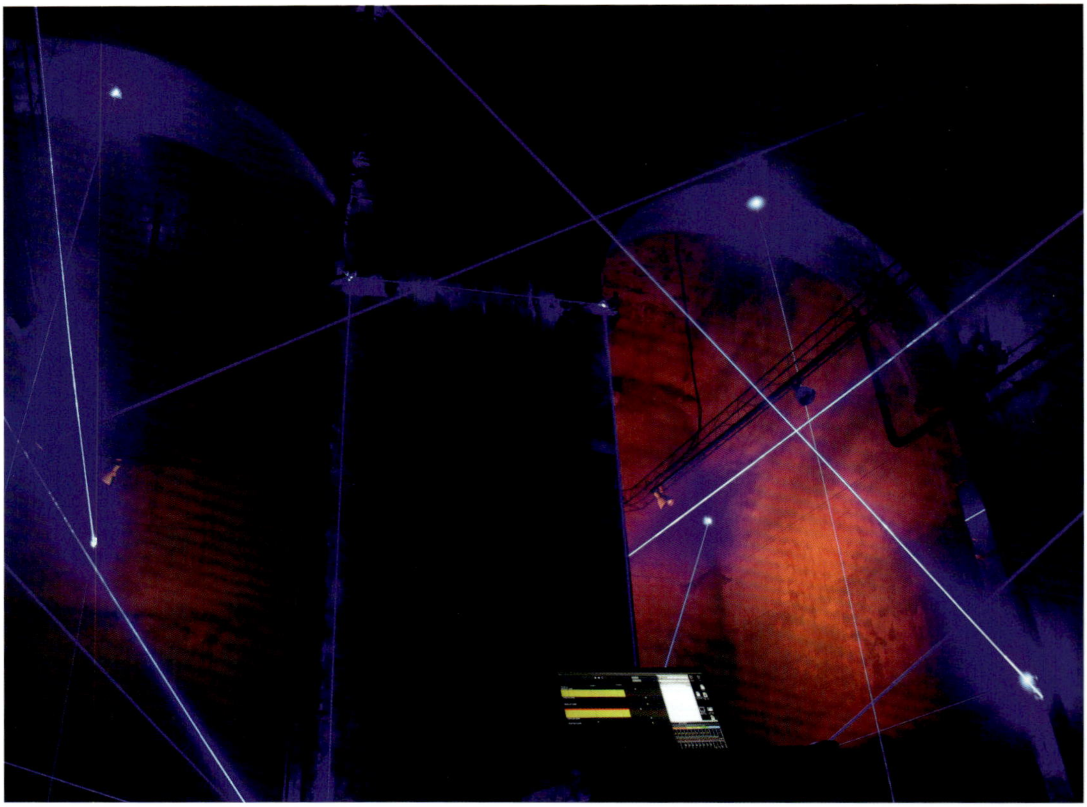

Blaus introduces us into the abstract realm of three-dimensional geometry in time. It can be a cube or a blossoming flower, a grid or a jellyfish; it is a mutant entity of reflecting lights which submerge the audience in a symbolic universe driven by hidden forces of the architecture. *Blaus* is an immersive space where light and sound relate intimately to impact on the visitor. Movement of light, sound and laser beams generates a kinetic atmosphere that transforms the architecture into the main character of a geometric play.

Blaus is a site-specific installation. The whole visual and sound creation is proposed by the architecture of the site where it is held. Through the use of self-made technologies, both hardware and software, *Blaus* re-draws the space by creating dynamic light figures which emerge from the architectural characteristics. The mix of DIY motorized laser beams and mirrors at key points of the room allows for multiple dynamic combinations of three-dimensional forms. The formal dramatism

Blaus gibt einen Einblick in die abstrakte Welt dreidimensionaler, sich in der Zeit entfaltender Geometrie. Sie kann die Form eines Würfels oder einer Blüte, eines Rasters oder einer Qualle annehmen, ist ein sich fortwährend veränderndes Gebilde aus reflektiertem Licht, das das Publikum in ein symbolisches, von den unsichtbaren Kräften der Architektur geprägtes Universum eintauchen lässt, einen Immersionsraum, in dem sich Licht und Ton auf das Engste verschränken. Die Bewegung von Licht, Ton und Laserstrahlen erzeugt eine kinetische Atmosphäre, in der die Architektur zum Hauptprotagonisten eines geometrischen Spiels wird.

Blaus ist eine ortsspezifische Installation. Die visuelle und akustische Gestaltung wird vollständig durch die Architektur bestimmt, in der sie stattfindet. Mithilfe eigens entwickelter Hard- und Software zeichnet *Blaus* den Raum in Form dynamischer Lichtfiguren nach. Bewegliche Laserstrahlen und an zentralen Punkten des Raums angebrachte Spiegel gestatten eine Fülle dynamischer Kombinationen von dreidimensionalen Formen. Die durch das RGB-Lichtdesign hinzukommende

formale Dramatik dient zur Verstärkung der den einzelnen Mutationen zugrundeliegenden Ideen.
Gleichzeitig wird die Architektur auch als Quelle für die Musik verwendet. Untersuchungen der Akustik und der Eigenfrequenz des Raums machen es möglich, den Raum als gigantisches Instrument einzusetzen. Seine Eigenfrequenz und Harmonien bildeten die Grundlage für eine Klangkomposition, die die Architektur auf ähnliche Weise wiedergibt und verstärkt wie die Laser und ihr damit eine Stimme verleiht.
Durch mehrere eigens programmierte Algorithmen auf komplexe Weise verschränkt, stehen Licht und Ton auf der Zeit-, Frequenz- und Wahrnehmungsebene in einem ständigen Wechselverhältnis.

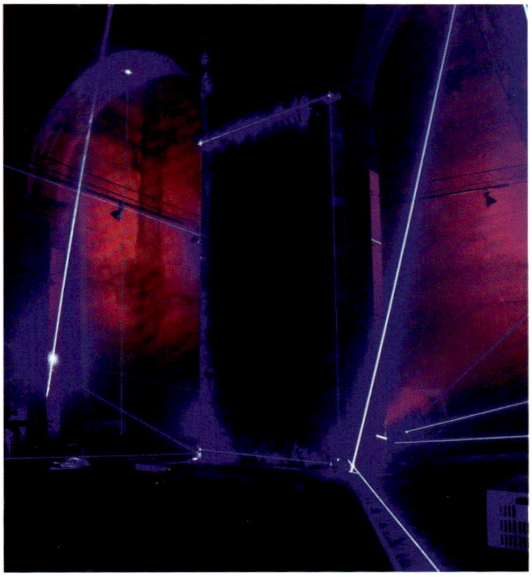

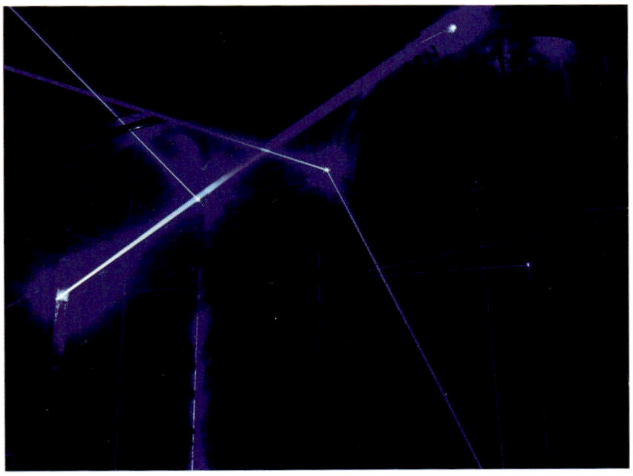

introduced by the RGB light design also helps to reinforce the concepts behind each mutation.
At the same time, architecture itself is used as a musical source, since the study of the room acoustics and its resonance frequency makes it possible to use the space as a giant musical instrument. Anchoring on this resonance frequency and its harmonics, a sound composition is generated that matches and reinforces the architecture in the same way that the laser does, allowing the space to speak. Light and sound are always related in time, frequency and perceptive domains, as several self-made software algorithms link light, sound and movement in an intricate manner.

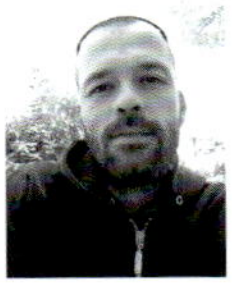

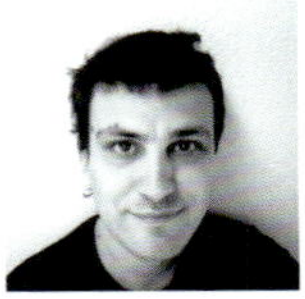

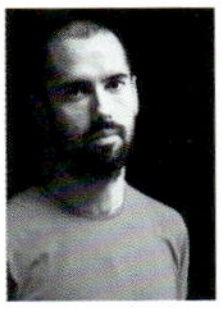

Playmodes (ES). Born in 2008, the fruit of a collaboration between Eloi Maduell and Santi Vilanova, Playmodes is a transdisciplinary studio focused on digital creativity. With a background in the fields of computer science and graphic design, we develop self-made digital technologies, both software and hardware, to create immersive interactive installations, projection mapping projects, stage scenography, still and motion graphics, audiovisual instruments, music and sound design. **MID** (ES) is an interaction design and technology studio developing installations in the boundaries of engineering, interactive design and new media. MID was founded in 2009 by Alex Posada, a digital creator, lecturer and researcher in the field of interactivity and new media. **Playmodes** (ES), hervorgegangen 2008 aus einer Zusammenarbeit von Eloi Maduell und Santi Vilanova, ist ein transdisziplinäres Studio für digitale Gestaltung. Aus der Computerwissenschaft und dem Grafikdesign kommend, entwickeln wir maßgeschneiderte Soft- und Hardware-Lösungen für immersive interaktive Installationen, Videomapping-Projekte, Bühnenbilder, Stand- und Bewegungsgrafik, audiovisuelle Instrumente sowie Musik und Sounddesign. **MID** (ES) ist ein Interaktionsdesign- und Technikstudio, das Installationen in den Grenzbereichen von Maschinenbau, Interaktionsdesign und neuen Medien entwickelt. Gegründet wurde das Studio 2009 von Alex Posada, einem Gestalter, Lehrer und Forscher im Bereich Interaktivität und neue Medien.

Descriptive Camera

Matt Richardson

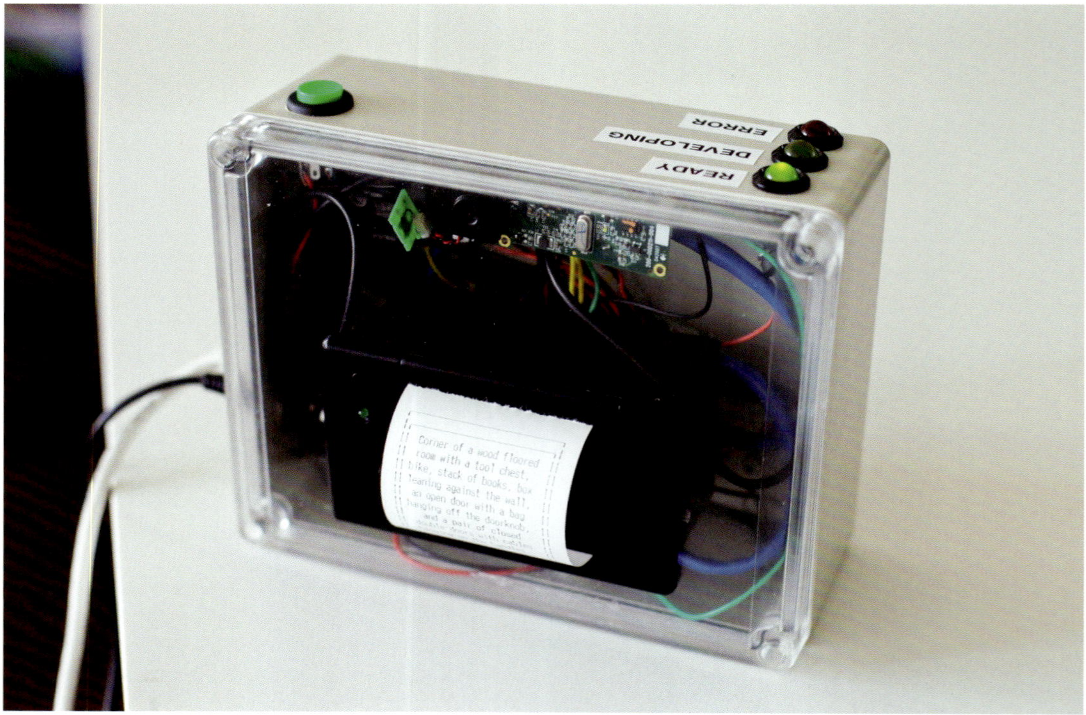

The *Descriptive Camera* works a lot like a regular camera—point it at subject and press the shutter to capture the scene. However, instead of producing an image, this prototype uses crowd sourcing to output a text description of the scene. Modern digital cameras capture gobs of "parsable" metadata about photos such as the camera's settings, the location of the photo, the date, and time, but they do not output any information about the content of the photo. The *Descriptive Camera* only outputs the metadata about the content.

Die *Descriptive Camera* funktioniert im Grunde wie eine normale Kamera. Man richtet sie auf ein Motiv und betätigt den Auslöser, um es festzuhalten. Die Kamera erzeugt allerdings kein Bild, sondern gibt das Motiv mithilfe von Crowdsourcing in Form eines beschreibenden Textes wieder. Moderne Digitalkameras liefern jede Menge „durchsuchbarer" Metadaten über Fotos wie Kameraeinstellung, Ort, Datum und Zeitpunkt der Aufnahme, aber sie geben keinerlei Auskunft über ihren Inhalt. Die *Descriptive Camera* liefert nur Metadaten über den Inhalt.

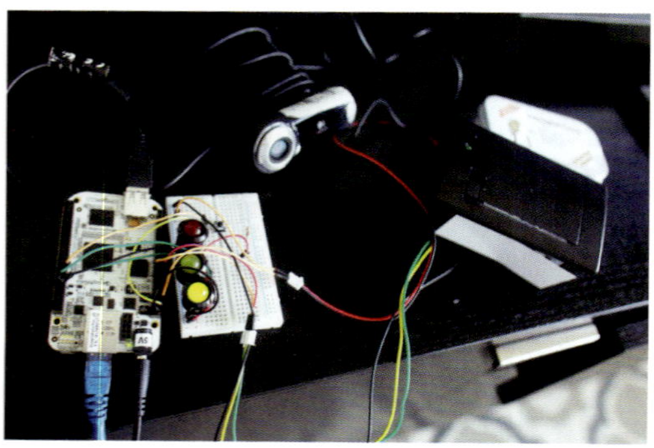

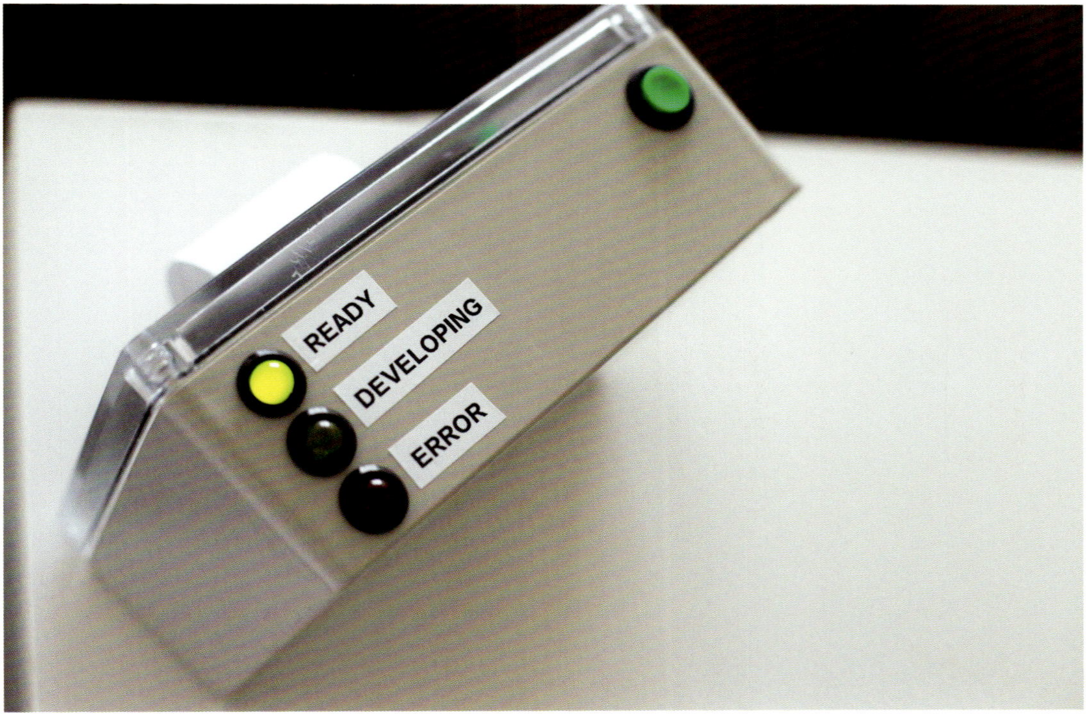

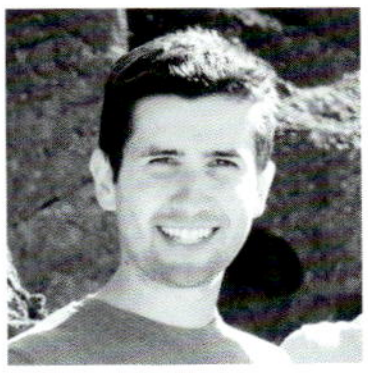

Matt Richardson (US) is an electronic artist working with networking, information display and electromechanics. Matt is also a contributing writer and video producer for *Make* magazine and *Makezine.com*, covering creative uses of technology within the maker community. He is currently a master's candidate at New York University's Interactive Telecommunications Program and owns a technology consultancy, Awesome Button Studios. **Matt Richardson** (US) ist ein Elektronikkünstler, der mit Netzwerktechnik, Informationsdisplay und Elektromechanik arbeitet. Außerdem schreibt er Beiträge und produziert Videos für die Zeitschrift *Make* und *Makezine.com* über den kreativen Umgang mit Technik in der Maker-Gemeinde. Derzeit schreibt er seine Masterarbeit am Interactive Telecommunications Program der New York University und betreibt nebenbei eine Technikberatungsfirma namens Awesome Button Studios.

Down with Wrestlers with Systems and Mental Nonadapters!

Dmitry & Elena Kawarga

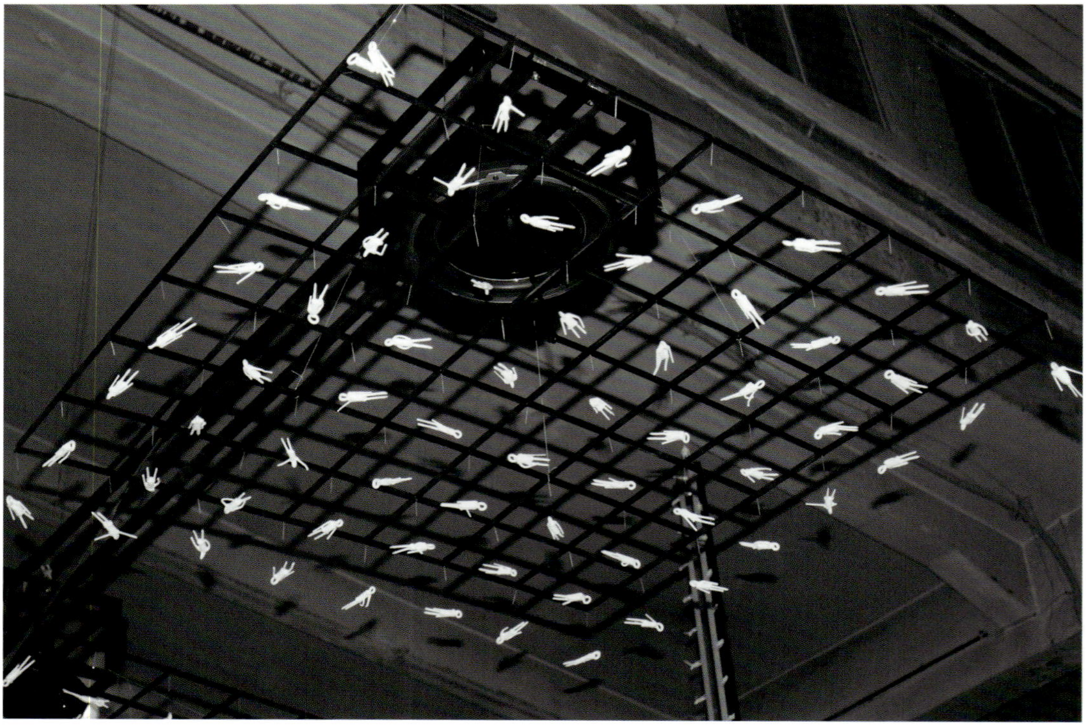

You need to go on a run-simulator to start up "a social mechanism." On the one hand you feel like God, because the movement of the mechanisms depends on your steps, and on the other hand you are only one figure among all the others. The consciousness of visitors bisects—is the society absorbing each of us? Or do we ourselves form this enslaving mechanism?

If you speak the "DaDa" manifesto into a microphone, the voice transmits a low-frequency impulse to the cellular structure, which begins to vibrate. As a result some figures fall off, liberated from the structure. One conveyor has a micro video camera, which shows a space inside a black box on a monitor—there is another reality in this box, the world of the artist.

Über ein Laufband setzt der/die BesucherIn einen „sozialen Mechanismus" in Gang. Dabei fühlt er/sie sich einerseits wie Gott, weil die Bewegung des Mechanismus von den eigenen Schritten abhängig ist, andererseits aber auch wie eine seiner vielen anderen Figuren. Der Besucher erlebt eine Art Bewusstseinsspaltung – vereinnahmt die Gesellschaft uns alle? Oder bilden wir selbst diesen Versklavungsmechanismus?

Spricht man das „DaDa"-Manifest in ein Mikrofon, wird ein niederfrequenter Impuls in die mehrteilige Struktur übertragen, wodurch diese in Schwingung versetzt wird. Das führt dazu, dass einige Figuren herunterfallen und sich vor der Struktur befreien. Eines der Fließbänder ist mit einer Mini-Videokamera ausgestattet, die auf einem Monitor das Innere einer Blackbox zeigt. In ihr befindet sich eine andere Realität: die Welt des Künstlers.

Organizers: Cabaret Voltaire, Zurich, Triumph Gallery, Moscow & Barbarian Art Gallery, Zurich. Curator of the exhibition: Adrian Notz, Cabaret Voltaire Zurich. Made in cooperation with the studio of roboto-technic, Moscow Polytechnic Museum.

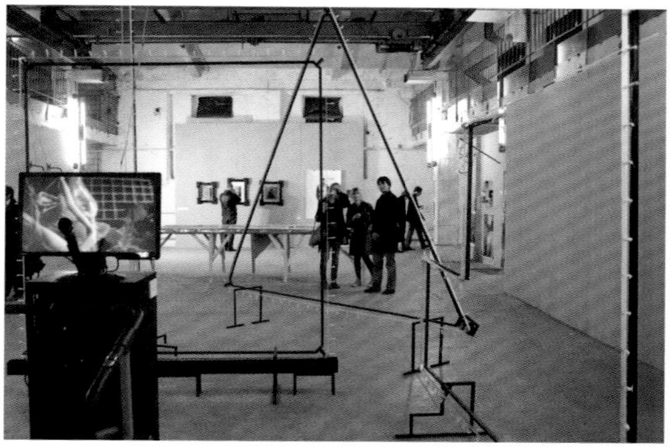

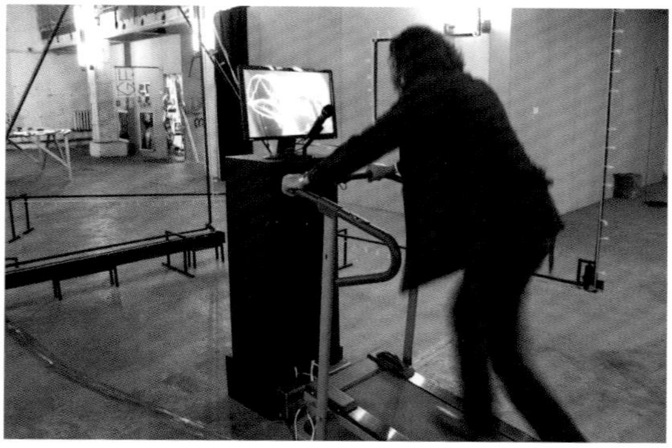

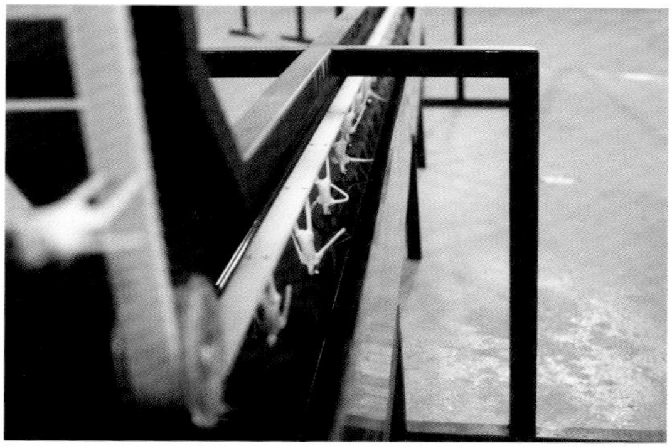

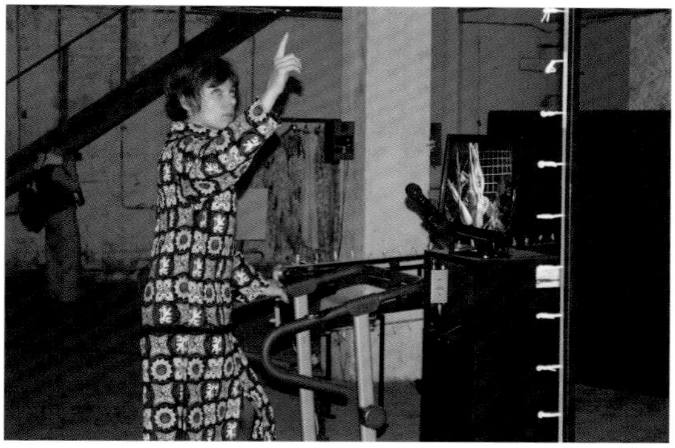

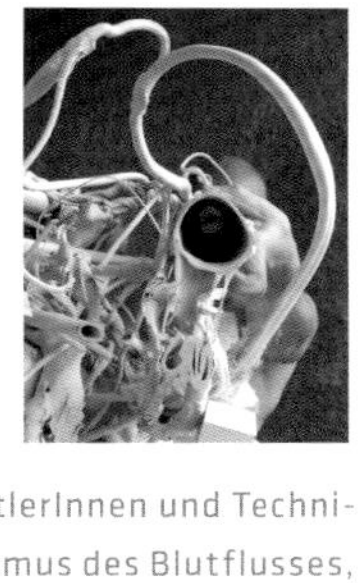

Dmitry & Elena Kawarga (RU) are two of the very few Russians artists who specialize in high-tech arts. The most significant recent works are based on science-art synthesis and created with scientists and engineers. Installations and objects imply a biological feedback; they respond to the touch, rhythm of human blood flow, voice, breathing and state of mind. **Dmitry & Elena Kawarga** (RU) sind zwei der wenigen russischen Künstler, die mit avancierter Technologie arbeiten. Ihre bemerkenswertesten neueren Arbeiten sind eine Synthese aus Wissenschaft und Kunst und entstanden in Zusammenarbeit mit WissenschaftlerInnen und TechnikerInnen. Installationen und Objekte arbeiten mit Biofeedback; sie reagieren auf Berührung, auf den Rhythmus des Blutflusses, Atem und die geistige Verfassung des Menschen.

Dronestagram

James Bridle

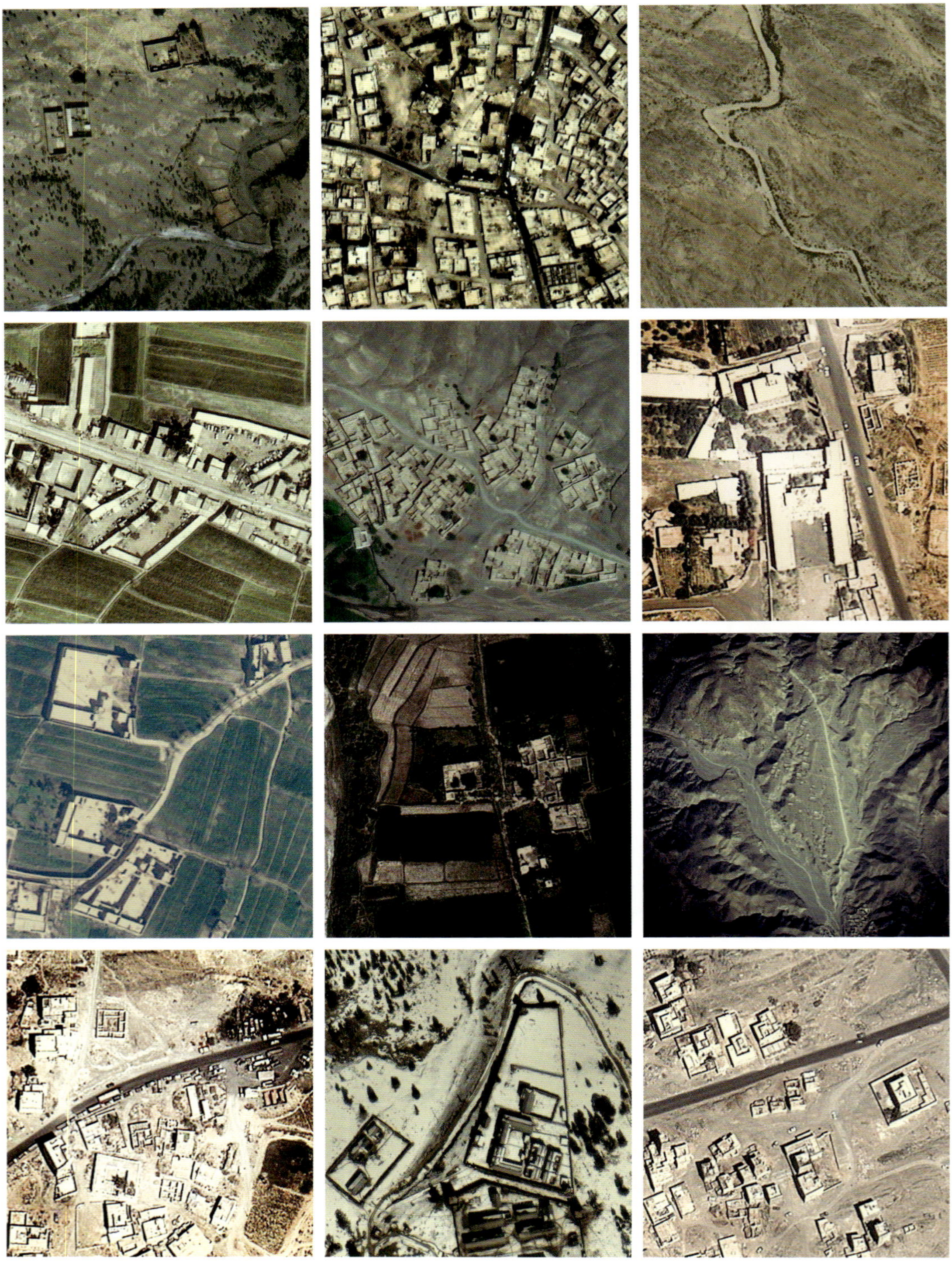

Dronestagram teilt mithilfe von Instagram und anderen sozialen Medien Bilder von Landstrichen, in denen Drohnenkrieg herrscht: illegale CIA-Angriffe mit unbemannten Fluggeräten in entlegenen Gegenden Pakistans und Jemens. Diese Landstriche bekommt man im Gegensatz zu den Schlachtfeldern konventioneller Kriege kaum je zu Gesicht und es wird selten von ihnen berichtet.

Politisch und praktisch ermöglicht werden Drohnenangriffe durch unsichtbare Distanztechnologien und eine technologisch entrückte Medienwelt und Gesellschaft. Ferne Kriege und fremde Leiber haben immer schon weniger gezählt, nun aber wird die Technologie, die uns einander näher bringen sollte, zum Verschleiern und Verdunkeln verwendet. Wir nutzen Militärtechnologien wie GPS und Kinect in Arbeit und Spiel, doch wird auch weiterhin mit ihnen verstümmelt und getötet – immer weiter weg und unsichtbarer. Zugleich versuchen wir, mit Satelliten- und Überwachungstechnologie eine 1:1-Weltkarte zu erstellen, mit der wir diese Landstriche sehen können, wenn wir sie bereisen wollen. Diese Technologien dienen nicht nur dazu, Information zu „ordnen", sondern auch dazu, sie sichtbar zu machen, uns etwas über die uns umgebende Welt zu erzählen, sie besser darzustellen.

Geschichte wird ebenso wie Raum durch uns und unsere Technologien mitproduziert. Zu diesen Technologien gehören auch Satellitenkartografie, von Mobilgeräten nutzbare Foto-Sharing-Portale und Flotten tödlicher Flugroboter. Wir sollten uns mit ihnen auf allen Ebenen auseinandersetzen. Dies sind trotz allem nur Bilder von fernen Landschaften; aber wir haben uns online in puncto Nähe und Unmittelbarkeit verbessert. Vielleicht verbessern wir uns auch in puncto Einfühlung.

Dronestagram uses Instagram and other social media to share images of the landscape of the drone wars: illegal CIA strikes by unmanned aircraft in the remote regions of Pakistan and Yemen. These landscapes, unlike the battlefields of more conventional wars, are rarely seen or reported from.

The political and practical possibilities of drone strikes are the consequence of invisible, distancing technologies and a technologically disengaged media and society. Foreign wars and foreign bodies have always counted for less, but the technology that was supposed to bring us closer together is used to obscure and obfuscate. We use military technologies such as GPS and Kinect for work and play; they continue to be used militarily to maim and kill, ever further away and ever less visibly. Yet at the same time we are attempting to build a 1:1 map of the world through satellite and surveillance technologies, which allows us to see these landscapes should we choose to go there. These technologies are not just for "organizing" information, they are also for revealing it, for telling us something new about the world around us, rendering it more clearly.

History, like space, is co-produced by us and our technologies: those technologies include satellite mapping, social photo sharing from handheld devices, and fleets of flying death robots. We should engage with them at every level. These are still just images of foreign landscapes; yet we have got better at immediacy and intimacy online: perhaps we can be better at empathy too.

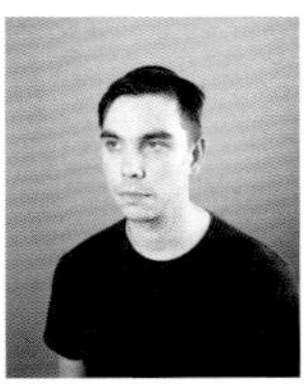

James Bridle (UK) is a writer, artist, publisher and technologist. His work covers the intersection of literature, culture and the network. He has written for *Wired*, *Icon*, *The Atlantic* and many other publications, and writes a regular column for the *Observer* newspaper on publishing and technology. James speaks worldwide at events including SXSW (Austin), dConstruct (Brighton), Lift (Geneva), Web Directions (Sydney) and Next (Berlin). In 2011, he coined the term "New Aesthetic", and his ongoing research around this subject has been featured and discussed worldwide. In 2012 he was adjunct professor on the Interactive Telecommunications Program at New York University. **James Bridle** (UK) ist Autor, Künstler, Publizist und Technologe. Er arbeitet an der Schnittstelle von Literatur, Kultur und Netz. Er hat Artikel für *Wired*, *Icon*, *The Atlantic* und zahlreiche andere Publikationen verfasst und schreibt eine regelmäßige Kolumne über Verlagswesen und Technologie im *Observer*. James war weltweit als Vortragender bei Ereignissen wie SXSW (Austin), dConstruct (Brighton), Lift (Genf), Web Directions (Sydney) und Next (Berlin) tätig. 2011 prägte er den Begriff „New Aesthetic" und wurde mit seiner weiterführenden Forschung auf dem Gebiet weltweit beachtet und diskutiert. 2012 lehrte er als Adjunct Professor am Interactive Telecommunications Program der New York University.

Exploded Views 2.0

Marnix de Nijs

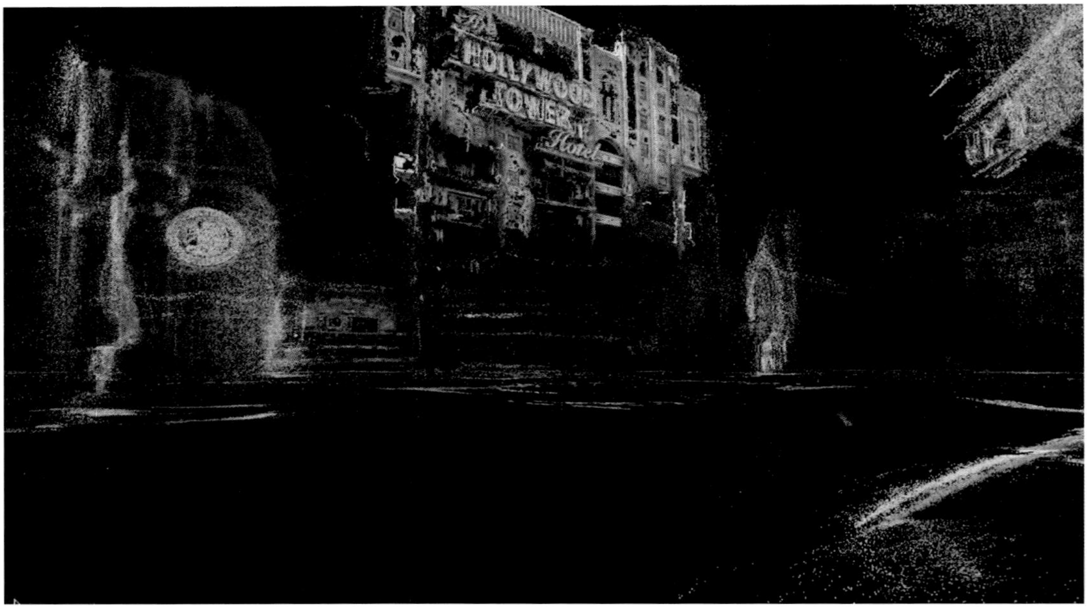

Exploded Views 2.0 is an interactieve installation where the visitor physically navigates through an audiovisual city landscape built up from "point clouds". These point clouds are generated from online web 2.0 photo collections like Flickr.

In *Exploded Views 2.0* the audience physically moves through an interactive audio-environment and interactive imagery projected on a large screen. The movement of the observer's body sets the 3D images in motion and reveals several cityscapes from all over the world. The city landscapes are scanned with an innovative 3D scanning technology that creates a surreal and dreamlike atmosphere. These 3D scans are meticulously built-up from an enormous pool of photographs, using complex algorithms. Playing with the possibilities offered by the combination of movement and 3D interactive imagery, this installation purposefully places the viewer in a strongly absorptive experience, but what is actually offered contradicts this positioning by mediating a disconnected dreamlike experience of the city.

Exploded Views 2.0 further investigates the representation of global urban environments and

Exploded Views 2.0 ist eine interaktive Installation, bei der sich der/die BesucherIn physisch durch eine audiovisuelle Stadtlandschaft bewegt. Die Stadtlandlandschaft besteht aus Punktwolken, die auf der Grundlage von Web-2.0-Fotoarchiven wie Flickr erstellt wurden.

Das Publikum bewegt sich physisch durch ein interaktives Audio-Environment und eine interaktive große Bildprojektion, wobei die jeweiligen Körperbewegungen verschiedene Stadtansichten aus aller Welt aktivieren und in Bewegung versetzen. Diese Stadtansichten wurden mit einer innovativen 3D-Scantechnologie entwickelt, die eine surreale, traumartige Atmosphäre erzeugt. Die 3D-Scans wurden jeweils mithilfe komplexer Algorithmen aus einem gewaltigen Fundus an Fotografien aufgebaut. Die Installation spielt mit den Möglichkeiten, die sich aus der Verbindung von Bewegung und interaktiven 3D-Bildern ergeben, und setzt den/die BetrachterIn bewusst einer immersiven Erfahrung aus, der aber das eigentliche Geschehen mit seinem losgelösten, traumartigen Bild der Stadt widerspricht.

Exploded Views 2.0 ist eine nähere Erkundung der Repräsentation globaler städtischer Umgebungen und ein Kommentar darauf, wie sehr das World Wide Web mittlerweile unser Bild von der Welt und letztlich unsere

Producer: Marnix de Nijs, Rotterdam; co-producer: V2_organisation, Rotterdam (NL). Scene-reconstruction: Mate Beljan, Sebastian Koch, Benjamin Lück, Prof. Dr.-Ing. Michael Goesele, TU Darmstadt (DE). Financial support: dKC, Rotterdam (NL); FBKVB/Mondriaan Foundation, Amsterdam; AFK, Amsterdam Fund for the Arts (NL)

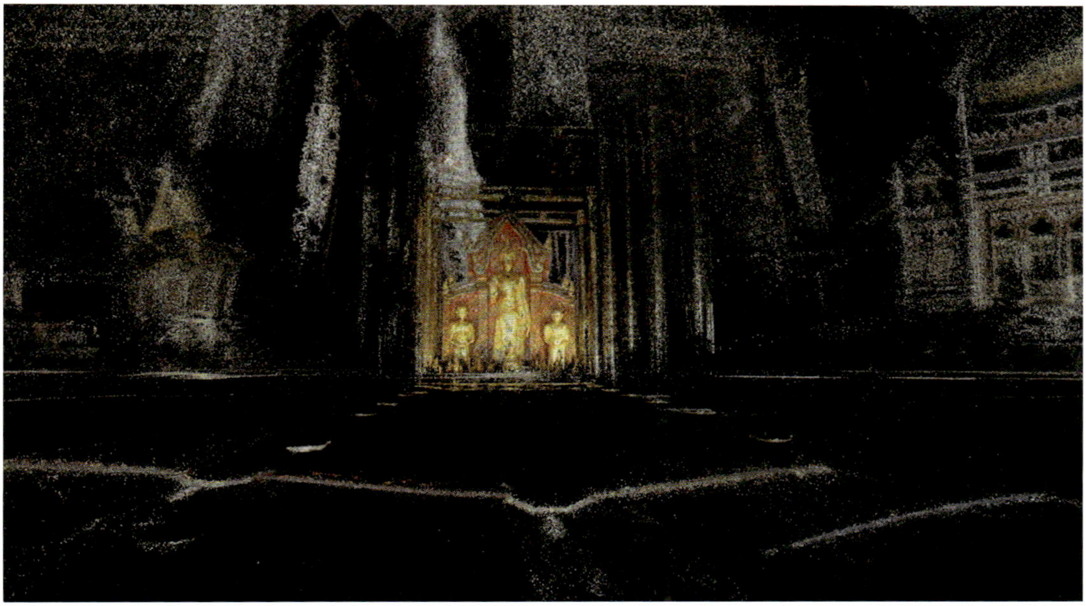

gesamte Realitätswahrnehmung bestimmt. Anders als bei der früheren Version der Installation stammt der Inhalt der Stadtlandschaften hier ausschließlich von den NutzerInnen sozialer Medienportale. Die Arbeit analysiert die GPS-Daten aller auf Foto-Sharing-Websites (wie Flickr) verfügbaren Bilder und rekonstruiert die 400 meistfotografierten Objekte in 3D. *Exploded Views 2.0* stellt die Welt so dar, wie sie fotografisch im Netz erscheint.

comments on the prominent role the World Wide Web has assumed in constructing our view of the world and ultimately, on what we perceive as reality. In contrast to the previous version of the installation, the content for 3D city landscapes is provided by users of social media platforms. The work analyses GPS tags of all the pictures available on photo-sharing community websites (such as Flickr) and reconstructs the top 400 most photographed locations into 3D. The work represents the world according to the way it is photographically represented on the web.

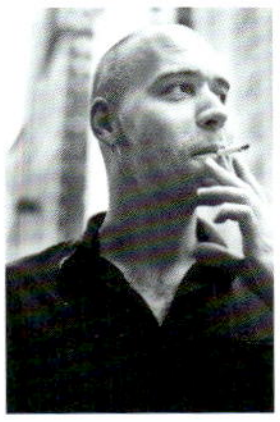

Marnix de Nijs (NL), born 1970, is a Dutch installation artist. Graduated as a sculptor in 1992, he focused his early career on sculpture, public space and architecture. Since the mid 90s, he has been a pioneer in researching the experimental use of media and technologies in art. Impelled by the idea that technology acts as a driving force behind cultural change and is therefore capable of generating new experiences where societal habits and communication are rethought, his work thrives on the creative possibilities offered by new media, while critically examining their impact on contemporary society and human perception. De Nijs' work has been widely exhibited at international art institutes, museums and festivals. In 2005, he was awarded the prestigious Dutch Witteveen+Bos Art+Technology Prize, for his entire oeuvre. **Marnix de Nijs** (NL), geb. 1970, ist ein niederländischer Installationskünstler. Nach Abschluss eines Bildhauerstudiums (1992) beschäftigte er sich zunächst vorwiegend mit Skulptur, öffentlichem Raum und Architektur. Seit Mitte der 1990er Jahre experimentiert er mit den Einsatzmöglichkeiten von Medien und Technologie in der Kunst. Ausgehend von der Idee, dass Technologie eine wesentliche Triebkraft kulturellen Wandels darstellt und damit neue Erfahrungen generiert, die soziale und kommunikative Gewohnheiten infrage stellen, nutzt er in seinem Werk gleichermaßen die kreativen Möglichkeiten der neuen Medien, wie er sich kritisch mit ihren Auswirkungen auf die zeitgenössische Gesellschaft und die menschliche Wahrnehmung auseinandersetzt. De Nijs' Arbeiten wurden vielfach international ausgestellt. 2005 wurde er für sein Gesamtwerk mit dem renommierten Witteveen+Bos Art+Technology Award ausgezeichnet.

Ishin-Den-Shin

Olivier Bau, Yuri Suzuki, Ivan Poupyrev / Disney Research Pittsburgh

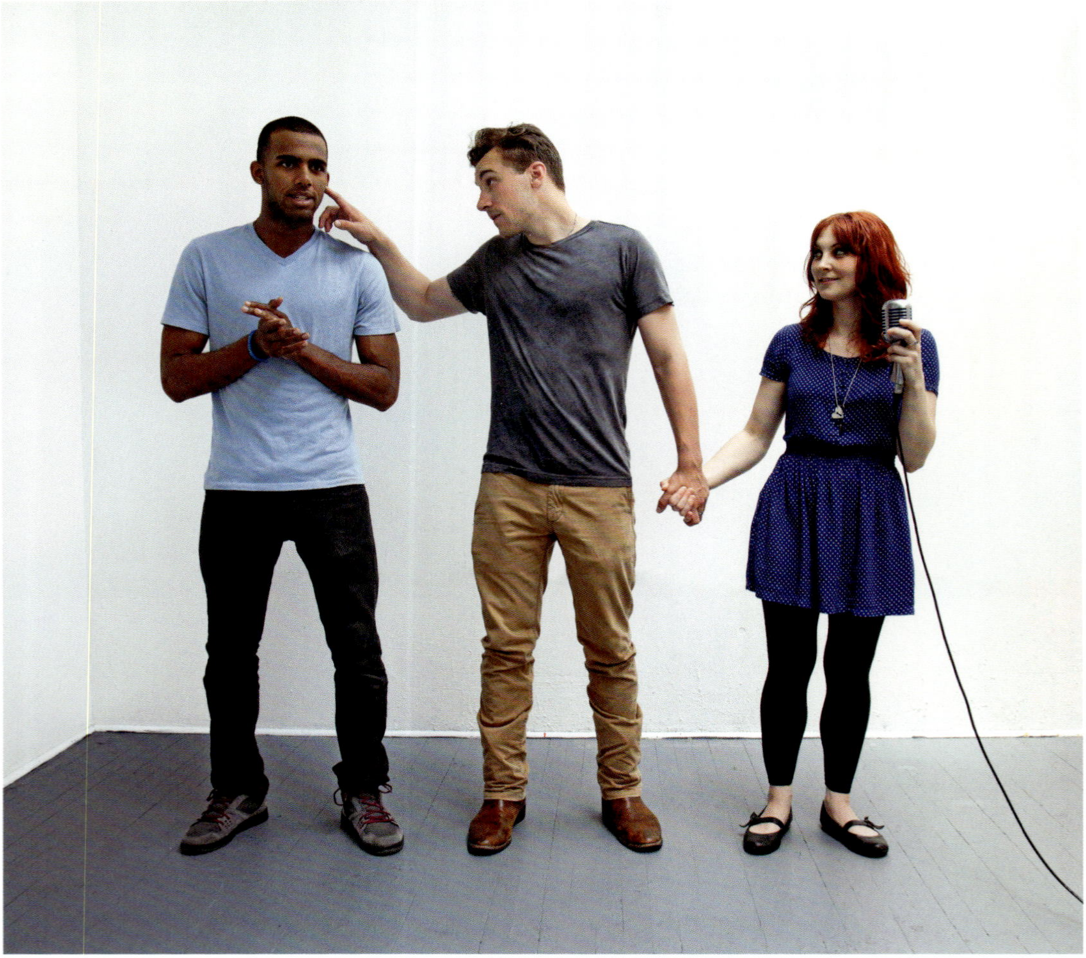

Ishin-denshin is a Japanese idiom which denotes the traditional concept of interpersonal communication through unspoken mutual understanding. This four-character compound, known as a *yojijukugo*, literally translates as "what the mind thinks, the heart transmits." Sometimes explained in English in terms of telepathy or sympathy, *ishin-denshin* is also commonly rendered as "heart-to-heart communication" or "tacit understanding." (Source: Wikipedia)

Ishin-denshin ist ein japanischer Ausdruck für die alte Vorstellung einer unausgesprochenen zwischenmenschlichen Kommunikation. Wörtlich übersetzt bedeutet dieses *yojigukugo* (eine aus vier Schriftzeichen bestehende Redensart): „Was der Geist denkt, überträgt das Herz." Oft auch als eine Art Telepathie oder Mitgefühl erklärt, wird der Ausdruck *ishin-denshin* meist als „ Herz-zu-Herz-Kommunikation" oder „stilles Einverständnis" wiedergegeben. (Quelle: englische Wikipedia)

Die Installation *Ishin-Den-Shin* thematisiert Körperlichkeit und Intimität in digitaler Audio-Kommunikation. Sie besteht aus einem Mikrofon, das Schallereignisse aufnehmen und haptisch übertragen kann. Das aufgenommene Schallereignis wird in ein unhörbares Signal umgewandelt und auf den Körper der Person übertragen, die das Mikrofon in Händen hält. Durch physischen Kontakt kann es von Körper zu Körper weitergegeben werden. Es wird nur hörbar, wenn man jemandes Ohr berührt. Es ist, als flüstere der Finger die aufgezeichneten Klänge und Geräusche ins Ohr der betreffenden Person. So lassen sich Geheimnisse und Nachrichten durch physischen Kontakt von Person zu Person übertragen. Der Körper wird zu einem Übertragungsmedium für intime akustische Kommunikation.

The *Ishin-Den-Shin* installation addresses physicality and intimacy in digital audio communication. It consists is a microphone that can record sounds and transmit them through touch. Once recorded, the sound is transformed into an inaudible signal. This is transmitted to a person's body when they hold the microphone. The signal can be transmitted by physical contact from body to body. The recorded sound becomes audible only when touching someone's ear. The sound can be heard only by the ear that is touched, as if the finger were whispering the recorded sounds. Secrets, messages and whispers can then be transmitted from person to person in physical contact with each others. Bodies become a broadcasting medium for intimate, physical, sound communication.

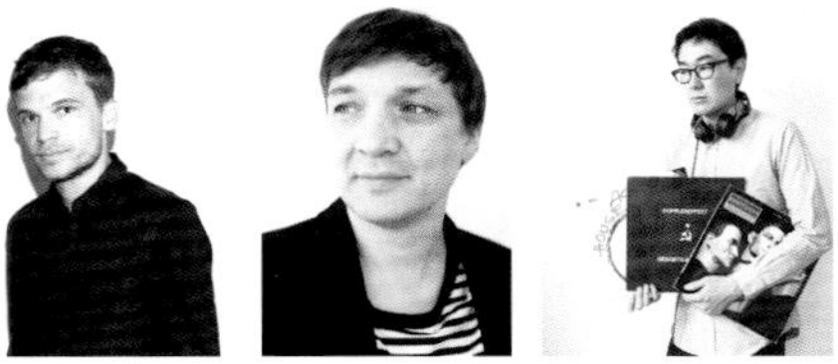

Olivier Bau (US/FR) is a researcher and designer working at Disney Imagineering, Research. His interests include augmenting the human body with new capabilities using wearable technology, creating installations and environments that engender unique and engaging experiences and developing interfaces that will enable us to take full advantage of advances in computing technologies. **Ivan Poupyrev** (US/RU) directs an interaction technology group in Disney Research's Pittsburgh Lab, tasked with dreaming up and developing future technologies for Disney parks, resorts, and cruises. His research focuses on inventing new interactive technologies for the seamless blending of digital and physical properties in devices, everyday objects and living environments. **Yuri Suzuki** (JP), born 1980, is a sound artist, designer and electronic musician who produces work that explores the realms of sound through exquisitely designed pieces. He worked for the Japanese art unit Maywa Denki, where he developed a strong interest in music and technology before moving to London in 2005. From 2011 he became designer and visiting artist in the Stockholm creative collective Teenage Engineering and the Walt Disney Research for Interaction design group. **Olivier Bau** (US/FR) arbeitet als Forscher und Designer bei Walt Disney Imagineering. Zu seinen Arbeitsschwerpunkten gehört die Erweiterung des menschlichen Körpers, um neue Fähigkeiten durch Wearable-Technologie, die Gestaltung von Installationen und Environments, die einzigartige und einnehmende Erlebnisse vermitteln, sowie die Entwicklung von Interfaces, die eine volle Nutzung der Fortschritte der Computertechnik gestatten. **Ivan Poupyrev** (US/RU) leitet die Interaktionstechnologie-Gruppe von Disney Research Pittsburgh. Ihre Aufgabe ist die Erfindung und Entwicklung künftiger Technologien für Disney-Freizeitparks, Resorts und Kreuzfahrtschiffe. Schwerpunkt seiner Forschung sind interaktive Technologien für die nahtlose Verbindung von digitalen und physischen Eigenschaften in Geräten, Alltagsgegenständen und Lebensumwelten. **Yuri Suzuki** (JP), geb. 1980, ist ein Klangkünstler, Sounddesigner und Elektronik-Musiker, der mit anspruchsvoll gestalteten Stücken verschiedene Bereiche der Akustik ergründet. Er arbeitete bei der japanischen „Kunsteinheit" Maywa Denki, wo er ein starkes Interesse für Musik und Technik entwickelte, ehe er 2005 nach London zog. Seit 2011 ist er Designer und Gastkünstler beim Stockholmer Kreativkollektiv Teenage Engineering und bei der Interaktionsdesign-Gruppe von Walt Disney Research.

Necomimi

Neurowear

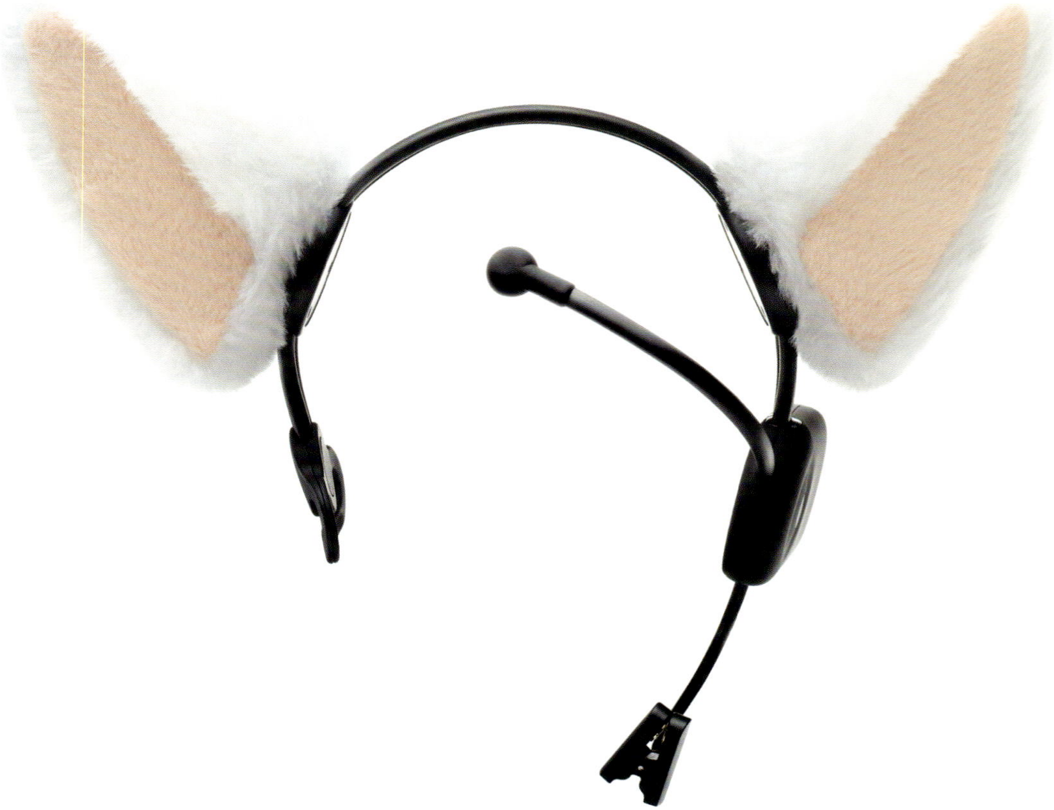

Our mission is to create an innovation in the communications area.
When we look at Japan and its people we see that many are very shy and have trouble expressing their basic feelings to others. We decided to invent a new communication tool for them using their brain waves. Brain waves refer to the change in potential when the human brain is active, and they express moods such as "focused" and "relaxed" states. They have recently been the center of attention as a method of clarifying the human mind and gaining insight into what people are thinking.
We have created a new augmented human organ that utilizes brainwaves for a new way of communication. This is the *Necomimi*—short for "neurocommunication machine."

Unser Ziel ist die Schaffung von Innovationen im Bereich der Kommunikation.
Betrachtet man Japan und seine Menschen, so sieht man, dass viele sehr schüchtern sind und sich schwer tun, ihre Gefühle zu zeigen. Wir beschlossen darum, ein Kommunikationswerkzeug für sie zu entwickeln, das mit Hirnwellen arbeitet. Hirnwellen zeigen Potenzialschwankungen der Gehirnaktivität an und bringen Bewusstseinszustände wie Konzentriertheit und Entspanntheit zum Ausdruck. Sie sind jüngst ins Zentrum der Aufmerksamkeit gerückt, weil sie als eine Methode angesehen werden, mit der man Einsicht in das menschliche Denken gewinnen kann.
Wir haben nun ein neues Organ namens *Necomimi* geschaffen, das mithilfe von Hirnwellen die kommunikativen Fähigkeiten des Menschen erweitert: *Necomimi* heißt soviel wie Katzenohren, steht aber auch kurz für

„Neurokommunikationsmaschine". Wir bedienten uns dieses in japanischen Mangas und Modeartikeln häufigen Motivs der Katzenohren, weil der Hirnwellensensor am Vorderkopf angebracht werden muss und es möglichst vielen Spaß machen soll, ihn zu tragen.
Durch die Sichtbarmachung der Gehirnaktivität sind wir in der Lage, daran einige Eigenschaften des Menschen abzulesen. Das bedeutet auch, dass TrägerInnen des Sensors ihre Emotionen direkt zum Ausdruck bringen und unabhängig von Sprache, Alter, Geschlecht und Rasse mit anderen kommunizieren können. Sind die NutzerInnen konzentriert, stellen sich die *Necomimi* auf. Sind sie entspannt, legen sich die Ohren flach an den Kopf. Sind die NutzerInnen, wie es bei vielen professionellen SportlerInnen der Fall ist, gleichzeitig konzentriert und entspannt, bewegen sich die Ohren rasch auf und ab. Am Anfang mag es einem seltsam vorkommen, die eigenen Gefühle direkt über die *Necomimi* auszudrücken. Aber man lernt schnell, die Ohren zu kontrollieren, und im Handumdrehen sind sie zu einem neuen Körperorgan geworden. In Japan jedenfalls haben die *Necomimi* sehr zu Verbesserung der zwischenmenschlichen Kommunikation beigetragen und waren ein Riesenhit.

Since there was a need to attach the brainwave sensor to the forehead, we used the cat's ears motif frequently used in Japanese manga and fashion items to make it fun for everyone to wear.
By visualizing the brain activities, we will be able to see people's various characteristics. This also means that users will be able to express their emotions straight from the brain, and it enables users to communicate with anyone, regardless of language, age, gender and race. When the user is "focused" the ears will stand up, and when the user is "relaxed" the ears lie down. If the user is simultaneously "focused" and "relaxed," as seen with many professional athletes, the ears move rapidly.
At first, expressing one's emotions directly by *Necomimi* may be a strange experience. But after a few minutes people could control the ears easily. It was a moment when we acquired a new, augmented human organ. After all, *Necomimi* has greatly helped the Japanese to communicate with each other better and has been an enormous hit.

Neurowear (JP), founded in 2010, is a project team based in Tokyo, focused on creating "communication for the near future." We design prototypes of new products and services based on biological signals such as brain waves, heartbeats etc. *Necomimi* was selected by *Time Magazine* as one of the top 50 inventions of 2011. **Neurowear** (JP), gegründet 2010, ist ein Tokioter Projektteam, das an der „Kommunikation der nahen Zukunft" arbeitet. Es entwickelt Prototypen neuer Produkte und Dienstleistungen auf der Basis biologischer Signale wie Gehirnwellen, Herzschlag usw. *Necomimi* wurde 2011 vom *Time Magazine* unter die besten 50 Erfindungen gewählt.

Perfume Global Site Project

Perfume (Aa-Chan, Kashiyuka, Nocchi), Daito Manabe, Mikiko, Yasutaka Nakata, Satoshi Horii, Hiroyasu Kimura

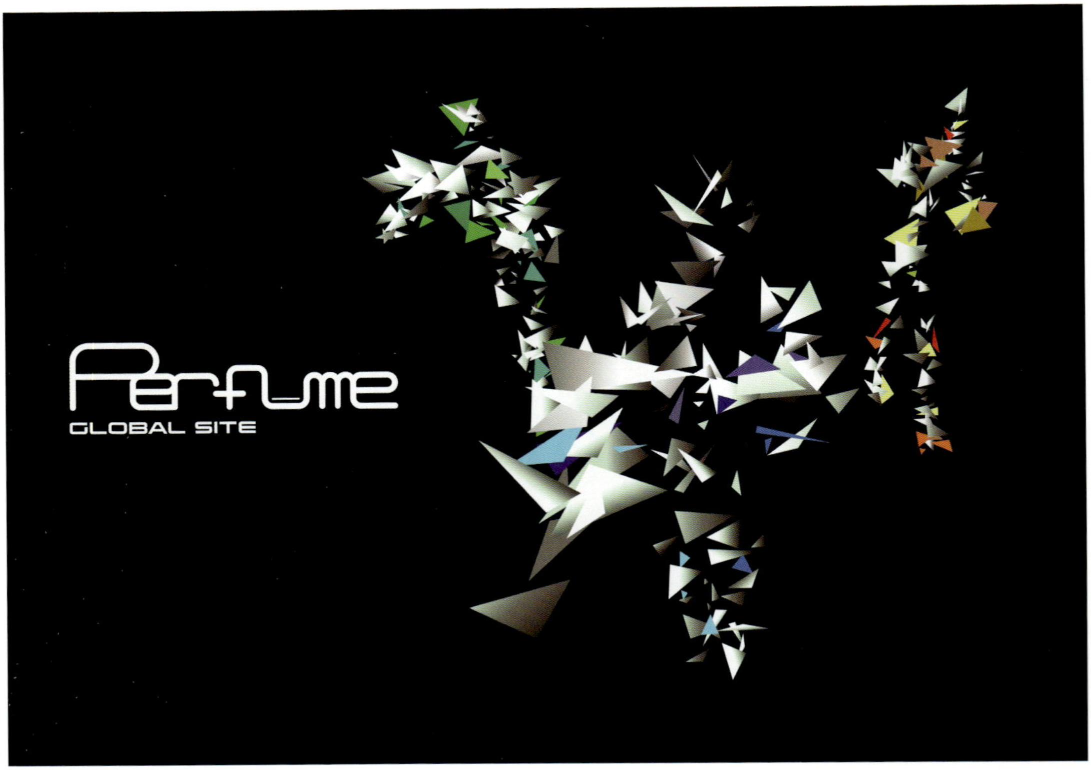

Perfume Global Site Project commemorates the global debut of the techno-pop group Perfume. Based on the concept of fans and creators launching the group into the world together, this massive project involved the planning and production of a teaser site, an open-source project and live performances by the members of Perfume. Following the site launch, the open-source project provided free distribution of original music and choreographic motion-capture data from the official website. Secondary creation by programmers was enabled by providing sample codes and extended features for the use of data via the social coding service GitHub. This gave birth to over 600 richly varied projects in countries around the world and six million total views of all films. On Perfume's global tour, works developed through this project were introduced and they performed compositions and choreography distributed through the site.

Das *Perfume Global Site Project* feiert den internationalen Auftritt der Technopop-Gruppe Perfume. Ausgehend von der Idee, dass Fans und Kreative die Gruppe gemeinsam in die Welt tragen, umfasst das Projekt insgesamt die Planung und Entwicklung einer Teaser-Website, ein Open-Source-Projekt und Live-Auftritte der Perfume-Mitglieder. Nach dem Start der Website wurden mit dem Open-Source-Projekt Originalmusik und choreografische Bewegungsdaten frei zur Verfügung gestellt. Die Bereitstellung von Mustercodes und erweiterten Datennutzungsfunktionen über den Social-Coding-Dienst GitHub ermöglichte überdies Sekundärkreationen durch ProgrammiererInnen. Das führte zur Entwicklung von über 600 unterschiedlichen Projekten in aller Welt, die alles in allem sechs Millionen mal aufgerufen wurden. Auf der Welttournee von Perfume wurden im Rahmen des Projekts entstandene Arbeiten vorgestellt und über die Website verbreitete Kompositionen und Choreografien aufgeführt.

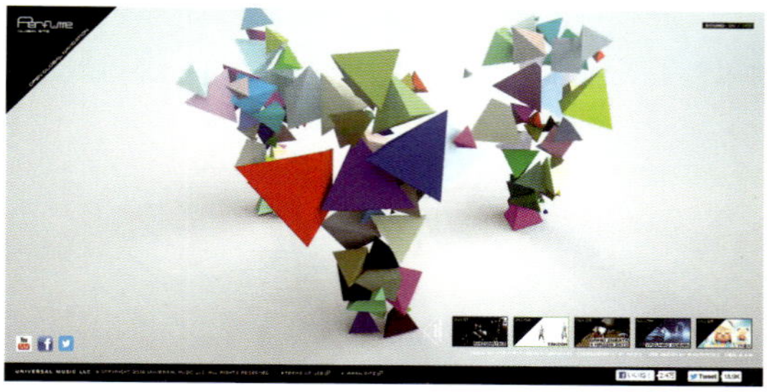
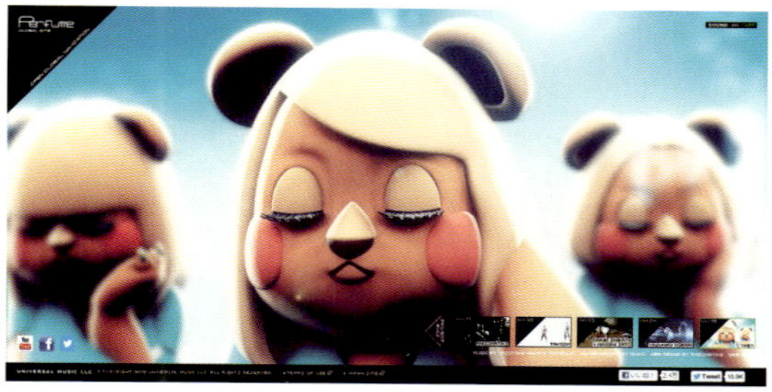
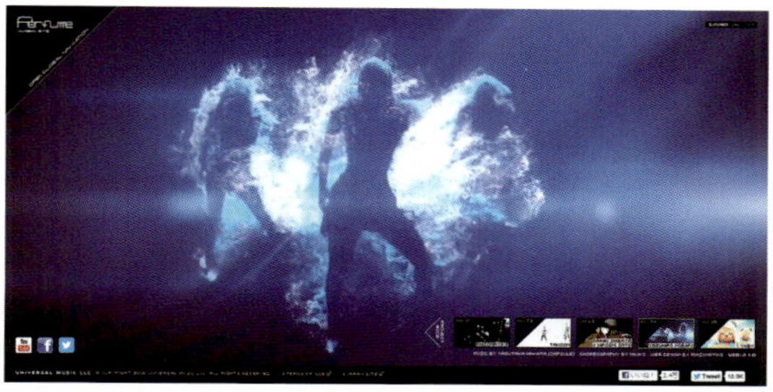
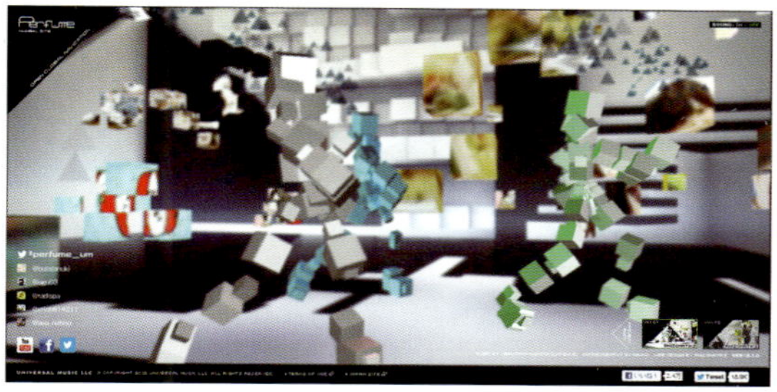
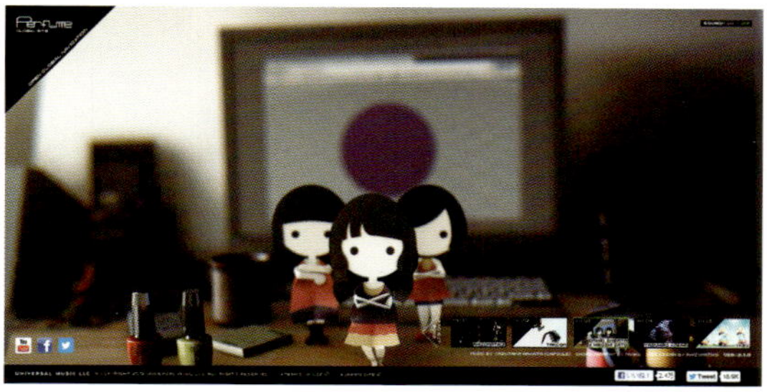

Perfume (JP) are **Aa-Chan (Ayaka Nishiwaki)**, **Kashiyuka (Yuka Kashino)** and **Nocchi (Ayano Omoto)**. Established in 2000, Perfume are the top techno-pop girl trio and one of the most influential girl groups in Japan. **Daito Manabe** (JP) is a pioneer in developing new forms of entertainment as well as a variety of other genres through sophisticated programming technology, thorough research and creative ideas. Founder of Rhizomatiks. **Mikiko** (JP) is a director and choreographer and handles the dance arrangements and live staging for Perfume, as well as choreography for numerous music videos, commercials and stage productions. **Nakata Yasutaka** (JP) is a music producer and composer who has produced Perfume and Kyary Pamyu Pamyu among other artists both in Japan and abroad. **Horii Satoshi** (JP) is active in programming-based image production and design. Member of Rhizomatiks. **Kimura Hiroyasu** (JP) is a designer and the art director of Rhizomatiks. **Perfume** (JP), bestehend aus **Aa-Chan (Ayaka Nishiwaki)**, **Kashiyuka (Yuka Kashino)** und **Nocchi (Ayano Omoto)**, ist ein 2000 gegründetes Techno-Pop-Trio und eine der einflussreichsten Girlgroups in Japan. **Daito Manabe** (JP) ist ein Pionier in der Entwicklung neuer Unterhaltungsformen und verschiedener anderer Genres mittels komplexer Programmiertechniken, gründlicher Forschung und kreativer Ideen. Gründer von Rhizomatiks. **Mikiko**, (JP) ist Regisseur und Choreograf. Er macht die Tanzarrangements und Live-Bühnenshows für Perfume und choreografierte für unzählige Musikvideos, Werbefilme und Bühnenproduktionen. **Nakata Yasutaka** (JP) ist Musikproduzent und Komponist. Er produziert u.a. Perfume und Kyary Pamyu Pamyu in Japan wie in Übersee. **Horii Satoshi** (JP) ist in der programmgestützten Bildgestaltung tätig. Mitglied von Rhizomatiks. **Kimura Hiroyasu** (JP) ist Designer und der Art Director von Rhizomatiks.

The Kuramoto Model (1,000 Fireflies)

David Allan Rueter

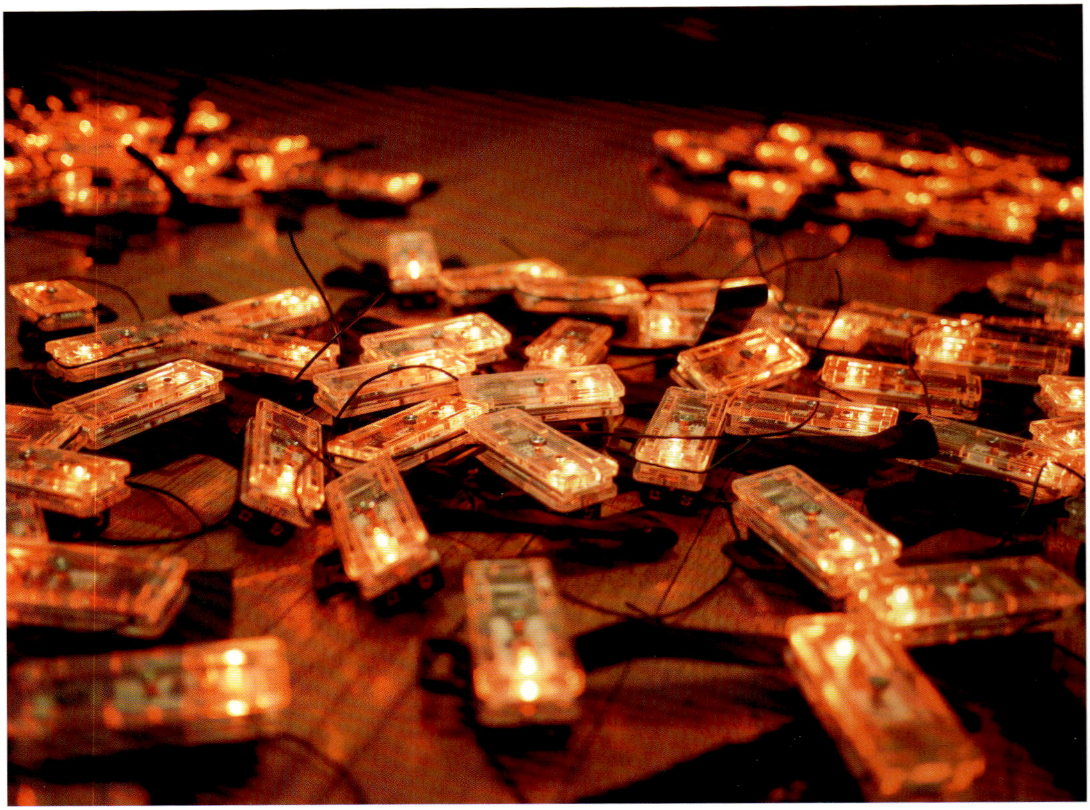

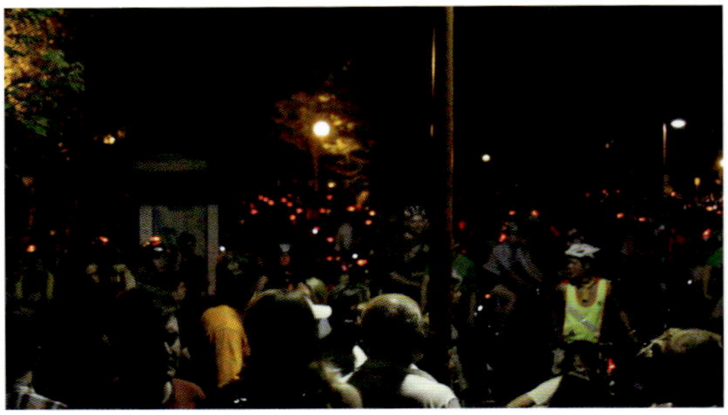

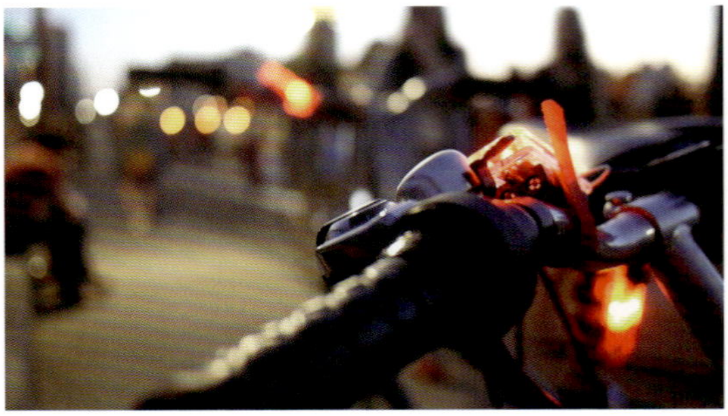

2012 erhielt ich von Northern Lights.mn den Auftrag, 1.000 spezielle Fahrradleuchten zu bauen, die bei einem Freiluft-Festival in Minneapolis, Minnesota, an RadfahrerInnen verteilt wurden. Mithilfe von Funkmodulen und auf der Grundlage von Erkenntnissen aus der Systemwissenschaft konnten diese Leuchten ihr Blinkmuster mit anderen in der Nähe befindlichen Leuchten synchronisieren, was die Spielregeln sozialer Nähe veränderte und ein über die Stadt verteiltes selbstorganisierendes System entstehen ließ.

In 2012, Northern Lights.mn commissioned me to build 1,000 custom bike lights to distribute to cyclists attending an outdoor arts festival in Minneapolis, MN. Using radio transceivers and insights gained from complex systems research, these devices synchronized their blinking patterns with other nearby devices, altering social rules of proximity and generating a citywide self-organizing system.

Commissioned by Northern Lights.mn for Northern Spark 2012.

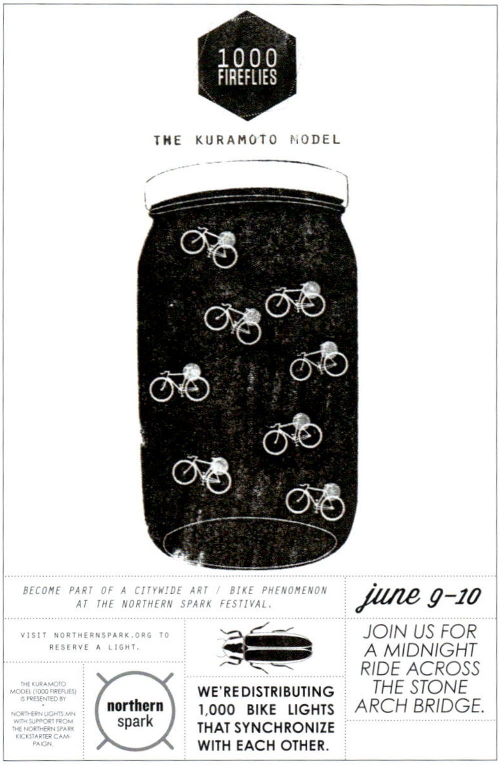

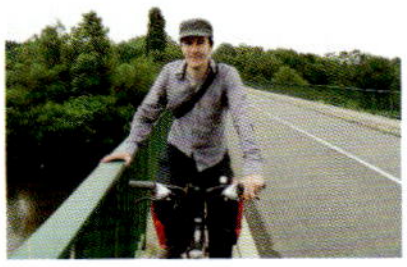

David Allan Rueter (US) is currently an MFA candidate in art and technology studies at the School of the Art Institute of Chicago. His work has been exhibited at galleries and festivals across the US, including ISEA and Northern Spark. He graduated from Oberlin College with a BA in politics and a focus in political theory. Before attending SAIC, David worked as a software engineer for ten years, designing and implementing tools for processing and transforming large sets of data. **David Allan Rueter** (US) ist derzeit Masterkandidat in Art and Technology Studies an der School of the Art Institute of Chicago. Seine Arbeiten wurden USA-weit in Galerien und auf Festivals gezeigt, u. a. auf der ISEA und bei Northern Spark. Er studierte zunächst Politikwissenschaft am Oberlin College und war dann bis zu seinem Masterstudium an der SAIC zehn Jahre als Software-Entwickler – insbesondere für Tools zur Verarbeitung und Umwandlung großer Datenmengen – tätig.

Voice Array

Rafael Lozano-Hemmer

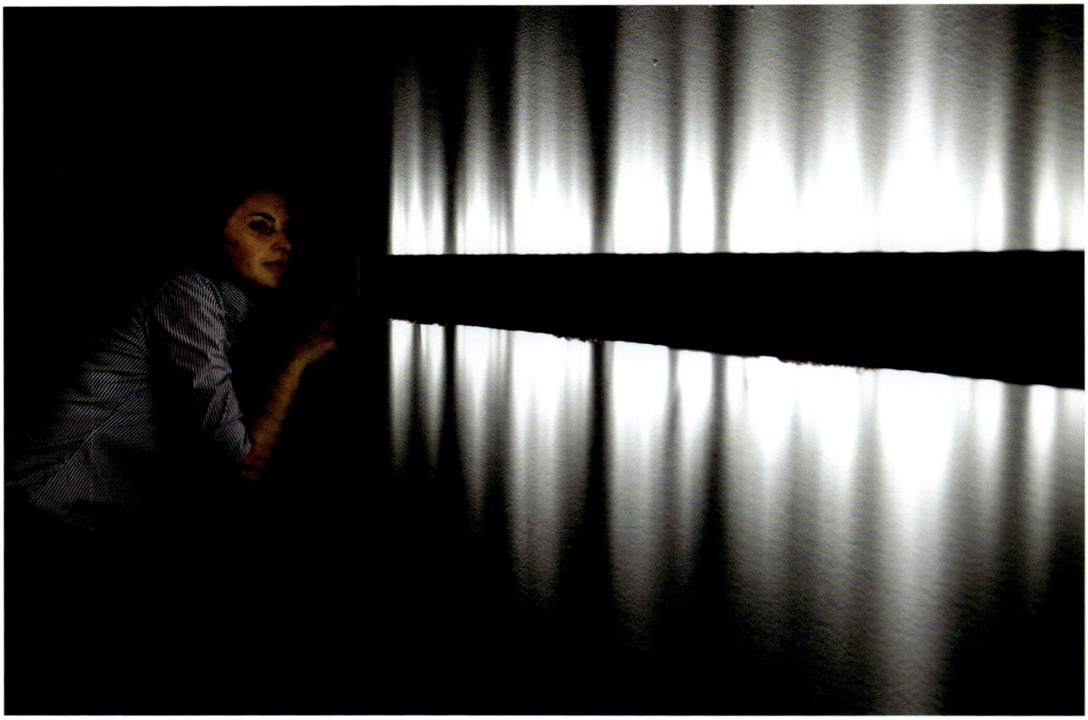

As a participant speaks into an intercom his or her voice is automatically translated into flashes of light and then the unique blinking pattern is stored as a loop in the first light of the array. Each new recording pushes all previous recordings one position down and gradually one can hear the cumulative sound of the 288 previous recordings. The voice that was pushed out of the array can then be heard by itself.

Spricht eine TeilnehmerIn in eine Sprechanlage, wird die Stimme automatisch in eine Serie von Lichtblitzen umgewandelt und das einzigartige Blinkmuster als Loop in der ersten Leuchte des Arrays gespeichert. Jeder neue Sprechakt schiebt alle vorangegangenen um eine Position weiter, sodass allmählich der Gesamtklang aller vorherigen 288 Aufnahmen vernehmbar wird. Die Stimme, die dabei aus dem Array verdrängt wird, ist schließlich alleine zu hören.

Rafael Lozano-Hemmer: concept, direction; Rahzel: beatboxing; Gideon May: programming, custom hardware and software; Stephan Schulz, Pierre Fournier, Sébastien Dallaire, Guillaume Tremblay, Tyson Parks: production support. Commissioned by the Museum of Contemporary Art, Sydney.

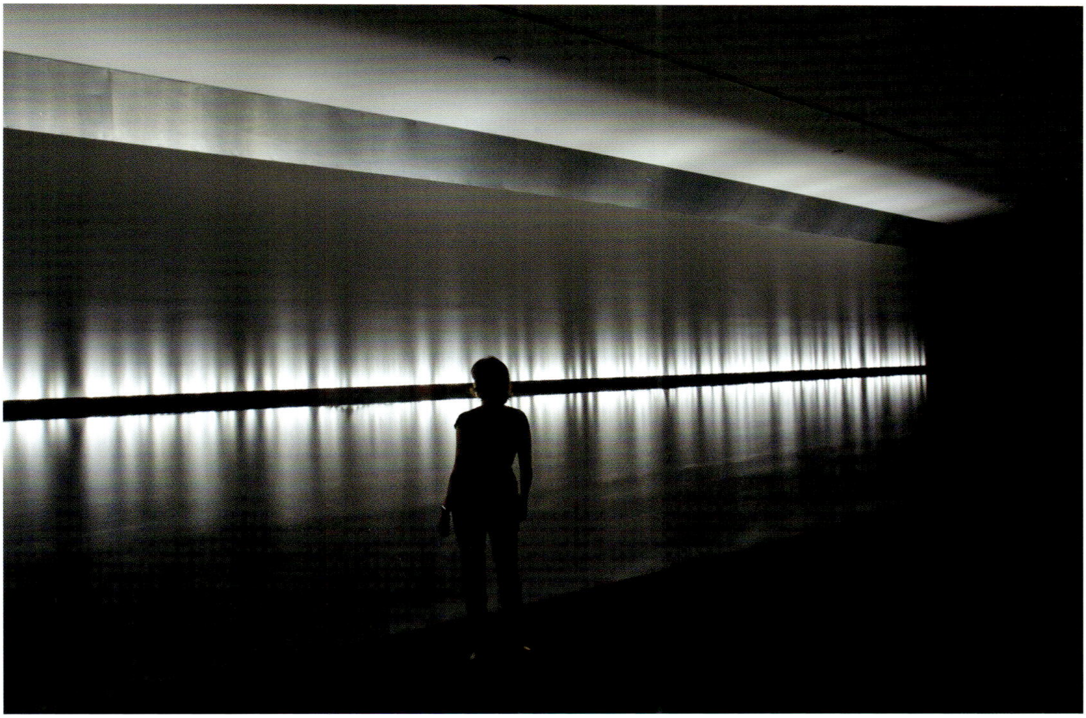

Photos: Antimodular Research

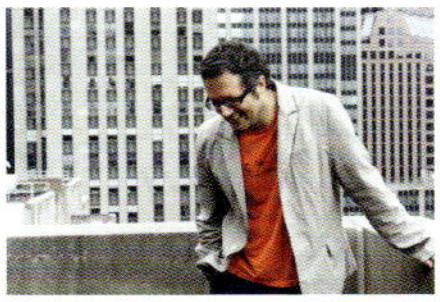

Rafael Lozano-Hemmer (MX/CA), born 1967. In 1989 he received a BSc in physical chemistry from Concordia University in Montréal. He develops interactive installations that are at the intersection of architecture and performance art. His main interest is in creating platforms for public participation, by perverting technologies such as robotics, computerized surveillance or telematic networks. Inspired by phantasmagoria, carnival and animatronics, his light and shadow works are "antimonuments for alien agency." His large-scale interactive installations have been commissioned for events such as the Millennium Celebrations in Mexico City (1999), the Cultural Capital of Europe in Rotterdam (2001), the UN World Summit of Cities in Lyon (2003), the opening of the YCAM Center in Japan (2003), the Expansion of the European Union in Dublin (2004), the memorial for the Tlatelolco Student Massacre in Mexico City (2008), the 50th Anniversary of the Guggenheim Museum in New York (2009) and the Winter Olympics in Vancouver (2010). **Rafael Lozano-Hemmer** (MX/CA), geb. 1967, studierte physikalische Chemie an der Concordia University Montréal (BSc, 1989). Er entwickelt interaktive Installationen am Schnittpunkt von Architektur und Performance. Sein besonderes Interesse gilt der Schaffung von Plattformen für Publikumsbeteiligung durch die Zweckentfremdung von Robotik, computerisierter Überwachungstechnik oder telematischen Netzwerken. Seine Licht-Schatten-Arbeiten sind von Phantasmagorie, Karneval und Animatronik inspirierte „Anti-Denkmäler für fremde Handlungsmacht". Groß angelegte interaktive Installationen entstanden u. a. für Ereignisse wie die Milleniumsfeierlichkeiten in Mexico City (1999), die Kulturhauptstadt Europas Rotterdam (2001), den UN-Weltgipfel der Städte in Lyon (2003), die Eröffnung des YCAM Center in Japan (2003), die EU-Erweiterungszeremonie in Dublin (2004), die Gedenkfeier für das Tlatelolco Studentenmassaker in Mexico City (2008), das 50-Jahr-Jubiläum des Guggenheim Museums in New York (2009) und die Winterolympiade in Vancouver (2010).

DIGITAL COMMUNITIES

The Muddy Camps of the Network Society
Die Niederungen der Netzwerk-Gesellschaft

Ian Banerjee, Leila Nachawati, Marcus Neustetter, Bruce Sterling, Lei Yang

We will offer a few words about the trends we observed in Digital Communities during 2013. The pace of change is rapid, and leads waves of development visible in societies worldwide.

- A desktop elite is replaced by massive mobility.
- Resilient local cybercultures, tied strongly to language and place, are outlasting technological fads.
- No major city anywhere lacks a "hackerspace" or "think-and-do lab," all busily taking open-sourced objects and services into the streets.
- Open-source hardware clusters around increasingly powerful and capable industrial devices.
- Broadband and cheap storage enable large, technically capable projects of community memory.
- Opened government databases are becoming immediate, useful, interactive and even interesting.
- Information visualization casts new light on old dilemmas, and is a novel method of advocacy.

How can one "judge" a community? Our criteria are as follows.

- First, and most importantly, is the context in which this Digital Community exists. Why are they there? What is the relevance of their activities? Do they inspire others around them? Are they a leading force within society?
- We deliberately privilege grass-roots communities over user-bases of commercial objects and services.
- Is this community vibrantly active? Does it inspire and involve people? Does it have a heritage and an established etiquette?
- Can this community grow? Could it change the texture of existence for many people in many situations? Might it represent a new way of life?
- Does this Digital Community demonstrate a humane spirit of citizenship within the so-called "smart city"?
- Is this an inventive learning community? Are ideas flowering here?

Wir möchten ein paar Bemerkungen zu den Trends, die wir in der Kategorie Digital Communities 2013 beobachteten, machen. Das Tempo der Veränderung ist hoch und treibt Entwicklungen an, die in Gesellschaften auf der ganzen Welt auszumachen sind.

- Eine Desktop-Elite wird schnell von massiver Mobilität verdrängt.
- Belastbare lokale Cyberkulturen, die eng mit Sprache und Ort verbunden sind, sind langlebiger als technologische Spielereien.
- In den meisten größeren Stadt gibt es inzwischen einen „Hackerspace" oder ein „Think-and-do Lab", die Gegenstände und Dienstleistungen, die nach Open-Source-Kriterien entstanden sind, unter die Leute bringen.
- Open-Source-Hardware dockt an immer leistungsfähigeren industriellen Geräten an.
- Breitband und billiger Speicherplatz ermöglichen große, technisch anspruchsvolle Projekte, die sich mit dem Gedächtnis einer Gemeinschaft beschäftigen.
- Offene Regierungs-Datenbanken werden direkt zugänglich, sind von hohem praktischen Nutzen, sind interaktiv und sogar interessant.
- Informationsvisualisierung wirft ein neues Licht auf alte Dilemmata und ist nun eine neue Methode der Advocacy-Arbeit.

Wie können wir eine Community „beurteilen"? Wir gingen von folgenden Kriterien aus:

- Das wichtigste Kriterium ist der Kontext, in dem eine Digital Community existiert. Warum gibt es sie? Wie relevant sind ihre Aktivitäten? Inspiriert sie Menschen in ihrem Umfeld? Ist sie eine treibende Kraft innerhalb der Gesellschaft?
- Wir haben bewusst Grassroot-Gemeinschaften gegenüber Usergruppen kommerzieller Projekte und Dienstleistungen bevorzugt.
- Ist die Community aktiv und dynamisch? Inspiriert sie, gelingt es ihr, die Menschen einzubinden? Gibt es ein Erbe, auf dem sie aufbauen kann? Existiert ein akzeptiertes Verhaltensrepertoire?
- Kann die Gemeinschaft wachsen? Könnte sie das existenzielle Gefüge vieler Menschen in unterschiedlichen

Situationen verändern? Könnte sie für einen neuen Lebensstil stehen?
- Bringt die Digital Community einen Sinn für humanes Bürgertum in die sogenannte Smart City?
- Ist die Community erfinderisch und lernfähig? Gibt es ein Feuerwerk an Ideen?
- Steht diese Gemeinschaft allen offen? Ist sie gerecht, integrativ und fair? Ist sie großzügig? Nimmt sie Neuankömmlinge mit offenen Armen auf?
- Wir sind überzeugt, dass Ästhetik in jeder Digital Community eine Rolle spielt. Wir alle verdienen ein elegantes Design und anwenderfreundliche Tools.

Es ist uns bewusst, dass die Zeiten hart und Gemeinschaften überall großem Druck ausgesetzt sind. Angesichts der dunklen Wolken, die der Finanzkollaps, die Wohnungskrise, die Flüchtlingsströme und eine archaische, korrupte Nationalpolitik aufziehen lassen, ist es wichtig, die konkreten Aktionen und die von Gemeinschaften übernommene Verantwortung anzuerkennen. Unsere Gewinner zeigen, welche Macht sich entfalten kann, wenn man für die Interessen von Bürgern eintritt und spontan, offen und ortsadäquat handelt, oder wenn es gilt, im Zuge von Kämpfen zerrissene Familien zu heilen. Sie sind ein Beispiel dafür, welche Kraft wohl überlegten Worten und Bildern innewohnen kann, selbst in den langwierigsten Kämpfen und Kriegen. Sie sind die Vorboten einer emergierenden Netzwerk-Gesellschaft des 21. Jahrhunderts.
Wir hoffen, dass die von unserer Jury vergebenen Preise all jenen, die bereits Mut gezeigt haben, noch mehr Mut machen. Gewinner der Goldenen Nica in der Kategorie Digital Communities ist *El Campo de Cebada* aus Madrid. Unsere Auszeichnungen gehen an *Refugees United* und *Visualizing Palestine*.
Digital Communities existieren dank der selbstlosen Bemühungen vieler Aktivisten auf diesem Gebiet, und einen davon möchten wir hervorheben: Aaron Swartz. Wir wissen, dass sich digitale Technologie auch weiterhin schnell verändern wird, aber wir vertrauen in die nicht versiegende Macht der Gemeinschaft.

- Is this community accessible? Is it just, inclusive and fair-minded? Is it generous in spirit? Does it welcome newcomers?
- We believe that aesthetics matters to any digital community. People deserve elegant design and usable tools.

We are sensitive to the fact that these are hard times and that communities everywhere are stressed. In a darkening atmosphere of financial collapse, crises in housing, flows of refugees, and archaic, corrupted national politics, it is important to recognize community responsibility and community action. Our winners demonstrate the power of citizen advocacy in spontaneous and open local action, in the healing of families torn apart by strife, and the power of well-considered speech and imagery, in even the most protracted scenes of war and struggle. They are exemplars and harbingers of an emergent 21st-century network society. We hope that our jury's award will further encourage those who have already shown courage.
The winner of the Golden Nica in the category of "Digital Communities" is *El Campo de Cebada* in Madrid. Our Awards of Distinction go to *Refugees United* and *Visualizing Palestine*.
Digital Communities exist through the selfless efforts of many activists in the field, among whom we specifically mention Aaron Swartz. We know that digital technology is and will remain in rapid flux, but we are happy to express our confidence in the lasting power of community.

El Campo de Cebada

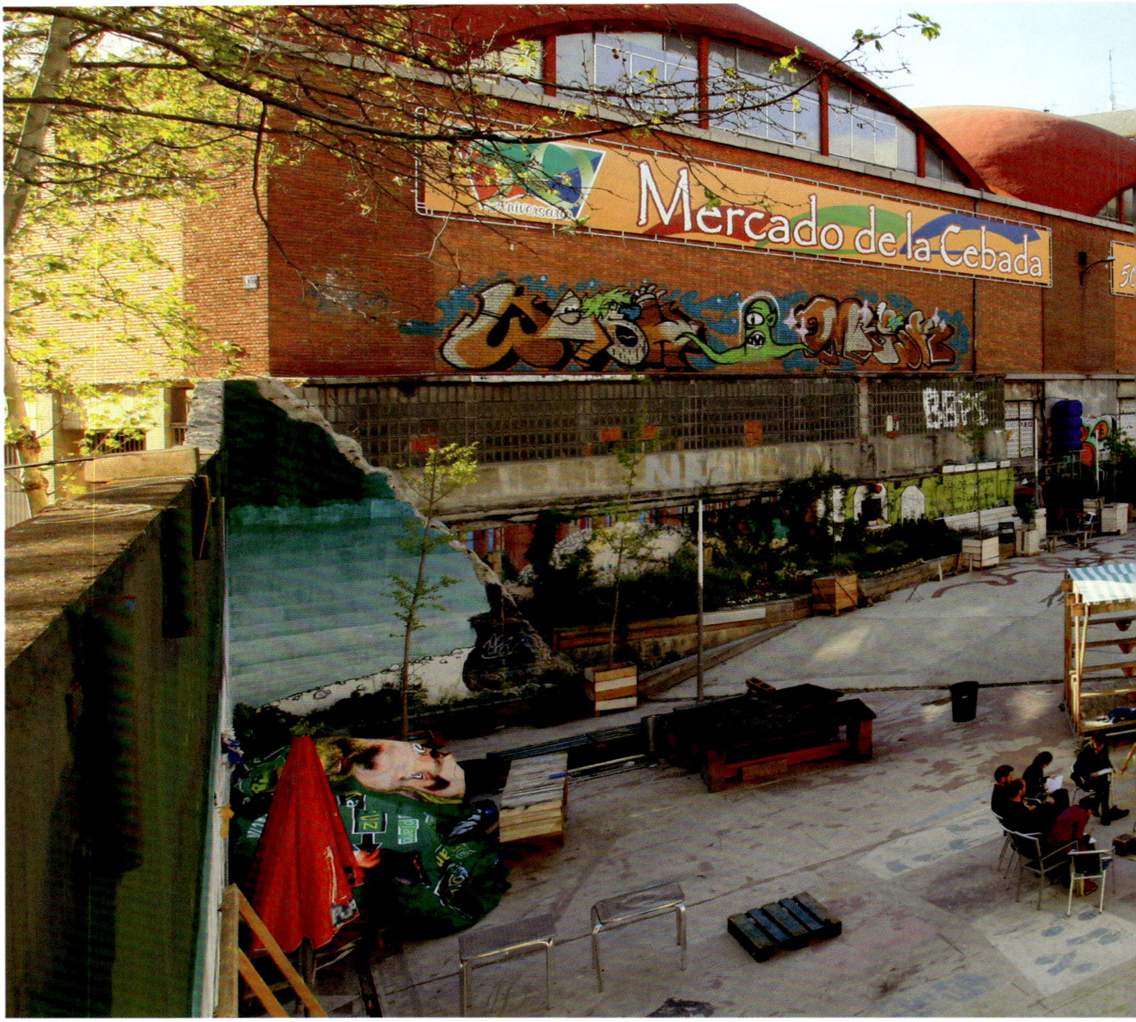

El Campo de Cebada is both a physical and a virtual space, an open-source square in the center of Madrid.

Two years ago it was only a void in the city, a hole where the local public swimming pool used to be. The city council demolished the pool to build modern new facilities, but then the economic crisis arrived and they found they had no money for the project. So the space was closed and fenced off. After a few months, and resulting from a conflict generated by a temporary activity held inside it during the celebration of Madrid's White Night, the local residents realized that it was a shame to

El Campo de Cebada („das Gerstenfeld") ist sowohl ein physischer als auch ein virtueller Raum, ein Open-Source-Platz im Zentrum von Madrid.

Vor zwei Jahren war dieser Platz der einzige leere Ort in der Stadt, ein Loch, wo einmal das öffentliche Schwimmbad war. Die Stadtregierung demolierte das Schwimmbad, um eine neue, modernere Einrichtung zu bauen, aber auf Grund der Finanzkrise gab es keine Gelder mehr für dieses Projekt. Daher wurde der Ort geschlossen und eingezäunt. Nach ein paar Monaten kam es zu einem Konflikt mit den Veranstaltern einer temporären Aktivität, die dort während der „Weißen Nacht" in Madrid abgehalten wurde. Da erkannten die Anrainer, dass es eine Schande

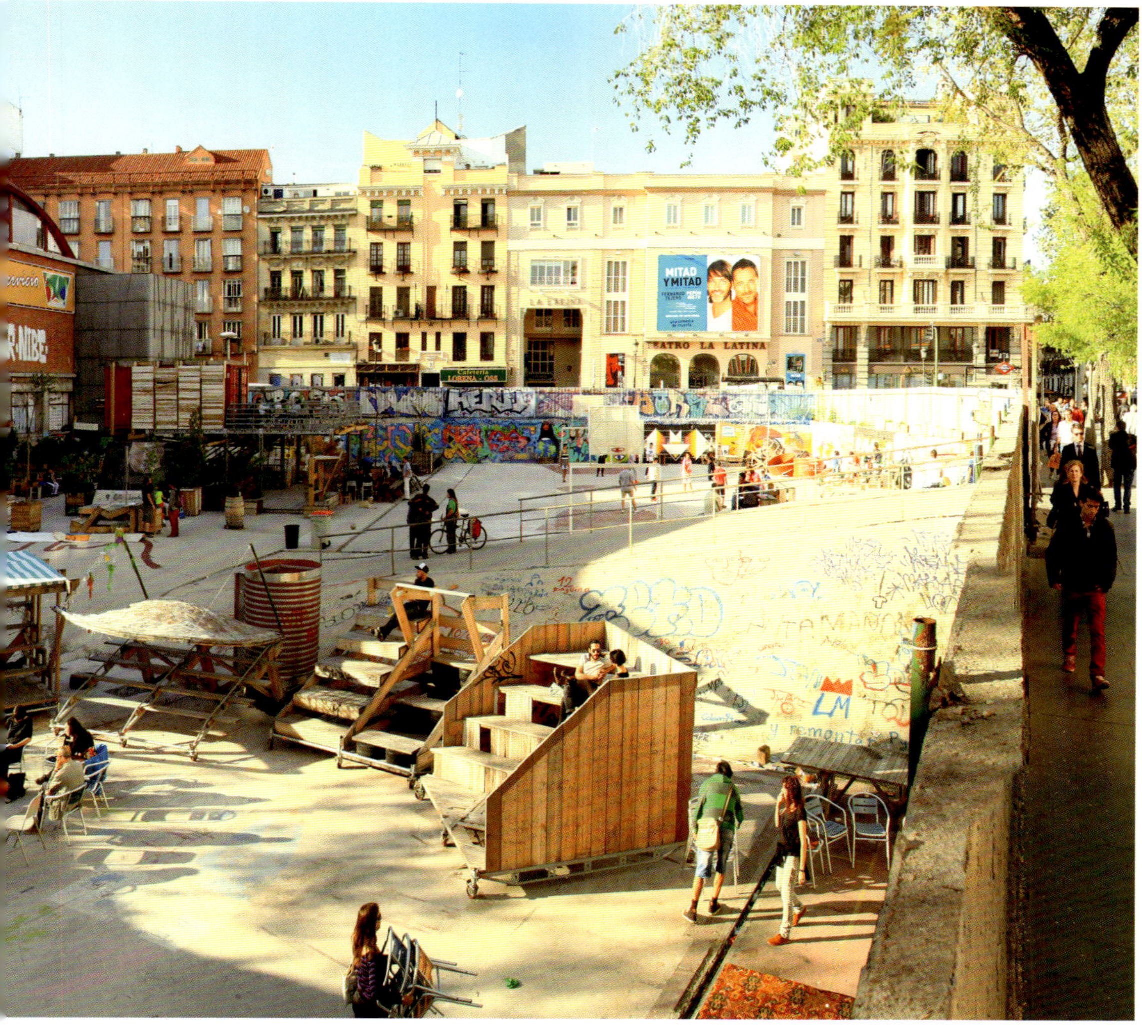

wäre, ein 3.500 Quadratmeter großes Gelände mitten im Zentrum von Madrid abgezäunt zu lassen. Sie sahen darin eine Chance, in ihrer eigenen Nachbarschaft aktiv zu werden, taten sich mit örtlichen Vereinen zusammen und begannen Gespräche mit der Gemeinde. Man kam überein, diesen Platz von den Anrainern gemeinsam mit der Stadtverwaltung managen zu lassen und die Energie der Menschen, die etwas für ihre Stadt tun wollen, mit den Tools und Experten der Stadtverwaltung zu kombinieren. Dies ist auch ein wichtiger Schritt, was die Legitimität des Projekts betrifft.
Nun wird dieser Raum von den Anrainern und der lokalen Verwaltung betrieben. Dabei kommen dynamische und

have 3,500 square meters of closed off land in the center of Madrid and thought it could be a chance for them to participate in their own neighborhood. So they came together with local associations and managed to talk to the government. It was agreed that the space should be managed by the local residents but in co-responsibility with the city council, combining the power of people willing to work for their city with that of the tools and experts that governments can deploy. This also works in the very important direction of legitimacy.
Now the space is co-managed by the residents and the local administration with dynamic and

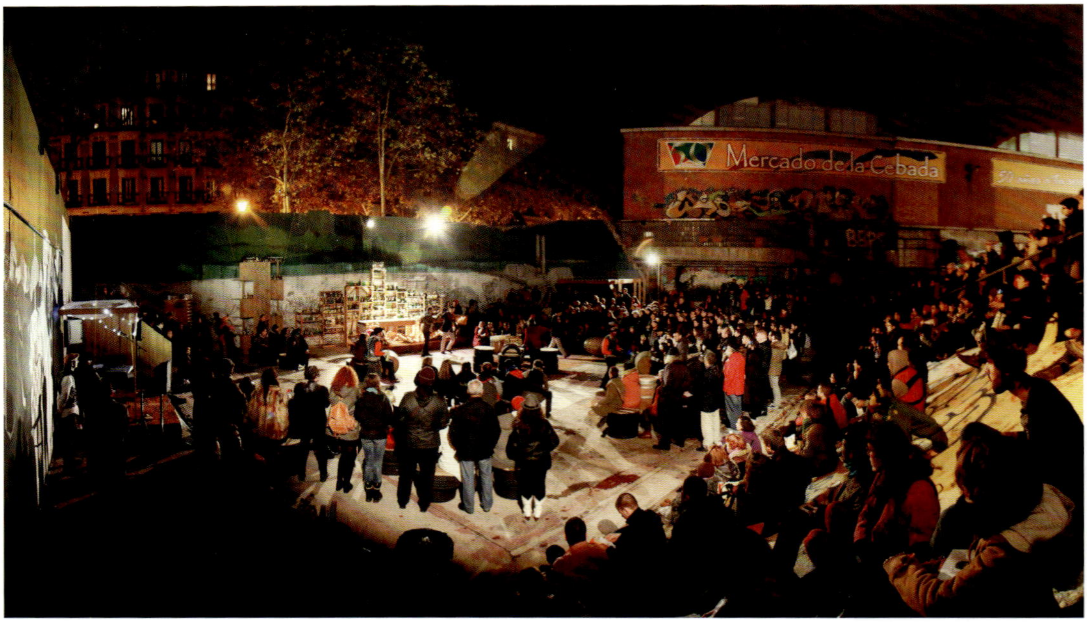

open tools to "save" the traditional understanding gap that often exists between them. It has a fully transparent open-data policy in both the virtual and real worlds, since all the meetings and assemblies are open to everyone, the resources management is published and can be always consulted. Everything is done through the effort of the individuals and collectives sharing their specific knowledge and all the designs are registered, uploaded and open for further improvement. It is a space to develop new ways of understanding and to construct an open-source urbanism based on ad-hoc solutions and common sense.

In all this, virtual space as important as the physical, with virtual players being related at the same level and creating this double support for a "community construction." It uses web 2.0 space, a common mailing system and traditional social networks such as Facebook or Twitter (@campodecebada), creating network dynamics with other community projects in the city, programming an open-source urban square.

The aim is to bring together the largest possible number of players to reach agreement between traditional "enemies." In this way *El Campo de Cebada* works differently to other current self-managed spaces, which reject government involvement. We think the government and its experts

offene Instrumente zum Einsatz, um traditionelle Missverständnisse, die oft zwischen diesen beiden Parteien existieren, zu überwinden. Sowohl in der virtuellen als auch in der realen Welt wird eine vollkommen transparente Open-Data-Politik betrieben: Alle Treffen und Versammlungen stehen jedem offen, das Ressourcen-Management wird veröffentlicht und kann jederzeit eingesehen werden. Alles geschieht dank der Anstrengungen von Einzelpersonen und Kollektiven, die ihr jeweiliges Wissen teilen. Alle Designs werden registriert, hochgeladen und sind für Verbesserungsvorschläge offen. Es ist ein Ort, wo neue Formen des Verstehens und ein Open-Source-Urbanismus entwickelt werden, der auf Ad-hoc-Lösungen und dem gesunden Menschenverstand basiert.

Hier ist der virtuelle Raum genauso wichtig wie der physische, wobei die virtuellen Player auf derselben Ebene mitspielen und die Bildung einer Gemeinschaft auf doppelte Weise unterstützen. Es wird der Raum des Web 2.0 genauso genutzt wie ein gängiges Mail-System und traditionelle soziale Netzwerke wie Facebook und Twitter (@campodecebada). So entsteht ein dynamisches Netzwerk, in das auch andere Community-Projekte der Stadt eingebunden sind und gemeinsam diesen Open-Source-Raum in der Stadt programmieren.

Unser Ziel ist es, die größtmögliche Anzahl von Akteuren zusammenzubringen, um einen Konsens zwischen traditionellen „Feinden" zu erreichen. In dieser Hinsicht unterscheidet sich *El Campo de Cebada* von anderen selbst organisierten Räumen, die jede Regierungsbeteiligung ablehnen. Wir glauben, dass die Regierung und ihre Experten die Verantwortung dem Aufbau einer Stadt des 21. Jahrhunderts mit den Bürgern teilen müssen. Indem wir visualisieren und abbilden, was wir tun und was wir bei diesem Projekt lernen, treten wir für neue urbane Modelle ein, in denen der Bürger nicht mehr bloß ein passiv Beteiligter ist, der über keine Entscheidungsmacht verfügt.

Die neue Weltlage verlangt nach solchen neuen Rollen; Stadtplaner und Architekten sind nun wichtige Experten, sie sind Mittelsmänner zwischen Bürgern und der Macht, zwischen der Verwaltung und den Nutzern der Stadt. Unser eigentliches Ziel ist es, Strategien zu entwickeln, die sowohl die physische als auch die digitale Welt hybridisieren können. Unserer Auffassung nach wird *El Campo de Cebada* gleichzeitig in beiden Welten „gebaut", und keine ist wichtiger als die andere. Sowohl in der physischen als auch in der digitalen Umgebung gibt es keine „Eröffnung", und das Projekt wird nie ein Ende haben, da es sich ständig aktualisiert – es ist ein Raum, der die Gelegenheit bietet, Dinge runterzuladen und – das ist wichtiger – raufzuladen.

must share responsibility with citizens in the construction of the 21st century city. By visualizing, mapping what we do and what we learn with this project, we can spread the idea of implementing new urban models in which the citizen is no longer a static agent with no decision-making power.

The new world context demands these new roles; urban planners and architects are now necessary experts, intermediaries between citizens and power, between administration and urban users. Our final aim is to implement strategies that can hybridize both physical and digital worlds. We understand that *El Campo de Cebada* is constructed at the same time in both worlds and with the same importance; in the physical environment just as in the digital one there is no inauguration day, and it never finishes because it is always updating—a space that provides the opportunity to download but, even more importantly, to upload.

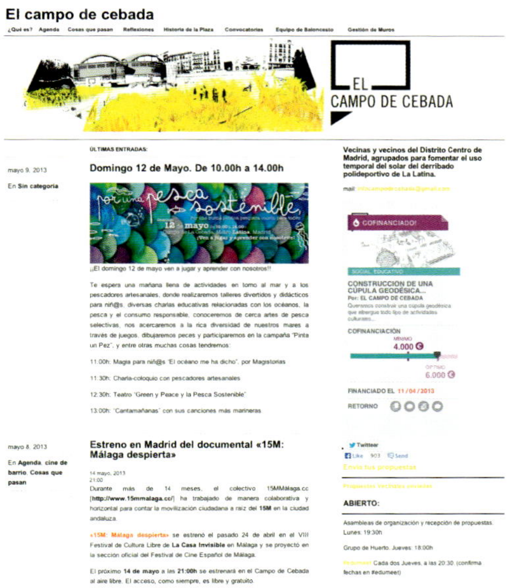

El Campo de Cebada consists of a large number of individuals and collectives, citizens, experts, administrative assistants and technicians involved in the management and development of *El Campo de Cebada*. They work voluntarily and for free for their neighbors, legitimated by their own work, hence increasingly feeling that they belong to a space that it is theirs because they look after it. They are curators of a city that they are helping to build through their own decisions. In this way everybody has authorship and yet nobody does. **El Campo de Cebada** besteht aus einer großen Anzahl von Personen und Kollektiven, Bürgern, Experten, Verwaltungsbeamten und Technikern, die im Management und der Entwicklung von *El Campo de Cebada* involviert sind. Sie arbeiten freiwillig und unentgeltlich für ihre Nachbarn, sie sind durch ihre Arbeit legitimiert, was das Gefühl verstärkt, zu einem Raum, der ihrer ist, zu gehören, weil sie sich seiner annehmen. Sie sind die Kuratoren einer Stadt, die sie durch ihre eigenen Entscheidungen errichten. In dieser Hinsicht hat jeder und niemand Urheberrechte inne.

Refugees United

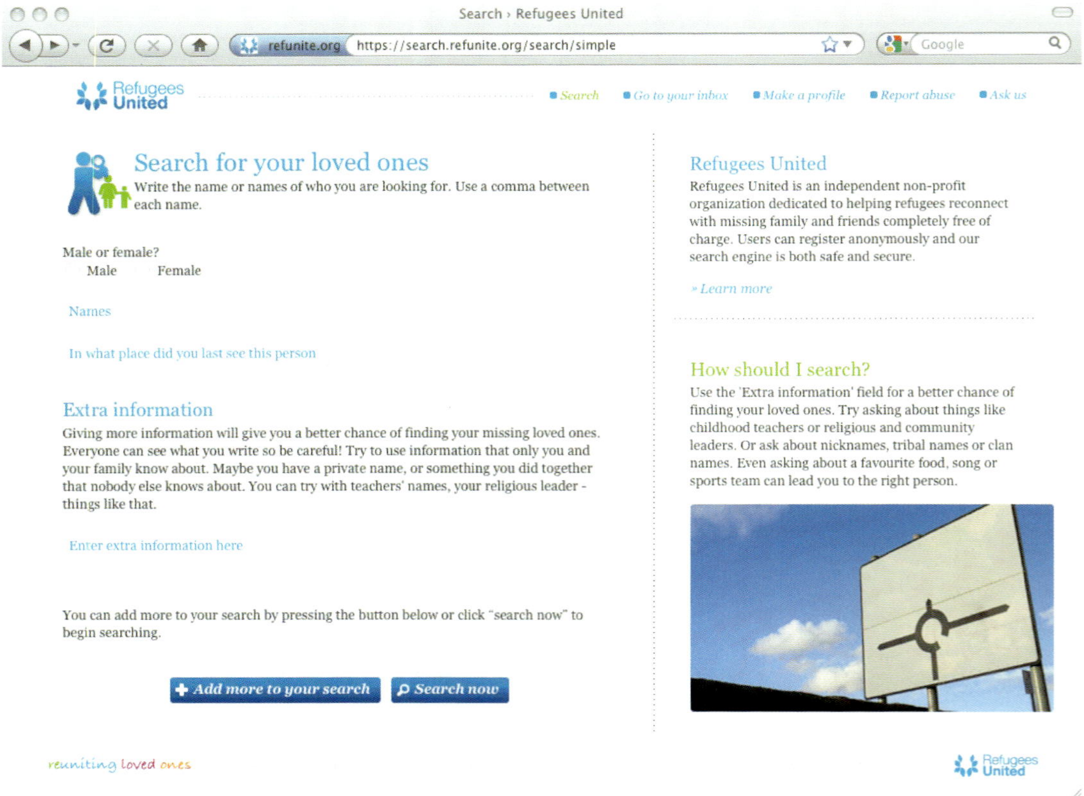

Refugees United is a non-profit organization working to provide refugee families with a global, anonymous and user-driven tracing system to help them reconnect with missing loved ones. *Refugees United's* platform and mobile tools were built via an open-source, collaborative approach to building an organization via partnerships with large corporate players as well as other non-profit organizations.

The platform empowers refugees to take the search process into their own hands and start looking for missing family and friends and it drastically streamlines the family-tracing process for both NGOs and individuals. Refugees can register on the *Refugees United* search site using information such as nicknames, scars, former

Refugees United ist eine Non-Profit-Organisation, die Familien von Flüchtlingen ein globales, anonymes und userbetriebenes Such-System zur Verfügung stellt, das ihnen hilft, Kontakt zu vermissten Angehörigen herzustellen. Die Plattform von *Refugees United* und die mobilen Tools verfolgen einen kollaborativen Open-Source-Ansatz, mit dem Ziel, eine Organisation in Partnerschaft sowohl mit großen Unternehmen als auch anderen Non-Profit-Organisationen zu errichten.

Die Plattform ermöglicht es Flüchtlingen, den Suchprozess selbst in die Hand zu nehmen und vermisste Familienangehörige und Freunde zu suchen beginnen. Dadurch vereinfacht sich der Suchprozess sowohl für NGOs als auch für den Betroffenen drastisch. Flüchtlinge können sich auf der Such-Seite von *Refugees United* registrieren und Informationen wie Spitznamen,

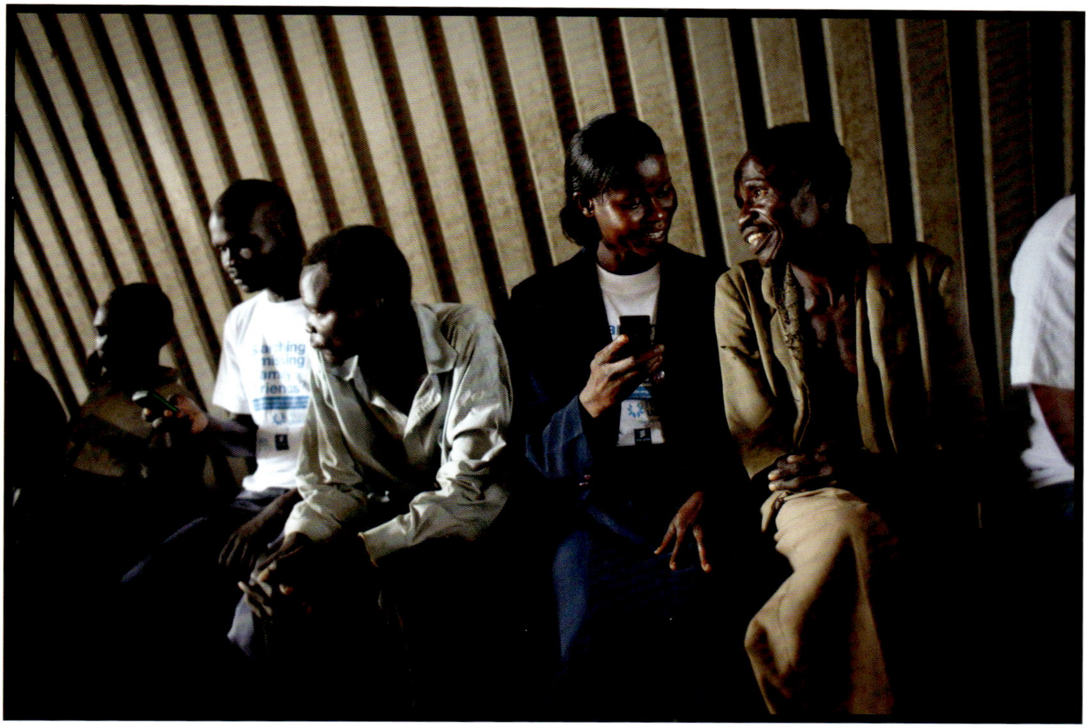

Narben, frühere Wohnorte und Ähnliches angeben, was nur Angehörigen und engen Freunden bekannt ist. Bei *Refugees United* ist weder in der Organisation noch im Betrieb und in der Betreuung des Such-Instruments eine dritte Partei involviert. Diese digitale Infrastruktur fördert nicht nur die Zusammenarbeit und ein ungehindertes Teilen von Informationen zwischen Institutionen, die sich bei der Suche und Zusammenführung von Angehörigen engagieren, sondern gibt den Flüchtlingen auch die Möglichkeit, die Suche nach vermissten Familienangehörigen mittels eines anonymen, sicheren Forums selbst in die Hand zu nehmen.

locations and the like that are recognizable only to family and close friends. No third party is involved in *Refugees United*, either in the organization or the running and supervision of the search tool. This digital infrastructure not only fosters greater collaboration and promotes unhindered sharing of information among family tracing and reunification (FTR) agencies, but it also gives refugees the ability to become directly involved in their search for missing family via an anonymous, safe forum with easily accessible tools.

Refugees United was founded by social entrepreneurs David and Christopher Michelson in 2008 based on a personal experience trying to reconnect a young Afghan refugee with his family. Today the team behind *Refugees United* consists of ten employees in two offices, in Copenhagen and Nairobi. The platform itself is open to everyone missing loved ones and currently has 185,000 registered users. **Refugees United** wurde 2008 von den Social Entrepreneurs David und Christopher Michelson gegründet, nachdem sie einem jungen afghanischen Flüchtling halfen, seine Familie zu finden. Heute besteht das Team hinter *Refugees United* aus zehn Angestellten und zwei Büros in Kopenhagen und Nairobi. Die Plattform selbst ist für jeden offen, der Angehörige vermisst, und verzeichnet zurzeit 185.000 registrierte User.

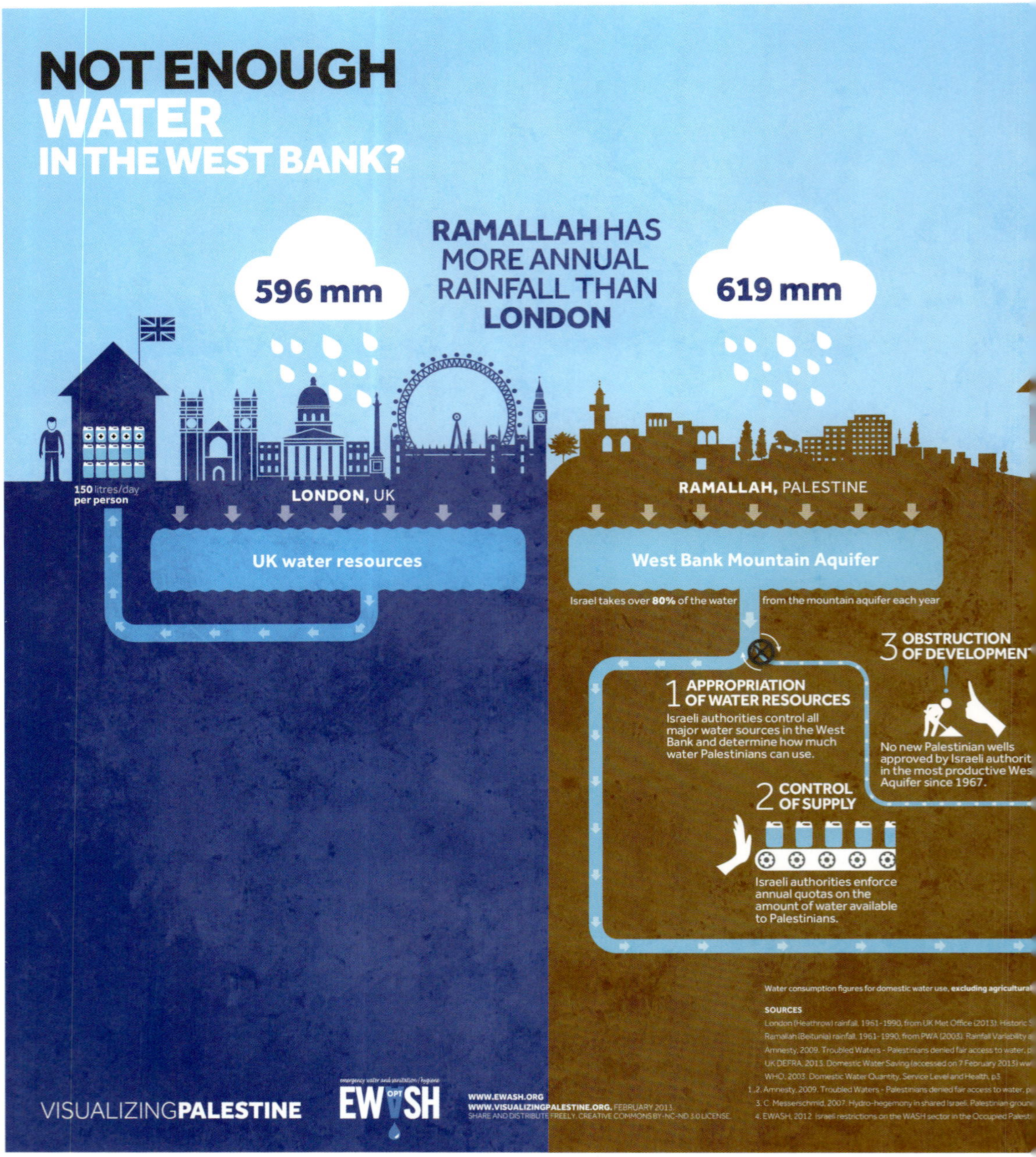
NOT ENOUGH
WATER
IN THE WEST BANK?
596 mm
RAMALLAH HAS MORE ANNUAL RAINFALL THAN LONDON
619 mm
150 litres/day per person
LONDON, UK
RAMALLAH, PALESTINE
UK water resources
West Bank Mountain Aquifer
Israel takes over 80% of the water from the mountain aquifer each year
1 APPROPRIATION OF WATER RESOURCES
Israeli authorities control all major water sources in the West Bank and determine how much water Palestinians can use.
2 CONTROL OF SUPPLY
Israeli authorities enforce annual quotas on the amount of water available to Palestinians.
3 OBSTRUCTION OF DEVELOPMEN
No new Palestinian wells approved by Israeli authorit in the most productive Wes Aquifer since 1967.
Water consumption figures for domestic water use, excluding agricultural
SOURCES
London (Heathrow) rainfall, 1961-1990, from UK Met Office (2013). Historic
Ramallah (Beitunia) rainfall, 1961-1990, from PWA (2003). Rainfall Variability
Amnesty, 2009. Troubled Waters - Palestinians denied fair access to water,
UK DEFRA, 2013. Domestic Water Saving (accessed on 7 February 2013)
WHO, 2003. Domestic Water Quantity, Service Level and Health, p3
1, 2. Amnesty, 2009. Troubled Waters - Palestinians denied fair access to water,
3. C. Messerschmid, 2007. Hydro-hegemony in shared Israeli, Palestinian
4. EWASH, 2012. Israeli restrictions on the WASH sector in the Occupied
VISUALIZINGPALESTINE
emergency water and sanitation/hygiene
EWASH
WWW.EWASH.ORG
WWW.VISUALIZINGPALESTINE.ORG. FEBRUARY 2013.
SHARE AND DISTRIBUTE FREELY. CREATIVE COMMONS BY-NC-ND 3.0 LICENSE.

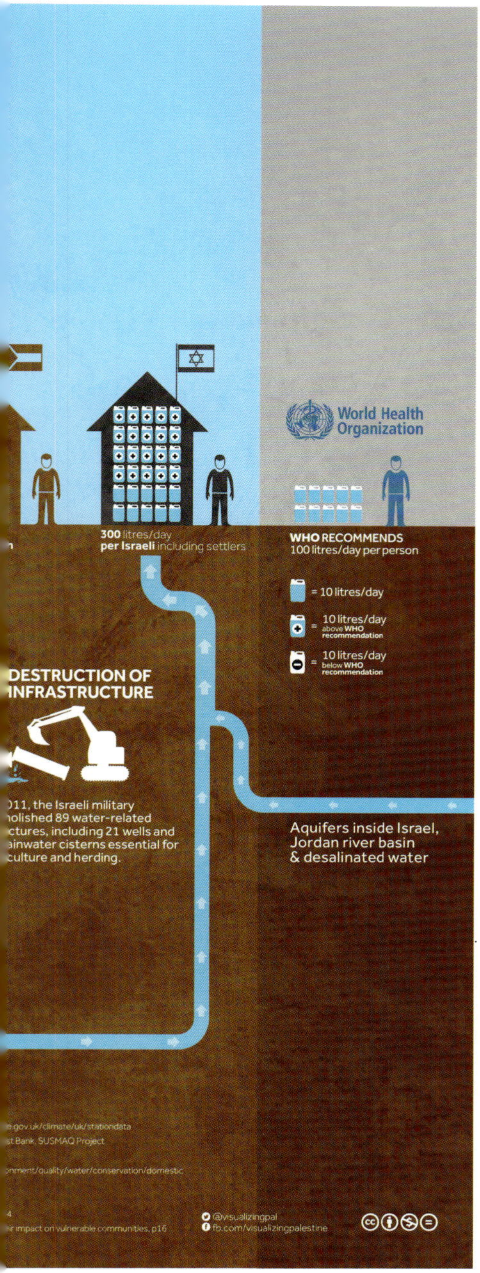

World Health Organization
300 litres/day per Israeli including settlers
WHO RECOMMENDS 100 litres/day per person
= 10 litres/day
= 10 litres/day above WHO recommendation
= 10 litres/day below WHO recommendation
DESTRUCTION OF INFRASTRUCTURE
Aquifers inside Israel, Jordan river basin & desalinated water
@visualizingpal
fb.com/visualizingpalestine

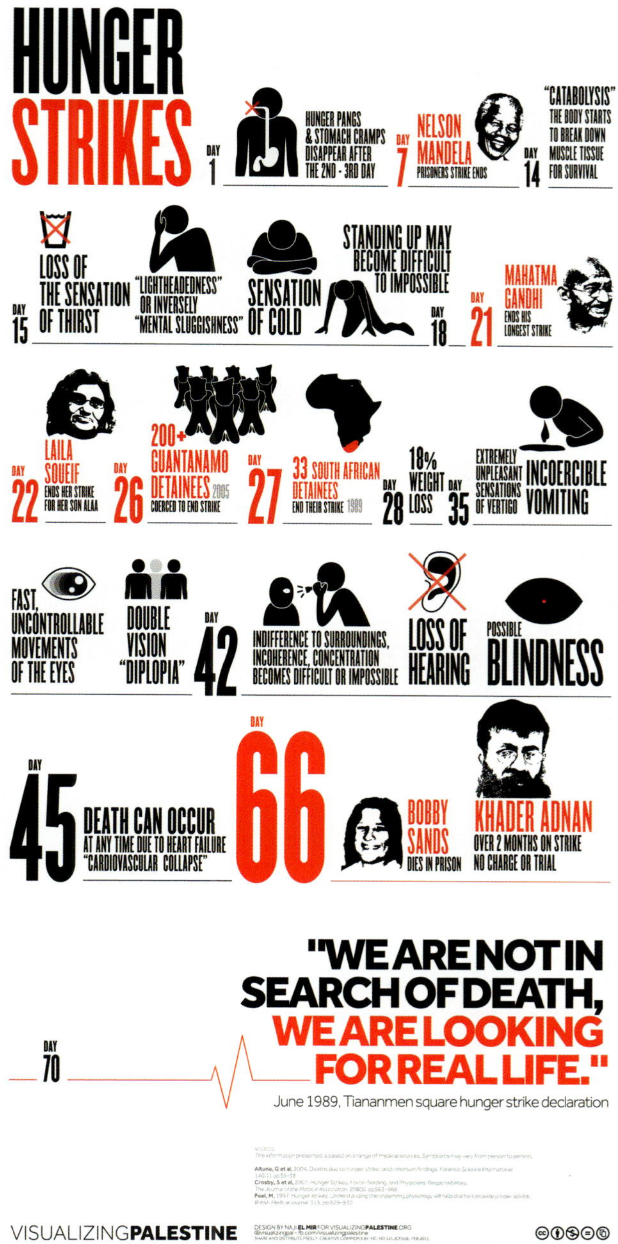

HUNGER STRIKES
DAY 1
HUNGER PANGS & STOMACH CRAMPS DISAPPEAR AFTER THE 2ND - 3RD DAY
DAY 7
NELSON MANDELA PRISONERS STRIKE ENDS
DAY 14
"CATABOLYSIS" THE BODY STARTS TO BREAK DOWN MUSCLE TISSUE FOR SURVIVAL
DAY 15
LOSS OF THE SENSATION OF THIRST
"LIGHTHEADEDNESS" OR INVERSELY "MENTAL SLUGGISHNESS"
SENSATION OF COLD
STANDING UP MAY BECOME DIFFICULT TO IMPOSSIBLE
DAY 18
DAY 21
MAHATMA GANDHI ENDS HIS LONGEST STRIKE
DAY 22
LAILA SOUEIF ENDS HER STRIKE FOR HER SON ALAA
DAY 26
200+ GUANTANAMO DETAINEES 2005 COERCED TO END STRIKE
DAY 27
33 SOUTH AFRICAN DETAINEES END THEIR STRIKE 1989
DAY 28
18% WEIGHT LOSS
DAY 35
EXTREMELY UNPLEASANT SENSATIONS OF VERTIGO
INCOERCIBLE VOMITING
FAST, UNCONTROLLABLE MOVEMENTS OF THE EYES
DOUBLE VISION "DIPLOPIA"
DAY 42
INDIFFERENCE TO SURROUNDINGS, INCOHERENCE, CONCENTRATION BECOMES DIFFICULT OR IMPOSSIBLE
LOSS OF HEARING
POSSIBLE BLINDNESS
DAY 45
DEATH CAN OCCUR AT ANY TIME DUE TO HEART FAILURE "CARDIOVASCULAR COLLAPSE"
DAY 66
BOBBY SANDS DIES IN PRISON
KHADER ADNAN OVER 2 MONTHS ON STRIKE NO CHARGE OR TRIAL
DAY 70
"WE ARE NOT IN SEARCH OF DEATH, WE ARE LOOKING FOR REAL LIFE."
June 1989, Tiananmen square hunger strike declaration
VISUALIZINGPALESTINE

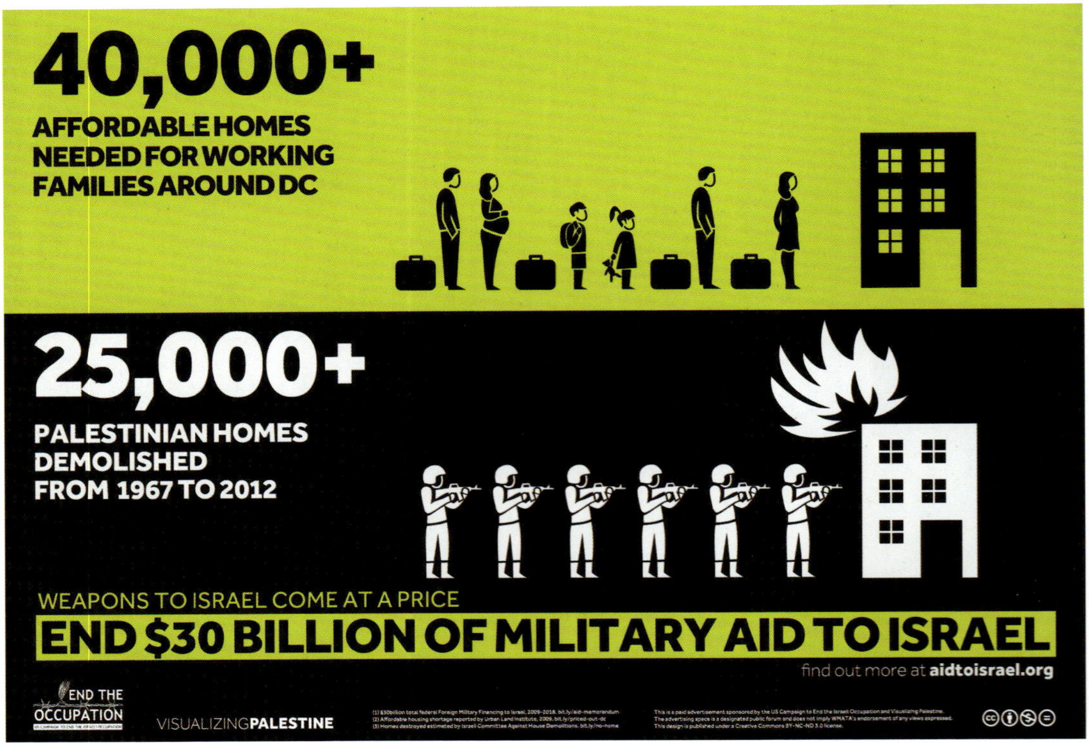

Visualizing Palestine is the intersection of communication, social sciences, technology, design and urban studies for social justice. We use creative visuals (infographics) to describe a factual rights-based narrative of Palestine/Israel. We envision a world in which people live in equality and dignity because they use communication tools to rally for positive change. We believe in the political potential of digital platforms and visual media to actualize a world in which people worldwide feel empowered to rally for positive change. We bridge the geographical digital divide by globally empowering communities and civil society (NGOs and rights organizations), giving them visual tools with which to transform information into positive change.

Visualizing Palestine creates a community of change-makers by addressing two key issues: the failure of organizations to use effective communication tools, limiting themselves to dry reports, data tables and primitive graphs; and the failure of the media to report without bias. Over-coverage of Hamas and under-coverage of the systemic

Visualizing Palestine ist an der Schnittstelle von Kommunikation, Sozialwissenschaften, Technologie, Design und Urban Studies angesiedelt und steht im Dienste sozialer Gerechtigkeit. Wir nutzen kreative Infografiken, um ein sachliches rechtebasiertes Narrativ der Situation in Palästina / Israel zu entwickeln. Unsere Vision ist eine Welt, in der Menschen in Gleichheit und Würde leben, weil sie Kommunikationswerkzeuge nutzen, um gemeinsam einen positiven Wandel zu bewirken. Wir glauben an das politische Potenzial digitaler Plattformen und visueller Medien bei der Verwirklichung einer Welt, in der sich Menschen weltweit befähigt fühlen, gemeinsam einen positiven Wandel zu bewirken. Wir überbrücken die geografisch bedingte digitale Kluft, indem wir Communities und der Zivilgesellschaft (NGOs und Menschenrechtsorganisationen) visuelle Werkzeuge zur Verfügung stellen, mit deren Hilfe sie Information in einen positiven Wandel transformieren können.

Visualizing Palestine baut eine Gemeinschaft von Change-Makern auf, indem es zwei Probleme anspricht: das Versagen der Organisationen, Kommunikationstools effektiv einzusetzen und sich statt dessen auf trockene Berichte, Tabellen und primitive Grafiken zu beschränken,

und das Unvermögen der Medien, unvoreingenommen zu berichten. Es wird verhältnismäßig zu viel über die Hamas und zu wenig über die systemische Ungleichheit berichtet, der sich Palästinenser gegenübersehen. Dies führte dazu, dass 57 Prozent der US-Bürger den Angriff Isreals auf Gaza im Jahr 2012 befürworteten. Selbst während der Angriffe, bei denen 25 palästinensische Kinder getötet wurden, betonten die wichtigsten Medien weiterhin die Rolle der Hamas und spielten den Verlust von Menschenleben und Infrastruktur herunter.
Unser Team identifiziert die wichtigsten Themen aufgrund eigener Erfahrung, aber auch in Kooperation mit Grassroot-Organisationen, Advocacy-Gruppen und einem Netzwerk von Journalisten und Bloggern. Wir generieren eine Geschichte, wobei wir die Absurditäten und Ungerechtigkeiten herausstreichen. Dann sammeln unsere Rechercheure Daten und Statistiken aus Berichten von Organisationen wie Amnesty International und der UNO. Unsere Datenanalysten aggregieren diese Daten, um Muster und Zusammenhänge deutlich zu machen. Unser Design-Team verwandelt diese Daten in aussagekräftige visuelle Darstellungen, die das Kommunikationsteam mithilfe unserer Partner sowie Mainstream- und sozialen Medien unter einer Creative-Commons-Lizenz veröffentlicht.

inequality Palestinians face led 57 percent of US citizens to support Israel's 2012 strikes against Gaza. Even during the strikes, in which 25 Palestinian children were killed, the major media continued to emphasize Hamas's role and downplay the loss of civilian life and infrastructure.
Our team identifies pressing issues through first-hand experience, partnerships with grassroots organizations, advocacy groups and a network of journalists and bloggers. We go through a process of story generation, highlighting the absurdities of the injustice. Next, our researchers collate extensive data and statistics from reports by organizations such as Amnesty International and the UN. Our data analysts then aggregate the data, exposing patterns and correlations. The design team then turns the data into powerful visuals, which the communications team publishes via our partners, the mainstream media and social media, under the Creative Commons license.

Visualizing Palestine began when Ramzi Jaber, a Palestinian from the diaspora, went back to live in Ramallah in 2009 to curate TEDxRamallah, the first event of its kind in Palestine. Since then, the project has evolved from an idea into a core team of designers, researchers, tech experts, communications specialists and strategists. *Visualizing Palestine* has produced 15 infographics and is in the process of being commissioned by the United Nations, the Emergency Water Sanitation and Hygiene Coalition and the Palestinian Business Committee for Peace and Reform. The infographics have been featured in *Al Jazeera English*, *The Daily Beast*, *Mondoweiss*, *Electronic Intifada*, and *Jadaliyya*. Its visuals have been translated into Arabic, Hebrew, French, Spanish, Finnish, Chinese and Korean. They have been used by universities, advocacy groups and organizations on four continents.

Visualizing Palestine startete, als Ramzi Jaber, ein Palästina aus der Diaspora, 2009 nach Ramallah zurückkehrte, um TEDxRamallah zu kuratieren, das erste Event dieser Art in Palästina. Seit damals entwickelte sich das Projekt von einer Idee zu einem Kernteam von Designern, Researchern, Technikern, Kommunikationsspezialisten und Strategen. *Visualizing Palestine* hat 15 Infografiken produziert und erhält Aufträge von der UNO, der Emergency Water Sanitation and Hygiene Coalition sowie des Palestinian Business Committee for Peace and Reform. Unsere Infografiken erschienen in *Al Jazeera English*, *The Daily Beast*, *Mondoweiss*, *Electronic Intifada* und *Jadaliyya*. Die Visuals wurden in Arabisch, Hebräisch, Französisch, Spanisch, Finnisch, Chinesisch und Koreanisch übersetzt und in Universitäten und Interessenvertretungen auf vier Kontinenten verwendet.

African Digital Art Network

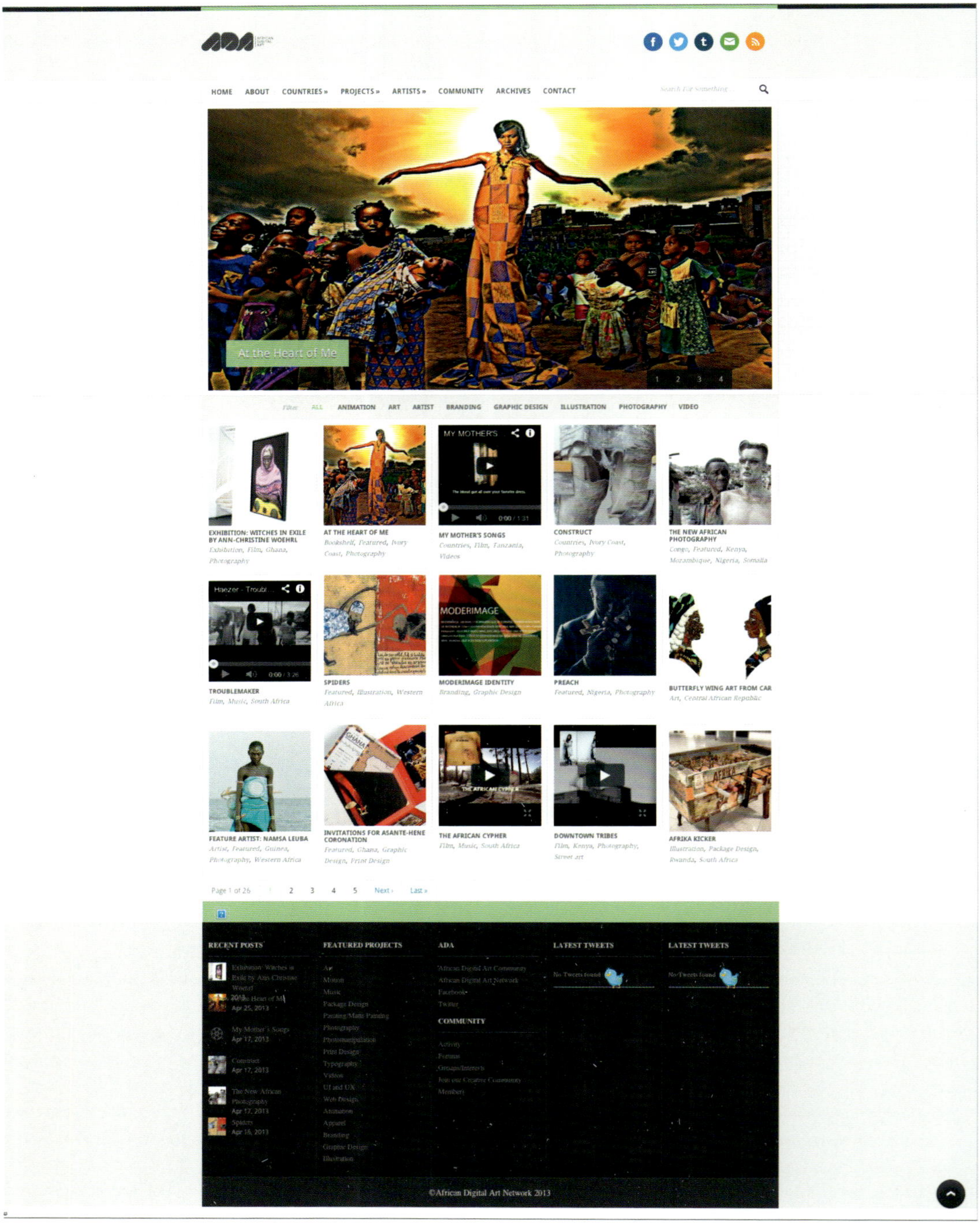

African Digital Art ist ein Online-Kollektiv, ein kreativer Raum, wo Künstler, Kunstliebhaber und andere in diesem Bereich Tätige sich inspirieren lassen, ihre künstlerischen Arbeiten veröffentlichen und mit noch unbekannten Künstlern in Kontakt kommen können. *African Digital Art* will die afrikanische digitale Wirtschaft unterstützen, wobei die Zielgruppe in erster Linie Kreative, Künstler und all jene sind, die eine Affinität zur Kunst haben. Wir sind überzeugt, dass Afrika bessere Lösungen für die Unzulänglichkeiten und Probleme des Kontinents finden könnte, wenn es eine gesunde Kreativwirtschaft gäbe und wir andere ermuntern könnten, sich in Design, Kunst und kreativen Institutionen zu engagieren.

Als wir *African Digital Art* starteten, agierten die Mitglieder der Plattform und unser Publikum in erster Linie online; es war eine winzige Gruppe von Künstlern, Fotografen, Filmemachern, Animationskünstlern, digitalen Künstlern usw. Es ging uns darum, jene zu ermutigen, die den digitalen Raum zur Partizipation nutzen, denn wir sind überzeugt, dass die Schnittstelle zwischen Kunst und Technologie ein Ort ist, der andere zu inspirieren vermag. Heute sind wir eine wichtige Inspirationsquelle auch für Künstler, die offline und außerhalb des Digitalen arbeiten, und wir entwickelten uns zu einem Archiv des sich wandelnden Afrikas.

African Digital Art will vor allem eine kreativere Partizipation fördern, um neue Vorstellungen von Citizenship zu entwickeln. Wir wollen verstehen, wie Design und künstlerische Lösungen neue Wege zu sozialer Innovation aufzeigen können. Wir haben über zehn Events, Workshops und Trainings in der ganzen Welt veranstaltet, die kreative Partizipation gefördert haben. Damit wollen wir zeigen, wie wichtig Design und Kunst für Gemeinschaften, Unternehmen, NGOs, Regierungen und Länder sind und dass sie überall einen Unterschied machen können, im Gesundheitswesen, Wissenschaft, Kunst usw. Wir haben auch eine Reihe von Video-Vorträgen mit afrikanischen Künstlern, die im digitalen Bereich arbeiten, veranstaltet, um angehende junge Künstler anzuspornen, mit digitalen Formaten zu experimentieren, die Bürgerengagement und -partizipation fördern.

African Digital Art is an online collective, a creative space where digital artists, enthusiasts and professionals can seek inspiration, showcase their artistry and connect with emerging artists. *African Digital Art* is dedicated to serve the African creative economy and mainly directed towards creatives, artists and those with an inclination towards the creative arts. We truly believe that with a healthy creative economy and by encouraging others to participate in design, art and creative institutions Africa can come up with better solutions to the myriad of limitations and problems we face.

When we began *African Digital Art* our audience and participants were mainly online, a rare group of artists, photographers, filmmakers, animators, electronic artists and more. We wanted to ensure that we encouraged those who were in the digital arena to participate, because we believed that the intersection between art and technology is a powerful place to inspire innovation. Today we have become a leading source of inspiration to other artists offline and outside the digital scope and we have become an archive of Africa's changing image.

African Digital Art is focused on encouraging more creative participation in ideas of citizenship by understanding the need for design focus and artistic solutions as it relates to social innovation. We have hosted over ten events, workshops and clinics around the world, which have encouraged creative participation to highlight the importance design and art plays in communities, companies, NGOs, governments and countries, and that it can make a difference everywhere, including in healthcare, science, art and so on. We also hosted a series of remote lectures with digital artists from Africa to encourage budding young artists to participate and experiment with a diverse range of digital forms that encourage civil engagement and participation.

African Digital Art Network was founded by Jepchumba, an African digital artist originally from Kenya. She begun the project while she was completing her master's degree in digital media. At the time she recognized that there were not any spaces for artists and creatives to participate in the digital arena. The discussion around art in Africa was often restricted outside the contemporary framework. Jepchumba has been listed by *Forbes* as one of the 20 Youngest Power Women in Africa 2012 and by the *Guardian* as one of Africa's Top 25 Women Achievers. **African Digital Art Network** wurde von Jepchumba, einer afrikanischen Künstlerin, die im digitalen Bereich arbeitet, gegründet. Sie startete das Projekt während ihres Master-Studiums in Digitalen Medien. Damals erkannte sie, dass es keine Möglichkeit für Künstler und Kreative gab, an der digitalen Öffentlichkeit teilzunehmen, da Diskussionen rund um Kunst in Afrika oft von der zeitgenössischen Kunst ausgegrenzt wurden. Jepchumba wurde 2012 von *Forbes* als eine der „20 Youngest Power Women in Africa" und vom *Guardian* als eine von „Africa's Top 25 Women Achievers" ausgezeichnet.

Casastristes

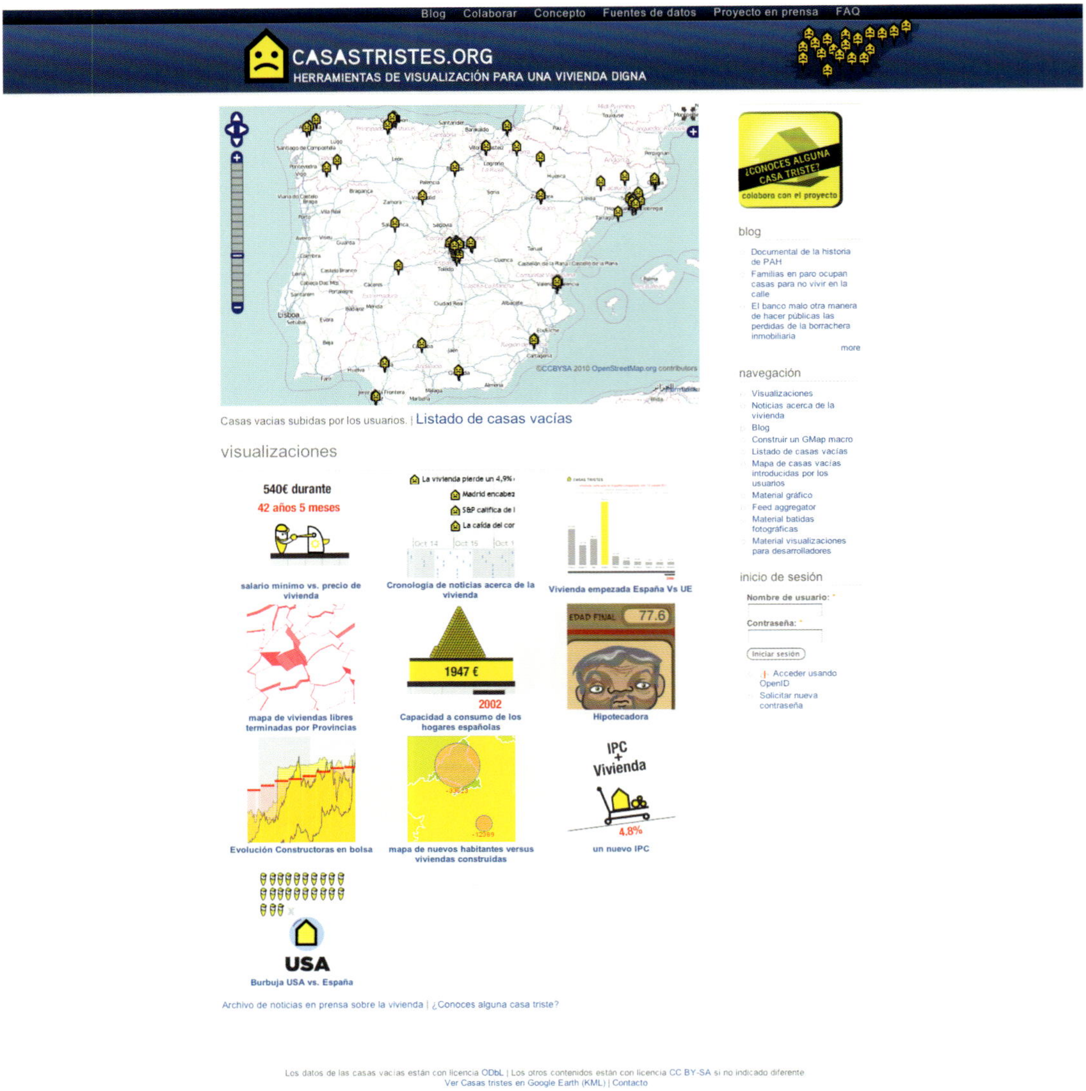

Casastristes, launched in 2007, explores housing problems in Spain. Its objective is to serve as an information- and resource-exchange platform through the creation of a reliable public database of empty houses in Spain. *Casastristes* highlights the abundance of empty houses in contrast to the generally accepted theory of "a lack of buildable land" and tries to explore the origins of the real-estate bubble in Spain. It also questions concepts such as "the advantages of buying a home instead of renting." Given the extremely high percentage

Das Projekt *Casastristes*, das 2007 begonnen wurde, beschäftigt sich mit dem Wohnungsproblem in Spanien. Es ist eine Plattform für den Austausch von Informationen und Ressourcen und erstellt eine verlässliche öffentliche Datenbank, die leer stehende Häuser in Spanien dokumentiert. *Casastristes* zeigt, wie viele leer stehende Häuser es gibt, kontrastiert dies mit der allgemein akzeptierten Theorie eines „Mangels an Bauland" und versucht, die Ursprünge dieser Blase des spanischen Wohnungsmarkts zu ergründen. Es hinterfragt auch Konzepte wie „Besser kaufen als mieten". Angesichts des extrem hohen

Leerstandes in Spanien will das Projekt Lösungen suchen und den Gründe nachgehen, warum so viele Menschen noch mit 35 Jahren bei ihren Eltern wohnen, und eine alternative Wohnungspolitik vorschlagen.
Auf seiner Webseite präsentiert das Projekt Datenvisualisierungen und eine Liste von Ressourcen, die unklare Konzepte erklären und das Netzwerk von Bürgern, Vereinen und Kollektiven stärken, die sich mit diesem Problem beschäftigen und nach neuen Wegen der Kommunikation untereinander suchen, wodurch sie größere Sichtbarkeit erlangen und auch Vorschläge unterbreiten können.
Der Launch der Web-Plattform und die ersten Visualisierungen zogen die Aufmerksamkeit der Medien auf sich: Es erschien eine Unzahl von Artikeln in den verschiedensten Medien. Kulturelle Institutionen luden uns ein, das Projekt auszustellen, wobei wir die Gelegenheit nutzten, Workshops zum Mappen leer stehender Häuser mit lokalen Bürgergruppen zu organisieren. Aber vor allem war es die Zusammenarbeit mit sozialen Bewegungen und Nachbarschaftsvereinen in ganz Spanien, die sich mit dem Thema auseinandersetzen, die das aktuelle Image von *Casastristes* formte. Gemeinsam wurden „Wohnungs-Safaris" organisiert, um leer stehende Häuser zu erfassen und Teilnehmern zu erklären, wie der Datenupload über unsere Plattform erfolgt.

of empty homes in Spain, the purpose is to look for solutions, evaluate the reasons why so many people are still living with their parents at the age of 35, and to propose alternative housing policies.
By providing data visualization and a list of references on the website, the project also aims to offer resources likely to help clarify ambiguous concepts and strengthen the network of citizens, associations, collectives etc. concerned about housing and searching for a way to communicate with each other, become visible and make proposals.
The launch of the web platform and the first visualizations attracted a lot of attention from the media, which is reflected in a huge amount of articles in all kinds of media. Cultural institutions invited us to exhibit the project, which was used to make workshops on mapping empty houses to involve local citizens' groups. But above all it was the collaboration with social movements and neighborhood associations around Spain working on the topic of the housing problem that shaped the actual image of *Casastristes*. Collaboration consisted in organizing housing safaris to map empty houses and teaching the use of our platform to upload the data.

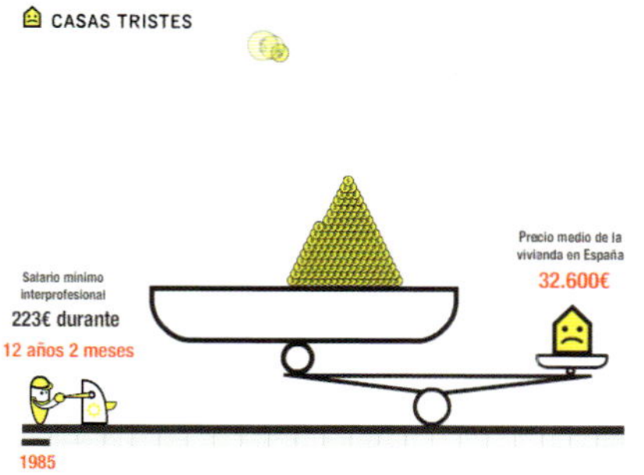

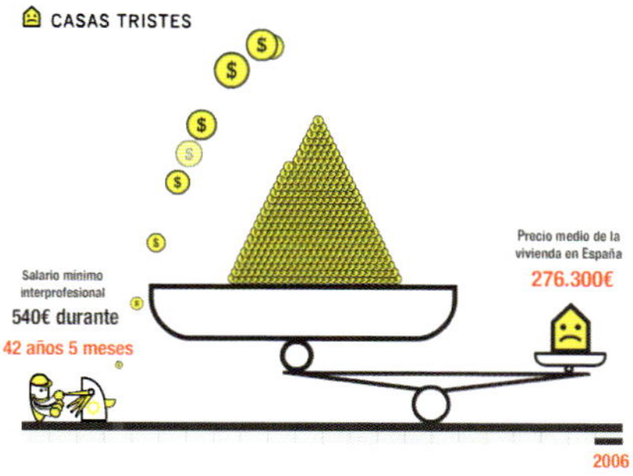

Casastristes is the original idea of Derivart, an interdisciplinary art group whose work focuses on the intersection between art, technology and finance. The project was developed by Mar Canet, Jordi Puig and Gerald Kogler during the Visualizar workshop at Medialab Prado Madrid and is currently being further developed and maintained by Gerald Kogler and Mar Canet. **Casastristes** geht auf eine Idee von Derivart zurück, einer interdisziplinären Künstlergruppe, die an der Schnittstelle von Kunst, Technologie und Finanzen arbeitet. Das Projekt wurde von Mar Canet, Jordi Puig und Gerald Kogler während eines Visualizar-Workshops im Medialab Prado Madrid entwickelt und wird im Moment von Gerald Kogler und Mar Canet betrieben und weiterentwickelt.

Indian Memory Project

INDIAN MEMORY PROJECT visual & oral history of the indian subcontinent via family archives

HOME ABOUT THE PROJECT CONTRIBUTE IMAGES, LETTERS & STORIES SUPPORT THE PROJECT COMMISSIONS PRESS & EVENTS CONTACT

Latest

108 – A batch of lost friends & acquaintances

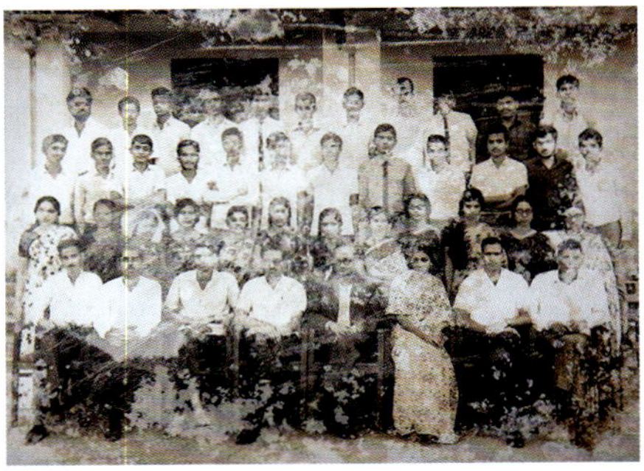

Class of B.Sc (Bachelor of Science), Poornaprajna College (PPC), Udupi district, Karnataka. Circa 1969

Image & Text contributed by Nishant Rathnakar, Bangalore

In 2010, while cleaning my wardrobe I stumbled upon my mother Ranjini Rathnakar's old autograph book dating back to the year 1970. This 40 year old book was filled with autographs and inscriptions of her classmates from her College, Poornaprajna college (PPC), Udupi. The ink and pencil writings in the book still dark and legible, as if it were written yesterday.

It wasn't the first time I came across the autograph book. In the past 29 years, I had found it time and again; and each time I was fascinated reading it. Some amusing inscriptions like *"First comes knowledge, next comes college, third comes marriage and finally comes baby in a carriage"* always made me laugh.

I would asked my mother if she was in touch with any one of her classmates and her answer was always a 'No', leaving me a little disenchanted. However, she would say that her best friend in College was a girl named *Rose Christabel*, but she never saw Rose after college. She had last heard that Rose had moved to Vellore in Tamil Nadu. That was 40 years ago. I made several mental notes that someday I'll find mom's old friends, maybe even Rose and make them meet again. I think that inspiration stemmed from my own experience because I was blessed with such good and decades old friendships that I recognised the value of having them around albeit we had the help of the internet & social media. A technological perk that wasn't available to my mother's generation.

For instance, one of my closest friends is *Santhu a.k.a Santhosh*. We have been friends for a decade now. We were in college together, worked as interns, and got our first tech jobs at IBM. Around the time I quit my job, I took-off on my first photography trip to the coasts of Karnataka, to our roots, our hometown, with *Santhu* as my accomplice. It was a special trip for both of us.

One evening, scouring over the pages of her college autograph book yet again, I froze, and I am very certain my heart skipped a beat too. I had gone through that book time and again, but I had never noticed one particular inscription -
"Best Wishes. Bhaskar Adiga K. Kuppar house, Shankarnarayana, Udupi (S.K)"

Now Santhu, my friend I just told you about, his full name is *Santhosh Kuppar Bhaskar Adiga*. Bhaskar Adiga being his father's name, and the house that I stayed at during the journey to our hometown was called the *Kuppar* house, and it was in a town named *Shankarnarayana*, in the present-day Udupi district of Karnataka.

With my heart bursting in anticipation, I asked my mother if she remembered Bhaskar Adiga, she had no clear recollection, but then she got up, went inside the house and came out holding this photograph in her hands. It was her only class photograph from college, taken during her graduation. A photograph she too had only come to possess a week ago, from my uncle while he was clearing up their now almost uninhabited ancestral home.

Humidity and lack of maintenance had damaged the photograph. In it few faces were recognizable, including my mom's (3rd from left in the row of women.) but Rose Christabel's face was crystal clear (2nd from right). Given that I was asking my mother to be part of an identification parade of faces that were hardly recognizable and that too 40 years later, she took sometime. Then, from left to right, slowly she named all the girls in her class. But the boys, she wasn't sure of. She said *"Maybe the 5th person from the left, on the top row, with a tie, could be Bhaskar."*

She didn't know him that well and his face was hardly recognisable. I too had met Santhu's dad many times, but could not picture his face with this one. I immediately emailed everything to Santhu and then called to ask him if his dad was a graduate from Poornaprajna college (PPC), Udupi, and if he had graduated in BSc, Zoology, in 1970. He cross-checked with his mother, and Hurray! the credentials matched –it was indeed Santhu's dad. The 5th person from left, on the top row, wearing a tie... he said, resembled his dad. After all, there where only two *Adiga* families in Shankarnarayana, and only one Bhaskar from the Kuppar house. It had to be him.

I do not know how Santhu processed this information; But we were both thinking the same thing – *"How I wish we had stumbled upon that page a couple of years earlier."* Santhu's dad Bhaskar Adiga had passed away a year ago. I was in tears. For my parents or even most parents at the time, meeting with an old friend or an acquaintance was a rarity. My mom and her best friend Rose didn't have the luxury of social media that I enjoy now. I was deeply disappointed . All along, I had wanted to gift my mother a small reunion with people from her younger days and her friends and I couldn't do that.

That night I slept with great anxiety. I dreamt of Santhu and I getting our families together. I dreamt of drinking with them, laughing and talking about life. I imagined my mom and Santhu's father recognising each other at the party, and talking about old times, about old friends, and about Rose Christabel. Maybe, Mr. Adiga knew where Rose might be. But I woke up to deep sadness and disappointment.

On the brighter side, Santhu was glad to see his father's calligraphy skills in my mum's autograph book. He said he would try hunting for the college photograph from his father's collection. It may be our last chance to have a proper photograph of our parents from their college. I think the chances are bleak, but we are glad to have uncovered a shared history.

Follow Us

Search

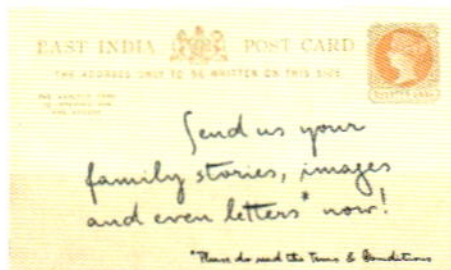

IMPORTANT

- Copyright belongs to the guardian of the photograph
- Pictures & Letters CANNOT be used for any reason whatsoever, without prior permission.
- Any unauthorised use will lead to prompt legal action.
- For Permissions, write at INDIAN MEMORY PROJECT

Indian Memory Project - YouTube Channel

SUBSCRIBE ON YouTube

Archives

Select Month

Categories

Latest

Most Mentioned

1920s 1930s 1940s 1950s 1960s 1970s Andhra Pradesh Bombay British Reign Calcutta Couple Delhi Doctor Education Family Portrait Fashion & Trends Fashion Accessories Friendships Furniture Hair Styles Head Gear Hinduism Indian Politics Jewellery Love & Romance Maharashtra Marriage Men's Clothes Migration Mustache Pakistan Partition Pre-1947 Indian Regions & States Pre Independence Props Sarees Sari Shoes Studio Portraits Teacher Uttar Pradesh Wedding West Bengal Women's Clothes Women Empowerment

Subscribe to our Mailing list

Your email:

Enter email address...

Subscribe

Das *Indian Memory Project* wurde im Februar 2010 von Anusha Yadav gegründet. Es ist ein kuratiertes, visuelles Archiv oraler Geschichte, das eine sehr persönliche Geschichte des indischen Subkontinent zeichnet, mit all seinen Völkern, Kulturen, Berufen, Städten, Entwicklungen, Traditionen, Zeitumständen und deren Konsequenzen. Es sammelt Bilder, Briefe und Geschichten aus Familienarchiven (die von Usern zur Verfügung gestellt werden) und rekonstruiert daraus eine visuelle Geschichte, die emotional, vielfältig, informativ und noch überraschender ist, als wir denken.

Persönliche oder Familienarchive, die Fotografien und Briefe enthalten, sind eine Fundgrube für historisch wertvolle Informationen. Sie bergen erstaunliche Geheimnisse, und wenn sie sich in Form von Narrativen offenbaren, stellen sie plötzlich eine Beziehung zur emotionalen und persönlichen Geschichte eines Landes dar, zur Vergangenheit, die wir fühlen und mit der wie in Beziehung treten können. Das *Indian Memory Project* ist auf der Suche nach dem Bemerkenswerten und Interessanten, dem Persönlichen, aber auch dem weniger Persönlichen.

The *Indian Memory Project* was founded in February 2010 by Anusha Yadav. It is an online, curated, visual and oral-history-based archive that traces a personal history of the Indian subcontinent, its people, cultures, professions, cities, development, traditions, circumstances and their consequences. Using images, letters and stories from family archives (submitted and collected from contributors), it reconstructs a visual history that is emotionally rich, vivid, informative and even more surprising than we think.

Family/personal archives of photographs and letters hold a treasure trove of incredible and historically valuable information. They contain astonishing secrets, and when they reveal themselves via narratives they become the missing links to a country's emotional and personal history. A past that we can actually feel, connect with and wonder at. The *Indian Memory Project* is now also on the lookout for the notable, the interesting, the personal and not so personal.

The **Indian Memory Project** was founded in 2010 by Anusha Yadav, a photographer, photo archivist and a book designer. She is a 2011 INK Fellow (in association with TED). Das **Indian Memory Project** wurde 2010 von Anusha Yadav gegründet, einer Fotografin, Foto-Archivarin und Buchgestalterin. 2011 war sie INK Fellow (in Zusammenarbeit mit TED).

I Paid a Bribe

I Paid a Bribe was launched as an India-wide online anti-corruption initiative on Aug 15, 2010–India's Independence Day. It is the Janaagraha Centre for Citizenship and Democracy's unique initiative to tackle corruption by harnessing the collective energy of citizens. Through its innovative, crowd-sourcing model, it has already collected a ground-breaking 22,491 bribe reports, has registered more than 1.8 million unique hits and in just over two years has become the largest online repository of bribe data in the world. Its work has been recognized in international media such as the *New York Times*, by global bodies such as the United Nations, the One World Foundation and the World Bank, and by Manthan–India's premier forum for public discourse.

I Paid a Bribe addresses India's endemic culture of transactional ("retail") corruption–the type that confronts ordinary citizens when availing themselves of government services. On the website, citizens report on the nature, number, pattern, types, location, frequency and values of actual corrupt acts, providing for the first time a snapshot of bribes occurring across India's cities. The IPAB team believes this type of corruption is the root cause of ongoing poor service provision in India, and a major impediment to the country's development. Critically, this system of retail corruption disproportionately impacts on the poor, as it places essential services beyond their financial reach. IPAB gives citizens a platform to publicly voice their corruption experiences and share them with the media, the Central Vigilance Commission (CVC) and concerned government departments–critical to bringing visibility and accountability to this destructive practice. Citizens across India can to access the site via the web, and on their phones through web browsers.

I Paid a Bribe also helps interested NGOs in other countries start their own *ipaidabribe.com* website. It shares its source code with interested partners and delivers ready-to-use platforms with all the requisite back-end support needed to launch. So far, replica sites have been built in Kenya, Greece and Pakistan, with conversations in progress with in a further 30 countries. The team seeks to drive the global momentum of anti-corruption crowd-sourcing sites through the Crowdsourcing Against Corruption Coalition–a community of practice conceived and administered by Janaagraha.

I Paid a Bribe wurde am 15. August 2010 – dem indischen Unabhängigkeitstag – als Online-Kampagne gegen Korruption in ganz Indien gestartet. Es ist eine Initiative des Janaagraha Centre for Citizenship and Democracy, die Korruption mithilfe der kollektiven Energie der Bürger bekämpfen will. Durch ein innovatives Crowdsourcing-Modell konnten bereits 22.491 Bestechungsberichte gesammelt und mehr als 1,8 Millionen Unique Users verzeichnet werden. In etwas mehr als zwei Jahren wurde es zum weltweit größen Online-Repositorium mit Daten zu Bestechungsfällen. Es wurde von internationalen Medien wie *New York Times*, von Institutionen wie den Vereinten Nationen, der One World Foundation und der Weltbank sowie von Manthan, Indiens wichtigstem Forum für öffentlichen Diskurs, gewürdigt.

I Paid a Bribe spricht die in Indien endemische Kultur der transaktionalen Korruption (Kleinkorruption) an, also jene Form von Korruption, mit der sich jeder Bürger, der Verwaltungsdienste in Anspruch nehmen will, konfrontiert sieht. Auf der Webseite beschreiben Bürger Natur, Anzahl, Muster, Typus, Ort, Häufigkeit und Wert des tatsächlichen Korruptionsaktes. Dadurch gibt es zum ersten Mal eine Momentaufnahme von Bestechungsakten, die in den indischen Städten stattfinden. Das IBAP-Team ist überzeugt, dass diese Art von Korruption die Ursache der nach wie vor schlechten Dienstleistungen in Indien bildet und ein wesentliches Hindernis für die Entwicklung des Landes darstellt. Entscheidend ist, dass dieses System der Korruption unverhältnismäßig stark die Armen betrifft, da essenzielle Dienstleistungen dadurch für sie unerschwinglich werden. IBAP gibt den Bürgern eine Plattform, wo sie öffentlich ihre Stimme gegen Korruptionserfahrungen erheben und sie mit den Medien der Central Vigilance Commission und den betroffenen Regierungsstellen teilen können – was wichtig ist, wenn Sichtbarkeit und Accountability in diese zerstörerische Praktiken gebracht werden soll. Bürger in ganz Indien können auf diese Webseite via Webbrowser oder Mobiltelefon zugreifen.

I Paid a Bribe unterstützt auch interessierte NGOs in anderen Ländern dabei, ihre eigene *ipaidabribe.com*-Website zu erstellen. Wir teilen den Quellcode mit Partnern und stellen auch fertige Plattformen mit dem für einen Launch notwendigen Back-End-Support zur Verfügung. Die Webseite wurde bis jetzt in Kenia, Griechenland und Pakistan repliziert, und wir sind in Gesprächen mit weiteren 30 Ländern. Das Team versucht, das globale Moment des Antikorruptions-Crowdsourcing durch die „Crowdsourcing Against Corruption Coalition", einer von Janaagraha konzipierten und betriebenen Community of Practice, zu nutzen.

http://www.ipaidabribe.com

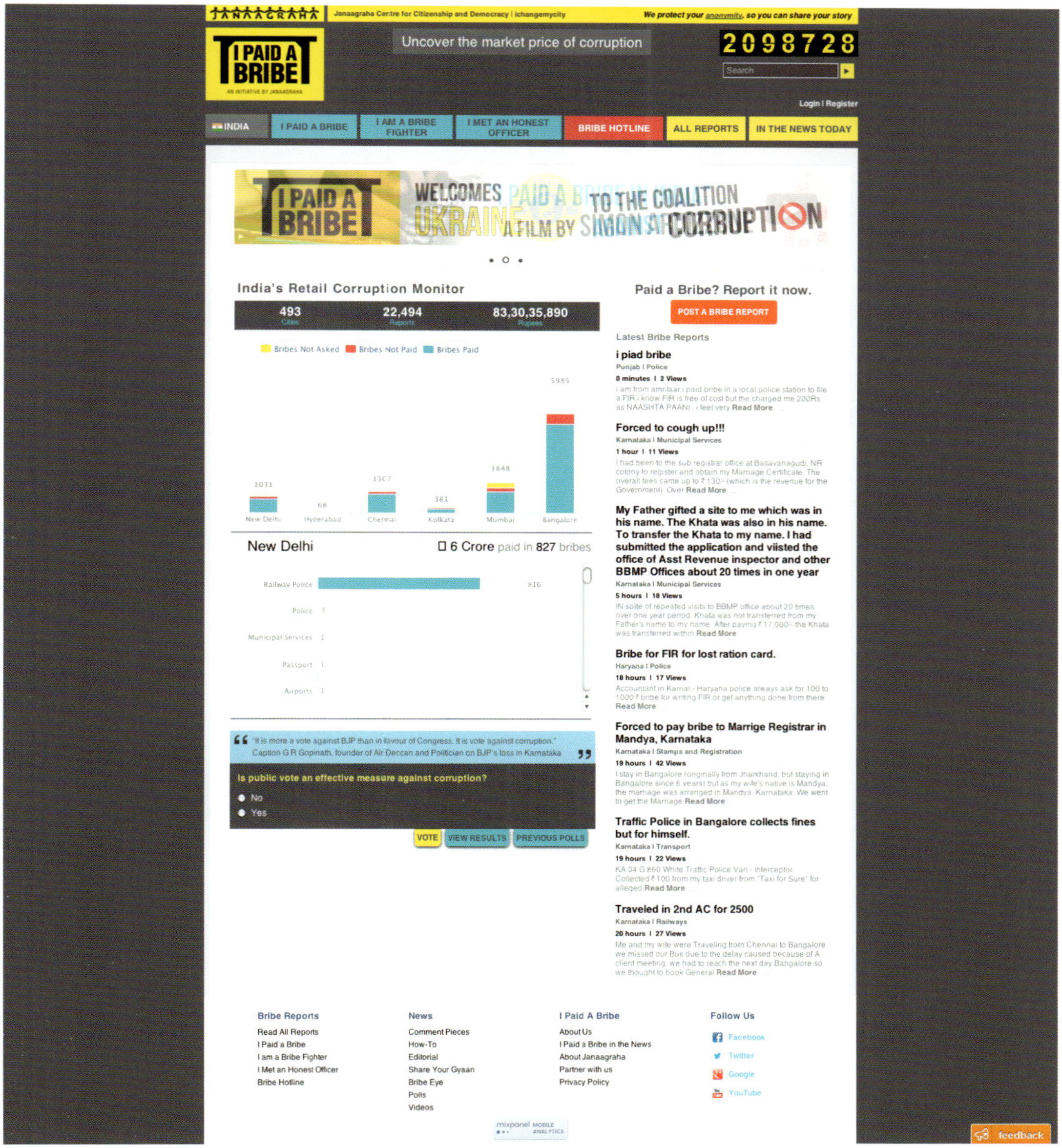

Special thanks: Joylita Saldanha, Gayatri Vijayan, Vidya Kumaraswamy. Logo by Fisheye Creative

I Paid a Bribe is an initiative of the Janaagraha Centre for Citizenship and Democracy. It was conceived by Swati and Ramesh Ramanathan and Sridar Iyengar and launched on August 15, 2010. **I Paid a Bribe** ist eine Initiative des Janaagraha Centre for Citizenship and Democracy. Sie wurde von Swati und Ramesh Ramanathan und Sridar Iyengar konzipiert und ging am 15. August 2010 online.

Kyberia

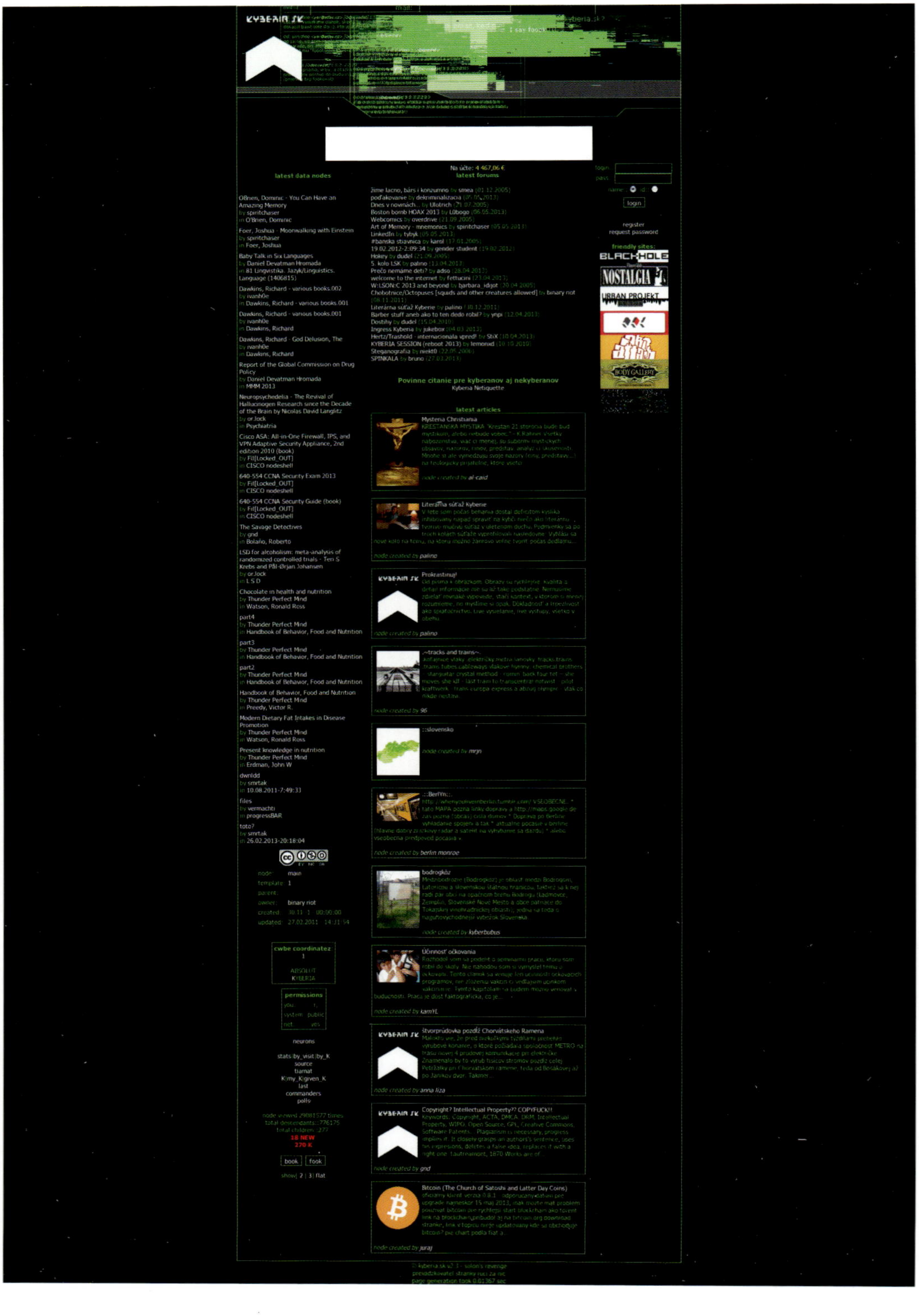

Kyberia ist ein unabhängiges, innovatives Archipel digitaler Gemeinschaften, das 2001 auf der slowakischen Domain *kyberia.sk* das Licht der Welt erblickte. Ursprünglich war es eine Webseite, die das slowakische Publikum über Themen informierte, die damals auf dem slowakischen Mainstream-Web ignoriert wurden (z. B. trans- und posthumanistische Philosophie, künstliche Intelligenz, Nanotechnologie, Entheogene). *Kyberia* entwickelte sich von einem klassischen Forum mit Thread-Struktur in eine wirklich digitale Gemeinschaft, wo Hacker, Künstler und Wissenschaftler miteinander in einem dicht hyperverlinkten Graph interagieren konnten. Die aktuelle Version wurde 2006 veröffentlicht und konzentriert sich in erster Linie auf interne Wissensökonomie und die Politik der Community. Konkret heißt das, dass ein Senat geschaffen wurde und wir versuchsweise ein Parallel-Democracy-Modell anwendeten, das es dem System erlaubte, sich selbst zu konfigurieren. 2007 gewann *Kyberia* beim größten je im slowakischen Web organisierten Wettbewerb den Preis für die beste slowakische virtuelle Community. 2010 wurde der Code der *Kyberia*-Engine auf GitHub veröffentlicht, und die Community weitete sich in den tschechischen Cyberspace aus, wo eine parallele Community auf der Domain *kyberia.cz* gestartet wurde.

Inzwischen hat sich *Kyberia* von einer Wissenschafts- und Hacker-Community in eine eher am Mainstream orientierte Gemeinschaft mit tausenden aktiven Nutzern verwandelt, die unzählige Themen in mehr als sieben Millionen paralleler Foren, Blogs und/oder Datenknoten diskutieren. Ein Faktor war unserer Ansicht nach ausschlaggebend dafür, dass sich *Kyberia* in einen sozialen Körper mit einer kollektiven Identität verwandelt hat, nämlich dass *Kyberia* eine semipermeable Membran hat (d. h. dass jedes Registrierungsansuchen eines neuen Nutzers von mindestens fünf Mitgliedern des *kyberia.sk*-Senats gebilligt werden muss) – ein Voting-System, das Jahre vor dem Like-Button von Facebook implementiert wurde. Andere bemerkenswerte Features sind z. B. ein flexibles (knotenspezifisches) System der Rechtevergabe, ein internes Bookmarking- und Mailingsystem sowie API-Templates – alles Funktionalitäten, die zur Zeit ihrer Entwicklung innovativ waren, auch wenn sie heute in allen sozialen Netzwerken zu finden sind.

Kyberia is an independent and innovative archipelago of digital communities that emerged in 2001 on the Slovak domain *kyberia.sk*. Initially a website informing the Slovak public about topics that were ignored on the Slovak web at the time (e.g. trans- and post-humanist philosophies, artificial intelligence, nanotechnology, entheogens). *Kyberia* swiftly evolved first into a threaded forum and subsequently into a fully-fledged digital community where hackers, artists and scientists were able to interact in a densely hyperlinked graph.

The current version released in 2006 focused more on internal K-economy and the politics of the community. More concretely, a Senate was created and first trials to allow the system to auto-configure by using the parallel democracy model were run. In 2007 *Kyberia* won the prize of distinction as a "best Slovak virtual community" in the biggest public competition ever organized on the Slovak web. In 2010 code of *Kyberia's* engine was released on GitHub under AGPL and the community was expanded into Czech cyberspace, where a parallel community was launched on the *kyberia.cz* domain. In over ten years of existence, *Kyberia* has transformed itself from a science and hackers' community into a more mainstream community of thousands of active users discussing myriads diverse topics in more than seven million parallel forums, blogs and/or data nodes. One of the most characteristic features that, we believe, transformed *Kyberia* into a social body with a collective identity is that *Kyberia* has a semipermeable membrane (which means that any registration application of a new user has to be approved by at least five members of the *kyberia.sk* Senate), a upvoting system implemented years before Facebook's "Like" button. Other features worth mentioning include a flexible (node-specific) system of access right attribution, an internal bookmarking and mailing system and API templates. These were innovative in the period when they were released, although today they are common in other social networks as well.

Kyberia was started in 2001 as a personal website of Daniel D. Hromada who is the officially elected consul and first senator of *Kyberia.sk*. Since then *Kyberia* evolved into a fully-fledged digital community, which has nonetheless succeeded in guarding its complete material independence from the external environment. **Kyberia** wurde 2001 als persönliche Webseite von Daniel D. Hromada begonnen, der der offiziell gewählte Konsul und erste Senator von *Kyberia.sk* ist. Seit damals entwickelte sich *Kyberia* in eine volle digitale Community, der es gelungen ist, sich ihre totale Unabhängigkeit von der äußeren Umgebung zu bewahren.

Labmovel

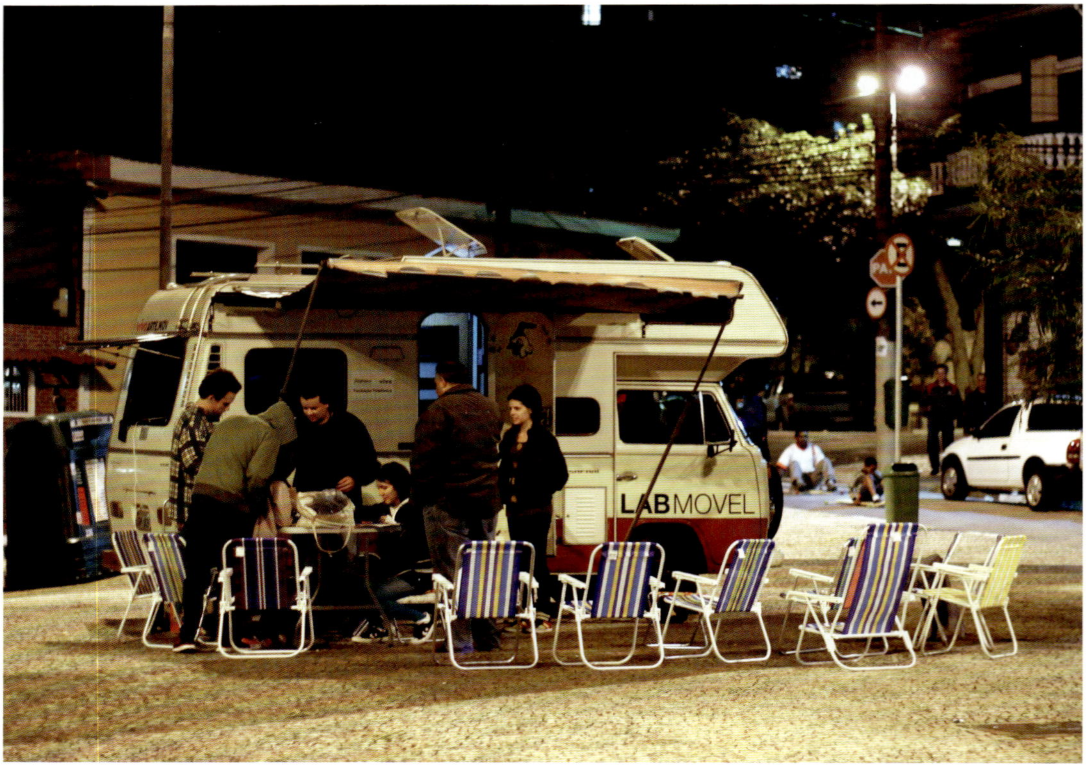

Labmovel creates temporary and mobile platforms that awaken the interest of the audience to media arts practice as the lab unit travels through outskirt locations lacking institutionalized art environments. During the *Labmovel* tours, guest artists offer workshops on open access technologies and showcase their works in ways that count with public engagement as a form of

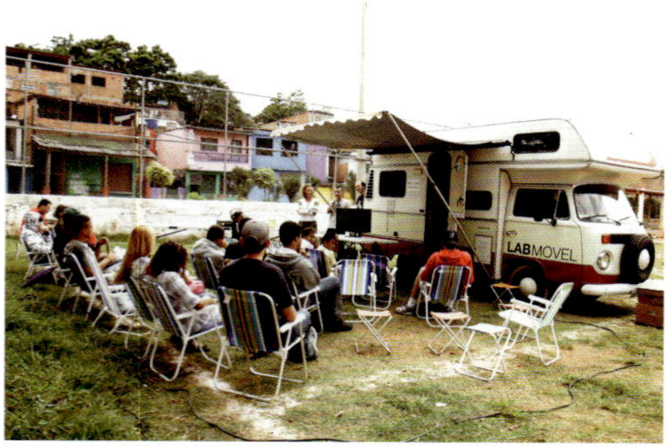

Gisela, Panetone and Lucas talk about the activities related to the workshop #4, *Creative Electronics* conducted at Casa do Zezinho, Capão Redondo south of São Paulo.

Labmovel kreiert temporäre und mobile Plattformen, die durch Vororte touren, wo es an einem institutionalisierten Kunstumfeld mangelt, um das Interesse der Öffentlichkeit an Medienkunst zu wecken. Während der *Labmovel*-Touren bieten Gastkünstler Workshops über Open-Access-Technologien an und zeigen ihre Arbeiten, bei denen die Einbindung der Öffentlichkeit Teil der kreativen Praxis darstellt. Das Resultat sind experimentelle und kontextbasierte Projekte, die vor Ort verwendet werden können, auf ein nicht spezialisiertes Publikum zugeschnitten sind und offene Formen der Zusammenarbeit zwischen Künstler und lokalem Publikum anregen. *Labmovel* begann 2012 und ist seitdem an der Peripherie von São Paulo und Belo Horizonte unterwegs gewesen. Es hat kulturelle Aktivitäten wie das arte.mov-Festival, Cidade Eletronika (BH) und Virada Cultural (SP) unterstützt. Es wurden gut ein Dutzend Grassroots-Workshops abgehalten, an denen Künstler wie Sander Veenhof, VJ Pixel, Radamés Ajna, Thiago Hersan, Mateus Knelsen, Ricardo Palmieri, Cristiano Panetone Rosa, Arthur de Leos, Lea Van Steen und Raquel Kogan, Denise Agassi, Vanessa de Michelis, Paloma Oliveira und andere teilgenommen haben.

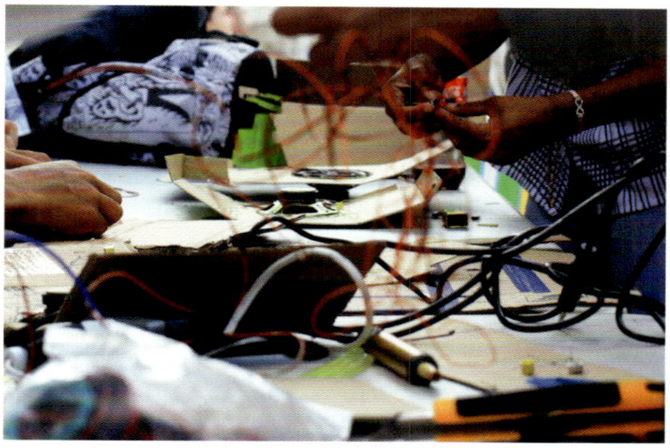

Hand-on lab: wiring electronic devices in the public realm.

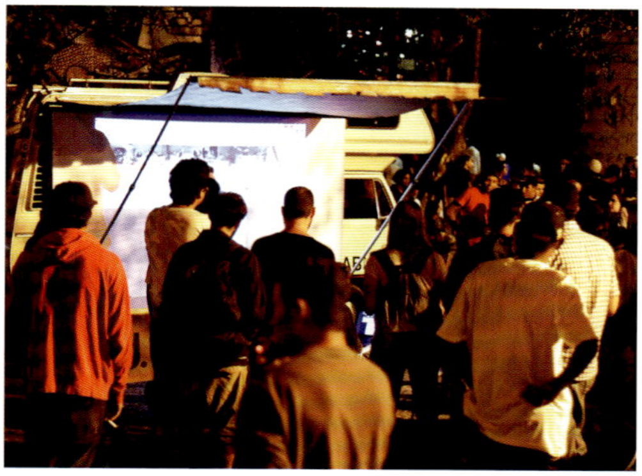

The Labmovel emppowering meetings and discussions at a downtown square in Belo Horizonte, during the Cidade Eletronika.

Coordination: Lucas Bambozzi; artistic direction: Gisela Domschke; production: Andrea Armentano, Luciana Tognon and Paloma Oliveira; video and documentation: Lucas Gervilla; administration: Diphusa Midia Digital e Arte Ltda.

Former support: Arte.mov group (Aluizer Malab, Rodrigo Minelli and Lucas Bambozzi), Fundação Telefonica, Nimk NL and Aaaan.Net (Annette Wolfsberger and Annet Dekker, NL)

Current support: Prince Claus Fund for Culture and Development (NL)

creative practice, leading to experimental locative and context-based projects that can be employed on the venues. The projects are usually available for a not specialized audience, also stimulating open forms of collaboration as the artists work with local audiences.

Labmovel started in 2012 and since then it has travelled to distinctive peripheries of São Paulo and Belo Horizonte, supporting and empowering cultural activities such as the arte.mov Festival (SP), Cidade Eletronika (BH) and Virada Cultural (SP). More than a dozen grassroots workhops have been conducted, involving artists such as Sander Veenhof, VJ Pixel, Radamés Ajna e Thiago Hersan, Mateus Knelsen, Ricardo Palmieri, Cristiano Panetone Rosa, Arthur de Leos, Lea Van Steen and Raquel Kogan, Denise Agassi, Vanessa de Michelis, Paloma Oliveira and other ones currently joining the program.

Labmovel has been initiated by Gisela Domschke and Lucas Bambozzi. Gisela Domschke (BR) is a media artist and independent curator, working in collaboration with cultural institutions, such as British Council, AHRC, Mondriaan Foundation, Virtuel Platform, Netherlands Media Art Institute, Vivo Arte.mov, FutureEverything and others. She led the media lab of Goldsmiths University in London as well as the media lab of the Museu da Imagem e do Som in São Paulo. *http://giselad.com* Lucas Bambozzi (BR) is a media artist producing installations, videos and interactive projects. His works have been shown in solo and collective shows in more than 40 countries. His recent work addresses issues related to immobility and contradictions on the urban context permeated by different kinds of media. *http://www.lucasbambozzi.net/* **Labmovel** wurde von Gisela Domschke und Lucas Bambozzi initiiert. Gisela Domschke (BR) ist Medienkünstlerin und freie Kuratorin, die mit Kulturinstitutionen wie British Council, AHRC, Mondriaan Foundation, Virtuel Platform, Netherlands Media Art Institute, Vivo Arte.mov, FutureEverything u. a. zusammenarbeitet. Sie leitete das Media Lab der Goldsmiths University in London sowie das Media-Lab des Museu da Imagem e do som in São Paulo. *http://giselad.com* Lucas Bambozzi (BR) ist Medienkünstler und produziert Installationen, Videos und interaktive Projekte. Seine Arbeiten wurden in Einzel- und Gruppenausstellungen in mehr als 40 Ländern gezeigt. Seine jüngsten Arbeiten beschäftigen sich mit Fragen, die mit Unbeweglichkeit und Widersprüchen im urbanen Kontext zu tun haben, der von verschiedensten Medien durchdrungen ist. *http://www.lucasbambozzi.net/*

Metropolitalia

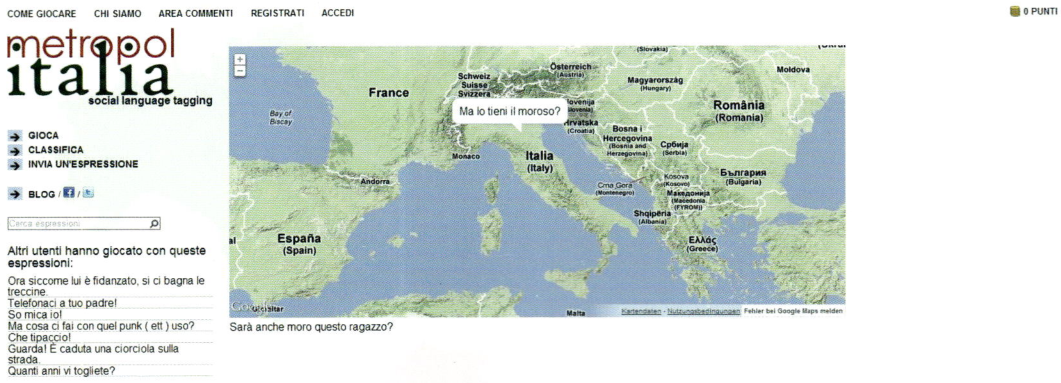

1. Startseite

Metropolitalia is an online platform where Italian native speakers can test their knowledge of their language. It is a so-called "game with a purpose" (GWAP), which means the community of users may, on the one hand, enjoy the game and compete with one another and, on the other hand, contribute to collecting and assessing language data (expressions in regional vernaculars and dialects). *Metropolitalia* is a platform for linguistic field research and its aim is to gather data from a large number of different speakers; in traditional field studies it is impossible to collect data from so many people. This platform may be used not only by researchers but also by the players themselves, as here they can check how the majority of speakers assessed specific expressions.

In each round, the player is presented with three examples, each consisting of a typical regional expression (phrase or whole sentence). By clicking on a map, the player assigns a location (supra-regional, regional or local) to an expression. At the same time, the player bets on how many other players share his or her assessment of a specific expression's origin. Bets are stored and compared to those of the other players; points are awarded according to the degree of agreement between the players' assessments. A player's points go up or down, depending on these assessments, as more people play. Hence the number of points awarded is not constant but varies depending on the community's assessments. The objective of the game

Metropolitalia ist eine Online-Plattform, auf der italienische Muttersprachler ihr Wissen über ihre Muttersprache testen können. Es handelt sich um ein sogenanntes „Game with a purpose" (GWAP): Die Gemeinschaft der Nutzer kann einerseits Spaß am Spiel und am Wettbewerb haben und andererseits zur Sammlung und Beurteilung sprachbezogener Daten (Ausdrücke in regionalen Umgangssprachen und Dialekten) beitragen. *Metropolitalia* ist eine Plattform für linguistische Feldforschung, mit dem Ziel, Daten von möglichst vielen unterschiedlichen Sprechern zu sammeln. In traditionellen Feldstudien wäre es unmöglich, Daten von so vielen Menschen zu sammeln. Diese Plattform kann nicht nur von Forschern genutzt werden, sondern auch von den Spielern selbst: Sie können hier nachschauen, wie die Mehrheit der Sprecher spezifische Ausdrücke beurteilt.

In jeder Spielrunde bekommt der Spieler drei Beispiele präsentiert, die aus einem regionaltypischen sprachlichen Ausdruck (Phrase oder ganzer Satz) bestehen. Der Spieler verortet den Ausdruck durch Klicken auf eine Karte (großräumig, regional oder lokal). Dabei schließt der Spieler eine Wette ab, mit der er einschätzt, wie viele andere Spieler wohl seine Einschätzung bezüglich der Herkunft dieses Ausdrucks teilen. Die Wetten werden gespeichert und mit denen der anderen Spieler verglichen; die Punktevergabe ergibt sich aus dem Grad der Übereinstimmung mit der Meinung der anderen. Mit zunehmender Spielerzahl erhöht sich bzw. sinkt die eigene Punktzahl, je nach den Einschätzungen der Spielercommunity. Die Punktzahl ist somit nicht konstant, sondern variiert je nach den Einschätzungen der

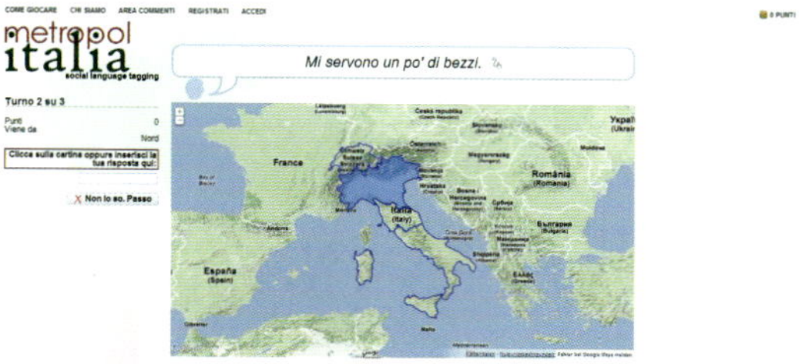

2. Beginn der Spielrunde: Verortung des Ausdrucks

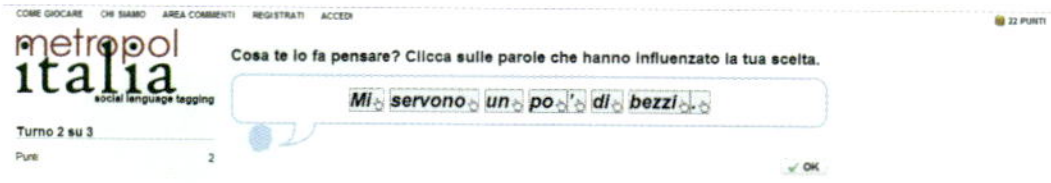

3. Sprachlich auffällige Elemente kennzeichnen

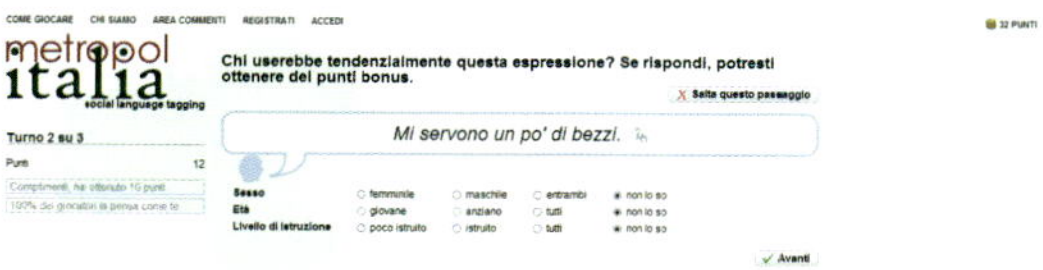

4. Persönliche Beurteilung des potentiellen Sprechers dieser Äußerung

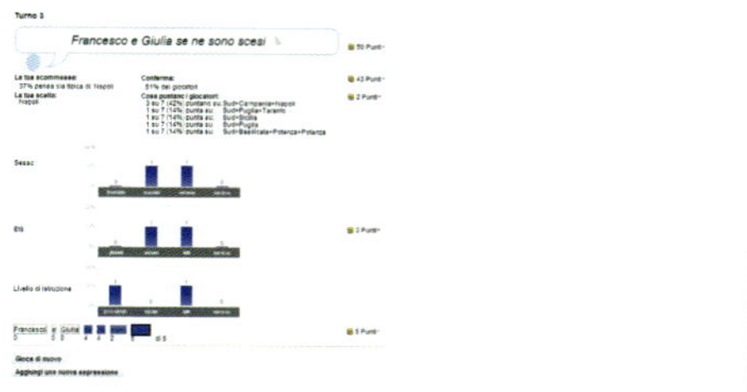

5. Ausschnitt aus der Darstellung der Ergebnisse aller drei Spielrunden

Crowd. Es gilt, so viele Punkte wie möglich zu sammeln (Bestenliste).
Ziel des Projekts ist die Erhebung authentischer Daten über die geographische Variation der italienischen Sprache, wobei weitere Parameter, die einen Einfluss auf den Sprachgebrauch haben (Geschlecht, Alter und Bildungsgrad der Sprecher), Berücksichtigung finden. „Unter" der Spieloberfläche wird eine Datenbank erstellt, die dazu dient, Primär- und Metadaten der italienischen Sprache im Bereich des Regionalitalienischen und der Dialekte zu erheben. Solche Informationen ergeben sich aus der Einschätzung der Spieler, die dadurch die entsprechenden Formen in der Datenbank taggen. So kann z. B. der prägende Einfluss der Großstädte auf die Dynamik der sprachlichen Variation untersucht werden, oder es können gängige Hypothesen zur mehr oder weniger starken Markiertheit von Ausdrücken überprüft werden.

is to accumulate as many points as possible and make the list of top scorers.
The objective of the project is to collect authentic data on geographic variation in the Italian language, while taking other parameters that have an influence on language usage (sex, age, level of education) into account. "Beneath" the game's surface, a database has been set up that collects primary and meta data from the Italian language, in particular, from the field of regional and social dialects. The data results from the assessment of the players who tag the appropriate forms in the database. This makes it possible to study, for instance, the formative influence of big cities on the dynamics of linguistic variation, or to reexamine common hypotheses on the degree of markedness of expressions.

Metropolitalia is an interdisciplinary initiative launched by the Ludwig Maximilian University of Munich (Institute for Romance Philology; and Institute for Informatics/Teaching and Research Unit Programming and Modeling Language) and aims, within the scope of the digital humanities, at harnessing the potential of "games with a purpose" for the humanities as a whole.
Metropolitalia ist eine interdisziplinäre Initiative an der Ludwig Maximilians Universität München (Institut für Romanische Philologie und Institut für Informatik, Programmier- und Modellierungssprachen), um das Potenzial der *games with a purpose* im Rahmen der Digital Humanities für die Geisteswissenschaften nutzbar zu machen.

NicoNicoGakkai Beta

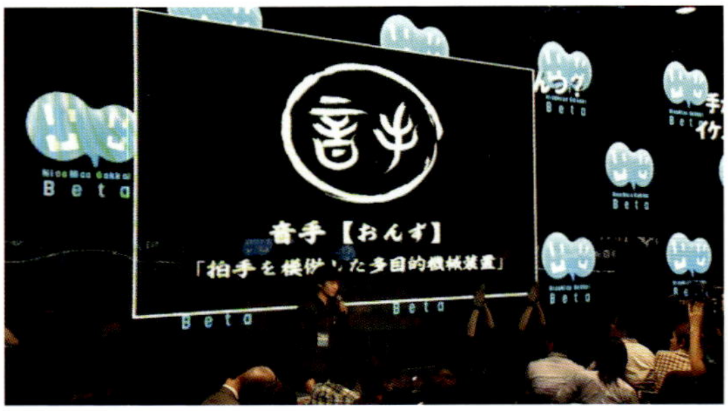

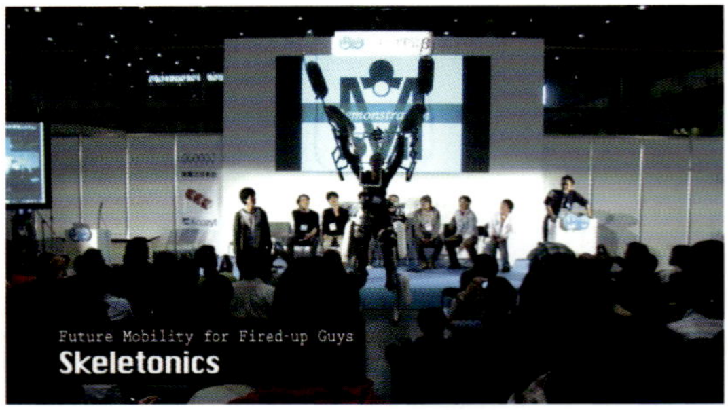

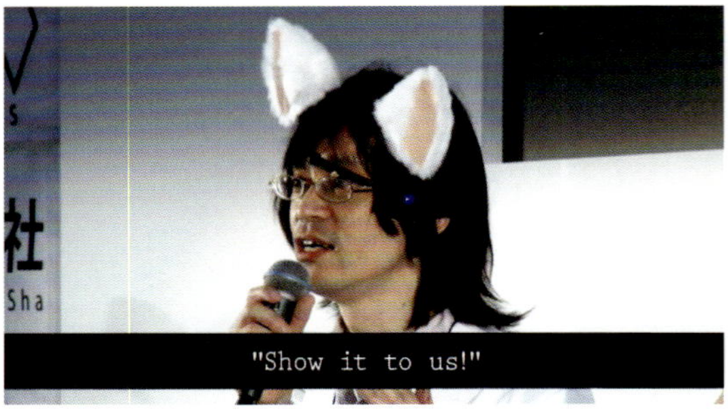

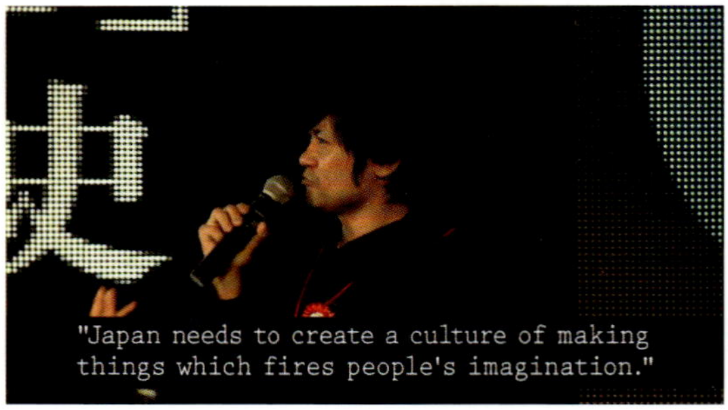

NicoNicoGakkai Beta is a new style of academy that emphasizes user-generated research. It is an online and offline research academy that recognizes research on a diversity of merits, from cultural and artistic values to academic and industrial strengths. The users of the video-sharing website *NicoNico Douga* include people who build robots or new user-interfaces and who share videos of their work on the web. Although their work is often unique and of a very high level, there are few opportunities for them in the traditional academic world. *NicoNicoGakkai Beta* brings these users, university researchers and researchers in the professional world together to hold open research presentations, aiming to deepen relationships and help to increase the level of research across the board. The presentations are broadcast live on *NicoNico Live* and the archives are available for anyone to view on the web.
There have been four *NicoNicoGakkai Beta* symposiums since 2011. For the first event there was an audience of over 110,000, who left a total of over 80,000 comments.

NicoNicoGakkai Beta ist eine neue Form von „Akademie", die usergenerierte Forschung fördert. Es ist eine Online- und Offline-Akademie, die die Verdienste von Forschung in vielerlei Hinsicht würdigt, seien es ihre kulturellen und künstlerischen Werte oder ihre akademische und wirtschaftliche Bedeutung.
Zu den Usern der Videosharing-Webseite *NicoNico Douga* zählen Menschen, die Roboter oder neue User-Interfaces bauen und die Videos von ihren Arbeiten im Web teilen. Obwohl ihre Arbeiten oft einzigartig und auf einem sehr hohen Niveau angesiedelt sind, gibt es für sie nur wenige Gelegenheiten in der traditionellen akademischen Welt. *NicoNicoGakkai Beta* bringt User, universitäre Forscher und Forscher in der Industrie bei offenen Forschungspräsentationen zusammen. Wir wollen damit die Beziehungen vertiefen und das allgemeine Niveau der Forschung steigern helfen. Die Präsentationen werden live auf *NicoNico Live* gestreamt und die Archive sind für jeden Internet-User offen.
Es hat seit 2011 vier *NicoNicoGakkai Beta*-Symposien gegeben. Das erste Event sahen über 110.000 Zuschauer, die mehr als 80.000 Kommentare schrieben.

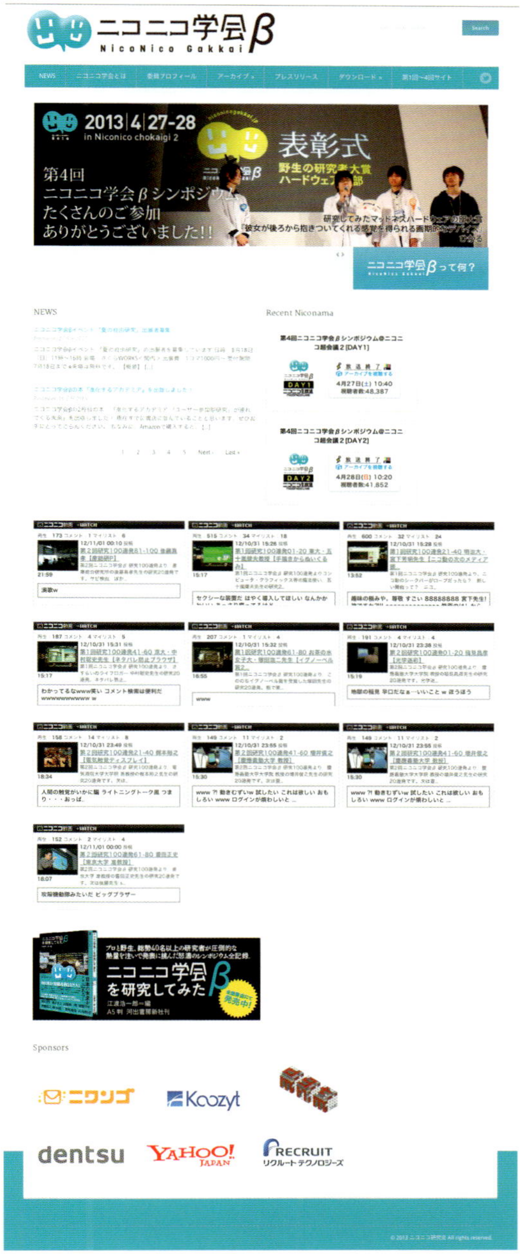

NicoNicoGakkai Beta has been initiated by Koichiro Eto. The core members are 28 people who are interested in user-generated content—researchers, university professors, media artists, engineers etc. The full team, including office staff, external collaborators and volunteers, is around 70 people. Presenters at the symposium are divided between invited guests and members of the public ("wild researchers"). **NicoNicoGakkai Beta**, initiiert von Koichiro Eto, besteht aus einem Kernteam von 28 Personen, die sich für usergenerierten Content interessieren: Forscher, Universitätsprofessoren, Medienkünstler, Ingenieure usw. Das gesamte Team, inklusive Büroangestellte, externe Mitarbeiter und Freiwillige, umfasst ungefähr 70 Personen. Die Moderatoren der Symposien sind sowohl eingeladene Gäste als auch Mitglieder des Publikums („wilde Forscher").

Numbeo

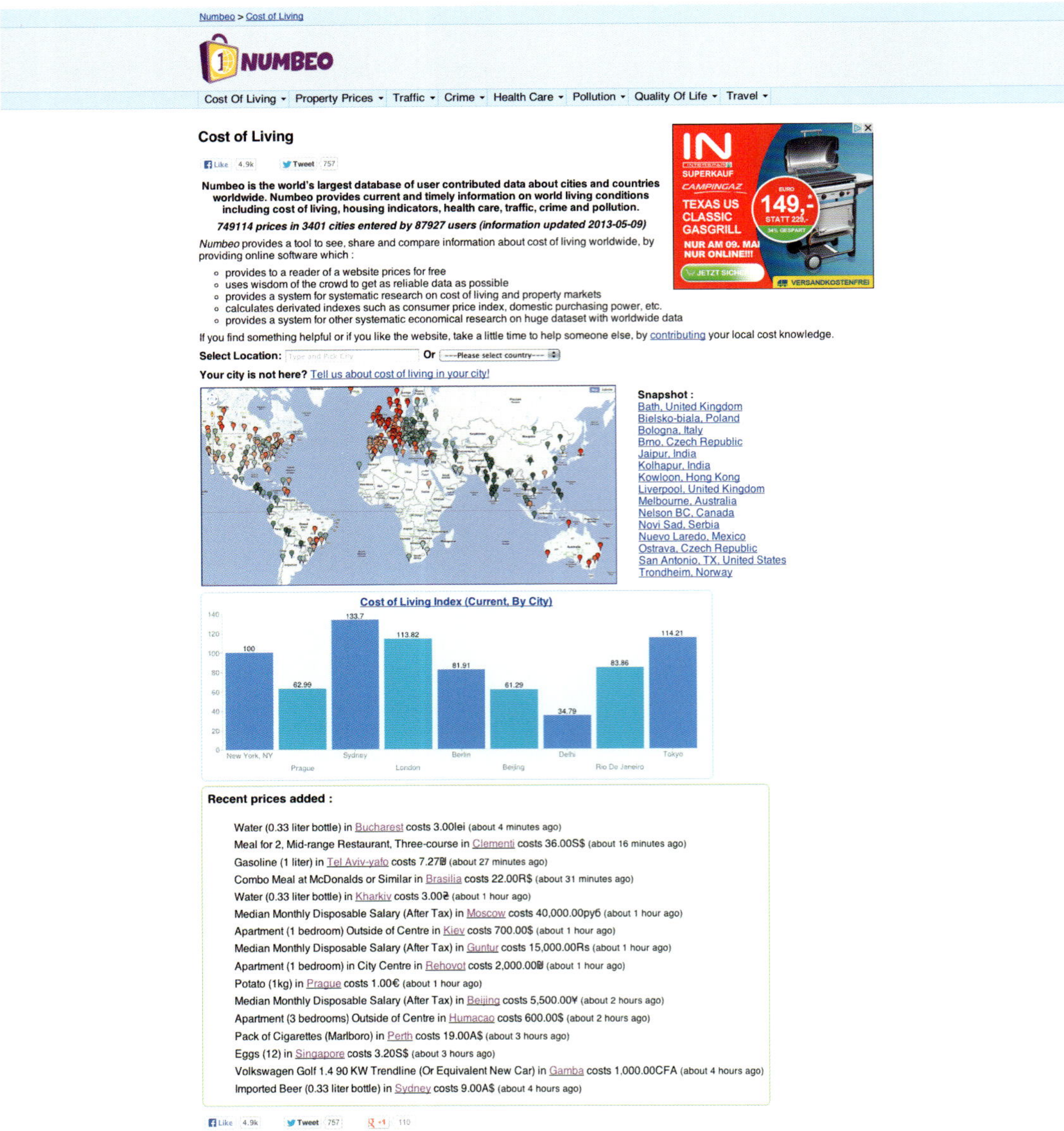
Numbeo > Cost of Living
NUMBEO
Cost Of Living
Property Prices
Traffic
Crime
Health Care
Pollution
Quality Of Life
Travel
Cost of Living
Like 4.9k
Tweet 757
Numbeo is the world's largest database of user contributed data about cities and countries worldwide. Numbeo provides current and timely information on world living conditions including cost of living, housing indicators, health care, traffic, crime and pollution.
749114 prices in 3401 cities entered by 87927 users (information updated 2013-05-09)
Numbeo provides a tool to see, share and compare information about cost of living worldwide, by providing online software which :
provides to a reader of a website prices for free
uses wisdom of the crowd to get as reliable data as possible
provides a system for systematic research on cost of living and property markets
calculates derivated indexes such as consumer price index, domestic purchasing power, etc.
provides a system for other systematic economical research on huge dataset with worldwide data
If you find something helpful or if you like the website, take a little time to help someone else, by contributing your local cost knowledge.
Select Location:
Or
---Please select country---
Your city is not here? Tell us about cost of living in your city!
IN
SUPERKAUF
TEXAS US CLASSIC GASGRILL
149,-
STATT 229,-
NUR AM 09. MAI NUR ONLINE!!!
VERSANDKOSTENFREI
Snapshot :
Bath, United Kingdom
Bielsko-biala, Poland
Bologna, Italy
Brno, Czech Republic
Jaipur, India
Kolhapur, India
Kowloon, Hong Kong
Liverpool, United Kingdom
Melbourne, Australia
Nelson BC, Canada
Novi Sad, Serbia
Nuevo Laredo, Mexico
Ostrava, Czech Republic
San Antonio, TX, United States
Trondheim, Norway
Cost of Living Index (Current, By City)
140
120
100
80
60
40
20
0
100
62.99
133.7
113.82
81.91
61.29
34.79
83.86
114.21
New York, NY
Prague
Sydney
London
Berlin
Beijing
Delhi
Rio De Janeiro
Tokyo
Recent prices added :
Water (0.33 liter bottle) in Bucharest costs 3.00lei (about 4 minutes ago)
Meal for 2, Mid-range Restaurant, Three-course in Clementi costs 36.00S$ (about 16 minutes ago)
Gasoline (1 liter) in Tel Aviv-yafo costs 7.27₪ (about 27 minutes ago)
Combo Meal at McDonalds or Similar in Brasilia costs 22.00R$ (about 31 minutes ago)
Water (0.33 liter bottle) in Kharkiv costs 3.00₴ (about 1 hour ago)
Median Monthly Disposable Salary (After Tax) in Moscow costs 40,000.00руб (about 1 hour ago)
Apartment (1 bedroom) Outside of Centre in Kiev costs 700.00$ (about 1 hour ago)
Median Monthly Disposable Salary (After Tax) in Guntur costs 15,000.00Rs (about 1 hour ago)
Apartment (1 bedroom) in City Centre in Rehovot costs 2,000.00₪ (about 1 hour ago)
Potato (1kg) in Prague costs 1.00€ (about 1 hour ago)
Median Monthly Disposable Salary (After Tax) in Beijing costs 5,500.00¥ (about 2 hours ago)
Apartment (3 bedrooms) Outside of Centre in Humacao costs 600.00$ (about 2 hours ago)
Pack of Cigarettes (Marlboro) in Perth costs 19.00A$ (about 3 hours ago)
Eggs (12) in Singapore costs 3.20S$ (about 3 hours ago)
Volkswagen Golf 1.4 90 KW Trendline (Or Equivalent New Car) in Gamba costs 1,000.00CFA (about 4 hours ago)
Imported Beer (0.33 liter bottle) in Sydney costs 9.00A$ (about 4 hours ago)
Like 4.9k
Tweet 757
+1 110

Numbeo ist die weltgrößte größte Datenbank mit usergenerierten Daten über Städte und Länder in der ganzen Welt. Sie liefert aktuelle Informationen über die Lebensumstände, inklusive Lebenshaltungskosten, Wohnungsmarkt-Indikatoren, Gesundheitsdienste, Verkehr, Kriminalität und Verschmutzung. Per 5. Mai 2013 enthielt die Datenbank 744.662 Preise in 3.390 Städten, die von 87.370 Usern beigesteuert wurden.
Numbeo stellt ein Online-Tool zur Verfügung, mit dem man Informationen über die Lebenshaltungskosten weltweit abfragen, teilen und vergleichen kann. Dank der Software dahinter kann man außerdem:

- eine Webseite mit einer Liste von Preisen abfragen
- die Weisheit der Massen nutzen, um möglichst zuverlässige Daten zu erhalten
- ein Instrument für systematische Forschung über die Lebenshaltungskosten und den Wohnungsmarkt nutzen
- abgeleitete Indizes wie den Verbraucherpreisindex oder die Kaufkraft eines Ortes usw. konsultieren
- ein System für weitere Recherchen im Bereich Wirtschaft über einen riesigen Datensatz mit Daten aus der ganzen Welt nutzen.

Numbeo is the world's largest database of user-contributed data about cities and countries worldwide. It provides current and timely information on world living conditions including the cost of living, housing indicators, healthcare, traffic, crime and pollution. By May 5, 2013, it had 744,662 prices in 3,390 cities entered by 87,370 users.
Numbeo provides a tool to see, share and compare information about costs of living worldwide, by providing online software which:

- provides a website with a free list of prices
- uses the wisdom of the crowd to obtain as reliable data as possible
- provides a system for systematic research on the cost of living and property markets
- calculates derived indexes such as the consumer-price index, domestic purchasing power, etc.
- provides a system for other systematic economic research on huge dataset of worldwide data

Numbeo was created by Mladen Adamovic in 2009. He has worked as a software engineer developing internal applications at Google Ireland (2007–2009), as a software engineer for Sungard (2010–2011) and as a project manager for Troxo (2011). He was a senior teaching assistant at the University of Banja Luka (2004–2007). He obtained a BSc in mathematics from the University of Belgrade in 2003 and an MSc in electrical engineering from the University of Banja Luka in 2006. **Numbeo** wurde 2009 von Mladen Adamovic entwickelt. Er hat als Software-Ingenieur interne Anwendungen bei Google Irland entwickelt (2007–2009), für Sungard (2010–2011) und als Projektmanager für Troxo (2011) gearbeitet. Er war Dozent an der Universität von Banja Luka (2004–2007). 2003 erwarb er einen BSc in Mathematik an der Universität Belgrad und 2006 einen MSc in Elektrotechnik an der Universität Banja Luka.

oiga.me

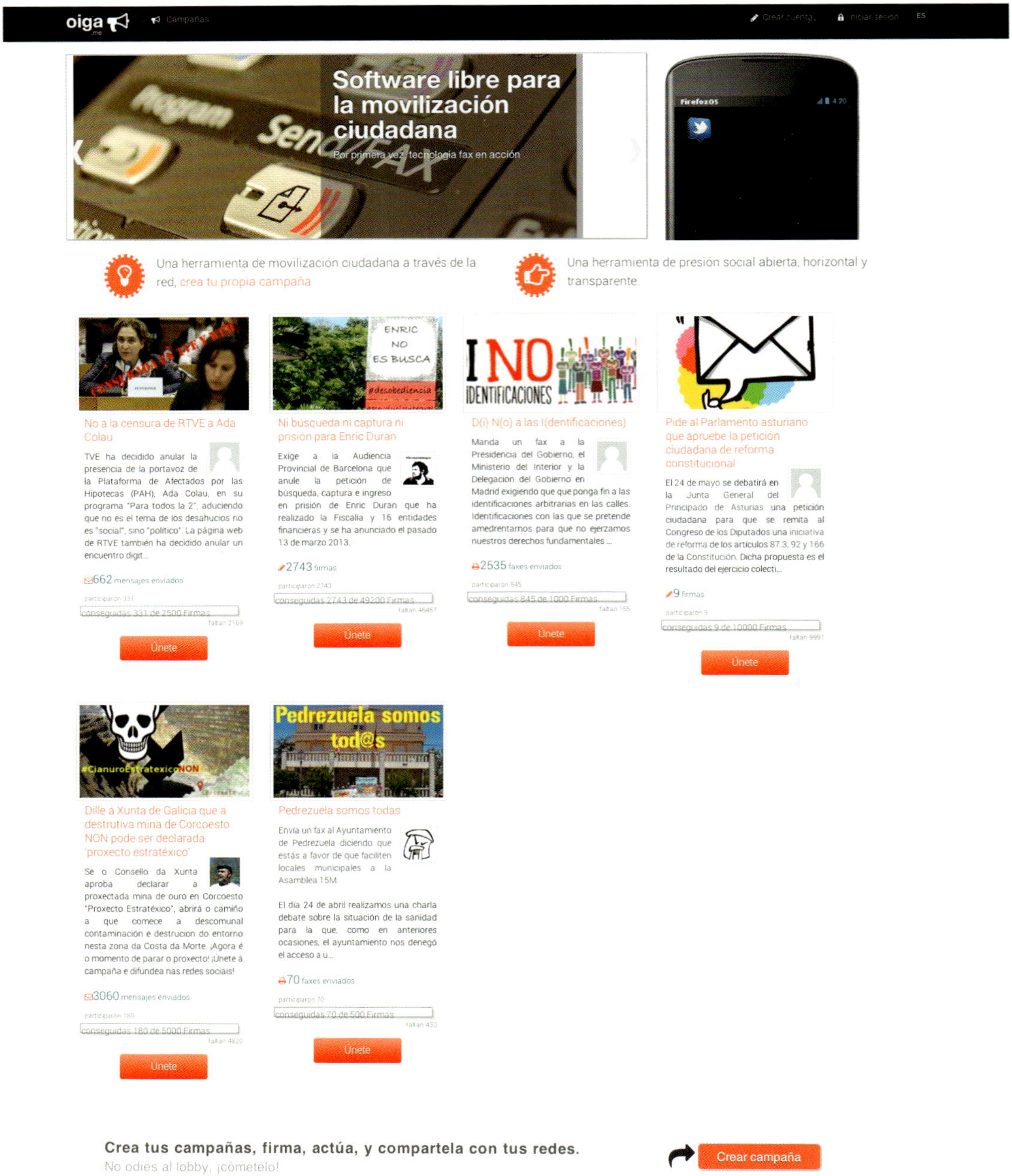

oiga
Campañas
Crear cuenta
Iniciar sesión
ES
Software libre para la movilización ciudadana
Por primera vez tecnología fax en acción
Una herramienta de movilización ciudadana a través de la red, crea tu propia campaña
Una herramienta de presión social abierta, horizontal y transparente.
No a la censura de RTVE a Ada Colau
TVE ha decidido anular la presencia de la portavoz de la Plataforma de Afectados por las Hipotecas (PAH), Ada Colau, en su programa "Para todos la 2", aduciendo que no es el tema de los desahucios no es "social", sino "político". La página web de RTVE también ha decidido anular un encuentro digit...
662 mensajes enviados
conseguidas 331 de 2500 Firmas
Únete
Ni búsqueda ni captura ni prisión para Enric Duran
ENRIC NO ES BUSCA
#desobediencia
Exige a la Audiencia Provincial de Barcelona que anule la petición de búsqueda, captura e ingreso en prisión de Enric Duran que ha realizado la Fiscalía y 16 entidades financieras y se ha anunciado el pasado 13 de marzo 2013.
2743 firmas
conseguidas 2743 de 49200 Firmas
Únete
NO IDENTIFICACIONES
D(i) N(o) a las I(dentificaciones)
Manda un fax a la Presidencia del Gobierno, el Ministerio del Interior y la Delegación del Gobierno en Madrid exigiendo que que ponga fin a las identificaciones arbitrarias en las calles. Identificaciones con las que se pretende amedrentarnos para que no ejerzamos nuestros derechos fundamentales ...
2535 faxes enviados
conseguidas 845 de 1000 Firmas
Únete
Pide al Parlamento asturiano que apruebe la petición ciudadana de reforma constitucional
El 24 de mayo se debatirá en la Junta General del Principado de Asturias una petición ciudadana para que se remita al Congreso de los Diputados una iniciativa de reforma de los artículos 87.3, 92 y 166 de la Constitución. Dicha propuesta es el resultado del ejercicio colecti...
9 firmas
conseguidas 9 de 10000 Firmas
Únete
#CianuroEstratexicoNON
Dille á Xunta de Galicia que a destrutiva mina de Corcoesto NON pode ser declarada 'proxecto estratéxico'
Se o Consello da Xunta aproba declarar a proxectada mina de ouro en Corcoesto "Proxecto Estratéxico", abrirá o camiño a que comece a descomunal contaminación e destrucion do entorno nesta zona da Costa da Morte. ¡Agora é o momento de parar o proxecto! ¡Únete á campaña e difúndea nas redes sociais!
3060 mensajes enviados
conseguidas 180 de 5000 Firmas
Únete
Pedrezuela somos tod@s
Pedrezuela somos todas
Envia un fax al Ayuntamiento de Pedrezuela diciendo que estás a favor de que faciliten locales municipales a la Asamblea 15M.
El día 24 de abril realizamos una charla debate sobre la situación de la sanidad para la que, como en anteriores ocasiones, el ayuntamiento nos denegó el acceso a u...
70 faxes enviados
conseguidas 70 de 500 Firmas
Únete
Crea tus campañas, firma, actúa, y compartela con tus redes.
No odies al lobby, ¡cómetelo!
Crear campaña

oiga.me ist eine Webseite, über die Online-Petitionen und Unterstützungskampagnen erstellt werden können, es ist aber auch eine Plattform für Bürger-Lobbying. Dank einer mächtigen Mailing- und Fax-Funktion (und bald auch IP-Telefonie) dient es als Katalysator für kollektive Forderungen und Petitionen, die die Energie von sozialen Netzwerken vervielfachen und transformieren. Personen oder Organisationen aus der Zivilgesellschaft können via *oiga.me* ihre Petitionen und Anfragen direkt an die verantwortliche Stelle richten: an Regierungen, Unternehmen, Lokalbehörden oder jede andere Art von Repräsentanz. Es ist ein Werkzeug für soziale Demokratisierung und Ermächtigung, ein Mechanismus, der die Stimmen der Bürger „verstärkt" und ihren Forderungen Ausdruck verleiht.

oiga.me begann im Jahr 2009. Während der Abstimmungen über ein Gesetz zur Regulierung des Internet im spanischen Parlament arbeitete *oiga.me* mit Xmailer. Nach diesem erfolgreichen Experiment entwickelten wir die erste Version, die im Oktober 2012 online ging und eine Mail- bzw. Online-Petitionsfunktion enthielt. Das Experiment war erfolgreich: Es verzeichnete 147.000 Besuche, 27.000 Mails und 9.500 Petitionen. Bei der zweiten Version (Januar 2013) kam eine Fax-Funktion dazu. Außerdem wurde eine Mikrospenden-Funktion implementiert und die Anbindung an soziale Netzwerke und andere partizipative Tools verbessert. Die gesamte Software von *oiga.me* ist frei, der Quellcode ist unter einer GNU Affero General Public Licence veröffentlicht, sämtliche Inhalte sind copyleft unter einer CC-By-SA-Lizenz.

oiga.me ist eine Non-Profit-Organisation, die auf Prinzipien der sozialen Ökonomie gründet. Sie wird von einem Social Council überwacht, der Unabhängigkeit, Privacy und Datenschutz garantiert. Der Social Council hat folgende Funktionen: Er muss den guten Einsatz der Plattform sicherstellen; die Unabhängigkeit von *oiga.me* garantieren; er hat Beraterfunktion im Entscheidungsprozess; er schlägt spezielle Kampagnen vor, identifiziert Verbesserungsmöglichkeiten und akquiriert Ressourcen für die Entwicklung und den Betrieb der Plattform. Der Social Council ist egalitär und repräsentativ für Organisationen aus der Zivilgesellschaft. Er verändert sich ständig und steht neuen Organisationen offen.

oiga.me is a resource to generate online petitions and support campaigns, but also a platform for citizenship lobbying. Through a massive mailing and fax-contact function (and soon IP telephone too) it serves as a catalyst for collective demands and petitions multiplying and transforming the energy of the social networks. Through *oiga.me* civil society individuals or organizations can communicate their petitions and demands straight to those responsible, such as governments, companies, local authorities or any other kind of representative. It is a tool for social democratization and empowerment that serves as a mechanism to enhance voices and express demands.

oiga.me started in 2009. During the Spanish parliamentary vote on the law regulating the Internet, *oiga.me* worked on Xmailer. After this successful experience, we developed the first version, which was released on October 2012. This included only the mail function and online petition form. The experience has proved great success: it has had attracted 147,000 visits, 27,000 mails and 9,500 signed petitions. The second version (January 2013) has added a fax function. It has also added a micro-credit donation system, better connection to social networks and more participative tools. All the software used by *oiga.me* is free and the application code is licensed under GNU Affero General Public License and all it contents are copyleft under CC-By-SA license.

oiga.me is a non-profit organization based on social economy principles that are monitored by its Social Council, which guarantees independence, privacy and data protection. The Social Council functions are: ensuring of the good use of the platform, guaranteeing *oiga.me's* independence, counseling on the decision-making process, proposing special campaigns, looking for improvements and obtaining resources for development and management of the platform. The Social Council composition is egalitarian and representative of civil-society organizations. It is also permanently under construction and open to new organizations.

oiga.me was developed by the aLabs association and managed by the *oiga.me* Social Council, which is composed of social organizations such as Ecologistas en Acción (NGO), the CGT (trade union confederation), the political platform of support of the Saharaui people, the organization ATTAC Madrid, the free association of lawyers (ALA), the Dabne cooperative, the MOC collective and the Multivalent Space Patio Maravillas, Xnet. **oiga.me** wurde von aLabs entwickelt und wird vom Social Council von *oiga.me* betrieben, der aus sozialen Organisationen besteht, u. a. Ecologistas en Acción (NGO), CGT (Gewerkschaft), der politischen Plattform zur Unterstützung des Saharaui-Volkes, ATTAC Madrid, ALA, der freien Assoziation von Rechtsanwälten, der Kooperative Dabne, dem Kollektiv MOC, von Multivalent Space Patio Maravillas und Xnet.

Seeed Studio

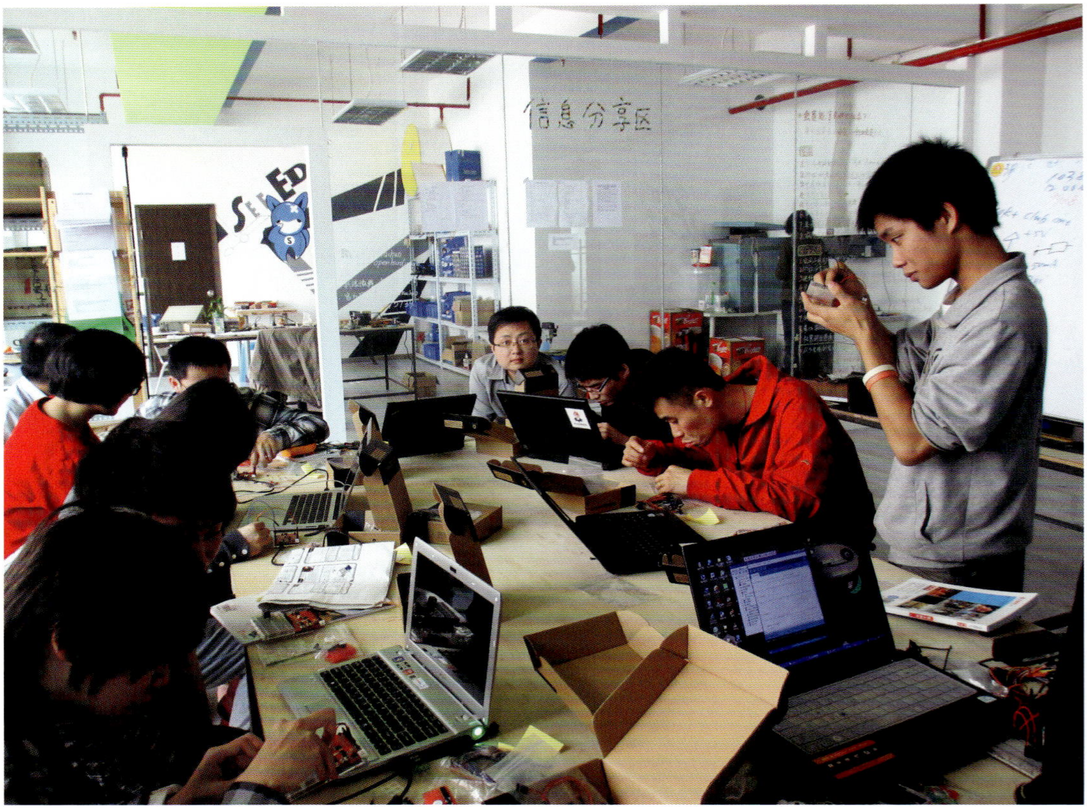

Seeed Studio is an open-hardware facilitator based in Shenzhen (China). Its goal is to promote the maker movement and the spread of maker culture (do-it-yourself, do-it-together, innovative spirit etc.).
We started *Seeed Studio* because we love the concept of open hardware. With the development of the maker culture and the upsurge in open hardware, we are taking advantage of the favorable situation to start research and development in open-hardware components and modules and then to provide them to the community. Communicating with the community members, we learned that one of the main problems for innovators is the difficulty of getting ideas into prototypes and from prototypes into production.
Hence we decided to support the community by providing innovative and cost-effective prototyping solutions for innovators. We help innovators turn their concepts into reality, shortening the time consumed in the idea-to-prototype-to-product

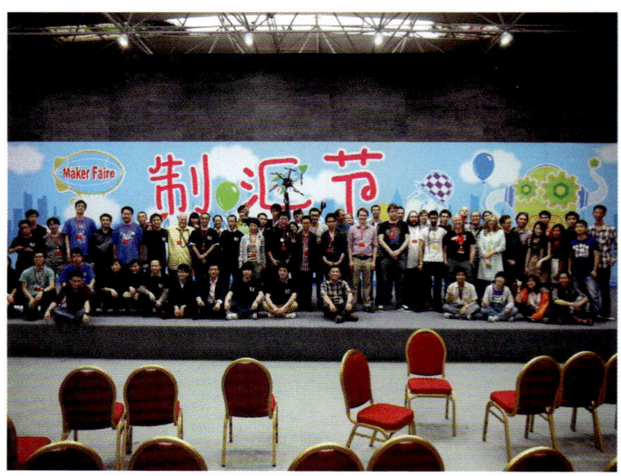

Seeed Studio ist ein Facilitator im Bereich offener Hardware, der in Shenzhen (China) angesiedelt ist. Sein Ziel ist es, die Maker-Bewegung und die Verbreitung der Maker-Kultur zu fördern (Do-it-yourself, Do-it-together, Innovationsgeist).

Wir begannen *Seeed Studio*, weil wir das Konzept der offenen Hardware gut finden. Wir nutzen die Entwicklung der Maker-Kultur und das Aufkommen offener Hardware, um Forschung und Entwicklung von Hardware-Komponenten und -Modulen zu betreiben und sie der Community zur Verfügung zu stellen. Im Austausch mit den Mitgliedern dieser Gemeinschaft wurde uns klar, dass eine der größten Hürden für Innovatoren darin liegt, Ideen in Prototypen zu verwandeln und diese dann in Produktion gehen zu lassen.
Wir beschlossen daher, die Gemeinschaft durch die Bereitstellung innovativer und kostengünstiger Prototyping-Lösungen für Innovatoren zu unterstützen. Wir helfen Innovatoren, ihre Konzepte umzusetzen und den Prozess von der Idee zum Prototypen zu verkürzen. Die Teilnehmer sind alle auch Mitglieder der Gemeinschaft: *Seeed*-Belegschaft, kooperative Designer, Künstler, Lehrer, Studenten und viele andere. Offene Hardware wird in vielen Bereichen eingesetzt, z.B. im Umweltschutz, beim Aufspüren von Schadstoffen, Near-Space-Erforschung, Internet der Dinge, Grüne Energie, Mode, Wearable Electronics, Kunst etc.
Wir organisieren oder unterstützen auch verschiedene Aktivitäten und Veranstaltungen, um die Community zu vergrößern und die Interaktion zu stärken. Im Moment ist *Seeed Studio* einer der wichtigsten Lieferanten von Open Hardware und einer der wichtigsten Verfechter der Maker-Kultur.

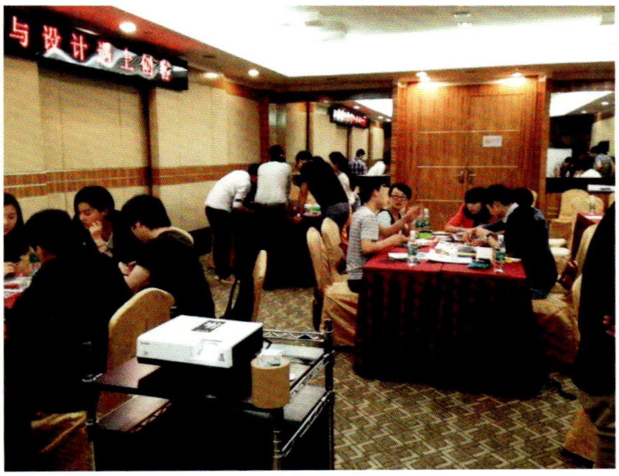

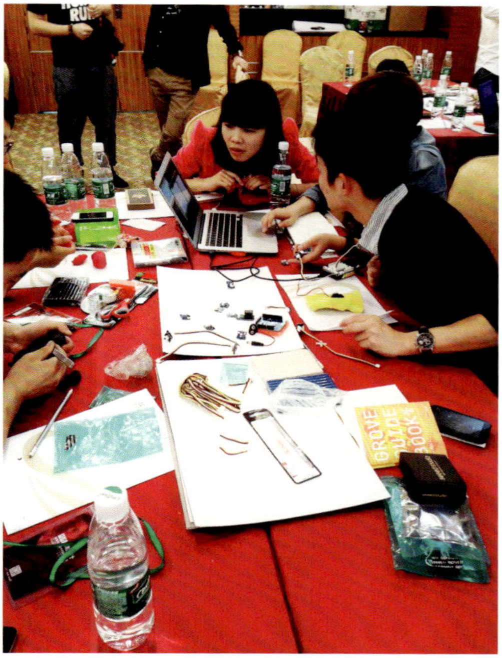

process. The participants are all the community members: *Seeed* staff, cooperative designers, artists, teachers, students, and many others. Open hardware is used in many fields, such as environmental detection and protection, near-space exploration, the Internet of Things, clean energy, fashion, wearable electronics, arts etc.
We also organize or support various activities/ events in order to expand the community and strengthen the interaction. Currently, *Seeed Studio* is one of the world's most important open-hardware providers, maker-event participants and maker-culture propagators.

Seeed Studio was founded in 2008 in Shenzhen. The open-hardware facilitator supports the community by providing innovative and cost-effective prototyping solutions to innovators. **Seeed Studio** wurde 2008 in Shenzhen gegründet. Der Open-Hardware-Facilitator unterstützt die Gemeinschaft, indem er innovative und kostengünstige Prototyping-Lösungen zur Verfügung stellt.

The East Japan Earthquake Archive

The East Japan Earthquake Archive is a digital archive using Google Earth to visualize and report on the real state of the damage from the earthquake in eastern Japan. Since data such as photographs, panorama pictures and disaster victims' testimonies are unified on Google Earth, users can browse all the data from a bird's-eye view. In addition, a time-stamp function is incorporated in this archive, so users can also browse all the data along with the time elapsed since the earthquake.

The East Japan Earthquake Archive offers a "mash-up" of content that users can explore to "understand the real state of affairs—that cannot be understood by inspecting individual photographs." The map shows over 100 photos from the *New York Times* overlapping with three-dimensional geographical features that offer comprehensive views of Sendai airport and the Fukushima nuclear plants. It includes 360-degree panorama images

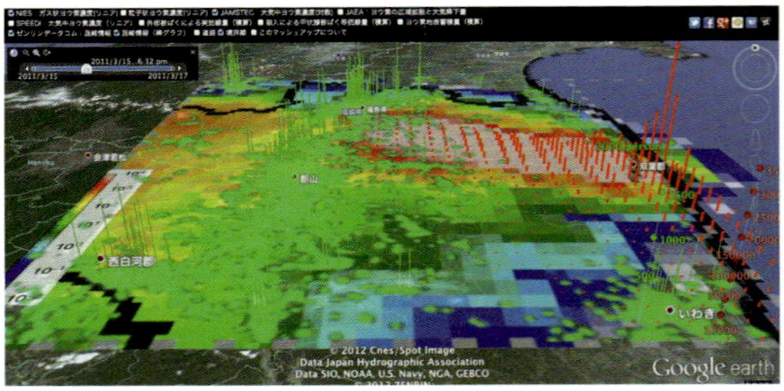

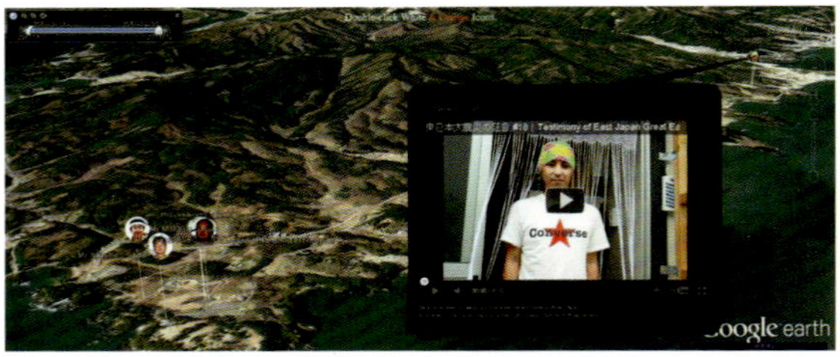

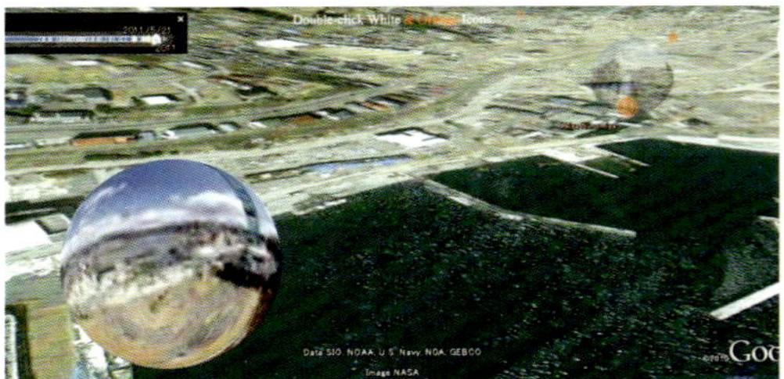

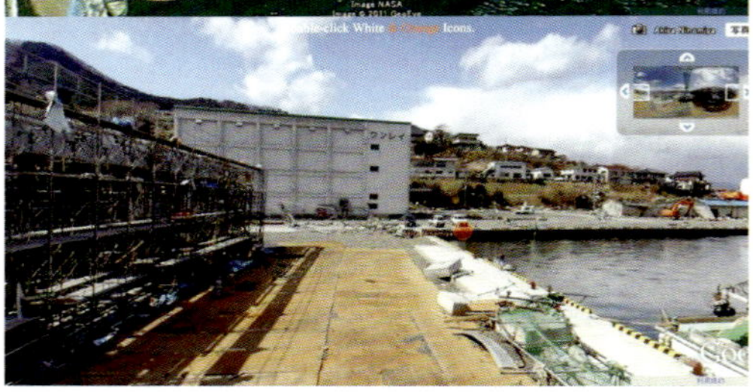

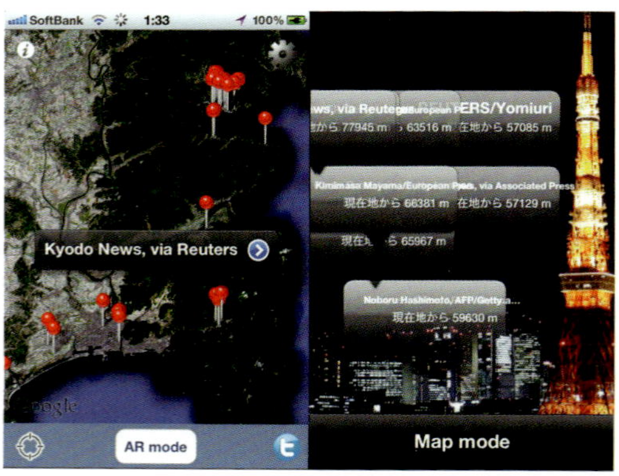

Das *East Japan Earthquake Archive* ist ein digitales Archiv, das Google Earth nutzt, um den wahren Zustand des Schadens, den das Erdbeben in Ostjapan angerichtet hat, zu visualisieren und zu dokumentieren. Da Daten wie Fotografien, Panoramaaufnahmen und Zeugenaussagen von Erdbebenopfern auf Google Earth versammelt werden, können die User aus der Vogelperspektive durch alle Daten browsen. Außerdem ist eine Zeitstempel-Funktion im Archiv eingebaut, sodass die User auch chrononologisch, beginnend mit dem Erdbeben, browsen können.

The East Japan Earthquake Archive bietet ein Mash-up an Inhalten, das User erforschen können, um „den wahren Stand der Dinge" zu erfahren, was nicht möglich ist, wenn man bloß einzelne Fotografien anschaut. Die Karte zeigt über 100 Fotografien aus der *New York Times*, die über die dreidimensionalen geografischen Merkmalen gelegt sind und so einen umfassenden Blick auf den Sendai-Flughafen und die Nuklearanlagen von Fukushima ermöglichen. Dazu gehören auch ein 360-Grad-Panorama und geografisch geordnete Videos von Augenzeugenberichten, die von der Zeitung *Asahi Shimbun* gesammelt, in Stereo von studentischen Freiwilligen aufgenommen und auf Google Earth abgebildet wurden. Die Film-Clips können über Sprechblasen mit den Gesichtern der Augenzeugen abgerufen, dazu ist auch das Sound-Environment eines Ortes in drei Dimensionenen reproduziert.

Das gesamte Material wurde von online rekrutierten Freiwilligen gesammelt. User können durch den Inhalt auf ihrem PC oder Smartphone stöbern. Das Projekt ist nicht abgeschlossen, es werden ständig neue Fotos und

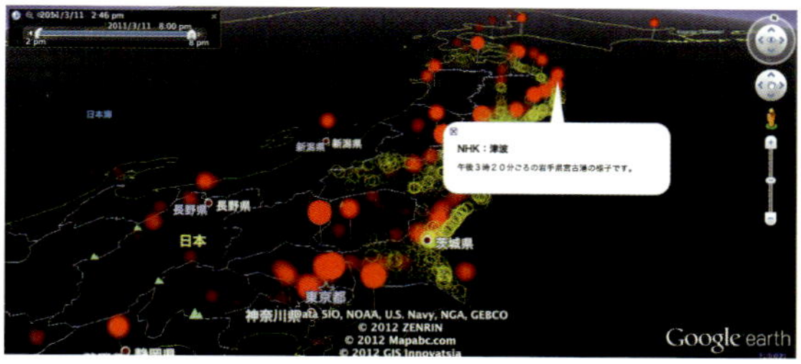

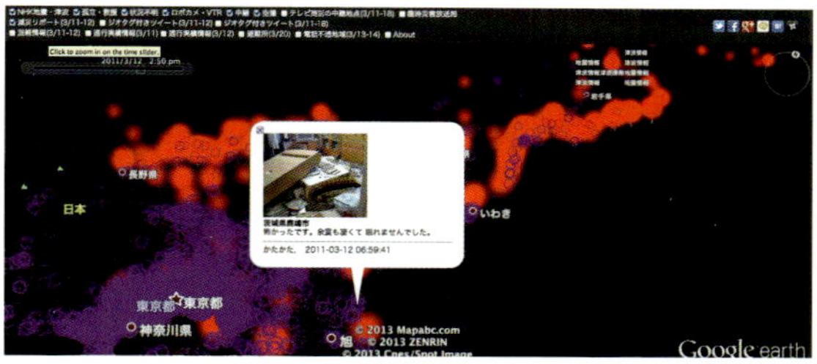

Informationen hochgeladen, die chrononologisch abgefragt werden können.
Beim „The Great East Japan Big Data Workshop-Project 311", einer großen Initiative zur Katastrophenbewältigung, die Technologie nutzt, um für zukünftige Unglücke besser gerüstet zu sein, haben wir zwei Mash-ups kreiert. Wir wollen eine legal saubere Entscheidungsgrundlage aufbauen, falls in Zukunft Schilddrüsenkrebserkrankungen auftreten sollten. Zweitens haben wir die Daten der Mainstream-Medien abgebildet, inklusive der Nachrichtentexte von NHK und crowdgesourcte Daten wie georeferenzierte Tweets und andere Crowd-Informationen, die der Gensai-Report von WeatherNews gesammelt hat.

and geographically arranged videos of victims' testimonies collected by the *Asahi Shimbun* newspaper and recorded in stereo by student volunteers and mapped on Google Earth. The film clips can be browsed in balloons by clicking face icons and the sound environment of a location is reproduced in three dimensions.
All the material was collected by online volunteers. Users can browse the content freely on their PCs and smartphones. The project is ongoing, constantly updated with the most recent photos and information that users can browse chronologically. We have also created two mash-up contents in "The Great East Japan Big Data Workshop-Project 311," a major post-disaster initiative designed use technology to help improve the preparedness for future natural disasters. We aim to establish a legally sound evidence base if cases of thyroid cancer arise in the future. Secondly, we have mapped out the mainstream media's data, including NHK's breaking-news coverage scripts and crowd-sourced data such as geo-tagged tweets and crowd information gathered by the WeatherNews' Gensai Report.

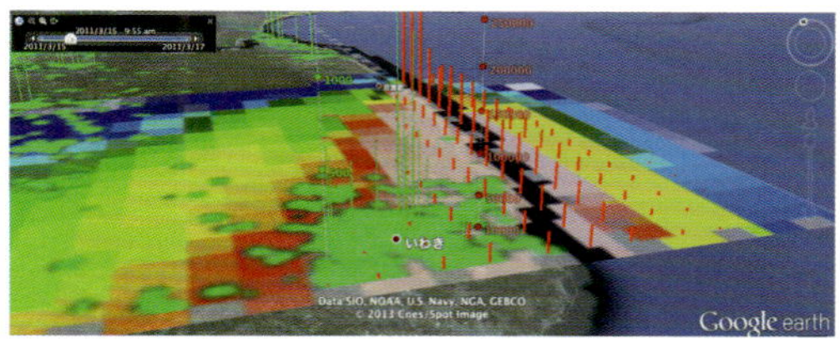

The East Japan Earthquake Archive was started by Hidenori Watanave on March 11, 2011, together with student volunteers from Tokyo Metropolitan University (Yusuke Ohta, Yoko Sasaki and Marie Nozawa). Its cooperators are Senhiko Nakata and Shiori Sasaki (Miyagi University), Akira Ninomiya and Taichi Furuhashi (panorama journalists). From 2012, offers of data started coming in from mass-media companies. Testimonies collected by *Asahi Shimbun* were added in August 2012. Movies collected by Fuji News Networks were added in September 2012. The radioactive-iodine diffusion simulation map, the mass media coverage map, and tweets with geotags were added in November 2012. The cooperation with the digital archives "Memory to the Future" by Google Japan began in February 2013. **The East Japan Earthquake Archive** wurde am 11. März 2011 von Hidenori Watanave gemeinsam mit freiwilligen Studenten der Tokyo Metropolitan University (Yusuke Ohta, Yoko Sasaki und Marie Nozawa) begonnen. Mitarbeiter sind Senhiko Nakata und Shiori Sasaki (Miyagi University), Akira Ninomiya und Taichi Furuhashi (Panorama-Journalisten). Seit 2012 wurden auch Daten aus Massenmedien berücksichtigt. Zeugenaussagen von *Asahi Shimbun* wurden im August 2012 hinzugefügt. Filme von Fuji News Network kamen im September 2012 dazu. Die Simulationskarte zur Verbreitung von radioaktivem Jod, die Karte zur Berichterstattung in den Massenmedien sowie Tweets mit Geotags wurden im November 2012 hinzugefügt. Die Kooperation mit den digitalen Archiven „Memory to the Future" von Google Japan begann im Februar 2013.

Aaron Swartz

Special Mention of the Jury

Digital communities exist through the selfless efforts of many activists in the field, among whom we wish to mention Aaron Swartz.

Aaron Swartz (November 8, 1986 – January 11, 2013) was a US-born computer programmer, writer and activist involved in countless Internet projects such as the development of Creative Commons, social news site Reddit and the web feed format RSS. He was an active defender of open access who at the age of 12 started writing programs to liberate information. A year later, he was working with Sir Tim Berners-Lee, creator of the World-Wide Web, and others on enhancing the Internet through the Semantic Web.

He devoted himself to protecting freedom of expression through initiatives such as Demand Progress and his tireless work against proposed legislation such as the Stop Online Piracy Act (SOPA). His digital political activism was work of genuine consequence; it was risky, and he suffered for it. Digital communities worldwide marked his passing as a watershed moment for the network society.

In the words of his friend and mentor Lawrence Lessig, "He was a hacker, someone who uses technical knowledge to make a better world." Aaron Swartz will be remembered for being at the forefront of Internet freedom.

Digitale Gemeinschaften existieren dank der selbstlosen Anstrengung vieler Aktivisten in diesem Gebiet. Als einen von ihnen möchten wir Aaron Swartz erwähnen.

Aaron Swartz (8. November 1986 – 11. Januar 2013) war ein in den USA geborener Computerprogrammierer, Autor und Aktivist, der an unzähligen Web-Projekten beteiligt war: an der Entwicklung von Creative Commons, von sozialen Webseiten wie Reddit und dem Webfeed-Format RSS. Er war ein aktiver Verteidiger von Open Access, der bereits im Alter von zwölf Jahren begann, Programme zu schreiben, um Information ihre Freiheit zu geben. Ein Jahr später arbeitete er mit Sir Tim Berners-Lee, dem Erfinder des World Wide Web, und anderen an einem Projekt, um das Internet durch das Semantic Web zu verbessern.

Er setzte sich für den Schutz der Meinungsfreiheit durch Initiativen wie Demand Progress ein und kämpfte unermüdlich gegen geplante Gesetze wie dem Stop Online Piracy Act (SOPA). Sein digitaler politischer Aktivismus war von seltener Konsequenz geprägt; er riskierte viel und er litt dafür. Für digitale Gemeinschaften auf der ganzen Welt war sein Tod ein Wendepunkt in der Netzwerkgesellschaft.

Mit den Worten seines Freundes und Mentors Lawrence Lessig: „Er war ein Hacker, jemand, der technisches Wissen nutzte, um die Welt besser zu machen." Wir werden uns für immer an Aaron Swartz als einen Menschen erinnern, der an vorderster Front für die Freiheit des Internet kämpfte.

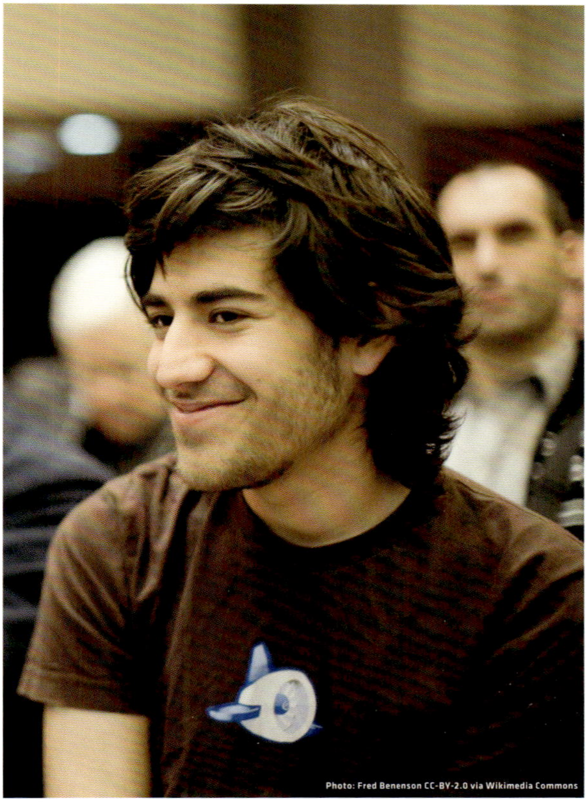
Photo: Fred Benenson CC-BY-2.0 via Wikimedia Commons

u19 – CREATE YOUR WORLD

Three Days of Astonishment
Jury Minutes: A Declaration of Love to the u19 Generation

Drei Tage des Staunens
Ein Juryprotokoll als Liebeserklärung an die u19-Generation

Sirikit Amann, Benjamin Brockhaus, Gerhard Funk, Conny Lee, Karl Markovics

For the past 16 years, the Prix Ars Electronica has been awarded in the u19 category to talented young people from all over Austria.

After years under the motto "freestyle computing", the competition was expanded in content in 2012. Now, under the heading CREATE YOUR WORLD, the Prix Ars Electronica singles out young artists, inventors, researchers and lateral thinkers who are shaping their world—and hence ours—with their ideas. They do so by altering our perspectives and widening our horizons.

Each year, a jury of five experts from different fields selects the prize-winners. Over the years, the u19 award has attained great renown not only in Austria but also far beyond its borders. People take note of the competition results and in many instances this helps the young winners to decide what they would like to pursue professionally. Moreover, the ever-larger number of submissions is an indication of the creative potential and interest of young people in current societal, artistic and social developments, and the consequences of them in the near future.

In 2013, the jury received some 650 entries. To select this year's winners of the Golden Nica, the two Awards of Distinction and 12 Honorary Mentions from the many different kinds of individual and group projects, a great deal of time and energy as well as empathy went into viewing and evaluating the submissions. This was particularly true because the jury wanted to give each project the attention it deserved.

This year, the task was carried out by cultural expert Sirikit Aman; radio-FM4 editor Conny Lee; actor, screenwriter and director Karl Markovic; Professor Gerhard Funk from the Art University in Linz; and youth-project expert Benjamin Brockhaus.

Already during the first viewing, the jury was extremely enthusiastic about the diversity of the entrants and entries. The young people submitting them ranged from an eight-year-old inventor to a 19-year-old filmmaker, from student collectives to small groups or individuals. And their works covered everything from classic shorts and experimental animated films, to robotics, interactive

Seit mittlerweile 16 Jahren wird der Prix Ars Electronica in der Kategorie u19 an junge Kreative aus ganz Österreich vergeben. Die Kategorie u19 wurde viele Jahre unter dem Motto „freestyle computing" geführt; 2012 erfolgte eine inhaltliche Erweiterung des Wettbewerbs. Seither werden unter dem Titel u19 – CREATE YOUR WORLD junge Künstler, Tüftler, Forscher und Querdenker ausgezeichnet, die mit ihren Ideen ihre, und damit auch unsere, Welt gestalten, indem sie unseren Blick verändern und unseren Horizont erweitern.

Jedes Jahr wählt eine Jury, die sich aus fünf Expertinnen und Experten aus unterschiedlichen Fachbereichen zusammensetzt, die Preisträger aus. Mit den Jahren ist der u19-Award nicht nur in Österreich, sondern weit über unsere Grenzen hinaus sehr bekannt geworden. Die Ergebnisse werden wahrgenommen und unterstützen in vielen Fällen die jungen Gewinner bei ihrer weiteren beruflichen Entscheidung. Die stetig wachsende Anzahl der Einreichungen zeigt das kreative Potenzial und das Interesse der Jugendlichen an den gesellschaftlichen, sozialen und künstlerischen Prägungen der Gegenwart und den Auswirkungen auf die nähere Zukunft.

2013 gelangten rund 650 Einreichungen in die Jury. Um aus so vielen sehr unterschiedlichen Einzel- und Gruppenprojekten eine Goldene Nica, zwei Auszeichnungen und zwölf Anerkennungen auszuwählen, bedurfte es auch heuer wieder Zeit, Energie und Empathie, um die Einreichungen sorgsam zu sichten und zu bewerten – vor allem da auch jedem Projekt die gebührende Aufmerksamkeit zukommen soll.

Dieser Aufgabe stellten sich in diesem Jahr Kulturexpertin Sirikit Amann, Radio FM4-Redakteurin Conny Lee, Schauspieler, Drehbuchautor und Regisseur Karl Markovics, Professor der Kunstuniversität Linz, Gerhard Funk, und Jugendengagement-Experte Benjamin Brockhaus.

Schon bei der ersten Sichtung waren alle von der Vielfalt der Einreichungen begeistert.

Das Spektrum reichte von der 8-jährigen Erfinderin bis zum 19-jährigen Filmemacher, vom Schülerkollektiv bis zu Kleingruppen- oder Einzelarbeiten, von klassischen Kurzfilmen bis zu experimentellen Animationen, Robotik, interaktiver Installation, Umweltprojekten, Fotoserien und und und ... Ebenso vielfältig wie die Art und Zahl der Einreichungen war natürlich auch deren Qualität. Da gab es Arbeiten von 8-jährigen, die durch ihre Kreativität und

Brillanz überzeugten, Werke von 14-Jährigen, die sich problemlos auch in einer der „Erwachsenen"-Kategorien des Prix Ars Electronica hätten sehen lassen können, aber auch Einreichungen, die bei der Jury Reaktionen wie „Da ist mehr drin; dran bleiben und im nächsten Jahr noch einmal einreichen!" hervorriefen.

Dieses breite Spektrum an Ideen spiegelt sich auch in den Top-15 wieder. Dieser Prozess der Verdichtung ist nicht nur schwierig, sondern erfordert eigentlich die Quadratur des Kreises. Bei der Auswahl wurden immer die jeweils besten Projekte aus den verschiedensten Gruppen von Einreichern und Einreichungen mit in die nächste Runde genommen. Wir wollten, dass alle – unabhängig von ihrem Alter und ihren Ausdrucksformen – eine Chance haben, es unter die Besten zu schaffen. Somit haben wir uns folgende Kriterien gesetzt:

- Die Preisträger sollten sich aus möglichst vielen verschiedenen Sparten zusammensetzen. Das heißt, wir wollten auch den Machern von Radiofeatures oder Fotokünstlern eine Chance geben, sich gegen die zahlenmäßig weit größere „Konkurrenz" der Filmemacher behaupten zu können.
- Wir haben darauf geachtet, dass möglichst verschiedene Schulformen gemäß der dort gängigen Möglichkeiten berücksichtigt werden.
- Wir legten besonderes Augenmerk auf ein ausgewogenes Verhältnis von Gruppen- zu Einzelleistungen und einer dem Alter der Teilnehmer gerechten Beurteilung.
- Außerdem hinterfragten wir bei jedem Projekt die Eigenständigkeit und Originalität der Idee, natürlich immer in Hinblick auf Alter und Möglichkeiten des/r Einreichenden.

Dieser Anspruch bedeutete für die Jury, erst einmal ein bisschen Ordnung ins wilde Durcheinander der Einreichungen zu bringen. So wurde zunächst eine Vorauswahl getroffen, bei der Projekte, die auf Grund ihrer Qualität bzw. ihres Umfangs nicht mit weiteren vergleichbaren Einreichungen mithalten konnten, aussortiert wurden.

Nach der ersten Runde blieben allerdings immer noch rund 150 Projekte übrig. Die größte Herausforderung, mit der die Jury während des Auswahl-Prozesses an diesem einen Wochenende zu kämpfen hatte, war, in kurzer Zeit die vielen Projekte zu sichten, sie auf sich wirken zu lassen und auf angemessene Weise zu bewerten.

installations, environmental projects, photo series and, and, and... The submissions varied not only in form and number but also, of course, in quality. There were works by eight-year-olds that impressed the jury with their creativity and brilliance, as well as projects by 14-year-olds that could have easily held their own in one of the other, adult Prix Ars Electronica categories. Then again there were also entries to which the jury exclaimed: "That's got potential, keep at it and reenter next year!"

The great diversity of ideas is also reflected in the top 15. The process of narrowing down the choice to achieve such a density was not merely difficult but was actually much like trying to square a circle. Only the best projects from the different groups of entrants and entries made it into the next round. We wanted every single one of them—independent of age or format—to have a chance of being among the best. For this reason we set up the following criteria.

- The prize-winners were to come from as many different areas as possible. In other words, we wanted also to give the makers of radio features or photo series the opportunity to assert themselves against the filmmakers, who, due to their large number, were their greatest competitors.
- The different types of schools had to be considered within the scope of the possibilities presently at their disposal.
- We paid special attention to achieving a balance between group and individual works, as well as to evaluating the submissions appropriately for the participants' age.
- In addition, we examined the degree of independence and originality of the idea involved in each project. Of course, this was done taking the entrant's age and possibilities into consideration.

To be able to apply these criteria, it was first necessary for the jury to put the wild potpourri of entries into a bit of order. A pre-selection was made by sorting out projects that, due to their quality or scope, could not compete with comparable entries.

Even so, there were still some 150 projects left after the first round. On this long weekend of deliberation, the greatest technical problem the jury had to deal with was how, in fact, to view all the projects—and then afterwards, how to digest what they had seen quickly and evaluate the works judiciously.
It would have simplified the jury's task if there had been short videos documenting the content and nature of larger-scale projects. For often there was little time to study longer texts or more elaborate radio features in detail. Thus in the brief breaks, the jurors had to quickly reread and reexamine many projects and documentations. Nevertheless, it took us two whole days to choose 35 projects out of the initial 150 entries. The even greater challenge was to select the finalists out of these 35 projects, as each of them was of remarkably high quality and would have deserved a prize. We debated each project in depth, compared them to one another, argued the pros and cons until finally, after another half day, we picked the top 15 winning projects.

GOLDEN NICA

With great enthusiasm, the jury unanimously voted to give this year's Golden Nica to *Visual:Drumset* by Dominik Koller. With the aid of vibration sensors, a control system he built himself, and software he programmed on his own, 17-year old Dominik Koller developed a projector system that projects freely adjustable light and color effects onto drumheads, making it possible to visualize the beats as they are played.
What especially impressed us about this project was the versatile and complex combination of sound, visuals, electronics, and self-developed software for laptop and smartphone, and how these components interacted to produce this splendid installation.

AWARDS OF DISTINCTIONS

An Award of Distinction went to the project *Soilution*, submitted by a team of environmental

Es hätte die Arbeit der Jury vereinfacht, wenn umfangreiche Projekte zusätzlich durch ein kurzes Video dokumentiert worden wären, in dem Inhalt und Art des Projekts erklärt werden. Denn oftmals blieb wenig Zeit für das intensive Studium langer Texte oder ausführlicher Radiobeiträge. In den kurzen Pausen musste oft noch schnell ein Projekt gelesen oder eine Dokumentation nochmals durchgeschaut werden.
Dennoch dauerte es volle zwei Tage, bis wir aus den ursprünglich 150 Einreichungen eine Vorauswahl von 35 Projekten getroffen hatten. Aus diesen 35 Projekten, die alle schon von sehr beachtlicher Qualität waren und jedes für sich einen Preis verdient hätte, die Endauswahl zu treffen, war *die* große Herausforderung. Wir diskutierten jedes einzelne Projekt im Detail, verglichen die Projekte miteinander, argumentierten „Für" und „Wider" und konnten schließlich nach einem weiteren halben Tag einvernehmlich die Endauswahl der 15 Siegerprojekte festlegen.

GOLDENE NICA

Einhellige Begeisterung herrschte in der Jury für das Projekt *Visual:Drumset* von Dominik Koller, der die diesjährige Goldene Nica erhält. Der 17-Jährige entwickelte mit Hilfe von Vibrationssensoren, einer selbstgelöteten Steuerung und einer eigens programmierten Software eine Beamer-Anlage, die beliebig programmierbare Licht- und Farbeffekte auf ein Schlagzeug projiziert und synchron die Rhythmen beim Spielen des Schlagzeugs visualisiert.
Das Überzeugende an diesem Projekt war für uns die vielseitige und zugleich komplexe Kombination aus Klang, Visuals, Elektronik und selbst entwickelter Software für Laptop und Smartphone, die erst im Zusammenspiel diese großartige Installation ergeben.

AUSZEICHNUNGEN

Eine Auszeichnung ging an das Projekt *Soilution* des 4. Jahrganges Umwelttechnik der HLFS Ursprung. Die Schülerinnen und Schüler entwickelten eine Methode zur Herstellung von „Terra Preta" – einer fruchtbaren Schwarzerde, die einen wertvollen Beitrag zum Klimaschutz leistet, da sie mit Hilfe von Kohle CO_2 im Boden fixiert und zugleich die Bodenfruchtbarkeit steigert – ein Projekt, das nach Meinung der Jury ein hohes Maß an Forschergeist und Initiative zeigt und das versucht, gemäß dem Motto CREATE YOUR WORLD durch einen verantwortungsvollen Umgang mit unseren Ressourcen, die Zukunft unseres Planeten mitzugestalten.

Von Anfang an beeindruckt zeigte sich die Jury von dem Können des 18-jährigen Filmemachers Isidor Dietrich, der eine ganze Serie von Kurzfilmen und Stop-Motion-Animationen eingereicht hatte, die allesamt durch ihre Lebendigkeit und Kreativität, aber auch durch technische Raffinesse überzeugten. Seine Filme zaubern wohl allen, die sie sehen, immer wieder ein Lächeln auf die Lippen. Deswegen erhielt Isidors Gesamtwerk ebenfalls eine Auszeichnung.

Für die Zukunft haben wir als u19-Jury folgende Wünsche: Um eure Arbeiten noch besser bewerten zu können, wäre es bei umfangreicheren Projekten und längeren Beiträgen sehr hilfreich, in Ergänzung zur eigentlichen Arbeit auch ein kurzes Video als Dokumentation und Erklärung des Projektes einzureichen. Außerdem möchten wir besonders die unter 10- und unter 14-jährigen Kreativen Österreichs ermutigen, sich mit ihren Ideen und Arbeiten zu bewerben, denn leider trauen sich das bisher nur wenige. Dabei werden ihre Leistungen besonders honoriert und gefördert.

15 Jahre der Kategorie u19 zeigen, dass es die richtige Entscheidung war, auf die Kraft der jungen Kreativen in Österreich zu setzen.

An all die tausenden von Einreicherinnen und Einreichern: Danke, dass ihr euch beteiligt und uns Jurymitgliedern drei Tage des Staunens schenkt. Und weil die 15 ersten Plätze nie ausreichen werden, um all die Leistungen zu zeigen, mit denen wir in der Jury konfrontiert sind, gibt es das u19-CREATE YOUR WORLD-Festival, bei dem zusätzlich zu den Ausgezeichneten weitere preiswürdige Projekte gezeigt werden. Mit *Young Animations* wurde im Rahmen des Ars Electronica Animation Festivals ein Format geschaffen, in dem Animationen von u19-Einreichern nicht nur in Linz, sondern auch international bei anderen Festivals gezeigt werden können.

technology majors from the 4th form at the HLFS Ursprung, a secondary school for agriculture and forestry. The students developed a method for producing terra preta—a very dark fertile soil and valuable contribution to climate protection. With its high charcoal content, it stabilizes the CO_2 in the soil, while simultaneously increasing its fertility. The jury appreciated the team's great passion for research and initiative, and how it strived, as fits the CREATE YOUR WORLD motto, to help shape the future of our planet by treating our resources responsibly.

From the start, the jury was impressed by the skills of 18-year-old filmmaker Isidor Dietrich, who submitted a whole series of shorts and stop-motion films. All of them are remarkable in their liveliness and creativity, as well as technical sophistication. His films succeed in bringing smiles to the faces of all those who watch them. This is why Isidor's work received the second Award of Distinction.

For future competitions in this category, we—the jury—have a number of requests: To enable us to evaluate your projects better in the future, it would be very helpful if larger projects and contributions were accompanied by a short supplementary video documentation and/or explanation. We would also like to encourage talented kids living in Austria who are under the age of 10 or under the age of 14 to enter their ideas and works. Unfortunately, to date, not many have dared to do so. We will honor and support their achievements in particular. Fifteen years of u19 have shown that it was the right decision to back the creative power of young people in Austria.

We would like to thank the thousands of contestants who have made entries for giving us three days of astonishment each year. And since the top 15 in no way suffice to show all the fantastic works encountered by the jury, there is the u19-CREATE YOUR WORLD-Festival at which, in addition to the prize-winners, many of the other projects deserving a prize will be displayed. Last not least: with the Young Animation Festival a format has been created to present animated works by u19 participants not just in Linz but also at other festivals worldwide.

Visual:Drumset

Dominik Koller

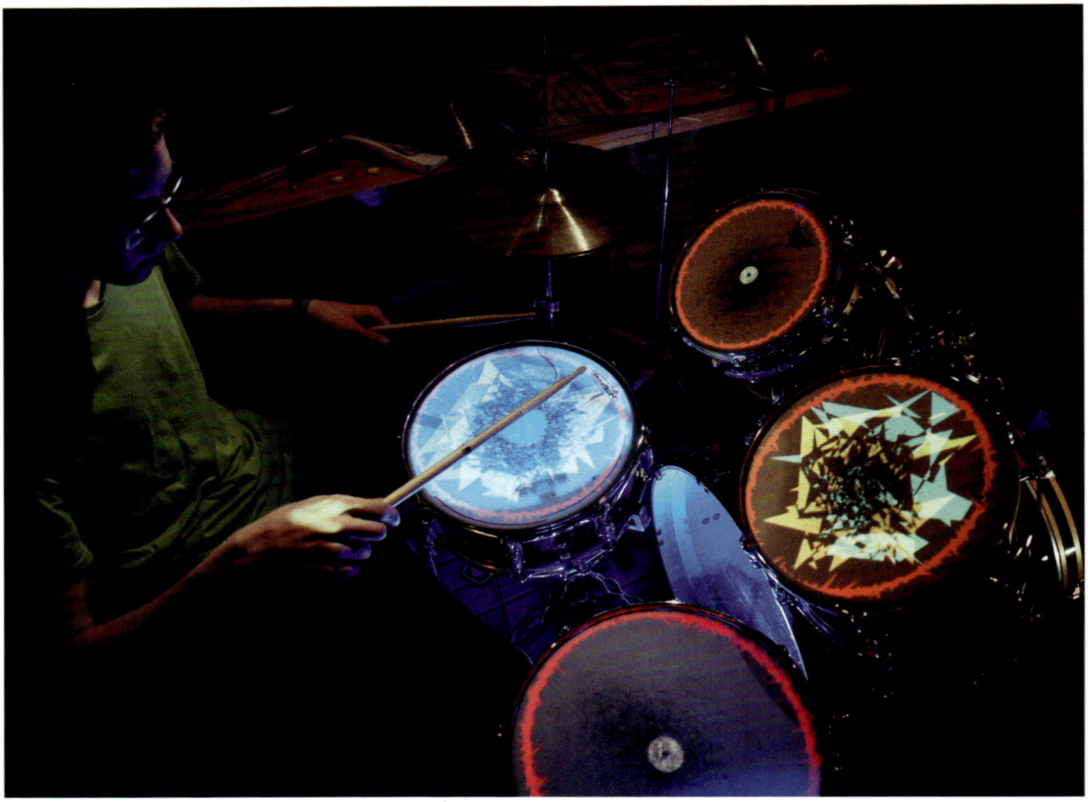

Visual:Drumset is a project that works by projection mapping, a technique that makes it possible to visualize drum beats directly on a set of drums. For instance, a projector projects a point onto each drumhead and whenever a drum is struck the point enlarges.
Vibration sensors are mounted on the underside of each drum. They register the drum beats, and the information is fed into an Arduino circuit board and then into a computer. Here the data is processed in a program developed using Processing and the results are then visualized via a projector directly onto the drumhead by projection mapping, a technique for projecting onto slanted and/or three-dimensional surfaces. The projector can be aimed at the drum set at any angle; the only prerequisite is that the line-of-sight to each drumhead is unimpeded. The visuals on the drumheads can be adapted and modified directly on the computer or via an Android-equipped smartphone. The color, form and animation of the effects are also easy to adjust.

Visual:Drumset ist ein auf Projection Mapping basierendes Projekt, bei dem man Schläge auf ein Schlagzeug direkt auf den Trommeln visualisieren kann. Mit einem Projektor wird ein Punkt auf jede Trommel projiziert, der sich bei jedem Trommelschlag vergrößert.
Mit Vibrationssensoren, die an der Unterseite jeder Trommel angebracht sind, werden die Schläge abgenommen, über eine Arduino-Platine eingelesen und an einen Computer weitergeschickt. Dort werden die Daten in einem in Processing entwickelten Programm verarbeitet und über einen Projektor mittels Projection Mapping, einer Technik zum Projizieren auf schiefe und/oder dreidimensionale Oberflächen, auf dem Fell der Trommel visualisiert. Der Projektor kann in einem beliebigen Winkel auf das Schlagzeug gerichtet sein; wichtig ist nur, dass er ungehindert alle Trommeln anstrahlen kann. Die Visuals auf den Trommeln können direkt am Computer oder über ein Android-Smartphone angepasst und verändert werden. Farbe, Form und Animation der Effekte lassen sich einfach einstellen.

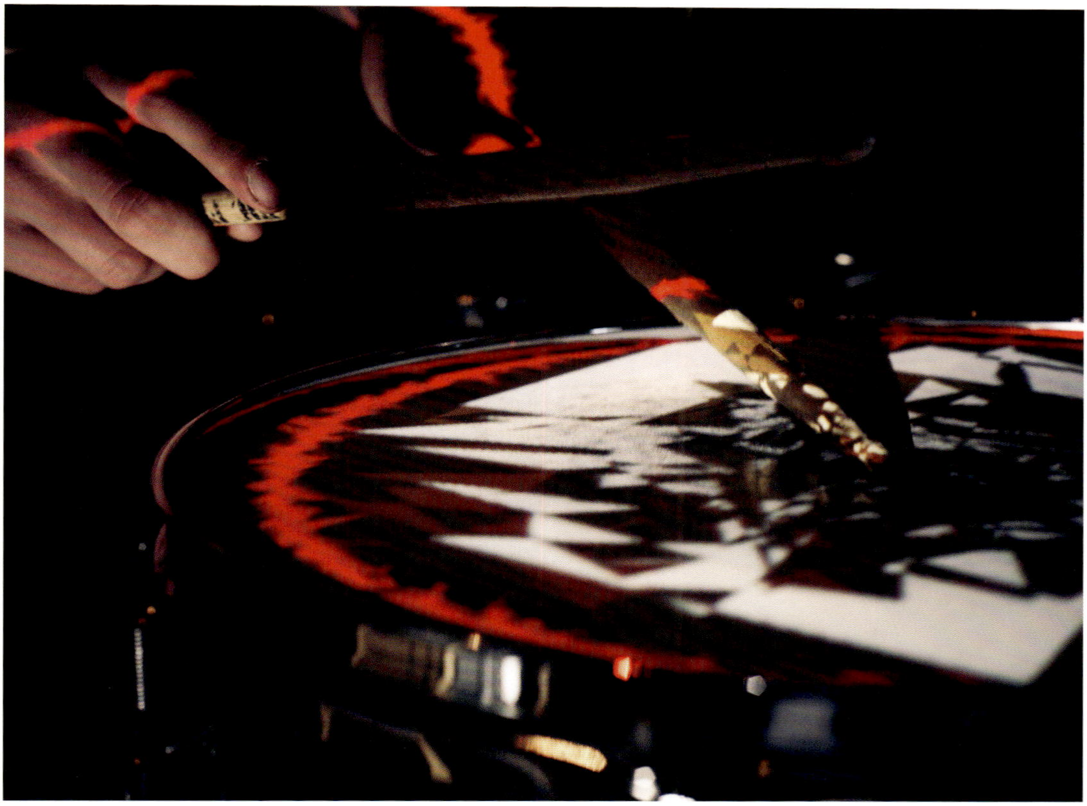

Visual:Drumset schafft somit ein visuell-interaktives Spielerlebnis für den Schlagzeuger und das Publikum und kann auch im Unterricht nützlich sein: Der Schlagzeugspieler spielt vor, das Gespielte wird aufgenommen, danach werden die Visuals als Orientierung für den Schüler wieder abgespielt.
Natürlich kann man die abgenommen Daten auch für Visuals aller Art verwenden, der Kreativität sind keine Grenzen gesetzt; bei Konzerten kann beispielsweise die Lichtshow direkt über das Schlagzeug gesteuert werden.

Thus *Visual:Drumset* provides an interactive, visual playing experience for both the drummer and the audience. The concept might also be useful for teaching: the drummer plays something and it is recorded and replayed in the form of visuals for the student's orientation.
The data that has been registered by the system may, of course, also be used for visuals of all kinds: creativity knows no bounds here. Light shows at concerts, for example, could be controlled directly via the drum set.

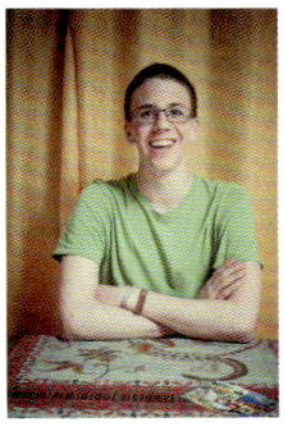

Dominik Koller (born in 1995) is currently attending the seventh form at the BORG, a college preparatory school in Mittersill, Salzburg. He spent two semesters abroad, one in Canada and one in Spain. In winter he enjoys freeride skiing and snowboarding; in summer his hobbies include the trampoline and mountain biking. In his free time he focuses on the computer and is especially interested in media design and computer science. He has been playing the drums for seven years now. Thus his project *Visual:Drumset* is directly related to many of his interests. **Dominik Koller**, geb 1995, besucht derzeit die 7. Klasse des BORG in Mittersill, Salzburg. Er hat zwei Auslandssemester in Kanada und Spanien verbracht. Im Winter ist er ein begeisterter Freerider; auch Trampolinspringen und Mountainbiken gehören zu seinen Hobbies. In seiner Freizeit beschäftigt er sich viel mit dem Computer und interessiert sich besonders für Medieninformatik und -design. Seit sieben Jahren spielt er Schlagzeug. Somit stellt das Projekt *Visual:Drumset* eine Verbindung seiner Interessen dar.

Destino / facebook / BluCar / Nur Kreide

Isidor Dietrich

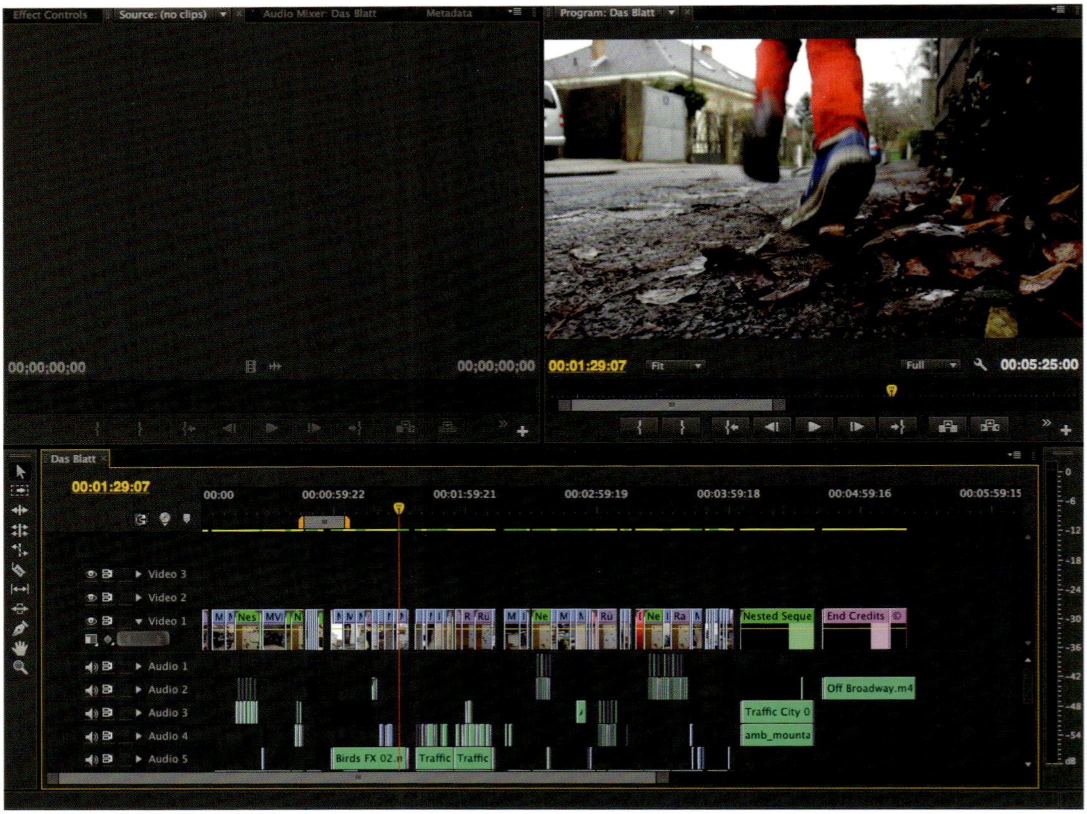

Usually, to begin with, I'm just trying to figure out how I might create an interesting effect, one that can only be realized using stop motion. Later I try to integrate this idea into a story. Then I start testing how I might make it look really good. To do this, I build a small set with two desk lamps and begin animating. Once I have the shots I need, I upload them to AfterEffects and set the frame rate (FPS). Normally I use 15 frames per second. In my film

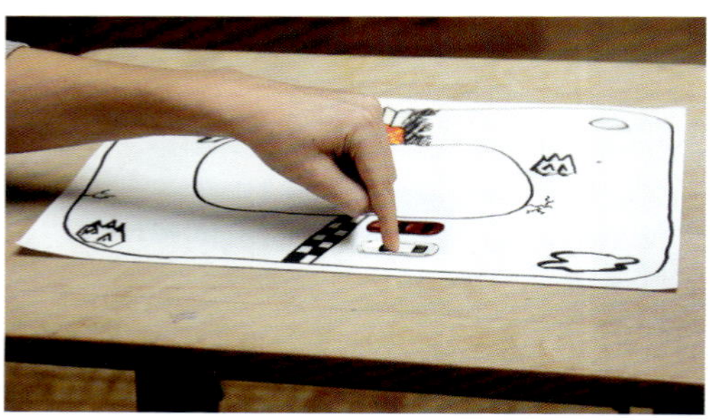

Am Anfang denke ich darüber nach, wie ich einen interessanten Effekt machen könnte, der nur mit Stop Motion realisierbar ist. Später versuche ich, diese Idee in eine Handlung einzubauen. Dann beginne ich zu testen, wie der Trick am besten aussehen könnte. Dafür baue ich ein kleines Set mit zwei Schreibtischlampen auf und fange an zu animieren. Sind die Fotos im Kasten, lade ich sie in After Effects und stelle die Bildrate (FPS) ein. Normalerweise liegt diese bei 15 Bildern pro Sekunde. Bei meinem Film *Destino* habe ich zum ersten Mal Computeranimation eingesetzt, womit ich mich wahrscheinlich weiterhin beschäftigen werde.

Wenn die Animation für meinen Geschmack gut ist, starte ich mit dem eigentlichen Film. Um die Clips zu schneiden, verwende ich Final Cut. Die Inspiration erhalte ich häufig beim Schauen von Videos auf YouTube. Oft kommen mir Ideen auch einfach so, ohne einen Anstoß. Manchmal entwickelt sich auch einfach aus einer ursprünglich als Test geplanten Animation ein Film, zum Beispiel *BluCar*. Bei diesem Film wollte ich anfänglich

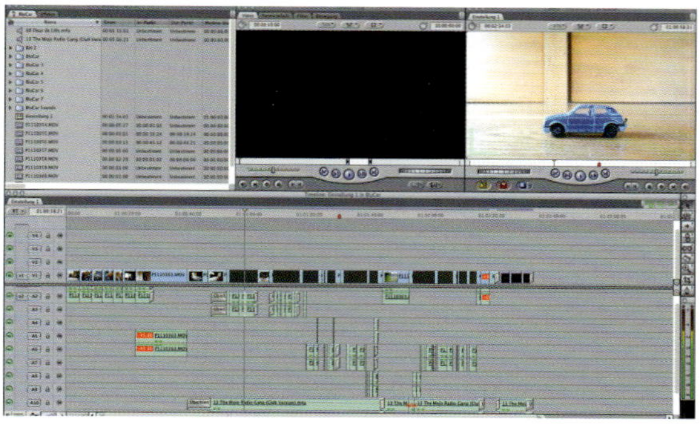

Destino I used computer animation for the first time; from now on I'll probably explore its use more. Once the animation is to my liking, I start making the actual film. To edit the clips I use Final Cut. I am frequently inspired by videos I see on YouTube. Though ideas often just come to me without anything triggering them. Sometimes, as with *BluCar*, a film develops from an animation that was originally intended as a test. With this film all I had initially wanted to do was to see what it would look like if there was something moving back and forth under the rug.

eigentlich nur sehen, wie es aussieht, wenn sich etwas unter einem Teppich hin und her bewegt.
In *Nur Kreide* erwacht ein Kreidemännchen auf einer Tafel zum Leben und malt sich Objekte, mit denen es interagiert. *BluCar* zeigt ein selbstfahrendes Spielzeugauto, das das Haus verwüstet, während die Bewohnerin beim Einkaufen ist. In *facebook* erlebt eine bunte Puppe die „Vorteile" des sozialen Netzwerks. In *Destino* findet ein Junge einen sogenannten „Blattracer", der sich als das beste Auto in einem populären Spiel in seiner Klasse herausstellt. Doch der Schein trügt ...

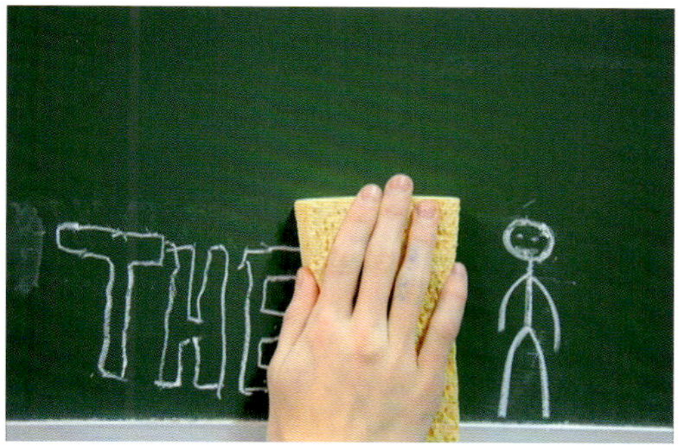

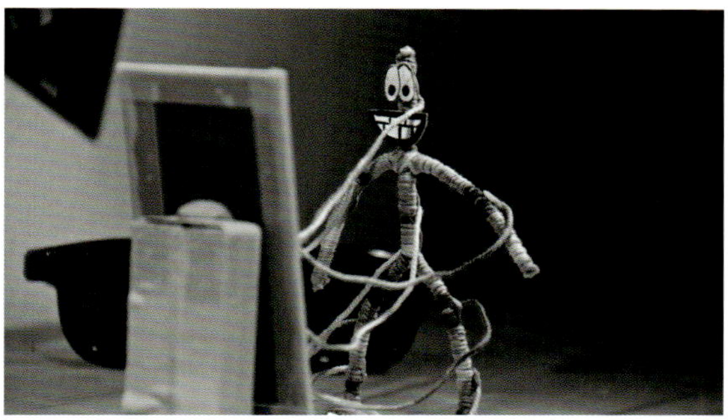

In *Nur Kreide* (Just Chalk) a stick figure comes to life on a blackboard and draws objects with which it then interacts. *BluCar* presents a toy car that can move all by itself and runs amok while the lady of the house is out shopping. In *facebook* a colorful doll discovers the "benefits" of this social network. In *Destino* a boy finds a "paper racer" that turns out to be the fastest at a game popular in his class. But appearances can be deceptive...

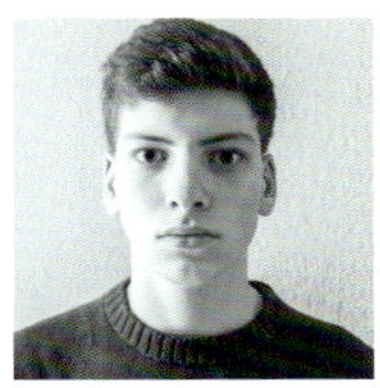

Isidor Dietrich (born in 1995) attended the lower forms at the BRG Marchettigasse, a college preparatory school. In 2009 he switched to another college preparatory school, the BORG Hegelgasse 12 in Vienna's first district. He did so because over time he had become ever-more interested in making stop-motion films and wanted to attend an art school with an audio-visual department. In 2013, after passing his college entrance exams, he will graduate. **Isidor Dietrich**, geb. 1995, besuchte die Unterstufe der BRG Marchettigasse. 2009 wechselte er in das BORG Hegelgasse 12 im 1. Wiener Gemeindebezirk, da er im Laufe der Zeit immer mehr Interesse am Drehen von Stop-Motion-Trickfilmen bekam und deswegen eine Kunstschule mit AV-Zweig (Audio Vision) besuchen wollte. 2013 wird er dort mit der Matura abschließen.

Soilution – Erde mit Zukunft

HLFS Ursprung

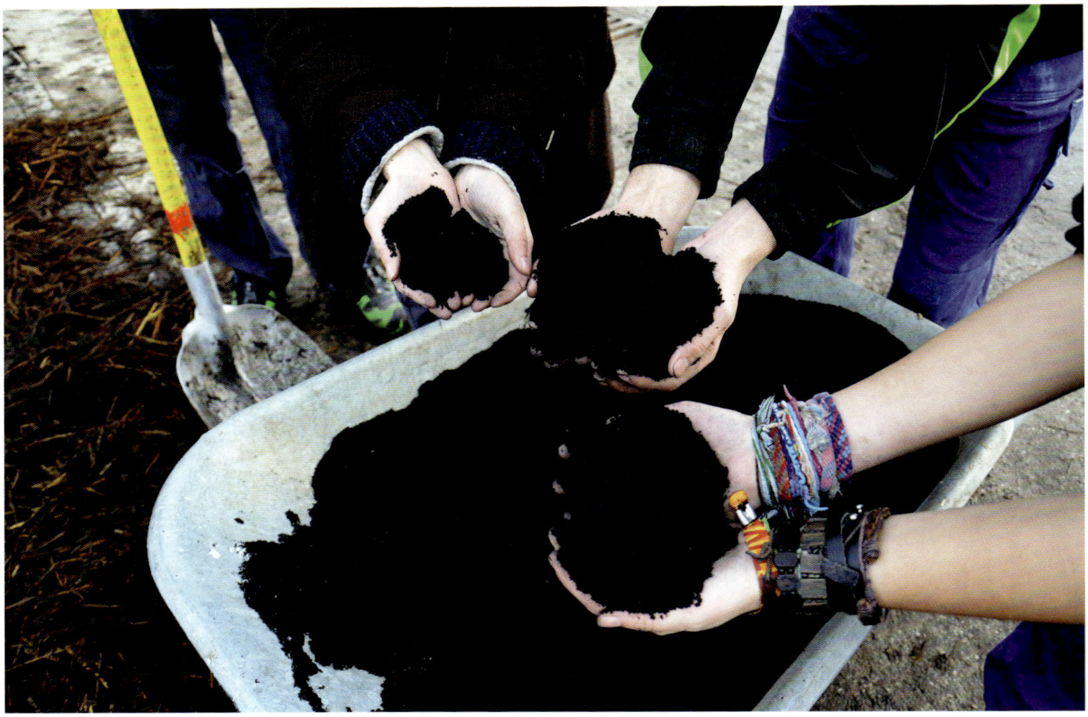

Inspired by a fascinating talk about *terra preta*, a sustainable, fertile, very dark soil from the Amazon Basin, we decided to launch a project on the subject. What is special about this soil is its very high concentration of organic charcoal and its ability to bind carbon—which would otherwise end up in the earth's atmosphere in the form of CO_2—for a very long time. These qualities enable it to contribute enormously to climate protection.

To make our research known to the public, we decided to develop garden soil with a high charcoal content, modeled on *terra preta*, in cooperation with a Bavarian company, EM Chiemgau. Our Soilution Junior Company has successfully marketed it to environmentally conscious gardeners.

To show that by using charcoal environmental protection is also possible in the home, we constructed a professional charcoal carburetor in collaboration with the Pergo-Gerätebau company.

Fasziniert von einem interessanten Vortrag über „Terra Preta", einer langfristig fruchtbaren Schwarzerde aus dem Amazonasgebiet, beschlossen wir, ein Projekt rund um dieses Thema zu starten. Das Besondere an dieser Erde ist die darin enthaltene Biokohle und deren Fähigkeit, Kohlenstoff, der sonst in Form von CO_2 in die Erdatmosphäre gelangen würde, für Ewigkeiten zu binden und dadurch einen enormen Beitrag zum Klimaschutz leisten zu können.

Um diese Idee publik zu machen, entwickelten wir in Kooperation mit dem bayrischen Unternehmen EM Chiemgau eine kohlehaltige Gartenerde nach dem Vorbild der „Terra Preta". Diese wurde erfolgreich durch unsere Soilution Junior Company an umweltbewusste GärtnerInnen vermarktet.

Um zu zeigen, dass der Umweltschutz mit Hilfe von Kohle auch zu Hause möglich wäre, konstruierten wir in Zusammenarbeit mit der Firma Pergo-Gerätebau einen professionellen Holzkohlevergaser. Neben der

Team: Magdalena Irnstötter, Magdalena Giesshammer, Doris Plasser, Elisabeth Winkler, Christina Proßegger, Theresa Eichhorn, Jessica Saria, Iris Rosenstatter, Lukas Schmidbauer, Christoph Unterraßner, Anna Greier, Daniel Groder, Florian Mackinger, Peter Schnitzhofer, Martin Pfaffinger, Sandra Mackner, Christiane Bachmann, Fabian Sanin, Martina Windsperger, Christina Zieher, Johannes Schmitzberger, Simon Kletzl, Philipp Klieber, Sebastian Perschl, Julia Karl

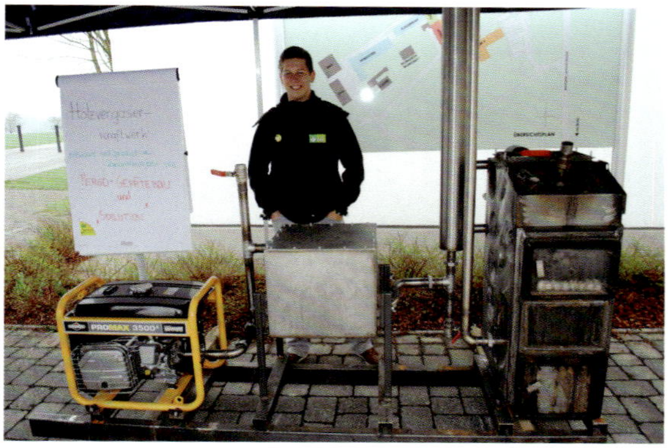

Kohleherstellung kann damit Strom und warmes Wasser erzeugt werden. Außerdem führten wir diverse Labor- und Pflanzversuche durch, um unsere Erde intensiv zu testen.
Das nachhaltig wirtschaftende Unternehmen Isocell erzeugt aus Altpapier einen Zellulosedämmstoff, der aus Brandschutzgründen mit Borsäure versetzt wird. Durch unsere umfangreiche Auseinandersetzung mit Kohleanwendungen im Boden inspiriert, tüftelten wir das innovative Konzept aus, das enthaltene Bor als landwirtschaftlichen Dünger zu nutzen. Nachdem der Dämmstoff aus recycelten Altpapier in drei Gebäuden hintereinander Heizkosten und somit CO_2-Emissionen erspart hat, soll er verkohlt werden und als wertvoller Spurenelementdünger in die Erde zurückkommen.

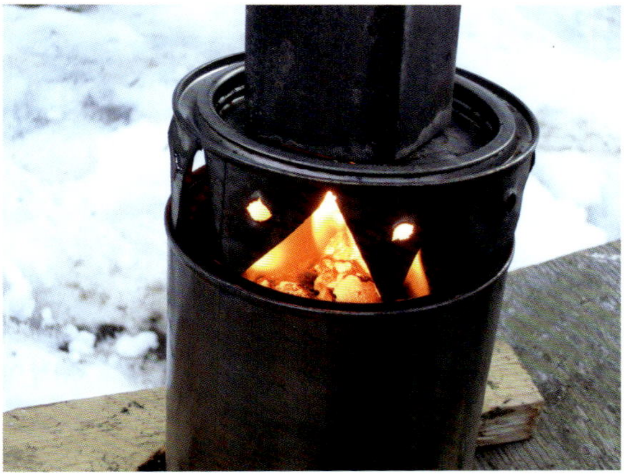

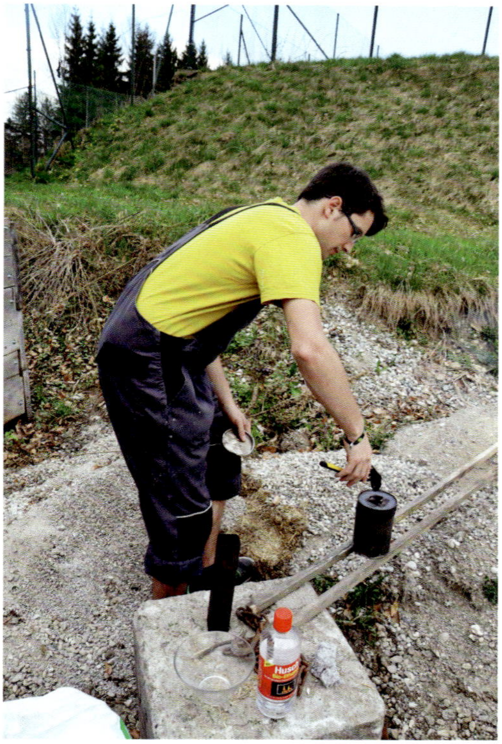

Besides producing charcoal, it can also be used to generate electricity and warm water. In addition, we conducted various laboratory and plant experiments to test our soil more intensively.
Isocell, a company run with sustainability in mind, produces cellulose insulation from recycled paper that is mixed with boric acid to make it fire resistant. Inspired by our extensive exploration of the uses of charcoal in soil, we worked out an innovative concept for using the boron contained in this product as an agricultural fertilizer. After this insulating material, made of recycled paper, has been used in three buildings to reduce heating costs and thus CO_2 emissions, it can be transformed into charcoal and returned to the soil as a fertilizer with valuable trace elements.

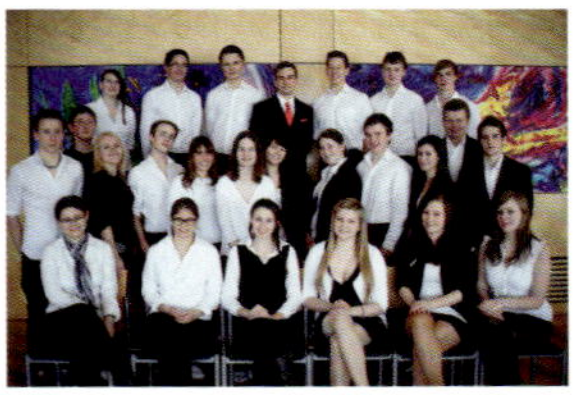

In fall 2012, 25 environmental technology majors from the 4th form at the HLFS Ursprung, a secondary school for agriculture and forestry, launched their sustainable project **Soilution–Earth with a Future** and founded the Soilution Junior Company. Im Herbst 2012 haben 25 SchülerInnen der 4. Klasse Umwelttechnik der HLFS Ursprung das nachhaltige Projekt **Soilution – Erde mit Zukunft** gestartet und die Soilution Junior Company gegründet.

Feldversuche

Florian Bührle

Surrounded by cold sterile walls, cubes break out of the structure: moving to the music, the cubes fall to the ground and shatter. They free themselves from the rigidity of the symmetry inherent in their cubic form.

I suddenly had the idea for this animated film a week before the submission deadline. As I had never worked with 3D software before, I quickly had to teach myself the fundamentals. With these new skills, I was able to realize my idea. I began modeling, animating and rendering. I used Blender for this. Rendering really tried my patience though, because it often took me more than ten hours a day. At last the final sequences were finished and I could start editing. It didn't take me long to find the right music: I had composed a short sound track for fun two years earlier, which I just happened to discover again. Right away I had the feeling that it fitted the video material. I edited the sequences so they harmonized with the music.

I certainly had fun working on this project, and I was even a bit sad that I had to get it done so quickly: with only one day left until the deadline, I really had to hurry.

Umgeben von sterilen, kalten Wänden brechen die Würfel aus diesem Schema aus: Sie fallen zu Boden und zerbrechen, bewegen sich zur Musik, sie entweichen aus der Starre der Symmetrie ihrer kubischen Form.

Die Idee zu diesem Animationsfilm hatte ich eine Woche vor Einsendeschluss. Da ich zuvor noch nie mit 3D-Programmen gearbeitet hatte, musste ich mir die Grundlagen selber aneignen. Auf dieser Basis konnte ich meine Ideen verwirklichen. Ich begann zu modellieren, zu animieren und zu rendern. Dafür verwendete ich Blender. Das Rendern war eine Geduldsprobe, denn es beanspruchte oft mehr als zehn Stunden. Schließlich waren die einzelnen Sequenzen fertig und ich konnte mit dem Schneiden beginnen. Die passende Musik war schnell gefunden: Ich hatte vor zwei Jahren aus Spaß einen kurzen Soundtrack zusammengebastelt, den ich zufällig wiederentdeckte. Ich hatte auf Anhieb das Gefühl, dass dieser gut zum Videomaterial passt. Die Sequenzen schnitt ich so, dass sie mit der Musik harmonierten.

Dieses Projekt hat mir sehr großen Spaß gemacht, und ich fand es fast ein bisschen schade, dass ich es schon fertigstellen musste, denn ich hatte nur noch einen Tag Zeit bis Einsendeschluss und ich musste mich wirklich beeilen.

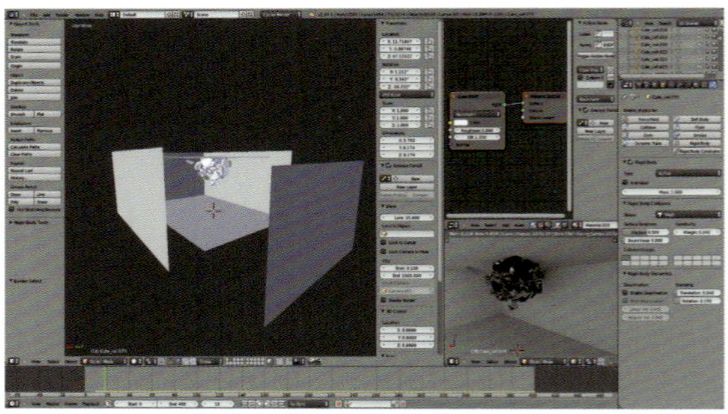

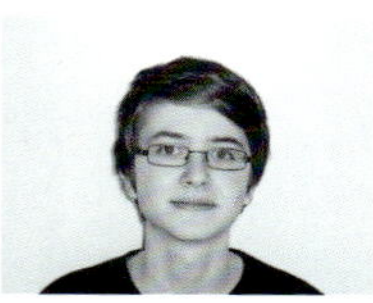

Florian Bührle (born in 1998) is currently attending the 4th form of the BG Gallus, a college preparatory school in Bregenz. His hobbies are computers, technology, electronics, reading and cycling. **Florian Bührle**, geb. 1998 in Bregenz, besucht derzeit die 4. Klasse des BG Gallus Bregenz. Seine Hobbies sind Computer, Technik, Elektronik, Lesen und Radfahren.

Lernprogramme für die Volkschule

http://members.aon.at/u19lernspiele

Sasan Hoseini, Arian Hoseini

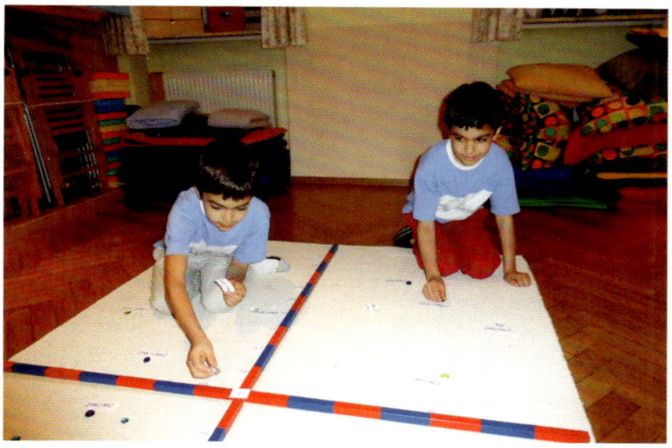

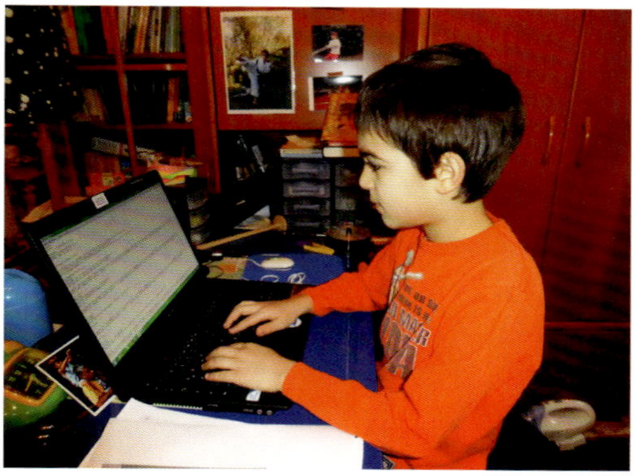

Eigentlich wollten wir Lego-Spiele programmieren. Wir hatten nämlich schon eigene Lego-Filme (Brickfilme) gemacht. Daher besuchten wir einen Programmierkurs für Kinder. Von unserem Programmier-Trainer erfuhren wir von u19 und überlegten, was wir denn machen könnten.
Wir selbst gehen ja nicht zur Schule, wir lernen zu Hause mit unseren Eltern. So haben wir auch die Möglichkeit, uns mehr mit den Dingen zu beschäftigen, die uns gerade sehr interessieren (Programmieren, Schach ...). Da wir viel mit CD-Roms lernen, kamen wir auf die Idee, für uns selbst und für andere Kinder Lernprogramme zu schreiben. Diese programmierten wir in Scratch – einer Open-Source-Software *(http://scratch.mit.edu)*. Man kann auch das Programm Scratch herunterladen und so den Quellcode der einzelnen Programm ansehen und sogar verändern.
Jeder von uns hat einige Programme und HTML-Seiten erstellt, die dann zu einem Ganzen zusammen gefügt wurden. Durch das Programmieren haben wir viel gelernt und wir verwenden selbst unsere eigenen Programme, um zum Beispiel das Einmaleins, Divisionen und Subtraktionenzu üben. Wir wollen in Zukunft noch mehr Lernprogramme erstellen.

Originally we had wanted to program some Lego games. We had already made a few Lego films (brick films). This was also why we were taking a programming course for kids. Our instructor told us about u19 and we began thinking about what we might do.
We do not normally go to school—we learn at home with our parents. That way we can focus more on what really interests us at any one moment (for example, programming or chess). Since we have learned a lot from CD-ROMs, we decided to write some learning programs for ourselves and other kids. We programmed them using Scratch—an open-source software *(http://scratch.mit.edu)*. You can download Scratch, too, and so look at or even change the source code of the individual programs.
First we each created a few programs and HTML pages. Then we assembled them into a complete program. We learned a lot by programming everything ourselves, and we now use our own programs to practice multiplying, dividing, subtracting and so on. In the future we want to create even more learning programs.

Arian (born in 2003) and **Sasan Hoseini** (in 2004) are brothers and live in Vienna. They worked on developing these learning programs together so that they and other primary school children can learn by playing computer games on the computer. **Arian** (geb. 2003) und **Sasan Hoseini** (geb. 2004) sind Brüder und wohnen in Wien. Gemeinsam haben sie an den Lernspielen gearbeitet, um sich selbst und anderen VolkschülerInnen das Lernen mit dem Computer spielerisch zu ermöglichen.

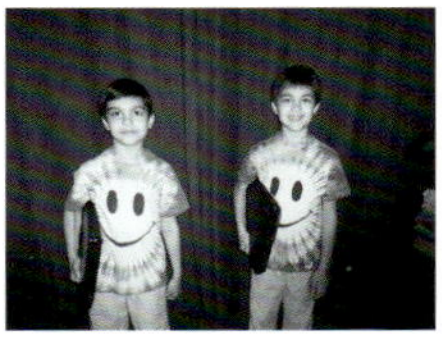

A Moving Picture

Elisabeth Bloder

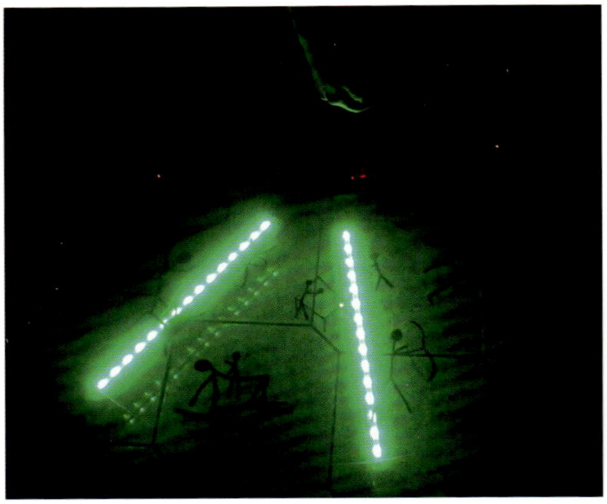

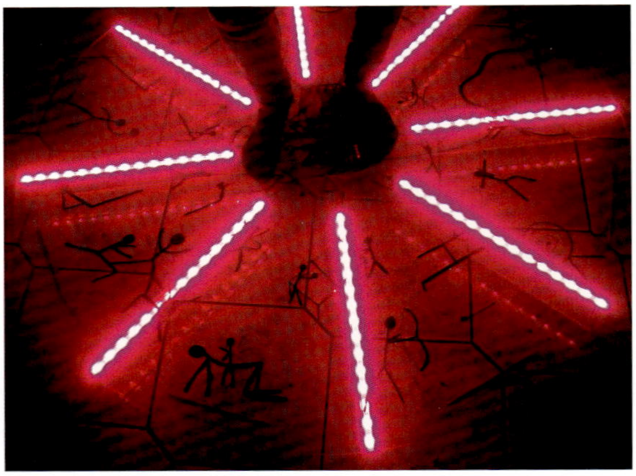

A Moving Picture unites the fields of light and art. The base is a 1.4-meter-diameter Plexiglas disk. Many different types of sports are symbolically displayed on its surface. LEDs connected to light sensors are mounted on the underside of the disk. If the circuit is broken, that is, if a hand blocks the sensors, then a certain section of the picture lights up. If the hand is withdrawn, then everything goes black again. This effect can be produced with each of the four light sensors. As icing on the cake, a clap switch has also been installed. Thus it only takes a clap for visitors to switch all the LEDs on and off.

Since light has neither a beginning nor an end, the artwork is circular. The lines of the stick figures relate to the LEDs, while their spiral arrangement refers to infinity. In addition, these figures symbolize people moving and should encourage viewers to move too. The light sensors used in the artwork allow us to give our body language greater scope for expression than we are usually aware of having. As people with speech impairments show, you do not always need words to communicate. Just by raising your arm, you can express something. Through my artwork, such small gestures are transformed into light effects.

A Moving Picture verbindet die Themenbereiche Licht und Kunst. Die Basis bildet eine große Plexiglasplatte mit 1,4 Meter Durchmesser, auf deren Oberfläche verschiedenste Sportarten symbolisch dargestellt werden. Unterhalb sind LEDs eingebaut, die mit Lichttaster verschaltet sind. Wenn man jetzt den Lichttaster, sprich den Schaltkreis, mit der Hand unterbricht, dann leuchtet ein bestimmter Teil des Bildes. Wenn man die Hand wieder entfernt, dann ist es wieder finster. Dieser Effekt kann bei vier Lichttastern vollzogen werden. Als Sahnehäubchen wurde noch ein Klatschschalter eingebaut. Dadurch werden entweder alle LEDs nur durch Klatschen ein- oder ausgeschaltet.

Das Kunstwerk ist deswegen kreisförmig, weil das Licht kein Ende und keinen Anfang hat. Die im Bild dargestellten Strichmännchen stellen durch ihre Linienform eine Verbindung zu den LEDs her und ihre spiralförmige Anordnung weist auf die Unendlichkeit hin. Zusätzlich symbolisieren sie Menschen in Bewegung und sollen dadurch die Betrachter anregen, sich auch zu bewegen. Die im Kunstobjekt eingesetzten Lichttaster ermöglichen uns, unserer Körpersprache mehr Ausdruck zu verleihen, als uns im ersten Moment bewusst ist. Am Beispiel spracheingeschränkter Personen kann man eindrucksvoll erkennen, dass man nicht immer Wörter braucht, um sich zu verständigen. Alleine durch das Heben eines Arms wird etwas ausgedrückt. Durch mein Kunstwerk werden diese kleinen Gesten in Lichteffekte umgewandelt.

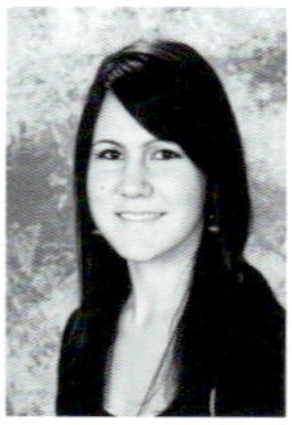

Elisabeth Bloder (born in 1996) lives in Frohnleiten near Graz and is currently in the 7th form of the BRG Kepler, a college preparatory school. Her hobbies are horse riding, winter sports, running and tennis. She has also played classical guitar for the past ten years and will graduate on the instrument at the end of the year.

Elisabeth Bloder, geb. 1996, wohnt in Frohnleiten bei Graz und besucht derzeit die 7. Klasse des BRG Keplers in Graz. Ihre Hobbys sind Reiten, Wintersport, Laufen und Tennis. Außerdem spielt sie seit zehn Jahren klassische Gitarre und schließt in diesem Schuljahr dieses Instrument mit der Abschlussprüfung ab.

Biogas für Burkina Faso

Johannes Egger, Patrick Maier, Dražen Petrović, Simon Zigala / HTL Anichstraße Innsbruck

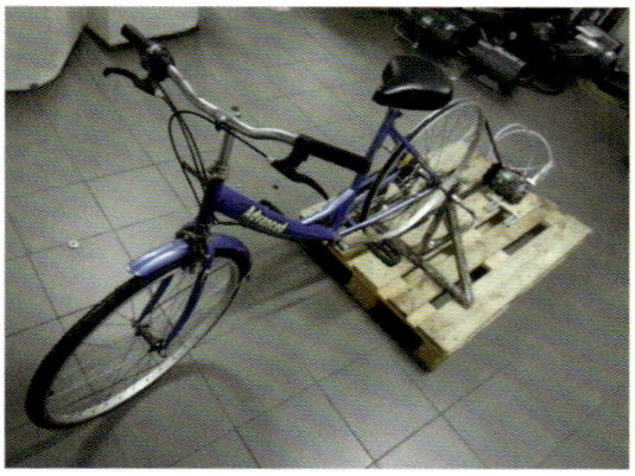

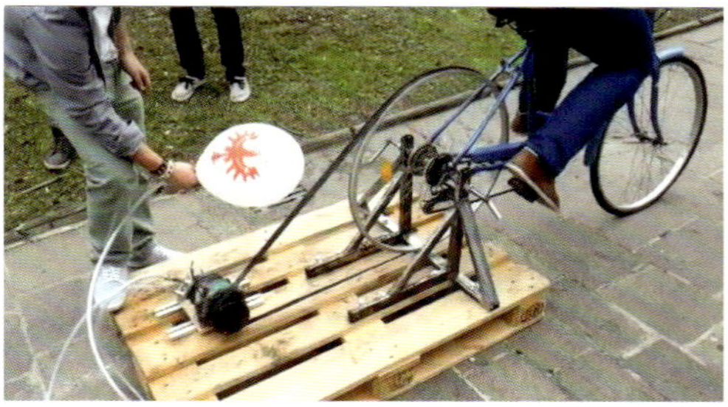

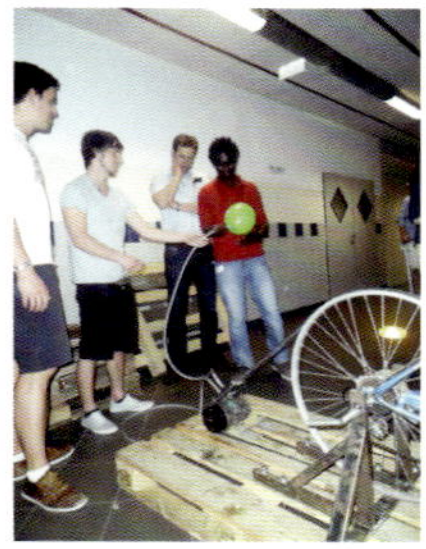

Das Projekt *Biogas für Burkina Faso* umfasst die Konstruktion und die Realisierung eines Pumpenprototyps, mit dem Biogas bzw. Holzgas komprimiert und transportiert werden kann. Es handelt sich dabei konkret um ein Projekt für ein Dorf in Burkina Faso. Die Menschen dort sollen das Biogas, das sich in einem Fermenter mit Abfall bildet, zum Kochen und Heizen nutzen können. Dies ist eine günstige und zugleich einfache Möglichkeit, ihnen das Leben zu erleichtern.

Die Pumpe soll das Gas vom Fermenter in beispielsweise einem LKW Reifen oder dergleichen zwischenspeichern. Daher soll sie einen Kompressionsdruck von ca. 3 bar aufbauen können. Da die Menschen in diesem Dorf allerdings keinen Strom haben, muss die Pumpe rein mechanisch betrieben werden. Des Weiteren musste sie natürlich vollkommen luftdicht abgeschlossen werden, da sich ansonsten schon bei geringstem Sauerstoffzutritt zusammen mit dem Biogas (zum Großteil CH_4) ein explosives Gemisch bildet. Ziel war also, eine sichere, voll funktionsfähige und mechanisch betreibbare Gaspumpe zu bauen, mit der Biogas transportiert und komprimiert werden kann.

Prinzipiell wird die Pumpe für Biogas ausgelegt, doch es soll, wie bereits erwähnt, genauso möglich sein, Holzgas zu komprimieren und zu transportieren. Da der Antrieb einfach durch ein Fahrrad erfolgt, kann auch viel Gas in kurzer Zeit befördert werden.

Wir möchten uns bei den Fachlehrern der Werkstätte bedanken, die uns speziell bei der Fertigung immer wieder wertvolle Tipps gegeben haben. Besonderer Dank gilt Herrn Professor DI Benedikt Frischmann für die exzellente Unterstützung und Hilfestellung.

The project *Biogas for Burkina Faso* involves constructing and producing a prototype for a pump that can be used to compress and transport biogas or wood gas. More concretely, this involves a project for a village in Burkina Faso. The idea is to enable villagers to use biogas, which is produced from organic waste in a fermenter, for cooking and heating. This would be an inexpensive and simple way to make life easier for them.

The pump should make it possible to store the gas from a fermenter temporarily, for instance, in a truck tire or the like. A compression pressure of about three bar should be attainable. But since the people in this village don't have electricity, the pump must be operated entirely mechanically. And of course it also has to be sealed air-tight as otherwise, if even a small amount of oxygen comes into contact with the biogas (which is largely CH_4), it will form an extremely explosive mixture. Hence our goal is to build a safe and very efficient, mechanically operated gas pump that can compress and transport biogas.

In principle, the pump is designed for biogas, but, as mentioned earlier, it should also be able to compress and transport wood gas. Due to the simplicity of using a bicycle to generate power, it is possible to transport a great deal of gas in a short time.

We would like to thank our teachers who as workshop experts gave us many valuable tips for implementing our ideas. Special thanks also to Professor Benedikt Frischmann for his excellent support and assistance.

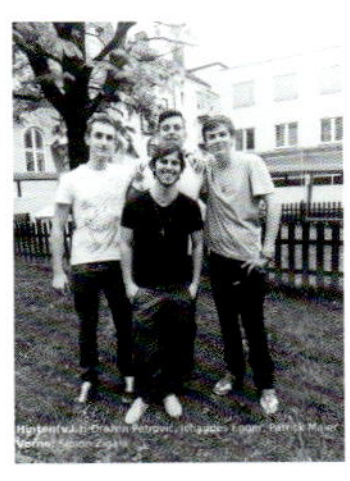

The project team consists of four students from the Department of Business Administration and Engineering at the HTL Anichstraße, a technical secondary school in Innsbruck. There was no strict division of the tasks involved; each team member had to research, plan, buy, construct or document certain items.

Das Projektteam besteht aus vier Schülern der Abteilung Wirtschaftsingenieurswesen der HTL Anichstraße in Innsbruck. Bei dem Projekt verzichteten sie auf eine strikte Aufteilung der Arbeiten. Jeder Mitarbeiter musste einmal gewisse Dinge recherchieren, planen, besorgen, fertigen bzw. dokumentieren.

Dictatorship of Perfection

Simon Stix

https://www.youtube.com/watch?v=eieV_jjGvog

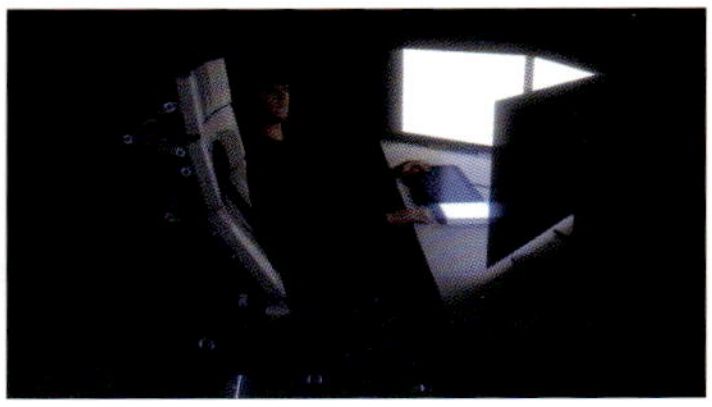
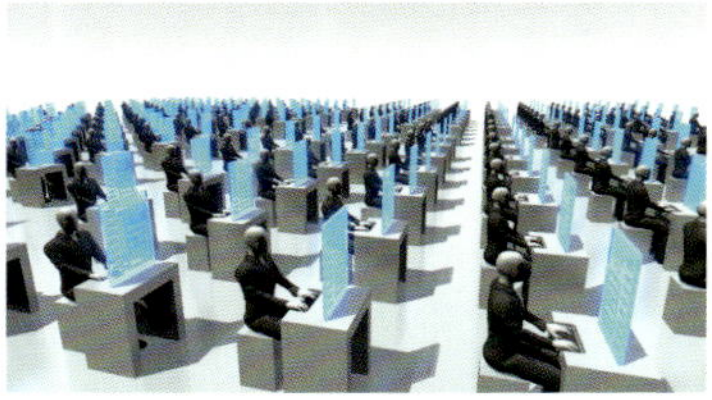
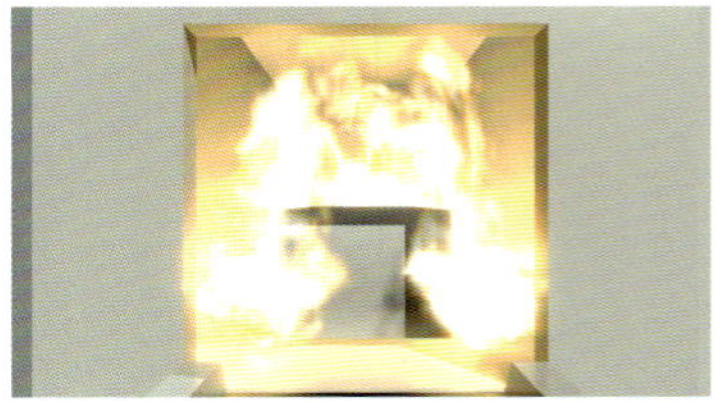
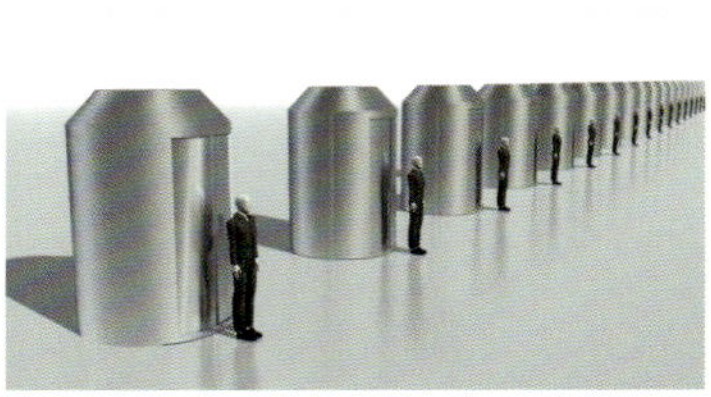
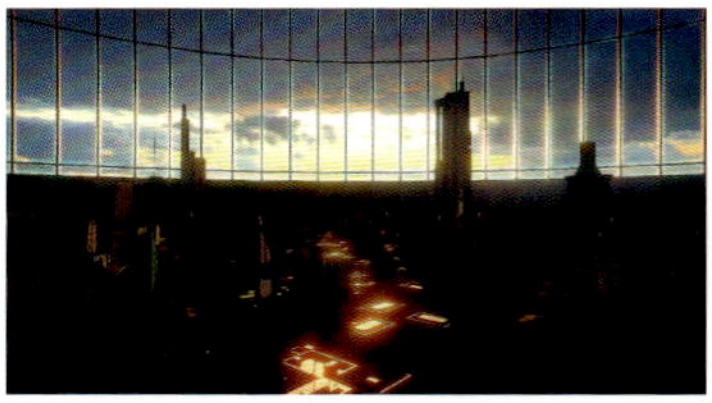
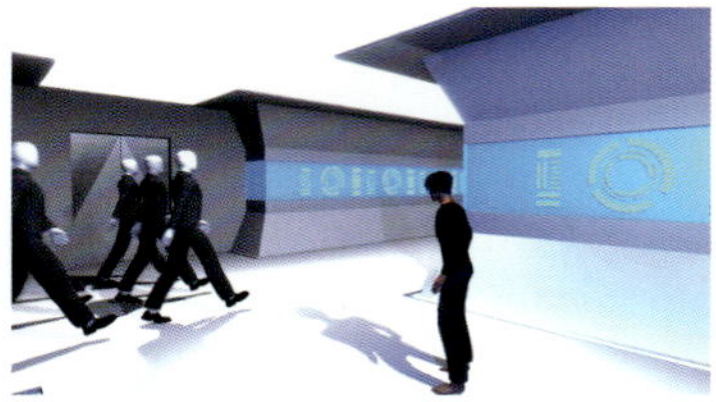
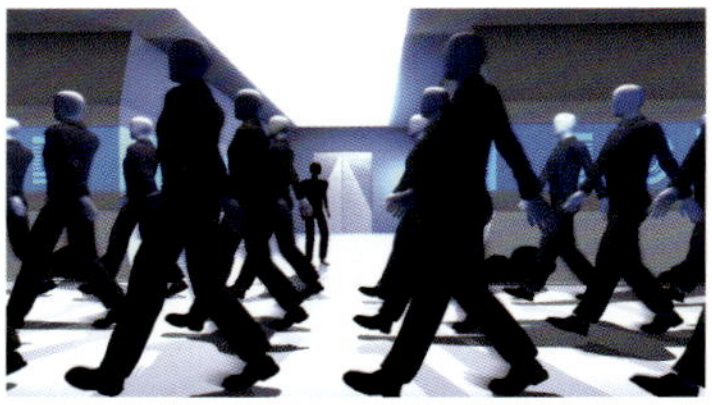
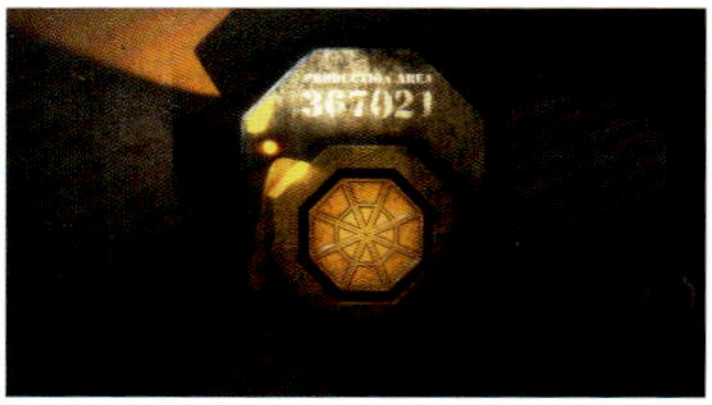

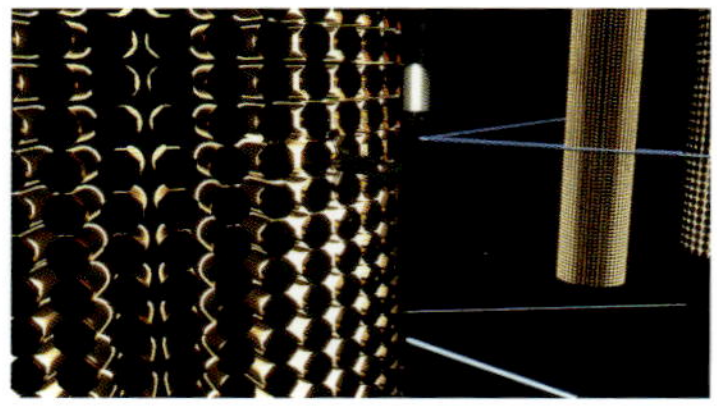

The ecological system of the earth was on the verge of collapse. Nobody could remember if this was because of a war, a natural catastrophe or people's destructive lifestyle. Almost everyone tried to adjust to a new life, to co-existing with nature. Yet those in power did not want to accept this turn of events and so they built a city where they would be protected from the consequences of their own actions. The facility was enclosed in a gigantic dome and was controlled by an artificial intelligence unit, which had the task of maintaining stability within this protected zone for the upper class. In the following centuries, this turned out to be its undoing. Most likely, the ecological system of the earth had in the meantime regenerated itself, but in the city there was nothing but stability and the dictatorship of perfection.

Das Ökosystem der Erde stand kurz vor einem Zusammenbruch. Niemand weiß mehr, ob der Grund dafür ein Krieg, eine Naturkatastrophe oder der zerstörerische Lebensstil der Menschen war. Die meisten Menschen stellten sich auf ein neues Leben, ein Zusammenleben mit der Natur, ein, doch die Mächtigen wollten den Wandel nicht akzeptieren und bauten eine Stadt, in der sie vor den Auswirkungen ihrer eigenen Taten geschützt waren. Die Einrichtung war von einer gigantischen Kuppel umgeben und wurde von einer künstlichen Intelligenz kontrolliert, der die Aufgabe übertragen worden war, die Stabilität innerhalb dieser Schutzzone der Oberschicht zu erhalten. Letzteres wurde in den folgenden Jahrhunderten zum Verhängnis. Das Ökosystem der Erde hat sich möglicherweise wieder regeneriert, doch in der Stadt existiert nur die Stabilität, eine Diktatur der Perfektion.

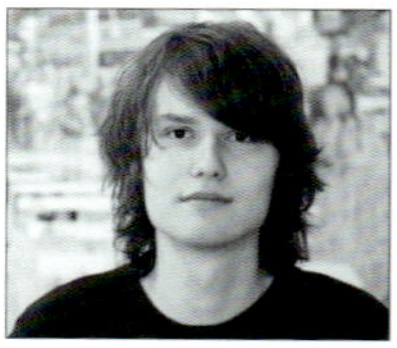

Simon Stix (born in 1994) graduated in 2012 from the BRG Fadingerstraße, a college preparatory school in Linz. In 2009, through the project "Schüler/innen an die Unis" (School Students at University), he studied computer science for a semester at the Johannes Kepler University in Linz. In 2013, he began doing his alternative service at the Media Culture House in Wels. His hobbies are programming, 3D modeling, composing soundtracks and, of course, computer games—both as a recreational pastime and source of inspiration for his own work. **Simon Stix**, geb. 1994, hat 2012 das BRG Fadingerstraße in Linz mit Matura abgeschlossen, aber schon 2009 ein Semester lang durch das Projekt *Schüler/innen an die Unis* an der Johannes Kepler Universität Informatik studiert. 2013 hat er mit dem Zivildienst im Medien Kultur Haus Wels begonnen. Seine Hobbies sind Programmieren, 3D-Modellieren und Soundtrack komponieren und selbstverständlich Computerspielen, sowohl als Freizeitbeschäftigung, als auch als Inspirationsquelle für seine eigene Arbeit.

Gekommen um zu bleiben: Zur falschen Zeit im falschen Land

http://www.schuelerradio.at/sendungen/2013-02-14

6B des Medienzweigs am BRG/ORG Henriettenplatz, Wien

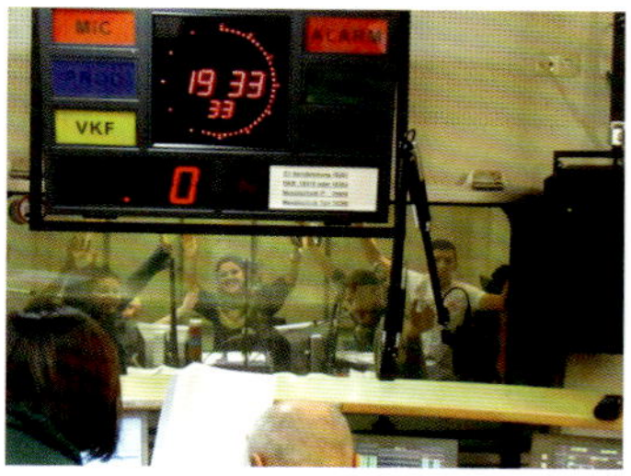

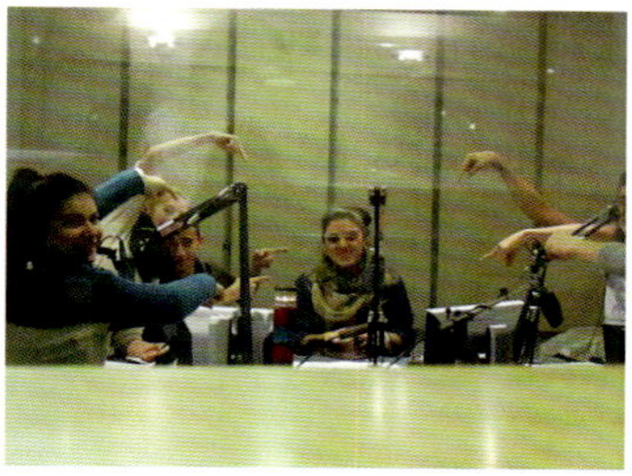

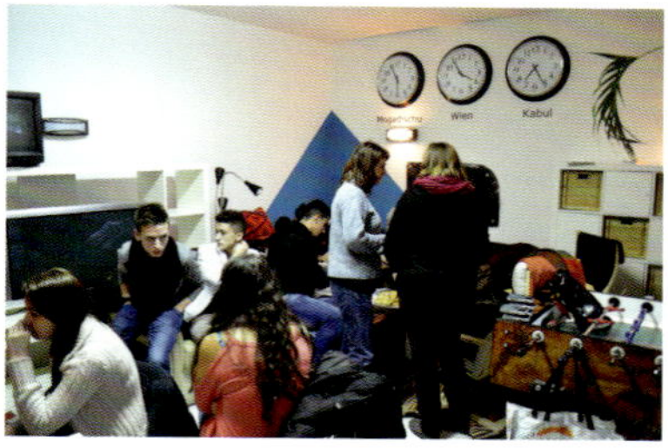

Um für unser Klassenprojekt zum Thema Flucht und Asyl eine Radiosendungen zu verschiedenen Aspekten der österreichischen Flüchtlingsfrage zu planen und live durchzuführen, besuchten wir die Laura-Gatner-Stiftung, die unbegleitete, männliche, minderjährige Flüchtlinge in Österreich bis zu ihrem 19. Lebensjahr betreut. Bei der Recherche war uns Paul Gulda (Verein Refugius) eine große Hilfe, da er uns während des ganzen Projektes mit seinem Wissen zur Seite stand. Bei unserem Besuch konnten wir Interviews mit vier Jugendlichen sowie zwei Betreuern durchführen. Besonders bemerkenswert fanden wir, wie sehr sich die Interviewpartner für dieses Zusammentreffen vorbereitet hatten. In den Gesprächen erfuhren wir sehr bewegende Geschichten seitens der Burschen und über die intensive Betreuungsarbeit des Teams.

Durch die sprachlichen Schwierigkeiten konnten wir die Interviews später nicht wie geplant als gebauten Beitrag in unserer Livesendung verwenden. So entschlossen wir uns, die gewonnenen Eindrücke in Form einer Studiodiskussion in die Sendung einzubauen. Ein Bestandteil der Sendung war auch ein Interview mit einem der Betreuer, das wir zu einem fertigen Beitrag zusammenschnitten. Weitere Arbeitsschritte umfassten das Aussuchen der zum Thema passenden Musik sowie die Recherche und das Verfassen sämtlicher Moderationstexte. Vor unserer Livesendung im Funkhaus Wien hatten wir noch eine Generalprobe in der Schule. Dann war es soweit, mit der Unterstützung der Medianauten konnten wir im Schülerradio On Air gehen und mit den Worten „Auf Sendung" lieferten wir eine halbstündige Performance ab.

For our class project *We Have Come to Stay: In the Wrong Country at the Wrong Time* on the topic of "flight and asylum", we wanted to plan and broadcast a live radio show on different aspects of the refugee issue in Austria. So we visited the Laura Gatner House, which cares for unaccompanied male minors (until they are 19 years old) who are seeking asylum in Austria. In researching the topic, Paul Gulda (from "Refugius") was also a great help, as he shared his knowledge and experience with us throughout the project. During our visits to the home, we were able to conduct interviews with four youths as well as two of their counselors. What we found remarkable was how well our interview partners had prepared for the meetings. During these talks, we heard very moving stories from the boys and learned much about the extensive support given to them by the staff.

Due to language problems we could not use passages from the interviews in our live broadcast as we had originally intended. Instead we decided to incorporate our impressions into the program in the form of a studio discussion. We also used an interview with one of the counselors, which we had edited into a finished piece. Before transmitting live from the Funkhaus Wien (broadcasting studios in Vienna), we had a final rehearsal at school. On the big day, with the assistance of the Medianauten (a group specializing in media education), we went on "Schoolkids Radio". When the words "on air" appeared, we delivered our 30-minute performance.

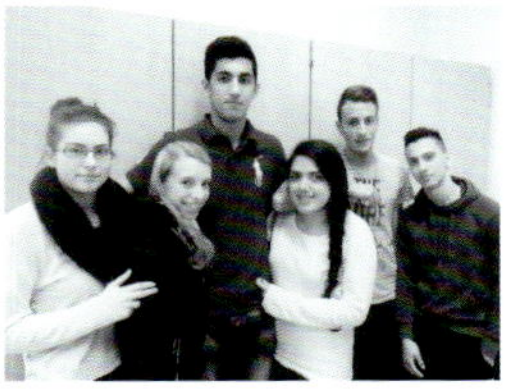

Kübra Börekci, Chiara Fürpass, Tunahan Harmankaya, Ali Özenir, Ana Protrka, Atilla Kahraman are media majors in 6B at the BRG/ORG 15 Henriettenplatz, a college preparatory school in Vienna. The team members are 16 and 17 years old and originally came from a number of different countries. **Kübra Börekci, Chiara Fürpass, Tunahan Harmankaya, Ali Özenir, Ana Protrka, Atilla Kahraman** aus der 6B des Medienzweigs am BRG/ORG 15 Henriettenplatz in Wien sind 16 bis 17 Jahre alt und haben verschiedene Herkunftsländer.

Kompositur

4C / BRG Horn

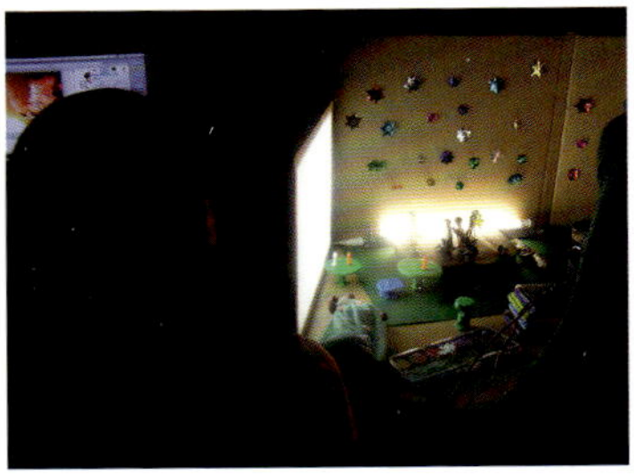

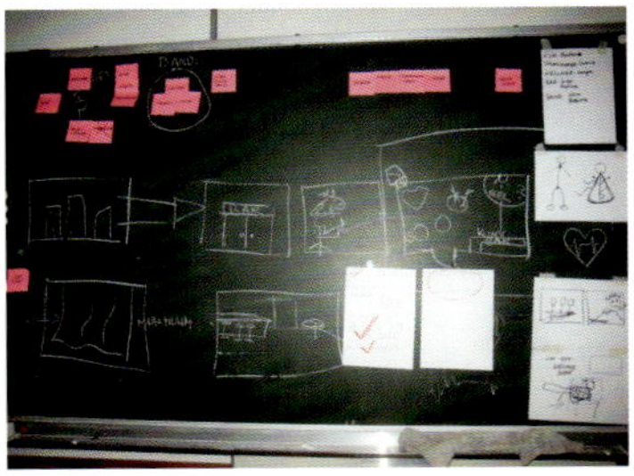

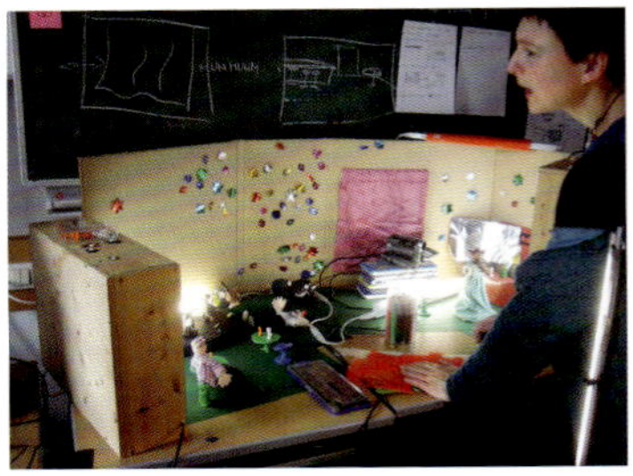

Kompositur, a short stop-motion film, was created during a three-day film workshop. On the first day we learned a lot about drawing comic characters from our workshop leaders. Since we already knew quite a bit about camera settings and angles from our art classes with Professor Gabriele Epp, we discussed these aspects only briefly. We picked a piece of music from the archive of "musik:aktuell" (a program on Lower Austria Radio Station) and then designed our short film to go with it. We sat down and thought up a story together. It wasn't easy, but after brainstorming a bit, we came up with some interesting content for the film: a crazy love story set in a bar.

The next day we began working. Ines and Melisa were in charge of the background scenery. We shaped the figures out of colored modeling clay. Sabine and Razija made the waiter as well as the sports teacher. Madlen made the cow; Barbara the cricket jazz musicians, and Karoline the musical instruments. We worked together on the props: cars, lights, animals, wine bottles, glasses and many other objects. Afterwards we were ready to begin shooting. Everyone took turns participating in the process. The last day we spent filming the rest. Our workshop leader Karo did the editing. Our film workshop was funded by the KKA (Ministry of Education, the Arts and Culture) and "musik:aktuell". We had a lot of fun on those three days and enjoy remembering our time together.

Der Stop-Motion-Kurzfilm *Kompositur* entstand im Rahmen eines dreitägigen Filmworkshops. Am ersten Tag erfuhren wir von den WorkshopleiterInnen viel über das Zeichnen von Comic-Charakteren. Da wir von Frau Prof. Gabriele Epp in dem Fach „Bildnerische Erziehung" schon viel über Kameraeinstellungen und Perspektiven gelernt haben, besprachen wir diese nur kurz. Aus dem Fundus von *musik:aktuell* wählten wir das Musikstück aus, zu dem wir den Kurzfilm gestalteten. Wir setzten uns zusammen und überlegten eine Geschichte. Es war nicht einfach, doch nach den ersten Ideen entstand ein interessanter Filminhalt: eine verrückte Liebesgeschichte in einer Bar.

Tags darauf machten wir uns an die Arbeit. Ines und Melisa waren für die Hintergrundkulissen verantwortlich. Die Figuren modellierten wir aus farbiger Knetmasse. Sabine und Razija formten den Kellner und den Sportlehrer, Madlen bastelte die Kuh, Barbara die Grillen als Jazz-Musikanten, und Karoline kreierte die Musikinstrumente. Gemeinsam arbeiteten wir an den Requisiten wie Autos, Laternen, Tiere, Weinflaschen, Gläsern und vielem mehr. Danach konnten wir mit den Aufnahmen beginnen. An diesen waren wieder alle Mitglieder beteiligt, immer abwechselnd. Den letzten Tag verbrachten wir damit, die restlichen Aufnahmen zu machen. Der Schnitt wurde von Workshopleiterin Karo erledigt. Finanziert wurden unsere „Filmtage" über KKA (BMUKK) und *musik:aktuell* (Land NÖ). Wir hatten an diesen Tagen sehr viel Spaß und erinnern uns gerne an diese gemeinsame Zeit.

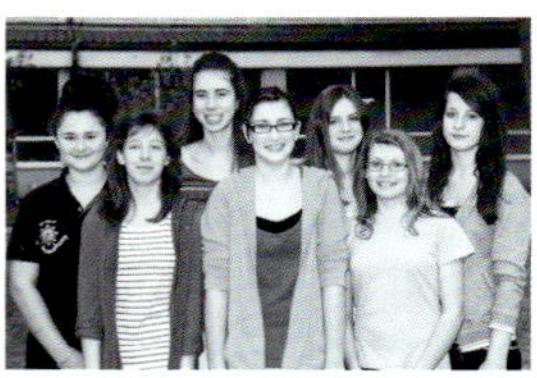

Sabine Bischinger, Barbara Pfaller, Madlen Weingartner, Razila Semic, Melisa Mujcinovic, Ines Tiefenbacher and **Karoline-Melpomeni-Hermine Schager** are all in 4C at the BRG Horn, a college preparatory school in Lower Austria. **Sabine Bischinger, Barbara Pfaller, Madlen Weingartner, Razila Semic, Melisa Mujcinovic, Ines Tiefenbacher** und **Karoline-Melpomeni-Hermine Schager** besuchen gemeinsam die 4C im Gymnasium Horn in Niederösterreich.

Konstruktion eines Fortbewegungsmittels nach dem Vorbild einer Ameise

Gabriel Krög

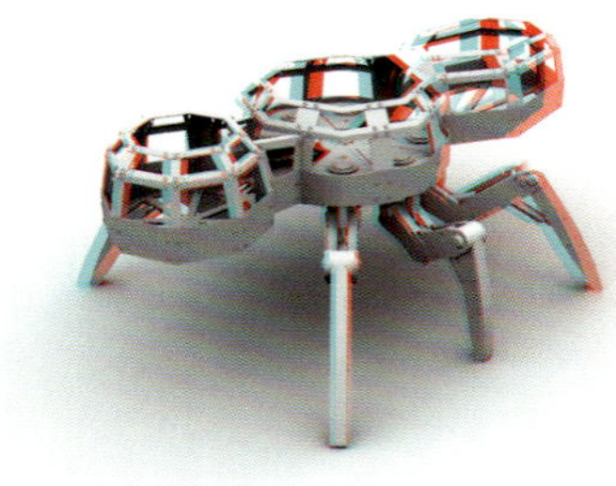

Fahrzeuge, die Räder oder Ketten zur Fortbewegung nutzen, haben den Vorteil, dass sie hohe Geschwindigkeiten ermöglichen und einfach aufgebaut sind, was sie in der Herstellung und Wartung sehr günstig macht. Sie haben jedoch den großen Nachteil, dass sie, um ideal zu funktionieren, Straßen oder zumindest einen befestigten Untergrund benötigen. Im Vergleich dazu muss ein Tier in der Natur mit fast jeder Art von Gelände fertig werden. Das Ziel dieses Projektes war es, ein Fortbewegungsmittel zu entwerfen, das sich, ähnlich einem Tier, auch in schwerem Gelände mühelos fortbewegen kann.
Dazu wurde die Ameise als Vorbild gewählt, die sich aufgrund ihrer Größe ständig in einer Umgebung befindet, die normale Fahrzeuge vor große Probleme stellen würde. Im Vordergrund steht die Konstruktion der erforderlichen mechanischen Bauteile. Das fertige Modell wird auf einem 3D-Drucker ausgedruckt.
Die Vorteile eines Fortbewegungsmittels, das Beine zur Fortbewegung nutzt, liegen auf der Hand: Es können wesentlich schwierigere Geländepassagen überwunden werden, als es rad- oder kettengetriebenen Fahrzeugen möglich wäre. Gleichzeitig wird auch der Untergrund geschont, da die Beine den Boden nur punktuell berühren und daher auch keine durchgehenden Spuren hinterlassen. Dies ermöglicht es, kleine Hindernisse einfach zu übersteigen. Anwendungen fänden sich beispielsweise in der Forstwirtschaft, wo es wichtig ist, den Untergrund so wenig wie möglich zu beschädigen. Auch in Katastrophengebieten, die für herkömmliche Fahrzeuge unzugänglich sind, wäre der Einsatz solcher Transportmittel denkbar.

Vehicles that use wheels or tracks to move have two advantages: they enable high speeds and are simple in structure. This makes their production and maintenance very inexpensive. Nevertheless they have the great disadvantage of requiring roads or at least firm ground to function ideally. In contrast, animals in the natural world have to be able to cope with almost any kind of terrain. The objective of this project was to design a means of transport that would also be able to move effortlessly, like an animal, over rugged terrain.
For this purpose, we chose an ant as our model. Due to its size, an ant constantly has to cope with an environment that would be very problematic for normal vehicles. Our main focus was to construct the necessary mechanical components. The finished model was to be printed on a 3D printer.

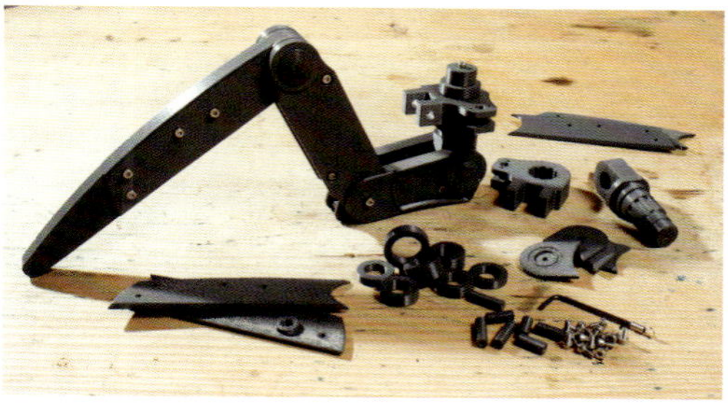

The advantages of a means of transport that uses legs to move are obvious: more difficult stretches of land may be negotiated than is possible with a wheeled or tracked vehicle. At the same time, it causes little wear to the surface on which it is moving, as the legs only touch the ground at single points, and thus do not leave a continuous track. It becomes an option to simply climb over small obstacles. Such a model might be used in forestry, for example, where it is important to do as little damage to the ground as possible. It would also be conceivable to use such a means of transport in disaster areas that have become inaccessible to conventional vehicles.

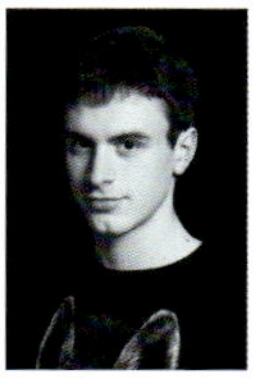

Gabriel Krög (born in 1993) is currently attending the HTBLA, a technical and vocational secondary school in Vöcklabruck. He is majoring in mechanical engineering. In his free time he is interested in 3D visualization and animation among other things. **Gabriel Krög**, geb. 1993, besucht derzeit die HTBLA Vöcklabruck mit dem Schwerpunkt Maschinenbau. In seiner Freizeit beschäftigt er sich unter anderen auch gern mit dem Thema 3D-Visualisierung und Animation.

Massageschulranzen

Lena Sophia Wagner

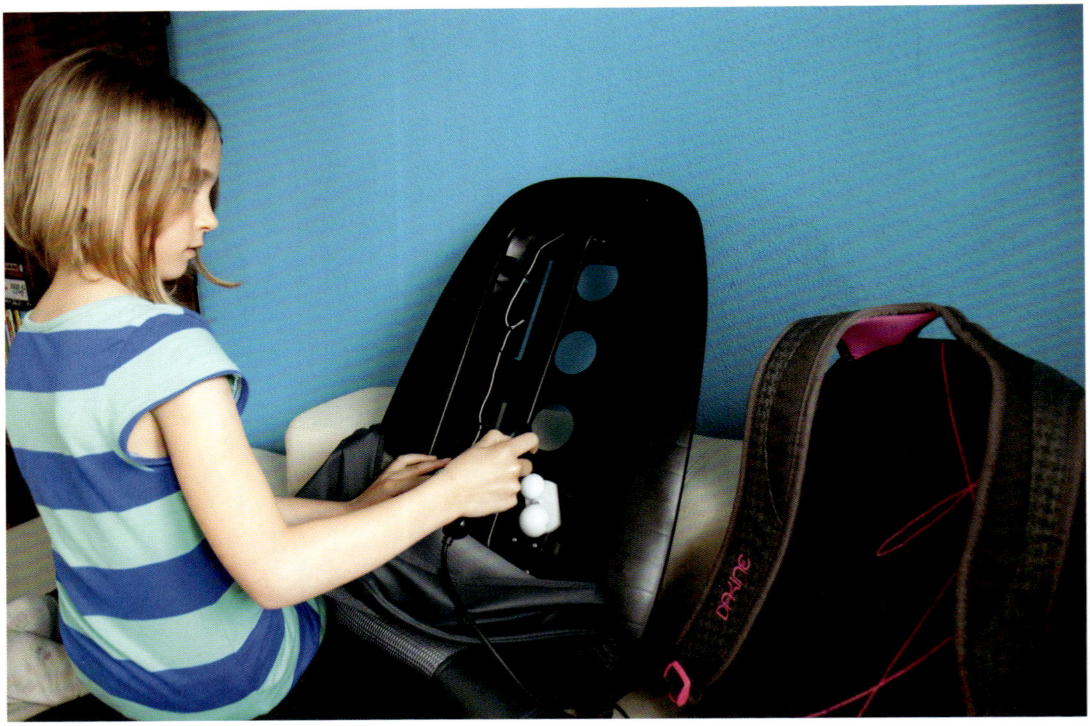

Every day I have to walk a long way to school. My schoolbag is very heavy. I wanted to construct a massage schoolbag so that my back would never hurt again. My idea was to dismantle the motor and rotating balls from a massage chair and attach them to my schoolbag.
With the massage schoolbag, my walk to school would be much nicer. My grandpa would also like a massage backpack for hiking in the mountains.

Ich muss jeden Tag ganz weit zur Schule gehen. Mein Schulranzen ist sehr schwer. Damit mir mein Rücken nicht mehr weh tut, würde ich gerne einen Massageschulranzen bauen. Man könnte dafür den Motor und die Drehkugeln von einem Massagesitz ausbauen und an meinem Schulranzen befestigen.
Mit dem Massageschulranzen wäre mein Schulweg viel schöner. Mein Opa würde sich so einen Massagerucksack auch für seine Bergtouren wünschen.

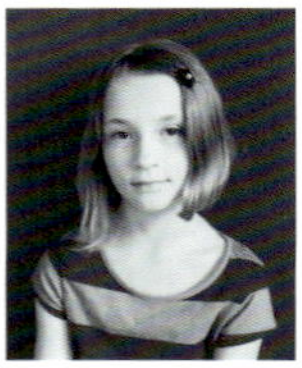

Lena Sophia Wagner (born in 2004) started at St Franziskus Kindergarten in Bernbeuren when she was three years old. Now she is in the third form at the Staufer Grundschule, a primary school in Schongau. Her hobbies are painting, jiu-jitsu, the flute and playing with her friends. **Lena Sophia Wagner**, geb. 2004, besuchte mit drei Jahren den Kindergarten St. Franziskus in Bernbeuren. Jetzt geht sie in die 3. Klasse der Staufer Grundschule Schongau. Ihre Hobbies sind Malen, Jiu Jitsu, Querflöte und mit ihren Freundinnen spielen.

Modern Media Guide

Informatikgruppe des BRG7 Kandlgasse

http://www.modernmediaguide.at

Der *Modern Media Guide* ist eine Internetapplikation, die den Besuch in Museen zu einem virtuellen Erlebnis machen soll. Dem Besucher werden Hintergrundinformationen, Bilder, Videos uvm. gezeigt. Des Weiteren haben die User die Möglichkeit, Inhalte am eigenen Mobiltelefon zu speichern.

Ein großer Vorteil des *Modern Media Guide* ist, dass dem User keine Provider-Kosten anfallen, d.h. der Besucher loggt sich direkt am Server des *Modern Media Guide*-Portals vor Ort ein. Mit professioneller Unterstützung der IT-Firma Datanet Solutions GmbH konnten die SchülerInnen des BRG7 Kandlgasse diese Idee umsetzen. Ein solch intensives und berufsnahes Projekt brachte für die SchülerInnen einen Mehrwert für ihre schulische und auch berufliche Zukunft. Sie konnten aktiv an der Entwicklung einer Software von Anfang bis zur Fertigstellung mitmachen. Die Motivation und das Selbstvertrauen der SchülerInnen stieg, da sie selbst an der Realisierung beteiligt waren und einen großen Teil selbst organisiert haben.

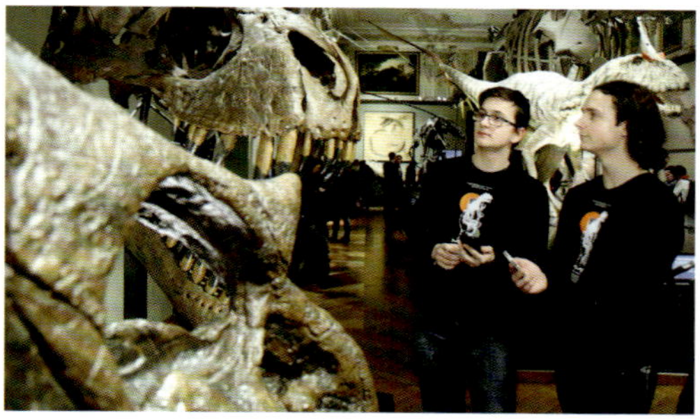

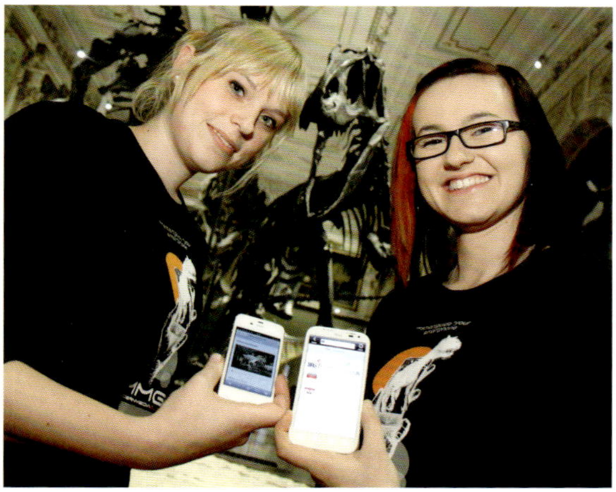

Sie waren für die Beschaffung der Hardware bis hin zum lauffähigen System verantwortlich. Mit der finanziellen Unterstützung des BMUKK konnten die Schüler einen leistungsstarken Server und weitere Hardware ankaufen, die anschließend von ihnen konfiguriert worden ist.

The *Modern Media Guide* is an Internet application that aims to turn a visit to the museum into a virtual experience. Background information, photos, videos, and more are shown to visitors, who can also store the contents on their own mobile phones.

A great advantage of the *Modern Media Guide* is that there are no provider fees for users, which means that they can log on to the server of the guide's portal directly on site. Professional support from Datanet Solutions made it possible for students from the BRG7 Kandlgasse to put their idea into practice.

The students gained valuable educational and vocational experience from this extensive and practice-oriented project. They were able to actively contribute to developing a software program from conception to realization. The students' self-confidence and motivation were given quite a boost as they implemented and organized this project largely on their own. They were responsible for everything from buying the hardware to getting the system up and running. With funding from the BMUKK (the Ministry for Education, the Arts and Culture), the students were able to get a powerful server and additional hardware and then configure them.

Christoph Auer, Kristina Cvetkovska, Melanie Eder, Nicolla Ivanov, Matus Porubsky, Fabian Zechmeister, Jan Kuschel, Raffael Hagleitner from the Computer Science Group at the BRG7 Kandlgasse, a college preparatory school in Vienna, realized the *Modern Media Guide* with the support of Datanet Solutions GmbH. **Christoph Auer, Kristina Cvetkovska, Melanie Eder, Nicolla Ivanov, Matus Porubsky, Fabian Zechmeister, Jan Kuschel, Raffael Hagleitner,** Informatikgruppe des BRG7 Kandlgasse, 1070 Wien, setzten den *Modern Media Guide* mit Unterstützung der IT-Firma Datanet Solutions GmbH um.

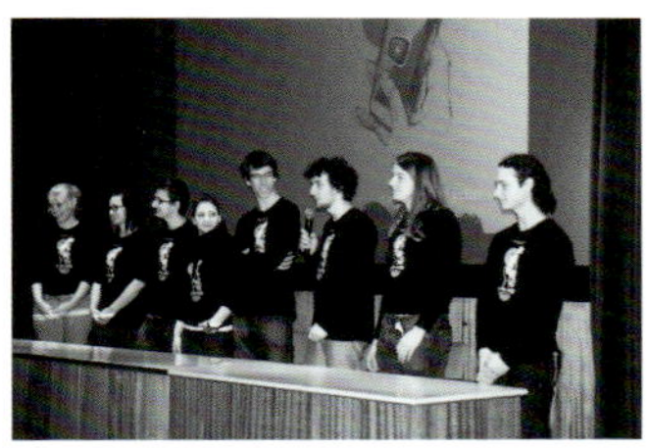

Schulgedächtnis – Eine interaktive Rauminstallation

HBLA für künstlerische Gestaltung Linz

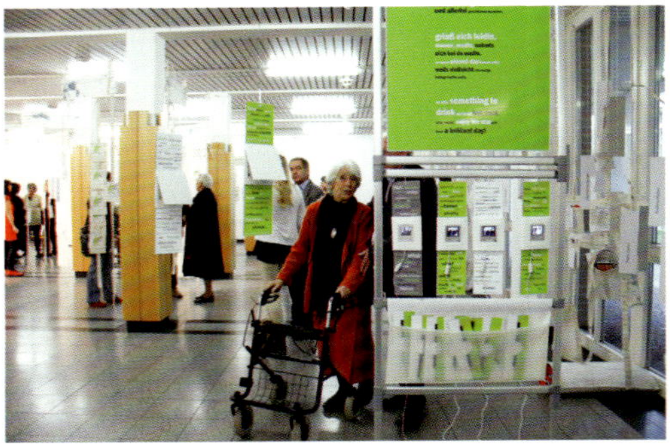

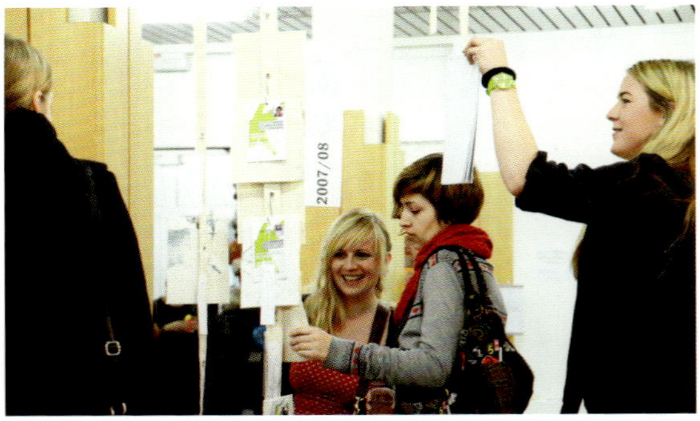

The basic idea of *School Memory–An Interactive Spatial Installation* is to enable visitors to have real-life encounters directly in an interactive format with a large number of people who have contributed to the 30-year history of our school, as well as to transfer and store everything in an archive. The exchange of memories and mementos and their accumulative presentation and mediatization creates a space of communication that can be used interactively, while simultaneously establishing the archive.
Schulgedächtnis (School Memory) strives to illuminate the patchy, incomplete yet authentic function of memory in different media. In doing so it transforms conventional spatial experience into an atmospheric one. This is possible because contemporary communication technologies are increasing despatialization: individuals, places, distances and memories condense in a metaspace where staged actuality and archiving are brought together.
Through social networks and the utilization of social media tools information material is made available and then, via new media, added to the installation and hence to the archive.

Der Grundgedanke besteht darin, dass die reale Begegnung sehr vieler Menschen, die unsere 30-jährige Schulgeschichte bisher mitgestaltet haben, in einem interaktiven Format sowohl direkt erlebt als auch ins Archiv übertragen und gespeichert wird. Der Austausch von Erinnerungsstücken, deren akkumulativer Zur-Schau-Stellung und Medialisierung schafft einen Kommunikationsraum, der interaktiv bespielt und zugleich zu besagtem Archiv wird.
Schulgedächtnis, der Name dieses Projektes, soll die lückenhafte, unvollkommene und trotzdem authentische Erinnerungsfunktion in verschiedenen Medien verdeutlichen und verwandelt dabei die herkömmliche Raumerfahrung in eine atmosphärische, weil die zeitgenössischen Kommunikationstechnologien für zunehmende Enträumlichung sorgen: Individuen, Orte, Distanzen und Erinnerungen verdichten sich in einem Metaraum, in dem inszenierte Aktualität und Archivierung zusammengeführt werden.
Durch soziale Netzwerke und Einsatz von Social-Media-Tools (Facebook, Twitter, Suchmechanismen im Internet) wird das Informationsmaterial bereitgestellt und mittels Nutzung neuer Medien inklusive kollaborativer Anwendungen in die Installation und somit ins Archiv eingepflegt.

Participants: Magdalena Barteder, Flora Besenbäck, Marina Burankova, Anna Döcker, Magdalena Gollner-Hollnbuchner, Anna Greifeneder, Andrea Grünstäudl, Martina Gundolf, Fabia Hahn, Luise Heininger, Johanna Hirth, Monika Huber, Thomas Kirchweger, Anja Labner, Valentin Lichtenberger, Orenda Mohan, Carina Oberleitner, Lisa Maria Palasser, Iris Piringer, Sandra Prandstätter, Jasmin Rammerstorfer, Kathrin Schinnerl, Cornelia Schraml, Laura Starsich, Lena Strasser, Bibiana Traxler, Theresa Winter, Birgit Wögerbauer, Sarah Zauner, Eva Zöchbauer, Nina Blaschke, Johanna Doblinger, Jana Katzlberger, Simone Hart, Alina Bittner

The **project group**, consisting of 35 students, was accompanied by teachers specializing in language, media design and design workshops. Great imagination, conceptual development and systematic planning came together in this group to yield a very productive collaboration. It was a matter of overcoming limits to meet the technical and artistic demands of the project. Die **Projektgruppe**, bestehend aus 35 SchülerInnen, sind unter der Begleitung von Lehrkräften aus den Bereichen Sprache, Mediengestaltung und Atelier für Gestaltung Phantasiereichtum, Konzepterstellung und systematische Planung eine sehr produktive Verbindung eingegangen. Grenzen mussten überwunden werden, damit sowohl die technischen als auch die gestalterischen Ansprüche erfüllt werden konnten.

stop war—start thinking

http://www.youtube.com/watch?v=oaP_uIQsmLA

Michael Dunkel, Nikolaus Müller, Georg Schneider, Philipp Unger

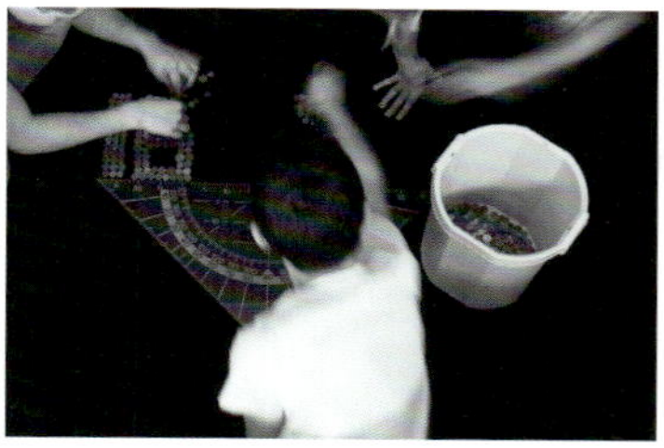

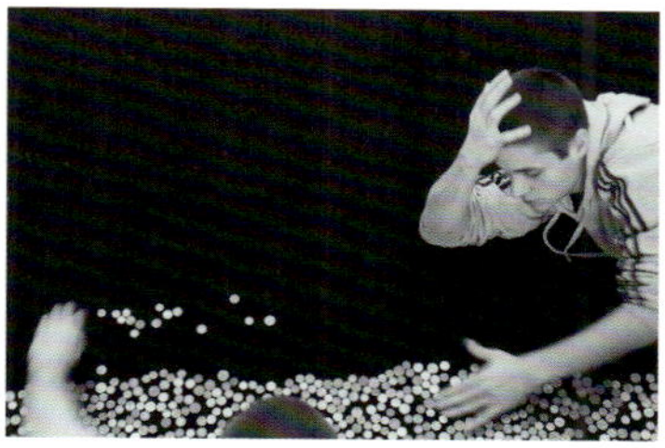

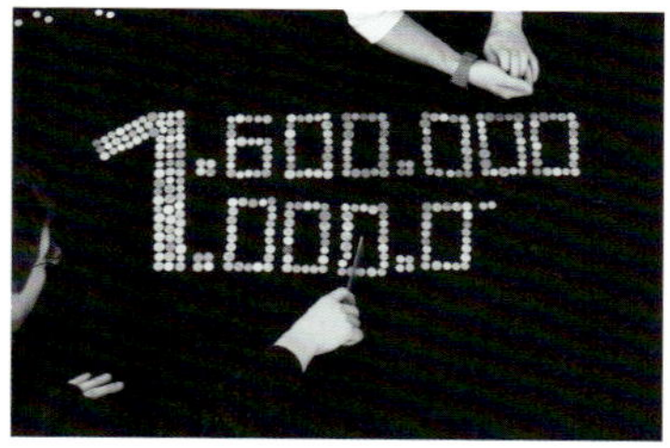

Die grundlegende Idee unseres Projekts ist es, die Problematik der Weltwirtschaft in der heutigen Zeit aufzugreifen und diese in Form eines Stop-Motion-Videos zu verdeutlichen. Da die Weltwirtschaft ein sehr umfangreiches Themengebiet darstellt, haben wir uns dazu entschlossen, uns nur um einen Teilaspekt, nämlich die Rüstungsausgaben, zu kümmern.
Zum einen haben wir uns dafür entschieden, in unserem Stop-Motion-Video hauptsächlich Münzen zu verwenden, um Schrift und Formen darzustellen und um die Thematik mit dem verwendeten Material in Verbindung zu setzen. Außerdem bieten sie viele Darstellungsmöglichkeiten in einem Stop-Motion-Video. Um eine gute Erkennbarkeit der Münzen zu gewährleisten, verwenden wir ein schwarzes Tuch als Hintergrund.
Zu Beginn des Videos wird eine Zahl mit Münzen aufgelegt, welche zeigt, wie hoch die Kosten des Krieges sind. Diese Zahl wird durch eine Bombe aus Münzen zerstört, wodurch die Münzen wild durch die Luft gewirbelt und verteilt werden. Während die Münzen wieder langsam zu Boden sinken, werden die ersten Fakten eingeblendet. In der nächsten Szene werden Soldaten, Panzer, und Flugzeuge aufgelegt, welche sich gegenseitig bekämpfen. Als Hintergrund wird ein Gebirge zu sehen sein, welches jedoch nicht von der Handlung ablenkt. Im Laufe der Szene werden die Soldaten immer weniger und die Leichen und Trümmer am Boden steigen rasant an, bis schließlich alles zerstört ist. Nacheinander werden nun erneut Fakten eingeblendet, welche veranschaulichen sollen, wie viel Geld in Krieg investiert wird, jedoch alternativ besser genützt werden könnte. Diese Vergleiche werden grafisch durch Hintergrundbilder aus Münzen unterstützt.

The basic idea of our project was to take up issues related to the global economy today and show them in a stop-motion video. But since the global economy is a very broad topic, we agreed to explore just one aspect, namely the cost of armaments.
Another thing we decided to do was to use coins for most of the lettering and forms in our stop-motion video, as there would then be a relationship between the topic and the material we were using. In addition, coins can be used in many different ways to represent things in a stop-motion video. To make the coins easier to see, we used a black cloth as backdrop.
At the beginning of the video, the coins are laid out in a multi-digit number that shows the high cost of war. A coin bomb destroys this number and causes all the coins to fly wildly through the air, spreading everywhere. As they slowly fall back to earth, the first facts and figures appear on the screen. In the next scene, soldiers, tanks and planes, also shaped out of coins, battle one another. Behind them is a mountain range, yet it in no way distracts from what is happening. As the scene progresses, more and more soldiers are killed, the corpses and rubble on the ground mount rapidly, until everything is finally destroyed. This is followed by a series of new facts and figures showing the sums invested in war and how they could instead be used for other, better alternatives. In the background, these comparisons are reinforced by illustrations made out of coins.

Michael Dunkel, Nikolaus Müller, Georg Schneider and **Philipp Unger** have been at the HTL Rennweg, a technical secondary school in Vienna, for five years. They have successfully completed three projects together and so want to start up a company with the same team in the future. **Michael Dunkel, Nikolaus Müller, Georg Schneider** und **Philipp Unger** besuchen seit fünf Jahren die HTL Rennweg, Wien. Gemeinsam haben sie schon insgesamt drei Projekte erfolgreich abgeschlossen und sich nun dazu entschlossen, mit all den Teammitgliedern und noch einigen mehr in Zukunft ein Unternehmen zu gründen.

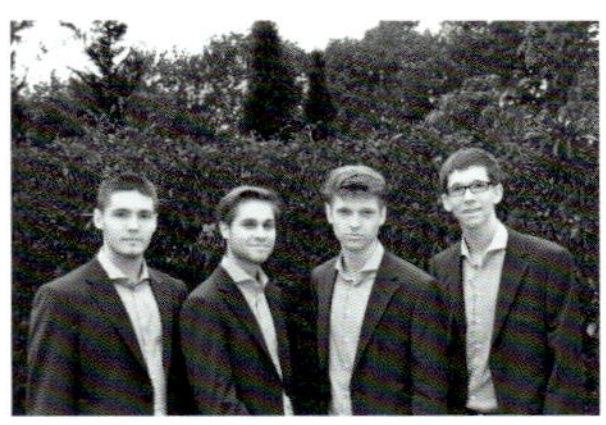

[the next idea]
VOESTALPINE ART AND TECHNOLOGY GRANT

Next Ideas

Michael Doser, Horst Hörtner, Ela Kagel, Gustav Pomberger, Michael Sterrer-Ebenführer

If one could talk about tradition in this comparably "young" Prix Ars Electronica category (launched in 2004), the "most traditional" element would probably be the great diversity of the entries submitted for [the next idea] voestalpine Art and Technology Grant.

The special challenge facing the jury each year is to choose one idea from this broad spectrum—it must be done based solely on descriptions and sketches and not, for instance, on material documenting a project that has already been realized.

Is an idea actually too ambitious? Or is the jury's attitude toward it too reserved? Is the proposed idea startling and spectacular in its initial effect, yet ultimately incapable of maintaining effectiveness beyond the first moment of surprise? Which potentials are inherent to the idea itself and which have been merely projected into it?

This is a difficult enterprise, not only for the jury but also and above all for those submitting their ideas. The "next idea" does not just fall into your lap. Sometimes enormous efforts (and expenses) go into making an idea clear to others—at the same, the jury's attention may hang for hours on a simple drawing on paper.

Particularly striking about this year's edition was that the category had "matured". Evidence for this was not only the substantial increase in entries from already established research groups and individuals from the academic world, but also the greater number of total submissions. What was also remarkable was the broader geographic and disciplinary range of the entries. Quantitatively, this category also reached an all-time high in parameters measurable in numbers: there were 156 entries from 32 countries. The diversity of organizational forms—entrants varied from individuals and artist groups to science buffs and

Wenn man in dieser vergleichsweise „jungen" Kategorie des Prix Ars Electronica (seit 2004) bereits von Tradition sprechen könnte, wäre wohl die Vielfalt der unterschiedlichsten Einreichungen das „traditionellste" Element beim [the next idea] voestalpine Art and Technology Grant.

Dieses breite Spektrum an Ideen und die Tatsache, nur aus Beschreibungen und Skizzen eine Idee auszuwählen—nicht etwa aus dem Dokumentationsmaterial eines bereits realisierten Projektes – ist die ganz besondere Herausforderung, der sich die Jury alljährlich stellt.

Ist die Idee tatsächlich zu ambitioniert, oder ist doch die Haltung der Jury gegenüber der Idee zu zurückhaltend? Ist die vorgeschlagene Idee spektakulär und überwältigend in ihrer Auswirkung, letztlich aber dann doch nicht in der Lage, über den Überraschungsmoment hinaus wirksam zu bleiben? Welche Potenziale stecken in der Idee selbst und welche werden vielleicht nur hinein projiziert?

Ein schwieriges Unterfangen nicht nur für die Jury, sondern auch und vor allem für die EinreicherInnen selbst. Die „Next Idea" fällt niemandem einfach in den Schoß. Mitunter werden enorme Aufwände betrieben, um die Idee deutlich sichtbar zu machen – und doch hängt die Aufmerksamkeit der Jury schon mal über Stunden an einer einzigen simplen Skizze auf Papier.

Zur diesjährigen Jury-Runde ist besonders zu bemerken, dass die Kategorie „erwachsen" geworden ist. Indiz dafür ist nicht nur die auffallend gestiegene Anzahl der Beiträge aus dem akademischen Umfeld von bereits etablierten Forschergruppen wie auch Einzelpersonen, sondern auch die zunehmende Gesamtanzahl der Einreichungen. Auch die steigende geografische und disziplinäre Reichweite fallen auf. Quantitativ war dies heuer das „All-Time High" der Kategorie in allen mit Zahlen messbaren Parametern: 156 Einreichungen aus 32 Ländern. Die Vielfalt der Organisationsformen der EinreicherInnen – von Einzelpersonen über Künstlergruppen, vom „Wissenschaftsbastler" zum Künstlerkollektiv, vom

Architekturbüro über Medienkunststudenten bis hin zu Startups – zeigt die große Bandbreite der Gesellschaftsgruppen, die sich von der Kategorie [the next idea] angesprochen fühlen.
So fällt es leicht, [the next idea] auch als Trendbarometer der künstlerisch-technologischen Auseinandersetzung zu bezeichnen. Viele der Einreichungen beschäftigen sich mit Maker-Communities und DIY-Konzepten, Open Source und Open Hardware. Ein besonderer Schwerpunkt der eingereichten Ideen lag auf der Nutzbarmachung biologischer Prozesse (z. B. Energiegewinnung aus Algen und Bakterien), der synthetischen Biologie und des Bio-Hacking. Anders als in den vergangenen beiden Jahren standen politisch motivierte, aktivistische Projekte diesmal weniger stark im Fokus der EinreicherInnen. Es marschierte ein sehr breites Mittelfeld auffallend guter Einreichungen und Ideen über die Ziellinie, doch wie jedes Jahr gibt es eine Einreichung, die die Nase vorne hat.

[the next idea] VOESTALPINE ART AND TECHNOLOGY GRANT

Hyperform

Marcelo Coelho, Skylar Tibbits, Natan Linder, Yoav Reches

Additive Manufacturing oder 3D-Printing ist nicht neu – lässt aber noch Spielraum für Innovation, wie diese Idee beweist. Sie reiht sich ein in die Serie der Erweiterung der Dimensionen in der Drucktechnik. Vom zweidimensionalen Druck hin zum dreidimensionalen Druck und jetzt auch die Integration der vierten Dimension, der Zeit! So ist es nicht weiter verwunderlich, dass die Einreicher selbst vom „4D-Druck" sprechen.
Das Gestalten von 3D-Prints bietet dem Anwender eine Vielzahl von Freiheiten, was Form und (mechanische) Funktion betrifft. Auch die Anzahl der 3D-druckbaren Materialien steigt laufend. Vom Kunststoff über diverse Metalle und Edelmetalle bis hin zu biologischen

tinkerers, from artists' collectives and architectural offices to media students and startups—demonstrates the wide range of society to whom this category appeals.
All this makes it easy to describe [the next idea] as a barometer of the latest trends in artistic, technological explorations. Many of the entries deal with maker communities and DIY concepts, open source and open hardware. A number of the submitted ideas concentrate on utilizing biological processes (e.g., generating energy from algae and bacteria), synthetic biology and bio-hacking. Unlike in the previous two years, the entrants were less focused on activist or politically motivated projects. A large range of outstanding submissions and ideas made it to the finish line, but as every year, one entry came in ahead.

[the next idea] VOESTALPINE ART AND TECHNOLOGY GRANT

Hyperform

Marcelo Coelho, Skylar Tibbits, Natan Linder, Yoav Reches

Additive manufacturing and 3D printing are not new, yet there is still plenty of room for innovation – as this idea shows. It is one of a whole string of efforts to expand the dimensions of print technology. From two-dimensional to three-dimensional printing, now a fourth dimension has been integrated: the dimension of time! And so it is hardly astonishing that these entrants actually speak of "4D printing".
Designing 3D prints gives users a great deal of freedom with regard to form and (mechanical) function. Moreover, the number of materials that can be used in 3D printing is continually rising. Prints

may now be made on everything from plastics, various metals and precious metals to biological cells. 3D prints are becoming more important in almost every conceivable field of work and discipline of science. But what if you don't want to print the end product—or can't? Be it because the printer which is at your disposal at any one moment is too small to produce the end product in only one step or the final form does not lend itself to assembly? In fact what you need is a form that assembles itself—over time—into the end product without requiring any additional work steps.
With Marcelo Coelho, Skylar Tibbits, Natan Linder and Yoav Reches's idea, this is possible!
Objects self-assemble after the actual printing process—by preparing the object mechanically (to print "joints" or "folds") and a chemical reaction (folding the joints in an alcohol bath), this work step is carried out, as it were, by the printed artifact itself. The final shape, which has been inscribed in the material during printing, results following a chemical reaction and via the fourth dimension—time. Comparable to a collapsible box that has to be folded into a container using only a few clever movements of the hand, all kinds of constructions can be thought up, printed and then folded into their final form whenever needed. The designer of a 3D model determines the individual folds in advance and "inscribes" them in it.
This year's [the next idea] voestalpine Art and Technology Grant goes to the group *Hyperform*. It will use its residency at Ars Electronica Futurelab to test the entire process in a variety of ways. Both the process and the test results will be made available in the public domain in documentations by/to the maker community so this idea can become a catalyst for further developments—the next ideas.

Zellen kann alles gedruckt werden. Der 3D-Druck spielt bereits in nahezu allen denkbaren Arbeitsbereichen und Wissenschaftsdisziplinen eine immer wichtigere Rolle. Was aber, wenn man nicht das Endprodukt drucken möchte – oder kann? Sei es, weil der gerade verfügbare Drucker zu klein ist, um das Endprodukt in einem Arbeitsschritt entstehen zu lassen, oder weil die Endform eventuell nicht zur Montage taugt und man eigentlich eine „Montageform" benötigt, die sich dann selbsttätig – über die Zeit – zur Endform formiert, ohne dass weitere Arbeitsschritte notwendig sind. Nach der Idee von Marcelo Coelho, Skylar Tibbits, Natan Linder und Yoav Reches ist das möglich! Eine Verformung nach dem eigentlichen Druck – ein Arbeitsschritt, der durch mechanische Vorbereitung (Drucken von „Gelenken" bzw. „Faltungen") und eine chemische Reaktion (Faltung der Gelenke im Alkoholbad) quasi selbsttätig vom gedruckten Artefakt vollzogen wird. Die Endform ist durch den Druckvorgang bereits in das Material eingeschrieben, wird durch eine darauf folgende chemische Reaktion abgerufen und über die vierte Dimension – die Zeit – erst erreicht, vergleichbar mit einer Faltschachtel, die erst durch ein paar geschickte Handbewegungen zu einem Behälter gefaltet wird, kann nun ein jedes beliebige Konstrukt erdacht und gedruckt werden, dass sich erst zu einem frei wählbaren späteren Zeitpunkt zu seiner Endform faltet. Dabei wird jede einzelne Faltung bereits vorab vom Designer des 3D-Modells festgelegt und in das 3D-Modell „eingeschrieben".
Der [the next idea] voestalpine Art and Technology Grant geht an die *Hyperform*-Gruppe, deren Residency im Ars Electronica Futurelab dazu genutzt wird, das gesamte Verfahren unterschiedlichsten Tests zu unterziehen. Das Verfahren und die Testergebnisse werden in Form von frei zugänglichen Dokumentationen der Maker-Community zur Verfügung gestellt, um diese Idee als Katalysator für weiterführende Ideen – the next ideas – nutzbar zu machen.

ANERKENNUNG

Gravity Light

Martin Riddiford, Jim Reeves

Die Suche nach der emissionsfreien Energiegewinnung, basierend auf erneuerbarer Energie, die jederzeit und möglichst unabhängig von äußeren Umständen weltweit sofort abrufbar ist, beschäftigt seit mehreren Jahrzehnten eine unüberschaubare Zahl kluger Köpfe. Dass diese Energie nun auch noch mit wirklich minimalem Aufwand an Investitionen in Infrastruktur zugänglich gemacht wird, ist ebenso verblüffend wie die Tatsache, dass dieser Lösungsweg nicht schon längst beschritten wurde.

Gravity Light ist ob seiner Simplizität die ideale Lösung für die unabhängige, erneuerbare und mobile Energiegewinnung und -nutzung. Vor allem die weniger entwickelten Landstriche fernab von Versorgungsanbindungen werden von der Realisierung dieser Idee enorm profitieren.

Gravity Light nutzt den von Kuckucks- und Pendeluhren bekannten Schwerkraftantrieb. Nur wird durch das am Seil oder der Kette hängende Gewicht nicht ein Uhrwerk, sondern eben ein Licht angetrieben. Ein Sack, gefüllt mit Erde oder Steinen treibt durch sein Gewicht ein Zahnrad an, an dessen Achse sich ein Generator befindet, der dann den Strom erzeugt. Um eine LED-Leuchte für etwa 30 Minuten betreiben zu können, reicht es, das entsprechende Gewicht etwa eineinhalb Meter über Boden zu heben und an das Seil zu hängen – den Rest besorgt die Schwerkraft. Nach dem Heben des Gegengewichtes geht aber nicht nur das Licht an – *Gravity Light* hat auch einen USB-Anschluss; etwa zum Aufladen des Mobiltelefons oder einer Taschenlampe oder eines beliebigen anderen Akkus.

HONORARY MENTION

Gravity Light

Martin Riddiford, Jim Reeves

The exploration of how to generate emission-free power, based on renewable energy, that can be tapped worldwide when needed, independently of the external conditions, has preoccupied many a clever mind over the past several decades. To discover that such energy may now be accessible with the bare minimum of investments in the infrastructure is just as baffling as is the fact that nobody hit upon this solution years ago.

Due to its simplicity, *Gravity Light* is the ideal approach to independent, renewable and mobile energy production and use. Especially less developed areas in remote off-grid locations will benefit enormously from the implementation of this idea.

Gravity Light uses gravity drive, a mechanism known to us from cuckoo and pendulum clocks. Though in this case, the weight that hangs on the rope or chain is used to power a light and not a clock. The weight of a sack filled with earth or stones powers a gear whose axle is equipped with a generator that produces electricity. To be able to operate an LED for approximately 30 minutes, the weight has to be lifted some 50 centimeters off the ground and suspended from a rope—gravity does the rest. Though raising the counterweight can power more than a light: *Gravity Light* also has a USB port that can be used to charge a mobile phone, a flashlight or any other device with a rechargeable battery/rechargeable batteries of all kinds.

Hyperform

Marcelo Coelho, Skylar Tibbits, Natan Linder, Yoav Reches

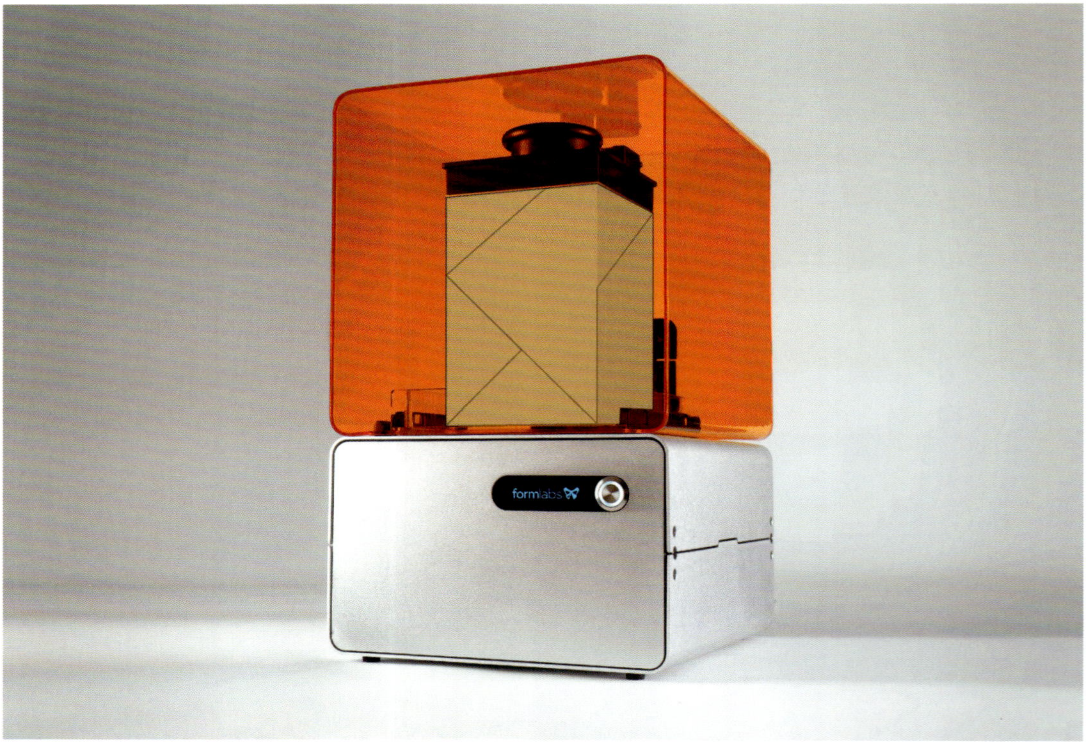

We are in the midst of a revolution that promises to forever change how we make things. At one extreme, software tools are empowering individuals to envision, create and share their own designs; while at another, low-cost digital fabrication machines are allowing these one-of-a-kind creations to be built and consumed from the comfort of our homes. However, while 3D printers are becoming increasingly accessible and capable of rivaling the quality of professional equipment, they are still inherently limited by a small print volume, placing severe constraints on the type and scale of objects we can create.

For [the next idea] we propose to address this problem by identifying computational and material folding strategies that will allow large-scale objects to be compressed into a minimal volume to maximize the printing capability of desktop 3D printers. The folding techniques we develop will be exemplified and embodied through a series of representative furniture pieces, and their fundamental principles and designs will be openly published and distributed to encourage others to learn from, use and modify our work.

Wir befinden uns mitten in einer Revolution, die verspricht, die Herstellung von Dingen für immer zu verändern. Einerseits ermöglichen Software-Tools die Erfindung, Schaffung und Verbreitung eigener Objektentwürfe; andererseits lassen sich diese individuellen Entwürfe nun mit preiswerten digitalen Fabrikationsmaschinen bequem zu Hause umsetzen und konsumieren. Doch auch wenn 3D-Drucker zunehmend erschwinglich werden und qualitativ an professionelle Geräte heranreichen, so ist ihr Bauraum doch immer noch ziemlich klein, was die Art der damit erzeugbaren Objekte erheblich einschränkt.

Für [the next idea] schlagen wir vor, die Printkapazität von 3D-Desktopdruckern durch die Entwicklung algorithmischer und materieller Falttechniken zu erhöhen, mit denen sich große Objekte auf ein möglichst kleines Volumen komprimieren lassen. Die von uns entwickelten Falttechniken wollen wir durch eine Reihe repräsentativer Möbelstücke veranschaulichen, und die ihnen zugrundeliegenden Prinzipien und Entwürfe sollen offen publiziert und gratis weitergegeben werden, damit andere von unserer Arbeit lernen, sie nutzen und weiterentwickeln können.

http://www.cmarcelo.com
http://sjet.us
http://formlabs.com

Faltung als algorithmische Entwurfs- und Fertigungsstrategie kommt nicht nur in allen natürlichen Systemen, z. B. in der Struktur der Proteine und der DNA, sondern auch bei industriellen Anwendungen vor, wenn es darum geht, die Effizienz zu steigern und zugleich ein hohes Maß an struktureller Komplexität, Interoperabilität und Wiederverwertung beizubehalten. Mit Unterstützung der Ars Electronica planen wir, eine Reihe von Falttechniken zu ermitteln und zu analysieren, Material- und Belastungstests durchzuführen, programmier- und in einem Stück ausdruckbare Universalscharniere zu entwickeln (die aber gleichwohl zerlegt werden können), und ein archetypisches Möbelstück zu bauen, um unsere Arbeit zu untermauern, zu evaluieren und zu kommunizieren.

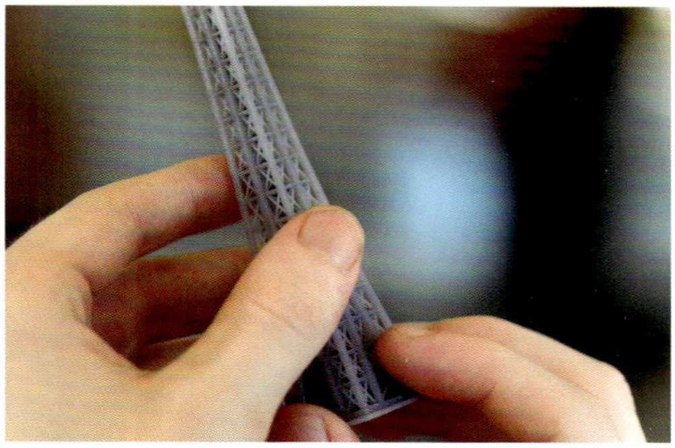

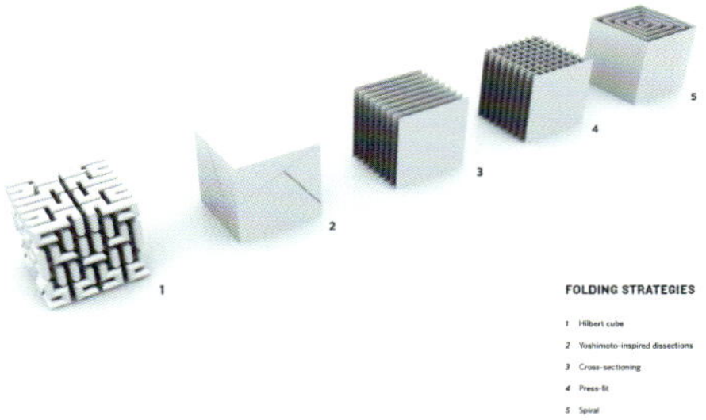

Folding as a computational design and assembly strategy can be found across natural systems, such as in the structures of proteins and DNA, and in industrial applications that seek to increase efficiency while supporting high degrees of structural complexity, interoperability and reuse. With Ars Electronica support, we plan to: identify and analyze a series of folding strategies; perform material and mechanical tests; design universal and programmable hinges that can be printed as a single piece (and be reversed for disassembly); and make a final archetypal furniture piece that can support, evaluate and communicate our work.

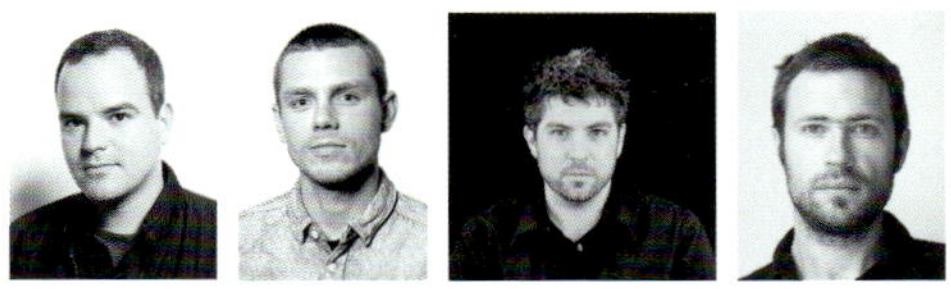

Marcelo Coelho (BR) is a designer and Research Affiliate at the MIT Media Lab, and his work explores how materials that embody computational properties can reshape the ways in which we design, interact and communicate. During his doctoral work, Marcelo studied how shape-changing materials can be used in the design of transformable surfaces in order to computationally reconfigure their topology, texture and permeability. **Skylar Tibbits** (US) is a trained architect and computer scientist whose research focuses on developing self-assembly and programmable material technologies for the built environment. Skylar is the director of the Self-Assembly Lab at MIT and is faculty in the Department of Architecture, teaching design studios and co-teaching *How to Make (Almost) Anything*, a seminar at MIT's Media Lab. **Natan Linder** (IL) is a co-founder of Formlabs and a PhD student in the Fluid Interfaces group at the MIT Media Lab. His work fuses design and engineering to create novel human experiences. Before joining the MIT Media Lab, he was the lead UI designer at Heartland Robotics. **Yoav Reches** (IL) is a London-based industrial designer and the designer behind Form 1. His multidisciplinary work explores the practical and conceptual applications of product design. **Marcelo Coelho** (BR) ist Designer und Research Affiliate am MIT Media Lab. Er untersucht, wie sich Materialien, die algorithmische Eigenschaften verkörpern, auf unsere Art des Gestaltens, Interagierens und Kommunizierens auswirken. In seiner Doktorarbeit erforschte er, wie Materialien, die ihre Form verändern, dazu herangezogen werden können, transformierbare Flächen zu gestalten und deren Topologie, Textur und Durchlässigkeit algorithmisch zu rekonfigurieren. **Skylar Tibbits** (US) ist studierter Architekt und Computerwissenschaftler, der sich vornehmlich mit der Entwicklung selbstassemblierender und programmierbarer Materialtechnologien für die gebaute Umwelt beschäftigt. Skylar ist Leiter des Self-Assembly Lab am MIT, gibt Design-Studio-Kurse am MIT-Architekturinstitut und unterrichtet im Seminar *How to Make (Almost) Anything* am MIT Media Lab. **Natan Linder** (IL) ist Mitbegründer von Formlabs und Doktorand in der Fluid Interfaces Group am MIT Media Lab. In seiner Arbeit will er durch die Verschmelzung von Design und Technik neue menschliche Erfahrungen vermitteln. Bevor er ans MIT Media Lab ging, war er UI-Designer bei Heartland Robotics. **Yoav Reches** (IL) ist ein in London lebender und arbeitender Industriedesigner und verantwortlich für das Design von Form 1. In seiner multidisziplinären Arbeit beschäftigt er sich mit praktischen und konzeptuellen Anwendungen von Produktdesign.

GravityLight

Martin Riddiford, Jim Reeves

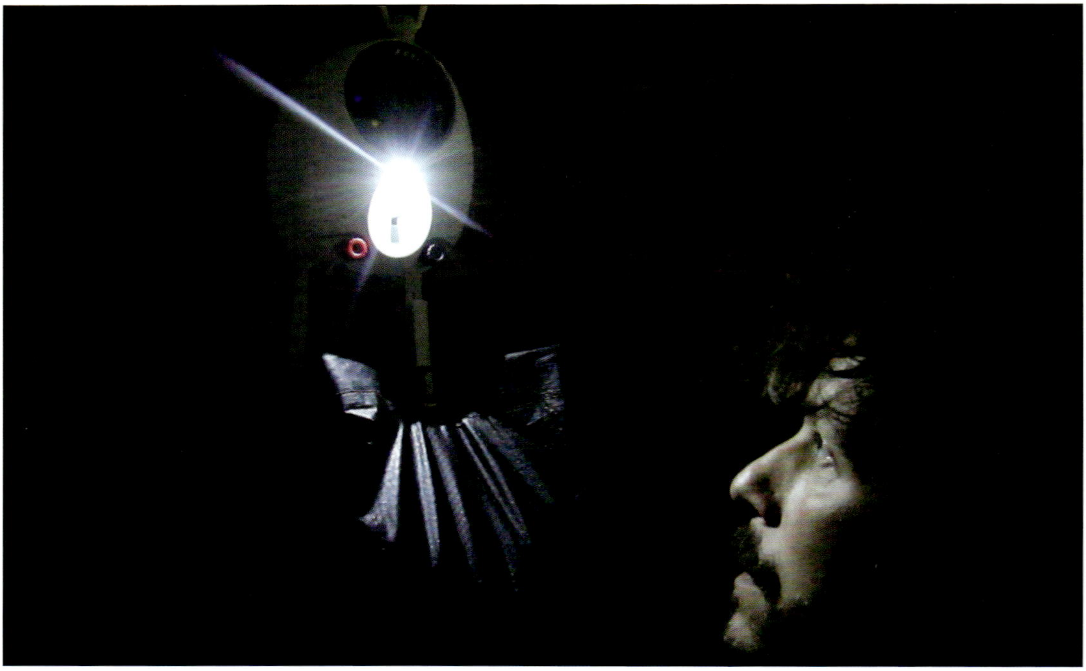

GravityLight is a revolutionary and sustainable approach to generating power and light. It eliminate the need for kerosene lamps, offering huge health, economic and environmental benefits.
It takes around three seconds to lift the weight that charges *GravityLight*, which will provide up to 30 minutes of constant light as the weight drops under the force of gravity. The weight is a bag (which doubles as the product packaging) that the user fills with 9 to 12.5kg of material (earth, rocks or sand). This connects to *GravityLight* via a plastic strap that passes through the generating mechanism. A series of gears and a generator inside translates this slow falling mass into electrical energy. The system can be varied to provide either task or ambient lighting, or both simultaneously at a lower level. It has terminals on the front to allow it to be used purely as a generator to top up batteries, or to power various low-voltage devices. *GravityLight* has no batteries to run out, replace or dispose of and has no reliance on the external environment, time of day, season or weather. As there are no running costs after the initial low-cost purchase, *GravityLight* has the potential to help lift people who would otherwise spend a large proportion of their income on kerosene for lighting out of poverty.

GravityLight ist eine revolutionäre und nachhaltige Methode der Strom- und Lichterzeugung. Sie kann Kerosinlampen überflüssig machen und hat damit enormes gesundheitliches, wirtschaftliches und ökologisches Nutzenpotenzial.
Es dauert etwa drei Sekunden, das Gewicht zu heben, das *GravityLight* mit Energie versorgt und etwa 30 Minuten durchgehend leuchten lässt, während es von der Schwerkraft wieder langsam zu Boden gezogen wird. Das Gewicht besteht aus einem (auch als Produktverpackung verwendeten) Säckchen, das vom Nutzer selbst mit 9 bis 12,5 Kilogramm Material (Erde, Sand, Steinen) gefüllt wird. Dieses ist über einen durch

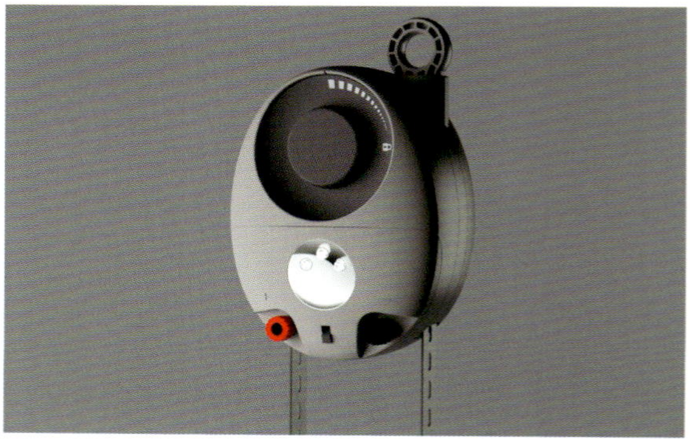

den Generatormechanismus laufenden Plastikriemen mit *GravityLight* verbunden. Eine Reihe von Zahnrädern und ein Generator wandeln die langsam fallende Masse in elektrische Energie um. Das System ist variabel und kann entweder Arbeits- oder Hintergrundlicht liefern – oder beides auf einem niedrigeren Niveau. An der Vorderseite besitzt es Buchsen, so dass es auch als reiner Generator zum Aufladen von Batterien oder zum Betreiben von Schwachstromgeräten wie z. B. einem Radio benutzt werden kann. *GravityLight* hat keine Batterien, die zur Neige gehen, ersetzt oder entsorgt werden müssen, und funktioniert unabhängig von äußeren Umständen – von Tages- und Jahreszeit oder vom Wetter. Es verursacht keinerlei Kosten außer dem niedrigen Anschaffungspreis und kann daher Menschen, die einen beträchtlichen Anteil ihres Einkommens für Kerosin ausgeben müssen, bei der Überwindung der Armut helfen.

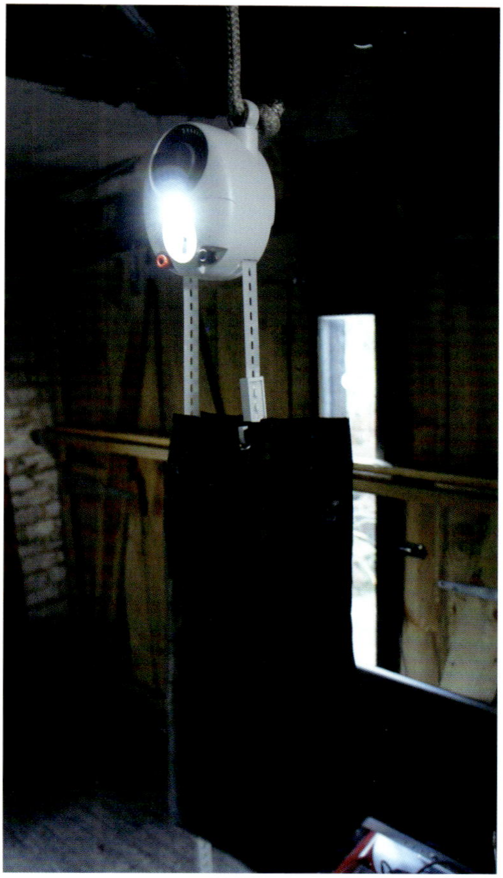

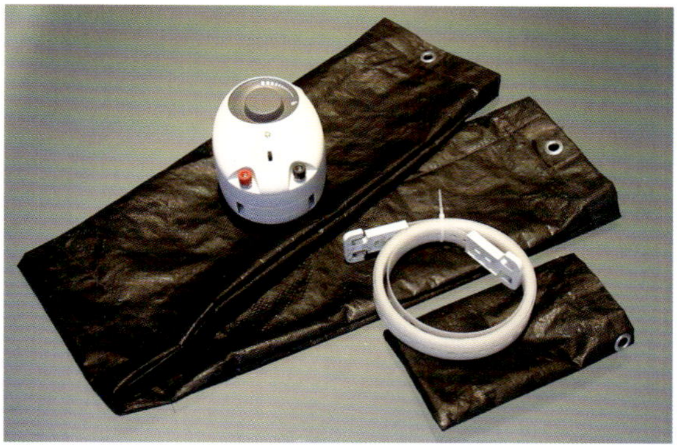

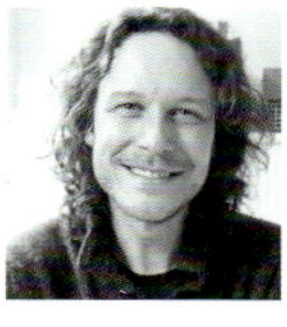

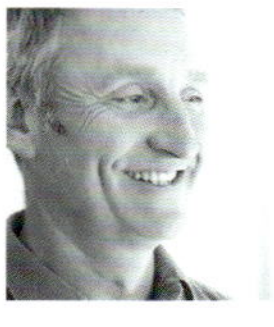

Martin Riddiford (UK) is a co-founder of London-based product-design firm *therefore* and also trained at Central School of Art and Design. He has been working in product design consultancy for 35 years. Martin's inventive approach to design and his immersion in new technology has contributed to the successful launch of important new-technology-based innovations on the consumer market, from Psion's original PDA to TomTom's satnav range. **Jim Reeves** (UK) has been working in product design consultancy for nine years. He is a design engineer and Associate Director at Therefore. He has undertaken in-depth engineering development on longstanding R&D projects at *therefore*, as well as extensive user-focused research. One of Jim's recent projects was *bednest*—a crib that facilitates safe co-sleeping. **Martin Riddiford** (UK) ist Mitbegründer der Londoner Produktdesignfirma *therefore*. Ausgebildet wurde er an der Central School of Art and Design. Er ist seit 35 Jahren als Produktdesign-Berater tätig und hat mit seinem einfallsreichen Zugang zum Design und zur Immersion in neue Technologien zur erfolgreichen Markteinführung einer ganzen Reihe wichtiger technologiebasierter Innovationen vom ersten Psion-PDA bis zum SatNav Range von TomTom beigetragen. **Jim Reeves** (UK) ist seit neun Jahren in der Produktdesignberatung tätig. Er ist Konstrukteur und Associate Director bei *therefore*, wo er für den technischen Aufbau langfristiger Forschungs- und Entwicklungsprojekte zuständig ist und extensive Forschung zur Benutzerfreundlichkeit betrieben hat. Eines seiner letzten Projekte war *bednest*, ein Kinderbett, das ein sicheres Schlafen bei den Eltern ermöglicht.

PRIX ARS ELECTRONICA COLLIDE@CERN RESIDENCY AWARD

Prix Ars Electronica Collide@CERN Residency Award

Michael Doser, Horst Hörtner, Ariane Koek, Gerfried Stocker

CERN's latest experiment in colliding the minds of scientists with the imagination of artists opened in 2011 with the Prix Ars Electronica Collide@CERN prize in digital arts. This was the first prize to be announced as part of the new Collide@CERN three-year artists' residency program initiated by the world's largest particle physics laboratory, located outside Geneva, Switzerland.

This international competition to win a funded residency at CERN and Ars Electronica Futurelab, marks the three-year science/arts cultural partnership and creative collaboration between CERN and Ars Electronica—which began with CERN's cooperation with *ORIGIN—how it all begins* the Ars Electronica festival, in September 2011.

Artists in any domain who work with digital media as means of creation and/or production, and who will be truly inspired by CERN and its science, are invited to submit their projects to the Prix Ars Electronica Collide@CERN. They have to show their desire to engage with the ideas and/or technology of particle physics or with CERN as a place of scientific collaboration, using them as springboards for the imagination that dare to go beyond the paradigm. They may be choreographers, performers, visual artists, filmmakers or composers—what they all have in common is that they use digital media as the means of making their work and/or the way of presenting it. The award includes prize money and a fully funded residency in two parts—with an initial two months at CERN with a CERN scientist as a dedicated inspiration partner. The second part is a month with the Futurelab team and mentor at Ars Electronica Linz, with whom the winner will develop an idea inspired by the CERN residency.

The first winner in 2011 was the German visual artist Julius von Bismarck, and the jury also awarded three honorary mentions. This first competition attracted 395 entries from over 40 countries around the world.

In November 2012, following the second Prix Ars Electronica Collide@CERN open call, the award was

Das jüngste Experiment des CERN, die Kollision von Wissenschaft und Kunst, startete 2011 mit dem Prix Ars Electronica Collide@CERN für digitale Kunst. Damals wurde im Rahmen des neuen dreijährigen Residency-Programms für Künstler Collide@CERN, das vom größten Teilchenphysiklabor der Welt in der Nähe von Genf initiiert wurde, zum ersten Mal ein Preis vergeben.

Der internationale Wettbewerb um eine finanzierte Residency am CERN und im Ars Electronica Futurelab steht im Zeichen der dreijährigen kulturellen Partnerschaft von Wissenschaft und Kunst und der kreativen Zusammenarbeit zwischen CERN und Ars Electronica, die mit der Mitwirkung des CERN beim Ars Electronica Festival *ORIGIN – wie alles beginnt* im September 2011 startete.

Künstler aller Disziplinen, die in der Produktion und/oder Entwicklung ihres Projekts digitale Medien verwenden und sich vom CERN und seiner wissenschaftlichen Arbeit wirklich inspiriert fühlen, sind aufgefordert, ihre Projekte für den Prix Ars Electronica Collide@CERN einzureichen. Sie müssen vermitteln, dass sie sich mit den Ideen und/oder der Technologie der Teilchenphysik oder mit dem CERN als Zentrum wissenschaftlicher Zusammenarbeit auseinandersetzen möchten und es als Plattform nutzen wollen, die die Fantasie beflügelt und ermutigt, über Paradigmen hinauszugehen. Ob Choreografen, Performer, bildende Künstler, Filmemacher oder Komponisten – allen Teilnehmern gemeinsam ist, dass sie ihre Arbeiten mit digitalen Medien kreieren und/oder präsentieren. Der Preis beinhaltet ein Preisgeld und eine zur Gänze finanzierte Residency in zwei Teilen. Diese besteht einerseits aus einem zweimonatigen Aufenthalt am CERN, wo dem Preisträger ein dort tätiger Wissenschaftler als Inspirationspartner zur Seite steht, und andererseits einem einmonatigen Aufenthalt bei Ars Electronica in Linz. Dort werden die GewinnerInnen gemeinsam mit dem Team des Ars Electronica Futurelab und einem Mentor die Idee weiterentwickeln, zu der er durch seinen Aufenthalt am CERN inspiriert wurde.

Der erste Preisträger im Jahr 2011 war der bildende Künstler Julius von Bismarck aus Deutschland, die Jury vergab außerdem drei Anerkennungen. Bei diesem ersten Wettbewerb wurden 395 Beiträge aus mehr als 40 Ländern aus der ganzen Welt eingereicht.

Nach der öffentlichen Ausschreibung des zweiten Prix Ars Electronica Collide@CERN wurde der Preis im November 2012 dem 65-jährigen amerikanischen Klangkünstler Bill Fontana verliehen. Die mexikanische Künstlerin Ale de la Puente erhielt eine Anerkennung.
Die Jury begutachtete Einreichungen aus einer Rekordanzahl von 49 Ländern weltweit, darunter erstmals Beiträge aus Nepal, Uruguay, Paraguay und Jordanien, was verdeutlicht, dass der Peis zunehmend internationale Aufmerksamkeit genießt. Wie im Vorjahr kamen die Einreichungen aus unterschiedlichen künstlerischen Bereichen – von Medienkunst, Bildhauerei und Malerei über Choreografie, Szenografie, Musik, Literatur bis hin zur Folkmusik.

MUT ZUR BESCHEIDENHEIT

Bill Fontana ist ein für seine wegweisenden Experimente in der Klangkunst international renommierter Künstler, der bereits in führenden Kunstinstitutionen der Welt, etwa der Tate Modern und dem Whitney Museum of American Art, zu Gast war. Er hat einige ikonische Gebäude in Klangskulpturen verwandelt – etwa den Arc de Triomphe in Paris, die Golden Gate Bridge in San Francisco und den Big Ben in London. Er studierte bei dem Komponisten John Cage und gilt als einer der Pioniere der Klangkunst.
Dass ein international etablierter Künstler wie Bill Fontana sich für den Prix Ars Electronica Collide@CERN bewirbt, zeugt von einem Mut und einer Bescheidenheit, die die Jury auf Anhieb beeindruckten. Diese Eigenschaften kamen auch deutlich in dem Präsentationsvideo zum Ausdruck, das Bill Fontana einreichte: „Als Künstler suche ich immer nach neuen Situationen, um meinen Horizont zu erweitern, diese Doppel-Residency erschien mir aufgrund der immensen Lernmöglichkeiten, die sie bietet, unwiderstehlich."
Bill Fontana demonstrierte der Jury in seinem Präsentationsvideo seine Offenheit für Neues sowie sein großes Interesse, mehr über die Teilchenphysik zu lernen und dadurch neue Dimensionen für seine Arbeit zu eröffnen. Er brachte auch deutlich seinen Wunsch zum

made to the 65 year-old American sound sculptor, Bill Fontana. The jury also awarded an honorary mention to the Mexican artist Ale de la Puente.
The jury met to assess entries from a record 49 countries, including new entries from Nepal, Uruguay, Paraguay and Jordan, showing how the award is increasingly attracting international attention. As in the previous year, entries came from very diverse artistic domains—ranging from media art, sculpture and painting, to choreography, scenography, music, literature and even folk music.

AUDACIOUS HUMILITY

Bill Fontana is an artist with an international reputation for his pioneering experiments in sound-art work, which has been featured in some of the world's leading arts institutions, such as the Tate Modern and the Whitney Museum of American Art. He has also turned some of the world's most iconic structures into sound sculptures—the Arc de Triomphe in Paris, the Golden Gate Bridge in San Francisco and Big Ben in London. He is known as one of the founding fathers of sound art and studied under the composer John Cage.
The audacity and humility of an international artist of Bill Fontana's reputation entering the Prix Ars Electronica Collide@CERN open call was a quality which first struck the jury when making the award. This audacious humility was clearly expressed in Bill Fontana's personal video testimony to jury: "As an artist I am always looking for situations to expand my horizons and this joint residency presents me with a tremendous learning opportunity, so it was irresistible."
In his video Bill demonstrated to the jury an eagerness and openness to learn about particle physics and to discover the new dimensions this might bring to his work. He also clearly detailed his wish to engage with the Large Hadron Collider (LHC)—one of the largest manmade machines in the world—by creating a series of acoustic experiments

and encounters. As he also clearly stated: "I may be 65, but I feel that I am still at the beginning of my artistic career and I enjoy testing myself with new challenges."
After they had made the award, the jury was also astonished to discover that, like the 2011 prize-winner Julius von Bismarck, Bill as a child was really interested in science and had considered it as a career. Instead, he began his career as a composer, became an artist in sound rather than a composer, being inspired to engage with sound by the late great John Cage, who showed him that listening is as creative as composing.

ACOUSTIC TIME TRAVEL

The working title of the sound sculpture Bill is developing at CERN during his residency and which he proposed in his application is *acoustic time travel*—showing how sound crosses time and space. As he says in his work at CERN, "I am in a sense mimicking the protocol of a scientific experiment. I plan to design a series of short soundbursts to test the sonic properties of various materials."
Bill began his residency by exploring the underground tunnels at CERN, playing back his recordings by using exciters and accelerometers mounted on the machinery and structures to explore how these sounds travel through the spaces. But his experiments at CERN began even before his residency started, when Bill came for his four-day induction visit in January 2013, designed to inspire his imagination before July.

SOUNDS LIKE CERN

In January 2013, Bill Fontana visited CERN with his mentor, Horst Hörtner from the Ars Electronica Futurelab, for his four-day induction visit specially designed and tailor-made for Bill's interests by Ariane Koek, the creator of the Collide@CERN

Ausdruck, sich mit dem Large Hadron Collider (LHC, Großer Hadronen-Speicherring), dem größten bislang gebauten Teilchenbeschleuniger der Welt, zu beschäftigen und eine Reihe akustischer Experimente und Untersuchungen im LHC durchzuführen. Auch für seine Motivation fand er klare Worte: „Ich bin zwar 65, habe aber das Gefühl, dass ich noch immer am Anfang meiner künstlerischen Laufbahn stehe, und genieße es, mich neuen Herausforderungen zu stellen und mich in neuen Zusammenhängen zu beweisen."
Wie auch bei Julius von Bismarck, der den Preis 2011 gewann, entdeckte die Jury nach der Preisvergabe mit Erstaunen, dass Bill Fontana bereits als Kind ein ausgeprägtes Interesse an Wissenschaft hatte und sogar eine Laufbahn als Wissenschaftler ins Auge gefasst hatte. Er entschied sich dann aber für eine Laufbahn als Komponist bzw. wurde – unter dem Einfluss des großartigen späten John Cage, der ihm offenbarte, dass Zuhören so kreativ ist wie Komponieren – Klangkünstler.

AKUSTISCHE ZEITREISE

Der Arbeitstitel der Klangskulptur, die Bill Fontana während seiner Residency am CERN entwickeln wird, lautet seiner Einreichung zufolge *Akustische Zeitreise* und bringt zum Ausdruck, dass Klang sich durch Zeit und Raum bewegt. Wie er bei seiner Arbeit am CERN erläuterte: „Ich ahme in einer gewissen Weise das Versuchsprotokoll eines wissenschaftlichen Experiments nach. Ich plane eine Reihe kurzer eruptiver Klangausbrüche, um die klanglichen Eigenschaften verschiedener Materialien auszuloten."
Bill begann seine Residency mit einer Erkundung der unterirdischen Tunnel am CERN, indem er seine Aufzeichnungen mittels Schwingungserregern und Körperschallmessern wiedergab, die auf der Anlage montiert waren, um zu untersuchen, wie sich diese Klänge durch die Räume fortpflanzen. Seine Experimente am CERN begannen sogar schon vor Beginn seiner Residency, bei seinem viertägigen Einführungsbesuch im Januar 2013, der dazu gedacht war, ihm Anregungen für den Aufenthalt im Juli mitzugeben.

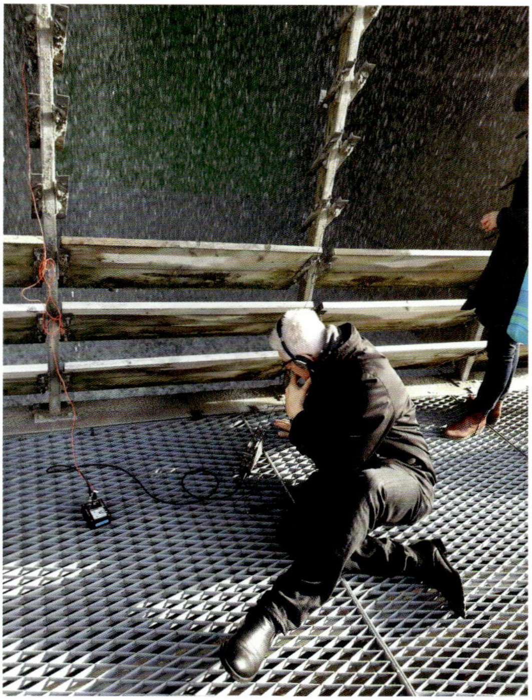

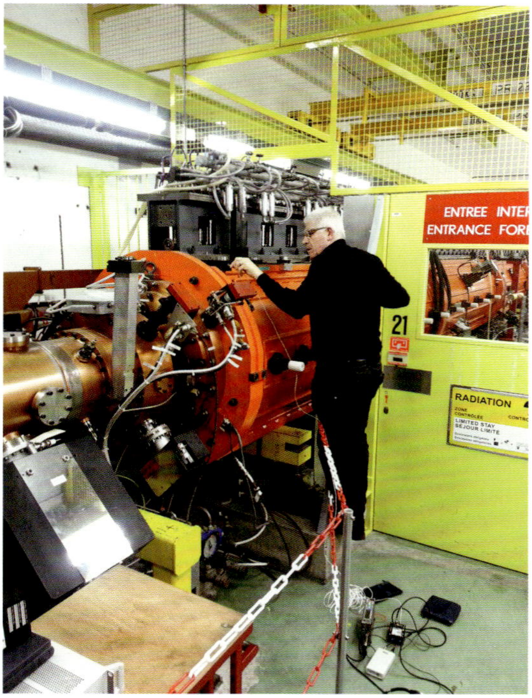

KLINGT NACH CERN

Im Januar 2013 besuchte Bill Fontana mit seinem Mentor Horst Hörtner vom Ars Electronica Futurelab das CERN zu einem viertägigen Einführungsbesuch, der von der Initiatorin des Collide@CERN-Programms Ariane Koek organisiert und speziell auf Bills Interessen zugeschnitten war. In diesen Tagen hatte Bill Fontana Gelegenheit, in einer Reihe von Seminaren und Treffen mit führenden Physikern des CERN die Welt der Teilchenphysik und auch die verschiedenen Räumlichkeiten des Labors kennenzulernen. Außerdem stellte ihm Ariane Koek seinen wissenschaftlichen Inspirationspartner am CERN vor, den Kosmologen und Marie Curie Intra European Fellow Subodh Patil, der in der Theorie-Abteilung des CERN tätig ist.

programs. During this time, Bill explored the ideas of particle physics with a series of one-to-one seminars and meetings with leading CERN physicists as well as exploring the different spaces of the laboratory. In this period, Ariane also matched Bill with his CERN science-inspiration partner, the cosmologist and Marie Curie Intra European Fellow Subodh Patil, who works in the CERN theory department.

Bill started making recordings almost immediately on his four-day visit, which also covered ten different locations on the vast CERN site. One of the first places he visited was the CERN proton source, the "magic bottle" where the particles begin their journey around the 27km circuit to just under the speed of light. He recorded the sounds of the magnets propelling the protons from the "bottle", which produces a rhythmic pulse every 1.2 seconds. This could be called the heartbeat of the LHC. The recordings were made using accelerometers mounted on the machines holding the magnets to pick up the sounds inside them. On the train to Paris at the end of his induction visit—even before his residency officially began—Bill was so inspired that he mixed a 24-track audio recording to create a new visual sound art work from the different sounds across the CERN site and the sounds of the machines while the LHC was running.

Bill said of his induction experience: "The visit to CERN was inspiring and renewing. It put me back in touch with myself. Being at CERN and having these conversations and then intensely listening and recording was like going on a spiritual retreat. I hope I can carry this inspiration forward to the Eiffel Tower."

Bill Fontana began his residency at CERN in July and is following this with his residency with the transdisciplinary team of the Ars Electronica Futurelab in Linz.

SCULPTING WITH SOUND

Bill Fontana

I have worked for the past 30 years creating installations that use sound as a sculptural medium to interact with and transform our perceptions of visual and architectural settings. These have been installed in public spaces and museums around the world including San Francisco, New York, Paris, London, Berlin, Venice, Sydney and Tokyo.

My sound sculptures use the human and/or natural environment as a living source of musical information. I am assuming that at any given moment there will be something meaningful to hear and that music, in the sense of coherent sound patterns, is a process that is going on constantly. My methodology has been to create networks of

Nahezu sofort begann Fontana bei seinem viertägigen Aufenthalt, in dessen Verlauf er auch zehn unterschiedliche Bereiche des riesigen CERN-Geländes in Augenschein nehmen konnte, Aufnahmen zu machen. Einer der ersten Orte, die er besuchte, war die Protonenquelle des CERN, die magische „Flasche", in der die 21 Kilometer lange Reise der Teilchen mit nahezu Lichtgeschwindigkeit beginnt. Er nahm die Klänge der Magneten auf, die die Protonen aus der „Flasche" feuern, wodurch alle 1,2 Sekunden ein rhythmisches Pulsieren entsteht. Man könnte es den Herzschlag des LHC nennen. Die Aufnahmen wurden mithilfe von Körperschallmessern gemacht, die auf den Halterungen für die Magnete angebracht sind, um die Klänge darin aufzunehmen. Fontana war von diesem Aufenthalt so inspiriert, dass er – noch vor dem offiziellen Beginn seiner Residency – während seiner Rückreise, im Zug nach Paris, aus den verschiedenen Klängen am CERN und dem Sound der Maschinen bei Betrieb des LHC eine 24-Kanaltonaufnahme für eine neue visuelle Klangkunstarbeit mixte.

Bill Fontana über diesen Aufenthalt: „Der Besuch am CERN war inspirierend und erneuernd. Er hat mich wieder mit mir selbst in Berührung gebracht. Am CERN zu sein, interessante Gespräche zu führen und dann der Prozess des intensiven Zuhörens und Aufnehmens waren wie ein Besuch in einem spirituellen Zentrum. Ich hoffe, diese Inspiration begleitet mich bis zum Eiffelturm."

Bill Fontana trat seine Residency am CERN im Juli an, im Anschluss folgte der Aufenthalt beim transdisziplinären Team des Ars Electronica Futurelab in Linz.

KLANG ALS SKULPTURALES MEDIUM

Bill Fontana

„Ich habe mich in meiner Arbeit in den letzten dreißig Jahren damit beschäftig, Installationen zu machen, die Klang als skulpturales Medium verwenden, um mit visuellen Elementen und architektonischen Räumen zu interagieren und die Wahrnehmung derselben zu verändern. Die Klangskulpturen wurden im öffentlichen Raum und in Museen der ganzen Welt, u.a. in San Francisco, New

York, Paris, London, Berlin, Venedig, Sydney und Tokio, installiert.
Meine Klangskulpturen verwenden den menschlichen Lebensraum und/oder das natürliche Umfeld als lebendige Ressource für musikalische Informationen. Ich gehe davon aus, dass es in jedem Augenblick Bedeutungsvolles zu hören gibt und dass Musik im Sinne kohärenter Klangmuster ein Prozess ist, der ständig stattfindet. Methodisch ging ich so vor, dass ich in einem Netzwerk simultane Hörplätze verband, die akustische Daten in Echtzeit in eine allgemeine Hörzone (Standort der Skulptur) übertragen. Seit 1976 nenne ich diese Arbeiten *sound sculptures*.
Ich habe viele Werke geschaffen, die die Idee von Live-Hörnetzwerken ausloten. Dabei verwende ich immer eine hybride Mischung von Übertragungstechnologien, die zahlreiche Klangpunkte mit einem zentralen Empfangspunkt in Verbindung setzen. Wesentlich bei diesem Prozess sind die konzeptuellen Zusammenhänge, die die Beziehungen zwischen den ausgewählten Hörplätzen und den standortspezifischen Qualitäten des Empfangspunkts (Standort der Skulptur) bestimmen. Zu den konzeptuellen Strategien zählten u.a. das akustische Gedächtnis, die totale Verwandlung des Sichtbaren (Retinalen) durch das Unsichtbare (Klang), zu hören soweit man sehen kann, die Beziehung von Klanggeschwindigkeit und Lichtgeschwindigkeit sowie die Dekonstruktion unserer Zeitwahrnehmung.
Von den späten 90ern bis heute habe ich in meinen Projekten die hybriden Hörtechnologien von akustischen Mikrofonen, Unterwassersensoren (Hydrophone) und Struktur-/Materialsensoren (Geschwindigkeits- bzw. Körperschallmesser) erforscht. Ich entwickle und realisiere auch Projekte, bei denen ich Zugang zu seismischen Netzwerken habe, um Meereswellen, deren Schallenergie sich unterirdisch über weite Distanzen fortpflanzt, akustisch zu erfassen.[1]

simultaneous listening points that relay real-time acoustic data to a common listening zone (sculpture site). Since 1976 I have called these works sound sculptures.
I have produced a large number of works that explore the idea of creating live listening networks. These all use a hybrid mix of transmission technologies that connect multiple sound retrieval points to a central reception point. What is significant in this process are the conceptual links determining the relationships between the selected listening points and the site-specific qualities of the reception point (sculpture site). Some conceptual strategies have been acoustic memory, the total transformation of the visible (retinal) by the invisible (sound), hearing as far as one can see, the relationship of the speed of sound to the speed of light, and the deconstruction of our perception of time.
From the late 90s until the present, my projects have explored hybrid listening technologies of acoustic microphones, underwater sensors (hydrophones) and structural/material sensors (accelerometers). I have also realized and am developing projects that access live seismic networks to explore the sound energy of ocean waves, traveling long distances underground.[1]

1 *http://www.resoundings.org/Pages/artists_statement.htm*, version of 27. 05. 2013

JURY

Computer Animation / Film / VFX

Tomek Bagiński, Chris Bregler, Suzanne Buchan, David O'Reilly, Anezka Sebek

Digital Musics & Sound Art

Ludger Brümmer, Electric Indigo, Emre Erkal, Jeff Mills, Pamela Z

Hybrid Art

Andrea Grover, Jens Hauser, Jurij Krpan, Arthur I. Miller, Karin Ohlenschläger

Interactive Art

José Luis de Vicente, Mariano Sardón, Olga Shishko, Jer Thorp, Maholo Uchida

Digital Communities

Ian Banerjee, Leila Nachawati, Marcus Neustetter, Bruce Sterling, Lei Yang

u19 – CREATE YOUR WORLD

Sirikit Amann, Benjamin Brockhaus, Gerhard Funk, Conny Lee, Karl Markovics

[the next idea] voestalpine Art and Technology Grant

Michael Doser, Horst Hörtner, Ela Kagel, Gustav Pomberger, Michael Sterrer-Ebenführer

Prix Ars Electronica Collide@CERN Residency Award

Michael Doser, Ariane Koek, Horst Hörtner, Gerfried Stocker

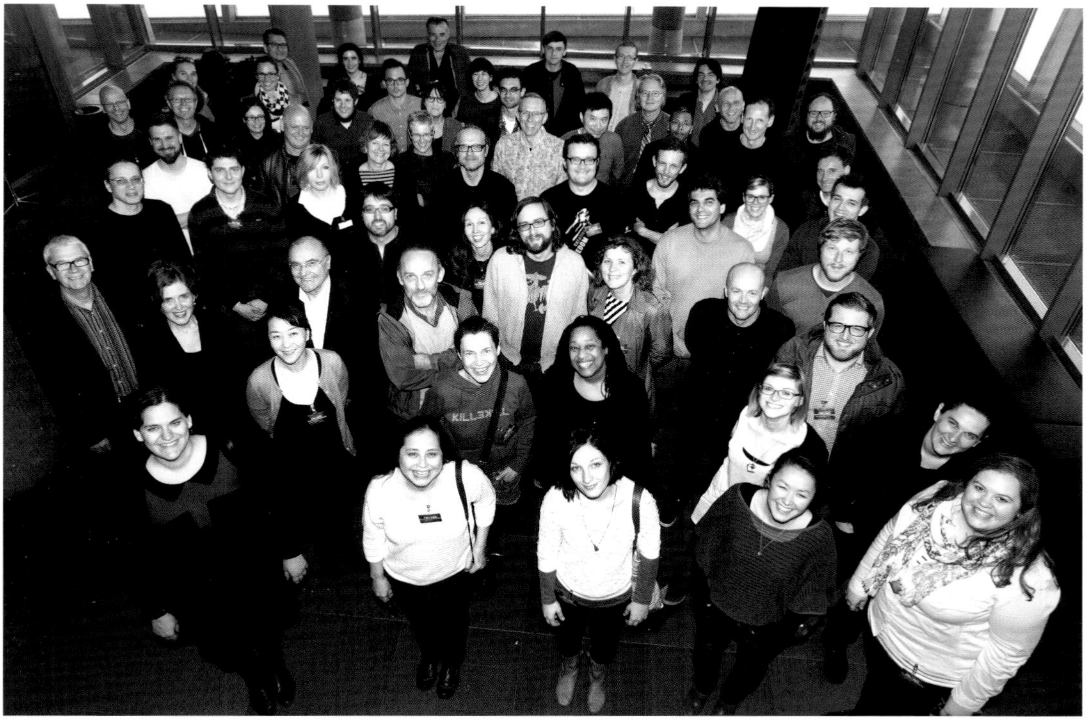

COMPUTER ANIMATION / FILM / VFX

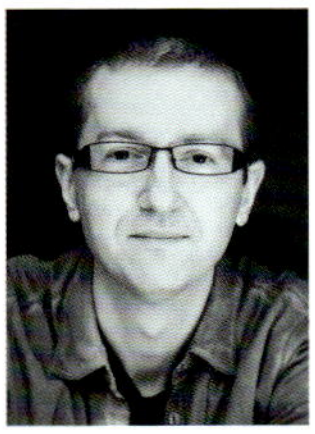

Tomek Bagiński (PL) joined Platige Image studio in 1997. Since then he has directed many game cinematics, animated shorts, and worked on multiple artistic projects. He is known and appreciated as the director of *The Cathedral*, *Fallen Art*, and *The Kinematograph*. His many awards for films include the Academy Award nomination, Best of Show award at Siggraph and a Bafta Award. Bagiński directed the animated set design for the Seven Gates of Jerusalem concert, which was nominated for an Emmy Award.

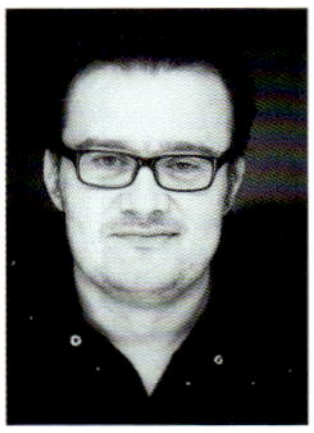

Chris Bregler (DE/US) is a professor of computer science at New York University's Courant Institute, director of the NYU Movement Lab, and CEO of ManhattanMocap, LLC. He has been on the faculty at Stanford University and worked for several companies, including Hewlett Packard, Interval, Disney Feature Animation, and LucasFilm's ILM. He was the chair for the Siggraph Electronic Theater and Animation Festival. He was the executive producer of Squidball.net, which holds several world records in the Motion Capture Society, and is the lead developer of ILM's Multitrack system, which has been used in many feature films. He has been named Stanford Joyce Faculty Fellow, Terman Fellow, and Sloan Research Fellow.

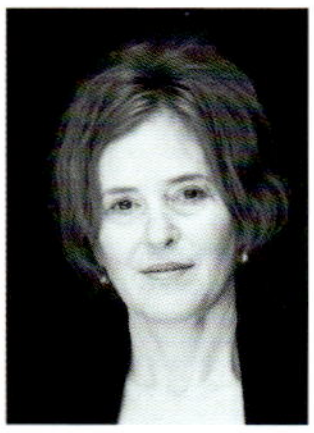

Suzanne Buchan (CH/UK) is professor of animation aesthetics at Middlesex University, London. She gained her PhD at the University of Zurich and was a founding member and co-director (1994-2003) of the Fantoche International Animation Film Festival (CH). She teaches, curates and advises internationally in her research field of a wide concept of history, theory and aesthetics of animation outside commercial canons. Books include *Pervasive Animation: an AFI Reader* (2013) and *The Quay Brothers: Into A Metaphysical Playroom* (2011). She is the founding editor of *Animation: An Interdisciplinary Journal* (Sage Journals). *adri.mdx.ac.uk.contentcurator.net/buchan-prof-suzanneanm.sagepub.com*

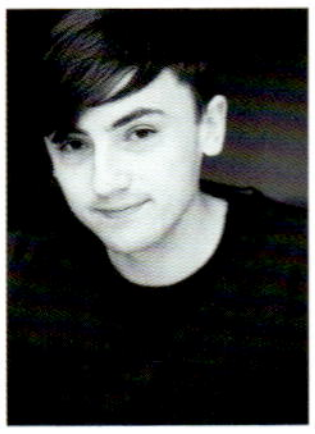

David O'Reilly (IE/US). David O'Reilly is David O'Reilly. *www.davidoreilly.com*

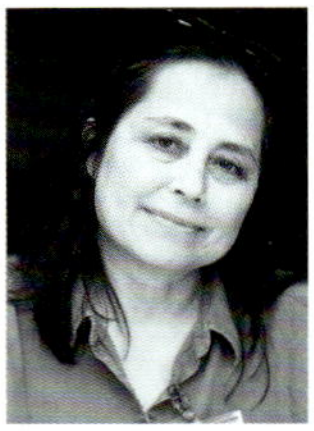

Anezka Sebek (US) has taught full time at Parsons in the MFA design and technology program since 1999 (program director from 2006 to 2010). She designs curricula in the BFA/MFA traditional, computer animation, and motion graphics courses as well as teaching in the BFA/MFA in design and technology studio courses. Before turning to teaching, her extensive career in the film industry included projects for television, advertising, documentaries and feature films for companies such as Kleiser-Walczak, R/Greenberg Associates, HBO, and Curious Pictures. She was best known as a visual-effects and computer-animation producer for technologically complex projects that combined live-action with digital effects.

DIGITAL MUSICS & SOUND ART

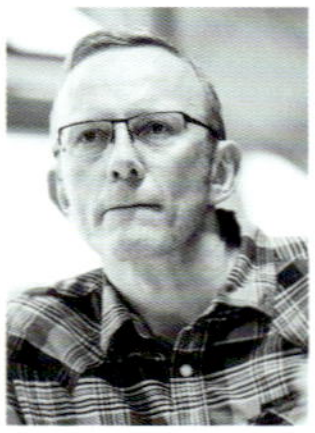

Ludger Brümmer (DE) studied composition at the Folkwang University of the Arts in Essen, Germany. Beginning in 2000, he was a research fellow at Kingston University in London and from April 2002 professor of composition at the Sonic Art Research Centre in Belfast. Since April 2003, he has been chairman of the Department of Music and Acoustics at the Center for Art and Media Karlsruhe. In 2009, he was elected to Germany's Academy of the Arts.

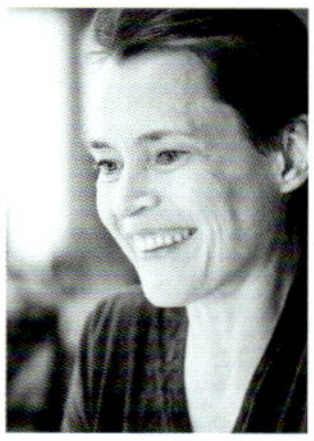

Electric Indigo (AT). DJ, composer and musician since 1989, has performed in 35 countries across the northern hemisphere. Clarity of vision as well as depth are characteristic of her music. As a composer and musician, she emphasizes the spatial-temporal placement of subtly textured sounds. She received the Outstanding Artist Award Musik 2012 for electronic and computer music and the 2013 national grant for composition from the Austrian Ministry for Education, the Arts and Culture. indigo-inc.at/

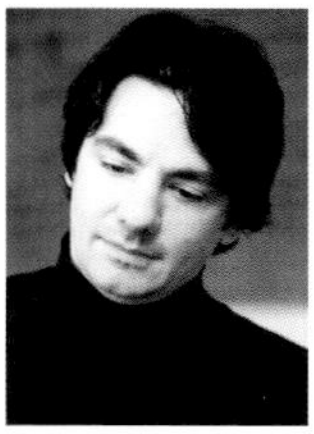

Emre Erkal (TR) is a practicing architect and a sound artist. After his electronics engineering degree from METU, he worked on research projects on computer graphics and cognitive science. He received his professional degree in architecture from Harvard Graduate School of Design, where he participated in research projects at MIT Media Lab. Venues where his sound art installations have been featured include the 8th Istanbul Biennial, ZKM in Karlsruhe, the Istanbul Architecture Festival, Mediamatic in Amsterdam, De Singel Conservatory in Antwerp, and NAiM. He has taught at several universities, including Bilkent University, Istanbul Technical University and Istanbul Bilgi University on sound and space, architecture and urbanism. Erkal is also co-founder of Nomad, an initiative for digital arts and culture in Istanbul.

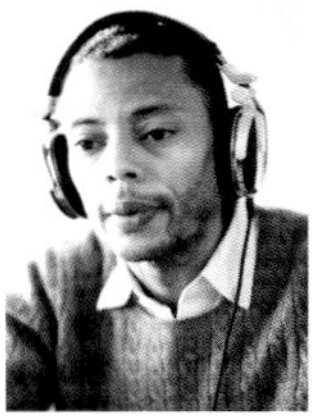

Jeff Mills (US) has been active in the electronic music industry by operating his own record label, Axis, and performing all over the world, an average 100 events a year. His specialty is conceptual music, mostly inspired by space and time travel. He also scores films such as *Metropolis, Woman in the Moon* by Fritz Lang, *Oktober* by Sergei Eisenstein as well as creating musical installations for museums such as the Museum Quai Branly, Centre Pompidou and Fondation Cartier, which led to him receiving the title of Chevalier des Art et des Lettres from French Government in 2007.

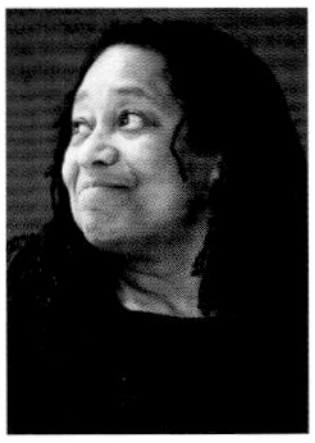

Pamela Z (US) is a composer/performer and media artist who makes works combining a wide range of vocal techniques with electronic processing, samples, video and gesture activated Midi controllers. She has toured throughout the US, Europe and Japan in concerts and festivals. She has also composed scores for dance, film and new music chamber ensembles, including the Kronos Quartet. Her installations have been presented in exhibitions in the US, Europe and Africa. Her awards include a Guggenheim Fellowship, Creative Capital, CalArts Alpert Award, and the NEA/JUSFC Fellowship. *www.pamelaz.com*

HYBRID ART

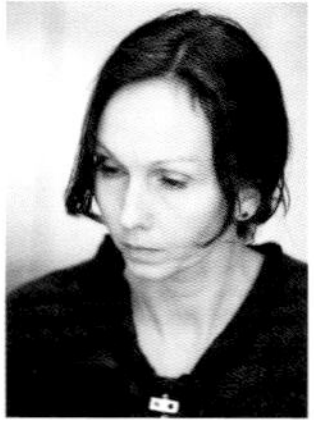

Andrea Grover (US) is the curator of special projects at the Parrish Art Museum, Water Mill, NY. From 1998–2008, she was director of Houston's Aurora Picture Show. In 2010, she was awarded a Warhol Curatorial Fellowship, hosted by the Studio for Creative Inquiry and Miller Gallery at Carnegie Mellon University, Pittsburgh, PA. The outcome of that fellowship is the 2011 publication, *New Art / Science Affinities*, co-authored with Claire Evans, Régine Debatty, Pablo Garcia and Thumb. The corresponding exhibition, Intimate Science, opened at the Miller Gallery in January 2012 and is touring the US.

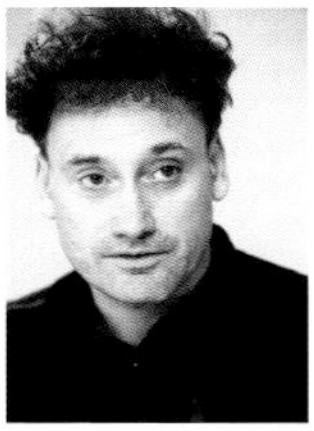

Jens Hauser (DE/FR) is a Paris-based curator, author and arts and culture critic. With a background in media studies and science journalism, he focuses on the interactions between art and technology, as well as on trans-genre and contextual aesthetics. He has curated exhibitions such as L'Art Biotech (Nantes, 2003), Still, Living (Perth, 2007), SK-interfaces (Liverpool, 2008/Luxembourg, 2009), the Article Biennale (Stavanger, 2008), Transbiotics (Riga 2010), Synth-ethic (Vienna, 2011) and Fingerprints... (Berlin, 2011/Munich, 2012). Hauser organizes interdisciplinary conferences and guest lectures at universities and international art academies.

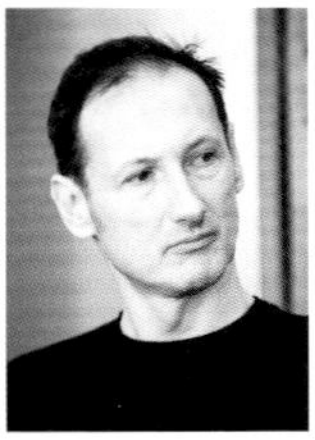

Jurij Krpan (SI) is artistic director of the Kapelica Gallery–Gallery for Contemporary Investigative Arts, Ljubljana, which was established in 1995. He is also art director of BioTehna, established in 2012. As curator he has participated in domestic and international festivals (organization and artistic management of the Slovenian pavilion at the 50th Venice Biennale in 2003, conceptual gallery Cosinus BRX at the European Commission building in Brussels 2006–2010: 5th Triennial of Contemporary Investigative Arts 2006 at the Museum of Modern Art, Ljubljana). He lectures on the artistic profile and curatorial practice of the Kapelica Gallery in Slovenia as well as abroad.

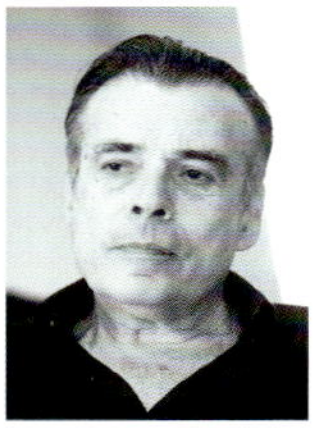

Arthur I. Miller (UK) is emeritus professor of history and philosophy of science at University College London. He is fascinated by the nature of creativity in art and in science—similarities and differences. His books include: *Jung, Pauli, and the Pursuit of a Scientific Obsession*, *Insights of Genius*, and *Einstein, Picasso*, nominated for a Pulitzer Prize. His forthcoming book is *The New Avant-Garde: Dispatches from the Edge of Science and Art*. *www.arthurimiller.com*

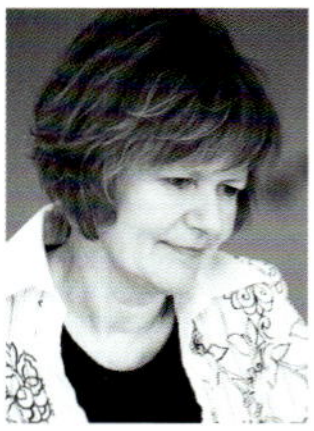

Karin Ohlenschläger (DE/ES) has been a critic and exhibition curator specializing in contemporary art and new media since 1985. She co-founded and co-directed MediaLab Madrid (2002-2006). She has directed various international initiatives, and her works have been shown worldwide. Karin Ohlenschläger teaches art, science and technology at the European University of Madrid and is the chairwoman of the institute of Contemporary Art (IAC).

INTERACTIVE ART

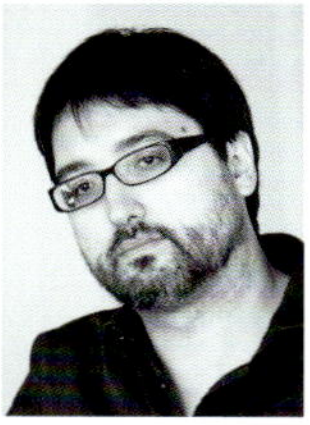

José Luis de Vicente (ES) is a cultural researcher, curator and writer working around the edges of new media, digital creativity and innovation in design and culture. He is the director of the Visualizar program on information visualization at Medialab Prado, Madrid, and one of the founders of Zzzinc, a cultural innovation consultancy in Barcelona. He has previously worked as curator for new media festivals such as Sónar, ArtFutura and OFFF. He teaches, lectures, and writes about new media in various Spanish organizations.

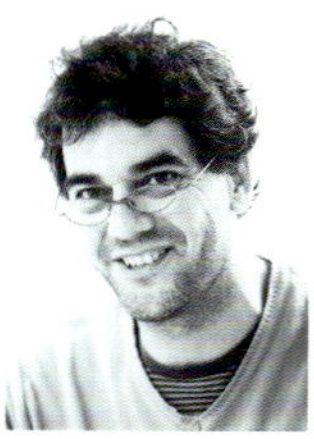

Mariano Sardón (AR) is professor and chair of the electronic art degree at the Universidad Nacional de 3 de Febrero. He is researcher in art and neuroscience at the same university together with the Laboratory of Integrative Neuroscience at the University of Buenos Aires. He is the academic advisor of the Interactive Art Program at Espacio Fundación Telefónica Argentina. He was consultant for the Daniel Langlois Foundation. He studied physics at the University of Buenos Aires and was a visiting scholar at UCLA. *www.marianosardon.com.ar*

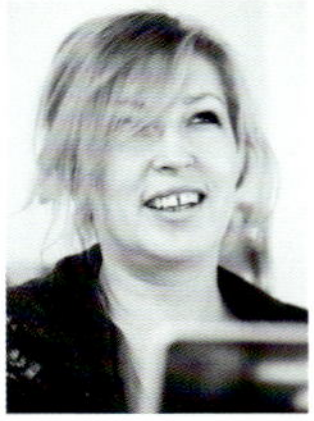

Olga Shishko (RU) is a curator and researcher of media culture. Founder (since 2000) and director (since 2006) of the Center of Culture and Art MediaArtLab, an integrated research within contemporary art involving media technologies. Her research activities focus on different aspects of contemporary media art. She has curated numerous international events, festivals and exhibitions and she is editor of catalogs, anthologies and books on contemporary media art issues published in Russia. *www.mediaartlab.ru*

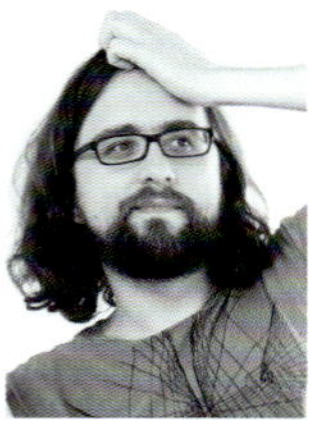

Jer Thorp (CA/US) is an artist and educator. Coming from a background in genetics, his digital art practice explores the multifaceted boundaries between science, data, art, and culture. Thorp's software-based work has been exhibited worldwide, including in the Museum of Modern Art in Manhattan. Jer is an adjunct professor in New York University's ITP program and a co-founder of the Office for Creative Research. From 2010 to 2012 Jer was the Data Artist in Residence at the *New York Times*. *http://o-c-r.org*

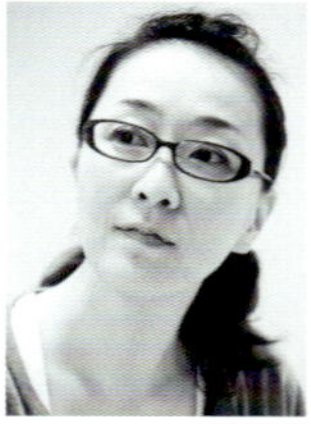

Maholo Uchida (JP) is a curator and exhibition development division manager of the Miraikan (National Museum of Emerging Science and Technology) in Tokyo, Japan. She started her career as a curator of new media art and design, producing several national and international exhibitions. She has developed a new style of science museum, where activities and exhibitions strongly orientated towards art, design, game, manga and other popular culture. She is a director of the Tsunagari Project, which is the symbol exhibition at the Miraikan and includes Geo-Cosmos—a six-meter-diameter interactive globe display.

DIGITAL COMMUNITIES

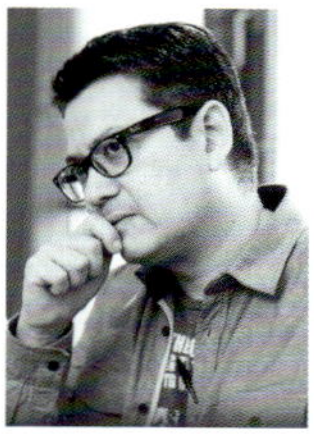

Ian Banerjee (IN/AT) is an architect, urban planner and educational researcher living in Vienna. He worked for several years for the Austrian Broadcasting Corporation (ORF) and the German satellite TV company 3Sat as a consultant on documentaries on urban innovations. Going back to academia, he joined the Centre of Sociology (ISRA) at the Vienna University of Technology as an assistant professor. Here he started researching radical innovations taking place in the educational sector—especially their virtual aspects. He is currently writing a book on emerging educational spaces.

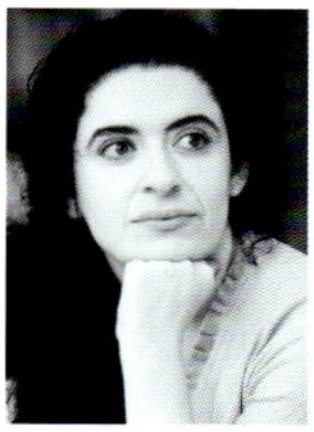

Leila Nachawati (ES) is a Spanish-Syrian communication strategist and human-rights activist. She is a professor of communications at Carlos III University in Madrid, where she has also started her PhD on new media and freedom of expression under authoritarian regimes. She contributes to several projects and online media, such as Global Voices Online, Global Voices Advocacy, Eldiario.es and Al-Jazeera English. She has degrees in English studies, Arabic studies, and a master's degree in international cooperation. *@leila_na*

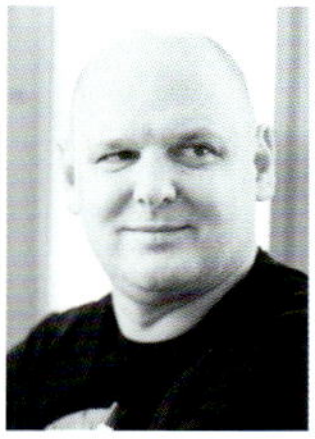

Marcus Neustetter (AT/ZA) is a Johannesburg-based artist, cultural activist and producer, who reflects critically and playfully on his context through his art and collaborative projects. Working in a multi-disciplinary approach in the fields of art, industry, science and technology, he has been finding context-specific strategies for working with artists and alternative audiences in developing his own work and platforms. He has been producing and exhibiting art internationally for the past 15 years *(www.marcusneustetter.com)* and, in partnership with Stephen Hobbs, has been active with the Trinity Session and in their collaborative capacity as Hobbs/Neustetter (*www.onair.co.za)*.

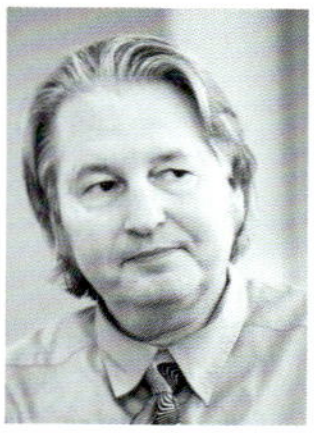

Bruce Sterling (US), an author, journalist editor, and critic, is best known for his ten science-fiction novels. He also writes short stories, book reviews, design criticism, opinion columns and introductions for books. His non-fiction works include *The Hacker Crackdown: Law and Disorder on the Electronic frontier* (1992), *Tomorrow Now: Envisioning the Next Fifty Years* (2003), and *Shaping Things* (2005). He is a contributing editor for *Wired* magazine and writes a weblog. During 2005, he was the "Visionary in Residence" at the Art Center College of Design in Pasadena. In 2011 he returned to Art Center as "Visionary in Residence" to run a special project on augmented reality.

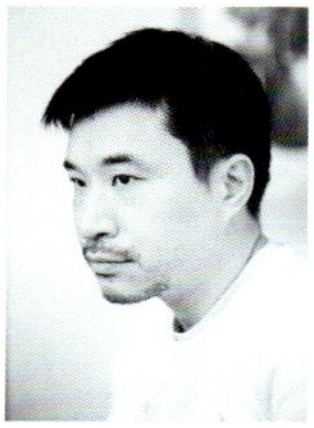

Lei Yang (CN) is the deputy director and chief curator at CMoDA (China Millennium Monument Museum of Digital Arts), Beijing. He is involved in exploring digital engagement to transform social life in China with the latest focus on the smart city / smart citizen movement. He founded the CMoDA CoINNO Lab on collaborative innovation on digital art and design in 2012. He is the founder, curator and producer of the Notch Festival on live media and social innovation. He founded Radio Take10, a collective internet radio co-curation project on net label and demo culture.

u19 – CREATE YOUR WORLD

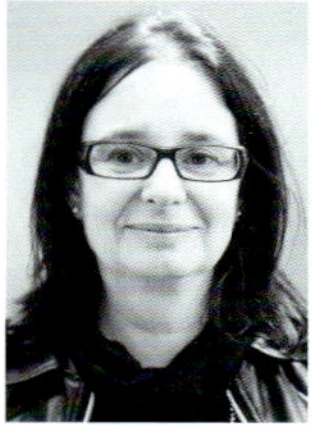

Sirikit Amann (AT) studied political science, theater and economics in Vienna, Munich and Boston. Since the 80s, she has been involved primarily with cultural education in the context of new media on the national and international level. Since 2006 she has been curating the film program Young Animations on behalf of Ars Electronica. In 2008, she took over the newly-founded Department of Artistic and Cultural Mediation at the Austrian Ministry for Education, the Arts and Culture.

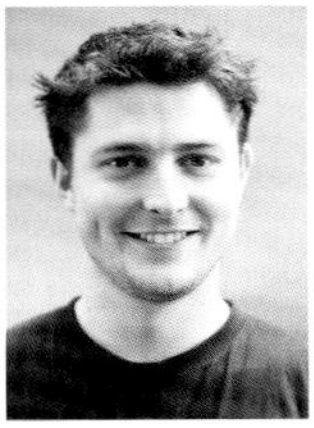

Benjamin Brockhaus (DE) worked as a ranger in a national park on the North Sea and graduated with a BSc in ecosystem management at the University of Goettingen (DE). Pursuing his personal goal, to empower young people in discovering and developing their potential as creators of our common future, he founded the Youth Future Project in 2009, which equips students and undergraduates with the knowledge and project-management tools which they need to initiate peace or sustainability projects. For this he arranges meetings between young people and role models such as Nobel Peace Prize winners.

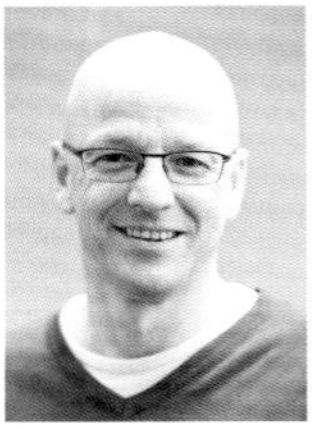

Gerhard Funk (AT) studied mathematics and art education in Linz and received his PhD in theoretical computer science. In 1993 he transferred to the Linz University of Art, where he established a course in digital media and developed the e-learning platform Digital Media for Artists–DMA. Since 2004 he has been a full professor at the Institute of Media and the head of the bachelor degree course Time-based and Interactive Media. Additionally he leads the web art and design course of the masters degree program in web sciences, which is offered together with the Johannes Kepler University, Linz.

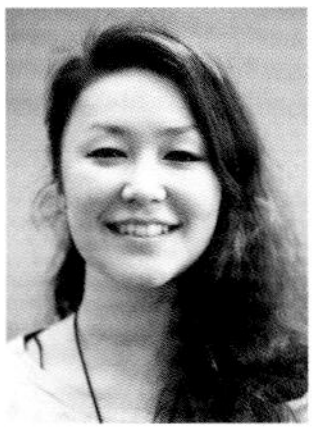

Conny Lee (AT) was born in 1985 with 50 percent South Korean genetic material from her father, raised in a tiny village far off in Lower Austria, moved to Vienna to attend university, completed the allegedly unpromising discipline of theatre, film and media studies, and since 2010 has been working as an editor for Radio FM4 on topics such as games, IT, literature and comics, additionally producing and co-hosting the Morningshow.

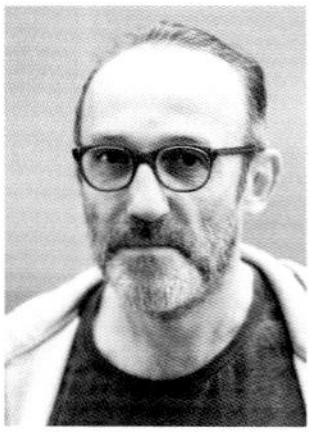

Karl Markovics (AT) is an Austrian actor and film director. He starred as Salomon Sorowitsch in Stefan Ruzowitzky's 2007 film *The Counterfeiters*, which won that year's Academy Award for Best Foreign Language Film. Prior to that, his most notable appearances have been in the highly-acclaimed Austrian (Viennese) black comedy *Komm, süßer Tod* (2001), his role as far-right terrorist Franz Fuchs in the 2007 TV movie *Franz Fuchs–Ein Patriot*, and in the police drama television series *Inspector Rex*. Markovics remains a frequent stage actor. He directed and wrote *Atmen* in 2011.

[the next idea] VOESTALPINE ART AND TECHNOLOGY GRANT

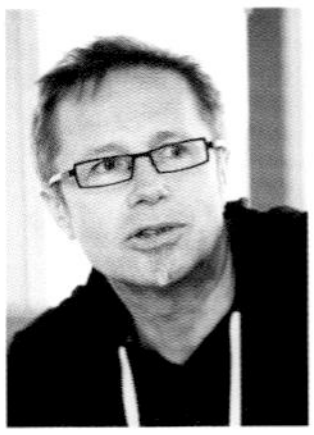

Michael Doser (AT/CH) has been working for Cern since 1991, where he is deputy department head of Cern's physics department. He has been working with antimatter since 1983, using it both as a tool and as an object of study, with the goal of understanding the first moments of the universe. In 2002, he was part of the team that made cold atoms of anti-hydrogen for the first time and he currently leads the Aegis experiment to measure the effect of gravitation of antimatter. He is the author of more than 250 publications related to his work and to the Aegis experiment.

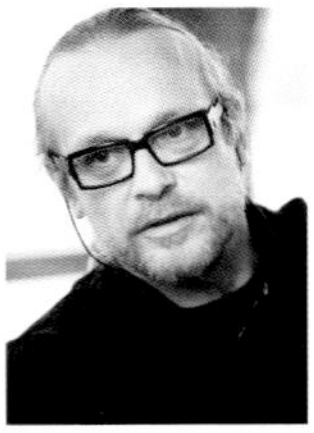

Horst Hörtner (AT) is a media artist and researcher. He is an expert in the design of human-computer interaction and holds several patents in this field. Hörtner was a founding member of the Ars Electronica Futurelab in 1996, which he has directed since then. He started work in the field of media art in the 1980s and co-founded the media art group x-space in Graz/Austria in 1990. Horst Hörtner works at the nexus of art and science and gives lectures and talks at numerous international conferences and universities.

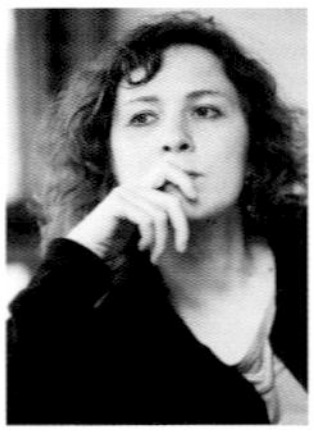

Ela Kagel (DE) is an independent cultural producer with a focus on open-source strategies, media activism and digital culture. As one of the Transmediale festival program developers, she initiated the Free Culture Incubator, a series of research events on the price and value of cultural work. Since 2005, Ela has been working with Public Art Lab and has initiated a broad range of media culture events. Since 2011, she has been the founder and managing partner of Supermarkt, Berlin's center for creative resources. She has an MA in European Cultural Planning from the De Montfort University in Leicester (UK). *@supermarkt, FB: supermarkt*

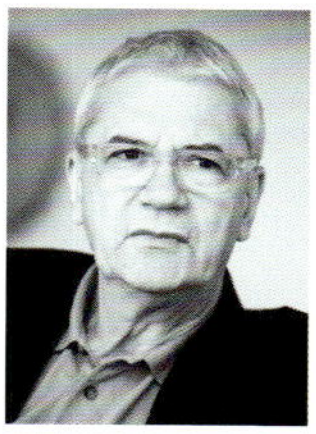

Gustav Pomberger (AT) is a full professor for software engineering and has been head of the Department of Business Informatics–Software Engineering at the Johannes-Kepler University, Linz, since 1987. In 1983 he was appointed professor of computer science at the University of Zurich. In 1987 he was simultaneously offered positions at ETH Zurich, the Technical University of Vienna and the Johannes-Kepler University, Linz. From 1992 to 1999 he led the Christian Doppler Research Laboratory for Software Engineering. His basic research focuses on the design of high-quality software development process. His applied research concentrates on the design of software architecture for augmented and virtual-reality-based embedded systems.

Michael Sterrer-Ebenführer (AT) is responsible for corporate communications at voestalpine AG.

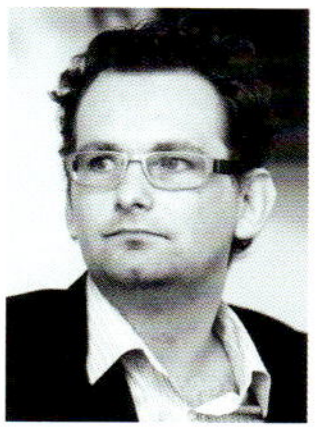

Prix Ars Electronica Collide@CERN Residency Award

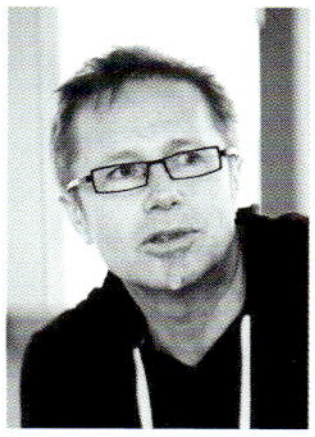

Michael Doser (AT/CH) has been working for Cern since 1991, where he is deputy department head of Cern's physics department. He has been working with antimatter since 1983, using it both as a tool and as an object of study, with the goal of understanding the first moments of the universe. In 2002, he was part of the team that made cold atoms of anti-hydrogen for the first time and he currently leads the Aegis experiment to measure the effect of gravitation on antimatter. He is the author of more than 250 publications related to his work and to the Aegis experiment.

Horst Hörtner (AT) is a media artist and researcher. He is an expert in the design of human-computer interaction and holds several patents in this field. Hörtner was a founding member of the Ars Electronica Futurelab in 1996, which he has directed since then. He started work in the field of media art in the 1980s and co-founded the media art group x-space in Graz, Austria, in 1990. Horst Hörtner works at the nexus of art and science and gives lectures and talks at numerous international conferences and universities.

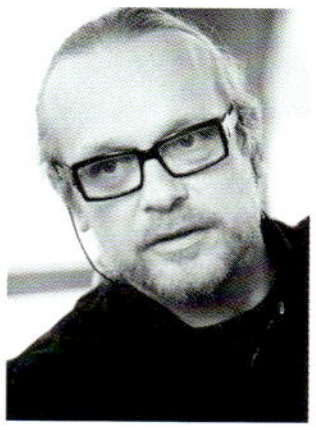

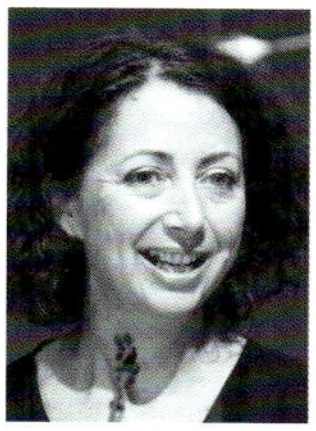

Ariane Koek (UK) is passionate about the power of the imagination and creativity across disciplines. She has worked extensively throughout the BBC as an award winning producer in radio and as a director in television, going on to become CEO/director of the Arvon Foundation for Creative Writing. Ariane was awarded a Clore Fellowship in 2009 supported by the Cultural Leadership Program, and she is currently working on International Arts Development at Cern.

Gerfried Stocker (AT) is a media artist and telecommunications engineer. In 1991, he founded x-space, producing numerous installations and performances featuring elements of interaction, robotics and telecommunications. Since 1995 he has been artistic director of Ars Electronica. In 1995-96 he headed the crew of artists and technicians that developed the Ars Electronica Center's pioneering new exhibition strategies. He has been chiefly responsible for conceiving and implementing the series of international exhibitions that Ars Electronica has staged since 2004, and, beginning in 2005, for the planning and thematic repositioning of the new, expanded Ars Electronica Center.

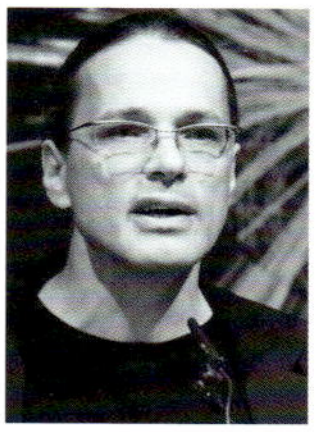

Digital Communities 2013—Advisory Board

Heitor Alvelos (PT) is professor of design and new media at the University of Porto, Portugal. outreach director at the UT Austin-Portugal program in digital media and principal curator of the FuturePlaces Digital Media Festival.

An Xiao Mina (US) is an artist, designer, writer and technologist. In her research and practice, she explores the intersection of networked, creative communities and civic life. *www.anxiaostudio.com*

James Burke (UK) is an advisor, product developer and designer with work spanning multiple genres from urban computational systems to self-quantification, from open-government data to exploring networks and their politics.

Tim Causer (UK) is a research associate at the Bentham Project, Faculty of Laws, University College London, where he has responsibility for running the public face of the double-award-winning, crowd-sourced transcription project *Transcribe Bentham*.

José Luis de Vicente (ES) is a cultural researcher, curator and writer. He is director of the Visualizar program on information visualization, Medialab Prado, Madrid.

Cyrus Farivar (US) is a journalist, radio producer and author. He is also the senior business editor at Ars Technica. He is the author of *The Internet of Elsewhere*—about the history and effects of the Internet on different countries around the world.

Carlos J. Gómez de Llarena (US) is a media architect and interaction designer working at the intersection of physical and digital experiences. His projects shape social interactions as well as our perceptions of spaces and have been awarded a Golden Nica, an artist residency at Eyebeam and a US Patent, among others.

Yesica Guerra (US) is a researcher in urban design with a master's degree in architecture and urban studies from MIT. She challenges the notion of conflict manifested in opposing relations between the needs, values, interests and concerns of the different constituents in communities.

Felipe Heusser (PE) is a researcher in the field of open government and a citizen activist using web technology as a mean for civic organizing and innovation. He is the founder and director of Ciudadanointeligente.org as well as co-founder of *Peepol.tv* and *Subela.cl*.

Mike Jensen (ZA) is an independent consultant providing advice on the use of information and communication technologies for development.

Jepchumba (KE) is an African digital artist and digital enthusiast who works hard to combine her two passions: digital media and Africa. Originally from Kenya she is the founder and creative director of the African Digital Art Network, an online collective space dedicated to Africa's growing tech and creative economy.

Peter Kuthan (AT) is a sociologist and specialist in the field of cooperative development. Since 1993 he has initiated a number of cultural exchange projects between Austria and Africa *(tonga.online)*.

André Lemos (BR) is an associate professor at the Faculty of Communication at the Federal University of Bahia, Brazil, and coordinator of the Cybercity Research Group (GPC). He is currently working on mobile communication and locative media studies.

José-Carlos Mariategui (PE) is a technology and media researcher and scientist. He is a founding member of Alta Tecnología Andina (ATA), an NGO for the development and research of art, science and technology in Latin America *(www.ata.org.pe)*.

Dietmar Offenhuber (US/AT) is a media artist with a background in architecture and a focus on spatial concepts of cognition, representation and behavior. He is a founding member of the Ars Electronica Futurelab and currently a researcher at MIT SENSEable City Lab.

Annalisa Pelizza (IT) is a media theorist and researcher in science and technology studies. Over the years her research interests have focused on the ethnography of contested urban spaces, DIY media education, the implications of tactical and citizens' media practices for urban planning.

The Public Laboratory for Open Technology and Science (US) is a community where you can learn how to investigate environmental concerns. Using inexpensive DIY techniques, we seek to change how people see the world in environmental, social and political terms.

Aniara Rodado (EC) is a choreographer, dancer and documentary film maker. She is also part of the programming and management team of the open-source culture reflection meta-network *labSurlab*.

Ulrike Reinhard (DE) is a consultant, author, free spirit and passionate digital native rolled into one. Her belief in the Internet's ability to empower people and change our lives and worlds for the better drives all her work. Currently she is building a school in rural India.

Clément Renaud (FR) investigates how online sharing practices are shaping new cultural forms of territories and understanding. He lives between France and China and can usually be found writing code, articles or research papers. @clemsos *www.clementrenaud.com*

TH Schee (TW) is a web veteran who has pioneered several social projects that have spawned dozens of startups and mayoral election web campaigns in Taiwan since 2002.

Mark Shepard (US) is an artist, architect and researcher whose post-disciplinary practice addresses contemporary entanglements of technology and urban life. He is an associate professor of architecture and media studies at the University at Buffalo, The State University of New York.

Rob van Kranenburg (NL) is the author of *The Internet of Things: A critique of ambient technology and the all-seeing network of RFID*. He is co-founder of Bricolabs and founder of Council. Together with Christian Nold he has published *Situated Technologies Pamphlets 8: The Internet of People for a Post-Oil World*.

PARTICIPANTS

COMPUTER ANIMATION / FILM / VFX

@c PT
7ate9 US
Abstract Birds IT
Aixsponza DE
Babis Alepis GR
Patrick Altmaier DE
Alessandro Amaducci IT
Francesca Amati IT
Edo Amin IL
Daniel Andersch DE
Christoffer Andersen DK
Gillian Anderson US
Stephanie Andreou CY
Brian Andrews US
Marcell Andristyák HU
Anthony Anthonny FR
Antoneta Antoneta Kusijanovic HR
Sandra Araújo PT
Tal Arbiv IL
Hugo Arcier FR
Johannes M. Arend DE
Lucio Arese IT
Art & Graft GB
Philipp Artus DE
Katerina Athanasopoulou GR
Elísabet Ýr Atladóttir DK
Mathieu Auvray FR
Bruno Aveillan FR
Manuel Azuela MX
Felipe Baeza Fuentes CL
Hugo Bailly Desmarcherlier FR
Alessio Ballerini IT
Yuuki Banno JP
Tibor Banoczki HU
Banzai Studio BR
Sebastián Baptista UY
Benjamin Bardou FR
Joey Bargsten US
Agathe Bascou FR
Rajeev Basu GB
Eric Bates CA
Mirjana Batinić HR
Simon Bau FR
Bauhausmaschine DE
Alexis Beaumont FR
BEELD. BR
Alberto Begueri US
Bastien Belvaux FR
Nicolas Benoit FR
Matt Berenty US
Robin Bersot FR
Ishac Bertran ES
Thomas Betrand Battle FR
Reinhold Bidner AT
Peter Bill US
Incredible Bob RS
Ivan Bogdanov BG
David Bokser US
Sara Bonaventura IT
Helena Bonham Carter GB
Pia Borg AU
Manfred Borsch DE
Zuzana Borysek SK
Martin Böttger DE
Charles Bouet FR
Jerome Boulbes FR
Maud Bourgais FR
Jeremi Boutelet FR
Box Team FR
Beyza Boyacioglu TR
Gizem Boyacioglu TR
Morrigane Boyer FR
Molly Bradbury US
Eni Brandner AT
Ulu Braun DE
Bernhard Braunstein AT
Scott Breen US
Yan Breuleux CA
Johan Bring SE
Christian Brinkmann DE
Bernardo Britto BR
Daniel Brkovic DE
Broken Team FR
Émilie Brout & Maxime Marion FR
Didi Bruckmayr AT
Marine Brun FR
Amy Brutton FR
Rob Brydon GB
Marilio Buelli IT
Julia Bueno FR
Gabriel Bulik FR
Jean Bultingaire FR
Fred Burdy FR
Carl Burton US
Kyra Buschor CH
Zhi-Ling Cai TW
Boris Cailly FR
Davide Cairo IT
David Calvet FR
Graciliano Camargo BR
Caminandes NL
Climent Canal ES
Ricardo Cancado BR
Raphael Cancellier FR
Francis Canitrot FR
Ivica Capan HR
Philipp Carbotta DE
Massimo Carrier Ragazzi IT
Josh Carroll & Scott McWhinnie US
Tonino Casula IT
Guillaume Cazabat FR
Osman Cerfon FR
Olivier Chabalier FR
Hui-Yi Chan TW
Tung-Chun Chang TW
Simon Chansard FR
Violaine Chapelain FR
Jeremy Charbonel FR
Dan Charit FR
Hui-Ming Chau MY
Mark Chavez US
Hsu Che-Yu TW
Ching-Heng Chen TW
Michael Chen AU
Ting-Yu Chen TW
Xiao-Ya Chen TW
Yi-Ting Chen TW
Zi-Ming Chen TW
I-Chun Chen TW
Ian Cheng US
Tao-Hsin Chiang TW
Lan Chi Chien TW
Tzu-Hsuan Chiu TW
Thibault Chollet FR
Clementine Choplain FR
Ting-Lin Chou TW
Jérémy Clapin FR
Thibaud Clergue FR
Joris Clerté FR
Martin Clunes GB
Ruben Cohen FR
Caroline Collinot FR
Robbie Coltrane GB
Philipp Comarella IT
Jérome Combe FR
Compositing DE
Ina Conradi-Chavez US
Grayson Cooke NZ
James Corden GB
Jean-Guillaume Culot FR
James Cunningham NZ
Peter Curet NL
Felipe Dacaret CL
DAf CL
Constantinos Daldakis GR
Katie Damien US
Ursula Damm DE
Valerio De Bonis IT
Anouk De Clercq BE
Mariska de Groot NL
Eric De Melo Bueno FR
Andreas De Ridder BE
Frederik de Wilde BE
Floriane Deal FR
decollage.tv AT
Aurelie Deconinck FR
Benoît Delaunay FR
Olivier Delequeuche FR
Camille Dellerie FR
Arno Deutschbauer AT
Maria Catena (Nuccia) Di Pasqua IT
Massimo Di Stefano IT
Lily Díaz US
Paolo Didier FR
Joachim Dieplinger AT
Alexander Dietrich DE
Silke Dietrich DE
Thomas Digiacomi FR
Digic Pictures HU
Patrick Doan CA
Domestic Infelicity HU
Temujin Doran GB
Barry Doupé CA
Olivier "HERO" Dressen BE
Yann Drevon FR
DSK (Juan Lesta & Belén Montero) ES
Nisha Duggal GB
Daniel Dugour NL
Aurelien Duhayon FR
Duke & Duke GB
David Dunne IE
Sarah Dupont FR
Robin Dupuis CA
Sébastien Dusart FR
Lucas Dworianyn FR
Marie Ecarlat FR
Christian Eckle AT
Dominic Eise DE
Gabor Ekes HU
Mikkel Mainz Elkjær DK
Leonard Ellis US
David Elwell GB
Audric Escales FR
Alain Escalle FR
Xárene Eskandar CA
Eventless Plot GR
experience-art.net AT
Andreas Feix DE
Letty Felgendreher DE
Ivonne Fernández y González DE
Guillaume Ferrachat FR
Pedro Ferreira PT
Vincent Ferrier FR
Conor Fin IE
Esben Fisker DK
Rune Fisker DK
Johannes Flick DE

Roch Forowicz PL
Antoine Foulot FR
Framestore GB
Lukas Franciszkiewicz DE
Eva Franz DE
Morgane Fraschina FR
Eddy Frechou FR
Louis Fremont FR
Iring Freytag DE
Fabian Fricke DE
Georg Frömelt DE
Snow Yunxue Fu CN
Hollie Gach FR
Clemens Gaisbauer AT
Jerry Galle BE
Arístides Job García Hernández ES
Emmeline Gautheron FR
Vaiana Gauthier FR
Charlotte Gayet FR
Thibaud Gayral FR
Adi Gelbart IL
Paolo Geminiani IT
Simon Geoffriau FR
Werther Germondari IT
Get Wild FR
Mohammed Ghanim AT
Helen Giokari GR
Pauline Giraudel FR
Theo Girettes FR
Thea Glad NO
Glassworks Amsterdam NL
Remi Godin FR
Clément Goffinet FR
Jeremy Goh SG
Lior Golan IL
Andreas Goldfuss CA
Harvey Goldman US
Milica Golubovic RS
Good Company Arts NZ
Andreas Goralczyk DE
Cameron Gough AU
Piotr Grabowski PL
Stephanie Grard FR
Green Trouble Team FR
Mitch Greer US
Simon Griesser AT
François Grumelin-Sohn FR
Eyal Gruß IL
Natalia Grzebyk PL
Xiaolin Guan CN
Christo Guelov ES
Brieuc Guenole FR
Benito Guyot Florent FR
Anna Habermehl DE
Eran Hadas IL
Ole Christoffer Haga NO
Harald Haraldsson IS
Jean-Baptiste Hardion FR
Mattias Härenstam SE
Constantin Hartenstein DE
Yasaman Hasani IR
Marion Hassan FR
Max Hattler DE
Sally Hawkins GB
Toru Hayai JP
Sachiko Hayashi SE
Julien Hazebroucq FR
Shirley Henderson GB
Eloi Henriod CH
Albane Hertault Lacoste FR
Don Hertzfeldt US
Rosanna Herzner DE
Colin Hesterly US
Floriane Hetru FR
Gael Heux FR
Shinsaku Hidaka JP
Ralf Hildenbeutel DE
Doug Hindson GB
Dániel Hodvogner HU
Brent Hoff US
Freya Holdsworth GB
Jonas Holmer SE
Al Holmes GB
Andreas Horvath DE
Octavian Horvath RO
Jamal Hosn LB
Szu-Yu Hou TW
Yu-Chi Hsiao SA
Cheng-Kai Hsiung TW
Lung-Kai Hsu TW
Tzu-Han Hsu TW
Ren Hsien Hsu FR
Andrew Huang US
Chien-Chieh Huang TW
Hsiao-Ya Huang TW
Pei-Chuang Huang TW
Scottie Chih-Chieh Huang TW
Wei-Jhe Huang TW
Gareth Hughes GB
Benoit Huguet FR
Benoit Huguet FR
Hannes Hummel DE
Margaux Huneau FR
Shih-Chieh Hung TW
John Hurt GB
Eric Hynynen FI
Dóra Ida Szűcs HU
Sebastien Iglesias FR
Igor Imhoff IT
intolight DE
Yuk Yiu Ip HK
Jochen Isensee DE
Island Keeper FR
Yuichi Ito JP
Faiyaz Jafri US
Shiang-Jie Jaing TW
Emmanuel Jambois FR
Edmunds Jansons LV
Rima Jastrumskaite GB
Miguel Jiron US
Andrew Ellis Johnson US
Cassandra C Jones US
Trevor Jones US
Andrew Ellis Johnson & Susanne Slavick US
Arnhild Jordet NO
Franck Jugdhurry FR
Márk Juhász HU
Patrick Jurányi AT
Kaeba IT
John Kahrs US
Monira Kamal DE
Shin-Yu Kao TW
Andrius Kauklys LT
Markos Kay CY
Kris Kelly IE
Daphné Keramidas FR
Jacques Khouri CA
Tehzeeb Khurana IN
Lexi Kiddo GB
Katarzyna Kijek PL
Hee Jin Kim KR
Shaun Seong-Young Kim KR
Tommy Kinnerup DK
Anna Kipervaser US
Ákos Kiss HU
Domonkos Kiss HU
Krzysztof Kiwerski PL
Pascal Klein FR
Yota Kobayashi JP
Kombinat DE
Michaela AT
Maria Korporal NL
Teppei Koseki JP
Stefan Kraus DE
Adrian Kresnik AT
Jan-Marcel Kühn DE
Hsiang-Hsu Kung TW
Eric Kunzendorf US
Sanja Kuveljić SI
La Mécanique Du Plastique FR
Shao-Tang Lan TW
Chris Landreth CA
Michael Langan US
Lani Pixels DK
Stephanie Lansaque FR
Boris Laprade FR
Alexandre Laroche FR
Stefan Larsson SE
Mickael Larue FR
Diego Lazzarin IT
Maïwenn Le Borgne FR
Mauri Lehtonen FI
Lei Lei CN
Cornelia Leichtfried AT
Emmanuelle Leleu FR
Stéphanie Lement FR
Thomas Lemoine FR
Catherine Lepicard FR
Francois Leroy FR
Bastien Letoile FR
Cheng Li FR
LIA AT
Kaun-Shiang Liao TW
Wan-Jan Liau TW
Gérald Ligonnet FR
Geoffrey Lillemon US
Daniel Pinheiro Lima BR
Thilko Limbeck DE
Chiao-Fang Lin TW
Fang-Yi Lin TW
Shu-min Lin TW
Yan-Yan Lin TW
Zhe-Xiao Lin TW
Shih-Tang Lin TW
Sebastian Linder DE
Yu-Jun Liou TW
Kuo-Hsi Liu TW
Ming-Zhong Liu TW
Te-Yu Liu TW
Chieh-Ni Lo TW
Nicolas Loesner FR
Michael Loithaler DE
William Lorton FR
Karina Løvslett NO
Yu-Ting Lu TW
Alexandru Lungu RO
Modesta Lupascu RO
Joanna Lurie FR
Pierre-Emmanuel Lyet FR
Diran Lyons US
M-I-E Studio GB
Zydrunas Maciulis LT
Michael Magario US
mahanaim 134 IL
Megan Maher US
Terah Maher US
Dominik Mahnič SI
Kostas Makrinos GR
Julie Manga FR

Scott Mannion AU
Olivier Martin FR
Aurélie Martin FR
Ludovic Martin FR
Elio Martusciello IT
Fabien Masson FR
David Mathews IN
Moritz Matschke DE
Charly Mauri FR
Martin Maxence FR
Isca Mayo IL
Andre Mayr AT
Evelyn McGrath IE
Maxime Mege-Ythier FR
Gaël Megherbi FR
Tristan Menard FR
Gottfried Mentor DE
Alyse Miller & Phillip Simon US
Nicoloas Millot FR
Rafael Miranda Huereca MX
Parag K. Mital US
Hans Mittendorf DE
Haruaki Mizutari JP
Mitja Mlakar SI
Nur Atikah Sari Mohamed SG
Thomas Mohr NL
Jolene Mok HK
Paul Monge FR
Adrien Montier FR
Lucas Morandi FR
Anaëlle Moreau FR
Michael Moreno FR
Marcella Moser CA
Daniel Moshel DE
Tal Moskovich IL
mostlikely AT
Kyle Mowat CA
Tara Mueller US
Dennis Müller DE
Kristin Müller DE
David Muth AT
Takeshi Nakatsuka JP
Natural.Code AR
Eugen Neacsu RO
Albert Negredo ES
Sonia Nelubina RU
Neon GB
Neon Golden AT
Nerdworking TR
Vincenz Neuhaus DE
Dennis Neuschaefer-Rube DE
Kingsley Ng HK
Duc Duy Nguyen FR
Serban Nichifor RO
Bo Juhl Nielsen DK
Tetsuka Niiyama JP
Yoshiki Nishimura JP
Jeanette Nørgaard DK
Jason Noto US
Till Nowak DE
Julia Ocker DE
William Ohanessian FR
Takashi Ohashi, Yuri Habuka,
Masumi Takino, Luschka, Kyojun
Tanaka JP
Helena Ohman McCardle SE
Masahiro Ohsuka JP
Sorin Oncu RS
One Day Group FR
Elizabeth Onofre Gonzalez MX
Javier Jesus Onofre Gonzalez MX
Galia Osmo IL
Magnus Östergren SE
Ouchhh TR
Marie Owona FR
Cosku Ozdemir TR
Irene Pacini IT
Simon Jaikiriuma Paetau DE
Jordi Pagès ES
Inès Pagniez FR
Baden Pailthorpe AU
Moritz Palnstorfer AT
Héloïse Papillon FR
Constantin Päplow DE
Dmitry Paranyushkin RU
Hyun Park KR
Parlez-moi d'amour FR
Michaela Pavlatova CZ
Carlos Pechant &
Sergio Martinez MX
Simon Pegg GB
Julien Perez FR
Camille Perrin FR
Batiste Perron FR
Peter Clausen Film &
TV Produktionsgesellschaft DE
Peter Petersen DK
John Pettingill US
Helen Petts GB
Marilyne Peyrichous FR
Micha Pichlkastner AT
Florian Pichon FR
Neon Pictures GB
Hugo Pievic FR
Victor Pillet FR
Alice Planes-Lavisse FR
Johannes Platzl AT
Johannes Poell AT
Tavo Ponce ES
Alexei Popogrebsky RU
Post TR
Eric Prah US
Robert Praxmarer AT
Manuel Preuß DE
Oleg Prodeus AT
Remi Prouzat FR
Alexia Provoost FR
Shuai-Cheng Pu TW
Casey Pugh US
Matt Pyke GB
Davide Quagliola IT
Cecile Rabhi FR
Nikola Radosavljevic RS
Christoph Rainer AT
Vid Rajin RS
Diego Ramirez MX
Marcela Rapallo AR
Guillaume Raynaut FR
Tim Razumovsky IL
Tobias Rehm DE
Ruth Reiche DE
Xiaoman Ren CN
Stefan Resch AT
Izabella Retkowska PL
Reverso Team FR
Rhapsodie Team FR
Luís Ribeiro PT
André Olsen Richard NO
Linda Riseley AU
Sébastien Roddier FR
Pablo Rodes ES
Thomas Rodriguez FR
Ana Rodríguez León ES
Julien Roguet FR
Sonja Rohleder DE
Tal Rosner GB
Rosto NL
Georgie Roxby Smith AU
Mischa Rozema NL
Krzysztof Rynkiewicz PL
Oda Ingrid Sæther NO
Hiroya Sakurai JP
Veronika Samartseva DE
Juan Carlos Sánchez Duque ES
Jeremy Sanchez-Romero FR
Mauricio Sanhueza PE
Chico Santos BR
Richard Sanz GB
Moritz Schneider DE
schnellebuntebilder DE
Keith Schofield US
Ida Maria Schouw Andreasen DK
Bastiaan Schravendeel NL
Christian Schulze DE
Lillian Schwartz US
Daniel Schwarz DE
Lorenz Schwarz DE
Secret Hand NL
Boris Seewald DE
Sehsucht Berlin DE
Robert Seidel DE
Daniel Semanas BR
Onur Senturk US
Jung Hee Seo KP
Aurélien Serres FR
Geoffrey Sexton US
Eddie Shearon IE
Ming Yee Sheh TW
Pei-Yu Shi TW
Prashant Shikare IN
Pernille Sihm DK
Guli Silberstein IL
Georg Simbeni AT
Edouard Sisternas FR
Joanne Smithies FR
Julien Soler FR
Julien Soulage FR
Eduardo Soutullo Garcia ES
Timothy Spall GB
Anne Spalter US
Nina Rike Springer AT
Jan Šrámek CZ
Jacob Stålhammar SE
Charles Stankievech CA
Dimitri Stankowicz FR
Marina Steck FR
Damien Steck FR
Lena Steinkühler DE
Viktor Stickel DE
Meghan Stockham US
Heidi Stokes GB
Axel Straschnoy AR
David Strindberg SE
Neil Stubbings CH
Sturqen PT
Masahiro Sugano JP
David Sullivan US
Matthew Sullivan US
Ting-Yu Sun TW
Otto Suuronen FI
Benjamin Swiczinsky AT
Sarolta Szabo HU
Loránd Szécsényi-Nagy HU
Mario Taferner AT
Aaron Tam NZ
Yoshimichi Tamura JP
Joshua Tan SG
Chiao-Wei Tang TW
Sachi Tanihara JP
Hong-Hong Tao TW

Simon Taroni FR
David Tart DK
AL Taylor GB
Huan Teng CN
Tennis and Barbecue Team FR
Andres Tenusaar EE
Natasa Teofilovic RS
Terraform Team FR
Alain Thay FR
The Animation School ZA
Louis Thomas FR
Myriam Thyes CH
Raphaël Tiellie FR
Teresa Timelthaler AT
Bin-Han To DE
Reda Tomingas LT
Paul Torris FR
Raffaele Totaro IT
Viktoria Traub HU
Benjamin Tron FR
Jean-Baptiste Trullu FR
Masahiro Tsutani JP
Florian Tuercke DE
Camille Turon FR
Maayan Tzuriel IL
Karl Überriegler AT
Taka Umemura JP
Anna Ursyn US
Remy Usson FR
Jan van Loh DE
Alec Vance US
Cecilio Vargas MX
Lucas Veber FR
Mathias Vef DE
Zoltán Végh HU
Santiago Vela Ruiz MX
Lea Vera Toro FR
Angel Vergara ES
Darko Vidackovic HR
Franck Vigroux FR
Leida Vincent FR
Virus Team FR
Carlo Vogele LU
Voile Noir FR
Lukas Vojir CZ
Sebastien Wackowiez FR
Atsushi Wada JP
Jelena Walf RU
David Walliams GB
Jing Wang CN
Meng-Han Wang TW
Wen-Hui Wang TW
Wung-Sing Wang TW
Zhipeng Wang CN
Gongjin Wang FR

Alan Warburton GB
Flora Watzal AT
Paul Wegschaider AT
Julika Welge DE
Regina Welker DE
Adam Wells GB
Weta Digital NZ
David Wexler US
Rob Whitworth GB
Susanne Wiegner DE
Paul Wiersbinski DE
Kasia Wilk PL
Tom Wilkinson GB
Leslie Wilson US
Mihai Wilson CA
Matthias Winckelmann DE
Clemens Wirth AT
Adam Witkowski PL
Wolf & Crow US
Chung-yu Wong CN
Gergely Wootsch HU
Hubert Wozniak US
Alexandra Wozniak FR
Stefan Wunsch DE
Yu-Ru Xu TW
Jing-Fang Yan TW
Ching-Chen Yang TW
Jen-Yi Yen TW
Tzu-Ying Yen FR
Davier Yoon SG
Lucas Zanotto IT
Kushtrim Zeqiri AL
Angelika Zieglerschick AT
Stephan Zlotescu RO
Sarah Zucker US

DIGITAL MUSICS & SOUND ART

[mo:ya] AT
@c PT
Jamal A-Hosn LB
Lucas Abela AU
Larry Achiampong GB
Giuseppe Acito IT
Monty Adkins GB
Angelo Airò Farulla IT
Memo Akten GB
Giulio Aldinucci IT
Ziad Alim BD
Edith Alonso ES
Leonardo Amico IT
Todd Anderson-Kunert AU
Iván Andrés Yagüe ES
Pablo Anglade AR
Thomas Ankersmit NL
Linda Antas US
Aikaterini Antouraki GR
Fernanda Aoki Navarro BR
André Aspelmeier DE
Atom™ & Marc Behrens DE
Andrew Au US
Kuai Shen Auson EC
Andrew Babcock US
Cecile Babiole FR
Ain Bailey GB
Andrej Bako GB
Dominique Balaÿ FR
Alessio Ballerini IT
Federico Barabino AR
Natasha Barrett GB
Adam Basanta CA
René Bastian FR
Fabio Battistetti IT
Jay Batzner US
BAW GB
Bay Players Experimental Music Collective US
Julien Bayle FR
BeatSneakers AT
Martin Bédard CA
Marc Behrens DE
Andrea Belfi IT
Antonello Belgrano IT
Konrad Belina-Brzozowski PL
Ludwig Berger DE
Vincent Bergeron CA
Nicolas Bernier CA
Pierre Berthet BE
Katrin Bertram DE
Sandeep Bhagwati DE
Ranjit Bhatnagar US
David Bird US

Black Biuti AT
Manuella Blackburn GB
Tim Blechmann DE
Olivia Block US
Per Bloland US
Evelyn Blumenau AT
Incredible Bob RS
John Bock US
Jason Bolte US
Bruce Bonnell CA
Lynn Book US
Pia Borg and Joel Stern AU
Mohammad Borzooeian IR
Alessandro Bosetti IT
Timon Botez NO
Xavier Bourassa CA
Adam Boxall GB
Gizem Boyacioglu TR
Michael Boyd US
Molly Bradbury US
Jens Brand DE
Marie-Hélène Breault CA
Matt Broach US
Roman Bromboszcz PL
Paul Browse GB
Julius Bucsis US
bugalta/owl yeah DE
Marcel Bühler DE
James Bulley and Daniel Jones GB
Arturas Bumsteinas LT
Sabine Bürger DE
Peter Bussigel US
Adolfo Luxúria Canibal PT
Rejane Cantoni BR
Brenna Cantwell US
Chris Carlson US
Lars Carlsson SE
Angus Carlyle GB
Io Casino AD
Ulysses Castellanos CA
Damian Catera US
Scott Cazan US
Mechi Cena IT
Aisen Caro Chacin US
Natalie Chami US
Chin Ting Chan HK
Esteban Chapela Gaxiola MX
Chasers US
Budhaditya Chattopadhyay IN
Chenchen Chen CN
Chen Chen CN
Bryan Christian US
Thanos Chrysakis GR
Marko Ciciliani DE
Marco Cinquegrana IT

Darius Ciuta LT
David Collier IE
Darren Copeland CA
Maxime Corbeil-Perron CA
Stephen Cornford GB
Juan Andrés Costa UY
Rupert Cox GB
Leonardo Crescenti BR
Catalin Cretu RO
Michael Cryne GB
Robert Curgenven AU
Julio d'Escrivan VE
Donald Daedalus US
Werner Dafeldecker AT
Diego Dall Osto IT
Darsha Darsha Hewitt CA
Yannick Dauby FR
Michaela Davies AU
Micha Dawid DE
Ricardo de Armas AR
Federico De Biase IT
Christoph De Boeck BE
Valerio De Bonis IT
Mariska de Groot NL
Leonardo de Melo BR
Fabio De Sanctis De Benedictis IT
Luca De Siena IT
Decibel AU
Christopher DeLaurenti US
Alexander Derben DE
Pascal Derycke FR
René Desalmand CH
Taylor Deupree US
Caroline Devine GB
Ruben Dhers VE
Maria Catena (Nuccia) Di Pasqua IT
Yorgos Diapoulis GR
Marco Donnarumma IT
Temujin Doran GB
Wolfgang Dorninger AT
DOS-F ES
Kevin Drumm US
Alexandros Drymonitis GR
Petra Dubach NL
Melissa Dubbin and Aaron S. Davidson US
Oliverio Duhalde AR
Andreas Dzialocha DE
Rudolf Eb.er CH
Jorn Ebner DE
Michael Edwards GB
Arne Eigenfeldt CA
Richard Eigner AT
Carrie Elston Tunick US
Roland Etzin DE
Jon-Carlos Evans US
Evidence US
Experiential Music Lab IT
FA TECH AT
Simone Faliva IT
Thea Farhadian US
Amiri Farris US
José Miguel Fernández CL
Marco Ferrazza IT
Michael Filimowicz US
Nirto Karsten Fischer DE
Rajmil Fischman PE
Peter Flemming CA
Eduardo Flores EC
Luca Forcucci CH
Ian M Fraser & Reed Evan Rosenberg US
Lee Fraser GB
Heribert Friedl AT
Benjamin Fuhrman US
Larry Matthew Gaab US
Andrea Gabriele IT
Richard Gadd AU
José Gallardo-Arbeláez CO
David Gann DE
Andrew Garbett GB
Scott Garner US
Gunnar Geisse DE
Moritz Simon Geist DE
Francesco Giannico IT
Stefano Giannotti IT
Stelios Giannoulakis GR
Bruce Gilbert GB
Matteo Giordano IT
Artemi-Maria Gioti GR
Lukas Girling GB
Ahna Girshick US
Ioni Gkliati GR
Gilles Gobeil CA
Harvey Goldman US
Daniel Gomes PT
Rui Miguel Gomes Amorim PT
German Gomez AR
Daniel González Franco CO
Good Willsmith US
Gerard Gormley IE
Annie Gosfield US
Suguru Goto JP
Rama Gottfried US
Panayiotis Goubouros GR
Zbigniew Gozdecki PL
GRAU/T DE
Antye Greie-Ripatti DE
Oliver Greschke DE
Brian Griffith US
Ragnar Grippe SE
Tobias Grosshauser DE
David Gutema HU
Gyre US
Moritz Haberkorn AT
Benjamin Hackbarth US
Gregory Haggard US
Nadine Haidenbauer AT
Hiroaki Haiyama JP
Sophie Marie Hammer AT
Byeong-Jun Han KR
Yoon Chung Han KR
Denis Handschin CH
Lars Lundehave Hansen DK
Jorge Haro ES
Nathaniel Hartman US
Miku Hatsune JP
Bjørn Erik Haugen NO
Lauren Sarah Hayes GB
Boris Hegenbart DE
Nigel Helyer AU
Douglas Henderson US
Robert Henke DE
Ron Herrema US
Kathy Hinde GB
Masahiro Hiramoto JP
Midori Hirano JP
Marlene Hirtreiter DE
David Hochgatterer AT
Elizabeth Hoffman US
Markus Hoffmann DE
Kurt Hofstetter AT
Pascal Holper AT
Akitoshi Honda JP
Andreas Horvath DE
Jamal Hosn LB
Brian House US
Earl Howard US
Feng Chen Hsieh TW
Lei Huang CN
John Hudak US
Yi-Ping Hung, He-lin Luo, Cheng-Xia Chang, Yi-Ting Tsai, Yen-Bin Tseng TW
Ignacy Ignacy Lukasiewicz PL
Interactive Institute SE
Intermedia Chef KR
Ipad Orchestra & App club FI
Daisuke Ishida JP
Shun Ito JP
Yuichi Ito JP
Daniel Jacobson IE
Viktor Jan KR
Paweł Janicki PL
Monique Jean CA
Sion Jeong KR
Luke Jerram GB
Ariane Jessulat DE
Manuel Jimenez Barrio ES
Kazuhiro Jo JP
Tarry Jon AU
Mikael Jorgensen US
Phil Julian GB
Kaeba IT
Timo Kahlen DE
Ai Kamachi JP
John Kamevaar CA
David Kamp DE
Thanasis Kaproulias GR
Bugra Karabey TR
Konstantinos Karathanasis GR
Zbigniew Karkowski SE
María Cristina Kasem AR
Simon Katan GB
Masayuki Kawai JP
Masayuki Kawai with Ryota Hamasaki JP
Chikada Kazuhisa JP
Eli Keszler US
Jusub Kim KR
Andrey Kiritchenko UA
Naoki Kita JP
Kleefstra|Bakker|Kleefstra NL
Karl Kliem DE
Jana Kluge DE
Ryoho Kobayashi JP
Yota Kobayashi JP
Andreas Kogler AT
Panayiotis Kokoras GR
Matthias König DE
Pavel Kopecky CZ
Hans-Henning Korb DE
Korinsky – Atelier für vertikale Flächen DE
Kotra UA
Marinos Koutsomichalis GR
Rico Krafft DE
Viola Kramer DE
Gintas Kraptavicius LT
Walter Kreuz AT
Roland Kuit NL
KUSC Interactive US
Peter Kutin AT
Slavek Kwi IE
Ursula Kwong-Brown US
Jakob Einar la Cour DK
La danse de l'ours FR
Miu-ling Lam HK
Michael Ka Yau Lau HK
Sebastien Lavoie CA

Gábor Lázár HU
Frédéric Le Bel CA
Ray Lee GB
Yann Leguay FR
Darr Tah Lei IS
Sjoerd Leijten NL
David Leone US
Jason Lescalleet US
David Letellier FR
Andrew Lewis GB
Grischa Lichtenberger DE
Signe Lidén NO
Jockel Liess DE
Stephen Lilly US
Anders Lind SE
PerMagnus Lindborg SE
Cort Lippe US
Yun Ting Lo HK
Jaime Lobato MX
Simon Longo IT
Carlos Edelmiro Lopez MX
Francisco López ES
Olivia Louvel GB
Love Cult RU
Menacho Luis AR
Stella Luncke und
Josef Maria Schäfers DE
Sergio Luque MX
Eric Lyon US
Rod Maclachlan GB
Ryan Maguire US
D. Burke Mahoney CA
Elena Maier DE
Byron Mallett NZ
Mark Malmberg US
Rodrigo Malvar PT
Ricardo Mandolini AR
Robert Mann US
Emmanuil Manousakis GR
Cedric Maridet FR
Jon Martin CA
Israel Martínez MX
Dylan Martorell AU
Wade Marynowsky AU
Doran Massey US
Eric Mathon FR
Robert Mathy AT
Piotr Matkowski PL
Seiichiro Matsumura JP
Matter IT
Antony Maubert FR
Daniel Mayer AT
Andre Mayr AT
Graham McDermott US
Markus Mehr DE
Lvis Mejía MX
Marcello Mercado DE
Edgar Merino MX
Christos Michalakos GB
Francesco Michi IT
Michiu & Fierbinteanu RO
Andrei Mikhailau BY
Vladimir Mikhailau BY
Cathy Milliken AU
Fabio Mina IT
Eduardo Miranda BR
Takuro Mizuta Lippit JP
Andrea Molino IT
Andrea Montalbano IT
Clio Montrey CA
Adrian Moore GB
Francisco Morales MX
Alejandro Morales Moreno ES
Hugo Morales Murguia MX
Weston Mossman US
mostlikely AT
Joao Martinho Moura PT
MU Collective FR
Markus Muench DE
Hilary Mullaney IE
Mihai Murariu RO
Simen Musaeus NO
Roberto Musanti IT
Roland Mylog SE
Yoichi Nagashima JP
Kosuke Nagata JP
Kera Nagel DE
Agoston Nagy HU
Elias Naphausen DE
Sehera Nawaz DE
Darren Ng SG
Serban Nichifor RO
John Nichols US
Click Nilson SE
Nobu_Lab IT
Yann Novak US
Aneta Nowicka PL
Alex Nowitz DE
Erik Nyström SE
Linda O Keeffe IE
Benjamin O'Brien US
Paul O'Donoghue IE
Mari Ohno JP
Masao Ohno JP
Junya Oikawa JP
Mark Oliveiro AU
Alessandro Olla IT
Opening Performance Orchestra CZ
ÖRF HU
Roberta Orlando IT
Ed Osborn US
Eirik Ostby NO
Matthew Ostrowski US
Yasuhiro Otani JP
otolab IT
Till Otto DE
ozmotic IT
Lefteris Papadimitriou GR
Zsolt Papp HU
Giovanni Parente IT
Thiago Parizi BR
Ake Parmerud SE
Claudio Parodi IT
Nye Parry GB
Javier Party CL
Fabrizio Passarella IT
Carlo Patrao PT
Pedro Patrício PT
Lee Patterson GB
Kevin Patton US
Dennis Paul DE
Miguel Pedro PT
Guilherme Pena Costa BR
Elisabeth Penker AT
Pedro Pereira PT
Felipe Perez Santiago MX
Tristan Perich US
Zoltan Peter HU
Raymond Pettibon US
Finnbogi Petursson IS
Andreas Pflanzl AT
Pieter-Jan Pieters BE
Antonella Pintus IT
Sergio Pirozzi IT
Renate Pittroff DE
Charles-Edouard Platel FR
Maria Ploskow DE
Neda Ploskow DE
Graham Plumb GB
Hans-Jürgen Poetz AT
Greg Pond US
Gianluca Porcu IT
Patricia Portela BE
Henrique Portovedo Marques PT
Post TR
Stefan Prins BE
Dyan Pritamo MX
Rostislav Prochovník CZ
Paul Prudence GB
Mykyta Prykhodchenko UA
Roberto Pugliese IT
Raffaseder / Hoerbst AT
Takayuki Rai JP
Bhob Rainey US
Robert Ratcliffe GB
MF Redman AT
Geo Reisinger DE
David Renault FR
ReVerse Bullets US
Michael Rhoades US
João Ricardo PT
Lasse-Marc Riek DE
Eric Glick Rieman US
Jane Rigler US
Lumi Charlotte Ripatti DE
Sasu Ripatti FI
Lucía Rivero ES
Arnaud Rivière FR
RIXC LV
Cendrine Robelin FR
Farkas Robert RS
Carol Robinson FR
Manuel Rocha Iturbide MX
Marco Rodriguez EC
Jean-Michel Rolland FR
Volker Rommel DE
Michael Rosas Cobian GB
Franz Rosati IT
Henrique Roscoe BR
Reed Evan Rosenberg US
Vanessa Rossetto US
Tim Otto Roth DE
David Rothenberg US
Christoph Rothmeier DE
Brian Routh GB
Joseph Butch Rovan US
Andrew Rowe GB
Timothy Roy US
Donika Rudi AL
Stefan Rudin CH
Edgardo Rudnitzky AR
Tonalli Rufino MX
Antonio Russek MX
Corrado Saija IT
Corrado Saija IT
Sam Salem GB
Karl Salzmann AT
Philip Samartzis AU
Dario Sanfilippo IT
Kyle Sanna US
Andrea Santini IT
Sergio Santoni AR
Donal Sarsfield IE
Ayako Sato JP
Dimitrios Savva CY
Giuliano Scarola IT
Janek Schaefer GB
Christian F. Schiller AT
Frauke Schmidt DE
Sebastian Schönfeld DE

Nichola Scrutton GB
Robert Seidel DE
Fabio Selvafiorita IT
Angelo Semeraro IT
Stefan Senf DE
Lorenzo Senni IT
Gautier Serre FR
Pei-Yu Shi TW
Chandra Shukla US
Balam Ronan Simon Delgado MX
Debashis Sinha CA
Stefanie Sixt DE
SjQ++ JP
Christian Skjødt DK
Ddominique T Skoltz CA
Vivian Sming US
Greg Smith US
Scott Snibbe US
Socic Mediation US
Fiona Soe Paing GB
Pia Sommer CL
Jan Peter Sonntag DE
Vanessa Sorce-Lévesque CA
Sound-A-Bout AT
Alexander Spechtenhauser AT
Spirograph Agnew US
Sam Spreckley GB
Roelf Staal NL
Carsten Stabenow DE
Adam Stansbie GB
Benjamin Staude DE
Phillip Stearns US
Tamás Stéger HU
Markus Steinkellner AT
Gerd Stern US
Daniel Strokis US
Sturqen PT
Dmitry Subochev RU
Surabhi Surabhi IN
Philipp Süß DE
Yuri Suzuki JP
Maria Swiecicka PL
Sz. Berlin GB
Yuji Takatsuka JP
Mirjam Tally SE
Kynan Tan AU
Zihua Tan MY
Sachi Tanihara JP
te_ri JP
Daniel Teruggi IT
Martin Tétreault CA
The Mustangs in
Social Modulator CN
The Resonance of
3 Meta-Energies PL
The Soundscape Project for Earth-
quake Disaster, 311 JP
Christoph Theiler DE
Dan Theorin SE
Bernd Thiele DE
Jo Thomas GB
Andreas Tilliander SE
Kasper T. Toeplitz FR
Francesca Sarah Toich IT
Isao Tomita JP
Dan Tramte US
Nikos Triantafillidis GR
Valerio Tricoli IT
Harry Triendl AT
Michael Trommer CA
Ioannis Tsirikoglou GR
Diogo Tudela PT
Florian Tuercke DE
Carrie Tunick US
Roxanne Turcotte CA
Typingmonkeys JP
Keiko Uenishi JP
Timo Ullmann CH
Carl Unander-Scharin SE
Luis Valdivia AR
Edwin van der Heide NL
Frank Van Duerm IT
Allard van Hoorn NL
Mario van Horrik NL
Kyle Vanderburg US
Nicolás Varchausky AR
Various IT
Evgeniy Vashchenko UA
vdrey feat schultz FR
Els Viaene BE
Andersen Viana BR
Benjamin Vida US
Franck Vigroux FR
Tadej Vobovnik SI
Sabine Vogel DE
Yuk Bun Wan HK
Jing Wang CN
Riccardo Wanke IT
Clinton Watkins NZ
Jean-Marc Weber FR
wechselstrom DE
Johannes Weinberger AT
Jonas Wendelin DE
Wei Weng CN
Michael Wertmüller CH
Simon Whetham GB
Frances White US
White Elephant AT
White Noise Generator IT
Duncan Whitley GB
David Wicks US
Boedi Widjaja SG
Jeffrey Wiley Jr US
Zackery Wilson US
Michel Winterberg CH
Amnon Wolman US
RD Wraggett CA
James Wyness GB
Xiao Xiao US
Ryota Yamamura JP
Yong Joon Yang KR
Toshitsugu Yasaka JP
Taro Yasuno JP
Cong Ye CN
Yi Yin CN
Kazuya Yokoi JP
Koji Yokoyama JP
Samson Young HK
Yurodny IE
Roberto Zanata IT
Rouien Zarin CA
Kevin Zhang US
Zimoun Zimoun CH
Rutger Zuydervelt NL

HYBRID ART

!Mediengruppe Bitnik CH
Romy Achituv IL
Elina Aho FI
Jean-Michel Albert FR
Amy Alexander US
James Alliban GB
Refik Anadol TR
Yuki Anai JP
Casey Anderson US
Rui Filipe Antunes PT
Marcel·lí Antúnez Roca ES
Raphael Arar US
Art of Failure FR
Nicky Assmann NL
Jean-Pierre Aube CA
Sofian Audry CA
Kuai Shen Auson EC
Adam Aw SG
Nurit Bar-Shai US
Koby Barhad IL
SE Barnet Barnet US
Emma Barrowman CA
Prokop Bartoníček CZ
Malte Bartsch DE
Bernhard Bauch AT
BeatSneakers AT
Philip Beesley CA
Nelly Ben Hayoun FR
Guy Ben-Ary AU
Todd Berreth US
Gondouin Bertrand FR
Julien Bezy FR
Ranjit Bhatnagar US
Martin Bircher CH
Martin Bircher CH
Joelle Bitton FR
Nikkel Blaase DE
Klemens Bobenhausen DE
Jacky Boen ID
April Bojorquez US
Balint Bolygo GB
Fedra Boscaro IT
Bosch & Simons NL
Mathieu Bouvier FR
Tega Brain AU
Jan Brand DE
Breeze Arts JP
Marco Brianza IT
Jason Brown US
Leonardo Budimlic Majnaric HR
Daniel Burkhardt DE
Peter Burr US
Davide Cairo IT
Graham Callister GB

Tania Candiani MX
Adolfo Luxúria Canibal PT
Daniel Canogar ES
Lars Carlsson SE
Mattia Casalegno IT
Karen Casey AU
Michael Casey GB
Scott Cazan US
Howard Chao TW
Wei-Ting Chen TW
ChenChenchen & ChenChen CN
Oksana Chepelyk UA
Nathalie Chikhi FR
Chi-Ping Chin TW
Javier Chozas ES
Shing Tat Chung GB
Paolo Cirio IT
Grisha Coleman US
Collectif Dardex FR
Dan Collins US
Company Adrien M / Claire B FR
Philipp Contag-Lada DE
James Coupe GB
Luisa Covaria CO
Catharina Cronenberger Golebiowska DE
Laszlo Csernatony Lukacs HU
Darija Czibulkova SK
Raffaello D'Andrea CA
Donald Daedalus US
Diego Dall Osto IT
Jan De Coster BE
Elout de Kok NL
Marta de Menezes PT
Marco De Mutiis IT
Laurent Debraux FR
Andy Deck US
Louis-Philippe Demers CA
Alper Derinbogaz TR
Frederic Deslias FR
Ronan Devlin IE
Heather Dewey-Hagborg US
Sandra Christine Dick DE
hernani dimantas BR
Ivor Diosi HU
Peleg Dishon IL
Evelina Domnitch NL
Marco Donnarumma IT
Adam Donovan AU
DPrime Research CA
drog_A_tek GR
DSK (Juan Lesta & Belén Montero) ES
Rob Dunne GB
Lígia Duro PT
Alexis Dworsky DE
ectoplastic DE
Jessica Edwards GB
Alicia Eggert US
Kate Ehrhardt ZA
Émilie Brout & Maxime Marion FR
Engelstrompete DE
Kerstin Ergenzinger DE
Stefanie Katja Ernst DE
Gilberto Esparza MX
Esther Polak and Ivar van Bekkum NL
Ichiro Esumi JP
Tobias Euler DE
Planquette Fabrice FR
Jo Fairfax GB
Gene Felice US
Marc Ferrario CH
Thomas Feuerstein AT
Francesca Fini IT
Nirto Karsten Fischer DE
Louise Flanagan GB
Mina France FR
Anna Frants RU
David Fried US
Paul Friedlander GB
Philipp Friedrich AT
Verena Friedrich DE
Sandra Fruebing DE
Shohei Fujimoto JP
Ken Fujiyoshi JP
Adam Fure US
Ashley Fure US
Ryu Furusawa JP
David Galbraith US
T. A. Gambarotto CA
David Gann DE
Leslie Garcia MX
Matthew Garcia US
Pablo Garcia US
Adriana García-Benítez MX
Nataly Gattegno GR
Caroling Geary US
Dmitry Gelfand NL
Amanda Ghassaei US
Allan Giddy NZ
GK TECH JP
Ioni Gkliati GR
David Glowacki GB
Rrebecca Comperts NL
Anthony Gonzalez US
Steve Goodman GB
Charles Goyard FR
Christian Graupner DE
Tobias Gremmler DE
Erica Gressman US
Grinder-Man JP
Franziska Grohmann DE
David Gross AT
Lukas Jost Gross CH
Benjamin Grosser US
Tobias Grosshauser DE
David Guez FR
Rodrigo Guinski BR
Uwe Haas DE
Ian Haig AU
Benjamin Hammerich DE
Dominic Harris GB
Reka Harsanyi HU
Bjørn Erik Haugen NO
Robert Henke DE
Verena Henn DE
Lily Hibberd AU
Muhammad Hidayat ID
Karin Hochstatter DE
Stuart Hodgetts AU
Kris Hofmann GB
Leo Hofmann CH
Peter Holden GB
HONF Foundation ID
Kohyo Hong KR
Matt Hope CN
Kurt Hörbst AT
Hörner / Antlfinger DE
Takayuki Hoshi JP
GH Hovagimyan US
Martin Howse GB
HR-Stamenov BG
Yi-Ching Huang TW
Kirsten Hudson AU
Jin-Kyoung Huh KR
Joseph Hyde GB
Mikko Hynninen FI
I.S.P. DE
I/O Collective HU
Salvatore Iaconesi IT
Jorge Isaac NL
Tomoya Ishibashi JP
Hiroshi Ishiguro JP
Yuichi Ito JP
Yannick Jacquet CH
Janez Janša SI
Charlotte Jarvis GB
Janet Jennings GB
Maria Johansson SE
Jason Kelly Johnson US
Eduardo Kac US
Yasuaki Kakehi JP
Ruslan Kamolov PT
David Kamp DE
Lambert Kamps NL
Liad Kantorowicz PS
Ajay Kapur US
Simon Karlstetter DE
KarmetiK US
Yum Keiko Takayama JP
Stephen Kelly CA
Denisa Ɲera CZ
Ozgun Kilic TR
EunJin Kim KR
Taeyoon Kim KR
Yunchul Kim KR
József Gergely Kiss HU
Ralph Kistler DE
Asanobu Kitamoto JP
Dustin Klein DE
Ullrich Klose DE
Sören Knöll DE
David J. Knowles IE
Elitza Koeva BG
Kenji Kojima JP
Vedran Kolac HR
Denis Kolokol UA
Kombinat DE
Michinari Kono JP
Stian Korntved Ruud NO
Yuri Kostenko UA
Dmitri Kourliandski RU
Egor Kraft RU
Oliver Kraft DE
Fred Ku TW
Ebru Kurbak TR
Hyungwoo Kwon KR
Yuni Kwon KR
Kundo Kyon DE
Lab Binaer DE
Laboratori del Caos ES
Laboratory for Adaptive Intelligence, RIKEN Brain Science Institute JP
Wan-Ying Lai TW
Steve Lambert US
Derek Larson US
Mark Lawson AU
Chia-Ying Lee TW
HeeWon Lee KR
Daniela Lehmann DE
David Letellier FR
Ellen K. Levy US
Jennis Cheng Tien Li DE
Carolin Liebl DE
Pei-Ying Lin TW
Robert Lisek US
Matthias Lohscheidt DE
London Fieldworks GB
Simon Longo IT
Mick Lorusso US

LoVid US
Benjamin Low SG
Penousal Machado PT
Maximilian Maintz DE
Mark Malmberg US
Maria Kong Dancers Company IL
Lida Marinkova AT
Mark Marino US
Marshmallow Laser Feast GB
Mario Martinez Santamaria ES
Tiago Martins PT
Amelia Marzec US
maschen AT
Atsushi Masumori JP
Keiichi Matsuda GB
Roland Maurmair AT
Nancy Mauro-Flude AU
Rachel Mayeri US
Lauren McCarthy US
Megan McMillan US
Murray McMillan US
Mikey McParlane US
Yiannis Melanitis GR
Achim Menges DE
Daniel Miller US
mischer'traxler AT
mobilitylab ES
Florian Model DE
Jin-Yo Mok KR
Carlos Molinero Brizuela ES
Max Mollon FR
Sean Montgomery US
Peter Moosgaard AT
Simon Morasi Pipercic HR
Juan Manuel Moreno Aróstegui ES
Caitlin Morris US
Iain Mott AU
João Martinho Moura PT
Federico Muelas ES
Rui Yi Mui SG
Simen Musaeus NO
Dionysia Mylo GR
Dionysia Mylonaki GR
Andrea Nagl AT
Yusuke Nakamura JP
Luca Nasciuti IT
Henrike Naumann DE
Kamil Nawratil PL
Anna Neizvestnova RU
Reinhard Nestelbacher AT
Neuhausen DE
Next Nature Network NL
Nika Oblak & Primoz Novak SI
John O'Shea GB
Arlette Ochsner CH
Hisato Ogata JP
Kohei Ogawa JP
Mari Ohno JP
Toshiki Okada JP
Zac Ong MY
Zac Ong SG
Noémi Ördög HU
Frederick Ostrenko US
Matthew Ostrowski US
Tsai Ou-Bau TW
Overpass Light Brigade US
Richi Owaki JP
Hiromi Ozaki JP
Thomas Papa DK
Lefteris Papadimitriou GR
Dmitry Paranyushkin RU
Raquel Paricio ES
Bauer Pascal FR
Pierre-Yves Paslier FR
Miguel Pedro PT
Fred Penelle BE
Claudia Pense DE
Tristan Perich US
Oriana Persico IT
Personal Cinema GR
Ivan Petkov BG
Bärbel Pfänder FR
Bundith Phunsombatlert TH
PlastikWorks DE
Sascha Pohflepp DE
Andrea Polli US
Joseph Popper GB
Irene Posch AT
Afroditi Psarra GR
pvi collective AU
Anne Quirynen DE
Jorge Ramirez MX
Laura Ramirez CO
Artur Rebelo PT
Alexander Reben US
Steffen Reichert DE
Simone Reis BR
Johann Reißer DE
Philipp Reist CH
Jacob Sikker Remin DK
LInda Riseley AU
RIXC LV
Cendrine Robelin FR
Matt Rogalsky CA
Ethan Rose US
Carl-Johan Rosén SE
Tapio Rosenius FI
Richard Rosenman CA
Philip Ross US
Frank Holger Rothkamm DE
Niklas Roy DE
Rafael Rozendaal NL
Annina Rüst CH
Tatsuya Saito JP
Julie Salgues FR
Chris Salter US
Mariusz Samól PL
Marcos Sanchez CL
Akiko Sato JP
Scenocosme Grégory Lasserre & Anaïs met den Ancxt FR
Andreas Schlegel DE
Nikolas Schmid-Pfähler DE
Antoine Schmitt FR
Bjoern Schuelke DE
Gerhard Schultz US
Stefan Schwabe DE
Tobias Schwall DE
Daniel Schwarz DE
Bill Seaman US
Nina Sellars AU
Rob Seward US
Erin Sexton CA
Elliott Sharp US
Kuai Shen DE
Yaniv Shentser IL
Keiichiro Shibuya JP
Alessio Silvestrin IT
Maja Smrekar SI
No first name Snow AU
Bogdan Soban SI
Karolina Sobecka US
Gustavo Sol BR
Gustavo Soriano Ariza MX
Oluwaseyi Sosanya US
Wolfgang Spahn DE
Ief Spincemaille BE
ss-io KR
Samuel St-Aubin CA
Jens Standke DE
Raycho Stanev BG
Charles Stankievech CA
Austin Stewart US
Bianca Stich DE
Kristina Stoyanova BG
Marek Straszak PL
Corinne Studer CH
Studiomobile IT
kathrin Stumreich AT
Junko Sugimori JP
sukebeningen JP
Yasuko Suzuki JP
Alasdair Swenson GB
Diana Szawłowska PL
Loránd Szécsényi-Nagy HU
Martin Szollos CZ
Szövetség '39 Association of Artists HU
Tiam Taheri DE
Keiko Takahashi JP
Hideaki Takahashi JP
Hiroya Tanaka JP
Curtis Taylor AU
TEAM[:]niel AT
teamLab JP
Ladislav Tejml CZ
Soichi Terada JP
The Erasers GR
The Living (David Benjamin) US
ThinkingSketch Unit JP
Nancy Tobin CA
Jacob Tonski US
Polona Tratnik SI
Terry Trickett GB
Isabella Trimmel AT
Yu-Chuan Tseng TW
ubermorgen AT
Maki Ueda JP
Anja Ulfeldt US
United Visual Artists GB
Urbanscreen DE
Filipa Valente PT
Allard van Hoorn NL
Willem van Weeghel NL
Dušan Váňa CZ
Dieter Vandoren BE
Koen Vanmechelen BE
Paul Vanouse US
Thomas Vaquié BE
Maria Pía Vasquez Cepeda CL
vdrey feat schultz FR
Tom Vens NL
Gilles Viandier FR
Videoliner CO
Mithru Vigneshwara IN
Vesela Mihaylova Vladimirova BG
Anatoli Vlassov FR
Sven Voelker DE
Nils Völker DE
Bill Vorn CA
Sam Walker GB
Jeffwery Wang TW
Tony Wang TW
Andres Wanner CA
Pierce Warnecke US
Brent Watanabe US
Philipp Weber DE
Penelope Wehrli CH
Rosmarie Weinlich DE
Felix Weinold DE

Stephen Weissberger US
Hans Wesker DE
Jake Williams GB
Francis Wilson US
Markus Wintersberger AT
Chris Woebken DE
Mini Wu TW
Shi-Yen Wu TW
Kuan-Ying Wu TW
Kai Yang CN
Wonbin Yang KR
Yuji Yasunaga JP
ycam interLAB JP
Masaki Yokobe JP
Pinar Yoldas TR
Young Poor Artists LT
Jinhui Yu CN
Roberto Zanata IT
George Zisiadis US
Konstantin K. Zlatev BG
Jacek Złoczowski PL
Walter Zurborg DE
Christiaan Zwanikken NL

INTERACTIVE ART

Illuminart AU
Richard Zetterberg SE
//////////fur//// art entertainment interfaces DE
1024 Architecture FR
74R505 consortium AT
Kaho Abe US
Abstract Birds IT
Advanced Media Lab NC State US
Joelle Aeschlimann CH
Aether & Hemera IT
Charuvi Agrawal IN
Radamés Ajna BR
Masayuki Akamatsu JP
Mert Akbal TR
AKQA London GB
Alexey Alexey Chebykin RU
Alkemie CA
Michael Allison US
Sebastian Alvarez PE
Refik Anadol TR
Yoko Ando JP
Caterina Antonopoulou GR
Mariadele Arcuri IT
Philipp Artus DE
Kim Asendorf DE
Ruben Aubrecht AT
AuroraMeccanica IT
Vasilis Avdelas GR
Axes US
Tetsuaki Baba JP
Lucas Bambozzi BR
Eduardo Barata GB
Sam Baron IT
Daniel Barry US
Piotr Barszczewski PL
Malte Bartsch DE
Chris Basmajian US
Raphaël Bastide FR
Olivier Bau US
BeatSneakers AT
Giselle Beiguelman BR
Kathryn Bell US
Adam Ben-Dror NZ
Yonatan Ben-Simhon IL
Damien Beneteau FR
Alexander Berman SE
Bertha Bermudez ES
Maite Bermudez VE
Gondouin Bertrand FR
Martin Bircher CH
Jean-Jacques Birgé FR
Svein Inge Bjørkhaug NO
Erik Björkland SE
Elie Blanchard FR
Blast Theory GB
David Boardman US
Matthieu Bogaert BE
Marc Böhlen CH
Haylee Bolinger US
Alejandro Borsani AR
Cati Boulanger FR
David Bowen US
Victoria Bradbury US
Yael Braha IT
Tega Brain AU
Jens Brand DE
Thibault Brevet FR
James Bridle GB
Roman Bromboszcz PL
Mateusz Brzozowski PL
Dmitry Bulatov RU
Alexandre Burton CA
Lucas Buschfeld DE
Joel Cahen IL
Martin John Callanan GB
Rejane Cantoni BR
Pierre Carniaux FR
Richard Carr IE
Rodrigo Carvalho PT
Ivan Cash US
CAVI DK
Daniel Cermak-Sassenrath DE
Changing Places Group, MIT Media Lab US
Gregory Chatonsky FR
Tosh Chiang US
Jongwon Choi KR
Jonathan Chomko CA
Anna Christoffer DE
Vincent Ciciliato FR
Günışığı Cihangir TR
circle side JP
Paolo Cirio IT
Sandy Claes BE
Nicolas Clauss FR
Sandra Coelho PT
Christopher Coleman US
James Connolly US
Grayson Cooke NZ
Mike Cooper GB
Anabela Costa PT
James Coupe GB
Luc Courchesne CA
CØV GB
Luisa Covaria CO
Leonardo Crescenti BR
Sterling Crispin US
Ryan Cronin US
Jeff Crouse US
Krzysztof Cybulski PL
Daily Tous Les Jours CA
Ed Dambik US
Ursula Damm DE
Mariska de Groot NL
Marnix de Nijs NL
Laurent Debraux FR
André Décosterd CH
Michel Décosterd CH
Arnaud Delorme FR
Alexandra Dementieva BE
Laura Devendorf US
Tim Devine AU
Joss Doggett NZ
Noa Dolberg US
Margaret Dolinsky US
Marco Dondana SE
Reynald Drouhin FR
Juliane Duda DE
Pascal Dufaux CA
Constant Dullaart NL
Bojana Dumeljic NL
Jesus Duran US
Tomáš Dvořák CZ
Grayson Earle US
EBMM (Émilie Brout & Maxime Marion) FR
Ernest Edmonds GB
Tobias Edwards AU
Alicia Eggert US
Electroland US
elevenplay JP
Marcus Englund SE
Kyle Evans US
Everyware KR
exonemo JP
Behnaz Farahi IR
FAT lab US
Antonio Fernandes PT
Luiz Gustavo Ferreira Zanotello BR
Valentin Fetisov RU
Andreas Nicolas Fischer DE
Roch Forowicz PL
Holger Förterer DE
Antonin Fourneau FR
Thierry Fournier FR
Francesca Pascquali, Carlotta Piccinini, Andrea Familari IT
Anaisa Franco BR
Lisa Frank US
Kostantinos Frantzis GR
Eva Franz DE
Janina Frau Schlichte DE
Tyler Freeman US

Aieda Freitas BR
Erik Freydank DE
Masaki Fujihata JP
Jun Fujiwara JP
Gints Gabrans LV
Vanessa Gageos RO
Gallagher & Associates US
David Gann DE
Pablo Garcia US
Benjamin Gaulon IE
Jane Gauntlett GB
Jenna Gavin AF
Knut Gerwers DE
Gijs Gieskes NL
Ioni Gkliati GR
Alan Gleeson IE
Ruairi Glynn IE
Alisa Goikhman IL
Krzysztof Goliński PL
Suguru Goto JP
Gotye AU
Panayiotis Goubouros GR
Charlotte Gould GB
Christian Graupner DE
Jeff Greenspan US
Dan Gregor CZ
Manon Greiner DE
Gareth Griffiths GB
Grönlund - Nisunen FI
Benjamin Grosser US
Jeff Guess US
David Guez FR
Maximilian Gurresch AT
Carles Gutiérrez ES
Hiromi Habuto JP
Jayson Haebich AU
Cosmin Haias RO
Eduard Haiman RU
Trevor Haldenby CA
Sanglim Han KR
Byeong-jun Han KR
Yoon Chung Han KR
Dominic Harris GB
Ellie Harrison GB
Haruma Kikuchi & Circuit Lab JP
Yuto Hasebe JP
Ai Hasegawa JP
Yasuhito Hashiba JP
Sunao Hashimoto JP
Toshiyuki Hashimoto JP
Bjørn Erik Haugen NO
Sachiko Hayashi SE
Sayuki Hayashi JP
He-Lin Luo & I-Chun Chen TW
Werner Heisse DE

Drew Hemment GB
Henrik Munch DK
Thiago Hersan BR
Thiago Hersan BR
Luke Hespanhol AU
Scott Hessels US
Muhammad Hidayat ID
Satoru Higa JP
Dolores Hilhorst NL
Masami Hirabayashi JP
Makoto Hirahara JP
Aleksandra Hirszfeld PL
Andreas Hjorth SE
Oliver Hödl AT
Brent Hoff US
Kurt Hofstetter AT
Marianne Holm Hansen DK
Toshiyuki Horie JP
Satoshi Horii JP
Christoph Höschele DE
Hosoya Schaefer Architects CH
Evelyn Hribersek SI
MinYen Hsieh TW
Bill Hsu US
Chin-Hsiang Hu TW
Hsin-Chien Huang TW
Scottie Chih-Chieh Huang TW
Caroline Huf AU
Tam Hunt US
Nick Hwang US
HYBE KR
Hypersonic Engineering & Design US
Etsuko Ichihara JP
IDEEA Lab JP
Daniel Iglesia US
Ayaka Ikezawa JP
Incredible Machines US
Shiho Ishizuka JP
ISO GB
Takayuki Ito JP
Mogens Jacobsen DK
Matthieu Jacquot FR
Arnim Jepsen DE
Nova Jiang NZ
Masaru Jingi JP
Daniel Julià Lundgren ES
ChangYong Jung KR
Hannes Jung DE
Boaz Kaizman DE
Yasuaki Kakehi JP
Jack Kalish US
Ksawery Kaliski PL
Akihiko Kaneko JP
So Kanno JP
Karen Lancel & Hermen Maat NL

Hirotaka Katakura JP
Yoshimasa Kato JP
Satoshi Kawabata JP
Dmitry Kawarga RU
Max B. Kazemzadeh US
Ellen Keith US
Matt Kenyon US
Hernán Kerlleñevich AR
Svenja Keune DE
Scott Kildall US
Christoph Kilian DE
Hyung-Gyu Kim KR
Minjee Kim KR
Hiroyasu Kimura JP
Yusaku Kimura JP
King Zog GB
Ryo Kishi JP
Markus Kison DE
Klangfiguren DE
Tobias Klein DE
Signe Klejs DK
Philipp Kliem DE
Karl Klomp NL
Urszula Kluz-Knopek PL
Marcin Kobylecki PL
Osman Koç TR
Raquel Kogan BR
Joyce Beetuan Koh SG
Michal Kohút CZ
Kollision DK
Keina Konno JP
Heidi Köpfer CH
Ralf Kopp DE
Julian Koschwitz DE
Tatiana Kovaleva RU
Jakub Koźniewski PL
Rico Krafft DE
Denise Kratzer CH
Lex Kravitz US
Sophi Kravitz US
Veronika Krenn AT
Tatsuro Kudo JP
Anna Kulik RU
Ebru Kurbak TR
KUSC Interactive US
Tsz Wai Alan Kwan HK
Elettra La Marca IT
David Labiano ES
Wan-Ying Lai TW
Tom LaPann US
Adam Laskowitz US
Caroline Laurin-Beaucage CA
Le Clair Obscur FR
Titus Leber AT
Byungjoo Lee KR

Jinha Lee KR
Joong Han Lee KR
Marc Lee CH
Mercedes Leipoldt NL
Joanie Lemercier FR
James Leng US
Jason Edward Lewis CA
WenChing Li TW
LIA AT
Hakan Lidbo SE
Geoffrey Lillemon US
Shu-min Lin TW
PerMagnus Lindborg SE
Jung-Hua Liu TW
Solimán López ES
Silvio Lorusso IT
Rafael Lozano-Hemmer MX
Jesse Lucas FR
Lucas Buschfeld & Markus Hoffmann DE
Felix Luque ES
Alexander Lysov RU
Dominik Mahnič SI
Eric Maillet FR
Małgorzata Kuciewicz & Simone De Iacobis PL
Laura Malinverni IT
Daito Manabe JP
Emmanuil Manousakis GR
Mark C. Marino US
Ana Catharina Marques BR
Matthew Martin AF
MASZ_IN PL
Lukas Matejka SK
Robert Mathy AT
Hiroshi Matoba JP
Katsufumi Matsui JP
Nancy Mauro-Flude AU
Kyle McDonald US
Natalie McKeever US
Laleh Mehran US
Jeremy Mende US
Neil Mendoza GB
Martin Messier CA
MID ES
Laurent Mignonneau FR
Milica Mijacevic-Carevic RS
Ivan Milas HR
Brad Miller AU
Ricardo Miranda Zuniga US
Daichi Misawa JP
mischer'traxler AT
Mikiko Mizuno JP
Mikołaj Molenda PL
Kasia Molga GB

Cristina Molina US
Anders Monrad DK
Dmitry Morozov RU
Takeshi Mukai JP
Kazushi Mukaiyama JP
Fumiaki Murakami JP
Mary Murray US
Roberto Musanti IT
Bruno Nadeau CA
Leila Nadir US
Yuji Nakada JP
Ken Nakagaki JP
Yoshihito Nakanishi JP
Yasutaka Nakata JP
Hye Yeon Nam KR
Su Hyun Nam KR
Ricardo Nascimento BR
Armine Nersesyan GE
Miguel Neto PT
neurowear JP
Simon Nielsen DK
Mani Nilchiani US
Miao Niu CN
Yasushi Noguchi JP
Marlena Novak US
Petr Novikov RU
Martin Očko SI
Kazunori Ogasawara JP
Soonmi Oh KR
Tetsuji Ohno JP
Maciej Olszewski PL
onformative DE
Kian Peng Ong SG
Zac Ong SG
Yoshito Onishi JP
Mizue Ono JP
Fernando Orellana US
Delfin Ortiz Djian ES
Johannes P Osterhoff DE
Frederick Ostrenko US
Erik Overmeire NL
Hiromi Ozaki JP
Guvenc Ozel TR
Maciej Ozog PL
Thomas Pachoud FR
Máté Pacsika HU
David Palazón ES
Karen Palmer GB
panGenerator PL
Maxence Parache FR
Dmitry Paranyushkin RU
Jun Park KR
Soo Sunny Park US
Chiara Passa IT
Dennis Paul DE
David Penuela ES
Cary Peppermint US
Perfume JP
Boris Petrovsky DE
Michał Piasecki PL
Playmodes ES
Plebian Design US
Matthew Plummer-Fernandez GB
Tsau Po-Yuan TW
Daphne Polyzos GR
Rehmi Post US
Lorenz Potthast DE
Ivan Poupyrev RU
Alex Prooper NL
Psychasthenia Studio US
Shuai-Cheng Pu TW
Jordi Puig ES
Jie Qi US
François Quévillon CA
Hansi Raber AT
Misha Rabinovich US
Erwan Raguenes FR
Vanessa Ramos-Velasquez BR
Kevin Raxworthy AU
Alex Reben US
Alexander Rechberg DE
Aaron Reed US
Lutz Reiter DE
Etienne Rey FR
Rhizomatiks JP
Maximo Riadigos AR
Russell Richards GB
Matt Richardson US
Morten Riis DK
RIXC LV
Niels Roensholdt DK
Grzegorz Rogala PL
Kevin Röhl DE
Daniel Rojas CL
Fred Romano FR
Daan Roosegaarde NL
Fraser Ross GB
Marc Roth US
Stephanie Rothenberg US
Rafael Rozendaal NL
Daniel Rozin US
Zsuzsa Rozsavolgyi HU
David Allan Rueter US
Adam Russell GB
Kimiko Ryokai JP
Maxim Safioulline US
Ozge Samanci TR
Davey Sams AU
Andrea Santini IT
Surabhi Saraf IN
Peter Sarkozi HU
Noah Sasso US
Mene Savasta Alsina AR
Scenocosme Grégory Lasserre &
Anaïs met den Ancxt FR
Vincenzo Davide Schinaia IT
Janina Schlichte DE
Markus Schmeiduch AT
Nikolas Schmid-Pfähler DE
Deborah Schmidt DE
Antoine Schmitt FR
Martin Schneider DE
Schnitt IT
Susanna Schoenberg IT
Philipp Schoessler DE
Tom Schofield GB
Stefan Schwabe DE
John Sear GB
Second Story Interactive Studios US
SEHSUCHT Berlin DE
Luca Serasini IT
Paul Sermon GB
Jack Shaw US
Inder Shergill IN
Aaron Sherwood US
Pei-Yu Shi TW
Shibuhouse JP
Motoi Shimizu JP
ShortKuts JP
Venelin Shurelov BG
Hanna Fidelis Siecke DE
SII Collective NL
Vygandas Simbelis LT
Gerald Simpson GB
SIProp JP
Eric Siu HK
Mats Sivertsen NO
Ante Sladic SE
Edwin Sloot NL
Vadim Smakhtin RU
Karolina Sobecka US
Michele Solinas IT
Christa Sommerer AT
Sosolimited US
Sound-A-Bout AT
Guilherme Souza BR
Judith Spang DE
Adam Sporne GB
Moritz Stefaner DE
Nathaniel Stern US
Nick Stevens GB
Damian Stewart NZ
Garry Stewart AU
Filip Strebeyko SE
Studio NAND DE
Superbe interactive BE
Yuri Suzuki JP
Synchrodogs UA
Szövetség '39 Association of
Artists HU
Yuta Takeuchi JP
Matthias Tarasiewicz AT
Shuntaro Tashiro JP
Team resonate DE
The Principals US
TheGreenEyl DE
Paul Thomas AU
David Tinapple US
Jonathan Tippett CA
Koki Toda JP
Martin Tomitsch AT
Spencer Topel US
Juan Carlos Toro Lecaros CL
Bartholomäus Traubeck DE
Terry Trickett GB
Guerlotte Tristan FR
Diego Trujillo MX
Tatsuto Tsuchishita JP
Yasuhiro Tsuchiya JP
Alexander Tuchacek AT
Hajnalka Tulisz SK
Fethi Can Tüzel TR
Jeroen Ubels NL
uh513 ES
Anja Ulfeldt US
Undendlich DE
Yolanda Uriz ES
Filipa Valente PT
Olav van der Doorn NL
Jochem van der Spek NL
Jasper Van Loenen NL
Mick van Rooijen NL
Nathan Van Schoote BE
Art Van Triest NL
Maartje van Zon NL
Evgeniy Vashchenko UA
Fernando Velázquez UY
Tom Vens NL
Tom Verbruggen NL
Bernardo Vercelli IT
Els I.R.L. Vermang BE
Aurélien Vernhes-Lermusiaux FR
Mithru Vigneshwara IN
Lilia Villafuerte PE
Jonathan Villeneuve CA
Vesela Mihaylova Vladimirova BG
Petros Vrellis GR
Addie Wagenknecht US
Wahlberg DK
Yandell Walton AU

Daan Wampers BE
Yufan Wang CN
Cheng-Liang wang CN
Brent Watanabe US
We Are Matik US
weAREmedienkuenstler DE
Pascale Weber FR
Chen Wei Ling TW
Where dogs run RU
Adam Wierzchowski PL
Marcel Wiessler DE
Wildbytes ES
Okke Willebrands NL
Michel Winterberg CH
Rob Wittig US
Spike Wolff US
Ming-Chang Wu TW
Xiao Xiao US
Aina Yamaguchi JP
Takahiro Yamaguchi JP
Junichi Yamaoka JP
Mika Yamauchi JP
Masasuke Yasumoto JP
YCAM InterLab JP
Muharrem Yildirim US
Jay Alan Yim US
EunKyoung Yoo KR
Hyeyoung Yoo KR
Sangjun Yoo KR
Shigeo Yoshida JP
Spiridoula Zachou GR
Jody Zellen US
Mushon Zer-Aviv IL
Arthur Zerktouni FR
Qian Zhang CN
Shanshan Zhou CN
Chris Ziegler DE
Witek Zimiszewski PL
Zimoun Zimoun CH
Enrico Zimuel IT

DIGITAL COMMUNITIES

Abstractorium https://www.youtube.com/feed/?feature=guide
Actipedia http://actipedia.org/
Activism Beyond the Interface: the Sandbox Project http://www.sandbox-prj.org/
Africa is a Country http://africasacountry.com
African Digital Art Network http://africandigitalart.com
AirCasting http://aircasting.org/
Akirachix—A revolution for African Women and Technology http://www.akirachix.com
Alchemy about the Poetry https://vimeo.com/61866678
Apps4Africa http://apps4africa.org
Arquivo Sonoro / Pernes / Sound Archive http://www.aspsa.tk
Bablrr http://bablrr.com/
Between the Bars http://www.betweenthebars.org
Bike Share Map http://bikes.oobrien.com/
BlogAdda.com http://www.blogadda.com
Botaniq http://www.botaniq.org
BudgIT http://yourbudgit.com
BundesGit http://bundestag.github.com/gesetze/
CAPE http://www.HiCAPE.com
Casastristes http://casastristes.org
Cenci Journalism Project http://www.icenci.com
CrisisMappers http://www.crisismappers.net
Critical Making http://conceptlab.com/criticalmaking/
Cryptagram http://cryptagr.am
CULTURESHUTDOWN http://www.cultureshutdown.net
Data Dealer—Legal? Illegal? Whatever! http://www.datadealer.net
Dérive app http://deriveapp.com
E-180 http://www.e180.com
ECO Chinese Website http://www.ecocn.org/portal.php
Ecofund—Our future is green! http://www.ecofund.org
El Campo de Cebada http://elcampodecebada.org
Emergent Mind of City and Qualia Landscapes http://www.cogart.org
Everyday Rebellion http://www.everydayrebellion.com
Fair Electronics https://play.google.com/store/apps/details?id=prosper.cornerstone.fairtech
Fantastic Futures http://www.fantasticfutures.fm
Fengmuqiao Farmer's Online Protest http://weibo.com/fengmuqiao
fhSPACE http://www.youtube.com/fhSPACEtv
Foldit http://fold.it
Free Weibo // Greatfire.org https://freeweibo.com/
Game Girl Workshop http://gamegirlworkshop.org
gANGA http://www.iganga.it
Gangway http://www.gangway.net/
Genspace Community Laboratory http://www.genspace.org
Gernot Untergruber http://gernotuntergruber.com/
Global Yodel—travel through a local lens http://globalyodel.com
HealthPhone http://healthphone.org
HONF Foundation—House of Natural Fiber http://ix.natural-fiber.com
I am we_interactive image http://www.interactive-image.org
Imaginary—open mathematics http://www.imaginary.org
Indian Memory Project http://www.indianmemoryproject.com
Information Bomb http://imedia.asp.krakow.pl
Inteligencias Colectivas 2.0 http://www.inteligenciascolectivas.org/
Interactive Virtual Video Library: Global Lives Project http://globallives.org
Interaktive Web 2.0 Literatur: „Zwirbler" - der weltweit 1. Facebook-Roman http://www.facebook.com/Zwirbler.Roman
Ipaidabribe.com—Crowdsourcing Against Corruption http://www.ipaidabribe.com
IRNAfrica Virtual Library & Learning Centre http://irnafricavirtual.org/
ISEA 2012: Machine Wilderness http://www.isea2012.org
Jaime Hernández https://www.facebook.com/#!/profile.php?id=100004837537492&fref=ts
Kamaloka (Hommage a Dante) http://www.hrom.de/kamaloka/
Kollabora—We are what we make! http://www.kollabora.com
Kyberia http://kyberia.sk
Labmovel http://www.labmovel.net
Laboratory of Patching http://www.rolandkuit.com/Laboratory.html
La cosa radiactiva (The radioactive thing) http://lacosaradiactiva.uncoded.es
LA Pools
Lasersaur http://lasersaur.com
LazyTruth http://lazytruth.com
Life Needs Internet http://www.lifeneedsinternet.com
Light is History http://designresearch.aalto.fi/projects/lih/
Lobbyplag.eu http://www.lobbyplag.eu
Locommun http://www.locommun.eu
MAMA (Mobile Alliance for Maternal Action) South Africa http://www.askmama.co.za
Manifestation http://www.adeptprojects.co.uk
Manushya http://www.hrom.de/manushya/
Meet Your Stranger http://meetyourstranger.com
Metropolitalia http://www.metropolitalia.org
Microbes and castles http://vimeo.com/50491192
Museu do Resgate (Museum of Ransom) http://www.facebook.com/museudoresgate
Musomap—The Global Map of Musicians http://www.musomap.com
Mustardland http://www.paranormal.org.uk/mustardland
netzpolitik.org http://netzpolitik.org/
New Media Nation STAND
Next City http://nextcity.org/
NicoNicoGakkai Beta http://niconicogakkai.jp/
Numbeo—cost of living http://www.numbeo.com
NYC Resistor http://www.nycresistor.com/
Odoygiant The New King http://www.odoygiant.com
oiga.me, a platform for citizenship's lobby https://oiga.me/
Open Government Data—data.gv.at http://data.gv.at

Openinspiration
http://www.openinspiration.com
Open Knowledge Foundation's Global Network
http://lod2.okfn.org/
OpenPositioningSystem
http://www.openps.info
Orçamento Participativo Digital de Belo Horizonte http://opdigital2011.pbh.gov.br/
OurGoods.org https://ourgoods.org/
PanSci http://pansci.tw/
PARK(ing) Day
http://www.parkingday.org
Parkins(on)line
http://www.parkinsonline.info/
Pause Festival
http://www.pausefest.com.au/
Petition Planet
Pijama Surf http://pijamasurf.com
Pinoccio http://pinocc.io
Public Lab's DIY Spectral Analysis Community
http://www.spectralworkbench.org
QRator http://www.qrator.org
Que Sabés? http://www.quesabes.org
QuintanaLibre: next-gen grassroots digital community network
http://quintanalibre.org.ar/
Refugees United
http://info.refunite.org/
Respekt.net http://www.respekt.net
Rights To Information–RTI India
http://www.rtiindia.org
Seeed Studio–Open Hardware Facilitator
http://www.seeedstudio.com/blog
Seven Sisters Project
http://www.sevensistersproject.org
Share Conference
http://www.shareconference.net
Smart Citizen. Open source hardware (and software) tools for the production of cities by citizens
http://goteo.org/project/smart-citizen-sensores-ciudadanos
SOS Sound of Sirens
http://www.sound-of-sirens.net
SQS & SQS.loc – Zukünfte digitaler Communities analog „erspielen"?
http://social-qs.net
Stadtwachewache
http://www.stadtwachewache.tk/
Stenstan Visitor Center
#StopTheTerror http://www.wegram.com/stoptheterror
Storage Room of the Museum of the Contemporary
http://www.mofc.org/
Subway
http://dwig.lmc.gatech.edu/projects/Quitmeyer/subway/main.php
Sunlight Foundation http://sitegeist.sunlightfoundation.com/
Swipp–Unlocking the wisdom of the world http://www.swipp.com
Tasty Pixels
http://jidori.me/works/tastypixels
Teatron http://www.tea-tron.com
Terms of Service; Didn't Read
http://www.tosdr.org
The Celebrity-Cluster Index
http://theclusterproject.com/bombs/celebrity-cluster-index/
The Community Currency Bitcoin
http://bitcoin.org
The Death of the URL
http://xxxxxxxxxx.xxxxxxxxxxxxxxxxxxxxxxxxxxxxxxxxxxxxx.xxx/xxxxxxxxxxxxxxxxx.xxxxxxxxxx/xxxxx/xxxxxxxxxxxxxxxxxxx_xxxxxxxxxxxxxxxxxxx/xxxxxxxxxxxxxx.xxxxxxxxx/xxxxxxx.xxxxxxxxxxxxx/
The East Japan Earthquake Archive
http://e.nagasaki.mapping.jp/p/japan-earthquake.html
The Garden Library
The Interaction Design Foundation
http://www.interaction-design.org
The Quintessential Revolution
http://youtu.be/0sIc3GqIG1I
The Restart Project http://therestartproject.org
The Universal Declaration of Urban Rights http://declaracionderechosurbanos.com/
The Void https://vimeo.com/43527997
The Widget Art Gallery http://the-widget-art-gallery.blogspot.it/%20
The Youth Republic
http://www.theyouthrepublic.com
The قلب Programming Language
http://qlblang.org/
Thinking Food Design
http://www.thinkingfooddesign.com
This Exquisite Forest
http://exquisiteforest.com
This is Roberto Delgado
https://vimeo.com/29201425
TradeSchool.coop
http://tradeschool.coop/
TurboVote http://www.turbovote.org
Universidade Livre Fora do Eixo
http://universidade.foradoeixo.org.br/
UpStage http://www.upstage.org.nz
UrbanLeaks http://urbanleaks.org/
Urban Legend Kampala
http://urbanlegendkampala.com
Urban Spirits
http://www.urban-spirits.com/
USEUM–The crowd-sourced museum of art http://useum.org
valeveil http://www.valeveil.se
Valo TV http://www.valo.tv
Visualizing Palestine
http://www.visualizingpalestine.org
Walking the Edit
http://walking-the-edit.net/en/
Walkonomics–How Walkable is Your Street?
http://www.walkonomics.com
Wasa2il
Watherweel http://water-wheel.net
Whatchado www.whatchado.net
White Sack
Wikipedia Illustrated
http://wikipediaillustrated.org
Wikirating–The Transparent World Credit Rating Organization
http://www.wikirating.org
Wiser.org http://wiser.org/
Women who Mentor & Innovate–Africa
Wooloo.org http://www.wooloo.org
XinCheJian
http://www.xinchejian.com
Yes Lab http://www.yeslab.org
Your Priorities
http://bulgaria.yrpri.org/
YourTurn! The Video-Game
http://yourturn.fm
Your World of Text
http://www.yourworldoftext.com
Youth Ki Awaaz: Mouthpiece for the Youth
http://www.youthkiawaaz.com/
ZED.TO http://zed.to/

[the next idea]

Air slaves HU
AMeBE IT
Sepand Ansari US
Najia Anwari AF
Atelier CMJN FR
Jaehyuck Bae KR
Nana Bagdavadze US
Courtney Bailey GB
Domenico Barra IT
Bastard DK
Woody Batts US
Sheldon Bess US
Laura Boffi IT
Agnieszka Ewa Braun PL
Eric Brittingham US
Martin Calvino UY
Ulysses Castellanos CA
Pei Hon, Seed Chen CN
Gimmy Chu CA
Sarawut Chutiwongpeti TH
Markéta Cilečková CZ
Chris Clavio US
Marcelo Coelho BR
Belinda Cullen GB
Gina Czarnecki GB
Ryan Davis US
Mike Dawson US
Senne Dehandschutter BE
Dibbital US
Roz Dimon US
Alexis Dworsky DE
Ento GB
Melody Eötvös AU
Gabriel Hainer Evansohn US
Anna Fatér HU
Rozita Fogelman US
Charles Fracchia FR
Anaisa Franco BR
Martin Fröhlich CH
Anna Gaik-Czasak PL
Mikhael Tara Garver US
Anita Giraldo US
Kosta Grammatis GR
Mara Haseltine US
Justin Hawkins US
Madeline Hawkins US
Marcel Helmer DE
Ivan Henriques BR
Garnet Hertz CA
Honf ID
Jannis Hülsen DE
Hoyan Ip GB
Marcin Jakubowski US
Christina Jauernik AT

Henry Jesionka CA
Lu Jin CN
Magdalena Kahr AT
Maxim Kamanin RU
Yoshimasa Kato JP
Courtney Katz US
Steve Keen AU
Kibu HU
Jonghwa Kim US
Olga Kisseleva RU
Sonja Maria Kröner DE
Wing Sze, kismet Kwong HK
Wolfgang Lehrner AT
Pei-Ying Lin TW
Alain Lioret FR
Bogdan Litescu RO
Jung-Hua Liu TW
Douglas Mallette US
Tobias Martens DE
Naho Matsuda JP
Milan Metthey FR
Chanwook Min KR
Andrea Müller DE
Jan Mun US
Dominic Muren US
Christian Buus Nielsen HU
Ole Stobbe Nielsen DK
Simon Oberhammer AT
Ruben Olguin US
Oxfam Novib / Team Kabul AF
Alejandro Palandjoglou AR
Nasser Palangi AU
Maxence Parache FR
Dmitry Paranyushkin RU
Cclaudia Pasquero IT
Timothy Payne US
Matthias Pázmándy AT
Iwer Petersen DE
Špela Petrič SI
Marco Poletto IT
Nelson Ramon CO
Gaurav Raut IN
Daniel Riegler AT
Nigel Roddy IE
Tomas Rodinger CA
Rafael Rozendaal NL
Atılım Şahin TR
Daniela Schiffer DE
Janina Schlichte DE
Uwe Schmidt DE
Markus Schulz DE
Robertina Šebjanič SI
Pei-Yu Shi TW
Stocznia CZ
Paul Strohmeier AT
Bartłomiej Święcki PL
Tacit Group KR
James Taylor US
Skylar Tibbits US
Stratton Tingle US
Wolfgang Tschapeller AT
Florian Tuercke DE
James Tunick US
Andrey Ustinov RU
Marco van Beers NL
jolan van der wiel NL
Merel van der Woude NL
Julio Velasco CO
Miguel Vidal ES
Lutz Waldenburger DE
Pascale Weber FR
Mario Werndl AT
Brian White CA
Juehui Wu CN
Christian Yan CA

u19 – CREATE YOUR WORLD

Agnes Aistleitner
Akram Abidi
Firat Aglamaz
Julia Aigner
Bernadette Aigner
Agnes Aistleitner
Bengisu Akbulut
Hacer Akogul
Bianca Albrecht
Yusuf Alimli
Mikail Altintas
Thomas Altmann
Michaela Altmann
Tansu Altun
Imal Amiri
Luzia Amon
Wendelin Angermann
Felix Anselmi
Patrik Arnberger
Dima Arutunjan
Betti Auberger
Raphael Auffahrt
Lukas Aufmesser
Lena Bachl
Klaus Bachmair
Tamara Barounig
Marlene Bartosik
Michael Bastirz
Lisa Baumann
Marco Baumgartner
Kilian Bayer
Selina Bayer
Christoph Berghuber
Julia Christine Bernhart
Christina Bichowez
Johanna Binder
Christoph Binder
Sandra Binder
Laurenz Birnbaum
Anna Birngruber
Nadine Birngruber
Anna Birngruber
Sabine Bischinger
Sebastian Blanka
Elisabeth Bloder
Xenia Bluhm
Jonas Bodingbauer
Luka Bogdanovic
Katharina Böhm
Tanja Böhm
Daniela Böhm
Kübra Börekci
Franziska Boschele
Hacibayram Bozdogan
Vanessa Brandi
Christian Brandl
Florian Brandl
Julia Brauneis
Isabel Brennsteiner
Stefan Breuer
Christoph Brodtrager
Mirjam Bromundt
Moritz Brosch
Kerstin Bruckner
Philipp Bruckner
Melanie Brugger
Stefan Brunner
Manuel Brunner
Florian Bührle
Felix Bürger
Anja Burgstaller
Ceyda Calisir
Tereza Cavarovic
Zoran Cavic
Vanessa Alina Cerny
Valentin Cizmas
Noah Coquet
Kerim Coskun
Georg Csarman
Georg Csarmann
Matthias Dafert
Emre Dag
Tobias Dam
Alexandra Dankl
Manuel Dattinger
Bianca Decker
Bilal Demirel
Esther Demuth
Jonathan Denz
Raphael Deschka
Simon Deutsch
Tobias Diestler
Isidor Dietrich
Esther Distlbacher
Matej Djekic
Marijana Djordjic
Astrid Dober
Selina Viola Doleschal
Aidan Don
Florian Draschbacher
Polina Dubova
Laurenz Dums
Simon Dutzler
Ingrid Ebel
Alexander Ecker
Sarah Eckerstorfer
Reinhard Edelmoser
Ruth Celine Eder
Sarah Eder

Hannah Eggenberger
Alexandra Egger
Johannes Egger
Katharina Egger
Johannes Egger
Alexandra Egger
Katharina Egger
Johanna Eichinger
Mert Ekmekci
Johannes Elsner
Magdalena Engl
Christina Engleder
Verena Claudia Engleder
Christina Engleder
Lisa Marie Ennemoser
Bettina Enzenhofer
Bernhard Ettinger
Victoria Ettl
Sonja Falkner
Arman Fazlijaj
Mona Felkl
Jakob Felner
Faruk Fetahagic
Felix Feuersinger
Fabian Fink
Nicole Fischer
Robert Fischer
Jonas Fölk
Jennifer Forst
Lorena Forster
Vanii Forster
Jenny Forster
Lorena Forster
Vanii Forster
Sophie Forsthuber
Michelle Forthofer
Kati Franjic
Valentina Franzzetta
Simon Freiberger
Laura Freidinger
Vanessa Friedl
Jaqueline Friedl
Sophie Friedrich
Jakob Fröhling
Alexander Fuchs
Markus Fuchsreiter
Chiara Fürpass
Christian Gaisl
Michael Gall
Kevin Gamper
Kathi Gärtner
Shereen Gassenbauer
Florian Gasser
Loretta Gassler
Sarah Gaßner

Maximilian Gattinger
Davor Gaura
Lukas Gegenhuber
Konstantin Georgoulopoulos
Melike Gercek
Sandra Gieringer
Magdalena Giesshamer
Andreas Glaser
Daniel Glaser
Andreas Glaser
Miriam Glatz
Aylin-Büsra Gökdal
Konstantia Gölß
Simone Goluch
Jakub Gora
Kathrin Göschl
Isabella Elena Göschl
Beate Gotthartsleitner
Manuel Graber
Stephanie Grabner
Lorenz Max Grabovac
Patricia Graf
Joachim Grassinger
Michaela Greil
Daniela Gressl
Kerstin Gressl
Lukas Greul
Matthias Grill
Rosi Grillmair
Michèle Grohs
Melanie Gruber
Jasmin Gruber
Gabriel Grünstäudl
Philipp Grünstäudl
Bertram Gschwandtner
Fabian Gtsöttnmayr
Betül Gül
Haydar Güler
Sophie Güntner
Alex Guppenberger
Hans Peter Guppenberger
Jonas Guru
Laura Haas
Roman Haberleithner
Katharina Hackl
Viktoria Hackl
Martin Hafner
Günther Hagenauer
Evamaria Hahn
Lisa Hahn
Lena Haidenthaler
Thomas Haider
Viktoria Haindl
Selina Halmetschlager
Benjamin Hammerl

Lena Hammerschmidt
Esma Han
Karin Haneder
Verena Hanny
Tunahan Harmankaya
Simone Hart
Florian Hartl
Maximilian Hartmaier
David Hartmair
Hannah Hasenberger
Viktoria Haslinger
Michaela Haumer
Markus Heiderer
Janine Heinzl
Sonja Heinzl
Bianca Heiss
Marie Hengsberger
Thomas Hennebichler
Gabriela Hennebichler
Armin Herbsthofer
Coletta Hermann
Gregor Hiemetzberger
Tobias Hinterlechner
Anna Hinterseer
Viktoria Hirl
Daniel Hirm
Lena Hirtl
Christoph Höbart
Viktoria Höbarth
Sabrina Hödl
Mirjam Hofbauer
Julian Hofbauer
Bernadette Hofbauer
Johanna Hofer
Kerstin Hofer
Madeline Hofer
Sebastian Höglinger
Kristina Hold
Samuel Holl
Georg Höller
Magdalena Höller
Rebecca Hollerer
Flora Nimue Hollinetz
Katharina Holzer
Kristina Holzinger-Neulinger
Romana Holzknecht
Sebastian Holzmann
Alexandra Holzschuh
Alexandra Holzschuh
Jacqueline Holzschuh
Matthias Honigschnabl
Philipp Hörandner
Lukas Hornegger
Arian Hoseini
Sasan Hoseini

Jolanda Huber
Johannes Huber
Anna Huemer
Laura Huemer
Manuel Huttegger
Tobias Hyde
Mathias Innerhofer
Florian Jachs
Thomas Jahn
Hannah Jaksch
Jaqueline Janschitz
Mike Johnson
Sarah Jovanovic
Daniel Judmaier
Nick Jurik
Atilla Kahraman
Ulrich Kaindlbauer
Simon Kalcher
Manuel Kaltenbach
Martin Kamleithner
Oguzhan Karadavut
Anika Kaserer
Amelie Kaserer
Benjamin Kasper
Jacky Kastner
Isabel Katzenschlager
Tanja Keczol
Max Kernmayer
Kevin Kirchmair
Christoph Kirchner
Manuel Kisser
Julia Klambauer
Sina Klapeer
Lucia Klecatsky
Siegfried Klecka
Lisa Kletzl
Milena Klien
Michele Corina Kloiber
Florian Kluibenschedl
Annabell Knapp
Lisa-Maria Knapp
Sarah Knapp
Victoria Knapp
Lisa-Maria Knapp
Julia Margaret Kober
Maria Koblmüller
Leon Kohlberger
Roman Kohlhofer
Dominik Koller
Marlene Kolm
Aida Koné-el-adji
Lukas Königsegger
Sarah Konrad
Markus Koppensteiner
Tobias Koppensteiner

Marcel Kosmaier
Felix Kotulla
Theresa Kramreither
Günter Kratochvil
Cosima Kristl
Gabriel Krög
Gregor Kronstorfer
Sandra Maria Kropik
Anna Krüger
Melanie Kšck
Eva Kubitschka
Raphaela Kucera
Daniel Kucera
Constantin Kuchler
Nina Kugler
Tobias Kühleitner
Diksha Kunj
Nikolai Kutsch
Phillipp Laabmayr
Maxi Laimbauer
Magdalena Lamprecht
Sabin Lang
Sabine Lang
Sabrina Lang
Nicole Larosch
Daniela Lehenbauer
Thomas Lehner
Ines Lehner
Verena Lehner
Maximilian Leithner
Michael Leitner
Stefan Lemmerer
Philipp Leonfellner
Christoph Leutgeb
Eric Lindenmayr
Selina Litschauer
Alexander Litzlfellner
Verena Löffler
Niklas Loidl
Ines Loimayer
Sarah Luef
Tobias Luger
Laurin Uriel Lux
Luisa Maier
Patrick Maier
Helga Maitner
Denis Maksuti
Martina Mallinger
Emir Mamou
Florian Manchen
Mathias Mannzberger
Stefan Marchsteiner
Antonijevic Marijana
Laura Marinkovic
Michael Mark
Terence Markov
Carina Martiner
Nadine Mauhart
Lukas Maul
Florian Mayer
Lydia Mayer
Angus Alfred Mayer
Wolfgang Mayer
Nadine Mayerhofer
Nicole Mayr
Nadine Mayr
Gregor Mayrhofer
Jakob Mayrhofer
Sara Mehadzic
Philipp Meisl
Lena Michel
David Andrew Miller
Martina Miritsch
Nina Mitterhauser
Josef Mitterhuemer
Marlene Mittermayr
Miriam Mohamed
Orenda Sophie Mohan
Arthur Mohl
Julian Möhlen
Verena Mold
Elias Monitzer
Johanna Möschl
Hannah Mösenbichler
Vanessa Moser
Stephanie Mösl
Gabriela Mruczek
Eva Mühlberger
Melisa Mujcinovic
Oliver Müller
Thomas Müller
Jasmin Müllner
Benedikt Müllner
Stephanie Munoz Visbal
Nadine Münzberger
Mucahit Mutlu
Daniel Nairz
Daniel Nemec
Daniel Netzer
Mario Neuhold
Julia Neumann
Birgit Neumüller
Selina Neuner
Patrick Neunteufl
Theresa Neunteufl
Petra Neureiter
Viktoria Neuschmid
Katrin Neuwirth
Christina Niedrist
Sandra Nikolic
Rachel Noble
Sabrina Oberdorfer
Max Obernauer
Theresa Obernosterer
Helmut Oberreiter
Mario Oberroithmair
Dominik Öckhl
Marcel Oelzelt
Selina Ofer
Emina Omerovic
Sarah Oos
Daniel Opacak
Katrin Oppeneiger
Nicolas Ormian
Halil Oyman
Ali Özenir
Christina Ozlberger
Pascale Palmetshofer
Veronika Palmetzhofer
Hanna Pammer
Sabrina Pannagl
Jennifer Pannagl
Emil Parth
Eric Paschinger
Denise Paukner
Sebastian Penz
Sophia Penz
Lisa Pernausl
Lena Pertl
Karin Peterschelka
Dražen Petrović
Barbara Pfaller
Lisa Maria Pfeiffer
Madleen Pfeiffer
Kerstin Pfeiffer
Jasmin Pichlmüller
Bernadette Pilar
Jana Pils
Lukas Pirerfellner
Thomas Pitter
Magdalena Pletzter
Martin Pöheim
Bianca Pokorny
Tanja Pöll
Fanny Popovic
Miriam Pötz
Corinna Pötzelsberger
Friedrich Pötzlberger
Martina Praxmarer
Sebastian Preuss
Oliver Prexl
Julian Probst
Jens Pröglhöf
Ana Protrka
Raphael Pühringer
Matthias Purker
Samuel Puttinger
Christoph Raab
Claire Rack
Valentina Rainer
Stefanie Ramler
Christian Ramljak
Lukas Rammerstorfer
Renate Ratzenböck
Katharina Rauch
Robert Rauch
Julian Rauchberger
Theresa Reichl
Sabrina Reigl
Teresa Reisinger
Jürgen Reitbauer
Melanie Reiter
Marlies Renner
Elisabeth Rensch
Julian Resch
Raffaela Ronja Ribel
Anna Rieder
Lukas Ritt
Martina Rohrer
Laurenz Roither
Maria Roithmair
Fabian Rosenkranz
Iris Rosenstatter
Kevin Sacher
Nadine Safron
Sarah Sailer
Marcel Sailer
Stefanie Salge
Patricia Salzer
Dragana Samcevic
Sarah Samel
Anant Sangar
Steven Sango
Thomas Sauerschnig
Matthias Schaffer
Karoline Schager
Laura Schamberger
Lukas Schaubmayr
Manuela Schauer
Natalie Schautzgy
Laura Schemberger
Peter Schernhuber
Ann-Kathrin Schickinger
Bernhard Schiefer
Astrid Schildberger
Carina Schimpl
Fabian Schindler
Dominik Schipany
Ludwig Schischka
Tobias Schleritzko

Mirjam Schmid
Sophie Schmid
Peter Schnitzhofer
Magdalena Schobesberger
Tanja Schöchtner
Sarah Schögler
Lukas Schürz
Kati Schuster
Nicole Schwab
Marissa Schwarz
David Schwarzenbacher
Stefan Schwarzenberger
Wolfgang Schweiger
Manuel (Secki) Secklehner
Vitus Sedmak
Hannes Seidl
Razila Semic
Cornelia Semper
Violetta Sevic
Stefan Christian Siedl
Lisa Simader
Enya Simic
Dominik Simon
Mario Josef Sinhuber
Omar Soliman
Julia Sommer
Eva Sonnberger
Udo Sorger
Bettina Stadlbauer
Tobias Stadler
Manuel Stadlinger
Stephan Stadlmair
Sarah Stadlmayr
Luisa Stangl
Lisa Stangl
Florentina Steindl
Ferdinand Steindl
Michelle Steindl
Elisabeth Steiner

Viktoria Steiner
Lena Steinhuber
Jakob Steininger
Michael Steininger
Thomas Franz Steininger
Daniel Steinkellner
Liam Stertzl
Valerie Stieger
Simon Stix
Theresa Stocker
Michele Stöckholzer
Christian Stockmaier
Daniela Stojkovic
Anna Catharina Stolz
Andrea Strasser
Lena Strasser
Christoph Straßer
Jennifer Straßer
Magdalena Strauss
Stefanie Streckfuß
Andreas Strobl
Stefan Strobl
Jasmin Stuck
Laura Stummer
Bettina Sturm
Christoph Süß
Daniela Süß
Tobias Süß
Sarah Szczepanik
Nadine Taibon
Melda Talas
Ines Tiefenbacher
David Tiefenthaler
Daniel Tomaschitz
Anita Topalovic
Cecile Trexler
Mathias Trölss
Kevin Trötzmüller
Laura Tschallener
Julia Maria Tüchler
Isabel Tureczek
Büsra Türkmen
Michelle Uitz
Patrick Ujvary
Patricia Ulbing
Theresa Unterberger
Maria Veit
Theresa Vogl
Bernd Von Gimborn
Angela Voss
Sandra Vuljaj
Jana Wachter
Aaron Wagner
Johanna Wagner
Lena Sophia Wagner

Paul Wagner
Vincent Walkolbinger
Tanja Wallner
Daniela Wallner
Jasmin Wally
Riccarda Wally
Julia Wannenmacher
Lisa Wartbichler
Michael Weber
Angelina Michelle Weber
Sabrina Weichselbaum
Laura Weichselbaum
Manuel Weichselbaum
Florian Weichselbaum
Isabella Weichselbaum
Jasmin Weichselbaum
Simon Weichselbaum
Tamara Weichselbaumer
Marlies Weidinger
Melanie Weidinger
Madlen Weingartner
Clara Weiss
Laura Weiss
Victor Weiß
David Weiß
Benedikt Weissinger
Jonas Weissinger
Nina Weissinger
Heinz Weissmann
Magdalena Weitgasser
Kerstin Weixelbraun
Claudia Wieser
Laura Wieser
Paula Wildbacher
Vera Willinger
Benjamin Wiltschnig
Brigitte Winkler
Anna Winkler
Maximilian Winter
Jan Winterauer
Laura Wishofer
Angelika Wlodarczyk
Julia Wojtkowiak
Manuel Wokac
Martin Woschank
Jakob Wundsam
Manuel Wutte
Lukas Zapata
Isabella Zauner
Bernhard Zdrazil
Michaela Zeilinger
Nadine Zeininger
Julian Zeller
Anja Zellhofer
Selina Zellhofer

Katharina Ziegler
Simon Zigala
Victoria Zinner
Julia Zlöbl
Nikolina Zunic
Simay Zwerger
Iris Zwölfer

SCHOOLS / INSTITUTIONS

AHS Rahlgasse Wien
AKS Kärnten Koroška Klagenfurt
Alpen-Adria Gymnasium Völkermarkt Völkermarkt
BBASOP St. Pölten St Pölten
Berufsschule für Bürokaufleute Wien
BG und BRG Zwettl Zwettl
BG/BRG Pichelmayergasse Wien
BG/BRG/SRG Reithmannstraße Innsbruck
BHAK Gmunden Gmunden
BHAK/BHAS St. Johann i. Pg. St. Johann im Pg.
BHAK/BHASCH Mistelbach Mistelbach
BHP HBLA Oberwart Oberwart
BORG 15 Henriettenplatz Wien
BORG Bad Leonfelden Bad Leonfelden
BRG 7 Kandlgasse Wien
BRG Horn Horn
BRG Pichelmayergasse Wien
BRG Schloss Traunsee Gmunden
BRG Traun Traun
Bundeshandelsakademie Eisenerz Eisenerz
Bundesoberstufenrealgymnasium Grieskirchen Grieskirchen
Christian-Doppler-Gymnasium Salzburg
Create Your Region Vorchdorf
eco telfs Telfs
Erzbischöfliches Privatgymnasiums Borromäum Salzburg
Europaschule Linz Linz
G19 Wien
Georg-von-Peuerbach-Gymnasium Linz
GRG 6 Wien
GRG Draschestraße VBS Wien
GRG Rosasgasse Wien
Gymnasium der Herz Jesu Missionare Salzburg
HAK 1 Salzburg Salzburg
HAK Baden Baden

HBLA für Künstlerische Gestaltung Linz
HLA für Umwelt und Wirtschaft
Stift Zwettl Yspertal
HLA Herbststraße Wien
HLFS Ursprung Elixhausen
HLW Steyr Steyr
Höhere Bundeslehranstalt für wirtschaftliche Berufe Linz
Hort St. Marien/KMS Wien
HS Stift Zwettl Zwettl
HS Zirl Zirl
HTBLuVA Salzburg Salzburg
HTBLVA Ortweinschule Graz
HTL 1 Bau und Design Linz
HTL 3 Rennweg Wien
HTL Anichstraße Innsbruck
HTL Mössingerstraße Klagenfurt
Impuls Schule Steyr, Mittelstufe 2 Steyr
IRC – International Regional College, Volksschule Liebhartsgasse Wien
Jubiz – Jugendbildungszentrum Wien
Jugendzentrum nang-pu Attnang-Puchheim
Kreativhauptschule Stift Zwettl Zwettl
Landesberufschule Baden Baden
Mädchentreff Marchtrenk Marchtrenk
Media Space Wels
MiM Wendstattgasse Wien
Modellschule Graz
MRG Mediengym Fadingerstraße Linz
Musik und Informatik Mittelschule Wien
Musisches Gymnasium Salzburg Salzburg
Neue Mittelschule Bürmoos Bürmoos
Neue Mittelschule Eberstalzell Eberstalzell
NMS Clemens Holzmeister Landeck
NMS Gramastetten Gramastetten
NMS Müllerstraße Innsbruck
NMS Reichraming Reichraming
NMS Salzburg-Lehen Salzburg
NMS Spittal/Drau Spittal
NMS Telfs Dr. Aloys Weißenbach Telfs
ÖGB OÖ Linz
Praxis HAK Völkermarkt Völkermarkt
RGORG 23 Wien
Schumpeter-Handelsakademie Wien
Sonderpädagogisches Zentrum Wien
Sonderpädagogisches Zentrum 2 Wien
Stiftung Talente Altmünster
TFBS für Handel und Büro Innsbruck
Vienna Business School – Schönborngasse Wien
Volksschule Alfred Bäck Taxham Salzburg
Volksschule Pettenbach Pettenbach
VS Neußerling Herzogsdorf
VS Oberlaa Wien
VS Viktorsberg Viktorsberg
Zentrum für Medienkompetenz Brunn am Gebirge

PRIX ARS ELECTRONICA COLLIDE@CERN RESIDENCY AWARD

21 IT
Pedro Aibeo PT
Lita Albuquerque US
Juan Gabriel Alzate Romero CO
Nikolai Antonie US
Jácome Armas PT
Association "Culture, Media and Education" - ARTHEA HR
Elodie Aubonnay CH
Sam Auinger AT
Saad Kamel Ayman EG
Girilal Baars SE
Marion Baeriswyl CH
Leah Beeferman US
Golnaz Behrouznia IR
Nick Belomatis GR
Reinhold Bidner AT
Sergio Bonilha BR
Liubo Borissov BG
Daniel Boschung CH
James Bridle GB
Kevin Bryce CA
Halsey Burgund US
Paul Bush GB
Alvaro Cassinelli UY
Philippe Chatelain FR
Oksana Chepelyk UA
Sarawut Chutiwongpeti TH
John Clavin US
Ryan Cockerham US
Stanley Cohen US
Chiara Cola IT
Eric Cordier FR
Xavier Cortada US
Layla Curtis GB
Darsha Darsha Hewitt CA
Arko Datto IN
Christopher Davidson US
Alejandra de la Puente Martinez de Castro MX
Stéphane de Gérando FR
Ivor Diosi HU
Evelina Domnitch NL
Adam Donovan AU
Josephine Dorado US
Mikhail Dyachkov RU
Mark Eaglen GB
Sam Falconer GB
José Miguel Fernández CL
Ruwan Fernando AU
Moritz Fingerhut DE
Nicholas Finocchio US
Florent Trochel FR
Bill Fontana US
Frédéric Curien FR
Iris Garrelfs DE
Dmitry Gelfand NL
Anita Giraldo US
Raphael Grascher AT
Eduards Griškevičs LV
Phillip Gulley US
Kunal Gupta US
H/A/D ID
Kerry Hagan US
Barry Hale GB
Katharine Hawthorne US
Johannes Heldén SE
Chris Henschke AU
Georg Hobmeier AT
HONF ID
Marc Horowitz US
GH Hovagimyan US
Eliane Huber-Irikawa CH
Salvatore Iaconesi IT
iFilms PL
Daniel Iglesia US
Pierre-Axel Izerable FR
Jean-Marie Dallet FR
Nova Jiang NZ
Philip Julian GB
Ricca Kawai-Kalderon JP
Jinku Kim KR
Maja Kirovska MK
Thomas Koener DE
Panayiotis Kokoras GR
Satya Surya Subrahmanya Sri Harsha Kolluru Venkata IN
Denis Kolokol UA
Marinos Koutsomichalis GR
Xu Li CN
Live Art Installations DK
Katiuscia Magliarisi IT
Alberto Magrin IT
marcella mandanici IT
Petra Lilla Marjai HU
David McCornack US
Lucy McKenna IE
Yiannis Melanitis GR
Alexander Mendelevich IL
Luc Messinezis GR
Ivelin Metodiev BG
Michael Michael Rhoades US
Angelika Middendorf DE
Drew Miller US
Miracle FR
Yasuno Miyauchi JP
François Moncarey FR

Ruben Naeff US
Robert Spalding Newcomb US
Luciana Ohira BR
Alessandro Olla IT
Fredrik Olofsson SE
Eirik Østby NO
Matthew Paradis GB
Joseph Paradiso US
Susana Perrottet PE
Eleni Phylactide CY
P o P _ X, Walter Biondani, la Tribu
Malù and The Nasty Power Bitch IT
Post Illusions TR
Lucy Pullen CA
Davide Quayola IT
Ariadna Rabago Snyder MX
Kevin Ramseier CH
Hillary Reeves Livingston US
Martina Reinhart AT
Jean-Michel Rolland FR
Roth Mobot US
Alexandre Rottolli FR
Simon Ryder GB
Ivan Safrin RU
Gordon Sasaki US
Tim Schwartz US
J. Scriba DE
Stuart Seaton GB
Semiconductor GB
Natan Sinigaglia IT
Ádám Siska HU
Pascual Sisto ES
Pipaluk Supernova DK
Debra Swack US
Sylvie Nigg CH
Ra'uf Tailony JO
Justin Tate CA
Caroline Teillier FR
Tobias Tiecke NL
tillsammans laboratories CH
Diego Trujillo MX
UBERMORGEN AT
Koert van den Beukel (K_Van) NL
Craig Vear GB
Ariel Waldman US
Chung-Kun Wang TW
Herwig Weiser AT
Paul Wiersbinski DE
Lior Yurfest IL
Chris Ziegler DE

Ars Electronica 2013
Festival für Kunst, Technologie und Gesellschaft /
Festival for Art, Technology and Society

Organization
Ars Electronica Linz GmbH

Managing Directors
Gerfried Stocker, Diethard Schwarzmair
Ars-Electronica-Straße 1, 4040 Linz, Austria
Tel: +4373272720
Fax: +4373272722
info@aec.at

Co-organizers

ORF Oberösterreich
General Director: Kurt Rammerstorfer

LIVA – Veranstaltungsgesellschaft m.b.H.
Directors: Hans-Joachim Frey, Wolfgang Lehner

OK Offenes Kulturhaus im OÖ Kulturquartier
Directors: Martin Sturm, Gabriele Daghofer

Partners
LENTOS Kunstmuseum Linz
Kunstuniversität Linz – Universität für künstlerische und industrielle Gestaltung
Tabakfabrik Linz
afo – architekturforum oberösterreich
MAERZ
Mariendom Linz
KIAVE
Bezalel Academy of Arts and Design, Jerusalem
Hamidrasha Art School am Beit Berl College
H.I.T – Holon Institute of Technology
Kibbutzim College of Art & Education, Tel Aviv
Shenkar College of Engineering and Design, Ramat Gan
Media Innovation Lab (miLAB) am IDC Herzliya
Musrara School, Jerusalem
Neri Bloomfield School of Design and Education, Haifa
Hadassah Academic College, Jerusalem
The College of Management – Academic Studies (COMAS)
FH Oberösterreich – Campus Hagenberg
Diakoniewerk
Japan Media Arts Festival
ikono.tv
Ministry of Culture, Republic of China (Taiwan) 中華民國文化部
The Association of the Visual Arts in Taiwan (AVAT)
SideBySide Studio e.V.
La Maison Laurentine
Ministry of Foreign Affairs, Republic of China (Taiwan) 中華民國外交部
Quanta Arts Foundation
MEGA - Museum of Electronic Games & Art
Austria Game Jam, Verein für Innovative Unterhaltungs-software
Andranik Ghalustians, Bildschirmsprünge

Directors Ars Electronica: Gerfried Stocker, Christine Schöpf
Head of Festival: Martin Honzik
Technical Head: Karl Julian Schmidinger
Internal Organization: Veronika Liebl

Production Team: Liam Achaibou, Laura Baumann, Katharina Bienert, Sigrid Blauensteiner, Stefan Brandmayr, Katharina Edlmair, Marlene Eggenreich, Hannes Franks, Stephanie Fuchs, Evi Garsleitner, Carmen Grabuschnig, Rosi Grillmair, Sarah Hellwagner, Simon Kopfberger, Alex Marasescu, Hans Christian Merten, Gerald Moser, Franziska Mucha, Kathrin Obernhumer, Emiko Ogawa, Maria Ogawa, Maria Pfeifer, Roland Ploner, Georg Pühringer, Miriam Schmeikal, Jutta Schmiederer, Florian Sedmak, Joschi Viteka, Susi Windischbauer, Michaela Wimplinger

Co-curators
Ars Electronica Animation Festival: Christine Schöpf, Jürgen Hagler
Big Concert Night: Dennis Russell Davies, Hans-Joachim Frey, Heribert Schröder
Campus Exhibition: Lila Chitayat, Yael Eylat Van-Essen, Sayfan G Borghini, Oren Zuckerman, Eyal Vexler
Featured Artist: Andreas Hirsch
Interface Cultures Exhibition: Faculty – Christa Sommerer, Laurent Mignonneau, Martin Kaltenbrunner, Michaela Ortner, Marlene Hochrieser, Georg Russegger
Pixelspaces: Horst Hörtner, Roland Haring, Veronika Pauser, Matthew Gardiner, Kristefan Minski, Johanna Mathauer, Michael Badics, Gabriele Purdue, Roland Reiter
Wir sind Hier: Salvatore Vanasco, Claudius Brodmann

Prix Ars Electronica 2013

Co-organizers

ORF Oberösterreich
Director: Kurt Rammerstorfer

LIVA – Veranstaltungsgesellschaft m.b.H.
Directors: Hans-Joachim Frey, Wolfgang Lehner

OK Offenes Kulturhaus im OÖ Kulturquartier
Directors: Martin Sturm, Gabriele Daghofer

Idea: Hannes Leopoldseder
Conception: Christine Schöpf, Gerfried Stocker
Coordination: Martin Honzik, Emiko Ogawa
Technical Management: Karl Julian Schmidinger

Production Team: Florian Bauböck, Bernhard Böhm, Viktor Delev, Stefan Dorn, Marlene Eggenreich, Christoph Einfalt, Ingrid Fischer-Schreiber, Gregor Göttfert, Sarah Stefanie Hellwagner, Michael Lettner, Veronika Liebl, Johanna Mathauer, Manuela Naveau, Kathrin Obernhumer, Johannes Ramsl, Remo Rauscher, Miriam Schmeikal, Florian Voggeneder, Susi Windischbauer

Press: Christopher Sonnleitner, Robert Bauernhansl, Michael Knoll, Raphael Gierlinger

Marketing: Sina Balke-Juhn, Cornelia Erber, Isabella Grünauer, Martina Huber

Ars Electronica Archive: Martina Hechenberger, Elvis Pavic, Christina Radner, Heinz Sambs, Jutta Schmiederer

Ars Electronica Linz GmbH

Ars Electronica Center: Andreas Bauer, Christoph Kremer, Renata Aigner, Viktoria Aistleitner, Reinhard Bengesser, Tamara Böhm, Sarah Breinbauer, Blanka Denkmaier, Wolfgang Deutsch, Hans Peter Ecker, Johannes Egler, Erika Eiter, Stefanie Farkashazy, Karl Federspiel, Julia Felberbauer, Melinda File, Evelyn Fränzl, Anna Friedinger, Andrea Fröhlich, Mitra Gazvini-Zateh, Christian Gerber, Elisabeth Gerhard-Mayrhofer, Nicole Grüneis, Ulrike Gschwandtner, Harald Haas, Gerid Maria Hager, Birgit Hartinger, Gerlinde Hauder, Florian Heiml, Martin Hieslmair, Thomas Hillinger, Denise Hinger, Gerold Hofstadler, Sri Rahayu Hofstadler, Katharina Hoffelner, Klaus Hollinetz, Lorena Höllrigl, Philip Huemer, Thomas Jannke, Erika Jungreithmayr, Elisabeth Kattner, Daniel Kern, Herwig Kerschner, Viktoria Klepp, Eva Klimesova, Michael Koller, Thomas Kollmann, Wolfgang König, Kristýna Krabatschová, David Lang, Andreas Leeb, Sabine Leidlmair, Juliane Leitner, Dominic Lengauer, Anna Katharina Link, Ulrike Mair, Reingard Medicus, Kathrin Meyer, Clemens Mock, Horst Morocutti, Marc Mühlberger, Daniel Murina, Heinrich Niederhuber, Michaela Obermayer, Benjamin Perndl, Svetlana Petrovic, Katharina Pilar, Armin Pils, Victoria Pilz, Andreas Plakolm, Anna Polewiak, Mathias Pöschko, Ulrike Rieseneder, Karl Hans Rois, Andreas Roth, Petra Saubolle-Hofmann, Alina Sauter, Birgitt Schäffer, Johann Schauer, Barbara Schmidt, Nina Schönberger, Markus Schwarzmair, Stefan Schwarzmair, Elio Seidl, Manfred Seifriedsberger, Margarete Stöttner-Breuer, Johannes Strasser, Lioubov Studener, Johannes Stürzlinger, Istvan Szabo, Bhoomesh Tak, Kerstin Tak-Wakolbinger, Michaela Maria Tanzer, Michael Thaler, Michael Trebo, Clarissa Ujvari, Linda Vankova, Thomas Viehböck, Florian Voggeneder, Karin Wabro, Florian Wanninger, Sebastian Zach, Silvia Zainzinger

Ars Electronica Futurelab: Horst Hörtner, Christopher Lindinger, Roland Haring, Roland Aigner, Tamer Aslan, Florian Berger, Bhavanesh Chamdal, Manuel Dobusch, Barbara Erlinger, Maria Eschlböck, Peter Freudling, Matthew Gardiner, Peter Holzkorn, Andreas Jalsovec, Michael Knoll, Anna Lucia Kuthan, Martina Mara, Johanna Mathauer, Benjamin Mayr, Michael Mayr, Kristefan Minski, Stefan Mittlböck-Jungwirth-Fohringer, Patrick Müller, Otto Naderer, Nicolas Naveau, Hideaki Ogawa, Veronika Pauser, Michael Platz, Erwin Reitböck, Deniz Saglam

Ars Electronica Festival: Martin Honzik, Karl Julian Schmidinger, Florian Bauböck, Laura Baumann, Katharina Bienert, Sigrid Blauensteiner, Stefan Brandmayr, Marlene Eggenreich, Stephanie Fuchs, Carmen Grabuschnig, Rosi Grillmair, Sarah Stefanie Hellwagner, Veronika Liebl, Michael Lettner, Hans Christian Merten, Franziska Mucha, Manuela Naveau, Kathrin Obernhumer, Emiko Ogawa, Maria Ogawa, Maria Pfeifer, Georg Pühringer, Miriam Schmeikal, Jutta Schmiederer, Susi Windischbauer

Ars Electronica Management Services: Elisabeth Kapeller, Markus Jandl, Sina Balke-Juhn, Sebastian Bauböck, Robert Bauernhansl, Bettina Danninger, Barbara Diesenreither, Bettina Gahleitner, Gerhard Grafinger, Michael Grausgruber, Isabella Grünauer, Martina Hechenberger, Gerald Hochhauser, Gerold Hofstadler, Martina Huber, Andrea Huemer, Heinrich Klambauer, Martin Kneidinger, Stephan Kobler, Zulfija Magomedova, Michaela Neunherz, Peter J. Nitzschmann, Elvis Pavic, Julia Rabeder, Christina Radner, Christopher Sonnleitner, Heinz Sambs, David Starzengruber, Michaela Wimplinger

Ars Electronica Solutions: Bernd Albl, Michael Badics, Lukas Bischof, Chris Bruckmayr, Cecile Bucher, Stefan Dorn, Stefan Fuchs, David Gann, My-Trinh Gardiner, Imanol Gomez, Yvonne Hauser, Barbara Hinterleitner, Christoph Hofbauer, Martina Karrer, Petros Kataras, Fadil Kujundzic, Kathrin Agnes Meyer, Harald Moser, Ali Nikrang, Benjamin Olsen, Dietmar Peter, Andreas Pramböck, Gerald Priewasser, Stephan Pointner, Gabriele Purdue, Roland Reiter, Vanessa Schauer, Markus Wipplinger, Claus Zweythurm

Spaxels Task Force: Horst Hörtner, Daniel Aigenbauer, Florian Berger, Chris Bruckmayr, Andreas Jalsovec, Martin Mörth, Benjamin Olsen, Michael Platz

OK Offenes Kulturhaus im OÖ Kulturquartier

OK CyberArts Team
Artistic Director: Martin Sturm
Commercial Director: Gabriele Daghofer
Curator: Genoveva Rückert
Public Relations: Maria Falkinger
Technical Manager: Rainer Jessl
Production: Martina Rauschmayer, Aron Rynda
Technical Head: Markus Wallner

Production Team: Jarno Bachheimer, Attila Ferenczi, Alfred Fürholzer, Martin Haselsteiner, Bernhard Kitzmüller, Andreas Kurz, Daniel Mandel, Gerald Schreilechner, Andreas Steindl, André Tschinder, Tom Vens, Hans-Jörg Weidinger, Gerhard Wörnhörer, Simon Wilhelm

Team: Verena Atteneder, Johann Aufreiter, Erika Baldinger, Renate Berger, Julia Brunner, Michael Dalpiaz, Walter Eckerstorfer, Max Fabian, Michaela Fröhlich, Andrea Gintner, Manuela Gruber, Dominik Harrer, Sabine Haunschmid, Evi Heininger, Robert Herbst, Maximilian Höglinger, Fritz Holzinger, Verena, Karner, Simon Lachner, Katharina Lackner, Elisabeth Lehner, Judith Maule, Franz Minichberger, Walter Mühlböck, Wolfgang Nagl, Josef Pfarrhofer, Franz Pfifferling, Wilhelm Pichler, Angelika Pöschl, Franz Quirchtmayr, Brigitte Rosenthaler, Gerda Sailer, Markus Schiller, Ulrike Schimpl, Alexandra Schlager, Helene Schoißengeyr, Ulrike Seelmann, Barbara Steindl, Marlies Stöger

Brucknerhaus

Wolfgang Scheibner, Wolfgang Schützeneder, Ursula Kislinger

afo – architekturforum oberösterreich

Architektur und Klang
Curatorial Head: Andre Zogholy
Co-Curator: Elmecker Ewald
Technical Team: Dietmar Elmecker Ewald, Hannes Franks

ORGANIZATION / VERANSTALTER

ARS ELECTRONICA

Ars Electronica Linz GmbH is a company of the city of Linz. Ars Electronica Linz GmbH ist ein Unternehmen der Stadt Linz.

ORF OÖ

BRUCKNER HAUS

OK im oö kulturquartier

COOPERATION PARTNERS / KOOPERATIONSPARTNER

LENTOS Kunstmuseum Linz
Kunstuniversität Linz – Universität für künstlerische und industrielle Gestaltung
Tabakfabrik Linz
afo – architekturforum oberösterreich
MAERZ
Mariendom Linz
KIAVE
Bezalel Academy of Arts and Design, Jerusalem
Hamidrasha Art School am Beit Berl College
H.I.T – Holon Institute of Technology
Kibbutzim College of Art & Education, Tel Aviv
Shenkar College of Engineering and Design, Ramat Gan
Media Innovation Lab (miLAB) am IDC Herzliya
Musrara School, Jerusalem
Neri Bloomfield School of Design and Education, Haifa
Hadassah Academic College, Jerusalem
College of Management – Academic Studies (COMAS)
FH Oberösterreich – Campus Hagenberg
Diakoniewerk
Japan Media Arts Festival
ikono.tv
Ministry of Culture, Republic of China (Taiwan) 中華民國文化部
The Association of the Visual Arts in Taiwan (AVAT)
SideBySide Studio e.V.
La Maison Laurentine
Ministry of Foreign Affairs, Republic of China (Taiwan) 中華民國外交部
Quanta Arts Foundation
MEGA – Museum of Electronic Games & Art
Austria Game Jam, Verein für Innovative Unterhaltungssoftware
Andranik Ghalustians, Bildschirmsprünge
Kinderfreunde Oberösterreich
LIFEtool gemeinnützige GmbH
LEGO
REHA SERVICE GmbH

ARS ELECTRONICA RECEIVES SUPPORT FROM / ARS ELECTRONICA WIRD UNTERSTÜTZT VON:

Linz verändert
Stadt Linz

LAND OBERÖSTERREICH
Land Oberösterreich

bm:uk
Bundesministerium für Unterricht, Kunst und Kultur

BMWF
Bundesministerium für Wissenschaft und Forschung

voestalpine EINEN SCHRITT VORAUS.
voestalpine

bfi
bfi

Hutchison 3

LINZ AG www.linzag.at | Immer bestens betreut.
Linz AG

Mercedes-Benz
Mercedes-Benz

SCHÄFER SHOP
SSI Schäfer Shop

LIWEST Ein Kabel Alle Medien
Liwest

ARS ELECTRONICA RECEIVES SUPPORT FROM / ARS ELECTRONICA WIRD UNTERSTÜTZT VON:

Sparkasse OÖ	Wirtschaftskammer OÖ	Ton + Bild	ÖBB
OÖ Nachrichten	Kronen Zeitung	Ö1	FM4
Standard	Arte	Smurfit Kappa	Casino Linz
Japan Foundation	EU-Japan Fest Japan Commitee	Quanta Arts Foundation	Messe Linz
LIVA	NTS	Trotec	Screenteam
Kuka	Studiolab	European Union	7th Framework Programme
Diakoniewerk	Pro Helvetia	Mondriaan Fonds	Jugend in Aktion
PH Oberösterreich	Rotes Kreuz	Cordial	USP

Triple A, Phoenics, Sony DADC, Sampad, Akademie des österreichischen Films

Additional Support: KulturKontakt Austria, Cubus

CyberArts 2013
International Compendium – Prix Ars Electronica

International Compendium - Prix Ars Electronica - Computer Animation / Film / VFX - Digital Musics & Sound Art – Hybrid Art – Interactive Art – Digital Communities – u19 – CREATE YOUR WORLD – [the next idea] voestalpine Art and Technology Grant – Prix Ars Electronica Collide@CERN Residency Award

Herausgeber / Editors: Hannes Leopoldseder, Christine Schöpf, Gerfried Stocker

Redaktion / Editing: Ingrid Fischer-Schreiber
Übersetzungen / Translations: Martina Bauer, Ingrid Fischer-Schreiber, Wilfried Prantner (Englisch-Deutsch / English-German), Catherine Kerkhoff-Saxon (Deutsch-Englisch / German-English)
Lektorat / Copyediting: Ingrid Fischer-Schreiber, Jutta Schmiederer, Dave Westacott

Grafische Gestaltung und Produktion / Graphic design and production: Norbert Artner, Mitarbeit / Assistance: Kathi Reidelshöfer
Schrift / Typeface: Klavika
Druck / Printed by: Gutenberg Werbering Gesellschaft m. b. H., Linz
Papier / Paper: BVS matt, 135 g/m², Galerie Vision, 285 g/m²
Herstellung / Production: Gutenberg Werbering Gesellschaft m. b. H., Linz
Fotos / Photos: S. / pp. 281: tom mesic; S. / pp. 282–287: Norbert Artner; S. / pp. 287: rubra

Erschienen im / Published by Hatje Cantz Verlag
Zeppelinstrasse 32
73760 Ostfildern
Deutschland / Germany
Tel. +49 711 4405-200
Fax +49 711 4405-220
www.hatjecantz.com
Ein Unternehmen der Ganske Verlagsgruppe
A Ganske Publishing Group company

Informationen zu dieser oder zu anderen Ausstellungen finden Sie unter www.kq-daily.de /
You can find information on this exhibition and many others at www.kq-daily.de.

Hatje Cantz books are available internationally at selected bookstores.
For more information about our distribution partners please visit our homepage at www.hatjecantz.com.

ISBN 978-3-7757-3631-2

Printed in Austria

Umschlagabbildungen / Cover illustrations:
Memo Akten, Quayola: *Forms*; Koen Vanmechelen: *The Cosmopolitan Chicken Project - Diversity and Dualism*; Thomas Feuerstein: *Pancreas*; Chris Carlson: *Borderlands Granular*

PEFC
PEFC/06-39-27 **klimaneutral gedruckt** CP IKS-Nr.: 53401-1307-1012